The Magical Training of Quareia

Volume II

The Tenth Anniversary Edition
Revised and Updated

Josephine McCarthy

Quareia Publishing

Copyright 1993 – 2025 © Josephine McCarthy
All rights reserved

Without limiting the rights under copyright reserved above,
no part of this publication may be reproduced, stored in,
or introduced into a retrieval system, or transmitted,
in any form or by any means
(electronic, mechanical, photocopying, recording or otherwise)
without prior permission of the copyright owner
and the publisher of this book.

First edition published by Quareia Publishing UK 2016
Second edition published by Quareia Publishing UK 2025
Exeter UK

www.quareiapublishing.com

A catalogue record for this book is available from the British Library

Hardback ISBN: 978-1-911134-77-0
Paperback ISBN: 978-1-911134-78-7
Ebook ISBN: 978-1-911134-79-4

Cover image by Stuart Littlejohn
Cover design by Stuart Littlejohn
Formatted and typeset by Quareia editor Liza Kalys

Dedication

This volume is dedicated to Gopal Slavonic,
flamenco guitarist extraordinaire,
who always argued with me on stage during performances.
He died suddenly and far too young while this volume was being created.
Good journey to you Gopal… The siguiriyas is playing for you.

And to Greg McComish,
who walked through the West Gate,
Under the watchful eye of Athena.

Acknowledgements

Thank you to the people who made this course possible
when it was first being written:
Stuart Littlejohn, Frater Acher, Michael Sheppard, Aaron Moshe,
Toni Paris, Christin C and SC.

And a big thank you to the Quareia volunteers
who tirelessly worked through these modules line by line
to bring the course up to date, tidy it up, re-edit, and to make it better:
Zoë, Liza K, Rebecca A, GF, Salem, Kirby, Cristina E,
Klex, Giulio F, JSVD, Liam M.

And a special thank you to Zoë and Rebecca A
for not only working on the editing
but also organising the rest of the volunteer team and collating the work.
Without you two and the rest of the team,
this updated version of the course would not have been possible.

And a massive thank you to all donors to Quareia over the last ten years;
without you the course would not have happened nor would it have continued.

And a special thank you to Liza Kalys,
her patience, amazing skill level, professionalism, humour,
and artistry in the design and typesetting of this book is just fabulous!

Contents

Introduction 15
Read before starting the course 16

Module IV Death, Birth, and the Underworld 19

Lesson 1   Overview   21

1. Death in general 23
2. Death and the Mysteries 24
3. Working magically in death while alive 29
4. The dead in the living world 29
5. The Underworld and the Abyss 29
6. Inner contacts and inner adepts 30
7. The Bound Ones 30
8. Summary 30

Lesson 2   Regular Death   33

1. Slow Death 33
2. Upon the threshold of death 38
3. Religious aspects of death 40
4. Energetic clinging 41
5. Death Parasites 43
6. Quick deaths 43
7. Comas 44
8. Task: Astrology 46
9. Task: Death chart practice 48
10. Task: Tarot and death 48

Lesson 3   The Magical Mysteries of Death   53

1. Religion versus the Mysteries 54
2. The Death Mysteries 54
3. The steps of the process: a brief overview 55
4. The Descent into the Underworld 57
5. The River and Judgement 58
6. The Key of the Scales 59
7. The Second Death 62
8. Fooling the Scales 63
9. The walk of the knives 63
10. The face of the angel 65
11. The Vista 65

	12.	Reincarnation	67
	13.	Summary	69
	14.	Task: Finding	69
	15.	Task: Reading	70

Lesson 4 — The Underworld and the Abyss — 73

	1.	Threshold of the Underworld	74
	2.	The first layer of the Underworld	77
	3.	The Goddess in the Cave	78
	4.	The Deeper Underworld	79
	5.	The Abyss	80
	6.	The Highway of the Abyss	81
	7.	About the practical work	82
	8.	Task: First Vision – The access to death through the Underworld	83
	9.	Task: Second Vision – Accessing the root ancient temples	87
	10.	The vision	88
	11.	Task: Working with the symbols	90
	12.	Task: Readings on the symbols	91
	13.	Summary	91
	14.	Task: Practice	92
	15.	Goddess	92

Lesson 5 — The Living Dead — 93

	1.	Ghosts	94
	2.	Recordings	95
	3.	Faery or land spirit haunting	96
	4.	Parasites and demonic beings	98
	5.	Real long-term hauntings: dead people and composites	100
	6.	Composites	102
	7.	Warning – Please take note	104
	8.	The dead that cling	105
	9.	Staying in the land	106
	10.	About the practical work	108
	11.	Task: Investigating sleeping warriors	108
	12.	Task: Investigating the Treasurer's House in York	112
	13.	Optional task: Your own investigation	114
	14.	Task: Clean up	114

Lesson 6 — The Thinning of the Veils — 115

	1.	Working the death cycle	118
	2.	Summary	120
	3.	The Lyke Wake Dirge	120

Lesson 7	Inner Contacts and Inner Adepts	121
1.	The process of becoming an inner adept	122
2.	The Inner Library	123
3.	Making contact with the Inner Adepts	128
4.	Task: Meeting the Inner Adept – the vision	129
5.	Task: Routine	132
6.	Task: Pondering	132

Lesson 8	The Bound Ones	135
1.	A hell of your own making	135
2.	Trapped in the sands	136
3.	Sinking into the Abyss	139
4.	Ritually Bound Ones	141
5.	Practical work	143
6.	Reading tasks: clips from classical and older religious texts	144
7.	Module Summary	147

Module V	The Magical Tools	149

Lesson 1	Introduction and Preparation	151
1.	The tools as vessels	151
2.	Tools and the Magician's Will	152
3.	The sword	153
4.	The cup or vessel	154
5.	The shield	155
6.	No wand?	156
7.	Tools that come to you	158
8.	Odd tools	159
9.	Practical Work	160

Lesson 2	The Sword and the Vessel	161
1.	Task: Empowering the sword and vessel	163
2.	Care of the tools	168
3.	Task: Research	168

Lesson 3	The Shield	171
1.	Task: The magical stone	173
2.	Task: The cloth shield	177
3.	About the cloth shield	180
4.	The cloth and the sword	181
5.	Task: Researching the stone and female Divinity	181

| Lesson 4 | Working with the Sword and Cup | 183 |

1. About the practical work 185
2. Task: Ritual: The Anchor 186
3. About the ritual of the Anchor 189
4. Task: Doing a job 190
5. The ritual vision of Unknown Service 190
6. Summary of the job 192

| Lesson 5 | Working with the Shield and the Cord | 197 |

1. The cord 197
2. Remaking the cord 199
3. The cloth 200
4. The stone 201
5. About the practical work 202
6. Task: The ritual of balancing the water 202
7. Task: Observing the results 205
8. Summary of action 205

| Lesson 6 | Lesser-known Tools | 209 |

1. Patterns 210
2. Watchers 211
3. Bottles and dilution 212
4. Short cords 214
5. About the practical work 215
6. Task: Working with patterns 215
7. Task: Working with watchers 219
8. Task: Working with bottles, dilution and succussion 226
9. Task: Working with strings, measuring a term of service 229
10. Summary 230

| Lesson 7 | Myths as Tools | 231 |

1. Two examples of myths as tools in action 233
2. The story of Ulster and Loughareema 234
3. The story of the monster in the lake and Beowulf 239
4. Beowulf: some keys 241
5. Dissection of events at the lake 243
6. How the magician can use this method 244
7. About the practical work 245
8. How to recognise and work within mythic patterns 245
9. Task: Research 246

Lesson 8	Travelling Tools	247
1.	The travel tools	247
2.	The travel sword	248
3.	The thread of the fate cloth	249
4.	The pattern of the Scales/Threshing Floor	249
5.	The shield of ancestors	249
6.	Issues when you travel	250
7.	Task: Creating a magical sword pendant	253
8.	Task: Creating the pattern of the Scales	254
9.	Task: Creating the Shield of Ancestors	255
10.	How to use the travel tools	256
11.	Summary	257
12.	Task: Documenting the process	257

Module VI	Different Types of Beings	259
Lesson 1	Deities	261
1.	Overview of Module VI	261
2.	Deities	262
3.	What is a deity?	263
4.	What is *not* a deity?	265
5.	How and why we work with deities	266
6.	Meeting the deities	267
7.	Task: Meeting the Deity of the East	268
8.	Task: Building the connection	270
9.	Task: Meeting the Deity of the South	272
10.	Task: Meeting the Deity of the West	273
11.	Task: Meeting the Deity of the North	273
12.	Summary	274

Lesson 2	Angels	275
1.	What are angels?	276
2.	Historical context	276
3.	Angels close to humans	279
4.	Threshold angels	282
5.	Angels and the Inner Desert	283
6.	Bound angels	284
7.	Developing a working method	285
8.	Task: Vision work	286
9.	Task: Tarot readings	287
10.	Task: Research and pondering	287

Lesson 3	Demons	289
1.	Biblical demons	290
2.	Demons, destroying angels and parasites – what is what?	293
3.	Ones that act on individuals	294
4.	The Destroying Ones of Nature	295
5.	Lilith – an example of a destroying power	296
6.	Talking to the Wind – The magical power of Lilith	299
7.	The Destroying Ones of Humanity	302
8.	Composters	305
9.	Choppers	306
10.	Guardians of sacred places and temples	308
11.	Exterminators	311
12.	Bullet dodging	314
13.	Having Pazuzu round for tea	315
14.	Other 'Demonic' presentations	316
15.	The Abyss	316
16.	Task: Researching a 'demon' of your choice	317

Lesson 4	Parasites	319
1.	Parasites and brains	321
2.	Physical doorways	322
3.	Example	323
4.	Breakdown of the picture	325
5.	Identifying the triggers of infestation	327
6.	Parasites and buildings	328
7.	Egregores	329
8.	Symbiotic relationships	331
9.	Task: Vision work	332
10.	Task: Preparing a report	334
11.	Task: Parasite research	334

Lesson 5	Titans/Primordial Deities and Vast Land Beings	337
1.	Titans	337
2.	Air	339
3.	Land beings	342
4.	Mountains	343
5.	Peeling the layers off the mountain	344
6.	Oceans	347
7.	Other land features	349
8.	The land beneath you	349
9.	About the practical work	351
10.	Task: Vision of the Pivot of the Mountains	351

11.	Task: Researching the Ogdoad	355
12.	Task: Faeries research	355
13.	Task: Research on connecting with faeries	356
14.	Optional task: Researching the bright light	356

LESSON 6 — SPIRITS OF THE BODY — 357

1.	Spirits of the organs	357
2.	Who are the organ spirits?	358
3.	Heart	359
4.	Intestines	360
5.	Brain	360
6.	Why we work with the organ spirits	361
7.	Our bodies and the land	363
8.	The power networks	365
9.	Task: Meeting the heart spirit	367
10.	About the previous exercise	369
11.	Task: Going into the inner landscape of the body	369
12.	Task: Mingling inner landscapes	371
13.	Task: Affecting your body by communing with the weather	372
14.	Task: Discover the other organ spirits using vision	373
15.	Task: Read the book *Magical Healing*	373
16.	Optional task: Read up on the five spirits	373

LESSON 7 — SACRED MONARCHS, SAINTS, AND PRIESTHOODS — 375

1.	Inner priesthoods	376
2.	Sacred/magical monarchs	377
3.	The priesthoods	381
4.	Saints	383
5.	Deities as saints	384
6.	Land powers/beings as saints	386
7.	Human saints	388
8.	About the practical work	390
9.	Task: Meeting a saint	390
10.	Task: Documenting your work with the saint	391
11.	Advice	392

LESSON 8 — APPRENTICE MIDTERM SUMMARY — 393

1.	Core skills: divination, inner senses, visionary skills, ritual skills	393
2.	Understanding of magic	396
3.	Operational methods	397
4.	What to do if you reach difficulties in your studies	399
5.	The inner contacts and keys	400
6.	Task: Review	400

Appendix A	Magical Healing	403
Chapter 1	**Knowing your body: part 1**	**409**
1.	What you need to know about engines	409
2.	'Power in'	410
3.	In the beginning	410
4.	Food and drink	412
5.	Carbohydrates	412
6.	Proteins	413
7.	Drugs, medicines and alcohol	415
8.	Antidepressants	416
9.	Hypnotics, opiates, alcohol, THC and medical marijuana	418
10.	Alcohol	420
11.	Visionary and hallucinogenic drugs	420
12.	Chemical shit-storms	423
13.	Summary	426
Chapter 2	**Knowing your body: part 2**	**427**
1.	Checks and balances: energy in, energy out	427
2.	Living or working in a city	428
3.	Empathy: other people and beings	431
4.	Inner alarms	431
5.	Energetic boundaries	432
6.	Talismans	435
7.	Protecting and healing within your sphere	436
8.	Sex	437
9.	Raising kids	437
10.	Summary	438
Chapter 3	**Energy and magic**	**441**
1.	Paying the piper: the price of advanced magic	441
2.	Magic and energy	441
3.	Visionary and inner magic	442
4.	Bridging	442
5.	Inner study	444
6.	Observing to bring change: magical exploration	446
7.	Power weaving	447
8.	Energetic consequences of working with deities	448
9.	Conditional magic and body effects	450
10.	Long-term projects	451
11.	Ritualising the action	452
12.	Retirement: knowing when to back out	453
13.	Summary	453

Chapter 4	Symptoms, reasons and power dynamics	455
1.	The reactor reaching critical mass	455
2.	Magical impacts	455
3.	Examples of impacts	456
4.	Magical imbalances	459
5.	Adrenals	459
6.	Thyroid	462
7.	Gland summary	464
8.	Magical catalysts	465
9.	Beings and the disturbance of the mind	466
10.	Intrusion	466
11.	Beings meet viruses in your body	468

Chapter 8	Visionary healing: part one	471
1.	Going down the rabbit hole	471
2.	When to use visionary healing	472
3.	Stillness	473
4.	Cleaning and vacuuming, sewing and patching	473
5.	The guardians of the organs	475
6.	Colouring with the organs	476
7.	Working with the endocrine system	477
8.	The inner landscape	479
9.	Working with the patterns of life force	481
10.	Summary	483

Chapter 9	Visionary healing: part two	485
1.	The call for help	485
2.	Working with Sekhmet	486
3.	Vision of Sekhmet	486
4.	Repairing the pattern	489
5.	Finding the right realm and contacts for the job	490
6.	Approaching a contact for healing	491
7.	Summary	492

Chapter 12	Approaches to self-healing and maintenance	493
1.	Magical, emotional, and physical considerations	493
2.	Emotional baggage	493
3.	Magical maintenance	495
4.	Keeping clear of tangles	495
5.	Everything has its own time for resolution	498
6.	Energetic resources	499
7.	Scapegoating	501

8.	Physical maintenance	502
9.	Getting maintenance work done	503
10.	Astrology	504
11.	Lose the New Age bullshit	504
12.	Summary	505

Appendix B	Magic of the North Gate	507

Chapter 5	Shrines on the land	509
1.	Faery/Land spirit work	509
2.	Deity shrines	514
3.	Known deity shrines	514
4.	Local deities and ancient powers	516
5.	Befriending local spirits and ancestors, and having them live with you	517
6.	Summary	520

Introduction

2024 is the tenth year from when I started writing the Quareia course. Ten years on, I am far more aware about how some text can be timeless, and some cannot. When I was writing the first couple of modules, I was oblivious to the temporary nature of websites: I put hyperlinks into the text, only for the sites to vanish a couple of years later. Some of the books that I recommended have now also become very expensive and inaccessible. And my regional Yorkshire sayings often confused foreign students. Moreover, when our small publishing team (Stuart, Michael, and myself) published the course as books, it was the first time that we had ever done such a thing, and we made lots of spacing, editing, and layout mistakes.

The final difficulty that we didn't see coming was the size and weight of the three big books that cover the three sections of the course: the Apprentice, Initiate, and Adept books. We only make our books available online, and due to rising postage costs they now often make a loss. The large Quareia books, however, now make such a loss that they have stopped being stocked at all in many countries.

I talked with Stuart and Michael and we decided that it was time to overhaul the course, tidy it up, future-proof it, and break it down into smaller books. We also decided, wherever possible, to include the chapters from my other books that are recommended reading, along with the Quareia Course Study Guide, and any other reading material that is now public domain.

A valiant team of volunteer Quareia students stepped up, many of them writers, academics, teachers, etc., and they have gone through the course line by line to spot mistakes, dead internet links, spacing errors, and anything else that needed addressing. The result is this 2025 edition of Quareia, printed in a more accessible size and with additional material.

The book series also has a new name. This is simply because the online retailer algorithms easily mix up any books whose titles begin with 'Quareia'.

None of the magic in this course has changed, but I have occasionally adjusted rituals to make them more relevant to the age we now live in and for what is to come. (For instance, in Apprentice Module One Lesson Seven, the cleansing ritual has been expanded.) I have also provided some additional explanations. But no change is so big that students would need to re-study anything. We hope we have made the course fitter and more on-point for the times ahead around the world.

I wish you well on your magical path of adventure.

Josephine McCarthy

Read before starting the course

Pace yourself and be realistic

This is a long and sometimes difficult course which will take years, not months. It is a full magical training that will teach you everything you need to know to be a fully competent magician who can work in any system and also *know how it works, why it works, what doesn't work, and why*. As you start the course you will realise there are some lessons, like for example the meditation lessons, where you can move on to the next lesson while still practising your technique or skills. However, this course is not a race. It is not something where you can complete all three sections in a year, or even three. It is likely to be the hardest and longest training you have ever done. Just like in bodybuilding or professional athletics, the power you will gradually encounter and work with can be exhausting. Quareia training will strengthen you, push you to your limits, and open a vista of worlds to you that you never realised existed. So take your time and enjoy it, instead of racing to the finish line.

The course is also designed so that you can leave your studies at any point to take a long break, and simply pick up where you left off when you return. You do not need to go back to the beginning, even if you had a break for many years. If you leave the course and do not return, then what you will have learned from the practical work will stay within you, like magical muscle memory, and it will be useful in whatever magical or mundane path you have decided to follow.

Work alone

Quareia training is specifically designed to be studied and worked with alone. In the last hundred and fifty years in the west, magicians have become used to having teachers at hand all the time, with group workings, lodges, etc. This has facilitated weakness in magical students, as a true and powerful magical path is essentially walked alone with only occasional input from an adept whose path you cross. At present (2024) mentoring is offered free to Quareia students who have completed the Apprentice section successfully and *who have had their work and journals checked by an adept*. However, Quareia mentoring is not about teaching, but checking that you have done the work you claim to have done, so that you can be fully recognised as a Quareia Initiate or Adept, should you wish that. In the longer-term future such mentoring may not be available, so it is important that a student can work alone, though with the inner contacts, spirits, and other beings that a magician meets through their training, they will never be truly alone. Do not be tempted by study groups: in such groups there is always someone who emerges as the dominant force that everyone else defers to. The inner pattern of Quareia is magically constructed for an individual to develop self-reliance and autonomous decision making, as well as magical skills. To defer to the guidance of another will disengage a student from this pattern, as well as weaken them magically.

Keep records and journals

You are prompted repeatedly in this course to write down your experiences and findings. Some are specifically outlined as 'tasks', but there are many other 'tasks' embedded within the main texts for which you should also keep written records. Keeping detailed notes and journalling is not just about wanting to be mentored later on in your training; it is also about establishing and keeping up with an important aspect of magical training and work. Often your experiences may seem trivial, strange, or even nonsensical, but later on as you become more experienced you will realise just how important some of these 'trivial' experiences actually were.

It is good practice to keep a separate exercise book/journal for each module. At first it will mean lots of blank pages in each one. But over time you will find yourself going back to those journals and adding in more writing about subsequent realisations, additions, and flashback visions. Your journals will become your own personal magical library.

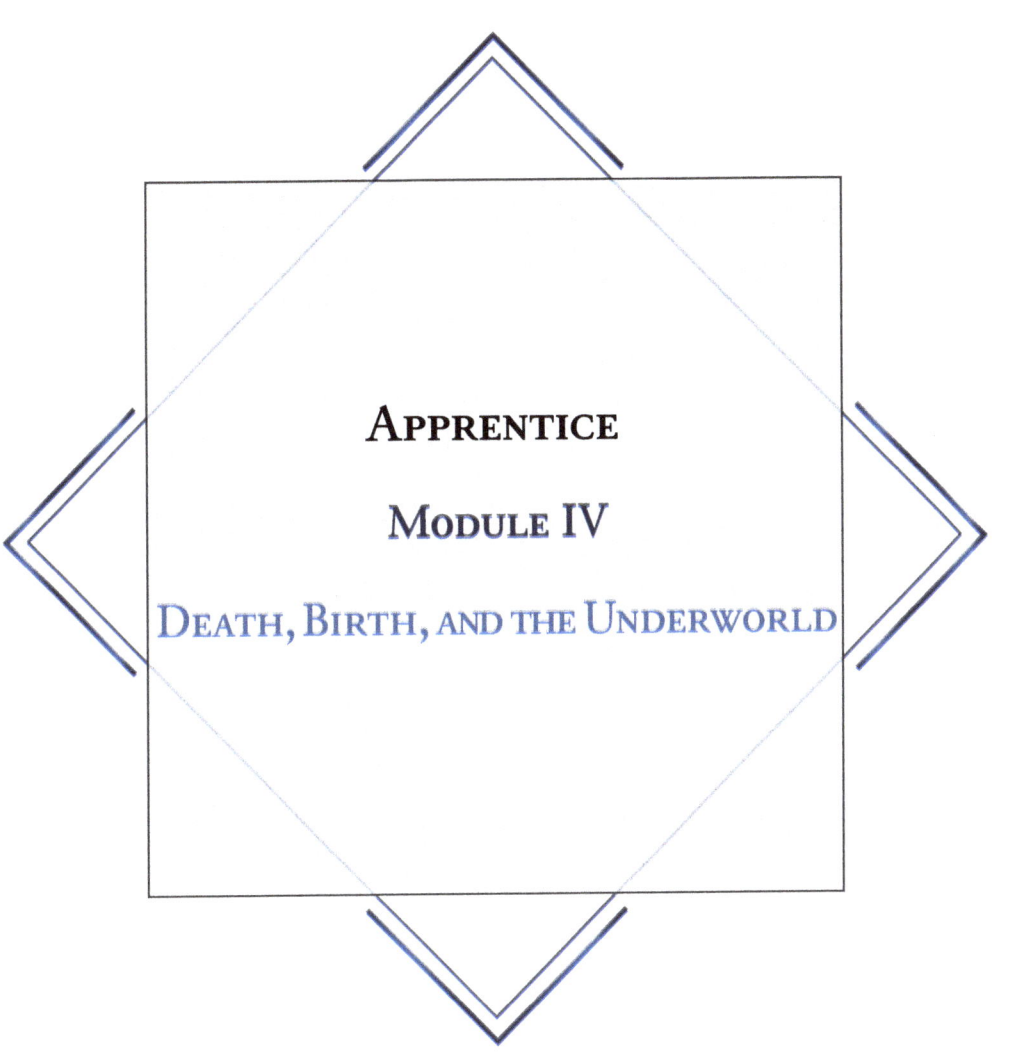

Apprentice

Module IV

Death, Birth, and the Underworld

Lesson 1
Overview

Before you move on to working with enlivened magical tools (your next module), and before you also begin the process of stepping into the inner realms in any depth, it would be wise to learn about the other side of the coin of creation. The opposing side of creation has two aspects: *death,* and *destruction.* Because they are so complex, I will address them in two separate modules. We will look at destruction a bit later in the apprentice section. In this module we will look at and work with death and the Underworld.

The reason it is so important to look at this subject matter before you get to tools, temples, beings, etc. is that understanding death is a major protector for a magician, and it helps you to spot those 'death hotspots' in your weave. When you wield an enlivened magical tool, you become visible to beings and powers that you were previously invisible to.

Interactions with those beings can inadvertently trigger one of those hotspots, and although triggering one will not necessarily put you in a death pattern, it can make your life a misery as it will cause discord in your pattern. That discord comes from not knowing certain powers that are coming at you, not understanding how to operate around those powers, and not being properly rooted.

The rooting of a magician is a key element in training that again, like many other aspects of magic, is woefully lacking in modern magical training. That rooting comes from understanding death, and magically going into the Underworld within life so that you understand and are familiar, through practical magical experience, with the Underworld and the powers that flow in and out of that realm. Through the rooting action, you are strongly anchored in the foundation of your ancestors, and anchored with an aspect of yourself in the Underworld: you have to go 'down' before you can go 'up.'

You have touched very briefly on this mechanism both in vision and in ritual, but now it is time to learn this aspect of magic in more depth, both in practical and theoretical terms. Once you come to wield magical tools properly, and step deep into the inner worlds, you will then understand why you had to do this work before you came to play with cool things like swords, wands, and all the glittery things that make magic so fashionable: if you are going to do it, do it properly!

Most (not all) of today's magical training puts tools into your hands in your apprentice stage, and does not begin to teach these Deeper Mysteries until much later (and most frequently these days, not at all). I have found that to be a self-defeating folly: know the powers *before* you work with them. Many magical systems train their initiates with these tools without the initiate being rooted, and without gnosis of what each tool truly is: what tends to happen in such circumstances is that either the work quickly devolves down into ritual drama with no power, or the magician slowly starts, mentally or emotionally, to fall apart. The other dangerous thing that happens, particularly if the initiate is a natural magician, is that they find themselves suddenly visible to all manner of beings, some of whom aggressively challenge them, and they have no knowledge of what to do, how to deal with it, or even what it is that is challenging them.

When you learn about and then work with death and the Underworld, it changes you at a very deep level: it completes a loop of power while you are still in life. That loop of birth and death is a pattern of all living things, but when a magician completes that loop in life, in gnosis, it takes them out of the uncontrolled endless pattern and puts them on a very different path. Passing through death while in life as an Initiate is a deep visionary process, and is one that is essential for any serious magician to do. The preparation for that visionary work comes during the apprentice phase of training.

I used to throw early students into the death vision when I trained groups, but I found that by doing it too early, it had a negative effect on their progress. Now, in hindsight, I have learned to tread a bit slower with students, to get them firmly anchored in mind, spirit, and body so that when they do step into the death realms as an initiate, they are truly solid and ready for work.

These days, many magical training groups have forgotten that the death-in-life work is an actual magical act, and instead they approach it as a 'self development' psychological ritual of a 'new start.' That is all well and good, but it is not the magical death within life.

As an apprentice, you learn to connect, recognise, and work with the beings that work in death; you learn to connect and work with beings that operate in the Underworld; and you learn to grow roots like a tree that hold you firm in the face of destructive power. These skills and keys put helpers and guardians in your path, and you learn to navigate, recognise, and work with the stronger powers, beings and deeper realms in a productive, safer way.

For this overview introduction lesson, we will look briefly at the various aspects of this subject matter that will then be addressed and worked with in detail in the lessons of this module, and you will be given some reading suggestions on some of the topics. I do not think it necessary, at this stage, for you to read in depth the various heavy tomes of death and the Mysteries at this stage of training, but it is necessary at least to be aware of the various writings, and have a basic idea of their approach, the reason for the writings, and a general understanding of the methods used in death (from a magician's perspective) by various ancient and not-so-ancient cultures. This in turn will prepare you for the coming lessons of this module that go into depth on the subject, so that you can get deeper into the subject matter, both in theory and in practical magical work: once you have a good basic understanding of the subject matter, you will find the coming lessons a lot easier to understand and work with.

You most likely will not understand much of anything in some of the suggested writings, and don't worry if that happens as it is expected. You do not read the suggested reading to learn them, you read them so that *the words connect with your deeper consciousness.* That is the first stage of magical learning. Later on when you have a good few modules that you have done, if you choose to, revisit those texts and you will be surprised by how much you do understand them, and how much you disagree with them in places.

In these short overviews, I will not go into explanations or discussions as such; rather it is just to outline the subject matter and give you chance to do a bit of your own research before you are plunged magically into the Death Mysteries.

1. Death in general

Before we get into the magical Mysteries of death, let's just ensure we are all on the same page, as there is so much bullshit written about death, and also so much religious programming that is warped and twisted.

The current Western religious view on death is that death is something to be terrified of, and that whether or not you were 'good' will determine where you go: either 'up,' or into holding, or 'down.' There is also an idea that if you confess your 'sins' on your deathbed, all will be well, which is not true. Death is seen as abhorrent, and very few Westerners have ever seen a dead body. When a person dies, they are whisked away, sanitised, held in a freezer, and then suitably disposed of without further family contact with the body. This is all very unhealthy for the living and the dead.

Most modern secular thinking is that after you die, it's lights out and goodbye. On the other end of the scale is the belief that you will 'pass down a dark tunnel' and emerge in a happy landscape with all your loved ones and live a surreal life with no mortgage. These different religious and secular views are degenerate, and they show just how low we have sunk into a magical/mystical dark age.

There is also a view of reincarnation that either plays into power games, "it's your lot to be poor; shut up and suffer", or into fantasy, "I was Mary Queen of Scots, you know...". The number of times I have heard that is enough to give me eye strain from rolling my eyes. Moving in magical circles, I sometimes have to venture into areas that wallow in New Age fantasy. In Glastonbury, for example, the number of folks who think they are the reincarnated 'Jesus,' Merlin, Morgan le Fey, etc. is hysterically funny and depressing at the same time.

As a people we have become disconnected from the experience of death, and of the experience of the Mysteries that lie beyond it. This disconnect becomes very apparent in magicians who have not managed to step outside of this soup of ignorance, and many leave themselves prey to fake mediums, spiritualists, or seers (which are many),

New Age nut-jobs, religious idiots, and wishful thinking. Some magicians and magical groups do work in death properly, but they are in the minority and tend to work under the radar.

We can also track, like many other things about the Mysteries, the evolution and devolution of death gnosis by looking at the texts, myths, belief systems, and artistic expressions of cultures. From the powerful mystical evolution expressed in the *Pyramid Texts*, through the less balanced but still interesting magic of the *Book of Going Forth by Day*, also known as the *Egyptian Book of the Dead*, to the degeneration in Christianity and beyond. This same evolution and devolution can also be tracked in Judaism, Greek Mysteries (before and after Greece's dark age), Tibetan, Indian, and so forth.

In Lesson 2 we will talk about death in general. We will look at the dying process from a magical perspective, track the post-death process from a magical perspective, and look into dismantling some of the dogmas we have clung to that serve only to bring difficulty and ignorance.

To help you prepare for that, look into different cultures and how they act with the body after death. Some cultures bury the body straight away, take down pictures of the dead person, and refuse to mention their name. Some cultures dig up the bones of their ancestors once a year to have dinner with them (yes... interesting). Some keep the body in the house and go through certain rites over a period of days before they are finally buried (how I grew up).

Find a way to research sensibly about different traditions and how they handle the dead. If you use the internet, use Google Scholar, if you do not, libraries that carry books on anthropology, social history, and religions can be a good source of information, as can talking to older people from different cultures. Don't be tempted to look at fantasy New Age books, or psychology books as it will not be helpful to you. You don't need to do any deep reading, just get an overview.

2. Death and the Mysteries

This is where death starts to get interesting. A magical understanding of death, and the ability to pass into the realm of death in order to work, is a major stepping stone for a magician. Every Mystery system around the world has, at some point or other, discovered, worked with, and then written about the realm of death. The realm of death is not a standalone realm; rather it is a part of a much bigger picture of a realm that exists within, around, and which is woven into the manifest world: it is the inner world of which the outer world is a physical manifestation.

Some ancient cultures worked within the inner realm as a part of their physical mystical life, while others strove to leave the physical world behind and step into the inner world as the 'real world.' The Greeks and early Christians were some who took this escapist approach. As an understanding of the guardians and gates of this realm became more known, the magician priests and priestesses of certain cultures figured out how to try and dodge these guardians and bypass natural spiritual evolution.

Whenever this manipulation appeared in a culture, that culture then began its descent into ignorance. The key is not to dodge, lie, trick, or bully your way through these guardians by having the right names, the right tale to tell, or the right ritual actions, but to enter these realms in a clear and balanced way so that the guardians recognise you and let you pass voluntarily.

One thing that does become apparent in virtually all of these ancient cultures is a similar attitude to rebirth: that reincarnation is for the lesser mortals. As one ancient Egyptian text put it:

"Being trapped in the net of souls[1] is for the common man."

The key was (and is) to develop well as a magician and a human being, to become recognised as such by the inner world guardians, and to flow through the inner worlds in magical work until you have a deep soul level understanding of how balance works (this is why the Scales feature so strongly in some ancient Mysteries).

Then, when the magician dies, he or she can make a choice, a conscious choice born out of necessity, and decide where and how they wish to move forward: do they need for some reason to come back into life, or do they wish to stay in the inner realms on the threshold of the manifest world in order to work with the living, or do they need to move deeper into the inner worlds and step out of the pattern of the manifest world completely?

Not only is it important, vastly important, for the magician to learn about death in life for his or her own death, but also because of the massive unfolding that triggers as a result of that work in the magician's life: essentially it is one of the key actions that plugs you in. This is why the 'death in life' features so strongly in ancient Mystery cults, where it either shows as death visions/rituals, or a 'passing into the Underworld and traversing of the stars.' Remnants of that can be seen in the well-meant but essentially useless psychodramas around death that we see in today's modern 'Mystery cults.'

Here is a list of things to read/look up. These are just a small selection of texts from around the world: should you wish to delve deeper/wider into more ancient cultures, read the list below first, as it will then help you to spot the Mysteries in other cultures. If these books have become expensive, then see if you can find the text on the internet, or if your local library can get you a copy. If the texts are inaccessible to you, don't worry about it, it will not affect your studies at this phase of your training.

---

[1] Rebirth

Browse through them so that you get an idea of what approach that particular culture is taking at that time. Some of the text and images you will now begin to recognise; many you will not at this stage of your training. Don't try to psychologise or philosophise around the texts; just let them sit with you and let the imagery surface in your mind, and compare it with what you already know. And you do not have to study these in depth or read them cover to cover as it is not necessary, and in my opinion would be counterproductive to you at this stage. Just look them over, dip in where you are drawn, and then ponder on the words.

The Tibetan Book of the Dead: The Great Liberation through Hearing in the Bardo

This is a complied book that tries to codify and organise what are essentially very different writings. When Walter Evans-Wentz came across these various writings, like every organised Westerner, he had to control it, bring it into order, and make it fit things he already knew. This book, which is presented as a coherent path through death, is not how it is, or was, used. Interactions between the living and the dead, and between the living and the inner worlds, are not neat and tidy, and do not follow a linear path that is easily mapped.

So when you come to look through this book, keep it in mind that these writings were, and are, used in a more fluid way (and the same goes for the Egyptian ones), and not all were used; nor is it a 'bible' of Tibetan Death Mysteries. Each area and each lineage had their own version, and in truth it is a series of scattered writings that are drawn upon.

Note, however, in the title the emphasis on hearing. Knowing what you now know about sound, utterance, and the power of the word, that will give you more insights. These texts are spoken to the body of the dead person, as the spirit/soul stays near the body for quite some time. Not only do they tell the spirit what to do, but the utterance of a Mystery also changes the web, the power, and the space around the newly dead person's spirit: it is also a form of assistance.

> **Note:** Originally in the course, I suggested the reading some of the *Utterances of the Egyptian Pyramid Texts*. However I have since found over the years that reading them only confused students more as the writings can be obscure and difficult to understand, so I have removed that suggestion. It is no loss to the student and will not affect their understanding of the subject.

The *Pyramid Texts* from the Old Kingdom period in Egypt's history are essentially a collection of utterances that guide the king through the Divine transformation. It is, as far as I know, the earliest text to talk about 'the Ladder' i.e. a mode of ascent from the land to the stars.

The Book of Coming Forth by Day (Papyrus of Ani)

You have already visited this text in the last module. Now you will look a bit deeper.

Whereas the *Pyramid Texts* outline the passage of the Divine Transformation of the King, and that transformation is very dependant on the king's upholding of Ma'at in his life and spirit, the *Papyrus of Ani* (one of many versions of the *Book of Going forth by Day*) is more about the transformation of the spirit by way of a journey through the Underworld, known in the Egyptian texts as the Duat. It emerged at the beginning of the New Kingdom period and has a strongly developed dynamic of judgement/being weighed on the Scales, and the passage through a series of gates in the Duat. Each gate has a guardian and the dead person must demonstrate that they have the right knowledge and the right utterances to say in order to pass through each stage of the Duat.

In utterance 125 of the *Papyrus of Ani*,[2] the dead person stands before the Gods of the Tribunal and declares his innocence in the form of 42 Negative Confessions i.e.

"O He-Who-is-Blood who came forth from the place of slaughter,
I have not done grain profiteering."

The 42 confessions declare the crimes he has not done. When I first read these, including ones like 'I never lied', I assumed they were about the whole life of the person: it is impossible to go through a whole life without one little untruth, for example. I still had this assumption when I first started writing the course, so I posited that the Negative Confessions were a form of magical manipulation: recipe magic or magical manipulation to dodge the guardians of the Duat. So in the original form of the course, in this lesson, I presented the *Book of the Dead* as powerful, but also as having magical manipulation within it. I saw it as a degeneration from earlier funerary texts.

However, with ten years more experience of focusing on Egyptian funerary texts, I realised it was not the texts that had degenerated, *but the humans who used them had*. Through life we are constantly presented with our weaknesses and given a chance to recognise them and evolve beyond them. What Ani was saying in his 42 Negative Confessions is:

"I have evolved and my evolved self has not broken these rules."

This is an important understanding and is still relevant for magical death today: have we evolved and has our subsequent behaviour changed?

When you read the 42 Negative Confessions, pay particular attention to them. Remember your work with the Grindstone and the Unraveller, with the Threshing Floor, and the practice of reviewing your mistakes and learning from them so that you learn to self-limit in life? What you are reading in The *Book of Going Forth by Day*

---

[2] Translation by Dr Raymond Faulkner 1972.

is the Egyptian version of the same magical dynamic. The dead person is declaring that they have been through the process, and their Threshing Floor has yielded a good Harvest of Truth.

The *use* of the *Book of Going Forth by Day* in Egyptian culture went from it being a text of guidance for the dead King, to a text that any rich noble could buy for their tomb from the priest scribes. This is apparent from the versions that have been found where the text is written by one hand, and the name of the dead had been inserted by another hand – the handwriting was different. By the time this was happening (later in the New Kingdom period) it reflected a slow point of descent of the Mysteries in Ancient Egypt. The layer of society in Egypt at this time that had wealth and status, obviously felt that by having the papyrus of *The Book of Going Forth by Day*, with its declaration of innocence, would protect them from the Underworld judgement of their life of many crimes. Except magic never really works that way. I find it interesting that such people didn't fear breaking the rules of Ma'at but did fear judgement enough to buy what would have been a very costly papyrus, to be buried with them. Unless of course by this stage of the society, it was simply a status symbol.

The Book of Am-Tuat

> *"He who knows these words will approach those who dwell in the Netherworld. It is very very useful for a man upon Earth."*
>
> — Concluding text of the Second Hour

The *Book of Am-Tuat* (Duat) tells the dead king about the various thresholds and guardians in the Underworld so that he may traverse them safely and ascend into the sky to traverse the sky like/with Ra. It is basically a *who is who* guide to the Duat that first appeared in its complete form in the tomb of Thutmose III.[3] At that point in time it was only used for the kings, and appeared in 20th dynasty royal tombs in parts, mixed with other funerary texts such as sections of the *Book of Gates* and the *Book of Caverns*. By the end of the New Kingdom period, the Am Duat was appearing on the tomb walls of anyone who could afford it – it lost its royal and sacred use, and became an obvious status symbol. Look through the text, which tells the king what, and who, resides in the Underworld, and see what you think about what was going on in the Mysteries at that time in Egyptian history, and *what was not*.

---

[3] 18th dynasty New Kingdom Egypt.

3. Working magically in death while alive

One of the things we will explore and work with at an apprentice level is working with and in death while still being alive. Although you will not step into death fully until you are at Initiate level, standing on the thresholds in vision, observing, and seeing the beings that work in death are major parts of your leap forward in the Mysteries. From there you learn to work with the newly dead in this realm, and also in the death realm. It is part of the work of a magician to work with the newly dead where needed and appropriate, and before you can get to that level of work, you first need to know how to ascertain if a newly dead person needs help, and when it is best to leave them to it.

Not quite on this topic, but related to everything within this module, is a short piece of writing by Plato that is very pertinent to this subject matter. That piece of writing is called *The Vision of Ayr the Armenian,* which appears in Plato's *Republic,* Book Ten (X). You may have already read this. If you have, then read it again in the context of the subject matter of this module. If you have not already read it, then now is the time to do that. It is not a long piece at all, but it is packed with very illuminating aspects, and you may recognise the roots of many magical concepts around fate.

4. The dead in the living world

One of the things that is really useful for a magician to learn about and work with is the knowledge of the dead in the world of the living. The most common ones that we in the Western world encounter are ghosts, sleepers, and ancient ancestors. We will look at the issues around hauntings, the various problems that arise when a spirit stays around the living, and how to recognise when there is a problem.

5. The Underworld and the Abyss

Knowledge of and practical familiarity with the realm of the Underworld is essential for all magicians, and the earlier you connect with it, the better. Volumes have been written about the Underworld and Abyss in modern terms, but few of those tomes even begin to touch on what the Underworld and Abyss is about. In ancient writings you have to stretch back pretty far to find a good outline of this realm, but another way of having a preview of it before we get to that lesson is to sit and look at the paintings of William Blake.

In fact, the works of William Blake are a wonderful example of magical art: he was touching into some very deep visions and realms with his work. The filter they flow through is Christian: Blake had a strong connection with the Divine as connected with via the Christian filter, and yet he considered the church and its structure to be not worth the time of day (sensible man). He was an eccentric and a visionary:

for you as an apprentice magician to spend time looking through his paintings would be time well spent indeed. You don't need to like them as this is not an exercise in art taste, it is an exercise in looking at how people from different cultures and religions envisioned God, the Underworld, death, angels, etc.

The paintings will not tell you directly about the Underworld and Abyss (or the inner worlds and angelic beings, of which he painted many), but the true inner knowledge and power that flows through these paintings will touch you deeply indeed whether you are aware of it or not – his paintings *mediate* magical power. The lesson on the Underworld will take you on your first steps of visionary descent into the Underworld so that you can begin the preparation process that will lead to the act of stepping into death while in life: something that you will do as an initiate.

6. Inner contacts and inner adepts

The lesson on inner contacts and adepts will take you through the process of how these people come to step into the inner worlds in service. These people, who once lived as adept magicians and priests/priestesses, are an invaluable source of support, advice, assistance, and guidance to any magician wishing to work with any level of power. You will also learn how to work in vision with these contacts, how to connect with them, and how to access and operate through the inner structure known as the Inner Library: a central and critical visionary interface for magicians.

7. The Bound Ones

The last lesson in the module looks at the phenomenon of the Bound Ones, humans and other beings who are bound up and held within the Desert and the sands of death. Although as an apprentice you will not work around this issue, it is an important one for apprentices to know about: it directly links in to what you learned in the last module and will deepen your understanding of some of the powers and dynamics that flow through life and death.

8. Summary

Read and take notes from the suggested texts wherever possible, and as I said earlier, there is no need to read all of the texts completely, other than *the Vision of Ayr* in Plato's *Republic*; read that whole vision, which is quite short. Rather it is just a matter of getting used to the texts if you can. It is really worth the effort if you can get a hold of them, and also worth the effort to read texts that are written in a way that you are not used to. They are not easy to read, and are even harder to understand. Don't worry about that, the texts are magical so what is necessary will flow into you energetically. One day, maybe years later, you will be surprised how much you understand the text when you remember or revisit it. It is also simply about getting more of an idea of what particular cultures were working on in terms of the Mysteries and death, and looking at how they approached them, for good or bad.

Once you have read what you need to read and have taken some notes for yourself, then it is time to move straight to the next lesson. Have your notes and the texts handy.

If you can, acquire a copy of *The Pyramid Texts:* of all the books listed in this lesson, this is the one to own in the flesh. Keep it close to you throughout this module, and if you wish to experiment with sleep/dream learning, place the book over your head (on a shelf) or under your pillow at night: sleep with the book. It is a strange and to many, incomprehensible book that seems to constantly defeat the reader. And yet, it is a bundle of pure magic that will jump out at you and reveal parts of itself to you when necessary. This is a very old-fashioned way of working, and one which recognises that some texts, just by their sheer subject-matter, carry power and connection with them.

I used to do this in my twenties when I could not penetrate the meaning of a text. I would sleep each night with the book, and slowly but surely a sort of strange understanding of the book began to surface in my mind. It was not that I read the book in my sleep; rather it was that my spirit interacted with the energies of the book and the energies of the Mysteries portrayed in the text: I 'got it' at a deep level. It works for some folks and not others, and can be a fun experiment.

Write down any pertinent things that come to mind, any 'ah-has,' and any understandings that come to you from reading the texts and looking at the pictures. Later, you can compare those understandings with what you have learned and discovered by the end of the module.

Lesson 2

Regular Death

Before we get to the Inner Mysteries, where we will look how magicians work and pass through death, let's first look at the actual dying and death process in general. What follows here is based on my own experiences of death and from working with people who are dying or who recently died. I realise that I probably only understand about 10% of what there is to know about the death process from an inner point of view, and I do not want to write from theory or conjecture. It is important that every step in this magical path of Quareia is rooted in experience, not theory.

There is a lot of theorising written about death in magical circles. Some of it touches upon real experiences, but a lot is theory from old texts and the conclusions drawn from those texts, along with a peppering of modern thinking. But as a magician, your work must always be grounded in direct experience, and by the time you come to the latter part of your training you will have had plenty of experience, both through this course and through things placed in your path that you can draw upon. So although I am writing from that 10% pot of experience, it is consistent experience, and working with that experience has brought profound change not only to me, but to those whom I worked with and around.

Most (but not all) death work, in magical terms, is vision work, divination, charts, and inner contacts. There is some ritual work, but not a lot: it is a process of interiorising for the spirit, not exteriorising. So the magician would not use a lot of ritual work other than to open and close gates, or to lay paths, give shelter, etc. Let's look at the process first from the act of dying and go in deeper a step at a time. I will give practical information for you, as you are very likely to be put in a position of having to deal with someone who is going through the death process: the more you do magic, the more you are put to work.

1. Slow Death

The first aspect of dying we will look at is the *slow death*. This is the most common aspect of death that you as a magician will likely be prompted to work with, particularly if you are also clergy of some sort. The majority of Pagan/occult ritual, like Christian ritual, and information about death tends to focus on the family left behind, but there is very little for the actual person who is on the threshold of death.

When someone is going through a slow death, for example someone with cancer, the spirit is usually already stretching itself out upon a web pattern of energy that is about *lives,* not merely this life. Remember your web of fate? There is another octave of this and that is the *web of lives.* Just as your web of fate has hotspots on it, the web of lives also has hotspots, and those hotspots are different lives.

As the body engages with the dying process, sometimes (not always) the spirit/soul starts stretching out in search of a new hotspot or life within its fate pattern that it can manifest through. This process shows very clearly in divination: the readings often show the new life and new parents lining up before the old life is completely finished. It seems to be an instinctive rather than a conscious impulse.

If a person has lived their life in a very closed-down mundane way that is totally devoid of any mystical, magical, or spiritual consciousness, they are prone to be constantly seeking a new life on the threshold of death. As the old life draws to an end, the soul desperately casts around its web of existence looking for a new life to connect into.

By 'closed-down' I mean someone who is wrapped up in their own life of consuming, and is totally unaware of anything else around them. It is not about religion or being a spiritual person or a mystical person; it is more a matter of them being either *switched on* at a deep level, or *switched off*. For example, someone who is non-religious, non-magical, etc. but has a sense of awe at life, who is aware that their actions affect others (not in a moral sense, but in a true sense), and feels at a deep level that there is something more – that is a *switched on* person.

By contrast, someone who is only out for themselves and is totally unaware of life around them, who fills their life with what suits them best to the detriment of everything around them, and who has no problem destroying others to get what they want when they want it – that is a *switched off* person. As they lie dying, their need to get what they want, life at all costs, drives their deeper spirit to cast around for another life to slip into. And so the pattern of life and death without any conscious engagement continues.

Someone who is *switched on* is less likely to line up another life while they are still dying, though it does happen, or else the stretching out comes a bit later when they are closer to the point of death. Someone who is very *switched on* will not cast about at all: the spirit stays still, waiting, and as they pass through the death process, *then* you start to see in divination the crossroads of choosing. It can be very apparent in readings to see a person like this spending time in stillness and waiting.

So let's get back to death. Even if the person is unconscious or in a coma, *they can still hear,* either in a physical way or in a spirit way. It is really important to communicate with the dying, as most people tend to be terrified at that point, regardless of their spiritual maturity. But it is the body that panics, not the person or the spirit of the person themselves. This is also a very important distinction to make. The brain puts out panic signals, the adrenals go nuts and the person may start panting quickly once they are very close to death. This is called Cheyne-Stokes breathing. It ranges back and forth from panting/hyperventilating to long drawn out pauses between slow breaths. The breathing may also become noisy which is known as the death rattle, as mucus builds up in the lungs and throat.

This can be seen in a person who is unconscious or semiconscious and is hyperventilating from fear: it is a common occurrence and causes a lot of unnecessary suffering. On the medical side, this should be immediately addressed with Valium or something similar to calm the person down. From the magical side of things, this should be addressed by talking to the person using mediated utterance. By that, I mean talking using empowered magical speech. It is important to address both the body panic, and the spirit that is panicking because the body is panicking. This can take the form of simply talking to them to calm them, and telling them it is going to be okay, but doing so with the gates open behind you, the contacts or Noble One beside you, or through mediating the Divine Breath as you speak.

This is at its most powerful when you are reading out loud or recounting a sacred text connected to death or prayer. By doing this, it stills the space around the dying person, reaches the deep spirit, and calms them to a point where they are less likely to rashly jump or cling to another life in panic: it gives them breathing space. The other thing to do is to hold their hand and allow your deeper spirit to talk to theirs. This is a good way to work if you are in a hospital room full of people and with a person trying to die peacefully amongst noise, family, and bustle.

Holding the hand of the dying person, while also mediating the void within you, and opening the gates in your mind while also chatting to the people around the dying person is a profound service to the dying: that takes skill and focus, but it is a great service. The chatting normalises the space for the dying person; the breathless reverent silence or whispers around a dying person can be counterproductive to a stressed-out spirit.

Normal chatting, while also conducting deep mediation across the thresholds, can make a major difference to a dying person. The reverse of this is true if the person is dying in gnosis: when a magician or priest is dying, often they need calm and quiet in order for their spirit to start lining itself up for death. Quiet companionship is a great service under such circumstances.

From the dying person's perspective, they are withdrawing more and more from the outside conscious world, and many drift in a semiconscious haze (if they are not in a coma), so bear that in mind. They will hear you and hear what is around them, but they often cannot respond. So do be careful about your words around the dying. One thing I have seen over and over again which I find interesting, is that many times, when a person is in a coma or unconscious, they sometimes wake up just at the point of death. If you find yourself at a bedside, just be ready for that, just in case, and be ready to hold the gate wide open for them (something you will learn later in this module).

Slow deaths of magicians, priests, and priestesses

If a magician (or priest/priestess) is dying, they should already know what they are doing and what is happening to them. What they will need, if you are in attendance, and if it is possible is this: the four directions lit, the gates wide open with the inner contacts on the thresholds, the underside of their feet anointing with consecrated oil, moisture upon their lips, and their enlivened vessel/cup/lantern in or by their right hand. If they do not work with or have such tools, just anoint the right hand with frankincense oil or similar sacred oil.

Let's take a moment to look at the 'whys' behind those ritual actions, and bear in mind that they all have a very good reason to be done. And this is why it is preferable to die at home if possible rather than in a hospital bed, so that the ritual actions can be attended to. First we will look at this from the perspective of the dying magician. The optimal situation for a dying magician or priest/priestess is a death that is not only medically eased (pain relief) but is also *magically* eased.

The gates should be open (the directions opened), and the gate of the west should be *widely* opened, which involves someone opening the gates, having two candles instead of one (a bit like landing lights on a runway!) to light the threshold, and the view of the death vision triggered beyond the gates. To do this, the carer 'sees' the vista of the death vision in their mind as they open the west gate and they keep that image strong in their heads as they sit by the dying person.

The anointing of the feet with consecrated frankincense oil is an old and deeply powerful but simple magical action: the feet carry the person into death, and the soles of the feet are anointed to ensure that they tread unhindered over the lights upon the path that are left there by the Noble Ones. This is not a symbolic action; rather it is a magical action. While the body and spirit are still connected (which can continue for days after death), what happens to the outer feet of the dying person affects the 'inner feet'. If you are sensitive and have good visionary technique, then when a person is close to death, if you place your hands upon their shoulder or head and 'feel' down the inner expression of the body, often the right foot cannot be felt: they have 'one foot in the grave.'

The slow death comes up from the feet, and the inner body of the person seems to withdraw from the bottom up. Using consecrated oil 'tunes' the spirit's footfall on its journey, and prevents any parasites sticking to them as they begin to journey through death (a problem that is very common in slow deaths).

Moisture on their lips is another outer action that affects the inner spirit of the dying person. There is a dynamic that happens with the element of water in death (covered in the next chapter), and the way this dynamic expresses to the spirit while it is still connected to the body is through thirst. The dying magician will know to 'reel' in the impulses of the body at this time, and that knowing has to be at a deep, unconscious level: chances are the magician will not be very conscious, hence certain

Mysteries have to be deeply embedded within the dying magician's psyche for them to activate in such circumstances: *the body and spirit have to know as well as the intellect.* And that comes from years of training and work as a magician or mystic.

The touch of moisture upon the lips, or the washing of the magician's face, triggers a response in the body which in turn alerts the spirit to what is coming and what to do. A switched off person newly arrived in death rages with a thirst that almost overwhelms them:

> *"They are the souls who are destined for Reincarnation;*
> *and now at Lethe's stream they are drinking*
> *the waters that quench man's troubles, the deep draught of oblivion…*
> *They come in crowds to the river Lethe, so that you see,*
> *with memory washed out they may revisit the earth above."*
>
> — Virgil, *Aeneid 6*

For a magician, mystic, or priest/priestess, the training of how to self-limit truly becomes a gift at this time, and the person knows, at the deepest most profound level, not to 'drink of the waters.' We see this, as living people working in vision, as a river that many have the compulsion to drink from. To a newly dead person, it is an energetic impulse that triggers at a deep level, but the trained or switched on person knows not to act on that energetic impulse.

The bathing of the dying magician's face, or the tracing of water upon their lips, reminds them of this impulse, and often, particularly with a magician or a switched on person, when they are offered fluid to drink when they are close to death, they will turn away or clamp their lips shut.

This happened when my mother was very close to death and I, along with other family members, was by her side. My sister kept trying to offer her fluid, as my mother's lips were very dry. My mother, who was semiconscious, kept turning her face away from the offer, which my sister found very distressing. My mother knew what she was doing; my sister did not. If you see this impulse in a dying person, to turn away from the offer of moisture, you know that they are clued in and the spirit knows what it is doing – you do not need to interfere.

The enlivened vessel in the hand is part of the Deep Mysteries, and is echoed in folk magic as placing a coin in the hand, mouth, or over the eyes of the dead person in order to 'pay the ferryman.' The enlivened vessel (or scales) that the magician worked with magically in life will hold (just as water holds) the sum *Harvest* of that magician's life. Remember the fragments on the Threshing Floor that the being of the vessel was picking through in your ritual vision work? Those fragments were your Harvest up to that point. Another way of looking at this, from a Judaic point of view, is the Book of Judgement: the sum total of your actions recorded.

The vessel, holding the energetic information of your scales, is what triggers different levels of guardians at the threshold of the death journey. This is not about good deeds and bad deeds: that is a degeneration of a much deeper knowledge. It is about what dynamics of balance that mind and spirit has learned and acted upon: the balance of Ma'at within life. Where the magician has not got their cup or didn't work with the cup, an anointed right hand serves the purpose. In the progression of the Mysteries, the adepts cup becomes a lantern, and the lantern eventually becomes a Light that shines in the Darkness. It is a still bright flame that appears in the palm of the right hand, and it is the light that is 'weighed' against Ma'at.

When the sum total of your Harvest is given/shown to the 'ferryman' or threshold keeper, it is not payment; rather it is showing the keys of your development in life as a human being. That is seen as different frequencies of energy, and those frequencies decide what level of the threshold opens for you.

At the point of death

At the point of death, if you are with someone at that point, your job as a magician is simply to *hold the space* in a clear, balanced, and powerful way.

Often this translates in practical terms to having to appear normal amidst a crying family while doing your magical work silently in your head and through your hands. And sometimes the point of death is not pretty. Sometimes death is fairly peaceful, with only a few tremors of the hand, or 'stoking'-style breathing just at the point of death. But at other times it can get messy, with vomiting or diarrhoea at the point of death. When this happens, your job is not to react, but simply to continue doing what you are doing. Let others worry about the mess of the body as you facilitate the separation between body and soul.

If you are at the beside of someone who is dying, particularly if it is a slow death from something like cancer, it might be an idea to gently warn the other family members that it could possibly get messy: we do not all have TV-inspired deaths.

2. Upon the threshold of death

At the point of death and shortly after, the dying person often has a slight recognition of the gates opening, and they perceive this as seeing light, or even seeing beings (who often cross-dress from the minds of the dying). More than once I have been at the point of death with someone who could speak, and they invariably became aware of the inner world as they died. I have found that immediately after the death it is as though the soul/spirit steps into a place of silence briefly: in vision this shows as if they have vanished, but it is short and temporary, like the resetting of a clock.

But I have also found that the body still continues to hear after death, which sounds bizarre, I know. The spirit and body do not fully separate straight away: it seems for many (but not all) to be a slow processes of disengagement that in our terms of time seems to happen over a few hours and days. This must be taken into consideration when you are around a newly-dead person: they still hear you. The spirit of the person often has an aspect that stays close to their body for a few days, and I have no idea how this mechanism of hearing in conjunction with a dead body works, only that it does in most (not all) cases.

There is an utterance that can be used immediately after the death while you are still with the body. But it is not an utterance for people you do not know, or who were simply acquaintances. It is an utterance for people who are very close to you such as a partner, child, parent, lover, sibling, or best friend, etc. The reason for this is that as a magician, uttering these words will connect you to the death process that the spirit goes through, and it can draw upon your vital force. That will manifest for you as sudden but profound moments of exhaustion or fear. So use it wisely. It is a beautiful utterance that is a part of chapter 43, the Book of Isaiah, and is occasionally used in Christian funerals, though rarely these days. It is a very old utterance that has its roots in the Egyptian temple practice, and while no magic runs through it when it is uttered by a mundane person, it can switch on powerfully when uttered by a magician:

> Fear not, for I have called you by your name and you are mine.
> When you pass through the waters I will be with you,
> and the rivers will not overflow you.
> When you walk through the fire you will not be burned,
> nor will the flame kindle upon you,
> for you are precious in my eyes, and honourable,
> and I have loved you.

As you can see, you are uttering protection to them, and that protection will partly come from you, so you have to be willing to take on that burden while they go through the early stages of death.

In the time between death and burial or cremation, the spirit often goes through a period of 'visiting' the people they were strongly connected to in life. Some people have a strong enough focus to be able to bridge between the non-physical world and the physical world to make their presence known. Other times they simply visit and then leave without being able to let you know they have visited you.

In my family, these visits do tend to bridge the physical and non-physical, and this often plays out through the blowing of light bulbs. When someone in my family who was close to me dies, they sometimes turn up in my house (and the houses of other inner-sighted women in the family) and all the light bulbs blow, one after the other. It can get rather expensive. My nephew's favourite action with his mother (my sister) was to visit and blow the TV up: he died in particularly difficult circumstances, and he continued to visit her for some years on the anniversary of his death.

This strong energetic output while trying to communicate, besides being very spectacular when witnessed, also gives us a little insight into the energies the dead can operate through: electrical things tend to be an easy and favourite way for the dead to try and signal their presence. Whether this is intentional or not, I don't know.

Because of these varied factors, learning to speak to the newly dead, both with your voice and your mind, can alleviate a lot of suffering, fear, and confusion not only in the newly dead person but also in the people around them. Often the dead person just wants you to know they still exist and that all is okay.

Some newly dead do not go through this, and seem to have stretched out so far during the last phases of their illness that they simply vanish deep into death straight away. Others, often magicians, immediately walk off into death with gnosis and purpose, often only visiting one or two people briefly to say goodbye, and some do not even do that.

When a properly prepared magician steps into death, they immediately drop all connection to the living world and move forward without looking back. That can be a painful thought for the living, but it is the healthiest of all actions for the dead. Again, we will look at that in more depth in the next lesson.

From a magical point of view, for the time between death and funeral/burial/cremation, the living magician who is assisting in this death has a few things they can do to assist the passage of the dead. One is to keep a space fully tuned, with gates open, flames going, and the magician's ritual tools out so that there is a temple space that the dead can come into.

This enables them to communicate with you in a more controlled way (through vision), but also gives them a holding place where they can stay, settle themselves, and prepare for the deeper walk into death. It also gives them a balanced space that is governed by Ma'at where they can go through their own life reassessment process before they step completely over the threshold.

But once the burial/cremation is done, the gates should be closed, the lights extinguished, and the dead soul should not be encouraged to hang around. If a soul chooses to hang around and not step further into death, it must be purely their own decision, and not one enabled by the living magician.

3. Religious aspects of death

Some religious ritual patterns for death can be very helpful, and some are totally useless and only there for the people left behind. A Catholic high requiem mass, for example, will often trigger the opening of the gates and ensure the dead person goes through them, often with a ritual firm hand just to make sure.

Some religious rituals, for example in Tibetan Buddhism and some other forms of Buddhism, talk to the spirit of the person to ensure they know what to do and where to go: reciting of texts reminds the spirit of what they had learned in life, and reminds them of the path that now needs to be taken.

Some people traversing death (and we get this report back from near-death experiences also) 'see' or encounter religious figures like saints, Jesus, prophets, etc.

These are the beings that work in death, and they will often cross-dress from the mind of the dead person in order to connect and communicate with a frightened and traumatised soul.

I have watched numerous times in death situations where a being, usually angelic, approaches a newly dead person, and as they get closer to the person, they transform into a human, usually dressed in a religious personality of some sort or other. Though I have also seen an angelic being transform into a heavily-breasted young blond girl in order to entice a comatose testosterone-fuelled teen into death (it worked: the teen died at that point as I was observing in vision). Religious and mystical texts either guide people through the death stages, or they give the mind something to cling to (imagery).

When people who are switched off die without any religious, mystical, or inner reference point it is often messy and traumatising for their spirit, and also for those left behind. However, I have seen very peaceful transitions done by people who are atheist scientists, who nevertheless understand the dynamics of energy, consciousness, vibration, and frequency: they are essentially understanding the Mysteries from an entirely different perspective, but it is a deep understanding nonetheless: they are switched on. And that understanding facilitates them through the death process.

4. Energetic clinging

This is a particularly distressing problem that happens in death and around death, and something that as a magician you really need to know about. This can happen around a slow death or a quick death.

The factors that trigger energetic clinging are being switched off, being terrified, and being used to not taking responsibility for oneself (again, the skills and maturing one acquires in life come in very handy at death). A person who dies unwillingly and who is absolutely terrified, and who is used to grabbing what they want, will instinctively *grab* for the nearest living human and cling to them. This creates an immediate and powerful energy drain upon the living person who is being clung to, and in some cases can drag them into death also. We see this as a sudden death in someone who is close to a newly dead person. When we die we revert to our unguarded selves. If the unguarded self is a mess, then this mess will come to the fore at the threshold of death. So a selfish, clinging person who is dying is very likely, upon death, to try and cling to someone near to them.

However, energetic clinging can also happen when the death is sudden, unexpected, or the spirit does not immediately realise what has happened. The instinct is to reach out and grab – a bit like grabbing for arms as you fall off a cliff. In this case it is not done out of selfishness, but out of sudden fearful instinct. This has happened to me a few times, so I tend to tread carefully around dying people I do not know.

A few years back, when I was in the States, I was driving through a junction and a motorist to the side of me slammed his brakes on for some reason and a motorcyclist ran straight into the back of him at quite a speed. The motorcyclist was catapulted off his bike and he went straight through the windscreen at the back of the car.

It all happened so fast, and I was trying to focus on the cars around me at the intersection, which was suddenly thrown into chaos. I saw the biker, his head stuck in the back window of the car beside me, and I instinctively went into the void as I pulled over. This is why it is important to practise these basic magical actions so they become instinctive responses, not conscious actions.

The ambulance and police were called. There was nothing more to be done, and standing around staring was not a good thing to do. People had gathered, and everything that could be done was being done. I was also tired and was just at the start of a long illness, so I drove back off after leaving witness details.

As I drove, I got more and more weary. And it was not a natural weariness: it was the feeling I have learned to recognise and know as the product of something seriously dragging on my life force. I staggered back to where I was staying and got into bed. It took me a little while to realise what was happening, and it was only when I noticed that my heart was racing and that I was not only shocked but terrified, and that this was not my own emotion that I realised I had picked up the biker as I drove past his moment of death. His spirit, in the sudden panic, had grabbed at the nearest thing he could: me. It took me a few hours to disengage him properly, but I essentially had to calm him down and then walk him into death.

Knowing about this dynamic is really important for magicians, as the deeper you go into magic practically, the more you become visible. It will be only a matter of time before you are *grabbed*, particularly if you work in a hospital or with the police, or anywhere where sudden death can occur. Knowing how to recognise this when it happens, and how to work with it and get yourself untangled, will get you out of danger. Then you need to know how to pick up the pieces of your own shocked body and spirit: the energetic impact of such a grab can have strong implications for your health.

I address inner and outer methods of putting your body back together at an inner and outer level in depth in my book *Magical Healing: a Health Survival Guide for Magicians and Healers*. This might be a very useful book for you to read, as among other things it has invaluable information within it about how to maintain your body from magical and energetic impacts. Chapters from *Magical Healing* can be found in the Appendix of this book.

You also need to know, as magician, how to keep an eye out for this happening to others, and to know what to do and how to do it quickly in the event that someone else has been grabbed in the middle of a death situation. The first action to do would be to give the affected person a ritual bath using the methods in Apprentice Module I, Lesson 7, and add on to the list of things removed from the bath (i.e. ghosts etc.)

the words *and any dead people clinging*. The ritual removal will not harm them if it works, but the spirit of the person will be catapulted into the darkness stage of early death. It is more important to focus on the health of the living person affected, as such clinging can drag a sick or weak person into death.

5. Death Parasites

When a person is dying slowly, particularly and most commonly when they are old, there is a major possibility that energetic parasites will have infested the weakened person and will be feeding off of their energy. The parasites will keep the person alive so that they can continue to feed, with the result that the person is held close to death in a weakened state.

This is something to keep a sharp eye out for when you are around someone who is dying, and if you spot it you will need to clean the dying person up energetically so that they can let go and die in peace. When this is the case, the death usually comes swiftly, often within hours, of the magical clean-up work.

There are also types of parasites that cling onto the newly dead and prevent them moving deeper into death, and feed off of the emotion/anxiety of the dead person. When the dead person has fully detached from their body, the emotion shifts its energetic form and becomes less about chemical bodily reactions and more about deeper spirit issues. The parasites cling to the energy outputted in its various forms in order to feed, and this prevents the spirit from moving deeper into death (and rebirth, if that is where they are heading). This is one of the reasons, wherever possible, to keep the space of a dying or newly dead person clean energetically, and to keep the gates open: that prevents any parasites either getting near or keeping hold of the person.

6. Quick deaths

Quick deaths have a very different dynamic from slow deaths and tend to be slightly less traumatic. We have already looked at what can happen with a quick death (the motorcyclist), and often, when the death is very sudden and unexpected (accident, massive heart attack), the spirit is sometimes catapulted away from the body, and yet still connected.

Within a few days in our time frame, the spirit seems to reorganise itself and either draws back close to the body or close to someone they are deeply connected to. Sometimes, if the trauma is great and the death was very sudden, they often do not at first realise they are dead. The spirit will be in a major panic, and they will thrash around energetically until they come to understand what has happened and what they need to do.

Often, particularly when young adults die suddenly, they will not accept death and will try very hard to cling to the world of the living. In these cases, the magician has to spend time talking in vision with the traumatised dead and giving them horizons in the death passage. Once you 'see' it in your head, they also begin to see it, and will eventually set off walking towards that horizon.

So often when someone dies these days, they have no religious, mystical, or cultural pattern for their consciousness to operate through, so you have to provide it for them, both ritually and in vision. Some spirits do not need this and seem to get themselves pretty well organised, and all they need is a 'good job' pat on the back.

This is also very true of children and babies: they very rarely need any help at all. It is as if they remember, as they have not lived a long life that will fill up their spirit with new patterns: they remember and get on with it quickly, and often painlessly.

7. Comas

The last thing I want to cover briefly before we move on to practical work is the issue of comas. There are lots of different types of coma, and people respond very differently from a spirit point of view. There are comas where the spirit is no longer there but is stretched already into death, still connected lightly to the body by an energetic umbilical cord, but they are beyond coming back into the body. There are some comas that are not connected to death at all, and there are some comas where the person is no longer there and something else has stepped into the body and is trying to operate it.

When a person is in a coma and their body is beyond real repair, often the spirit will stand upon the threshold of death, unable to move forward into death as the body is being kept alive artificially; or else they don't wish to continue living in a body that does not work, but they are also scared of death. There are also times when the spirit is starting to move towards death but a parasite is keeping the body going, which in turn makes it difficult for the spirit to really move on.

Working with people in comas is a fascinating experience, and is a major service to all concerned. The first thing for a magician to ascertain is whether the spirit/person is still properly anchored in the body and is 'there,' or if they are on their way out, or have already gone. This is done via visionary work on the threshold of death, and also by going into the vessel (body) of the person to see who or what is still there.

More often than not, the person is still there but unable to operate the body. Under such circumstances it is a simple waiting game, and the magician's job is to ensure there is nothing else in the body with the person and vying for residence. Parasites are the most common squatters, and whatever the magician finds in there, he must remove in order for the spirit to have full, proper residence. With the use of functional MRI's, the incidences of switching off life support to people who are still 'in' are becoming less frequent.

I remember when I was a little girl and my mother was working on a ward of people with head injuries and/or who were in comas. (Her speciality was in infectious/tropical disease, but as the call for that grew less in the 1960s she moved sideways in her work.) She told me of a situation once where she, medical students, and doctors were gathered round a coma patient. The person was being reviewed for turning off life support and the consultant had come to the conclusion that the person was brain-dead.

My mother could feel the person still in their body, trying to look out. She had a twenty-four hour window to figure out what was going on before the person was going to be switched off. She poured over his medical records and also looked up his drug regime in detail. He had been brought to the ward after a bout of meningitis (her home territory) and had fallen into a coma just as he was winning the fight with the infection.

She noticed he was on a drug that in a very small number of people could cause total paralysis. She discussed it with the consultant and asked if they would take him off the drug and wait forty-eight hours to see what happened. After a battle of egos, the consultant agreed. The patient woke up within twenty-four hours.

It was not her medical expertise that first led to that recovery; it was the fact that as a natural psychic she could 'feel' him alive, in panic, trying to communicate. It was also her willingness to take time and pour over drug formularies while paying close attention to detail that also saved the patient. Both of those skills are born out of *perception,* one of the core skills in magic.

Few people have such natural psychic ability, but a magician trains to be able to do essentially the same thing: talk in your mind to the body and see if there is still a person trapped in there. The moral of the story is: always check the lights are truly out before you go disconnecting someone.

For many people, though, the prognosis is not so good. And that is where the magician comes in. The job of the magician is to trigger change: that change could be the patient waking up or the patient dying. And the hardest part of that job is to not get involved with the emotion of the situation: the magician should always remain neutral.

That is why, as an apprentice, you spend so much time learning to be still, learning about the balance of powers, learning to let go of things, the balance of influences, and about your own Harvest. Emotion rules our culture and causes untold damage out of good intent.

Without going into detail which will come later in your training, with most comas the magician works with the body and also with the spirit in vision during the death process. The body is first checked and cleared of all parasites, is harmonised and balanced, and then the magician goes into death in vision to talk to the spirit. If the spirit wishes to let go, the magician asks if there is anything that the spirit wishes to convey to the family, and then the umbilical cord is cut. The cutting of the cord does not cause an immediate cessation of life; rather it triggers the body and spirit's own disengagement process. The spirit is then shown how and where to begin the walk into death. When a magician who knows what she is doing does this, death usually follows naturally within twenty-four hours: the heart gives out or just stops. This can bring to an end a long cycle of suffering for both the spirit and the family.

In one such coma case I worked on at an intensive care unit in North California, the message that the spirit wanted conveying was that if he could not be who he really was, then he did not want to come back into consciousness. The man had been in a coma for around a month and they wanted help reaching him. I went in vision into death and found him, but could not get him to communicate with me. He would not respond to me or even react. But then he visited me in my dreams that night and conveyed his rather cryptic message, *If I cannot be who I really am, then I do not wish to come back.*

I was not sure what it meant, but I thought it had something to do with the very strict Christian family he lived in. When I conveyed the message (and it must be done word for word; *never* interpret) the father burst into tears and nodded. The patient had massive brain damage that I was not told about (they thought I would not work on him if I knew how bad the injuries were) and if he had survived, he would have been totally paralysed or worse. I went back to the hospital the following morning, worked on him to 'line him up,' and he died that night.

This is a difficult area of magical healing to work in, and it is very likely that few of you will follow that specialisation in magic, but having a rudimentary understanding of the dynamic is important should you at some time in the future be put in the position of needing to try and reach someone who is deep in a coma.

8. *Task:* Astrology

When we look at a chart, we not only look at the natal planets and the current transits, but we also learn as magicians to look at the 'sigils' that the alignments make, particularly when it comes to specific events that we are looking at. This can be particularly helpful when looking at a death chart.

When we look at a death chart, we are not looking at the person's astrology; rather we are looking at the planetary influences at the point of death. The death chart will tell us a lot about the timing of a person's death, and whether that death was their true, final, appointed time, or whether they had died during a hotspot. If a spirit is properly attuned, is magical, mystical, or a priest in the real sense of the word (in true communion with Divinity), then we will see the spirit using the optimum time to pass into death.

This is very well demonstrated with the death of Pope John Paul II. Regardless of what we think of religious leaders, this man was a true priest in every sense of the word, and died at a time when the planetary alignments over Rome were in a position where the gates were wide open. We can see this clearly in his death chart, which was cast for the location and time of his death. Look at the following chart, and see the four directions open and the planetary gates held open:

LESSON 2 – REGULAR DEATH

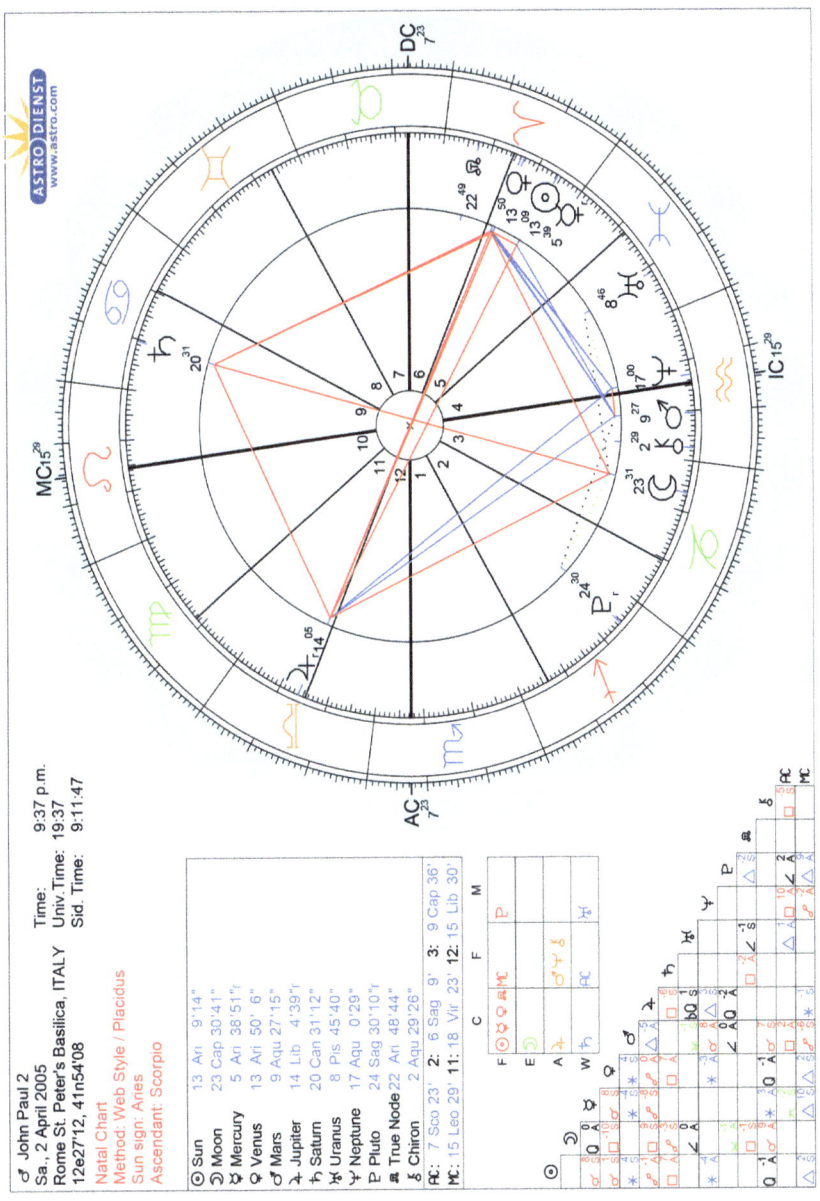

Figure 1: Pope John Paul II's death chart.

47

Module IV – Death, Birth, and the Underworld

See how clearly the gates are shown, and how many of the planets are down below his horizon; all the activity is in the Underworld. This is a very poetic way of reading an event chart, but it gives you a clear view of patterns of power in action.

A magician's death chart will either show the four gates, or a great triangle.

9. *Task:* Death chart practice

Using the free chart drawing facility at `astro.com`, choose ten people, either known to you or public figures, where you can get the time, date, and location of the death, and run death charts for them.

Look at their charts, the shapes of the lines generated from the planets' positions, and see what sort of patterns were around them astrologically when they died. Take computer notes: using Word or something similar, embed the charts and write your observations, ideas, and what you know of the person, and compare what you know to what the chart reflects. Keep the file, as it may need to be submitted later.

10. *Task:* Tarot and death

Using the same ten people, you are going to do a series of readings to look the state of the spirit/soul of the person at the point of death, and then also track them through the early stages of death. You will use the FOUR-DIRECTIONAL LAYOUT, and also a new layout that is more focused on the inner landscape of a person.

Four-Directional readings

For the FOUR-DIRECTIONAL READINGS:

The **first card** (centre) tells you about the state of the **body** itself at the point of death;

The **four directions** tell you the **influences** that are flowing around the spirit of the person at that time as the gates open;

The **final card** that crosses the centre card tells you about the **power/contact** that the person is having a direct **relationship/contact** with at the point of death.

The question you will ask for each person is:

> *"Show me this person at the point of their death, and show me the inner power influences that were flowing around them at that time."*

Write down the card positions of each reading and your conclusions. When you have all ten of them, compare the readings to the death charts. Look at the planetary influences at that time and compare them to the four directions in the readings, and see if there is a correlation between the planets, the houses they are in, and the powers flowing out of the directions. Don't try and do all of the readings in one session, as it would tire you out. Spread them out over days.

The Inner Landscape/Desert Layout readings

This is an abridged version of a larger layout that gives you more details as to the passage or state of a spirit and what influences are flowing through their situation, where those influences come from, and where the spirit is going.

You may have worked with this layout already from my books, or it may be totally new to you. Either way, it is a key layout for magicians, and you will learn a lot more about it in this course, and also work with it in its full expression.

Learn the layout first, map it out on paper, and have the map at your side so that you can work with it. As with all new layouts, fix the layout in your mind as you shuffle so that both you and the cards know what pattern it is you are reaching for. It is a magical layout that is very versatile and can be used for all sorts of magical questions: it is not geared specifically to death readings, so bear that in mind as you interpret the positions.

The following image shows the magical pattern structure of the LANDSCAPE LAYOUT.

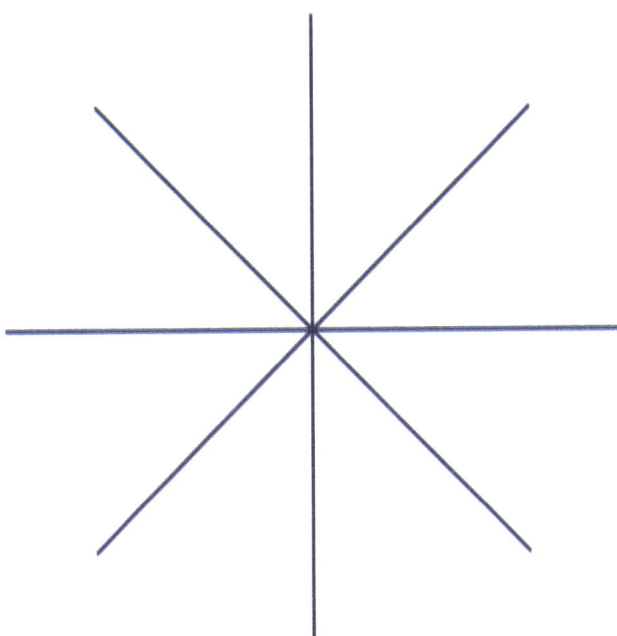

Figure 2: Magical pattern structure of the Landscape layout

The full layout (*Figure 3*) is overleaf.

Module IV – Death, Birth, and the Underworld

Figure 3: The Inner Landscape or Desert Layout

Position meanings:

1. The first position is the **body** or **land**.
2. The second position, that crosses the first, tells us what **power** or **people dynamics** we are currently **dealing with**.
3. The third position tells us what is coming in the **long-term future**, a pattern that is still being formed in the stars. If resolution is on its way, but will take some time, then that will show here; however, if the problem is going to be prolonged, then that will also be indicated here.
4. The fourth position shows us what has already **passed away** down into the depths and **will not be returning** any time soon.
5. The fifth position shows us the **gate to the past**: this is the threshold of what is now in the immediate past. Whatever is in this position of the threshold has the potential to return at some point in the future, but for the moment is considered past.
6. The sixth position is the **current pattern of fate** or **action** that is playing out: that could be a struggle, a cycle of magical work, a period of renewal, etc. This is the path you are currently on, unless you do something to change that path's direction.
7. The seventh position is **hardships** and **difficulties** that **must be overcome**. On the current path (indicated in the sixth position) there are bound to be hardships, difficulties, and barriers that must be overcome: these are shown in the seventh position, and must be endured if you are to continue in the fate direction you are currently travelling.
8. The eighth position shows what is coming directly into your landscape from the **inner worlds**. All magical attacks, inner contacts, work programs, inner support, deities, etc. will show here.
9. The ninth position shows you what **influence in your inner landscape** is potentially **affecting your home/family surroundings** or vice versa. If there is a haunting, bad energy, or difficulty in the home environment it will show here.
10. The tenth position is what **is falling away** or **starting to go into decline**. If you have defeated something, or it is starting to leave your body or fate path, it will show here. It is travelling towards the gate of the past and will finally vanish into the depths. If, however, you do not meet the challenges that appear in the seventh position, then any difficulties that show in the tenth position will come right back to challenge you until you get the message.
11. The eleventh position is **dreams and sleep**. This position tells you what your deeper unconscious mind is dealing with, and what is happening to you in your sleep.
12. The twelfth position is the way ahead, and tells you the **immediate outcome** to your question. For a longer-term outcome, look to position three.

Module IV – Death, Birth, and the Underworld

Do the **Desert layout** for each of the ten deaths you are looking at. The question you will ask for each person is:

"Show me the death of person X, their point of death, and what happened to them as they went through the death process."

This spread will show you **how the body dealt with death** (**1** is the **body**, **2** is their **relationship** with death).

The reading will also show you their **short-term movement** into death and how they are handling it (**6**);

It will show you what they have to **overcome** in their journey (**7**),

What inner, deeper powers are flowing to them from the **inner worlds,** i.e. angelic, or human or priesthood guidance (**8**),

What **effect** the **family** left behind is having on them (**9**),

What is **falling away** from them/what they are letting go of (**10**),

What they are **dreaming** for the future (**11**),

What their **short-term future** is: is it resting, balancing, cleaning up, or are they struggling, or looking to jump back into life (**12**)?

Position **3** will tell you whether they are going back into life (and may show what sort of life), or it will show if they are going to step into the inner worlds to be a contact, or if they are going to rest.

As with the charts, write it all down, and then compare each reading to the other readings and the death chart of each person. Take your time to ponder over each person, and look in depth at the little details. If something confounds you, put it to one side and go back to it later.

This process of charts, readings, and conclusions should take you three weeks to a month, which gives you time to do the readings, look at the charts, meditate on each person, and let the story slowly unfold for you. Also take note of any unusual dreams or encounters at this time, as some of it may filter through your dream world.

Lesson 3
The Magical Mysteries of Death

Now that you have a basic background idea of death, it is time for us to look a bit closer and find out about some of the deeper mysteries that surround death. As you will have seen from the Egyptian texts, constant rebirth was/is considered the lowest common denominator, not only in the Egyptian Mysteries but also in the Buddhist Mysteries.

You will find, as you expand your reading list further over the span of the course, that many of the ancient and not-so-ancient Mysteries have the same core to them. That is because they are expressing what is there, not because they are copying or sharing.

The writings of the various versions of the Mysteries around the world, particularly when it comes to the subject of death, usually have two layers to them: one for the everyday person and one for the initiates/priests/magicians. The one that is aimed at the common man (a switched off person) tends to be simplistic, moralistic, and full of threats. A deeper layer of such writings also hides profound aspects of the Mysteries that someone who is both switched on and has knowledge of the Mysteries (through direct experience, not academia) will spot and can learn from.

It is the common, moralistic writings that tend to become popular and well-known to the various populations, and many of our world religions are based upon those moral writings and stories. Initiates of the Mysteries often reject those writings or dogmatic systems in search of something else: an initiate knows in their very depths that there is 'more.' And there is.

But it is wise to understand that the outer writings aimed at the common man serve a multi-fold purpose: first to ensure some societal boundaries, but also to bridge the common man from being switched off to being switched on. They either get it at a deeper level, or they stay switched off and follow the shallow moral code slavishly. Or of course they will ignore everything.

This is important for magicians to understand, as, for an adept working in the depths of death and dying, knowing that bridging aspect helps the magician to work with the dying person in their 'reality' and not the reality of the initiate.

If a religion connects a person to a sense of Divinity, to a sense that even slightly approaches balance, then it is a religion that is serving that person. If the religion locks down the dying person (overly dogmatic), then there is nothing that the magician can do to change that – all you can do is to hold the space.

Before we go on to look at the Deeper Mysteries, let's first look at religious dogma and how it affects the passage of the soul through death.

1. Religion versus the Mysteries

Most religions have a version of heaven and hell, of judgement, of helpers, and of the angel of death. In the past, before more advanced education was the norm, this gave a switched off person a compass of behaviour that was easy to understand and follow. This in turn helped to build a society and avoid total chaos and anarchy. But most religions in their everyday sense have degenerated to the point that they simply express as manipulation and encourage the devolving of personal responsibility, along with having a 'God' who is humanlike and parental. A person within a religion learns to manipulate the system for their own ends, and devolves responsibility for themselves to a 'higher power.'

For example, if a person wants something, they will pray to a saint, to God, or to a religious symbol. The mantra of 'it's God's will,' or doing something 'in God's name,' or blaming God when things go wrong, are all degenerations and serve to switch the person off even further. The summary of all religions is: be good and you get to have an easy life after death; be bad and you will burn. And if you say sorry at the end, or pay enough money into a religion, you will be saved. Within that unbalanced, dogmatic view, there are fragments of cause and effect, and of the Mysteries themselves, but they are so far buried as to make them almost unreachable.

For people who gain a good education, and who tend to be thinkers, they look at this pattern, they see how silly, empty, and degenerate it is, and they walk away from it. Some eventually delve into the Mysteries, but most do not. This is the human melting pot that the magician confronts when they work in death.

So why did it get like that? Human nature. Working within the depths of the Mysteries is hard work indeed. Very few people are drawn to such work, and even fewer are able or willing to withstand the hard work. Just remember as you read through these stages, that the beings, landscape, actions, etc. that we see as living magicians, is not what is really there, and over time the presentation for the newly dead also starts to fall away. *What is really there is energy, frequency, patterns, vibration, sound, and our own minds.*

2. The Death Mysteries

Let us have an overview of the Death Mysteries, and as we go through it you will start to see the roots of certain dogmas and beliefs, see how they have developed out of context, and how they have developed in a degenerate, manipulative way. It is pertinent to point out that however much an adept learns about these Mysteries there will always be aspects of them that we cannot understand, grasp, or even find. What we have as magicians and mystics is a small section of understanding; nothing more.

First I will briefly outline the steps within the Mysteries that deal with death, and then we will look in more depth at key aspects of them. Bear in mind that the imagery in these steps is how the living, conscious mind perceives energy dynamics:

on the side of the dead person, the imagery is more a matter of processing energy, emotion, power, and balance. The deeper into death the deceased goes, the less they perceive in terms of imagery and the more they perceive in terms of energy responses. The images are our interface for recognition and understanding, and it is important to work within them as they are patterns that are strongly held in the collective consciousness and they also act as an energetic filter for the living to work through *safely*.

3. THE STEPS OF THE PROCESS: A BRIEF OVERVIEW

The first step of a person when they step onto the threshold of death is to begin the process of disconnection from their body, and their spirit stays in our world for a brief time. We have already looked at this. Suffice to say, this is the stage where the newly dead can influence the physical world and reach out to the living. However, for most people this period is fairly brief.

The vast majority of the newly dead begin their 'descent into the Underworld' fairly quickly, often at or just after funerals. In life, we perceive this as 'down'; in religion it is often termed as 'hell,' and subsequently fills many with fear or the more adventurous with curiosity. We will look in depth at the Underworld and the Abyss in the next lesson.

It is at this stage of the Underworld that the process of 'awareness of self' begins. In some Death Mysteries, this is depicted for us as the newly dead walking across a desert towards a river in the Underworld, where some cross the river, some stay at the side of it, and some attempt to avoid going deeper into death by immediately grabbing for a new life: unconscious reincarnation.

For those that do not immediately grab for new life during that walk, a deeper process triggers for the person which is the process of *the Scales*. The desert is the Inner Desert; or to be more precise, it is an aspect of that vast inner territory that adepts learn to operate within for lots of different reasons.

The triggering of the Scales is sometimes depicted in Mysteries as the opening of the Book of Judgement, or of facing judges, or a literal weighing of scales, or crossing a bridge over a river, or being confronted by demons with sharp pointy weapons. What they face in death in terms of how it presents to them is largely influenced by culture and thousands of years of human made imagery that instills itself into the deep subconscious of the person. It is basically an overview of their life. The outcome of this process defines what stage the spirit moves on to next: deeper into the Underworld, back into life through rebirth, etc.

So far this all sounds very neat and tidy, and yet the reality is far more complex. For instance, spirits that are deeply disturbed can often be observed, while in the Underworld, suddenly being absorbed into a deity, or becoming trapped in the sands of the Desert. Some stay in the Underworld, trapped, until they find manipulative ways to access the living, manifest world. Some descend deeper into the Underworld and a few pass through the Underworld and into the Abyss.

For some who descend into the Underworld, there comes a point where they emerge from the Underworld out into the stars and go through a process where they either choose web patterns of fate within the stars that they can step into, or they learn to navigate around those webs and complete the journey of the stars, which brings them back to a centre point. Reaching that centre point is one of the goals of an adept of the Mysteries: it brings the spirit in direct, face-to-face contact with a vast angelic being. This process is depicted in many different ways in the Mysteries, but the dynamic is the same.

From that centre point, the adept chooses either to move deeper into the depths of Divinity (depicted as heaven, which is a total degeneration of the idea), to stay in the inner worlds in gnosis and/or in service, or to step into life in full gnosis in service, or to step into the Underworld. For the adept, all of these options are conscious decisions that have specific reasons attached to them. The key point being that nothing is moved towards from impulse, desire, fear, or any other emotive or manipulative reason.

So in a moment we will look at these key steps in detail from the view of a magician. Most of those keys can be read about in various Mystery texts around the world, but few who look at them intellectually actually understand what it is they are looking at as they browse through these texts. Just before we get to those keys, let's look at why it often goes so badly wrong for people, or why they cannot access the keys properly as they traverse through death. The understanding of these problems will help you to understand the keys better.

The majority of people who travel through death as a spirit either approach it blindly (no religious map), or in dogmatic ignorance (the dogmatic map), or with a focus on manipulation (using spells/magic to dodge the guardians). All of these approaches fail and can sometimes result in intense suffering for the spirit (not the suffering of hell's damnation, but the suffering of being stuck and not knowing a way out).

If the spirit approaches death blindly (no religious map), then the deeper instinct of that spirit leads the way. The success or failure of that approach largely depends on the balance of the person in life. If the spirit approaches death through religious dogma, the spirit quickly learns that such dogmas are for the large part meaningless in this realm (as you will see when we get to the keys).

As for the manipulator, this is often the spirit of a person who followed a magical or religious path. They sometimes get a bit further in and then are confronted by the degeneracy of their action. That confrontation is often aggressive for the spirit and deeply counterproductive: they get stuck with no way forward and no way back, and potentially have a nasty-looking being with sharp knives following them around. The being with the sharp knives, which I call 'Choppers' are energies that forcibly strip away what should have been voluntarily let go of by the dead person, such as physical appearance, personality, emotions, belongings, etc.

When people make these mistakes, sometimes the process of death itself unfolds them, and the deeper aspect of their spirit emerges and propels them forward. However if that deeper aspect is very unbalanced then the spirit experiences many difficulties that could have been avoided.

The one point to remember in all of this, before we reach the keys, is that there is no moralistic or punishment/reward dynamic involved: the process of death is one of finding (or not) balance. That balance is an energy harmonic that allows the consciousness to flow freely and to interact with its environment in a conscious way.

So let us look a bit closer at some of the key aspects of death, and the Mysteries of death. Through that understanding, not only can you help yourself, you can also help others.

4. The Descent into the Underworld

The Descent into the Underworld is a purely natural action that creates separation between the dead person and the land of the living. This natural impulse is sometimes mirrored by the living in the action of burying the dead, which also protects the living from disease.

We call it 'Descent' because in our living worldview, density, age, and the layers of the past are 'down' deep in the land. This is mirrored in the inner landscape of the Desert, as we see the past as being down in the sands, and the future as being up in the stars. As the body decays and becomes part of the dirt and rock of the earth, the spirit too, on its initial journey, moves into this vast processing system. For the spirit it is less a sense of 'down' and more a sense of 'forward.'

This stepping away from life triggers a deep inner response, and that response is the first major key of the Mysteries. A major part of the learning process within the ancient Mysteries was geared towards preparing the spirit at a very deep level, while in life, to respond appropriately to this response.

In the early development of most Mysteries, that in-life preparation was about changing first the individual's behaviour, and then their knowledge and understanding. That deep shift over a lifetime enabled the spirit to move through the death process with ease and in a conscious, active way.

As the Mysteries began to degenerate for one reason or another depending on the culture, that process of deeply shifting over a lifetime turned into the rote learning of a series of spells to dodge the process, and finally a series of dogmatic threats, scary stories, and hints of great 'rewards.' Both of these degenerations resulted (and still result) in spirits having great difficulty in death.

The first trigger response from the inner world for the spirit in the death process is known by a number of names, the most common one being *Judgement*. Many spirits do not get this far (to Judgement), as many rush impulsively back to life before ever properly entering the death process. But in this lesson we are focusing on those who do manage to step forward and onto the Deeper Mysteries.

5. The River and Judgement

The River and *Judgement* are the first and most important keys; and of all of them they are the ones most badly misunderstood and misinterpreted, both in religion and in the modern study of the Mysteries and magic. On average, fewer spirits get to the Judgement point in the death process; many dive straight back into the rebirth cycle in an unconscious, impulsive grab for life at any cost.

That is one of the reasons that many Death Mystery writings talk about the Death Mysteries in terms of 'not for the common man.' This is not a class discrimination; it is merely an observation from adepts of the Mysteries: many people do not even get to the door of the Death Mysteries.

The River stage of death is depicted in ancient texts, and can also be observed in vision as people in a desert running towards a river and drinking great quantities of its waters. That is how we the living 'see' this process. From an inner point of view, what is happening is that a switched off person, driven only by instinctive *thirst* for life, reaches out for an energy that will *blind* the spirit from its memories, allowing it a clean slate free from the pattern of the last life. This in turn enables the spirit to lunge forward unconsciously back into life, so that the cycle begins all over again.

Those who value life at any cost see this wiping of their slates as a boon, a great way to get back to where they want to be. Ghosts who cling to the material world and their past life/family/belongings, try hard to not be drawn to the river: once they have drunk and forgotten, they are cast back into a new life.

For those who have trodden the path of the Mysteries in some form or other, such unconscious lunging blindly back into life is seen as an undesirable action that will lead to more blindness and less advancement into being one's true self.

This first step is written about in virtually all Mysteries in the form of the warning:

"Do not drink of the River of Oblivion."

> *"Men, driven on by thirst, run about like a snared hare; let therefore the mendicant drive out thirst, by striving after passionlessness[1] for himself."*
>
> — Ch 24, *Dhammapada*

The initiate learns first to be aware of their deeper impulses in life, and then to turn those impulses into a conscious act of choice. Through developing that conscious ability in life, it becomes second nature in death. The adept or mystic reaches this first threshold and makes a conscious choice that is not dictated by desire or emotion. If the adept chooses not to drink of the river, or not even to wash their face, they move forward deeper into the realm of the death aspect of the Desert. This is where they reach the key of judgement, also known as the *Weighing of the Scales*.

---

[1] Not driven by emotions or impulse.

The choice of the spirit to step into judgement is a conscious one, and is a decision made by a mystical or adept spirit who wishes to progress deeper into the Divine Mysteries that can only be reached through the passage of death. It is a decision that involves a great deal of danger for the spirit, and is a choice that is not taken lightly: hence the training in life.

If a spirit does not feel ready, or knows that they are not ready to move forward into Judgement, as they still have work to do on themselves and in the world around them, they will not drink of the River: they may wash their face in order to rid themselves of the memory of their physical image, which if left may pull them backwards rather than forwards. The adept would then step into the next life, while still retaining a deep memory of what they learned.

Those who feel they are ready, forge forward towards Judgement. Those who feel they have enough magical skill to manipulate their way through the process will also, foolishly, step forward.

A wise adept/mystic knows what submitting to the Judgement of the Scales entails: potential annihilation is the worst case scenario (the Second Death). An unwise adept or mystic will try to manipulate their way through this process, only to be potentially caught by the guardians beyond the threshold. The spirit that decides it is ready for Judgement makes a clear decision and then steps forward. This is depicted in the Greco-Roman Mysteries as the Bridge across the River (the Bridge is a being of the Scales, not an actual bridge).

6. The Key of the Scales

This is the major step, the major filter that decides where and how the spirit of the dead person moves forward in their journey. In Egyptian texts this is depicted as the Scales of Ma'at weighing the heart of the dead person. To the Egyptians, the heart was the seat of the soul/spirit and is shown as being placed upon the Scales of Ma'at and weighed against the white feather of Ma'at. If the heart weighs less than or equal to the feather of Ma'at, the guardians will part and allow the dead person to begin their deep journey through the inner processes of death and renewal. The feather is also an indicator of air, utterance, and the heart spirit of the dead can be questioned by the judges – the heart spirit is the deep aspect of the eternal soul of the person and always utters Truth.

So what is it that is being weighed? This concept is where a lot of degeneration of wisdom has happened in religion and the Mysteries over time. In most of today's religions, and also in some magic, what is perceived as being judged/weighed is the life deeds of the individual in relation to the morals and cultural norms of a particular society. Sometimes those morals/norms cross paths with balance, but most often they do not.

There is also a get out clause in many religions nowadays, that if you 'confess', or pay money to a shrine, or go on holy war, etc., then you will be judged lightly. That is not the case. These get out clauses developed within religious systems as a method of control and manipulation. So people feel they can behave badly and then make up for it: it plays to the wish of people to have their cake and eat it.

For the magician, the process of balancing the scales is a lifetime of evolution and development. We are driven by our hormones, by our bodies, by our relationships, and by society, and each of these things gives us both difficulties to overcome and also excuses: "it was not my fault."

As a magician progresses, it becomes less about struggling to 'behave' in a certain way, and more about coming to know yourself, taking responsibility for yourself and your own actions, and realising that development of the spirit is all about "the responsibility starts and ends with you."

> *"By oneself the evil is one, by oneself one suffers:*
> *by oneself evil is left undone, by oneself one is purified.*
> *Purity and impurity belong to oneself, no one can purify another."*
>
> — Chapter 12, *Dhammapada*

We have already looked into this process in a previous lesson, so I do not need to go over it again. That process slowly changes how we live, how we act, and how we treat everything around us, and it is that adjustment in how we exist as human beings, how our deeper responses change, that is weighed.

It is not about actions or lack of actions; it is the deepest part of us, how we are on a day-to-day basis, both consciously and unconsciously, that is placed on the Scales. How the Scales react defines what then happens to the spirit.

As an aside, there is a stunning example of a deep mystery of adept service that is found in Old Kingdom Egypt, a dynamic that began to fall apart by the time to kingship had reached king Unis. The dynamic was this: the king was also a priest (sacred kingship), and the king worked deeply in mystical magic to take on the role of *Scapegoat* and 'Heart upon the Scales' for the nation and the land.

While the king worked with total balance (Ma'at) for the good of the land and the people, and kept himself balanced, the nation and the land would all collectively enjoy the benefits of the king's balance.

This takes us back to the Sword of Damocles hovering over the head of the king. The king had to tread a very thin line of self and behaviour, constantly striving to be in balance, self-aware, and in harmony with the land. By doing this he took on the burden of the spirits of the people, and the whole nation and land benefited from this kingship of Ma'at. In return, the king enjoyed the help and assistance of all the deities.

At the end of his life he would be placed before the Scales: it was not a choice the king had. By taking on that role he submitted to the lesser judgement in life which would ensure that upon death he or she would be immediately placed before the Scales to finish the job.

This worked well for a few generations of kingship, but soon human nature reared its ugly head and we got to a king who thought he could dodge his way around it. The moment the king steps off that very thin line, the sword falls, the connection to the land and people is cut, the deities withdraw their support, and chaos ensues.

We see this pattern over and over again in Egyptian history, with successive kings trying to reestablish that balance. But every time human nature crept in or the rules of Ma'at were manipulated, the sword would fall once more and the nation would be plunged into war, famine, etc.

If you read the following clip of text from the Dhammapada in the context of Ma'at and not morals, you begin to see the dynamic within this text:

> *"All that we are is the result of what we have thought:
> it is founded on our thoughts, it is made up of our thoughts.
> If a man speaks or acts with an evil thought, pain follows him,
> as the wheel follows the foot of the ox that draws the carriage."*

It demonstrates so clearly that the thought, the first impulse, that only you know, is the root of the balance or imbalance of the spirit. The action follows the thought and creates a good or bad effect. Modern religions judge upon effects; the Mysteries realise that the Judgement is upon the spirit itself, and that is founded in the thought impulse.

This theme of sacred kingship, and the failure or success of the sacred king, is found repeatedly in Egyptian and also Biblical texts. It is also probably at the root of the role of Jesus as the saviour of mankind: he takes on the suffering of the people, acts in balance, and descends into the Underworld in order to release those in suffering.

It is also very possible that it is this dynamic that is behind the tales of Solomon the king. The more you look at Biblical text and the ancient texts and stories from the Near and Middle East, the more you begin to see this role in action. The other and very important ancient aspect of the Mysteries that the sacred kingship shows us as magicians is the most forgotten one: as adepts we are all potentially those sacred kings and queens.

In Egypt this was ritualised and formalised, but it is in fact a natural magical dynamic that does not need one to be a king or a queen to practise – and nor does it *make* one a king or a queen. It is a dynamic that wherever there is a person (usually an adept, priest/priestess, or mystic) who is fully immersed in Ma'at and lives within the narrow boundary of Ma'at, so too will you find a land or part of a land (where the person lives) that is healthy and balanced, or is moving towards balance. How you are affects everything around you. The energetic frequency that you generate by living within that dynamic affects the Divinity within substance all around you: that frequency triggers rebalance and regeneration actions in whatever way it needs to express in order to bring balance.

7. The Second Death

If the Scales tip against the spirit being weighed, it is cast aside and torn apart, or is hacked at. This all sounds very final and not very pleasant, but it is the risk that the adept or mystic takes. The Scales are a major step, so to speak, of the spirit, which is why so many in death choose not to invoke it but rather choose to step back into life without the potential benefits that the Scales can bring.

The Second Death, where the spirit is totally composted, is something I have little understanding of, and is possibly connected to the idea of the soul first being cocooned and then bound into the Underworld, something we will look at in Lesson 8. The closest I have seen, apart from the 'cocoons' which may have been what I was observing and didn't realise, was something I saw in vision when working deep in the Desert. I wrote it into a chapter in my novel *The Last Scabbard*.

I had requested and triggered judgement in life (the Lesser Judgement, a bit like an exam pre-run) as part of my role as an exorcist. I did not do it lightly, but I realised that my work was taking me into very deep and dangerous waters, so I needed to make a decision: either stop that work, or surrender to judgement.

I needed to surrender to judgement, as the work I was doing in service as an exorcist was at a critical point and I could not just drop my responsibilities; but to continue working without a Scales assessment would have put my life in danger: by submitting to the Lesser Judgement and surviving, the adept then enjoys greater support and help from the deities.

So I triggered the process and stood before the vast being that 'weighs the Scales.' As I stood there, I realised another spirit was standing at the side of me. I had no clue who or what it was, and was prevented from looking at the spirit. A 'sword' came out of nowhere and sliced into the spirit next to me, and the spirit vanished. I started to get a bit worried, and then the sword came down on me. It hit me in the shoulder very hard, and I fell out of the vision. Looking back, years later, I began to wonder if the spirit that vanished had undergone a Second Death and had ceased to be.

I also understand now why the sword hit my shoulder (and physically injured me). I was not really ready for Judgement: I still have blind spots and unbalanced parts of myself that I have slowly become aware of, and I now know how much more work I have to do in order to lighten the spirit to that of a feather (huge mountain to climb). Putting myself up for Judgement at that time was both necessary, and was also folly. It was one of those moments where you look back in time and think... *moron*. But the process did speed along my self-reflection process, and since that day I have become more and more aware of what I need to do to work towards the Greater Judgement, if I truly want to opt out of the continuous cycle of life.

8. Fooling the Scales

In ancient Egypt (yeah, them) as the civilisation developed and the temples gained more power, manipulations crept in. This manipulation can be seen very clearly in the Egyptian funeral texts (*Papyrus of Ani*) where spells abound that attempt to dodge, manipulate, bind, or lie to the guardians and the Scales.

One spell in particular works upon the heart of the deceased spirit and forces it to lie or be silent on behalf of the dead person. When the heart is placed upon the Scales, it is depicted in Egyptian texts that the spirit has to undergo the forty-two Negative Confessions: declarations of the heart that tells what sins they have not committed.

There are spells in the text which force the heart to lie in order not to be judged harshly. This is a degeneration in so many major ways: not only does it not work, but it shows just how badly this society had degenerated. It had gone from the sacred king upholding Ma'at for the whole of society, and in return having the help of the gods (and the help of the *Pyramid Texts* to guide the king through death). The process was for the king and the occasional high priest/priestess only: not from class distinction, but from necessity.

To live a life of Ma'at and be immersed in the Mysteries is a hard life indeed. Very few can be expected to live such a life, so in practical terms, it was left to the king and the occasional magical priest/priestess to live such a life for the good of all. As the society degenerated, two things happened. The vast magical power that flowed in harmony with Divinity and the land was cast aside (too much hard work), and a lesser, though still very powerful magic of manipulation, bargaining, and binding replaced it. This immediately caused an imbalance in the Ma'at of the land and the nation.

The second thing that happened, as a result of that magical degeneration, is that the rich aristocrats wanted their chance at passing by the Scales and moving deep into harmony (heaven). So they paid priest magicians to work with scribes to paint the spells on the walls of their tombs, so that their spirits would have all the spells ready in order to dodge their fate and judgement. Of course it does not work, but hey, if a corrupt priesthood is offered enough money, they will tell you anything. I think also that the Mysteries had begun to degenerate to a point whereby the priesthood believed such behaviour would work.

9. The walk of the knives

Once the Scales have been dealt with, the spirit begins its walk through the Desert towards the Abyss and to Divinity beyond. If the spirit weighed badly, the blade would fall. If the spirit weighed a bit off but not enough for a Second Death, nor enough to pass deeper into the process, then the blade would cut into the spirit to disable, but not enough to destroy. This is depicted in Egyptian funeral texts as demonic or Underworld deities who carry long, sharp blades and cut into the spirit as it journeys through the Desert. Some spirits are cut deeply and some are not.

When I was a young woman and working in vision in death, I would work within a landscape of desert, river, bridge over river, plains, mountain, and mists beyond. I worked with that visionary system for many years until I realised it was only a fraction of what was actually there.

The Bridge is the Scales (the bridge is a being, not a structure). When I was working in this vision and was learning about it as I pushed deeper and deeper into the vision, I noticed that many who crossed the bridge (and some did not cross, but vanished in the middle of it: Second Death?) and began walking towards the mountain had bits dropping off of them. At the time, and for years later, I thought they were just dropping their attachments to the life they had just left behind. As the years went by, I realised that they were having their bits sliced by the guardians. These were spirits preparing to climb the mountain who had gone through the Scales, and what I was seeing was the result of that judgement: they were sustaining injuries that were triggering the process of Ma'at so that as they went forward (to life or whatever) they had these injuries not to punish, but to trigger an awareness and understanding of their imbalance that they then could work with.

It then dawned on me that as a young woman, I had done something terrible in ignorance and arrogance. When I worked in the death vision, I got it into my head that a major job was to assist people across the bridge so that they could go back into life. I noticed that multitudes of people simply sat at the side of the river and I became evangelical about hauling them over the bridge, sometimes kicking and screaming.

It was only in the last few years that I got to see and then realise a dynamic that I was interfering with: if a soul crosses the bridge under its own steam, when it is ready, it may or may not trigger the Scales on the bridge depending on what that spirit is doing. Some pass over the bridge and continue without triggering the Scales, and eventually go back into life. Some trigger the Scales by themselves as they pass through this stage of death.

But by forcibly putting people on the bridge, or pushing them towards it, I was obviating their own natural process and also triggering the Scales for every spirit I pushed onto the bridge. I do not know why it triggers the Scales if a soul is forced; only that it does. I was horrified when I was finally able to see this: the implications of my actions were far reaching indeed.

Which takes us back to the Mystery wisdom: you are responsible for yourself. Everything starts and ends with you. Everyone has to walk their own path and take the consequences of their own path upon themselves. By forcing people over the bridge I had interfered with that process: I was trying to sort everyone else out instead of minding my own business and sorting myself out.

The old maxim that people should not start Mystery training until they have reached forty began to make more and more sense to me. Before that age we are too dumb, too full of hormones and everything else that goes with that (ego, emotion, impulse). And yet I have learned far more from my mistakes than I have learned from my successes. So it is a two-edged sword, really. And what I have seen of others on magical paths, is that magic seems to find people at the right time in their lives regardless of their age. The struggles, mistakes and missteps that the young magician makes are all part of the path that can either strengthen them and build their wisdom brick by brick, or unravel them out of magic for their own good.

10. THE FACE OF THE ANGEL

Once the spirit has crossed the plains of the Desert and overcome many challenges,[2] it comes face to face with a vast angelic being *whose face shines with the light of Divine Being*. That is to say, an angelic being that is a direct mediator of the powers of creation and destruction: the angel of glory.

This encounter is a deep mystical version of 'looking in the mirror.' The spirit is given a brief look at Divine Being and also of their true self at a soul level. This enables the soul to make a choice, and it is this choice that adepts of the Mysteries strive for, and thus work hard to learn the powers of the Scales in life and death. You see, life is not the be-all and end-all, or the 'true existence'; it is more like going to the gym to get strong and fit.

Those who have been through this process once or more remember it at a deep level and strive in life not only to repair and renew the 'cuts' they received, but also to pass on guidance to others in order to point the way. However, there is a difference between guidance, i.e. pointing the way ahead and giving them just enough of what they need for them to self develop/learn, and 'teaching' a person. The adept must be careful to not expose too much information or knowledge that could forestall the progress of others. We see this throughout history as magicians, mystics, priests/priestesses who spend their life pointing the way through texts and teachings. Or they simply write/paint or express their experience so that others may have a step upon the road.

The experience of looking into the face of the vast angelic being triggers a deeper understanding of their eternal self and what it is they need to do. Once they have settled on what they need to do, the angel opens up a *Vista* of options that would facilitate that process.

11. THE VISTA

The *Opening of the Vista,* in magical terms, is something that happens when the spirit is shown a variety of options that are open and accessible to them in order to do whatever it is they need to achieve. This could be a life or series of lives, and often the spirit is shown a variety of lives. Or it could be passing into the inner worlds (inner temples, for example) in order to work as an inner contact; it could be rest in the arms of a deity power that holds the spirit in sleep for a while; it could be service

---

[2] In the Greek Mysteries that is depicted as a mountain that must be climbed.

in the Underworld; or it could be, if the spirit did not sustain injury from the blades and is therefore complete, the option of the *ladder of angels,* which takes the spirit into a deep, Divine state of balance and union (going home).

The choice is for the spirit to make, and as soon as that decision is made all other options close off and the spirit falls into the option that they reached for. If the option was life, the angel withdraws and the spirit falls into life. This action is a much higher and vastly more powerful dynamic of the one that you learned a little about in the last module when you stood in the centre of the web of lives/fate and looked around that web for hotspots or lives. This is the same mechanism, but at an infinitely more powerful level.

What fascinates me is that I have often come across this mechanism in action not only in deep vision, but in people who remember this process at a deep level. They will dream it, taste it, feel it: a deep part of them remembers, but the everyday consciousness tries to suppress the memory (for good reason). As the person gets older, and I have come across this not only in priests/priestesses or adepts, but also in seemingly everyday folks, they slowly remember more and more fragments of the event. Of course there are always the silly people who read about events like this and then loudly declare that they remember in total, that their spirit was the spirit of Cleopatra/Jesus/Buddha/whatever, and that they were sent back on the earth to be a messiah (what, another one??). Those you can discount as just being nuts.

I remember a conversation with one person, who wasn't magical or religious but was a deeply profound human, after they had surgery (which can sometimes trigger deep memories). About a month after the surgery he had a vivid dream that not only was powerful, exhausting, and terrifying; it also 'woke him up' and changed his life forever.

He dreamed of standing before a vast, shining face, and beyond the face was a parade of many lives. He was missing a foot and a hand (action of the blades?), and felt a total failure. But the angel smiled and nodded towards the parade of lives. He looked, and saw a life that pulled at him deeply. He fell towards it and woke up with a bump. There was nothing untoward in the dream, but it shook him to the core: his spirit recognised and remembered.

He came to me to chat, as he was still shaken days later and could not understand why. I told him about the Death Mysteries process and when we came to the Opening of the Vista, his face lit up. He said he remembered, and he also remembered what it was he needed to do to feel complete, and off he went. He left his job and travelled half way round the world to go work on the top of a mountain with a tribal community. He never told me what it was that he needed to do, and as I moved around we slowly lost contact.

This act of remembering also brings me to another aspect of the Death Mysteries, and that is reincarnation. So let's have a look at the many twists and turns that are relevant to the Mysteries.

12. Reincarnation

Reincarnation is something that happens either unconsciously or consciously. I do not mean that in a sense of remembering past lives, but in a sense of whether it was by conscious choice of the spirit (at the Vista) or whether it was an unconscious, impulsive grabbing for life.

The unconscious reincarnation is something that virtually everyone has an idea about, but the conscious action of reincarnation is not so widely known. It has come to the public's attention in the last few decades through the actions of one particular spirit who chooses conscious reincarnation: the Dalai Lama. Whether or not we think his actions have been of use is irrelevant – the fact remains that here is a soul that chooses to come back and live within the same pattern over and over. My personal opinion is that such action is degenerate and counterproductive for so many reasons, regardless of the good intent of the spirit. And as I write this lesson, the Dalai Lama has announced that he (or the line of consciousness that flows through him) will possibly not be coming back. Wise choice.

Many in the modern world get very hung up on reincarnation and devolve into a fantasy world of past lives – this is just silly. It does not matter who or what you were in another life; what you do, how you evolve, and how you move forward in *this* life is what is important. Memories are truly fleeting, and can serve only to weigh us down.

One thing that has become apparent to me over the years is that sometimes spirits choose consciously to come into life to rebalance themselves by serving in a life that triggers a rebalancing for a wider group of people or a nation. Sometimes these lives they step into are not pleasant, or they step into a fate role that will result in them being a hated person. I came across this purely by accident many years ago. I was teaching a group different tarot techniques, and we were looking at deeply unpopular political figures.

Once we had looked at their current situation, we then looked at their whole life pattern, and finally at their deeper spirit. One particularly nasty politician[3] who has caused immense suffering through his warmongering caught my attention. His outer life showed a story of destruction. His deeper self showed a profound soul in service. I was deeply shocked.

Once the class was over, I delved deeper into investigating this. Sure enough, this vile warmonger had a great and balanced spirit, and had consciously chosen to step into the fate pattern of destruction in order to bring balance and change: he was a soul in Divine service.

Subsequently, I came across more of these people, and it really changed how I viewed people in general. I did not wholly trust my results, so I asked other adepts to look

---

[3] Still living, so I will not name him.

as well, without telling them what to look for, just to check out the deeper spirits of a group of people. They came back with the same results and the same sense of astonishment.

Sometimes it takes destruction to bring regeneration, and the key players in that destruction, often reviled, are sometimes (not always) profound spirits who stood at the Vista and agreed to take on the burden of such a life in order to bring balance to themselves and everything around them. Divine service indeed. To knowingly step into a life pattern that brings intense suffering and destruction to others, to be hated and reviled, is a sacrifice indeed.

> Note: In the original version of the Quareia course, this part had a link to a 1970's documentary on the research of an Australian clinical psychologist who accidentally stumbled across examples of women who, under hypnosis, described lives and places that at that time they could not possibly have known about. The documentary was banned in many countries, but I had found a link to it on the internet where someone had kept it up in the public eye. It is now much harder to find, so I have taken that link and paragraph out of this lesson. Instead, I will give you a short example of one of my own experiences with someone and reincarnation.

My mother died while I was still working on the course, and I was beside her as she died. She had a good death and was a woman who was very aware in terms of 'otherness' as she called it. Two years later I had a powerful vivid dream that woke me up. A couple I knew with a small child had come to visit me. The child who was about five years old stood and looked up at me, and I recognised something in this child. And the child said, "Josie, it's me, I am coming back." I recognised instantly that this was my mother. Three months later, a couple who are close friends of mine told me they were having a baby. I thought that was a funny coincidence but nothing more. They had a beautiful baby, and they would send me regular photos as the baby grew. When the baby got to the age of four they sent a picture that stopped me in my tracks. The child looked exactly like the child in my dream, even down to the outfit the child was wearing.

It is an interesting situation for magician to be in. I met the child when she was three, and I knew her energy straight away, but said nothing. Nothing can be said – the child must grow and develop in this life, not the old life. And it is irrelevant to try and prove it, what would be the point? What I can say is that my mother had a very tough life with a lot of suffering, and now her eternal spirit is in a life that is wonderful. That is good enough for me.

The obsession with trying to prove reincarnation is pointless and can often be counter productive for the person. It is better to acknowledge it to yourself when you see it, and learn what you can from it through observation for the sake of your own personal learning. The same is true if you have your own memories from another life. Take note, and move on as it is far more important to focus on who you are to become, not what has been.

13. Summary

Because the main body of this lesson is about the first steps of learning about these Mysteries and this is an apprentice section, there will be no visionary work attached to this lesson: it is far too dangerous for you to wander off into these Deeper Mysteries. But knowing about them is important for your progression, even at this early stage of training. That knowing triggers deep changes within you that will surface in your more advanced work, and at that point it will be time to delve a little deeper in a practical sense.

In the meantime you can explore for yourself through research. I will not set you specific research tasks for this lesson; it is up to you to decide how much more you wish to look into this. If you do wish to research, then look at depictions of funeral imagery in ancient texts, and go back over the ones you have already looked at. You may well spot more things now you know a bit more of the Mystery. Also look at visionary paintings by past mystical painters, and wall paintings in various temples.

14. *Task:* Finding

By now you should have your scales and they should be somewhere in the west part of your house or working room. Now it is time to find the feather. This is not something you can buy, or go to someone who keeps birds and get one: you have to come across it yourself, out in nature.

Over the next couple of weeks, go out for walks (in nature if possible) and as you walk, mull over in your mind the concept of the Scales, the Judgement, the passage of the spirit through death, and how the way you live potentially affects that process. As you walk and think, keep an eye out for a white feather. It must be pure white, and must be either on the ground already or falling down to you in the air. It cannot have been placed somewhere by human hands.

When you find it, place it upon your scales. Do not place it in the cup of the Scales (the trigger of Judgement) but place it at the top of one arm of the Scales (where the chain of the cup and the arm of the Scales meet, thread it into the chain). By placing it there and not in the cup, it serves as an indicator that you are beginning to walk within the Death Mysteries and are striving to learn and evolve, but you are not yet asking for Judgement in life, nor are you ready yet to have Judgement in life or death.

Once it is there, just leave it there. Always keep your Scales where they cannot be knocked or tampered with, and if they cannot be visible in the house, then they can be set up in a cupboard, so long as they will not be knocked. They are slowly, magically, becoming an exteriorisation of your evolution of Ma'at, of balance, and of your Harvest.

Over your years of magic, you will energetically bond more and more with the Scales, and you will work with them magically as an adept. Should they ever become damaged, simply repair them and put them back where they belong. There will come a day, usually as an adept, when you get a strong feeling to dismantle them and put them in a box. That is when they have done their job and the rest is up to you.

Don't move onto the next lesson until you have found your feather. It seems like such a simple thing, but there is a powerful magical action behind this, and having the feather you are given by the land fixed to your Scales before you go in vision deeper into the Underworld (next lesson) is very important.

15. *Task:* Reading

Read the following passage below (*Aeneid* extract from Chapter 6) which is about the Death Mysteries. Read it a few times so that some of its more hidden meanings can come to light in your mind. It is the Greco-Roman version of part of the Death Mystery.

Revisit *The Vision of Ayr the Armenian* from Plato's *Republic* – you should have recently read it. Read the section about the passage of souls flowing down to the land and Underworld, and others flowing up into the stars. This passage of souls is the spirit in conscious choosing where it needs to be next. It is not the spirits of the switched off, but the spirits of the switched on as they choose the next place from the Vista and go to where they need to be.

Extract from Chapter Six of *The Aeneid*, Virgil

> *And, just before the confines of the wood,*
> *The gliding Lethe leads her silent flood.*
> *About the boughs an airy nation flew,*
> *Thick as the humming bees, that hunt the golden dew;*
> *In summer's heat on tops of lilies feed,*
> *And creep within their bells, to suck the balmy seed:*
> *The winged army roams the fields around;*
> *The rivers and the rocks remurmur to the sound.*
> *Aeneas wond'ring stood, then ask'd the cause*
> *Which to the stream the crowding people draws.*
>
> *Then thus the sire: "The souls that throng the flood*
> *Are those to whom, by fate, are other bodies ow'd:*
> *In Lethe's lake they long oblivion taste,*
> *Of future life secure, forgetful of the past.*
> *Long has my soul desir'd this time and place,*
> *To set before your sight your glorious race,*
> *That this presaging joy may fire your mind*
> *To seek the shores by destiny design'd."*

"O father, can it be, that souls sublime
Return to visit our terrestrial clime,
And that the gen'rous mind, releas'd by death,
Can covet lazy limbs and mortal breath?"

Anchises then, in order, thus begun
To clear those wonders to his godlike son:
"Know, first, that heav'n, and earth's compacted frame,
And flowing waters, and the starry flame,
And both the radiant lights, one common soul
Inspires and feeds, and animates the whole.

This active mind, infus'd thro' all the space,
Unites and mingles with the mighty mass.
Hence men and beasts the breath of life obtain,
And birds of air, and monsters of the main.
Th' ethereal vigor is in all the same,
And every soul is fill'd with equal flame;
As much as earthy limbs, and gross allay
Of mortal members, subject to decay,
Blunt not the beams of heav'n and edge of day.
From this coarse mixture of terrestrial parts,
Desire and fear by turns possess their hearts,
And grief, and joy; nor can the groveling mind,
In the dark dungeon of the limbs confin'd,
Assert the native skies, or own its heav'nly kind:
Nor death itself can wholly wash their stains;
But long-contracted filth ev'n in the soul remains.
The relics of inveterate vice they wear,
And spots of sin obscene in ev'ry face appear.
For this are various penances enjoin'd;
And some are hung to bleach upon the wind,
Some plung'd in waters, others purg'd in fires,
Till all the dregs are drain'd, and all the rust expires.
All have their manes, and those manes bear:
The few, so cleans'd, to these abodes repair,
And breathe, in ample fields, the soft Elysian air.

Lesson 4

The Underworld and the Abyss

With an understanding of fate and death under your belt, it is now time to learn a bit more about the Underworld. In texts it is mainly touched upon in relation to death, but it is much more than that.

The Underworld, in its deepest, most abstract form, is the *compression of manifestation*. As consciousness crosses over the threshold into manifestation, the body that houses that spirit/consciousness begins its long march to destruction and breakdown. We talked briefly in the module on creation about how the Divine Breath issues out an energetic impulse that, as it moves towards manifestation, is slowed down by the beings that interact with that energy so that it can manifest.

That same action of slowing down continues throughout the physical manifestation until it becomes so slow and dense that it eventually ceases to be a vehicle for living consciousness: the spirit releases and the body/substance composts, finally becoming dense substance. We see this in geology and archaeology, and from a magical perspective we call this process the Underworld.

If we look at it from a different angle, we can also see this process in action in the Inner Desert: the realm where nothing lives. This is the back room of creation and destruction, and the template for time, manifestation, and destruction is held in the Inner Desert. When you stand in the Inner Desert in vision, 'up' is the future, the desert is the present, and beneath the sands is the 'past' (the Underworld).

If we look at the Underworld from the point of view of our physical existence on the earth as magicians, the Underworld is beneath our feet and is the realm of ancient deities, ancestors, the death landscape, the sleepers, and vast beings from the distant past.

Magicians access this realm for many reasons: working in death, connecting with the ancient powers of the land, working with ancient deities, ancient temples, and our distant, long gone relatives of humanity. There is also another very important reason why magicians work with this realm: it is an anchor. One of the dynamics you have already begun to learn about is the energetic balancing that occurs for a magician if they go into the past before they go into the future, and if they go 'down' before they go 'up.'

Magicians also learn about the various types of beings that can be found in the Underworld, beings that are often treated with fear and revulsion, usually because of a lack of knowledge and direct experience. What some call demons can be accessed through the Underworld and the Abyss, but the term 'demon' is laden with misunderstanding, fantasy, and fear.

We will look at demonic beings (along with angelic beings) a bit later in the apprentice section. Suffice it to say that although these beings are dangerous and should not be lightly messed around with, they are not 'evil.'

The whole concept of good and evil that has been promulgated by some more recent religions (Christianity, for example) is designed to steer you away from danger, but it has also instilled a simplistic duality into the minds of generations which only serves to cut people off from the deeper aspects of creation and destruction.

So let us have a look at the different layers of the Underworld, what one would expect to find there, and how a magician would work there. Then we will look briefly at the Abyss, a connected realm that links directly into the Underworld. In this lesson you will also visit the Underworld in vision to begin your first real connections with this realm, but you will not be going down the Abyss just yet: to access such a place needs knowledge and skill to keep you from destruction – it is not a place to play in.

1. Threshold of the Underworld

The first layer of the Underworld is the threshold between the living and the dead. It is also a layer that appears in the inner landscape of a land, and is the place where the dead, the living, faery beings, and land spirits all interconnect and intersect. This is the layer of the Underworld most known to various types of magicians and which is worked with to access the faery realm, recent ancestors who have remained connected to the land (rather than gone in to rebirth), and to access the first layer of older deities.

This aspect of the inner realm is very interesting and is a space where magicians are very active. If a magician wishes to learn about the land around them, its fairly recent history, or about the faery beings and land beings that are all around us, the magician would work in this threshold place. It is pretty close to our own consciousness, therefore the rules of safe engagement are very close to the rules you would apply in your everyday physical life when you are in a place unknown to you.

The threshold of the Underworld can be accessed through the inner landscape of the land: they overlap and are of one another. In this crossover space, we find faery beings, land beings, ghosts, recent ancestors, and all manner of different beings.

You have already begun to work in the inner landscape, and if you move into the inner landscape with intent to interact with this crossover threshold, it will open up to you. We will spend a bit more time looking at this crossover place and the beings within it (mainly faery beings) in another lesson.

Faery beings are not nice little sweet things with wings: they are strange, powerful beings with a twisted sense of humour and no particular love of humanity. But once the magician earns the trust of these beings and learns to work sensibly with them, they can become powerful allies in your life and magical work. They are essentially much smaller versions of land beings, which are large beings that reside in rock outcrops, mountains, and forests; for example, whereas a faery being can be found in a forest, the land being is the consciousness of the whole forest itself.

If in your work as an apprentice you cross paths with one of these beings, be very honourable, honest, straightforward, and respectful – regardless of how you are treated or approached by them. These beings will test you, harass you, or try to beguile you to see what your deeper self is like. They will watch how you treat the land and creatures around you, how you interact with the land, the elements, animals, birds, spiders, etc., and they will form their opinion of you from how you act towards everything around you.

The other type of beings you are likely to come into contact with in this threshold space are the *sleeping dead*. Basically, there are two different types of sleepers that you will encounter upon the land and in this realm: working sleepers and waiting sleepers. A *working sleeper* is usually an ancestor that is deeply (tribally) connected to a land area, and went into death, sometimes ritually, with the intent to work as an interface between the land and the tribe. The incidences of these sleepers are getting rarer as archaeologists dig more and more of them up.

Not every ancient burial is a sleeper; it is often just a body. But sometimes they are, and if you wish to work with an intentional tribal sleeper, you need to know the rules of engagement: something you will learn fairly soon. Most countries have some sort of intentional sleeper present upon the land, as this was a widespread practice in many different cultures.

Another type of ancestral consciousness you will potentially come across in this threshold space are the *waiting sleepers*. These are people who upon death believed that they had to stay asleep in the land until the time of judgement arrived. This is particularly common in pre-twentieth century Catholic communities. The religious pattern was so strong in the life of the person that upon death they immediately fixed themselves to their body in burial and simply stayed there.

One way to spot this in a culture is where the idea of cremation or exposure of the body to the elements is abhorrent. In the Catholic communities, it was felt that keeping the body as preserved as possible would enable them, upon judgement, to rise in body and ascend to heaven. In terms of the death realm, they would not really appear, or only appear in that realm briefly as they held on tightly to their bodies in the belief that this would guarantee them a place in heaven.

As an aside, but one very relevant to you, there is a strange phenomenon that I have observed that is probably the fragmented root of this belief. Over the last few years I have observed waves of 'Judgement' flowing over the land of the living, and other people who are sensitive have also been picking up on this. It seems to affect those who do pick up on it, triggering an impulse to either magically engage with the Lesser Judgement in life, or triggering an unconscious impulse to 'clean up their act.' In the northern hemisphere it seems to trigger once a year, and over the last few years it has gotten stronger and stronger.

I became very curious about this, as so many magicians from around the world were contacting me about this experience, and were seeing what I was seeing. So I decided to investigate further. I worked in the inner realms to try and watch this impulse as it flowed out onto the land, and asked a being standing beside me what the hell was going on. This was an angelic being, a type very close to humanity (a Noble One) and therefore easy to converse with.

The being showed me cycles of this type of event happening every few thousand years, usually when large parts of humanity had become 'rotten.' Essentially, what the being conveyed was that as a nation or group of nations devolves (which is a natural progression in most nations), the people engage less and less with any mystical, religious, tribal, or magical patterns. Some who are removed from such patterns still live in relative balance for generations, and some do not.

The groups that do not live in balance tend to react in a particular way in death: they are fearful and immediately grab for another life without going through the process of the Scales, or even attempting to evolve towards that process. When there are large numbers of people circumventing this natural process, it causes a deficit, an imbalance of some sort, which in turn automatically triggers a deep energetic response.

That imbalance seems to be the result of not enough people going through the natural progression in death, which in turn results in too many living humans in general (if they are not going through the full death process, which slows them down), and too many that are deeply unbalanced: the species becomes self-destructive. That response is, to put it bluntly:

"If you will not come to us, then we will come to you."

The process of balance through the Scales flows out of death and into life instead, and affects every living thing. I asked the being to show me the process, but what I was shown didn't really fully translate for me: I didn't fully get it and still don't. But I will outline for you what I did understand and what I observed, so that you can ponder over it for yourself.

What I was shown was waves of energy sweeping over the land, and the humans it flowed over seemed to be deeply affected by it. Some were affected physically, and some were swept into death. Some whom I observed seemed to recognise what was happening and intentionally engaged in the Lesser Judgement process, and in those cases, the wave of energy seemed to enliven them.

As I write this, (September 2014) we are currently in a phase of this 'wave.' Just from chatting lightly to the local villagers where I live, I have found that many are having sleepless nights, some are feeling a sense of doom, and others are furiously spring cleaning. Interesting.

I have been working with the self-assessment process, as have other magicians I know, and the energy does seem to get up behind that conscious engagement. It is not a wave of 'God's punishment'; rather it seems to be a very natural response to the state of our species at this time and its effect on the land around them. We really need to get away from this dualist and simplistic religious dogmatic thinking that infects everything that we do as magicians.

Observing this process, and also thinking about it, it makes me wonder if this natural response/process is behind some of the Biblical stories that run along similar veins, and also the ideas of the Essenes, who felt that Judgement was at hand. The Essenes felt that they needed to prepare for Judgement and therefore had to live their lives in a particular way. If we take the religious dressing out of the picture, what we are left with is a group of people who were picking up on this wave of the Judgement process and tried to live their lives in a way that would positively engage it. But as always with everything connected to humanity, dogmatic thinking quickly moves in and the process begins to fall apart.

And in that, I think, is a major lesson for us at this time in our own history: do not try to box, organise, and systematise too much. We all need some structure, but there has to be fluidity in thinking that allows the consciousness of an individual person to connect fully with these inner impulses in their own way. That translates to *walking your own path in gnosis*: we are truly unique as individuals, and what is the right approach for one may not be the right approach for another person.

Back to the Underworld. (By the way, these little diversions are intentionally put into these lessons so that they cannot be easily found by those simply dipping into the text out of curiosity. What an apprentice can take away from these texts is vastly different to what a casual reader will understand.)

2. The first layer of the Underworld

The first true layer of the Underworld is where you find deities that are still active in the outside world, deities that are connected to the Underworld in terms of death, destruction, the cycles of species, etc. It is also the layer where the magician finds access to the realm of death. This is also the realm where we find the ancient dynamic of prophecy: going into an Underworld cave to meet an oracle or goddess who heals, curses, or prophesies is an ancient pattern indeed.

In most ancient cultures in the northern hemisphere, we have many examples of stories of Underworld goddesses who sit at the first layer of the Underworld and interact with the living world. The goddess Sul in Bath, England is a prime example. She is also known as Sulis Minerva, and was a goddess of cursing, blessing, and healing. Glastonbury in England is another place that is an ancient entrance to this first layer of the Underworld.

Sadly, these days fantasy has overtaken reality with regards to Glastonbury, and it abounds with Merlins, people dressing as faeries, and various women play-acting in a generic 'goddess' community.

Glastonbury is an entrance to the realm of death, to the Underworld, and to the powers that surface into our world from the Underworld: the power of destruction.

These days it is covered with a crust of commercial messiahs, wannabe 'wizards,' and tons of escapism.

One way to sidestep a lot of this type of 'crust' that seems to cover the Underworld, and one of the major keys to working with this realm and the deities, powers, and beings that inhabit this realm, is to work with the beings without attaching 'names' or dogmas to them. One way to do this, and it is an ancient way of working, is to work with and connect with the beings as they appear, without all the dogmatic dressing, and to not work with 'known names' but to address them in relation to their function. A goddess of the Underworld is just that. She does not need the names that humans have given her, nor the dressings that they have attached to her.

Before we move on, let's just look a bit closer at these different goddesses of the Underworld, as you will be soon meeting one.

3. The Goddess in the Cave

The Goddess in the Cave is an ancient expression of the female deities that reside in this first layer of the Underworld. It is a visionary interface that I have used with students for decades as it is so stable and predictable. It is not 'one' goddess that is connected to when magicians work in vision with this being; rather it is the female deity of a particular land that is contacted.

Overall, though, the interface is the same throughout the northern hemisphere (I have no idea if the same pattern exists in the southern hemisphere) and that is to say: cave, goddess, pool or river of water.

It seems to be a particular pattern that allows the individual female deity of a particular land to interface through. So for example, if you have been working with the goddess in the cave on your own land for a while and then move to another country, it is likely that the same visionary pattern would work, but the actual being you meet, while still being a goddess, is different. They are heavily interwoven with the landmass, and seem to be expressions of the female power within that land.

By using the stripped-down interface, the magician is able to use that pattern to connect with the goddess in the land where they are and work with them without having to resort to using names/dogmas or human constructed patterns.

It is very much a fashion these days to take goddesses out of their natural environment and shoehorn them into a modern role which is often far removed from who and what they actually are. And while some goddesses do *travel* i.e. you can connect to the exact same goddess regardless of what landmass you are on, there are many who do not travel. The usual rule of thumb is the deeper in the Underworld they reside, the more likely they are to travel. This is for a lot of reasons which we will cover later in another lesson.

The reason the magician connects with these 'Goddesses in the Cave' is that such a connection helps to open up a lot of the Underworld for the magician, makes it more accessible, and also can afford a deep level of protection: you work for her, she will work for you. The work trade-off changes somewhat according to where you live and what exact power it is you are tapping into. And even within your own land, there are various layers of these goddesses.

For example, where I live there is a layer of this cave goddess that is very specific to the valley that I live in. If you go just a few miles down the road, she vanishes. But if you go a little deeper into the first layer of the Underworld, where I live, you hit another layer of goddess that is specific to the island of Britain, but does not appear, for example, in the USA.

So it would seem we are connecting with various frequencies and more surface expressions of a deeper power, and it is that deeper power that we will look at next.

4. The Deeper Underworld

Once you pass through the first layer of the Underworld and continue moving downward, you come to a deeper layer of the Underworld where ancient powers reside and are still accessible to the magician.

These realms work very much along the lines of *as above, so below,* in that the patterns and layers mirror each other. Just as the magician reaches 'up' and finds primal deities, mediators of Divinity, angelic beings, etc., so the Underworld, too, has its own mirrored layers. The Deeper Underworld and the powers that reside there mirror the deeper powers of creation that flow into manifestation.

In practical terms of an apprentice and initiate, that means finding and being able to work with powerful deities that once were widely worked with in the ancient world. Although some of these deities still have a presence in their temples in the manifest worlds, their roots and deeper selves reside in the Underworld, anchoring them as they bridge between the past and the present.

The ancient deities, and also the roots of the ancient temples that are still partially or fully operating in the manifest/surface world, create a bridge between their outer existence in the surface world, their original outer structure in the Underworld, and their inner templates in the Desert. The surface world is a fulcrum for them, and the power flows in a constant stream from the inner world, out into the surface manifest world, and then flows down into the Underworld.

This constant stream of energy creates a highway for power and consciousness to travel along. We as living humans can flow into the inner realm as magicians to access the inner temple, and we can also flow down into the Underworld to reach the patterns of its original existence. This pathway of power is also utilised by spirits, and this is demonstrated, for example, by the *Vision of Ayr* that you read in Plato.

These pathways can be utilised not only to access these powerful deities and their temples, but they are also highways to realms that these temples and deities are connected to and plugged into. So now you can begin to see how knowledge of this realm is so vital to the work of a magician. They are more than just realms in themselves; they are also highways to the depths of creation and destruction itself.

Rather than ramble on for hours about this realm, it will be easier for you to just visit it in vision, passing through the layers and going into an ancient temple to stand before one of the very powerful goddesses that reside in this deep realm. This interaction will trigger the creation of your deep tap root that will anchor you in the depths of the Underworld in order to prepare you for the work to come in the future.

Before you get to that practical work, I want to also outline another major aspect of this subject matter for you (though it will not be something you visit or work in for quite some times in your studies, for safety's sake), and that aspect is the Abyss.

5. THE ABYSS

There has been quite a lot written about the Abyss over the last century, but most of it is vague, or is written from a place of 'not knowing,' where the writer draws on other texts and forms a theory based upon them. Others have written about the Abyss, inspired by Crowley, and place personal psychological meaning to the Abyss and the magical act of crossing the Abyss. Still others deny it altogether as they have not had any experience of it, and the writings they have read make no sense to them. There are some modern writings out there on the Abyss that actually do tackle it from the writers' direct experience, but for the most part, much of what is readable and truly is about the Abyss can be found in ancient and mystical texts.

It is not that magicians don't know about it: many do but they choose, for good reason, to be silent about it. I thought long and hard about how best to approach this for the apprentice section, as I have written about the Abyss before, which has helped some people but has also triggered truly disastrous experiments in others. I came to the conclusion that it would be wise to give the apprentice an overview, with the appropriate health warnings, so that the apprentice at least has a basic understanding of what it is, why it is, and how it works.

Later, in your training, you will learn how to work in the Abyss and how to cross the Abyss, and most important of all, why a magician crosses the Abyss, what it does, and what effect it has on the rest of your life. Too many people play around magically in and around the Abyss, and the result of such curiosity and experimentation tends invariably to result in death or mental illness.

So what is the Abyss? Moving away from all previous writings, the following is what I have discovered through decades of magical visionary work.

My earliest encounter with the Abyss was as a young magician. I was working down in the Underworld in ritual vision when a being appeared and guided me down a tunnel which opened out over what appeared to be a vast crack that ran through all the worlds. Something within me knew what it was and what I had to do. I knew that what I was about to do could potentially kill me, but I also knew deep inside that it was something I needed to do. I had to step off the cliff I was standing on, and put my trust in my own soul and in Divinity. I crossed the Abyss by stepping out into the nothing and not falling, but reaching the other side. It changed my life in every way possible.

After that event I spent years exploring and discovering the Abyss, and then more years of working in service both down and up in the Abyss. I finally had to stop working in the Abyss when I hit the menopause, as my body could no longer handle the huge physical and energetic impact that such work involved.

So now let's go over what I found, so that you have a good idea of what it is we are talking about.

As an aside, for a time after my first experience, I did not realise that what I was working with was the Abyss – it was only after lengthy discussions with Jewish Kabbalists and mystical visionaries that they finally drilled into me what it was I was doing and looking at.

In retrospect I was very lucky to survive unscathed: I was very young and foolish, but I was also well grounded and was working deeply with the Noble Ones. I think I owe my life, or at least my mental health, to their attentive guidance in those early years.

6. The Highway of the Abyss

The Abyss is found in the Inner Desert and appears to us in a visionary context as a vast, seemingly bottomless crack in the earth. If you look up (it took me some years to realise that there is an 'up' also) the crack also runs through the 'sky': it is a 'highway' that flows from the stars to the bottom of the Underworld and cleaves the Inner Desert in to two parts. What we see as the Inner Desert that we can access is one side. The other side of the Abyss appears misty: the knowledge of what lies beyond is obscured with mist. If you look down the Abyss, you will see ledges and tunnels, and sometimes you will also see beings looking back at you. If you look up, it tends to be obscured by mist: most of the time you are only able to see the Desert (our own time) and down (our past).

And that brings me to the dynamics that flow through this place: up is future, surface is now, down is past. What is coming into formation (life, substance, time) flows down from above, and also concurrently from across the Abyss (Divine utterance across the Abyss): those two streams of power meet on our side of the Abyss and immediately filter through a pattern which begins the process of shaping something for creation (something you will learn a lot more about in the Initiate section).

When something is breaking down, it stays in the manifest world and sinks into the Underworld. If it is a power or energy or being/soul that should not be coming back into manifestation, it sinks deeply into the Underworld and finally passes into the Abyss. The Abyss is a place where manifestation is suspended: beings sleep here, or are bound here, to keep them out of the circulation of physical life or the manifest world.

When a being (or species, even) is or becomes very imbalanced to the point of being overly destructive, it is withdrawn from the cycle of birth/death and is essentially put into storage. (This also makes me wonder if this is where the 'Second Deathers' go.) The beings found down the Abyss are not just humans pulled out of circulation, but also many other types of beings that are destructive and seriously out of balance, or simply do not fit in the pattern of life any more.

Very ancient deities can be found sleeping or even bound into the Abyss, as are demonic beings, i.e. beings that are solely destructive and no longer have a role in the composting/necessary destruction process in life, along with the consciousness of ancient dangerous diseases, the spirits of ancient sentient beings that have been taken out of the loop of creation (like some dinosaurs, for example) – you get the idea.

The layers of the Abyss that are nearest to our layer of the Desert (fairly recent past – last few thousand years) have beings that are not fully locked down or sleeping, but they cannot leave the Abyss. These beings can be worked with in times of major crisis, as they hold ancient knowledge and have excellent guarding skills.

However, a magician who does that really needs to know what they are doing and have a very good reason for doing it. If one of these beings bridges through a human (hitches a ride) and into the manifest world, our world, they can do untold damage: as it is with disease, so it is with these beings. If they have been out of circulation for a few thousand years and are suddenly inadvertently released back into the world, we have no natural immunity to them. The consequences of that can be horrifying.

The Abyss has a vast angelic being that is essentially the 'doorkeeper' of the Abyss. For some reason, some magicians seem to think that this being is a demon… no it is not, it is just a vastly powerful, non-fluffy angelic being that keeps and guards the threshold. When as magicians you come to learn how to work with the Abyss, first you will learn to work with this keeper, who will ensure you do what you are supposed to do and don't do what you are not supposed to do.

On the other side of the Abyss is the source of Divine Breath: the Universal Power of Divine Being. The other side of the Abyss is the realm that has no time, no structure of manifestation; it is a place beyond creation, a place of eternal being, and is the source of the impulse that crosses the Abyss and begins its journey into creation and manifestation. Heavy stuff indeed! So let us get back to the topic of the Underworld and on to the practical work.

7. About the practical work

The practical work in this lesson, for the most part, will be visionary work.

It is important, really important, for your own safety, that you do not step out of the boundaries of the vision and go off exploring on your own. When worked with correctly, this visionary work is perfectly safe and will give you more information on some aspects of the Underworld than a pile of books could. However, if you step outside of or over the thresholds outlined in the vision you are very likely to injure yourself: this is where the apprentice has to be a responsible adult and not a curious, foolish teen.

The act of doing these Underworld visions will trigger the establishment and growth of your own 'tap root' that will seat strongly in the Underworld, giving you a strong foundation and anchor for your future work.

It will, for some, also trigger the slow process of 'remembering' for those of you who have stepped into the inner worlds in other lives. If this triggering happens, do not get hung up on it and start to identify with that remembering. You do not make a big deal out of your childhood memories, and these are the same. They are past: remember, and then move on.

Advice:

Do these visions when you have time to relax or sleep afterwards. If you are not good at remembering the directions or details of the path through the vision, then record the vision in your own voice and listen to it as a guide as you do the vision. Plan ahead, and ensure that you have plenty of time to process the vision work through your sleep and through your body. After you have been in the Underworld, eat something solid that will ground you. Do this every time you go into the Underworld, as it will help your body deal with the impact.

Have your journal to hand in the room with you so that you can take notes as soon as you come out of vision. Always write up your findings, impressions, and consequent dreams, and also note any bodily effects afterwards, or strange happenings around you. Write them in a computer log so that they can be submitted.

Like all other visions on this course, learn the key elements and steps to each vision before you attempt it. Read it repeatedly, like a story, until you are familiar with each part of the vision. Then, and only then, if you wish, record the vision so that you can listen to it as you work and have it guide you.

If you do record it, make sure you put in the breaks of silence where you are doing something (like climbing) that will take a bit of time. Do not add anything to it, do not embellish or dress the vision in any way. It is a specific map to follow, not a psychological pathworking.

8. *Task:* First Vision – The access to death through the Underworld

Before you start the vision, open the directions, see the contacts on the thresholds, and then sit before the central altar with your back to the east, so you are facing west with the central flame before you. Do not lie down for this work: it is very important that you stay awake.

Meditate for a few minutes to still yourself, and when you are ready close your eyes and see the central flame in your inner vision. Hold the clear intention that you are going to go into the Underworld to visit the threshold of death. As you watch the flame, an entrance to the land beneath you opens up, and the flame falls down into the Underworld.

In vision, stand up and look down the hole that has appeared in the room. It will be dark, and you will just be able to see the light of the flame in the darkness. You will also see rough stone steps leading down into the darkness, and they curl around the hole to form a stone spiral stairway.

Step onto the first step, holding your hand to the wall for support, and begin to climb down the steps. Even though it is dark, you will be able to just see enough to climb safely down. Climb down and down, moving deeper and deeper into the darkness. Take your time and run your hand over the rough stone walls as you climb down, feeling the stone, its moisture, and the occasional tree root. Eventually you come to an area where there is a floor, and an entrance covered in fabric and moss.

Pull the fabric to one side, and step into a cave that seems to be dimly lit by a light of its own and which has a pool of water in it. The water seeps out on the far side of the cave, vanishing down a dark tunnel, and the wall on the opposite side of the cave has a large stone high-backed seat that is naturally formed out of the rock.

Upon the seat sits an old woman who is asleep. Her long hair grows into the rock beside her and down into the floor like roots. Around her, upon her lap, in her arms, and tucked into her clothing are many creatures and birds, also fast asleep. You also begin to notice the occasional human also sleeping on the floor beside her and curled around her feet, and in the edges of her long cloak that spills out onto the floor.

Tiptoe quietly towards her, as you intend to pass by her and into a tunnel that leads deeper into the Underworld.

As you get closer to her you recognise her: you have already met her, given her a gift, and honoured her. When you draw close to her, lean or kneel down and touch the hem of her cloak to honour her: this is the *Mother*, the goddess who holds the threshold between the living land and the Underworld. As you touch the hem of her cloak, she opens one eye and looks at you. Bow to her and ask her permission to pass beyond her and into the tunnel of the Underworld.

She nods her permission, closes her eye, and goes back to sleep.

See the tunnel that leads into the darkness, and as you step into the tunnel, you realise you are walking in ankle-deep water. Walk along the stream-bed and listen carefully for any sounds that you may hear. Take your time walking down this tunnel.

The tunnel eventually opens out in a vast cavern that holds shallow water and ancient trees growing out of the water. The place is lit with strange green light that flows from the trees, the water, and the very air in this strange place. This Underworld is the head of the River of Death that flows through the Underworld and emerges in the Plains of Death.

Wade through the water, walking among the trees, and as you walk, sing. The trees are the guardians of the river, and the thing they love above all else is the sound of singing. Single lullabies, childhood songs, or simply hum as you weave in and out of the trees. Take your time walking through the forest.

Should you develop a thirst as you walk, *do not drink of the water at all*. Be disciplined and continue walking.

As you make your way further into the Underworld Forest you begin to see a faint light that grows brighter the closer you get to it. As you emerge from the forest you see a large opening, an entrance of the chamber you are in, and it opens out onto a bright, sunny desert where the waters of the Underworld come together to form a river. Do not step out of the Underworld cavern; do not step over the threshold of the cavern into the desert. Stay within the cavern, but draw close enough that you can see the desert, the river, and everything in that landscape.

Look out over the desert, see the river flowing from the cavern, and see it flow into the desert and off into the horizon. See people gathered by the river, and look closely at the people. Some will look 'different' energetically: they are the angelic beings that work in death and 'dress up' to appear human in order to connect with humans more easily. Watch for other beings coming and going; watch what the people do, how they are, how they are reacting, and what actions they take, if any. Take as long as you need to observe. When you are ready to leave, step back and turn around.

Look at the vast cavern with the Underworld Forest and all the water, and look around the edges of the cavern. You will see, off to one side and partially hidden, a rough stone stairway that climbs up the side of the cavern and vanishes up into the darkness. Climb onto the stone stairway and ascend to the top of the cavern. Take your time and watch your step as you climb.

Once you reach the top you will find a tunnel with yet more stairs leading up. Climb those too, with the intention of returning to the surface world. As you climb those steps, you will hear voices or mumbles, and the stone walls of the stairwell begin to turn to compacted earth and tree roots. Climb slowly, and listen as you climb: there are various voices one can find in this space. Some are ancestors in the land; some are faery beings. Do not try to connect with them, just be aware of them as you climb.

As you climb, you begin to see light up above you. Climb towards that shaft of light, and you will find yourself emerging out of a hole in your working room. Climb out of the hole and as you step out of it, the hole closes up and all that is left is the central flame burning in the centre. Before you open your eyes, go over in your mind everything you saw and experienced. Ensure you have recalled the memory, and once you are clear, open your eyes and write down key words or notations in your journal that will remind you once you come to type up the details on computer.

Always, whenever you do involved visions like this, have your journal before you and write down notes as soon as you come out of vision, as often visionary contact fades in the memory much quicker than ordinary memories do. From those notes you can then type up in more detail and keep it in a computer file.

About the vision

This vision took you down through the cave of the goddess; this is a place you can visit often if you wish, to go be there, talk to her, sleep, wash, learn, and observe. When I was a young magician I visited her often and learned a great deal from talking with her, from watching, or just being there.

From her cave you moved into a slightly deeper part of the Underworld, which often appears as a partially submerged underground forest: the head of the river Lethe. This is also a place you can work regularly to observe (nothing more) as spirits of many different species pass through on their journey in and out of death. There are quite a few different rivers that flow from this place, but simply stay with the one that you have worked with and now know. Don't try to over-organise it in your mind: it is tempting to decide what rivers flow out of this place and what their names are (there are quite a few ancient texts about this place). That is a bad road to go down early in your magical training: learn to keep an open mind that is about direct experience, and don't try to map these realms. They will eventually reveal themselves to you directly over time.

The threshold between the Underworld Forest/Cavern and the Plains/River of Death is a good place to go and observe. You can watch the dead as they go through their various processes, and also observe the angelic beings that work in depth from a safe distance. Do not be tempted at this stage in your training to step over that threshold. Be patient, learn to observe, and learn to rein in the curiosity or impulse to step over into the death realm.

Notice that you did not return the way that you came. This is slowly introducing you to a very interesting dynamic in visionary work whereby you always have to take your time going to a realm, letting the body, mind, and spirit adjust to the different energies, and also ensuring that the right steps take you to the right place. But coming back sometimes you do not need to take such a convoluted route. You needed to go through the Cave of the Goddess to trigger her protection, but to get home from the Underworld, you simply go 'up.'

So now let us move on to the second vision in this lesson, which is to go deeper into the Underworld and connect with the very ancient and powerful goddess power that resides there. Notice that in this lesson you are connecting with goddesses and not gods: you are learning about the power of the vessel before going on to learn everything that the vessel contains. There are male powers also in the Underworld, of course, and once you have learned one side of the coin, then you will learn the other and balance the two together.

9. *Task:* Second Vision – Accessing the root ancient temples

This vision takes you down into a very ancient layer of temple culture so that you can interact with the consciousness still residing there.

As an aside, these ancient temples are also found in the Inner Desert: the Underworld version is on our 'side of the fence,' the remnants of the physical manifestation of the temple. And the temple found in the Desert is the remains of the inner construct of the same temple that is found in the Underworld – the Inner Desert version is the back room, so to speak, of the physical temple.

The more you work in the Desert and the Underworld (and upper worlds) as the course goes on, you will find that mirror images of places, beings, and people appear not only in the various realms, but also in the Desert. To access the manifest history or future potential of a place or being, you go to the realms that hold the outer pattern. To access the timeless inner construct, spirit, or consciousness of a place or being, you go to the Desert.

Over the span of the course, you will learn carefully how to access these different realms individually and eventually learn how to work with them together. But to stay solid, safe, and sane, you need to learn, visit, and interact with these different aspects in slow, careful steps.

This next visit is a key step in that process. This specific ancient temple that you will be visiting has roots far back in human history, and over the millennia has become a composite made up of different temples that worked with the same power. This composite action happens to places and also beings when there is a vast span of time where they have been or still are active. So for example, the powers you experience and interact with in this temple will be recognisable when you then go to visit (in the flesh) some of the still-standing very ancient temples that worked with the same deep goddess power.

It took me a while to figure this out. After working in depth for a few years with these places, and then going to an ancient temple site, I immediately recognised the power signature and aspects of the building. But then I went to an ancient site of the same power but in a different land, and the same thing happened. It took me a while to realise that over time, as the inner aspects of the temples sink into the Underworld, those that were working with the same power fused together somehow and became a 'root' temple.

In the vision I will not name the goddess you are going to work with, as there is more than one name for her. But once you have worked with her, you will recognise her in slightly different forms, and one of those forms will gravitate to you in your magical work. The other thing to understand about working with this deep temple is that this particular vision is the one that really roots you into the Underworld and gives you a powerful anchor to work with. The deeper you go 'down' in your practice, the further you will then be able to go 'up' in your ritual visionary work.

10. The vision

Prepare yourself in the same way that you did for the previous vision, but for this vision sit with your back to the central altar, facing north. The ground will open up the same way, but this time it will be the north flame that falls down into the Underworld.

In vision, follow the flame in exactly the same way, and take the same route through the cave of the goddess and through the Underworld Forest. When you get to the forest, walk through the water again with the intention of going to the deep, ancient temple of the goddess in the Underworld. (Your clear intent and focus allows the entrances to appear in the vision – the beings know from your intent where you want to go.)

As you walk through the Underworld Forest, keep a lookout for the temple guardian. This guardian can appear in many different forms, but you will know them when you see them. When you find the guardian, bow, tell them who you are, and ask permission to enter into the deep Underworld temple of the goddess. The guardian will look at you, and you will notice that they have quite a few eyes around their form that open and look at you in detail. The guardian will see that you have already worked with the goddess in the cave and are therefore suitable to access deeper into the Underworld.

When the guardian is happy with what they see (that you are who you say you are) the guardian will either point you to a hidden entrance, or they will take you by the hand and lead you to an entrance you would not have seen had you not been shown it. The entrance will have water from the forest flowing into it, and will most likely be partially submerged.

Get into the water and dive down under the water, swimming forward towards a light that will have appeared. You will swim under the entrance and emerge in a tunnel with low light and lots of ancient paintings on the walls of strange-looking demon guardians.

Stand up in the water and follow the tunnel, staying within the shallow water, and look at the paintings as you walk. As you follow the tunnel, you will notice that the water is starting to get deeper again. Continue to walk until it has become too deep, and you can no longer see anything in front of you. At that point, dive back down into the water, swimming forward underwater again towards a light.

When you reach the light, swim up to the surface and you will find yourself in an underground lake with stone steps at the side that you can use to climb out. Once you are out and have stood up, you realise you are standing at an entrance to a vast stone temple with a doorway so big you can barely see the capstones. It looks like it was built for giants.

Pass through the entrance and walk into the rectangular outer court which has huge columns on either side of you. As you continue, you see a slightly smaller doorway before you with vast wooden carved doors covered in strange signs and symbols, faces, and shapes. Place your hands upon the door so that the door can feel you. After a moment, the doors swing slowly open and you feel like you are propelled forward with an invisible push from behind.

You are pushed into a vast inner sanctum of the temple. It is cubic in shape, with a ceiling almost a hundred feet high (about 30 meters). At the far end sits a vast statue upon a throne. The statue is of a black lioness goddess seated upon a stone throne, with two bronze doors between her feet and a bowl of fire before her. The power emanating from this statue is so strong that it takes your breath away. Take a moment to simply stand in its presence and let your mind, spirit, and body adjust to the power of this goddess.

Slowly walk to the feet of the statue and touch them lightly with respect and recognition. As you touch the foot it moves, and you realise this is not a statue but a living being. You step back, and the doors between her feet open: out walks a priest or priestess of this temple, and they stand before you. Bow to the priest/priestess, tell them your name, who you are, what time you come from, which land, city, and that you are there to make connection with this ancient place. Tell them that you are studying as an apprentice in magical training and wish to learn.

The priest/priestess may talk to you briefly, and try to remember what they say. The contact then points down to your feet and asks you to take off your shoes or socks. Even if you are physically sitting with nothing on your feet in this vision, see your everyday footwear on you in vision, and take them off until you are standing on the stone floor in bare feet. Feel the sense of your skin on the stone. Feel the temperature (hot or cold?) and feel the energy of this place through your feet.

The contact then points up to the roof. Be aware of your upper body in the surface world while you are still standing in the Underworld. Imagine your upper body in the surface world and your feet/legs in the Underworld: get a sense of stretching between the two places. Take as long as you need to in order to get this sense, and don't worry about the visuals; simply recover the feeling or sense of this stretched position: your feet upon the stone in the Underworld and your body in the surface world; imagine it as if you were standing up.

Once you have a sense of the stretch, now bring your focus back to the contact and the goddess before you. The priest/priestess tells you that this ancient lioness goddess is vital for the northern hemisphere of the earth: she is the guardian and protector of balance, or Ma'at. She is fierce, destructive, and yet compassionate and healing: whatever is needed to bring balance.

The contact reaches out and gets a hold of your left arm, and begins to draw out a small number of shapes, sigils or hieroglyphs on your skin. It will be a fairly simple shape or shapes, and work very hard to see them *and remember them*. Once that is done, the contact leads you back to the foot of the statue and asks you to once more place your hands upon the foot of the goddess. Keep your hands there and feel her power: it is a very specific power that has a very distinct feel or sense to it. Remember that feeling or sense.

When you are ready, remove your hands, bow to her, and step back. Kneel down and look at the floor. It is dusty. Write your full name in the dust, the name you were born with. In the dust you see a small but very sharp blade. Pick it up, cut your finger, and drip a few drops of blood on your name written in the dust: you are leaving your unique identity at her feet, deep in the Underworld.

Once you have done that, the great goddess moves, leans over, and places her hand by you in order for you to step up onto her hand. The priest/priestess bows to you and tells you that you can come back here as often as you like simply to be in the presence of this power, to root yourself, and also to come here if you wish to learn about your own need for balance: the priesthood here will place within you the knowledge that you need in order to facilitate that balance. That knowledge will then appear in your mind unbidden when it is needed.

Step onto the hand of the goddess, and hold on as she holds you up to her face. Feel her lion breath upon your face; see the endless stars in her eyes, the sharp power of her teeth, and the softness of her fur. She looks into your eyes and blows gently over you: the breath of the goddess. She then holds you up, higher and higher to the roof of the temple, where you see a small opening to a stair well cut into the stone. Climb onto the stairs and ascend without looking back.

As you climb, you come to a break in the steps which you recognise as the stairway from the Underworld Forest to the surface world. Keep climbing up and up until you emerge back into your work space, and step gently back into your body. Before you open your eyes, once more remember the shapes that were drawn upon your arm. Once you have a sense of them, open your eyes and draw them in your journal.

Once you are finished and are ready to close the work space down, when you come to stand before the northern altar, before you blow out the candle, stand for a moment in silence with your eyes open. Be aware of the sense of your feet upon the stone, deep in the Underworld before the goddess, and your upper body here in the surface world. From now on, every time you still yourself to light the first candle in the ritual space, do this brief meditation of your feet on the stone in the Underworld and your body in the temple.

11. *Task:* Working with the symbols

The shapes that were written on your arms may very possibly become working shapes for you in the future. For some, simply having them written on their skin in vision is enough; for others the images will be useful in meditation or to use as seals in work related to that specific goddess power, or they may be shapes that directly mediate power to you for you to work with. They can also be 'marks' left upon you that will identify you in other realms and mark you as 'protected by the great lioness goddess.' These are magical working marks. So you need to learn what to do with them.

The first step is to write them in your journal and then redraw them over and over until you can draw them from memory, accurately. If you cannot work out what the shapes were and cannot retrieve the memory, don't panic. That also happened to me years ago. Many years later I saw them on a temple wall in a ruin that I was exploring while on holiday. The wall was full of different symbols but two, very insignificant ones, suddenly lit up and I remembered.

A year later it became very apparent to me what they were doing on me, why they were there, and what they did. They had been asleep up to that point, and then they suddenly leaped to action. So just go with the flow.

Once you have a clear image of them in your mind and can draw them with ease, then you need to do a series of readings to find out what the next step for them is. If you get no clear readings and cannot interpret them properly, just give it time for the dust to settle, and then revisit the reading exercise in the future.

But do not skip over this task of doing the readings. Not only is it important to know what to do with the symbols, but you must practise your reading skills regularly: don't be put off from lack of skill... it does not drop out of the sky, it comes with practice and focus.

12. *Task:* Readings on the symbols

Use the **Tree of Life layout** for the following questions and write up each reading on your computer log.

"Are these symbols already active in my energy field?"

"Do I need to do anything with them at this point in my training?"

"Do I need to draw them out and place them near the north altar?"

"Can I use them as a protective seal (on a talisman, or on a door for example)?"

"Should I just leave off working with them for now and let them surface later?"

If all the answers are negative, then you simply wait and move on in your studies. Not everyone works with these signs; simply having them on your inner pattern is enough.

And always with magic... *if you are in doubt, wait.* Do not take a magical action if you are not clear about what you are doing or it does not feel right. Learn to work with your instincts.

13. Summary

There are many different aspects to the Underworld, and in magical terms you have barely scratched the surface. These vast realms can take lifetimes to learn about in full, but the key aspects that you have learned about in this lesson will give you a good, simple, but very powerful foundation to stand upon as a magician. The Cave of the Goddess, the threshold between the Underworld Forest and death, and the deep temple are major elements in magic, and before you go on to learn about any other aspect of working in the Underworld (or the Abyss) you need to have a strong solid connection to these places.

14. *Task:* Practice

Go into both visions each week for four weeks. (You should still be doing your daily meditations too!) Get used to going in and out of these places, learn to observe, to acknowledge the contacts, and be respectful of the goddesses you encounter there: these are ancient and very powerful beings, so watch your manners. They are not figments of your or anyone else's imagination, and they operate in very different cultural ways to what we are used to. Respect is a major thing for these goddesses, and any disrespect will potentially be met with aggression (which will affect your physical as well as mental health).

The priesthood contact in the deep temple will probably be willing to guide you gently in how to be around these goddesses, but do not treat that contact as 'support' or badger them with questions, or ask them to do things for you that you should do yourself. They will immediately close down on you, and 'sorry' does not cut any ice in this place.

Your job is to learn to get in and out of these places, to learn how to be there and observe only (**no work at all**), and to learn how to stretch yourself (feet in the Underworld). Do not try and skip ahead in your actions by exploring or pushing boundaries in this deep place – you will regret it.

15. Goddess

You may, after working with these visions a few times, come across an image or a statue of a goddess that triggers the same sense/feeling of the power of the lioness goddess in the Underworld. Do not go searching for one, but should one cross your path, take her home and have her in the north of your working space.

You do not need to do anything special (it is best and safest at this point just to let her be) other than find a space for her, cleanse the space with frankincense smoke, and occasionally burn frankincense before the image.

This is about tuning, clearing, and establishing. There is no deity worship – you are a magician, not a priest. But there is a deep respect, honour, and awareness of her presence. Rather than thinking in religious terms, think in terms of having a very old professor with old-fashioned ways of doing things sitting in the corner of your room. You would make sure they are happy, listen to them with respect, and treat them with the honour they deserve: she is the elder of all elders.

Lesson 5
The Living Dead

Now that you have a better idea of the death process in general, it is time to take a closer look at the people/spirits that do not go through the usual death process but stay connected to the physical world for one reason or another. Not every spirit that stays attached to the living is a 'ghost' or in distress, or is dodging the whole death process.

As a magician, it is important to know the difference between who is choosing to stay and who is stuck or clinging to the living world, so that you do not inadvertently haul someone into the death process against their will. It is also important for a magician to know the difference between a real ghost and something else: most hauntings are 'something else.'

A lot of magicians these days have very little understanding of these phenomena. As a result of that innocent ignorance, all sorts of problems can kick off in a house where magic is being worked with. So this basic background knowledge can become invaluable should you inadvertently trigger a pissed-off being or get an unwanted lodger. Also, you will find that the deeper you get into magic, the more you will be placed in situations where you have to deal with these types of issues. It is a matter of the universe saying "oh good, you have switched on, now go solve this problem!" A magician should never go looking for issues to solve, nor advertise such, and never ever charge money for solving these issues – is a part of the adept service. Something is fatefully placed in your path and it is made very clear that it is something that you need to deal with, *if you have the knowledge and experience* to deal with it.

This particular subject can be very difficult for a lot of apprentices, as the film and TV industry has used 'ghosts' as a major theme in movies to shock and horrify people. Add this to numerous old stories and taboos around death, and what results is generations of people in the West who are terrified by the very idea of a ghost. Our TV station listings are crammed full of B-rate movies, docudramas and psychic questing programs that play on fear and rely on pseudoscience to try and discover ghost activity.

Trust me, if you had real ghost activity, you would know about it. You would not need an instrument to measure a change in electromagnetic fields or anything like that – if a ghost wants your attention, it will get it.

Let us first have a close look at the 'ghost' phenomenon: what ghosts are, what they are not, how ghosts get your attention, and why. If you are a magician, particularly if you are also sensitive or psychic, then as soon as you start to work magically in a space you will light a beacon in the inner worlds. Many things come to investigate, and ghosts are one of them.

1. Ghosts

A fair number of people, upon death, tend to want to touch base with the living they have left behind to let family members or friends know that they still exist and that they are okay. I have already talked about the visits that tend to happen in my family, particularly when one of the women dies, and the resulting blowing of light bulbs.

These are the most common forms of *haunting*. They are harmless and all they require is recognition, conversation, and then moving on. Sometimes these visits manifest as aromas, noises, 'feelings,' or electrical disturbances. This is a time when the living can say goodbye and the dead can move forward knowing that they will be remembered, and that they have been acknowledged as still existing. This period of disengagement with the living is usually short and fades off after the funeral rites.

Sometimes a spirit will hang around a little longer if they have specific things they wish to convey – and they will try very hard to get attention. A quite dramatic and humorous example happened once when I visited a friend for a discussion.

My friend had recently lost a work colleague who had died of cancer. We were sitting chatting about life in general when the room started to feel a bit strange. I asked how the kids of the dead colleague were coping (they were fine) when suddenly my friend's cell phone launched itself off the fireplace, across the room, and landed at his feet. We all sat stunned in silence for a moment: the dead colleague was trying to tell my friend that he wanted to talk to him.

This is a good example of a spirit trying to get attention and get a message across. The phone being launched, as opposed to something easier, was the only way the dead person could say that he needed to talk. My being in the room triggered and bridged the contact. When a natural psychic (or a magician who is psychic) is in a space, they generate a slightly different energy to most people. That different energy can be utilised by the dead to enable them to try and bridge a contact: we are like batteries, and we are also very visible in the inner worlds.

For some magicians who are not natural psychics, this phenomenon of different energy can develop as a result of magical training and practice, whereas others, like me, are born with it. We must learn how to work with it, or else we would plagued by it (and it tends to run in families).

From early childhood I was followed around by newly dead people, and that also happened to my eldest daughter when she was little – she is also a ghost magnet (I used to have to evict them out of her bedroom so that she could get to sleep). In our modern culture we see this as extra-ordinary, weird, and something to be dramatic about, but in fact it is a perfectly normal phenomenon. It is not that people like us are weird or special in any way; it is more that we are people who have not 'forgotten': I feel it is a normal survival mechanism that most of modern humanity has filtered out through the evolutionary process. In effect, we are throwbacks.

Through finding someone who can pick up on them, ghosts are able either to get a message across or just to have recognition of their existence. Once they have achieved that, they begin to relax and not panic so much – our culture has no pattern or mechanism of understanding for the newly dead: they have no compass, no idea of how to behave, of what to do, or any idea of what is going to happen to them.

The kindest thing a magician can do under these circumstances is to not whip out some equipment to prove that they are there, or to banish them, but simply to acknowledge them, ask if they need help (communing in vision is an easy way to find out what they need), and let them know they can hang out with you for a while until they feel ready to move deeper into death.

There are various things that you can do as a magician to help the dead (outlined in the next lesson). The basic rule of thumb for how to behave as a magician is: if it finds you, do the work. Don't go chasing after it or looking for jobs. Modern ghost hunting clubs and TV shows cause so much distress in the newly dead, and they only serve to perpetuate nonsense as fact. But if a dead person turns up at your home or you trigger one somewhere, then you need to deal with it. There are various ways of doing that, which we will look at in the next lesson.

Some cultures have a place within their society for these newly dead people: some Buddhist temples hang wind-chimes outside the temple for the dead. If a ghost is lost and distressed, they hear the chimes and seek refuge at the threshold of the temple for the night – a bit like a homeless shelter for lost ghosts.

Problems really start to occur when you have a true haunting of a spirit that is not newly dead and that is trapped in this world, or is clinging furiously to life. This causes all manner of problems, not just for the living but also for the dead: they become exposed to the danger of composites, something we will look at in a moment. If a magician walks into a problem situation, it is wise to know first what it is you are dealing with. We have looked at the newly dead, which is pretty straightforward. Now let us look at the longer-term dead, and other types of haunting events that are not always human spirits.

2. RECORDINGS

What people generally think of as hauntings are actually a mix of a many different phenomena that can be caused by a dead person, a faery or land being, a composite, a demonic being, a parasite, or a *recording* (a situation where a certain event in time has become embedded or impressed upon a building or a place). The phenomenon of a recording is the simplest type of haunting, so we will look at that first and get it out of the way. Sometimes these recordings are volatile events where the energy becomes impressed into substance and keeps replaying over and over again. They are sometimes triggered into replaying by the moon's cycles, astrological events, a sensitive person visiting a place, or a sudden burst of energy caused by changing the structure of a building. Often they appear as seemingly unimportant events which, for some reason or another are recorded and play back over and over again.

There is a very famous account of one of these recordings in the ancient city of York in Britain, a well-documented haunting in the cellars of the Treasurer's House. Here is a clip from an article about the hauntings:

> *Workmen repairing the cellars in 1953 reported seeing and hearing a group of Roman legionnaires marching along, though only visible from the knees upward as though marching behind a low wall. Later excavations discovered a Roman road running beneath the cellar floor, at the very spot of the apparition. Were these the ghosts of the 9th Roman Legion who went missing without trace?*
>
> `www.jorvik.co.uk/treasurers-house/`

These types of recordings are mostly harmless and serve only to shock people when they experience them. There are no dead people involved: it is simply a scene from the past that keeps replaying. These types of hauntings cannot be interacted with, as no dead person is actually still there, and they are easily identified by the fact that the scene never changes, and the apparition cannot be interacted with. They cause no harm and are really just a curiosity.

If there is more than one of these recordings in a building or space and they constantly replay, then it is very likely that the land is seated upon an energy vortex or anomaly that causes certain events to be recorded and impressed into the building. If it is an energy anomaly, then there is nothing you can do about it and it will continue to record events through time.

3. Faery or land spirit haunting

This is actually the most common occurrence that people mistake for a haunting. They are also often described as poltergeists. The more that land is gobbled up by houses, towns, businesses, etc., the more the faery and land beings of an area are going to surface or clash with local inhabitants. In fact, a fair percentage of what people think of as violent or aggressive hauntings is in fact these beings.

This type of 'haunting' can manifest as poltergeist activity (throwing stones, moving things about, scratching people, pushing people down stairs, etc.). The thing that marks them out from other non-human hauntings is that land or faery beings do not try to get into the heads of the occupants living in the space: they will attack a person, but they will not attempt to move into a person's body or mind.

There is usually a combination of factors that trigger this type of event, and those triggers tend to be:

Location + particular human + the behaviour of that human = the triggering of a Poltergeist

The location aspects tend to include things like having a well, waterway, or spring under or very close to the house, and/or the house being built upon a particular faery spot or over an inhabited stone outcrop, an active fault line, or a nearby cave.

The particular human aspect that triggers such a haunting is often a high-testosterone male living over a faery-inhabited spring, a psychic female child hitting puberty (massive energy output), or someone who is mentally unbalanced. The human behaviour triggers tend to be a male being violent, a psychic teen meddling in occult games, construction workers adding to a building or rewiring a house, the house's owner disrespecting a local faery site, or a person living in the house who is very hostile to nature in general. When these elements (and there are more, but these are the most common ones) come together, it triggers a hostile response.

The activity of faery beings is very clear in some hauntings, such as the Bell Witch in Tennessee. A lot of fantasy has slowly been added to that story, to the point that I was extremely sceptical of the whole situation until I actually went and spent some time in the area around the old house, the local graveyard, and the cave area. As with all these stories, it is sometimes hard to spot the truth buried under the fantasy, but this story had enough specific aspects that are known to be connected with faery activity that I had to go and take a look for myself.

The noises, slapping, pinching, throwing things around, pulling off bedding, touching people and then talking out loud to them are all signs of a powerful faery contact, and not of a ghost. Of course, these stories are then embellished with fantasies like levitating, being stuck to a ceiling, vomiting porridge, and all the other visuals that Hollywood loves so much.

When I visited the spot it became immediately apparent as soon as I got close that this was a very active area energetically. That was the first real clue: this was not just centred on a house, but a whole area. After spending a day in the area and feeling the beings there for myself, it was very clear that this was no haunting.

What happens with these situations is that when a being gets disturbed or has its territory invaded, or is awoken from a deep sleep by human activity, or when a line of land/faery beings become hostile to particular types of humans on their territory, then they surface and start trying to attract attention.

While faery beings do not operate in the same emotional paradigm as humans, and do not live to the same social rules that we do, they are not usually just hostile for no reason: they are often willing to communicate, adjust, and negotiate a little if the humans are willing to respect them and take them into consideration.

Usually though, because of the humans' fear of haunting, which is what they think the contact is, the humans' response to the first contact (sounds, tapping) is full of fear and aggression (often followed by lots of religious ranting and prayers). This in turn triggers an aggressive response, and it usually degenerates down from there.

In Iceland, when it comes to the Huldufólk (Icelandic faery beings), the people in general have learned to communicate with these beings, or at least take them into consideration when it comes to building projects and major changes. They are treated respectfully, so the incidents of aggression are kept to a minimum.

Knowing what it is you are dealing with is fifty percent of the problem already solved, as you can then act appropriately, without fear; with such an approach the problem usually becomes a non-issue. However, where a being has been awoken, is hostile, and is connected to a particular aspect of the land that the house is standing upon, then unless the occupants are willing to drastically change how they live in the building and understand that they are essentially interlopers on someone else's land, the violence will continue indefinitely. Houses built upon springs and wells are particularly prone to this.

4. Parasites and demonic beings

These are the types of hauntings that tend to be most depicted in movies. And yet they are pretty rare, particularly in countries that have long-established civilisations with religious centres. Places that have fairly recent human communities (only a few hundred years old), like the USA and Australia, are the most common places where these events occur.

And the one thing that really marks them out from all other types of hauntings is that these beings *get into the heads and bodies* of the people who are victims of the hauntings. Sometimes the beings get into the fabric of the building itself, but more often they move into a human and begin a process of possession.

These beings are often not locked to a particular place, and if the person moves out, they will move with them, hounding them often to death. Of the two types, the parasitical being is the more common of the two, but saying that, the line between what is a powerful parasite and what is a demonic being is a thin one. The only real discernible difference between the two, and one that we can often pick up on as magicians, is that a parasite infests for its *sustenance* whereas a demonic being infests in order to cause *destruction*.

We will look at demonic beings in more detail later, in the Initiate section, particularly in light of their potential for destruction: there is a lot of misunderstanding about what is or is not a demonic being, and religious programming has so overtaken the Western psyche that sensible discussion is virtually impossible. But knowing the difference is of vital importance to a magician in order to ensure that a situation can be properly dealt with. Religious ranting at a parasite will do nothing, but cutting off its food supply will. Cutting off a food supply to a demon will not work, as it is not their attractor: a totally different approach is needed (and religious ranting does not work on them, either).

So for this lesson we will concentrate on the parasitical element. Parasites are usually the cause of a haunting when there has been a very nasty incident which drew them there in the first place: a violent rape that brought death, a murder, a mass murder, seriously mentally ill people who are violent, or a concentrated disease outbreak; the attractors are usually violence, sex, and/or painful death.

The particular aspects of the energy released by these occurrences provide a major feeding station for parasites. Once the meal is over they will sometimes wait until more humans come along, and if that human or humans do not display behaviour that feeds them, the more intelligent parasites will badger the humans or break down their resistance until they can get into their heads and push them into behaviour that feeds them.

A good fictional representation of this extreme, and thankfully not common, sort of situation is presented in the film *The Amityville Horror* (2005 version). The film itself is fiction, but it had some good consultants for the film who knew just how these beings can behave. They are often mistaken for demonic beings purely because of their power and ability to manipulate the minds of humans, and their ability to affect physical objects in the house. If you wish to watch a good depiction of this sort of incident, watch that film (and then have a salt bath afterwards – read the warning lower down in the lesson and take the advice!).

Bear in mind that it is a Hollywood movie with all the accompanying shock horror dressing, but the baseline theme and the way it is presented regarding the mind of the male in the story is spot on. Also the point made in the film, that the problem originated with a mass murder, is spot on: those are often the original feeding attractor.

A *parasitical haunting* will present itself as slow changes in the personality of one or more occupants and a heavy feeling in the house that builds at certain times of the day/night and which also changes with the moon's cycle. The changes in the person will take the form of either sexual or violent presentations, or both, or sudden unexplained suicidal tendencies.

As the parasite feeds more from the mind of the victim and gets stronger, or moves closer in to feed (or more parasites move in), the parasite will be able to use any surplus energy from the feeding to affect physical change in the house: shutting down the electrics, setting fires, dropping or smashing things, throwing weapons, psychically raping the women or children, strangling people, etc. – anything that generates a lot of fear. The more fearful the people, the stronger the parasites get, as they feed on the emotion.

At this stage in your training it is unwise to learn how to deal with this, or even how to look at it properly as a magician, because you do not have the skills and tools to deal with such a dangerous situation (and trust me, large, clever parasites are far more dangerous than real demons in a one-to-one situation: most of what people think are demons are in fact these types of parasites).

You will learn in the Initiate section how to deal with these beings, but for now it is important that you do learn to recognise them in all their different forms.

Often a parasitical haunting is not quite so dramatic, but it still has the same elements: the victim has changes in their thoughts and behaviours, the house is affected or things in the house are being tampered with (one of the clues that it is not just mental illness in the victim), and other people who stay in the house start to exhibit the same odd behaviour.

As with all types of body infestations (bacterial, fungal, etc.) there is not a simple cure, but the right approach will first weaken, then disable, and finally purge such an infestation from the house or family. Demonic beings, however, are another matter entirely hence they will be looked at later. But bear in mind that a problem with a demonic being is very rare indeed.

5. Real long-term hauntings: dead people and composites

Now we get to the actual real hauntings, which are one of the rarest events. They do tend to happen in clusters of specific areas, as the energy or a land area plays a major part in the ability of a dead person to remain present for long periods of time after death. Also note that wherever there is a properly tuned sacred place (cathedral, synagogue, Hindu temple, etc.) it is very rare to get a long-term haunting.

A real haunting of a dead person is either just the dead person themselves (the rarer of the two), or is something known as a *composite*, which is more common. A composite is where you have a dead person who is also infested with a parasite, or the 'shell' of a dead person that a parasite has completely moved into (and has pushed the dead spirit out of the shell) and which it is operating as if it was the dead person.

When a long-term dead person (with no parasites) stays in this world, they are either trapped/bound to this realm by something or someone, or they have serious issues and are badly out of balance. There is an easy way to tell if they are simply stuck here, in that their apparitions are often expressions of suffering, of being unable or unwilling to move forward out of fear, or they just prefer to stay and hang out with the living. All of these are ultimately unhealthy and need working with, but such spirits are rarely, if ever, destructive or violent.

If there is a specific thing that is binding them magically, all that needs doing is to unbind them and let them go. If they are not moving forward by choice they must not be forced: they need time and help to come to the right decision themselves.

When I was a young mother, the house where I lived had an elderly man in residence who had died some years before. He could be heard walking around the house at night, checking on the children or standing in the corner of their bedroom watching over them. At first I was freaked out that he might harm the children, but once I came to know him, I discovered that he simply wished he'd had children when he was alive, and wanted to make sure that the girls would be safe.

During the daytime, if someone came into the house who he didn't like or who he perceived as a threat to the family, he would throw things about: books would fly off shelves and hit people, and his favourite trick was throwing pot plants. It became a problem, as babysitters would not come to the house, neighbours would not cross the threshold into my house, and visitors were sometimes assaulted.

At that time (I was twenty-two and clueless) I did not know what to do, so we moved house. But looking back, he was right about every person he perceived to be 'bad.' I eventually learned the hard way that those people he attacked were indeed not good people. I should have listened to him better. I revisited the house many years later, (same neighbours still there) and he is still there, watching over the kids in the current family.

With what I know now, I should have talked to him, shown him how death worked, and how he could travel through death and back into life if he wanted to have a family for himself. He was stuck in a Christian mindset of only one life and desperately wanted the experience of raising his own children. The role of the magician in such instances is to open the Vista for them, show them that more lives are potentially there, and that it is a natural process, not one to be scared of. Then they usually move forward.

If a long-dead person is aggressive, they are often like terrified, wounded animals and need the magician simply to show them the way forward and then to keep the space tuned to stillness to give them healing time. Then they usually move forward under their own steam eventually.

Occasionally you get nasty, aggressive spirits who were just total nasty assholes in life and they are terrified of going into death and onto judgement. Many people who behave very nastily in life think that death is the total end, and that they can be as destructive as they want. When they die and realise they still exist, they panic, and in that panic the deeper nastiness and manipulative personality comes to the fore.

When there is such a situation, you should not force them, as you short circuit their own development. But you can limit them by boxing them into a corner and constantly keeping the space tuned to stillness. Open the gates and let the inner beings deal with them.

If they come to a realisation that they have to move forward and there is no other option, then they will begin the process of self-examination. This in turn allows their step into evolving, which is a major service on the part of the magician. Cutting off their access to other parts of the house so their actions towards others are severely limited, and keeping the space tuned so that no parasites can latch onto them and make the situation worse, are the best options. But that is not always possible.

Sometimes, if the spirit is very destructive to the living, particularly if children or the elderly are being affected, then you have to detach them from the building and take them to the plains of death and leave them there. The key is to try everything possible first to get the spirit to move under its own steam, as that way they have a chance at improving. But when the living are under threat, then it is time to intervene. The main thing to remember with this sort of situation is that such spirits are rarely dangerous, just bloody annoying.

Remember, at this stage of your training, this is outlined for your information only: it is not yet time for you to dive in and work with any of these more difficult situations as you do not know how to protect yourself and your family enough for such work.

I once had to drag a spirit into death after a particularly nasty haunting in New York. A Mafia type had died suddenly and was angry that his wife had inherited all of his wealth (he was divorcing her when he died). He harangued her night after night until I intervened and hauled his ass into death.

The woman was terrified, sleep deprived, and at the end of her tether. Catholic priests had tried to help, with no success, and I was the last resort. I was not sure if I could move him or not, as he was so filled with hate and rage, but as I started the process, many other beings that work in death suddenly turned up to help.

This is a dynamic worth remembering: the magician is the *catalyst,* and if you start an action that will lead to a balanced resolution, then as soon as you start the work, any help that you would need will turn up. And it is only what you need: if you are capable of doing the work, however hard it is, you will not be helped. But if it is a bit too much for you, all hands will come on deck.

6. Composites

When we see scary haunting movies or possession movies, what is generally being depicted (often in silly, over-the-top scenes) is what is known as a *composite,* usually mislabelled as a demon.

A composite is where a long-dead person who is seriously out of balance and hostile becomes inhabited by intelligent parasites that move in, take over, and run the show. This creates a very nasty situation where you have a spirit that is seriously unbalanced, often aggressive and hostile, and a parasite that has intelligence, is manipulative, and uses the imbalance of the spirit to trigger destructive situations that feed the parasite.

These usually present as hauntings where fear is a major factor, as is physical violence, and the parasite uses the life experience of the spirit to target the other humans in the space.

So, for example, if the dead host was a rapist, the parasite would drive the spirit to continue that behaviour, which in turn gives the spirit an energy boost to help further their invasive behaviour, which in turn creates situations where the parasite can feed. That manifests as a haunting that targets women living in the house: they have nightmares of being raped, sometimes they get physically assaulted in their sleep, and they are kept in a constant state of fear. Don't forget: rape is rarely about sex, and more about power/control.

A composite can also get into the heads of the residents of the house, and the parasite uses the knowledge within the personality of the dead spirit to project specific behaviours into the minds of the people in the house. The ideas the composite gets from the mind of the dead person/host are impressed into the mind of a vulnerable living person in the house, and the composite attempts to drive the living person to behave in a way that will produce energy to feed from. This can all get very nasty and very destructive.

The knee-jerk reaction of most exorcists is to tear the composite out of the situation and cast it, complete, into the Abyss. The only problem with that method is that the dead spirit then has no chance at evolution or development, which in turn makes the magician responsible energetically for the stalled progress of that spirit. So the magician has to weigh up the consequences of such an action against the current danger of the situation.

Sometimes you just have to do it. But wherever possible the parasite should first be detached from the dead spirit and composted, and then spirit should be marched into death and handed over to the beings that work there. After that, the future of the spirit is not your responsibility: the magician's job will then be to deal with the house or invaded living person and get them cleaned, sealed, and balanced so that the situation cannot repeat.

And this brings me to another aspect of this situation that apprentices need to be aware of: once a vessel (a person, a house, a land area) has been breached and occupied, that vessel is vulnerable to further infestation if it is not cleaned, strengthened, and balanced. A pattern of behaviour becomes impressed upon the person or place that makes it easier for future parasites or composites to move in.

The media's depictions of exorcisms, where it is done and dusted and everyone moves on, is a fallacy: to truly rid a place or person of a composite and make sure it never happens again is a long, drawn-out job. The immediate act of getting rid of the composite is just the first step. The cleaning and balancing is the second step, and identifying how it happened in the first place is the third.

Often you will find that the building, the land, the person, or all three have an inherent weakness that enabled such a situation to occur in the first place. That weakness needs to be identified and strengthened, any natural portholes (wells, springs, burials, etc.) need to be tuned and properly guarded (working with land beings or deities), and the pattern of behaviour or weakness in the human (feeding potential) that may have attracted the parasite in the first place needs to be addressed.

So you begin to see how complicated this can get, and knowing what type of haunting you are dealing with specifically dictates how it must be dealt with. The first step towards being able to deal with these sorts of situations is knowing all the different types of beings, the different presentations of hauntings, and knowing how energy, land, and spirits operate.

And you will now see how a generic 'exorcism,' blessing, or clearing will for the most part be ineffectual. You will also now begin to understand just how dangerous these psychic 'reality shows' and 'quests' can potentially be. If the haunting is a composite or a standalone parasite, or a seriously disturbed dead person, then such playing about is only going to feed the situation and make it worse.

7. Warning – Please take note

> I do not post this warning lightly, so please read it carefully, as it comes from years of direct experience as an exorcist. Simply reading about composites and parasites can draw you into a pattern where you become more visible to these types of beings. These are beings and situations that you will not have anything to do with magically until you are an adept, when you will know what you are doing and have the tools to deal with them.

Simply discussing *specifics*, or watching the films, or doing readings or visions around these situations can put you in a direct line of connection with them. I have seen this over and over again, and while it is not my job to dictate to you what you must or must not do, watch, or investigate, it *is* my job to outline for you the inherent dangers, after that, it is your own choice (and I will not clean you up from your mistakes if you do not follow advice).

My job is also to teach you basic skills but in a safe way, so while we will do practical work around 'recordings' and simple dead people hauntings, you will do no practical work around the more dangerous types of beings until you are an adept. So if you choose to look deeper into the murkier side of this subject matter before you are ready, then it is on your own head.

The deeper into magic you go, the more visible you become, and the more careful you have to be. Watching some of these films or going to some badly infested sites may or may not affect a curious ordinary person, and indeed some people develop a thick skin of natural immunity from exposure. But some do not and become infested.

For the magician, the training tunes you, which in turn can make you more visible. When you are working within the confines of balance and common sense, other beings step up to help you and keep an eye on you. But if you step away from that common sense and dip your toe into murky waters simply out of curiosity, knowing that it is a risk, then you are on your own: inner guardians will not help you.

Reading through parts of this lesson will be a minor risk to you, even though it is just words. But it is time for being grown up and not overprotected. **At the end of this lesson, do the ritual salt and water bath and also use the ritual salt and water cleanse for your work space.**

After the cleansing and before you do anything else, any other lesson, meditation or exercise, do the Hexagram ritual to tune yourself and the space, and when you come to stepping into the empty hexagram in the ritual, face south, be aware of your feet on the stone in the Underworld, of the Divine Breath above you, your sword in your left hand and your vessel in the right hand (the stance of the pentagram) and your flame in your centre. Anything that even remotely tried to connect with you will be swept away as the frequency of the ritual will make it hard for things to hook into you.

These simple basic acts of ritual cleaning and re tuning that you learn in the early part of your training may be simple, but they are not ineffective. The more magical experience you have under your belt, the stronger these simple steps become. The depths and layers of those ritual actions open out and expand as you evolve and develop as a magician. They are in reality, adept steps; the power is drawn from the magician not the steps themselves. Whenever you get yourself, as an Apprentice, into a difficult spot or get infested or get covered in energetic dirt, the ritual acts of cleansing as laid out in Apprentice Module I Lesson 7, and the retuning with the Hexagram ritual, will restore you. They are core skills that you carry with you as a magician throughout your magical life. All the skills learned in the first few modules are skills that adepts use, it is just that adept power takes such skills to a whole different level. And that should teach you another magical truth: fancy rituals are often for show only. More complexity doesn't mean more power. Magical 'simple' often hides great strength behind it.

Anything that you watch, hear, or read, will, now that you are a magician, have an effect on you in some way or another. The key is not to get paranoid or avoid everything and get fearful; rather it is to be aware of how things can potentially affect you subtly, and if you feel that effect, to move away from whatever it is that is causing such a feeling.

Cleaning and retuning yourself is something you should learn to use whenever you get that energetic feeling of intrusion or imbalance. These beings work through your mind: thought is everything, and the imagination is the vehicle for everything: media affects and triggers your imagination, and this in turn creates a door that things can step through if you are not careful. The more you work with your imagination, the more you have to be careful what you expose that imagination to.

If you watch the movie I suggested earlier in the lesson, make sure you clean and rebalance yourself and your space properly afterwards. Even if you are used to watching such films, as is commonplace these days, as a magician you are stepping into a whole different ballgame and you need to be aware of that and act accordingly.

8. The dead that cling

Before we move on to other Living Dead situations, there is something that is pertinent to the subject matter that an apprentice should be aware of, and that is a newly dead person clinging onto a living person.

Usually it is the person closest to them, like a parent, a partner, or a child. When someone dies in state of shock, or they were a person who was clingy, vulnerable, and fearful, they sometimes reach out for the closest person and *cling* to them. They will attach themselves to the inner spirit of the living person and will not let go. This creates an energetic drag on the spirit of the living person they cling to, and the living person not only processes their own emotions, but also the emotions of the dead person.

This most commonly presents as the living person having grief beyond what would normally be expected. Now I know everyone deals with death differently, but when you get a bereaved person who is not going through the different stages of processing grief, but is instead stuck in one expression of it in a major way, then the magician should suspect a *clinger*. This is easily identified in vision: you will see the dead person stuck to the living person.

This often presents from an outer perspective as someone displaying extreme grief, who is unable to function at all, who wants to die (sometimes the dead person wants to pull them into death with them, to keep them company), and has no resolution at all – the grieving person does not go through any stages of coping, and they get stuck in a very dark place emotionally. This can go on for years if it is not dealt with.

Gently detaching the clinger and accompanying them in vision on a daily basis to the plains of death slowly allows the dead to let go, and the improvement in the living person is often quite stunning: they start to go through a healthier period of grief and resolution, and can move on.

9. Staying in the land

I have already touched upon aspects of this phenomenon in other lessons, and have also written quite a bit about it in my books, so I don't wish to repeat myself here. But what would be useful is to outline for apprentices how these spirits present and under what conditions, so that should you come across this sort of situation you will recognise it. From there you can do further reading for yourself.

We have already looked at dead people who sleep in the land waiting for judgement, and also at working sleepers. There are also burials whose occupants have stepped into the sacred king or queen pattern and sleep in the land for the good of the people and the land, keeping balance simply by their presence.

Most of these types of spirits just get on with their job and are rarely connected accidentally with the living. But sometimes circumstances do occur where they are disturbed or have reached the end of their 'term of duty' and are ready to move deeper into death. It is useful to know which is which, as both situations often need the assistance of a magician.

Where a sleeper has been disturbed, either by building construction, digging such as happens in archaeology, or farm clearing of the land, they will start to appear to people in the vicinity. They often are tightly bound into a small, specific area, and will appear to the local people within that boundary.

Sometimes they simply project an image of themselves to those who can see: they expect you to know what to do. Often when these sleepers died, their spiritual society was vastly different to our societies today, and they are often not aware of such a shift and the modern lack of knowledge.

When the people to whom they appear do not do what is expected of them, the spirit can become frustrated and sometimes angry. The way to discern that it is indeed one of these disturbed sleepers that is causing the issue is that they will simply keep appearing, projecting an image, and trying to/asking the living to do a specific thing.

If something like this does occur, the first thing to do is to research the land and find out if any major building, excavation, demolition, or similar work has been done or is being done locally. In such circumstances the solution is usually easy: open all the gates, light a fire outside as close to the disturbed burial as you can, and, working in vision, build a bridge for them through the fire to the gates.

They cannot go back to sleep, so they need someone to open the doors for them. This is not usually a job for an apprentice, but should you be directly presented with such a situation, then it is a job that you cannot do much harm to yourself with.

The thing to remember is that all you do is hold open gates – never ever try to force a sleeper into the death pattern. The same is true for a sleeper that has reached the end of their term of sleep: they will present asking for help, and all you need to do is light a fire and open the gates.

Sometimes, however, these spirits will present around a particular site, and it is not that they have awoken: what you can be seeing is a guardian projecting an image of the sleeper to basically tell you to go away. They can also present as black dogs, strange-looking cloaked/hooded men, or warriors.

If that happens, usually it is because a sleeper has been threatened in some way, or someone is trying to dig into the mound. If this happens, see if there is anything you can do practically to help. Are kids messing about around a burial? But most of the time there is nothing we can do, or it is that a house is on top of the burial. If that is the case, the issue can be resolved by incorporating the house into the role of guardian: the house becomes a part of the mound.

But in all circumstances of sleepers or guardians appearing, trying to banish or exorcise such a spirit is not only fruitless but hostile, and it will only aggravate any guardians connected to the site. Later in the course, you will learn skills to be able to deal with such issues; for now, knowing about them will not only lay a foundation for the future work, but it will also help you to spot these various situations in texts and histories, which in turn will give you a deeper understanding of those histories and texts.

As you go through your training and learn more skills, you will recognise which skills can be applied in haunting situations as well as very different circumstances. As an apprentice magician, you are very unlikely to be placed in a situation where you would have to deal with something dangerous, and of course, never go looking for it!

The other type of Living Dead that you can come across is what is known as an inner adept, inner priest, or inner contact. Because this type of spirit is very important for the work of a magician, they will be dealt with in their own lesson, Lesson 7.

10. About the practical work

This practical work will be cautious because of the potential dangers in the subject matter for apprentices, so stay within the confines of the task boundaries and don't be tempted to peer into the murkier waters of this subject matter.

You are going to find, through research, certain haunting situations, and look at background information, presentation, and then do tarot readings around the situation to try and ascertain what in fact is/was going on.

This will teach you a basic process of investigation that any magician would do when presented with a potential haunting. It will help you to learn how to look, what to look for, and what to cast aside.

We will only look at the safer aspects of haunting, and we will not delve into demonic, parasitical, composite, or violent hauntings, as such investigation would open you up to the contact and place you in danger (even if it was a past event, it could potentially drag you back energetically into that pattern).

11. *Task:* Investigating sleeping warriors

The following is a folk tale from Wales that emerged during the 19th century Druid Revival movement, and was written by a Welshman called Edward Williams, A.K.A. Iolo Morganwg.

A lot of Williams' work is considered to be *total construct* ('made up') by scholars, but some anecdotal evidence of his stories in much earlier texts has been emerging recently. So we have an uncertain situation. What is most likely is that he found old folk legends, clothed them in an Arthurian dressing (which was fashionable at the time), and adapted them to fit his agenda.

Your job is to find out what is behind this story. This will teach you the basic steps of investigation as a magician, in a safe way. This story could be about faery beings, it could be about ancient sleepers, ancestral sleepers, or something else.

Different versions of this story, or similar versions of it, appear throughout northern Europe, which would point to either a faery type of contact or to a pattern of behaviour in ancient tribal people, or both. Also keep in mind as you read the story that there is more than one cave in Wales called Craig-y-Dinas. Read the story, and then follow the tasks that come after the story.

This story is taken from Elijah Waring's *Recollections and Anecdotes of Edward Williams,* Iolo Morganwg (London, 1850), pp. 95-8, where it is headed *A popular Tale in Glamorgan,* by Iolo Morganwg.

A Popular Tale In Glamorgan, By Iolo Morganwg.

A Welshman walking over London Bridge, with a neat hazel staff in his hand, was accosted by an Englishman, who asked him whence he came.

"I am from my own country," answered the Welshman, in a churlish tone.

"Do not take it amiss, my friend," said the Englishman; "if you will only answer my questions, and take my advice, it will be of greater benefit to you than you imagine. That stick in your hand grew on a spot under which are hid vast treasures of gold and silver; and if you remember the place, and can conduct me to it, I will put you in possession of those treasures."

The Welshman soon understood that the stranger was what he called a cunning man, or conjurer, and for some time hesitated, not willing to go with him among devils, from whom this magician must have derived his knowledge; but he was at length persuaded to accompany him into Wales; and going to Craig-y-Dinas,[1] the Welshman pointed out the spot whence he had cut the stick. It was from the stock or root of a large old hazel: this they dug up, and under it found a broad flat stone. This was found to close up the entrance into a very large cavern, down into which they both went. In the middle of the passage hung a bell, and the conjurer earnestly cautioned the Welshman not to touch it.

They reached the lower part of the cave, which was very wide, and there saw many thousands of warriors lying down fast asleep in a large circle, their heads outwards, every one clad in bright armour, with their swords, shields, and other weapons lying by them, ready to be laid hold on in an instant, whenever the bell should ring and awake them. All the arms were so highly polished and bright, that they illumined the cavern, as with the light of ten thousand flames of fire. They saw amongst the warriors one greatly distinguished from the rest by his arms, shield, battle-axe, and a crown of gold set with the most precious stones, lying by his side.

In the midst of this circle of warriors they saw two very large heaps, one of gold, the other of silver. The magician told the Welshman that he might take as much as he could carry away of either the one or the other, but that he was not to take from both the heaps. The Welshman loaded himself with gold: the conjurer took none, saying that he did not want it, that gold was of no use to those who wanted knowledge, and that his contempt of gold had enabled him to acquire that superior knowledge and wisdom which he possessed.

In their way out he cautioned the Welshman again not to touch the bell, but if unfortunately he should do so, it might be of the most fatal consequence to him, as one or more of the warriors would awake, lift up his head,

---

[1] "Rock of the Fortress".

and ask *if it was day?*. "Should this happen," said the cunning man, "you must, without hesitation, answer *No, sleep thou on*; on hearing which he will again lay down his head and sleep."

In their way up, however, the Welshman, overloaded with gold, was not able to pass the bell without touching it—it rang.

One of the warriors raised up his head, and asked, "Is it day?"

"No," answered the Welshman promptly, "it is not, sleep thou on."

So they got out of the cave, laid down the stone over its entrance, and replaced the hazel tree. The cunning man, before he parted from his companion, advised him to be economical in the use of his treasure; observing that he had, with prudence, enough for life: but that if by unforeseen accidents he should be again reduced to poverty, he might repair to the cave for more; repeating the caution, not to touch the bell if possible, but if he should, to give the proper answer, *that it was not day*, as promptly as possible.

He also told him that the distinguished person they had seen was ARTHUR, and the others his warriors; and they lay there asleep with their arms ready at hand, for the dawn of that day when *The Black Eagle* and *The Golden Eagle* should go to war, the loud clamour of which would make the earth tremble so much, that the bell would ring loudly, and the warriors awake, take up their arms, and destroy all the enemies of the Cymry,[2] who afterwards should repossess the Island of Britain, re-establish their own king and government at Caerlleon, and be governed with justice, and blessed with peace so long as the world endures.

The time came when the Welshman's treasure was all spent: he went to the cave, and as before overloaded himself. In his way out he touched the bell—it rang—a warrior lifted up his head, asking *if it was day*—but the Welshman, who had covetously overloaded himself, being quite out of breath with labouring under his burden, and withal struck with terror, was not able to give the necessary answer; whereupon some of the warriors got up, took the gold away from him, and beat him dreadfully. They afterwards threw him out, and drew the stone after them over the mouth of the cave. The Welshman never recovered the effects of that beating, but remained almost a cripple as long as he lived, and very poor. He often returned with some of his friends to Craig-y-Dinas; but they could never afterwards find the spot, though they dug over, seemingly, every inch of the hill. He lived in this crippled and poor condition very long, a warning to all, of the evils which result from a want of knowledge and prudence, teaching not to be covetous, not to neglect good advice, and never to trust that they can, without danger, give way to their own wishes, except one *the wish to be good*.

---

[2] The Welsh.

Tasks

Geography and history

Look on a map of Wales, or use the internet to look up places called Craig-y-Dinas. Look and research as to what natural features surround these places: springs, rivers that go underground, caves, ancient forest, or fault lines. Then research the ancient history of these places to see if any of them were the site of any battles between the Celts and the Romans (such as Anglesey).

Folklore

Do a search for local legends throughout Europe of caves or hills that have stories of sleeping kings and warriors, with stories that they will once again rise at some point in history. Compare the stories to the one you are working on. And for the ones that leap out at you, research further into the land features of those sites. Take computer notes of what you find.

Readings

Get your tarot deck and use the T ree of L ife layout. The first skill you will practise is the skill of locking on to a partially or unknown element/place.

We do not know exactly which Craig-y-Dinas the writer was talking about, so you have to go by *what he was thinking of.*

Your first reading would be to ask:

> *"Does the place Craig-y-Dinas that Williams was specifically writing about actually exist?"*

If the answer is **no** (either a card that denotes separation such as the Three of Swords, or the Fool, for example) then you know straight away that this legend does not track back to a specific story of a burial in Craig-y-Dinas.

Then you need to ascertain if the story is about ancient tribes/a sleeper, or faery beings.

Ask first:

> *"In this story, there are sleeping warriors and a sleeping king; are they, in this particular story, the spirits of long dead people?"*

If the answer is **no**, ask the same question, but ask if they are faery beings.
If the answer is **yes**, ask if they are still sleeping in the cave.
If the answer is **no**, ask if they have gone deeper into death.

Write down your findings in a computer log. From the answers you get, think about what these stories are telling us. Are they telling us about ancient faery contacts? Or are they telling us about ancient burials?

These investigations will show you how stories repeat across different lands, sometimes because they are stories carried by travellers, and sometimes because they are patterns of behaviour found throughout tribal territories or faery territories.

If you want to, do further tarot readings around any other sleeper stories you came across in your investigations. Take good notes for you to return to in the future.

Interactions with humans

Choose one of the burial stories you have been researching, and ask, again using TREE OF LIFE LAYOUT:

> *"Are these burials (or faery areas) any problem to humans living on top of them or very nearby?"*

From your answers, you will be able to see (or not) the potential issues with humans living closely to these places. If you get a **yes** answer, use the INNER DESERT/ LANDSCAPE LAYOUT and ask:

> *"Show me why they are a problem for humans."*

Read the results in context to a human community living on the site of one of these situations.

12. *TASK:* INVESTIGATING THE TREASURER'S HOUSE IN YORK

We looked at the incident of time recording in the Treasurer's House in York. The whole of York is one big ghost playground: there are so many layers of conquest, history, and successive waves of different inhabitants all *within a fully walled city* which contains it all, that it is a ghost hunters paradise. There are more than three thousand years of human settlement history in that area so it is rich in 'happenings' indeed. It was founded in AD 627 and was frequently expanded upon for another six hundred years.

Also, because of the strong influence of the Minster, it is relatively free of parasites, and the turnover of ghosts is pretty quick: few long-term hauntings tend to survive the influence of the Minster, so most hauntings there that are active are fairly recent.

York Minster is ancient indeed, and is kept very well tuned, which means the general muck of a city does not tend to accumulate: it is not a good feeding ground for parasites, so there is little if any issue with these beings in the walled city. So you can do readings around this place safely. You will look at some various 'haunting' situations to see what information you can get on the different various presentations that York tends to get.

Romans in the cellar

Using the INNER DESERT/LANDSCAPE LAYOUT from this module, Lesson 2, we are going to look at the 'Romans in the cellar' haunting.

Your first question is:

> *"With the apparitions of the Romans in the cellar of the York Treasurer's House, show me what is happening energetically when that apparition appears."*

What you are looking for in the reading is specifics:

What happened **in the past** to cause that apparition to become recorded in the first place (positions 4 and 5),

What the **trigger** is (position 6),

What is it that is actually **appearing** (position 8),

What is still trying to **resolve** (position 7),

How is it **affecting** the living world (positions 9 and 11),

What is **falling away** from the situation (position 10),

How long into **the future** is it going to keep appearing (short-term future 12 and long-term future 3).

Now you will start to understand how this layout gives you so much information and what a valuable tool it is.

Write down your findings and your conclusions in a computer log.

Anyone else there?

Your second question to do with the Treasurer's House is (and use the TREE OF LIFE LAYOUT for a yes/no answer):

> *"Was there another dead person haunting that building at some point in the past?"*

There have been various hauntings over time in that house, but they were never able to stay for too long, as they were dispatched by the frequencies emitted from the Minster at various times in history when it was well maintained. However, it is possible to get a look at one of them.

The way to do that is to ask:

> *"Show me the strongest haunting of a dead person who has haunted or stayed in the Treasurer's House in the past that I can look at."*

It may show a male, female, a child, the lovers (more than one strong person). If it shows a trump personality (Hierophant, High Priestess, Emperor) than it is likely that you are getting a clergy member, or a Royal court dignitary, or a Roman in a position of authority.

This particular building has many layers to it, so you are likely to hit at least one of them.

If you totally draw a blank, it is not because is it was never haunted, but because you are being blocked for your own safety. If that happens, either you are about to get sick (get a cold) which would make you vulnerable, or you are too sensitive and would likely tap into some of the deeper layers of this place without realising it. Such a thing at this stage would be counterproductive for you.

The other reason you could get blocked is that you are not able, as yet, to reach the layers where these different 'hauntings' are. Simply write up your reading and take notes from the reading as to how you came to your conclusions.

If you get a **yes** answer, then use the **Desert layout** and ask:

> *"What was the situation for that dead spirit that caused it to stay connected to that building?"*

The **Desert layout** will show you how that person came to stay behind in death, and how the dead person came to be moved on.

13. *Optional task:* Your own investigation

If you know of a story of a non-violent, non-aggressive haunting or apparition in an area local to where you live or in a place that you know fairly well, go through the same process (research, land survey, and readings) to look at that haunting. Write down your findings and your conclusions in a computer file. It is really important that you do not dip into any sort of apparent haunting that is any way aggressive, parasitical in nature, or potentially dangerous. You do not have the skill as yet to get yourself out of a mess if you stick your energy into a badly unbalanced situation (and I will not rescue you... you're all grown up now!).

14. *Task:* Clean up

Now do the clean up outlined in the warning I gave you earlier in the lesson, and make sure you do it without delay. Do not put it off, and once you have cleaned up, do not go back to the subject matter until you are visiting it again in another future lesson. You will have learned what you need to know, gained the investigative skills you need, and you will be able to apply them to different things as you progress in your studies.

Lesson 6

The Thinning of the Veils

Within Autumn (Fall) there is a time where 'the veils thin' throughout the northern hemisphere. Why this happens I have no idea, other than that it is a time where things are dying back for the winter. Nature has a series of tides that ebb and flow through the world, bringing in energy and taking out energy. It is a time where the various worlds seem to draw closer, and the thresholds between the living world and the Underworld become thin and permeable for a short time (one cycle of the moon).

Casting various traditions and their stories aside, over the years I have observed these tides and the effects they have on the inner worlds and on the outer world that we live in. As I looked through various traditions around the world, the one thing that stood out was times spanning October and November that were marked with light or fire festivals.

For the tides in my own land, Britain, I did notice from quite an early age that around this time there is an upswing in spirit activity and it becomes easier to connect to and with the newly dead: it was like a lot of people were hanging around, became more visible, and were badgering me to do things for them, to help them.

In my early thirties I still worked very much by instinct, and around that time of the year I would have the urge to light candles after dark and keep them burning all night. By the middle of November the urge would fade, and everything would settle back down. But one incident marked a turning point in my understanding, and gave me something more solid to work with.

It was the end of October, and I was living in a small town in Wiltshire. I lived with my family in a house that was very old, parts of it dated back to the fifteenth century. It was dug into an ancient, un-excavated burial mound, and in general was a very busy house in terms of spirits.

It was a few days before the full moon, and I got an irresistible urge to go and lay out on the mound one night (like you do). As I lay there, I looked up at the stars. It took me a moment to realise that I was lying on the mound directly under the constellation of Orion, which was lying across me in exactly the same position as me: head where my head was, feet where my feet were.

Suddenly I got a strong flash-vision of a man lying in the burial mound who was waking up. I was fascinated. It felt strange: the vision was strong, but I was still too young and dumb to realise what was happening. I went back into the house, and that night I dreamed of a man waking up and finding himself not only alone, but trapped.

Out of sheer curiosity, every night for three nights I went out and laid on the mound, with Orion over the top of me and the sense of the man awakening deep in the mound.

I did not get the message, I can be a bit slow, until the fourth night, the night before the full moon (which was the thirtieth of October that year), that I was being asked to do something to help this awakening sleeper.

But I had no idea what to do. I laid and stared at Orion until a flash of fire dropped into my mind. Then I remembered the autumn fire festivals and the fact that although Bonfire Night (fifth of November) in Britain was supposed to be a tradition that only went back to the 1600s, there had been a bonfire at this time of the year on the town's common land for nearly a thousand years: a much earlier folk fire festival.

So I built a small bonfire and, as the full moon did its thing, I lit the fire and sat in front of it on top of the mound. Beyond lighting a fire I had nothing planned and had no idea what to do next. So I just sat there. After an hour or so I was about to go back in the house when a huge pressure started to build up within me: something was happening. The pressure built and built, and I simply sat and watched the fire until the feeling became unbearable.

Without any warning, it felt like I was about to vomit into the fire when something passed through me and into the fire. At the same time I suddenly became aware of the gates: they were open, very present, and very strong. It was hard to stay sitting still, as my body was struggling with the sensation which I know now to have been a bridging action. I was hit with waves of nausea, sweating, and dizziness.

Suddenly the pressure released and something moved quickly through one of the gates: the spirit of the man in the mound had bridged through me and used the fire as a porthole to access the gates into death. I sat stunned for a short while, and as I sat I became aware of other spirits drawing near to the fire and then passing through it, heading west as they began their journey deeper into death. Many came, passed into the fire, and then vanished.

When I finally went back inside, I felt like I had been sitting on the mound for about an hour; but in fact, once I looked at the clock, I realised that I had been out there for six hours.

For days afterwards I was exhausted, nauseous, and felt deeply bruised. But I had learned a lot. Also, the mound became very quiet after that night, which in turn brought peace and quiet to the house.

In subsequent years I worked with the idea of a fire as a gate for the dead at that time of the year, and I discovered that it was much easier on the body to work with a fire to do bridging if it was done over a three day period, or with a group of people all doing the same thing.

A few years later, when I lived in California, a small group of us decided to work with the same tide, and with a fire. We waited until the full moon that fell between the middle of October and the middle of November. On the days leading up to it, we visited the hill where we planned to do the work and we sat there each night, just keeping vigil with the intent of helping any lost souls wandering around the area.

On the full moon, we lit the fire and sat around it, at first chatting, until finally we fell silent and settled into our own thoughts. One woman, on instinct, starting singing a death song I knew from my childhood, the *Lyke Wake Dirge*.

This old remnant of heathen folk tradition from Yorkshire was a song that was sung as the body was carried from the church for burial. It was often chanted without instrument but to the slow beat of a large drum, like a slow, deep heart beat.

As she chanted (it is more spoken than sung), we started to pick up on spirits drawing near, attracted by the singing. Over the span of about two hours, spirit after spirit drew near to the fire and then passed through it, vanishing through the fire and into the west: their deeper journey into death and separation from the living world had begun. They didn't pass through us this time; rather they gathered around us and then plunged into the fire.

We expected a handful. Two hours later they were still coming: it felt like hundreds of spirits had passed through the circle of women and plunged into the fire. None of us could move, speak, or break the pattern: we had to stay there, silent, until it was done.

We were all impacted for a few days afterwards, but we recovered quickly enough, and it gave us all a lot to think about. What we had intended, in a rather naive way, was to hold the gates open for a lost soul or two. We didn't expect half the dead population of the area to turn up; nor were we prepared for the amount of energy it would take.

The reason I tell you this story is because it is important to understand that while we as magicians think we have it all sussed out in our different traditions, with rituals for this and visions for that, to be honest, we do not have a clue, we are barely scratching the surface. We may have evolved technologically as a species, but when it comes to magic, inner worlds and power, we are still struggling to climb out of a dark age.

Because of that, while there is a lot of organised magical learning to do as an apprentice, there is also a lot for you to learn using your own intuition and instincts, and learn to listen to everything around you. Sure you will make some mistakes, and some of those may be major ones, but you will also have breakthroughs, make connections, and stumble across things that move you forward in your development. The key is to try and stay in one piece throughout the process, and that in turn comes from using your common sense.

In the decades since those events, I have observed more and more tides that flow across the land and that seem to do different things. I have learned not to try to over organise them in my mind, but just to be aware of them, and to be acutely aware of how they make me act, am I suddenly needing to spring clean, or sleep a lot, or stay in after dark, or keep lights on?

The ancient wisdoms around these tides will not be found in books but in our ancestral knowledge that is buried deep in our blood; in our DNA. That knowledge can surface if you let it, and stillness is one of the keys, as is knowing what is your own imagination and what is something deeper. That comes from practice, common sense, and discernment.

When it comes to these tides of death, tides of scale-balancing, and tides of renewal, always observe and keep diaries of how they affect you. If you find yourself feeling out of character, or feel something strange happening to you, look around you. Is everyone else acting up, or is it just you? If everyone else seems to be going through the same thing, the chances are that a tide is flowing through to bring change or shake things up a bit. If you do observe something like this happening around you, simply take notes: write down the date, the moon cycle, the moods and actions of the people around you, and what is happening in the news (sudden increase in violent crimes or natural disasters?).

It is about learning how to observe for yourself rather than stick your head in a text: everything that is written in ancient texts comes from the direct experience of the people: it all started with someone taking note, someone observing and experimenting. Become a part of that process in magic by slowly becoming more and more aware of what is happening around you.

There are a lot of magical rituals, visions and so forth that can be used to work with a lost soul or a problematic spirit, but it is not yet a safe time in your training to dive into that. However, you can start that working process by tuning in to the next autumn death cycle, if you so wish. And this is something that you can do each year if you wish to, as a service to the land and to the people where you live. If you do work with this cycle, then work with your instincts and write everything down.

1. Working the death cycle

From what I have observed over the years in different countries, the tide seems to start with a new moon in October and finish with the new moon in November; and it peaks with the full moon in the middle. I find it interesting that at this time of year, lighting fires and lights in the window to guide the dead should come straight after a time of harvest, both of food and of the weighing of Scales/opening of the Book of Life in Jewish traditions. They dovetail together quite nicely.

What you can do as a magician is to start working with this autumn cycle on the new moon: start by keeping a candle burning at night, potentially where its cast of light can be seen from a window. Hang wind chimes outside near to the window where the light can be seen, and when you do your daily meditations, think about the many souls who get lost in the death process because they have no compass, noway of knowing what to do or where to go. Many figure it out for themselves, but some do not.

I would not use religious texts for reciting at this time; rather it would be better to learn to work with the tides of nature, to learn for yourself how to work and be with the dead.

A compromise could be to go out each night and talk to the dead, spend a few minutes each night standing in the darkness, and speak to the wind (the magical power of utterance): tell the dead who can hear you not to be afraid, that a fire will be lit at the full moon and the gates to death and renewal will be open for them. Tell them that in the meantime they are safe near you, and can rest a while around the outside of your house until it is time for the fire.

The fires for the dead, I have found, are most effective and have least impact on the worker if they are lit over three nights: the night before the full moon, the night of the full moon, and the night after. Either light a fire on the ground or in a fire bowl, and just sit with the fire each night, *with the intent of providing a gate for the dead*. As you light the fire, be aware of where the west is, and simply see in your mind the west gate. That is as much as you need to do magically.

This passive way of working can be a major lesson: often our rituals, visions, and actions can get in the way of a natural flow of power, and there are times when it is very powerful simply to turn up somewhere with intent, light a flame, and just be present. There is no need to behave as if you are in a church, with whispers and reverence. Just as it is with the dying, often simply being there, chatting, or singing is enough, if the sacred intent is held.

The major magical trigger is the lighting of the fire: treat the fire as if it was the central flame in your work space. Ground yourself with your feet upon the stone in the Underworld, the stars above you, the ancestors behind you, the Noble Ones before you, and with your intent of service and compassion. Then light the fire. That simple tuning will trigger a cascade of events that will culminate in the spirits drawing near and knowing it is safe to pass through the west gates via the fire. Some may bypass the fire and walk straight into the west.

You will know when you have done enough: the atmosphere will change and become more normal again, you will be sleepy, and you will feel that it is okay to leave. While you sit around the fire, take note of everything that happens around you (and turn your phone off!): watch nature, watch the stars, listen to the sounds, and listen to how your body reacts. Let your mind wander as you observe, learn to *be* without entertainment of a phone or music.

Those of you who are sighted will have more than enough to keep you busy. For those who are not naturally sighted, learn to listen to the slightest whisper on the wind, the slightest change in how you feel, in what is happening around you. Don't, however, get jumpy and dramatic, nor think that everything around you is a sign: be grounded, be open, be aware, and use your common sense. None of this is paranormal; it is in fact perfectly normal.

If you are interested, do some research on old folk traditions about this time of the year. Don't fall into the trap of looking only for death-related traditions: cast your net wider and you may find some interesting things around the theme of fire, light, darkness, and a soul finding its way home.

2. Summary

As you will have noticed, this is not a heavy-duty lesson and there are no practical exercises or tasks for you to do. This is one of those lessons that is here for you to read, take note of, and then file away so that when this time of the year comes around you can revisit this lesson and decide if you wish to work with the idea of holding the fires of death.

3. The Lyke Wake Dirge

(Written in old Yorkshire dialect.)

This ae nighte, this ae nighte,
Every nighte and alle,
Fire and fleet and candle-lighte,
And Christe receive thy saule.

When thou from hence away art past
To Whinney-muir thou com'st at last
If ever thou gavest hosen and shoon
Sit thee down and put them on;

If hosen and shoon thou ne'er gav'st nane
The whinnes sall prick thee to the bare bane.
From Whinny-muir when thou may'st pass,
To Brigh o' Dread thou com'st at last:

From Brig o' Dread when thou may'st pass,
To Purgatory fire thou com'st at last;
If ever thou gavest meat or drink,
The fire sall never make thee shrink;

If meat or drink thou ne'er gav'st nane,
The fire will burn thee to the bare bane;

This ae nighte, this ae nighte,
Every nighte and alle,
Fire and sleet and candle-lighte,
And Christe receive thy saule.

Note:

I have never found a recording that sounds anything like how it was back when I was a kid. Most recordings in the last few years all track back to a group from the 1960s called the *Young Tradition* and are very much styled in the 1960s folk revival. Traditionally it was more spoken to a drum than sung, with only the refrain sung ("And Christe receive thy saule" – and Christ receive your soul).

Lesson 7
Inner Contacts and Inner Adepts

We now get to, from a magical perspective, one of the most interesting aspects of death and the sort of variables that we see in death, and that is the subject of the inner adepts.

The phenomenon is as old as temple culture itself, and examples of people who once lived and who opted out of the usual cycles of birth and death in order to serve can be spotted in most ancient and not-so-ancient cultures. The one thing they all have in common is that they tend to come out of temple cultures of one sort or another.

More recent inner adepts are the product of mystical, spiritual, and magical traditions that keep a continued sense of service in their line. Like all things connected to humans, it sometimes goes wrong, but for the most part if you aim in the right direction in terms of contacts, these inner adepts can be very valuable. Just don't assume that every inner adept is wise or has your best interests at heart. Often their own agenda's and interests, or those of their magical line comes first. So treat each inner adept you come across in the same way you would a stranger who has approached you – be cautious, use common sense, and think about it carefully if any inner contact asks you to do something. And also be aware that sometimes parasites can dress as inner adepts. The best way to avoid any such issues, is to stay within the pattern of the vision or ritual without variation or addition which gives you protection. Later as an adept, you can make far more informed choices about evolving a piece of work.

In the last hundred years, and particularly in the last forty or fifty years, this aspect of human service, i.e. inner adepts, has been co-opted by the commercial New Age and 'magick' community in order to sell product. It is not that the inner adepts themselves have been co-opted; rather that the concept has been misused and in a dishonest way. People channelling 'ascended masters' are more common these days than plumbers, (and have about the same magical skill as the average plumber) and for the right price there are many 'teachers' who will connect you or initiate you into the 'Inner Order of Melchizadek' – something that does not exist.

Many esoteric orders have tried to pin these contacts down and organise them (giving them fancy names, imaginary lines of initiation, and made-up histories), something which never works and always ends up messy.

But the inner adepts themselves have throughout time interacted with various magical and mystical orders, working on the thresholds, and working in the inner realms with magicians who work in vision. So what are these inner adepts/masters/elder brothers and sisters?

1. The process of becoming an inner adept

We looked at the death process, the process of the Scales, and how some spirits who stand before the angel decide not to come back into life, but are not yet ready to go deeper in to the process, so they choose to serve in the inner worlds for a time. The spirit of the person steps into the inner worlds and operates through an inner structure that can be used as an interface with the living: inner temples, inner libraries, thresholds, and so forth.

Usually the personality that they last held in life is jettisoned before they step into the inner realms, so as not to cause a back-drag on the spirit or create a cult-type situation with the living humans with whom they will work. This is one of the hallmarks of knowing when you have gotten a real inner adept contact: **you will never know who they are/were.** Any inner contact that appears as a known human or declares to be a certain person is most likely not, and is something else masquerading as them.

This can be for good reasons for dressing up: an inner being trying to get a specific way of thinking across will pluck from your mind, or from the collective mind of the group, a person that they can dress up as who represents what they are trying to teach. Just be aware that what the spirit thinks is good teaching, may actually not be for us in modern times.

The bad reason would be a cross-dressing parasite. In such a case, anything transmitted from the contact to the living is usually banal or total drivel dressed up with light, aliens, crystals… you get the idea.

Sometimes fairly recently dead adepts will try to contact other magicians and work with them, but that is not the same thing. They are still going through the death process and have not yet moved deeper into the aspect of death that we looked at (the angel and the Vista). This is the most commonly mistaken type of contact: an adept in death who is waiting around, connecting with the lodge or other magicians, and who retains the personality/image from their life in clear terms is in fact, technically, a haunting. And they can be very annoying.

Many of these types of magicians who hang around after death can become a bit of a problem as their ego and personality is still driven by a sense of control. We see this when lodge leaders die who cannot let go. They badger the living magicians, gatecrash into the temple, and generally become a nuisance. It is understandable: when a magician has spent their whole adult life trying to build something, to then feel in death that those left behind are not doing it properly must be frustrating.

But the dead magician has failed at the first post: upon death, everything that you held dear must be released and let go of: you cannot cling to a past life in death and still expect to be balanced. The net result of this type of behaviour tends to be the living magicians having to banish the dead magician from the temple or lodge. Very sad.

In such a situation (a magical leader/teacher dying), it is important for both the dead magician and the living ones left behind to realise that their old era is now over. Some living magicians, upon the death of a beloved teacher, will try to hold on to them, desperately trying to contact them and draw them back into the temple. Not only is that seriously unbalanced, it is also magically immature and a sign of bad or inadequate training.

A true inner adept will have shed their life identity, and what is left is the deeper knowledge, wisdom, skills, and intent to serve. Many will purposely not give a name, or if badgered by an inexperienced but psychic magician they will give a totally meaningless name. This is for good reason: this is not a personality show; it is deep reserves of service in action without ego attached. But most sensible adept leaders will cut loose from the lodge upon death and will leave the new generation to make of it what they will, for good or bad.

The interactions I have had over the decades with this type of inner contact have usually involved me learning, or being shown something, or being asked to bridge something from the outer to the inner. I have never known who they were, where they lived in their life, or what they did. But they all bear the hallmark of the inner priesthood, the inner adepts; an inner frequency that becomes easily recognisable to the living magician.

And inner adepts do not always appear as humans, even though they once were. They can appear in different forms: the one I found the weirdest to get my head around for a long time was the inner adepts who were presenting as 'books' in the Inner Library.

Before we go any further, now would probably be the best time to start to look at the Inner Library in depth, as this inner construct is key to the understanding of inner adepts and how to work with them.

2. The Inner Library

The Inner Library is an ancient interface that has been known by various terms over the millennia, but what it is stays the same: an inner place where knowledge and the knowledgeable can be accessed. You are already familiar with the idea of the inner temples: inner structures that feed through and into an outer structure. The inner temples and the Inner Library are not naturally-occurring inner places (obviously), but are inner templates that were constructed using magical technique which were tied into or simultaneously created as their outer temples were built. However, moving the construction to one side, the power that the constructs hold *is* natural. What the books in the library in fact are, are the condensed learned skill and knowledge of a person who once lived.

The person themselves has no presence or connection with the 'book', rather it is the jettisoned energetic pattern of the practical side of the evolution of that person's expertise. Another layer of meaning is the energetic pattern of the sum total of that person's spiritual evolution through the development and practice of skills. This in turn is connected to the Ancient Egyptian concept of the Ka – the part of a person that through their work, *and* through their love of the Divine in any of its forms, evolved. The meaning of Ka is both worship and work, and the two are deeply entwined.

The main difference between inner temples and the Inner Library is that there are quite a few different inner temples (which are connected to outer world temples), whereas there is only one Inner Library and it is not connected to an outer library; rather it is *the root source of knowledge for all the inner and outer temples.*

All the acquired knowledge and wisdom that has passed through temples and through magical, mystical, and spiritual institutions or individuals is stored in the Inner Library, and it is also a major access point to virtually every inner temple, or even deeply spiritual or magical place that can still be reached.

Every true temple from any culture anywhere connects to the Library in one way or another, and when a temple finally breaks up, all of the knowledge held in that temple remains in the library. As an inner temple falls into disuse from an inner point of view, it slowly breaks down and eventually sinks into the sands of the Inner Desert, or tips into the Abyss if the structure it maintains is to be composted permanently; only the knowledge of its people remains as 'books' or 'scrolls' upon the shelf.

My earliest direct contact with an inner adept when I was a young magician was in the Inner Library, which is a safe and solid structure for a young, inexperienced magician to work in. I did not go into the Library with the specific intent to make a connection with an inner adept, it just sort of happened. The time that I spent going into the Inner Library and working with this inner adept was invaluable to me in terms of learning and experience.

A few years later I was to connect with inner adepts that were not in the Inner Library, but were in a very ancient temple that was preparing to tip into the Abyss. There was a sense of great urgency, almost desperation, in their contact with me. I wanted to know who they were, what temple culture they came from, and what I could learn on the spot from them (typical youngster attitude). In turn they wanted me to shut up and to simply take what they had to give so that I could bridge, process, mediate, and then externalise what it was they wanted to pass on. I was expecting a sudden download of instant knowledge (idiot that I was), but what happened was something far more profound and which is still unfolding for me to this day.

In turn, each of them, men and women, stood in front of me in the ancient temple and literally shoved 'something' into me. Some of whatever they were placing within with me appeared to me as books, and some of it was, well, I could not even begin to describe it. And then they were gone.

At the time when this happened in my early thirties I felt special, a superior feeling that was very quickly slapped down by the inner adepts I worked with in the Inner Library. It was made very clear to me that I was an idiot, a novice in their eyes, and it was more a matter of me being the fool in the right place at the right time who was willing to take the burden on. Once I was quite rightly cut down to size, I slowly learned how to access what was in me and work with it. I was no more special than a library assistant helping to sort books.

Over the years I worked more and more with inner adepts, both in the temples and the Inner Library, until I came to a point where part of me is now always there as well as here: I don't have to *go* to these places any more, I carry them around with me always; you eventually become part of the 'hive.' And again that is not being special; it is just something that slowly develops over decades of work.

In the library, these inner adepts can appear in many different ways. Some appear as librarians or priests/priestesses within the Inner Library itself, and these are inner adepts who have stretched beyond the structure of the temple line they came from. They have become *generic* in that they no longer belong to any single stream of magic, spirituality, or structure: they are mediators of knowledge, plain and simple.

A deeper version of this generic knowledge contact appears in the Inner Library as a book or scroll. This is where the personality and the human dressing has fallen away and all that is left is the core energy and knowledge of that adept. This appears to us as a book (pure knowledge), but it is not *actually* a book and cannot be read as a book. This is a mistake that many magicians make: they go to the Inner Library, pick up a book, and expect to be able to 'read' the knowledge contained within it. But it doesn't work that way; this is not a movie with instant results.

The books in the Inner Library are energy patterns that hold knowledge and wisdom. To access that knowledge, the magician *takes the book into themselves* and gives that energy and knowledge a vessel that it can unfold within and bloom through. By taking the book into yourself, you literally absorb the knowledge of an inner adept, a knowledge that will unfold within you as time goes on. And boy does it unfold!

So you begin to see how the inner masters who are worked with in lodges, such as 'Plato' and 'Socrates,' are not *actually* Plato and Socrates: that grandiose claim is a dressing that tells you what sort of frequency that being is operating at, and what they are trying to convey to you. And when a true inner master dresses up, it is because they feel they have to 'talk slowly' to you; they have to dress up so that you will accept what they have to say.

But as always with 'personalities,' more often it is an intelligent parasite that is cross-dressing. That tends to happen most often if someone is using scrying methods, or brings the contact to them in their work space.

Working within the specific confines of the Inner Library or an inner temple gets rid of all of those and other issues – parasites just cannot get into these inner constructs. Occasionally you will come across a dead adept still holding on to their life persona in the Inner Library, but it is unusual and can often lead to issues as they want to connect to 'their magicians' through you. But such an occurrence is rare.

As an apprentice, the safest way for you to connect with and learn from an inner adept is to work with them in the Inner Library. If you work as an apprentice in vision in the Inner Library and you perceive a grandly dressed adept who is talking at length to you giving you 'wisdoms,' it is most likely that it is your own mind that is talking to you.

For the most part, contact with inner adepts can be a bit weird, particularly if they are from a very distant past: it is difficult with such a contact to have a communal language as their concepts and ours are so vastly different. So a sort of pidgin sign language, symbolic displays, and lots of pointing at things tends to happen.

You can converse with some of them, but such conversation is usually quite simple, and yet profound. They will reach into your mind to look for a visual vocabulary, so be aware of that: they are looking for a common form of communication.

Teaching tends to come in the form of showing you things, pointing at things, shoving things into you, pulling things out of you, and/or taking you to different parts of the library and pushing you into side rooms to observe, or just simply to be there. Eventually over time you gain a common language so that communication between you flows better and you learn to trust the contact.

The first inner adept from the library that I worked with communed fairly well with me, but would only give me lectures about food. We could have fairly clear basic conversation, but it was always lectures about what I should not eat. I became frustrated because I wanted magic, not dietary counselling. And yet at that time, in my early thirties, it was exactly what I needed. I was being cleaned up, my body was being prepared to cope with high levels of power, and as someone with an autoimmune disease (at that time undiagnosed), the adjusted diet was spot on. My body coped well with the work thanks to the adept's advice. So don't dismiss seemingly non-magical conversation.

Working in the library should be a long-term, consistent discipline over decades, which in turn will change how the interface works for and with you: it gets to a point where a part of you is constantly in the Inner Library and the Inner Library is constantly in you. When you reach that point, it is made clear to you that you no longer need to work in vision in the library: you become a part of the interface at a deep level. When you die as an adept, your stored wisdom, experience, and knowledge will be released into the library for future magicians to access.

The appearance of the Inner Library varies according to the lines of culture that the person comes from: its appearance to a magician is shaped by the collective consciousness of their culture. Someone accessing the Inner Library from a Hindu culture, for example, will see an Inner Library with the hallmark shape, but the dressing will look more like something from the ancient temples of the Indian subcontinent, whereas Western magicians will see something akin to the Great Library of Alexandria: it is the collective memory within your own culture and blood that often dictates how your brain will interpret the surface dressing.

One constant, though, is the shape of the Inner Library: it has a central circular area with four wings, like an equal-armed cross with a circle in the middle. Regardless of how it is dressed, it holds the same shape: the shape dictates how the power flows through it, how the temples connect into it, and also how all of those things come together (think back to your lessons on magical patterns and the four directions). The fine detail of the decor, dressing, etc. is what varies. But what it is and who is in it does not vary from person to person; it is itself, and the inner adepts, or whatever different traditions call them, are always the same.

It is also good to bear in mind that when you do make a contact with an inner adept, that the meeting is specifically relevant to you, to what time, culture, and mystical or magical system you are operating in. You are led to or introduced to an adept who is deeply connected to the line of magic/mysticism that you are studying. This ensures that the inner adept can pass their knowledge on to someone who can actually make use of it, and the magician receives something that they can actually do something with.

Saying that, I have had some very culturally different contacts in the library, and at times it was a bit of a struggle. But eventually it made sense as to why I was guided to such diverse contacts.

As an apprentice, it is time for you to start this connection process and learn how to first connect with an inner adept and then work with them. By now, after reading so far into this lesson, you should be aware that if any contact shows up in, say, Golden Dawn robes, or in white robes and tells you that they are Papus, then your mind is playing up and you need to clear your mind and focus. If you get an adept that looks very weird and unexpected, then chances are you have a very ancient contact.

The main thing to remember is that by staying within the confines of the Inner Library (and later the inner temples) most of the crud that is of any danger is filtered out. If, over time, you have become used to working in the Library and you come across a known dead magician, the best advice I can give you is to quell your curiosity and steer around them – they are always trouble.

3. Making contact with the Inner Adepts

The way to initially make a contact with an inner adept that you can work with and learn from is to go in vision to the Inner Library. Before we get to that, here are the basic rules that will keep you safe, and help you to process what knowledge you are given. And don't forget, if it is a grand presentation, it is likely fake or coming from your own head, as inner adepts tend to be very simple, focused, powerful, and unfussy.

Don't expect to open a book and be able to read it. You take the energy into yourself, absorb it, process it, and the knowledge contained within it springs to life when you start working on something that is relevant to that knowledge.

Don't be fooled by the apparent simplicity of the vision. Sometimes a powerful contact can seem easy while you are going through the process, but it will hit you like a wall afterwards. Everyone processes power in a different way, so when you come to do the visionary work, make sure you have some hours afterwards for downtime.

If you find it very difficult to form the images or make sense in vision of what is happening, don't over force it: some people are strong visualisers, some magicians are not. You need to learn how *your* mind and body processes information and power. For some it is sensations, for others it is like a movie. Neither is better than the other; just do the work and see how it unfolds for you.

Now is also the time in your training to learn how to cope should you be suddenly disturbed in the depths of vision. If that should ever happen to you (the door bursts open and the dog leaps on you), learn to simply open your eyes while holding the energetic sense within you. Sort out the disturbance as simply as possible and return back to the vision: learn to put your mind on hold. It does not always work at first, but trying opens the pathways in your brain for doing that. Having kids is a good trainer: I learned early on to switch on and off according to which child was catapulting themselves at me while I was in vision. I would put the vision on hold, sort out the issue, and then pick up where I left off.

Learn the access points of the vision by heart, really well, before you start to actually do the vision. Learn the paths, and then visualise each step in your head before you eventually sit down to the do the vision. The key steps are: knowing where you are going, how to get there, what the layout of the place is, how to make the contact, and then how to get out again. The rest is just details. But in all visions always remember how to get out again!

4. *Task:* Meeting the Inner Adept – the vision

In your work space, light the directions including the central altar, see the gates open, see the Noble Ones in the south, and go around the directions at least once, seeing the gates open, seeing a contact standing on the thresholds, and then once you have finished in the north, stand with your back to the north in front of the central altar.

Spend a moment tuning in to the sense of your feet in the Underworld, the stars/Divine Breath above you, the sword to your left and the vessel to your right, and the path with the Noble Ones before you. Once you feel fully tuned and ready to work, walk a full circle around the directions and finish at the east. Sit down with your back to the central altar, with your body facing east, and close your eyes.

With your inner vision, build up an image of the east altar with the open gates behind it. Still yourself, be aware of your central flame, and when you are ready see yourself in vision standing up and going to the east altar. Bow before the altar and then walk through the altar. (See the note on walking through altars below).

As you walk through the altar see the gates wide open and see that they lead to a long tunnel cut out in stone that leads off into the distance. As you step through the gates, a person steps forward: the guardian of the library. They look at you and you must simply stand and wait as they look at the marks upon you and around you. They look into your eyes and may ask you why you are here. Simply reply that you wish to access the Inner Library in order to learn. The person will look into your eyes again, and when they are satisfied that you are indeed an apprentice they will step aside and let you pass.

Walk down the long tunnel, and as you walk, think about the main thing that you think you need to learn from an inner adept. It will not be necessarily what you want to learn, but rather what you need to learn. You will not get that learning upon first contact, but it is important to have at least some idea formed in your mind as to areas of your magical or mystical life that needs focus: this creates something that the inner adept can work with. If you just flounder in without a clue, or with the wish for power, they will not waste their time with you. Think about what it is that you struggle the most with in your practice and study as a magician.

As you walk down the tunnel, you can feel all sorts of things happening around you, but there is nothing to see: it feels like the tunnel cuts through a vast building that has lots of things happening in it. That is exactly what the tunnel is. In the distance you see a light shining through a half-open door. Walk towards the door, and take your time.

Once you arrive at the door, carefully step through it, and you will find yourself in a wing of a vast library that seems to stretch in all directions. The shelves go up so far that the tops are veiled in mist. In one direction the wing vanishes into mist, but to the left of the door you emerged from, you see a vast circular foyer.

Walk to the foyer, and you find yourself in a large, circular library space. In the centre is a large ornate pedestal that holds a huge book, and in each of the four directions are entrances to wings of the library that stretch off so far into the distance that you cannot see the ends of those sections of the building. The building is very bright, light, and airy, and after the darkness of the tunnel it takes you a moment to readjust.

As your eyes adjust to the brightness, you notice that the library foyer is full of people milling around. Some are seated and reading, some are tending to books, some are chatting to each other, and some seem busily to be going somewhere. One of the people in conversation spots you, breaks away from their conversation, and comes over to greet you.

This is a Keeper of the Library. She asks you what you want, why you are here. Tell her that you wish to learn and you wish to meet an inner adept. Tell them that you are in magical training and wish to develop more.

She will indicate for you to follow her to the very centre of the library where all the directions come together. There in the centre is the very large and ornate pedestal with a vast book upon it. The woman stands up on the pedestal and asks your name. Tell her the name you were born with, your full name.

The woman sifts through the pages of the book, looking for your name. When she finds it, she reaches into that page and pulls out another much smaller book. She opens that book and then looks again at you to check that you are who you say you are. She is holding your Book of Life. She leafs through it, seeing everything you have done, good and bad, indifferent and odd, what you have studied, what your fate pattern looks like: all the things that make up your life so far. She checks to see if indeed you are working magically, how your work is going, and what you need next in terms of learning.

Instead of placing your Book of Life back in the vast book, she holds it up directly above her. A large hand comes down from the mists above that obscure the top of the library and takes the book from her before vanishing back into the high mist. She nods at someone in the distance and then climbs down from the pedestal and walks away, leaving you standing at the pedestal. Stay where you are and just wait.

In time, someone walks up to you from behind, male or female, and places a hand upon your right shoulder. Turn around and greet them: this is an inner adept.

The opening of your Book of Life, and the handing up of your Book, signals a point in your life when your real learning begins in magic. That in turn *marks* you as a magician: you become visible to the inner adepts.

Let the person look at you, think at you, and interact with you. They may place books within you, they may talk with you, or show you things. Remember, this is a first meeting: it is about getting used to being in the presence of an inner adept and learning how they communicate. They may be able to converse well with you or they may not. Spend as much time as you need to interact with them, and take note of everything that happens, however minor or strange it may seem.

When you feel it is time to go, or they indicate to you that it is time to leave, bow to the adept and thank them. They will walk away from you, and as you watch them go you will notice that the majority of the people in this place are now looking at you. Take a little while to look at them. You will slowly notice that they are from many different times, cultures, religions, and some of them will look very strange to you indeed.

You will also notice that they seem to group near each of the entrances to the four wings of the building that lead from the central podium. They do not seem to go down the wings of the building much; rather they stay in the central foyer, but browse the shelves close to a specific wing. Each wing corresponds to a direction, and the books that are held in that wing hold all the knowledge and wisdom that flows from the powers of those directions.

Now it is time for you to leave. You need to find which is the east wing, as it will lead to the tunnel that will take you back to the east altar in your work space.

Stand in the centre by the podium and look at each wing in turn. Look at the people, the magicians, priests and priestesses, the scholars, composers, writers, thinkers: you will notice that in one of the directions there is a debate going on, and people listening to the debate are writing down notes from what is being said. They are working with the power of the east.

Walk towards them, and as soon as you start to walk towards the east you will feel a slight wind on your face: you always get an elemental confirmation of the direction you are approaching in the Inner Library. As you pass by the people gathered at the entrance to the east wing, stop and bow to acknowledge them: these are all inner adepts, magicians, or priests/priestesses. They acknowledge you with a smile, and some may bow back: these are teachers who are acknowledging your path as a magician. Pass by them and go down the east wing.

Part of the way down you will see a wall to your right that has many small doors in it. One of them holds a symbol you recognise: the X with a line through the middle of it. Go through that small door, and you will find yourself back in the tunnel. Walk back through the tunnel until you pass over the threshold, through your east altar, and back into your work space.

Sit back down into yourself, and when you are ready, open your eyes. Immediately write down everything in your journal that you can remember, even the smallest detail and things you may normally discard – they could be important in the future. Then go around the directions starting in the east, bow, say thank you, see the gates partially close, and put the flame out, leaving the centre candle until last.

If anything pops into your memory later in the day, go back and write it in your journal, along with drawings of any symbols you see. Type up a summary for your computer log. Don't fixate on the presentation of the contact you made: it does not matter what they looked like, what their name is, or where they came from in life – what is important are the interactions between you in the library room.

5. *Task:* Routine

Do the Library vision once or twice a week for four weeks, and keep computer notes of the encounters. Also spend some time in each of those visions handling the books in the Library, feeling, them and interacting with them.

Once your month of working in the Library is up, set up a schedule to go into the library at least once a month for a year. Working in the Library in vision is a major foundation feature of magical training. Throughout your training, you will work with the Library in various ways, learning more and more about its depths, its connections, and how it links into so many different things.

As you go back and forth into the Library, you begin to change at a deep level and wake up to dormant knowledge stores within you, as well as learning how to tap into the collective knowledge of humanity. It is a slow but steady evolution in how you learn, and it is not about learning facts or intellectual knowledge; rather it is a connection to very deep reserves of wisdom and knowledge that come from generations of experience. It will slowly unfold over your lifetime and will surface in every aspect of your life when needed.

6. *Task:* Pondering

Remember at the podium, your Book of Life, that the Library Keeper handed it upwards into the mist? Think about what was happening to the book.

The Book of Life is not actually a book; we just see it that way in vision. The Book of Life is the same as the contents of your vessel, your Harvest so far: it is an energetic pattern that is constantly evolving according to what you do, how you do it, why you do it. It is woven tightly into your web of fate, and together they make a complex mix that is unique to you.

You will find throughout your magical work that this complex, ever-changing pattern that you create through your life actions and evolution appears in different magical realms in different forms. Learning the different ways it can appear will tell you a lot about the varied aspects of it and how it can be worked with in different ways.

Think about why it was handed upwards. There is a very specific reason for this, and it marks a turning point in your magical training. Think about what you have learned about the directions, what is up and what is down, and why the book would have been handed upwards. Note any thoughts in your computer log.

A note on walking through altars

By now you should be used to passing through an altar. There is a very specific reason for doing this in vision. When you pass in vision through an altar that physically exists and has been worked with repeatedly in ritual tuning, it becomes a guarded gateway: all the power that has built up over the time of your work is embedded within the altar, and also that direction in your work space. This in turn creates a membrane or filter that acts as a protection and a landing strip.

By walking through the east altar, not only are you protected by the power of the sword that you have been building up in that direction, but also by the nature of the contacts and the focused energy of the east that you have slowly been building. By walking through the east, you are guided to inner realms directly connected to the east: i.e. the Inner Library, inner temples, etc. It is a very safe, well guarded, and well trodden path that you can walk without having to worry about protecting yourself.

Study note

While you are doing the month of visions in this lesson, you can also move on to Lesson 8 which is a reading/study lesson and can be done concurrently with this lesson.

Lesson 8

The Bound Ones

There is an aspect of death that is not widely known about or generally discussed in magical circles, but which does appear in dogmatic terms in some religions, and that is the aspect of death that deals with the souls/spirits of the dead who are bound through a natural process or a ritual process.

We have looked at souls who stay close to the living, that is to say, a haunting; but there is also a deeper process whereby souls can become trapped in a cage of their own making, which prevents them from progressing through death or returning back into life. That process can also be exploited by skilled magicians, though it is uncommon in Western magic. We will look first at the sort of binding that is the direct result of the actions/inaction of the person who has stepped into death; then we will briefly look at the magical aspect.

1. A hell of your own making

There are some people that step into death and seem neither able to reach the living, nor willing to move forward into death properly, and end up trapped in a cage of their own making. Their inability to let go of the things that they clung to in life, and their inability to self-assess or to even be self-aware, slowly traps the spirit in a loop of obsessive frustration. It can also happen when the person has been very seriously out of balance to the point of total destruction.

In the last module we talked about the Grindstone and the Unraveller. These natural angelic forces that flow throughout creation can have a direct continuum effect in the dying and death process. We looked at how immersing oneself in the actions of the Unraveller can sometimes trigger an opposing action of the Grindstone in life.

If, however, the person dies in the midst of a serious immersion in the Unraveller, a much deeper opposing power can be triggered, and that is the *Binder*. When something has unravelled to the point of dissolution, or to the point of seriously destructive spirit imbalance, the power of the Binder is triggered and the spirit becomes trapped. They are not bound against their will; rather the deep unbalance within the spirit affects such binding for itself.

I confess that I do not deeply understand this process myself, but I have observed it enough times to know that it exists, it happens, and that there are many different variables around it. So rather than theorise around it, I will lay out what I have discovered and seen in vision, so that maybe that will provide a stepping stone for others to take it further. It is a mechanism that is reflected in Jewish Kabbalah, and is a major aspect of the creation/destruction process, so those of you who have studied Jewish Kabbalah (not Hermetic Qabalah) will recognise the Sefirot at work in this mechanism.

I think the best way to approach this, as it is a complex issue that I don't have a wide understanding of, is to explain it in terms of the sequence of discoveries I made over the decades. It is part of the death process, and as such is pertinent to apprentices should you come across it in your own work over time. I also feel that it would assist your understanding of the various dynamics involved in death, the evolution of the human spirit, and their relationship to themselves and the Divine.

2. Trapped in the sands

Decades ago, when I first started working within the various death visions, I noticed an area away from the river, deep in the sands on our side of it, where many souls were trapped in the sands. Some were trapped up to their waists, and some were trapped up to their necks. Some were asleep, some were talking, and some were really angry. Some were cocooned and looked like larvae, and they had angelic beings that seemed to be tending and watching over them. I was fascinated.

After watching this process for a while when I was working in vision, I approached one of the angelic beings who was tending a cocoon and asked them what it was and what they were doing. The angle placed a hand over my eyes so that I could see through their filter, and I saw into the cocoon. Inside was a human who was full of destructive rage, imbalance, and fear. Every emotion of the person inside was heightened to a destructive level and they were completely engrossed in their turmoil: they were not aware of anything or anyone around them.

I asked if they were all like that and the angel said 'no,' and showed me another one. Inside was a person who exuded so much suffering that it caught my breath. The suffering of the person in the cocoon was so great that it hit me in the chest like a punch and I started physically crying. As I watched, my body and mind felt assaulted and I quickly pulled back out of vision. I realised that whatever I was observing, it was seriously energetically imbalanced, and if I wanted to learn more I would have to do this in short bursts of visionary work and not stay too long in any of the visions. So over a period of months, I went in and out of this part of the death vision and simply watched.

I slowly began to notice that those who were up to their necks in the sand were totally wrapped up in themselves: they talked and talked to themselves, shouted, gossiped, spat, struggled, and were generally very unpleasant. Some were shouting threats and some just raged, full of hate and spite.

Over time as I went in and out, some of them slowly quietened and began to look around them. As they did this, the sands seemed to withdraw a little bit and more of their 'bodies' became exposed.

The ones who were buried up to their waists were still very negative, but they were looking around more, and were trying to communicate with the angelic beings. I noticed something that struck me quite strongly: as some of them tried to communicate with the angelic beings and the beings communicated back, some of the trapped people immediately rejected whatever was said to them and went back to ranting to themselves. As they did this, the sand seemed to tighten around them.

In the vision, I got a sudden flash of people I knew in life who were like that – very negative, very dismissive and insular, and very self-destructive with it. These are qualities that we all have to a greater or lesser degree, but in these people they were so intense that they were the overriding qualities that ruled them.

At this point, I started to try and make sense of it in terms of the living, and why/how this binding happens to some people and not to others, and I just ended up tying myself in knots. So I gave up trying to rationalise it, and just went back to observing, which as an aside is a good way to operate as a magician if you want to learn about something: don't theorise, just observe.

As the months went by, some of the souls slowly released themselves out of the sands and began to walk towards the river; others seemed to dig themselves deeper or stayed in exactly the same state.

But the most curious group of all was the souls in the cocoons: some of them stayed there unchanged, some slowly became unbound, but some vanished in increments down into the sands. I asked the angelic being where the cocoons were going, and the angel just pointed downwards. I asked if they were going to hell (I know... I was still young at that time) and the angel had no idea what I was talking about (and I am sure the Catholic visuals in my head did nothing to help its confusion).

After a few months of looking into this, I seemed to get no further other than understanding that some souls got released, some stayed put, and some went 'down.' I became frustrated because I didn't fully understand why some people where there and others were not, nor could I figure out what (if any) role a magician would have in the process. I was too young really to grasp it, and did not at that time have any deeper experience in the death, creation, and destruction cycle. So I left it and moved on.

A year later I had started working in the Inner Desert in vision in a limited way. During one particular visionary session in the Desert I was walking with the Sandalphon when I noticed, off to one side in the Desert, people and other types of beings trapped in the sand and seemingly asleep. I asked if I could look closer, and the angel nodded. So I wandered over to these trapped souls and walked around them. Some were obviously people, buried up to their shoulders deep in the sand (just like in the death vision), and they looked to be deeply asleep.

Some were not human. I saw what looked or presented to me like angelic beings sleeping standing up, buried in the sand up to their waists or necks, and other strange, powerful-looking beings were in a similar bound state. Some had what appeared to me to be 'mummy bindings' on them, some had layers of sacred script around them like bandages, and all of them were deeply asleep.

They reminded me of the people in the death vision, and I had not at that point connected up the dots – that the sands of the death vision and the Inner Desert were different layers of the same inner realm. I asked the angel why they were there, and the reply that I got was that these beings of different types had no place in the living, manifest world at this time. I asked if they would ever be released, and the angel said that some would eventually, and some would not. The some who would not would slowly descend 'down,' and again the angel pointed 'down.'

I was getting a bit fed up with this 'going down' malarkey, as I did not understand it and was therefore dressing it in my mind in the dogmatic dressing of 'Catholic hell,' which I knew instinctively was not true. I asked about the angels that were bound. And I was told that they would be released from the sands when it was their time to be active: they were very destructive and would be released when the time for that massive destructive period arrived. I was then unceremoniously booted out of vision. After that, I gave that area of the Desert a wide berth for a while.

Moving on a few years, I was back working in the death vision when I saw some activity around one of the cocoons. A few angelic beings were waiting around a cocoon that was slowly cracking open. I asked if I could watch, and when it seemed that it was okay, I moved closer to watch. Inside the cocoon was a human that exuded the energy of a psychotic mass-murderer. I took a few steps back, but an angelic being came up behind me and pushed me forward again to watch. As I looked closer, I saw something inside the human, as though the human's energy was a cocoon in itself.

Fascinated, I watched as first the outer cocoon and then the human structure cracked open, and a bright, beautiful spirit stepped out and began a walk towards the river of death. I followed. The spirit went to the river and drank deeply before climbing on to the bridge. Fascinating.

I went back to the shell of the cocoon. The angelic beings were busy breaking it apart and composting it into the soil. I asked what that was all about. I was shown the physical shell of the human and told to look closer. Its structure, besides giving off the energy of a mass killer, was badly put together: the bits did not seem to fit. I was confused. I asked the angelic being for clarification and it immediately grabbed me by the hair and 'transported' me to a living scene.

In the scene was a psychotic killer pacing around a room fighting an urge to kill. I immediately thought of a parasite driving it. I was shown that although there were parasites around this person, a parasite was not what was driving them. I was pushed to look closer. I then spotted the spirit of the person within the body.

It was a good energy, intelligent and bright, but it did not fit in the body properly, and the body looked strange, mismatched, as though it was not a good fit. The angelic being once more put its hand over my eyes so I could see better. The body was inherently flawed: the brain, the gut, and the whole of the structure was so badly deformed in its development that it was like a feral car plummeting over a cliff with the driver unable to stop it.

I was then immediately back in the death vision, and I got it. The damage to the body, whatever had caused it, created a situation where the spirit or soul of the person was not in control of the impulses of their body. Their brain was so badly damaged or unbalanced that the soul could not operate properly through the body, and the body's impulses were so strong that it was driving itself. The spirit in the body watched helplessly as the outer person wreaked more and more destruction.

That in turn damaged the spirit, plunging the spirit into deep trauma. The spirit had to slowly, carefully detach from the outer personality driven by the body, and that took time. Once the spirit was able to disentangle itself from the outer personality, it could begin the process of breaking out of the cocoon.

This radically changed how I thought about 'good' and 'bad' spirits/people, and made me realise that sometimes the issue was far more complex than I had understood it to be. It was also the time when I realised that being judgemental about a person and a spirit was limiting my understanding, and was also at times just plain wrong.

I then swung the other way for a while, and assumed that every cocooned spirit was simply a victim of their body. This was also a wrong assumption, as some were indeed just deeply imbalanced and destructive spirits. So I eventually learned to take a 'wait and see' approach.

3. Sinking into the Abyss

I spent quite some time observing these souls and cocoons held in the sands, and after seeing some of them sink beyond trace, I wanted to know where they went and what happened to them.

Eventually I managed to figure out how to track them, and I watched as they sank into the Underworld and became trapped in the substance of the rock. Slowly the rock would absorb them and they would become unreachable even in the Underworld. For a few years I was unable to ascertain what happened then. Did they stay in the rock? Did they dissolve? If so, what happened to the idea of an 'eternal spirit'?

I got no answers for the longest time, but years later, I was working down in the Abyss and had to go down one of the tunnels for the work I was doing. At the end of the tunnel was a small cavern, and in that cavern was what looked like a stone cocoon. I asked the being I was working with what this was, and the being told me it was a spirit that was suspended in stone, and that while ever the planet existed, it would be held in that stone, taken out of circulation until living physical beings no longer existed. Hell indeed.

This was a turning point for me in a lot of ways. As a young teen I had rejected the religious dogmas I was raised in, but I also knew there was a grain of truth within them; I just could not find that grain or understand it. After total rejection and then spending my late teens and early twenties searching, the shift into deeper magic took me down this road of discovery that I still walk to this day.

I learned that some of the dogma in all religions is just made up for the sake of various agendas. Some dogmas have their roots in folk myths that in turn developed from direct communion with the vast array of spirits within nature, and some of the dogmas were the tiny fragments of a much more profound understanding. Those tiny fragments had survived in the human consciousness and had been dressed in layer after layer of dogma, agenda, and just plain silliness.

What was once ancient magical knowledge that emerged out of the Mediterranean areas, North Africa, and the Near/Middle East has over millennia been reduced down, through generations of ignorance, to dogmas designed to control.

What I have observed, for example, with the Bound Ones, is I think the root of the Christian concept of hell. A lot of Christian structure is cobbled together from Egyptian, Greek, and Babylonian streams (as well as many other influences), and if we look deeper into those ancient structures, we see the seeds of magical wisdoms that were converted into shock horror tactics that in turn controlled the believers.

So we go from an understanding of natural tides and forces, of the dynamics of cause and effect, until, through the dogmatic development of religion, we end up with stories which tell us that if we do not adhere to that religion's particular laws, we will 'burn in hell' or be 'trapped in hell.' Yes, a spirit can be trapped in the Underworld, but not from punishment; rather because that is the safest place for it to be for all concerned.

I have to say that after decades of exploration around these subjects, the older I get, the less I know, and the less I understand. And I think that is a good thing. This magical universe is far beyond our understanding: we do what we can to understand what is relevant to us and to interact with it, but the more you dig, the bigger it gets.

The best advice I can give at this point in my life – and I do hope I progress more so that my understanding changes over time – is that when you come across something in magic that you do not understand, don't try to theorise and fit it into something. Just watch it, observe, follow it around, and let whatever understanding you can grasp rise up to you through exploration.

4. Ritually Bound Ones

This is something else for you to begin learning about, but which you should not be working with as an apprentice for obvious reasons. All magical technique is a structured application that has its roots in a natural process: the magician uses a mechanism that is already inherent within nature and then applies it in a ritualised, visionary way.

One of those ritualised mechanisms that has been used in magic is the process of the Bound Ones. Where nature cocoons, locks in, and binds something that is a potential threat (and the human body does the same), so too the magician follows that same mechanism in order to bind something out of the life cycle. This is pretty nasty magic for the most part, and when it is necessary to ritually bind something using magic, the magician forestalls what would otherwise be a natural process.

There is a middle ground in this, and that middle ground comes into play when magic is the catalyst which caused the problem that subsequently needs to be bound up. If a spirit needs binding, nature responds and deals with it – though often not in the time frame humans would like. But if a magician releases a destructive and powerful being that would not naturally have been released, then the natural process does not always seem to respond properly.

To fix this magically by using ritual binding opens the door for lots of things to go into disarray: as humans, we do not always get the right picture, or our intentions are not always what they should be, and many times it becomes an ego issue for the magician. Nevertheless it is possible to ritually bind something that should not be out in the world, and to do it without upsetting the balance even more. The Egyptians were pretty good at this.

But the middle ground is where something has already been triggered and released by magic: the magician can work within the natural process along with the beings who would normally work with this issue, and as a combined team, it is possible put the being back and seal it back up. Under such circumstances, the human magician does only what is needed in proportion to the original magical act, and the rest is dealt with by the beings who take over nature's side of things.

This is something that is really important to grasp as apprentice magicians: ninety percent of your magical work as an adept is collaborative, and is often work where you only play a limited part: the angelic and other beings do their bit, and you do yours. This means you often do not get to see the finished results, or at times even get to see what it is you are doing: you become a bit-part actor in a massive blockbuster movie (alternatively, you can stay in control and be a leading actor in an amateur production at the local village hall). It's all about ego and control.

When you get to work as an adept, if you cannot get past yourself and your own need to control, your work will be limited. If you can learn to do your job and let others do theirs, you become part of a major team. This lesson about the Bound Ones is a very good example of a natural and powerful process that can potentially be reduced down to petty magical acts of revenge or control, and the common denominator in those petty acts is the limited thinking and ego of the magician.

The ritual binding of a soul/spirit is something that has been used in various religions, particularly ones that have reincarnation as a mainstay of their system. And of course, wherever you get magicians of great skill, corruption can so easily creep in, and those skills end up being used to bind souls into their bodies and into the land in order to make sure that an agenda is followed.

There is no practical magical work that an apprentice can do around this theme, as it is a mechanism that is energetically dangerous to be around in its natural inner form, and fraught with serious difficulties in its ritual presentation. But as apprentices it is wise to know about these dynamics early on in your training, as spotting them in different texts around the world will tell you about the depths of understanding in the roots of that religion/culture, so that you can then understand what it is that the religion stands upon as a foundation. In turn, it tells you about the magical skills of the early priests/priestesses who operated within that religion.

It is also handy to know about ritual binding early on in your training so that you can spot inherently imbalanced and flawed magical systems that incorporate such methods. In the early days of magical training it can be a bit of a minefield when you read and research, and often an apprentice magician has no reference point to be able to measure the balance, knowledge, or degeneration of a system.

By casting your net of understanding to the peripheries of magical texts, myths, legends, and systems, you will slowly learn to spot where a system's problems are, where its weaknesses are, and where there are gems hidden within the dogmatic bullshit. So your task for this lesson will be to hunt down these ancient wisdoms hidden in ancient texts so that you can see the fragments of knowledge and magical wisdom buried among the dogmas and agendas.

The best way to approach this is to be able to read texts without getting drawn into their dogmas and manipulations: look for the magical keys in words, images, statues, and architecture. Look for the fleeting mentions or clues in images or shapes, of deeper more ancient magical powers at work, and learn to extract from the dogmas the roots and foundations of older wisdoms however fragmented they may be: and by 'older' I mean going back up to five thousand years or more. By 1500 BC the rot had already set in, and by the time the Greeks had come along after their dark age, it was well and truly over. But fragments of knowledge and wisdom from those very ancient times have continued down to us in a variety of texts, images, statues and architecture.

5. Practical work

What follows are clips from various religious texts. Read through them, wade through the dogma, and see the dynamic you have been reading about in action. You have a choice once you have read through them:

Either choose one of the texts/authors and read/research further into those writings to spot the various creation and death dynamics that you have been learning about.

Or, once you have read the texts, use key words to do a search for similar presentations in other cultural myths, legends, and religious texts. They will of course present in many different ways but the foundation mechanism will be the same.

If you are interested in tracking the dissolution of understanding of the Mysteries and the rise in dogma with the Abrahamic religions, first read further into the texts that I have outlined, and then read the various gospels and epistles in the New Testament around the same subject matter. You will immediately spot the loss of the ancient fragments of knowledge and the rise of hellfire agenda-driven dogmas designed to frighten and subdue the masses.

Some of the New Testament writers still carried through the more ancient wisdom fragments in their writings, while others display a sad degeneration into fear-mongering and flashy visuals, probably co-opted from the Greeks (hellfires). This also marks the rise of the idea of hell as a place of punishment as opposed to a deep Underworld place where things are taken out of circulation: similar, and yet very different.

As you read, take computer notes about anything that leaps out at you and any connections you make. It is up to you how much or how little you explore, but it is an important skill to acquire – learning how to learn about magic by reading non-magical texts.

Don't forget that the separation between magic and religion is not that old; many ancient texts are stuffed with magic hidden away in the corners. The skill of the magician is to be able to spot those hidden gems and to read around them to see what else can be discovered. This method of reading old texts is also a very useful habit to get into when you work as a visionary magician. Often what you see in vision appears strange and can make no sense. But once you then visit ancient texts that talk around that topic, you find your weird contact, and it is often written in a context that helps you understand it a bit more.

Many young magicians fill their shelves with tons of magical books. But in fact the best magical library is stuffed with ancient and religious texts, myths, and folk legends: that is where a lot of the real magic hides. But often these days people expect everything in bullet points and laid out in obvious paths for them. The real Mysteries are found by working in ritual vision, and then reading ancient texts which then give you a clue as to the next step. This module has been the beginning of that process for you.

6. *Reading tasks:* clips from classical and older religious texts

The Book of Enoch, Chapter 10

> And again the Lord said to Raphael: "Bind Azâzêl hand and foot, and cast him into the darkness: and make an opening in the desert, which is in Dûdâêl, and cast him therein. And place upon him rough and jagged rocks, and cover him with darkness, and let him abide there for ever, and cover his face that he may not see light. And on the day of the great judgement he shall be cast into the fire...
>
> ...And when their sons have slain one another, and they have seen the destruction of their beloved ones, bind them fast for seventy generations in the valleys of the earth, till the day of their judgement and of their consummation, till the judgement that is for ever and ever is consummated. In those days they shall be led off to the Abyss of fire: and to the torment and the prison in which they shall be confined for ever. And whosoever shall be condemned and destroyed will from thenceforth be bound together with them to the end of all generations."

The Book of Jubilees, chapter five

> And it came to pass when the children of men began to multiply on the face of the earth and daughters were born unto them, that the angels of God saw them on a certain year of this jubilee, that they were beautiful to look upon; and they took themselves wives of all whom they chose, and they bare unto them sons and they were giants.
>
> And lawlessness increased on the earth and all flesh corrupted its way, alike men and cattle and beasts and birds and everything that walks on the earth— all of them corrupted their ways and their orders, and they began to devour each other, and lawlessness increased on the earth and every imagination of the thoughts of all men (was) thus evil continually.
>
> And God looked upon the earth, and behold it was corrupt, and all flesh had corrupted its orders, and all that were upon the earth had wrought all manner of evil before His eyes.
>
> And He said that He would destroy man and all flesh upon the face of the earth which He had created. But Noah found grace before the eyes of the Lord.
>
> And against the angels whom He had sent upon the earth, He was exceedingly wroth, and He gave commandment to root them out of all their dominion, and He bade us to bind them in the depths of the earth, and behold they are bound in the midst of them, and are (kept) separate.

And against their sons went forth a command from before His face that they should be smitten with the sword, and be removed from under heaven. And He said "My spirit shall not always abide on man; for they also are flesh and their days shall be one hundred and twenty years."

And He sent His sword into their midst that each should slay his neighbour, and they began to slay each other till they all fell by the sword and were destroyed from the earth. And their fathers were witnesses (of their destruction), and after this they were bound in the depths of the earth for ever, until the day of the great condemnation, when judgement is executed on all those who have corrupted their ways and their works before the Lord.

Epistle of Jude

These people are blemishes at your love feasts, eating with you without the slightest qualm—shepherds who feed only themselves. They are clouds without rain, blown along by the wind; autumn trees, without fruit and uprooted—twice dead. They are wild waves of the sea, foaming up their shame; wandering stars, for whom blackest darkness has been reserved forever.

2 Peter 2:4

For God did not forgive the angels that sinned, but cast them down into the deepest Abyss (Gr. Tartarus) and delivered them into chains of darkness, to be reserved unto judgement.

The Theogony of Hesiod II

And amongst the foremost Cottus and Briareos and Gyes insatiate for war raised fierce fighting: three hundred rocks, one upon another, they launched from their strong hands and overshadowed the Titans with their missiles, and buried them beneath the wide-pathed earth, and bound them in bitter chains when they had conquered them by their strength for all their great spirit, as far beneath the earth to Tartarus. For a brazen anvil falling down from heaven nine nights and days would reach the earth upon the tenth: and again, a brazen anvil falling from earth nine nights and days would reach Tartarus upon the tenth.

Round it runs a fence of bronze, and night spreads in triple line all about it like a neck-circlet, while above grow the roots of the earth and unfruitful sea. There by the counsel of Zeus who drives the clouds the Titan gods are hidden under misty gloom, in a dank place where are the ends of the huge earth.

And they may not go out; for Poseidon fixed gates of bronze upon it, and a wall runs all round it on every side. There Gyes and Cottus and great-souled Obriareus live, trusty warders of Zeus who holds the aegis.

And there, all in their order, are the sources and ends of gloomy earth and misty Tartarus and the unfruitful sea and starry heaven, loathsome and dank, which even the gods abhor. It is a great gulf, and if once a man were within the gates, he would not reach the floor until a whole year had reached its end, but cruel blast upon blast would carry him this way and that. And this marvel is awful even to the deathless gods.

There stands the awful home of murky Night wrapped in dark clouds. In front of it the son of Iapetus stands immovably upholding the wide heaven upon his head and unwearying hands, where Night and Day draw near and greet one another as they pass the great threshold of bronze: and while the one is about to go down into the house, the other comes out at the door.

And the house never holds them both within; but always one is without the house passing over the earth, while the other stays at home and waits until the time for her journeying come; and the one holds all-seeing light for them on earth, but the other holds in her arms Sleep the brother of Death, even evil Night, wrapped in a vaporous cloud.

And there the children of dark Night have their dwellings, Sleep and Death, awful gods. The glowing Sun never looks upon them with his beams, neither as he goes up into heaven, nor as he comes down from heaven. And the former of them roams peacefully over the earth and the sea's broad back and is kindly to men; but the other has a heart of iron, and his spirit within him is pitiless as bronze: whomsoever of men he has once seized he holds fast: and he is hateful even to the deathless gods.

There, in front, stand the echoing halls of the god of the lower-world, strong Hades, and of awful Persephone. A fearful hound guards the house in front, pitiless, and he has a cruel trick. On those who go in he fawns with his tail and both his ears, but suffers them not to go out back again, but keeps watch and devours whomsoever he catches going out of the gates of strong Hades and awful Persephone.

And there dwells the goddess loathed by the deathless gods, terrible Styx, eldest daughter of back-flowing Ocean. She lives apart from the gods in her glorious house vaulted over with great rocks and propped up to heaven all round with silver pillars. Rarely does the daughter of Thaumas, swift-footed Iris, come to her with a message over the sea's wide back.

"Sigh... they are all such happy souls..."

— Josephine

7. Module Summary

This has been a tough, though interesting module for apprentices, as it has been less about ritual and magical learning, and more about visionary and textual exploration. Setting down this foundation before you move on to work with ritual tools is important, and it will help you to understand the deeper powers at work as you begin to learn about ritual tools, what they are, and how to work with them.

Now you are at this stage in your training, you have worked with a variety of different magical skills, and I am sure you find some easier than others. Some will struggle with meditation, some will struggle with tarot, and others will struggle with visionary work. What is crucial is that you do not give less attention to one skill and more to another: learn them all equally, practise them, and do not give up or let one slip to one side if you find it difficult. Magic is not easy, and all the skills in this course are necessities.

Keep up with your regular meditations, keep working with your tarot deck, and keep your working space and yourself clean and tuned. Keep up with your journals and computer notes.

The idea I suggested in an early lesson that you have a journal for each module (use thin exercise books) is so that you can go back to that journal later on in the course, and add notes around the subject matter. Your learning will expand, your understanding will deepen, and as you revisit a topic, the new layer of learning can be compared to your old notes, and then added on. At the end of your training, these journals will be like unique textbooks that you can then use in so many different ways as an adept.

Apprentice

Module V

The Magical Tools

Lesson 1

Introduction and Preparation

Note 1: Lesson 2 will involve going out in nature for a few hours (during daylight, preferably early morning). You will need to be by a river, lake or stream of water, and where you can briefly bury the tools near the water. A public park is probably not a great idea, find a wilder place if you can. So start planning now by looking for somewhere and making time in your schedule to do it. You will also need a small engraving tool to mark a sigil on your sword. Small electric ones can be bought very cheaply online. If it is not possible to find a place that is near water where you can also bury the tool, I will give alternative directions in the lesson.

Note 2: Remember the work you did with the stone in Module II, Lesson 5? (Finding a stone, working on it, and then putting it back.) In Lesson 3 of this module you will need to go back there and find a bigger stone to work with for your shield; so plan ahead.

The tools of the magician are deeply embedded within the psyche of modern magic, and their roots go back into history as far as we can reach. But over time what were at first tools became necessities instead of assistants, and with the rise of the mindset developed by the *Scuole Grandi* in Venice, and later the Freemasons, these tools also became symbols of office and power. Today in magic they are often used as accessories, and one only has to look at the dazzling array of fancy, flashy, and often gaudy tools to see how far magic has devolved.

In this course you will learn about the tools in depth and how to work practically with them, but as assistants, not necessities: it is time to put magic back on its proper foundation and steer it away from the mishmash that has developed in our age. I am sure that this will prove unpopular in many quarters, but it will lead the apprentice away from 'fashion magic' and 'control magic' and towards the Greater Mysteries, so that you can learn the full depth of magic in all its glory. So let us look at the magical tools in general, what they are, how they work, what they do, and what the magician does with them.

1. The Tools as Vessels

The classic Western magician's tools are the sword, wand, cup, and shield. In some modern magical schools they have devolved down to 'representing something' or being a prop or accessory in ritual. Nothing could be further from the truth. This locking-in of the four classical tools has also narrowed down the modern magician's idea of what tools are: there are far more tools than these classic ones and those other tools are often either misunderstood or completely ignored.

Later in the module we will look at these other tools, and later on in the apprentice section you will also learn about the elements as tools. But first let us look at the classic tools that are pivotal in the ritual and visionary work of the magician.

The classic tools are essentially *vessels* and *bridges*. They can be permanent containers or they can be temporary containers depending on what you are working on and why. They can also bridge contact, power, and patterns from the inner worlds into the ritual space. You have already begun the process of awareness of the tools as vessels by nature of the inner beings connected to the sword and the cup/scales that you have slowly become aware of.

The outer shell of the tool, its shape, its nature, (blade, cup, etc.) defines what sort of power and consciousness will flow into that tool and what it will do, how it will work, and why. A true magical tool is a clear outer shell into which the magician pours or bridges power and consciousness: the tool becomes enlivened and becomes a being in its own right. Just as our bodies house our spirits, so too the tools house a spirit or being that will operate alongside the magician as an assistant. They also become deeply connected, over time, to the fate pattern of the magician, and slowly become extensions of the magician's wider pattern of energy and fate.

You will also find, as a magician, that the tools have deeply interconnected relationships with each other, creating patterns of balance within the forces that you work with. As the magician progresses in their work, they come to realise that the tools are not just active when they are being used in a ritual or vision: they become assistants who are constantly working in the background and bring change just by their very presence.

2. Tools and the Magician's Will

This is one of the many stumbling blocks on the road of magic: the tool has come to be seen as something that bends to the will of the magician, that it does what the magician wants and demands. Why is that such a mistake? This forcing of the will of the magician upon everything is one of the things that has brought magic down to its knees. It is a misunderstanding of an ancient method, and also a misunderstanding of what is meant by *will* in magic. Hopefully by the time you have worked with a few more modules and had direct experience, you will understand that mistake, and also how long that mistake has been embedded within magical systems. Learning by personal experience and observation is the finest method of learning such things in magic.

By now you will have begun, through your studies, to see that the powers of the universe are far beyond the understanding of a human. Fate, power, energy, and the forces of nature are not trifles to be dabbled with in an effort to control; rather they are forces that we as magicians consciously join in with, like members of a large, powerful orchestra. We become players, not the conductor.

That enables us to partake, as magicians, in a conscious interaction with vast powers: we learn to navigate the 'turbulent river' to get where we need to be, rather than being swept away by it. And we certainly do not stand in the midst of the 'river' and demand that it stops – such an action will sweep away the magician. And this wish for total control, for bending tools to do our will, not only puts us at odds with the vast forces, but it also locks us out of the deeper powers that are potentially available for us to work with.

History is littered with the tales of grand magicians, their tools bent to their will, spirits forced to behave a certain way: it is all very impressive but it always ends in tears. It took me many years of working as a magician to realise these mistakes, and slowly but surely I dropped my old methods of working with the tools and opened myself up to relearning, listening, and watching. I learned a very different way of working with the tools, a way that is far more profound, powerful, effective, and full of co-workership, not control. Because of what I learned, and what came out of that learning, I now approach working with the tools in a very different way, a far more effective way, and that is the way you will learn in this course.

3. THE SWORD

The sword or blade is a sharp vessel, a vessel of metal that is essentially a guardian. It is also a limiter, something you have already been introduced to. Like all the magical Mysteries there is an outer, popular idea about the sword and a deeper, hidden wisdom. The deeper wisdom of the sword has many layers to it.

The sword *mediates the power of the word,* the utterance of power, and that is the sword at its most powerful. It becomes a bridge, a mediator of the pure power of utterance between the inner worlds and the magician. No amount of vocal ritual posturing and the waving around of a sword can outdo the sheer power of a mediated, simple utterance breathed down the blade of a true magical sword. This connection between the breath, the utterance, and the sword goes far back in our history, and the utterance with the sword is inextricably linked with the magical Threshing Floor (the harvest of the soul).

Here is a striking example of this ancient mystery surfacing in early Christianity:

> *"And out of his mouth proceedeth a sharp two edged sword;*
> *that with it he may strike the nations.*
> *And he shall rule them with a rod of iron;*
> *and he treadeth the winepress of the fierceness*
> *of the wrath of God the Almighty."*
>
> — Revelations 19:15

The dynamic that you have been working with (of the Sword in the east, the Utterer, the Limiter, connected to the Grindstone) and its opposing power, (the Vessel that holds the Harvest, holds the being of the Scales and is the vessel of the Threshing Floor) is clearly defined in that one clip of text: the uttering of the Word (the Sword and the Word are the same thing), the rod of iron (the Grindstone power) and the treading of the winepress (triggering the Scales of Judgement/the Threshing Floor so that humanity reaps what it has sown).

Immediately you begin to see the ancient roots of that dynamic, and the further back you go in ancient texts the more you will see it now that you know what you are looking at.

The sword also *guards*. It guards the magician who works in balance, but it does not guard against the results of a magician's unbalanced acts, nor does it guard against lesser things that the magician should deal with themselves. It guards against powerful unnecessary destruction, against powerful overwhelming attacks, and it also guides the magician, warning them against imminent danger. It is also the companion of the utterance: if you work with the magical power of the utterance, having the sword nearby will ensure that it guides you and guards you as you work.

It also *oversees the balance of the magician:* remember the sword of Damocles? The sword becomes an all-pervading presence in your life, and the deeper the magical powers you work with, the more the sword becomes an ever-present limiter in your life: this is to ensure that you tread a clear path through the Mysteries if you heed its warnings.

If you do not heed its warnings, the power of the limiter will kick in and put pressure on you until you get yourself back on track. In this respect the sword works in conjunction with the Grindstone: the power of Saturn that ensures you tread a disciplined path of the art.

4. THE CUP OR VESSEL

Traditionally in magic the tool of the west/water is the cup/grail, and it is used as a communion cup, a balance to the fire of the wand, and a receiver of the dagger. In many magical systems it is connected to the idea of compassion, feminine qualities, redemption, and the angel Gabriel (the connection being via water/Mary/the annunciation). Once more, like the sword, the surface presentations used in modern magic dance around the deeper mysteries, but often the true depth of power of the vessel is missed as it becomes a ceremonial cup, and is also used as a symbolic representation of feminine qualities. Once more, this tool is far more than that.

The vessel (it can be a variety of things) has three actions: *containing, recording,* and *dispensing.* Its most profound act is as a recorder of deeds, hence the connection to the Scales in the west. As a container, the water within the vessel receives and then holds a magical pattern which is then dispensed out into the world either by pouring the contents out in nature, or by consuming the transformed liquid.[1]

---

[1] Transubstantiation.

It is the pinnacle tool in magic, in that the vessel comes into play once the magical pattern has been formed in the east, and is rooted in the north: first the vessel collects and holds that magical pattern, then it dispenses it into the future, the present, or the past. The role of the feminine power, which in truth is the power to contain and then dispense power/life, is so often reduced down to watery, passive, feminine, gentle qualities, and it is this misstep in magic which has in turn reduced the understanding of the sheer power and central role of the vessel.

As apprentices you will learn to work with both the vessel and the Scales: separating the two powers out not only helps you to develop a deeper working knowledge of the two vessels, but it also sets up a working pattern whereby one vessel (the Scales) is working quietly in the background recording the actions of the magician, while the other tool is worked with in ritual and vision.

Another way that you will learn to work with the vessel is via an obscure technique whereby a pattern is magically worked with to become a container or vessel for magic: the pattern is created, the magic is infused into the pattern which in turn then contains/holds the magic so it can be worked with.

5. THE SHIELD

Like the other tools the shield is not a simple, straightforward representation, nor it is simply a badge or shield; rather it is a complex weave of magic that serves a multitude of purposes. Some magical systems reach 'up' for power to draw into a shield, and will work with the hexagram, along with entreating angels and divine names to protect them. Others work with the pentagram drawn out on the floor, or on paper; and some work with a breastplate in a cruciform shape. What a lot of magical schools have in common in their use of the shield is that it is only used for protection and is always drawing on power from 'above.'

The shield at its most profound is the rock deep within the earth that you stood upon in vision before the lion goddess in the Underworld. It is also the rock of the earth beneath you that through your left foot mediates the power of the Grindstone, and through your right foot mediates the power of the Threshing Floor. It is the stone altar, the bones of the ancestors beneath your feet, and the substance that you as a human are made from: the pentagram is the sum total of your human vessel.

The shield *protects* you not by way of divine and angelic names, but by nature of the strong stone foundation you stand upon, the clarity and strength of your conscious engagement with your fate and with your body, and the positioning of all of that in the centre of the directions, with all the powers around you. The shield is the floor that you stand upon, it is the stone that blocks destructive power barrelling towards you, it is your anchor, and it is the cloak of the magical pattern of your own existence that you wrap around yourself.

And the shield is also far more than protection, which is probably its least profound action. The shield is also the *tap root* into your ancestral knowledge and the knowledge that lies within the land. It is the focal point for all of the knowledge and magic that has gone before you, and most of all, it is the focal point for the Garden (the true balance of nature).

The shield is like a tiny, low octave of the world of creation: as a magician you stand upon or before the shield, with your actions in your left hand and your results/ Harvest in your right hand, facing the future. That might not make much sense to you at this stage, but once you are ritually placed within that pattern, then it will make sense. Like the vessel, the shield has two presentations: the *cloth* that holds your central *pattern* of existence and fate, and the *stone* that is your *anchor*.

The stone works closely with the vessel, and the cloth becomes the scabbard of the sword: the cloth is an extension of you, and in essence, you become the scabbard for the sword. I will go into this in more detail in the coming lessons, but it is a part of the mystery that the magician and the tools are essentially one hive being: they become a part of you.

6. No wand?

This is where we get into controversy, and where Quareia departs completely from the dogma that has become entrenched in magic. Students of Quareia will not work with wands. Why? There is no need to, and one of the things that Quareia is about is that you work with what is necessary, so that your magical foundation is a strong rock with no Achilles heel.

The traditional belief is the wand is the pinnacle of fire power, of kingship, control, and intent: it is the 'pointer' of the will and command of the magician. Yawn.

As is always the case, if you use a magical tool simply as a tool, it is powerless in truth. If you work with the tools collaboratively, as beings, then you are into a whole different ball game. The wand/fire/south in its most natural and powerful form is the future: it is the direction of formation. That is a direction and power whereby a magician can make some very dangerous mistakes, and it is the directional power that is most likely to blow a magician up – or at least facilitate a good wallow in stupidity/arrogance.

The wand directs power into the future: the magician works magically with an intent to change something, forms the power of that change, and aims that power of change into a situation/person, using the wand, to bring about a result. However, the knowledge and understanding of the flow of time, power, and the patterns of fate is severely limited in a human. So the magic is aimed and dispensed without knowing all the parameters: the magician essentially shoots blindfolded and hopes to hit the target without doing any collateral damage. Working that way ensures that the magic is only as effective as the magician is competent.

However, working with the other tools to limit, guard, and balance; to contain, form, and dispense; and working with the inner contacts to target and exteriorise the magical power creates a magical form that is ready for action. The wand is not used to form or direct the power as the magic is already 'programmed': the combination of the three tools, the fate pattern of the magician, the power raised, and the team of inner contacts all come together to create a formed action. The beings and contacts the magician works with ensure that all the parameters are covered, the magician does the formation, and then it is released into the future/south to do its job. (Notice it is *released,* and not *sent,* there is a big difference).

The magician actively weaves the power of the elements of air, water, and earth; and the inner beings, contacts, and deities add in the element of fire, not the magician. The magic then flows out through the south into the future and forms its own path as directed by the inner contacts. There is no need for a wand as an Apprentice. Using a wand is equivalent to manually navigating a supersonic missile: it is much more efficient to use the on-board targeting system that can think and act far faster than you can.

Also, fire as a magical element is the most unstable of the four. We are constantly surrounded by air, earth, and water, but fire needs a power component and a fuel to manifest.[2] For that reason, and many others, fire is a magical element that needs treating with a great deal of caution and respect. In nearly all the stories of magnificent disaster, and the destruction of magicians or magical priests, it is the fire temple, fire power, wand/control/fire magic that was usually the thing that went badly wrong.

There will be many times during your training as a magician that you will work with fire, but to do so successfully and safely it is important first as an apprentice to root yourself in the three stable elements. By that time, you will fully understand the issues of fire/the wand in magic, and you will have gained that understanding through direct experience. Stable, powerful magic is a combination of *power in, power anchored,* and *power formed:* it is then sent out into the world under its own steam to go do its job. It does not need pointing and commanding; it already knows what it is doing.

Waving a wand around commanding power is where the magician oversteps the mark and ceases to be a fellow player and becomes a control freak, which is one of the hallmarks of magicians who focus on fire power. The future is not ours to lock down, and absolute control belongs with the Divine, not with the human. We can work with the future, but we cannot block it. This is not something I have just made up: this is an ancient pattern, and once again we are reaching back to the roots of magic. (Remember Moses using his staff/wand to hit the rock? We discussed it in Module II, Lesson 7).

The magician *works* with east, west, north, and below and their magical powers and patterns; above is *acknowledged* and *invited*; and the south is the open gate through

---

[2] Lightning, a volcano, etc.

which the magic flows into the future. Once the magic is formed and released, it is up to the powers of fate to decide how it will fully unfold in the future. If the magician also tries to form, command, and control the power of the south/fire it immediately triggers a massive imbalance just by the sheer nature of our own limitations.

However, the staff, which is the ancient root and source of the wand concept, *is* a powerful tool, and is one that Quareia Magicians learn to work with later on in training. It is not waived about, rather it is a really powerful vessel for serpent power, companion workers of the magician.

7. Tools that come to you

In this course you are working initially with tools that you have made or purchased. This is so that you can directly learn the techniques that apply to these tools, and it will trigger the deeper learning process for you around these magical implements.

However, in their most powerful state, the tools come to you in various unusual ways. This may have already happened to you, or it may happen to you decades from now. The *true* magical tools find you when the time is exactly right, and not before.

So you may find yourself working with a variety of sets of tools over the decades: the ones we buy and work with usually have a limited working life (although that is not always the case), whereas the ones that find you are often (not always) for life.

And then there is the more obscure and less-known aspect of the magical tools, which is where the inner tool leaves its outer shell and migrates into a new shell, for example the power of a sword leaves the physical sword and transfers into a new sword. The outer sword is new and different, but the power residing in that sword is the same one that the magician has always worked with. That is something that you will learn how to work with in the later sections of the course.

Often the tools come to you in ways that you do not recognise, and sometimes they have been with you for years before you realise what they actually are. It was like that for me with most of my tools. My sword came to me when I was very young, and for years I had no idea what it was. But it worked quietly in the background, guarding me from very dangerous situations, and slowly nudging me towards magic.

My shield also came to me as a gift, and once again I had no idea that it was a magical tool (it was not a defined magical shield; it was a natural substance). It was a few years before I realised what it was doing and how it was working with me.

The same, too, with regards to the vessels, two of them: one a bowl, and one a set of scales. All these tools came into my possession before I was ready to work with them, and they patiently waited, working in the background, until I was ready to 'see' them and understand the power that flowed through them.

I also came across a wand in the weirdest of circumstances, which was also the start of my lesson about how wands should not be used. Within a short time of gaining the wand, I was told very clearly in vision to return it to nature. I had to walk out into the woods and 'plant' the staff back in nature. I was reluctant to do this, as it was indeed a powerful fire staff, but once I had caved in and released its power back into nature, and thus handed over my sense of control as a magician, then I really started to learn about the sheer magical power that flows when you drop those reins and let that aspect of magic do its own thing.

As an adept you will learn how to spot these tools that come to you, and you will also learn how to transfer, if necessary, the power of one tool into another.

The whole dynamic around the tools, how they come to you, how you trigger the deeper aspects of the tools, and how you migrate from working with tools you have forged to tools that come to you, are all fluid, mutable forces of fate that you learn as a magician to bend and flow with. This in turn teaches you about how the forces of magic and of nature are not a straight, dogmatic path that can be marched by a magician, tool in hand, but are in fact a series of convolving rivers that you swim in.

8. Odd tools

There are other tools, not often mentioned in magic, that can become a bedrock of your magical family of tools. Again these tend to find their way to you, or you pick them up unknowingly in a yard sale, or out in nature, or often in seemingly-random circumstances, only to slowly discover that here is something that is working away powerfully in your work space. They are often not 'magical' in the sense that they are not covered in known magical regalia, nor do they even look magical in any way. But they slowly unfold themselves to you for the powers that they are.

These objects need no consecration or ritual work to wake them up or fill them: they come to you as objects already filled with a consciousness that is willing to work with you. As an apprentice it may be difficult for you to spot them when they come into your life, but as you progress in magic you will slowly start to 'hear' them as they work around you and attempt to communicate with you.

A common one that turns up for people is *eyes*. The eye is a powerful magical tool for obvious reasons in a magical space: they watch, warn, and frighten intruders. If you go out and buy an eye for this purpose (very popular in the Near and Middle East) it will be less likely to work dependant upon how you came across it. They find you, not the other way around. Here is an example.

There was a period of my life when I was in a lot of danger (I won't go into details) both physically and magically. I was also quite sick and weak at the time, so my defences were stretched to their limit. My sword was very active, as were the other magical tools around the house, along with the spirits and deities. I was driving out one day when I was told very clearly by an inner contact to pull over, climb a fence and go into a field, as there was something there that I needed to 'keep an eye on me.' I dug around in the field and found a small piece of facing stone with an eye painted on it in Roman style: it was most likely from a Roman ruin under the field.

I took the eye home and put it on my shelf, and it most certainly did keep an eye on me: I started to find more and more eyes, always ancient, until it became a bit of an in-joke among my friends. I would go to ancient ruins abroad, and find... an eye. Now the eyes are all over the house, unseen, undramatic, but ticking away in the background and warning me if something untoward is coming my way.

These unseen, unrecognised tools come to you when needed, and just get on with their job. You can work with them magically and ritually to form a more engaged relationship with them, or you can just let them get on with their work. The key is to recognise them in the first place, and that ability comes with knowing your magic and knowing your tools. By the end of this module, I hope that you will be well on your way to such knowledge.

Other such unusual but powerful tools that can come your way are shapes that hold various ritual patterns and which reflect that pattern into the space where you live and work (that is how a Christian crucifix works, for example). In a non-magical home they do little, but when brought into a magically-tuned building they spring to life and get on with their job.

9. Practical Work

In this lesson, I have outlined for you the outer details of these tools. Before you actually start to bring the tools to life, you need some inner details, too. This is very simply done. In your work-space, light the directions and open the gates. Go into the Inner Library, find the inner adept that you have been working with and ask them to place within you whatever you need to know about the magical tools.

The adept will place within you whatever you need in terms of deeper learning, either in the form of a book or in the form of a bundle. Let that sink into you, and it will slowly surface over time as you work with the tools, and it will guide your hand.

Your next lesson is the one where you will bring the sword and vessel to life. To prepare them you will need to be out in nature, by water and earth. As soon as you set the place and time to go out with them, the inner process will begin and the beings connected to the sword and vessel may become more active, so in the intervening time, don't be surprised if they start turning up in your meditations and/or dreams. Just let them get on with their job. Note down any strange dreams or anything else you notice happening: you can look back on these notes later to understand the process that was set in motion.

Also, be aware that in some countries (like the UK, for example), wandering around with a sword can get you arrested. Wrap it well in a blanket and tie it up like a bundle, so that if you are stopped and searched it will be obvious that you could not access it quickly as a weapon. If you are in a car, stick it in the trunk and try to plan to do the outdoor work in as remote an area as possible. Also plan, if possible, to do it very early in the morning, so that there is less chance of someone stumbling across you.

Lesson 2

The Sword and the Vessel

This lesson teaches you how to bring your sword and vessel to life. It moves away from the dogmatic representational rituals that call upon the elements and named beings to work and enliven the tools, and takes the magic back to its roots.

For those of you who have already had ritual magical training it could be a bit of shift in thinking, but this method takes the control out of the magician's hands and puts the job back where it belongs: working directly with the land, the spirits, and the deities inherent within a land area.

This also means that the magician has to get out of the way of the magic and surrender control: you do your job, they do theirs, and together you make a powerful working magical tool. Because of this surrender of control, more power is allowed to flow into the tools, and with this comes the necessity to be respectful of the beings that you will work with.

This method links the tools into the land and the beings and powers that flow through it, and connects you directly to the deity powers that flow through the land. There is no grand posturing, there are no great speeches: outwardly it all looks a bit boring, but under the surface the power rises to meet the tools and fills them with consciousness.

From there, the tools do their job and you do yours. However if you misuse the tools you will most certainly know about it. The powers that flow into them are what you need in order to make your next steps into magic, but instead of just having a power tool in your hand, you hold a living being that will work in harmony with you if you work in balance. If you go off the rails and misuse the tools, they will either abandon you or they will fight you.

Because you are working with other beings and are allowing them to join in the alchemical process of bringing the tools to life, there has to be a two-way exchange. You need to take gifts for the land spirits and deity that you are going to be working with. The land itself prefers simple gifts, like honey, a song, picking up litter, a gift of fruit: things that nourish.

The water, however, is a different ballgame. This is not a spirit you will work with, but a deity. Bodies of fresh water such as rivers, springs, and lakes all have inherent goddesses that flow within them, and if you wish them to work with you then they must have a suitable gift. You do not need to know the name of the goddess; names are created by us for us to use, deities do not 'name' themselves. The only time a name is useful is when it is well known and has been used for centuries, and even then it is not necessary. All you need to know is that wherever there is a natural flow of fresh water there is a goddess – and they are not sweet, gentle, flowing females with silken robes and loving smiles. The female power that flows through water is powerful and can heal or destroy. She is the power that tempers a sword, a power that records the contents of a vessel, a power that can hold blessings or curses, a power that can send men mad and strengthen a woman for battle: in short, she is not a power to be messed with.

The Celts knew this, as did the Romans and the Greeks. Rivers were treated with the greatest of respect and were given the finest gifts. We see aspects of this today in Britain, where we still have sacred springs and wells that are respected, loved, and cared for by the local villagers. We also see remnants of this in the tradition of throwing coins into wells and fountains for good luck.

The gift that you take to the river for your magical work must be a special gift indeed. The river goddesses like jewels, jewellery, or precious metal things that are precious to you. It is not the worth of the precious metal that is the issue; it is what it is worth to you that is important. You have to be willing to give something of great worth to you in order to receive something of great value. That way there is no debt on your part, *something that is very important with these goddesses*. So do not shirk at this.

I have lost count of the gifts I have given rivers: diamond rings, twenty-four carat gold rings of exquisite design, gold and diamond necklaces, rubies, garnets: over the years all the jewellery I had of value has gone into the rivers. Some of them were heirlooms; some were valuable antique pieces. But that is of no matter – letting go was important, as was giving the river goddess her due. And what I received in return has far outweighed the value of any bauble.

So find something of great value to you that is precious metal, i.e. gold, silver, platinum; something that would be hard to let go of. If you have nothing like that then you must buy something. This must cost enough that you have to forgo decent food, treats, and entertainment for a couple of weeks or a month, depending on how often your pay check comes to you. Its cost must bite into your daily life so that for the period your pay packet normally lasts you and after you have paid your bills, fed your children, etc., you cannot afford your usual recreations, nice or good quality food or drinks, meals out, movies – whatever you usually do to make life pleasant or at least liveable.

It does not matter if that means you have to spend $10, $50 or $500 on this gift, only that it is a cost that is great to you personally. And if you try to dodge around that one and get a cheap bauble so that you can continue to live as you usually do, it will insult and enrage the river goddess – which is not a good idea. Remember the connection to the vessel/west/water and the Scales/Harvest? This gift is connected to your Harvest: you give the best as a gift of your Harvest. It is because of this dynamic that when the Romans invaded Britain, they had already negotiated who would get which river, as they knew the rivers were full of gold and silver.

As well as your gift for the river you will need some honey, and also either fruit, good quality bread, or nuts: look to what is harvested in that area, and if you can, take some of that harvest back. If it is a wheat growing area, take bread. If it is a fruit growing area, take the fruit, and chop it up so that creatures can eat it. If it is not an agricultural area, take honey, organic wine, bread, a bit of salt, berries or grapes chopped up, and some olive oil. If it is on American land, also take organic tobacco. And take a pin to prick your finger with, or an auto lancet such as diabetics use.

Read through the ritual so that you know what is involved, and what other things you will need. Be aware that towards the end of the work your tools will be left on altars with candles burning. For safety reasons, use tea lights or small but fat candles placed in small bowls of water for safety. But the safest is a tea light in a holder with a protective mat under it. When power begins to rise in a ritual, sometimes the candles can flare, fall over or spit. So always be aware of fire potential.

If there is absolutely no way you can get to a place where there is a river, spring or lake, and a place to bury your sword briefly, at the end of the following ritual you will find an alternative, but do be aware it is a poor second choice compared to the ancient ritual.

1. *Task:* Empowering the sword and vessel

Get your sword, your vessel/cup, and your gifts. Go to the area that you have chosen that is out in nature and by water. This can be a spring, river, stream, or lake – just ensure that it is fresh water, not seawater, and that there is earth nearby with which you can cover over your tools for a brief time. Take a book with you, turn off your phone, and give yourself time to spend a few hours doing this job. Take a strong hand spade or gardening tool so that you can dig into the earth.

When you get near the water unwrap your sword and get your vessel out. If there is a lot of ground to choose from, wander around and talk to the earth, trees, and rocks. Tell them you are looking for the best place for your sword, and see where that takes you. If you do not have much choice, go with what is there; and again, quietly use your voice to tell the earth that you are going to put your sword and vessel into it for a short while.

Once you have identified where you can work, and before you start digging, pour honey on the ground, scatter the fruit/food around the area, pour oil upon the earth, and find a small stone a little way away from where you are about to dig and put a tiny bit of salt on it. Do not put a lot of salt down as it can poison both the land and creatures. A pinch is all that is needed.

If you are also working with tobacco, take a pinch and face east, thank the sun for rising and the wind for all that it brings, and release some tobacco to the wind/air. Then turn south and thank the future for all that it brings and release some tobacco to the air; turn west and thank the rain and water for gracing the world and all that it brings; turn north and thank the powers of the land for everything that they do; release some tobacco to all four directions. And once you dig the earth for the sword, add some tobacco onto the earth before you put the sword in.

Dig into the earth so that you can lay the sword on the earth or in a shallow trench. Before you cover over the sword, place your right hand over the sword and recite:

"You came from the earth,
I return you to the earth,
and from the earth you will be reborn."

Cover over the sword with the earth. Now do the same with the vessel/cup.

This is where you wait. It is preferable to leave the tools in the earth for a few days, but that is not always practical or safe in the modern world. If it is a place where you can leave them, cover over the graves of the tools with brush and leaves so that they will not be found by anyone else. When you should return depends on the land, and it can be twenty-four hours or a few days: you will know/feel when they are 'cooked', as you will feel a strong pull to go get them.

If this is not practical, don't panic. This is a first step of learning with the tools, and you will most likely repeat this in many different ways over your lifetime of being a magician. If you have to stay and guard them while they sleep and clean, take a book and read, lie down and snooze, or just watch nature.

In our fast modern world, being silent and still can be very hard as our brains have become wired for constant fast input. As a magician it is important to be able to slow down, observe, keep vigil, listen, and experience the more subtle powers around you. Watch the birds, watch the insects, watch the trees move with the wind; learn to slow your mind down and quieten it as you wait. It is a form of meditation and can be a form used as your regular meditation if the beginner method doesn't work well for you.

Reading stories or poetry to the land always goes down well with local land spirits, as does singing. If you are alone, use your voice to learn how to communicate with the land. It is not so much what you say or sing that is important as the frequency, melody, thoughts, and emotions that flow with the words: these alert the powers of nature to you. A beautiful poem, prayer, or song uttered to the wind, the trees, and the birds will have far more effect than any magical incantation. If you do this, just make sure that whatever you say or sing is neutral: there must not be any appeal or asking, nor any mention of God or deities: just stories or songs that evoke a love of the land, of nature, of the elements... you get the idea.

This might all sound very romantic, but it is not. It is the pure dynamic of utterance, emotion, and intent from a human voice that awakens and alerts the powers around you. This is how the ancient priests/magicians worked, and the use of magical incantation with its entreating, flattery, control, and threats is a sad degeneration of this power. Remember the connection with the sword and utterance? By doing this action of talking or singing, you are also passively awakening with the sword within the land and creating a bond between you, the land and the sword.

It may take a few hours until the tools are ready. If you are not sure whether they are, place your hand on the earth where they are buried or covered over, be still, and see how you feel. If any resistance to digging them up comes into your mind, back off and wait a bit longer. However, there are also modern practicalities. If it gets to a time when you *have* to dig them up, tell the earth that you have to dig the tools up soon, that you have little choice, and then wait a few more minutes for the message to get through. Don't use this as an excuse if you are bored. Get over it. If you can wait, then wait.

Once it is time to dig the tools up, get them out of the ground. Then prick your finger and drop blood into the land before replacing the earth. If you have a fear of blood or needles, well, this is a time as a magician you need to be able to override such fear. There are many times as a magician you will need to override fear and face it, so get used to it. We have all gone through this and faced our fears in small and big ways. If you cannot override fear in order to do your work, that creates a weakness that is visible, that hostile beings will see in you and will use it as leverage against you.

Now it is time to work with the river/water. Take the tools to the water and lay them down. Take out your gift for the river and think about what it is worth to you.

When you are ready, hold the gift out of the water and say:

> "Goddess of the waters,
> I give you this gift which is precious to me.
> It is the best that I can give you.
> Thank you for flowing across the land,
> thank you for all that you bring to all living beings,
> and thank you for your power that is in our world."

Bow to the river to honour her, and drop your gift into the water.

Now take the sword. Bathe it in the water. If it is a spring that you cannot fully immerse the sword in, put the sword into the spring and wash it all over. Make sure that every part of the sword is washed, and that it remains standing or lying in the water for a short period of time. As you wash the sword, be aware of the guardian of the sword standing nearby.

Take the sword out of the water and hold it up to the air in front of you, not pointing it up but pointing it away from you. Hold it by the handle in your left hand, with your right hand under the blade to support it.

You are going to breathe down the blade. Be aware of your inner flame, be still, and feel your feet and legs stretch down through the land and into the Underworld. Keep your mind silent and still. Take a deep breath, and slowly breathe out, aiming your breath down the blade of the sword. As you breathe let nothing pop into your head. Have no thoughts other than your breath. Say no words or sounds: it must just be a clear air. Now place the sword on the ground and pick up the vessel.

Take the vessel to the water, wash it in the river, then fill it with water. Prick a finger and drop a drop of blood into the water-filled vessel.

Once more still yourself and take a deep breath. Close your eyes, keep a still mind, and breathe out over the surface of the vessel and the water contained in it. Hold it up, and then pour the contents into the river. This is your first harvest of the vessel: the gift of the water goddess held within the water, and the gift of your blood.

Now get your sword and the vessel and wrap them up. Bow to the river, bow to the land, say thank you, pick up your tools, and leave. Go straight home. Do not divert or go visit anyone: go straight home and put the tools in their directions. As soon as possible, light the directions, open the gates, have the central altar and flame burning, place the sword on the east altar with the blade pointing to the central altar, and place the vessel on the west altar. Now leave the room with everything working.

Leave the room to itself for an hour or so. This is a very old way of magical working; you do your part, and then you leave the space for the beings and spirits to fully do their job without human interference or presence.

While you wait, get your engraving tool ready. If the vessel you are working can be engraved, you will do the vessel as well as the sword. If it cannot, you will need some acrylic paint or something similar and fine brushes to mark your vessel.

When you are ready, return to the room. While the directions are still open, engrave the sigil, the one that has been waiting that you wrote down, on the sword and then engrave or paint the sigil on the vessel. If you have never used an electric engraving tool before, hold it lightly, don't hold it tight like a pen as it will jump around more. It does not need to be a work of art, it just needs to be recognisable to you. And do not add anything extra.

Once you are finished, close everything down in the proper way. Put the sword back in its resting place in the east and the vessel in the west near your scales. If it is not possible to have the tools out, put them in a cupboard in the east direction of your space, or place it behind something. You will also notice, as you close things down, that the guardians of the sword and vessel are no longer around.

Alternative method

If there is absolutely no way you can work with the earth at the side of a natural water feature like a river, stream, spring, or lake, then the following is an alternative, but it very much is a poor second choice in terms of power and contact. But that would be better than nothing. Read through the original main ritual a few times so that the small details get into your mind. And try to maintain as much of the original ritual as possible.

You would need to first find a place where you can lay the sword on the earth and cover it over and stay with the sword, or where you can cover and leave it for a few days safely. If you have a garden, that would work, so long as the garden is not on top of concrete or has a membrane under the soil. A membrane is where gardeners place a large material sheet over the land to block down weeds, and then put topsoil over it. The sword needs to be able to be in contact with the land underneath the garden.

For the water part of the ritual, if there is water that you can take the sword to once you have dug it up, then continue with the original ritual. If you find the water but you cannot take the sword there, then you will need to bring the water to the sword.

Go to the water source, take the vessel/gifts, and take one or two large containers with you to fill with the water. Do the work with the vessel, water and blood, and also speak to the river in your mind and tell her what you are trying to do, and that you need her water to cleanse and awaken the sword. Give the gift to her, and fill the two large containers with her water. Bow to her and thank her. Take the containers of water back to the sword and use a large bowl, or even a child's paddling pool, and pour the water into it. Remember the water is connected to the goddess in the river/lake, and that water travels (by air as clouds and rain, or through the earth). Treat the water in exactly the same way as if you were by the water source, and cleanse your sword. When you have finished working with the water and sword, pour the remaining water onto the ground and say thank you to it. Use your voice, and not just your mind, so that the vibration and frequency of sound follows the water.

Notice how throughout this your job is essentially to get out of the way in terms of magic. You provide the physical work only: digging, giving gifts, uttering, putting things in and out of water. There is no ritual, no incantations or invocations, and no visionary aspect other than silence and stillness. This is what is missing from modern magic: letting the elements and land beings, spirits, and deities do their job while you are simply the person who does the physical lifting. This can be a bit of a shock for those people who have already trained in a system that puts control firmly in the hands of the hapless magician.

Learning to let go, to trust, to let power do its thing, and to trust in the alchemical process of nature and power is a tough lesson indeed. We have grown a mentality over the millennia that we are the controllers of magic: we are not. We are the *catalysts*. Often intent and then physical action alone is enough; sometimes we have to do more. The trick is to know what to do and when.

Throughout this course you will be put in situations where sometimes you are the *weaver* of power, and other times the *pointer* that points the way. Other times you will simply be a *catalyst* – and this is one of those times.

Everything you have been doing in your ritual work has been building up to this point: the magic has already been done. All you need to do with the tools now is to seal that magic with the outer actions of the elements. Something that you will slowly come to understand is that sometimes *very simple* is the most powerful, and that is because we have gotten out of the way of ourselves and the process, allowing things to form properly and naturally.

2. Care of the tools

Caring for the tools is very much about respect. Each of those two tools is now a being in its own right, like a newborn baby. It will take time for the sword, the cup, and you to learn the language of mutual work. They will grow as you grow.

Treat them as you would any living being: with respect and with attention to their needs. The scabbard for the sword is something that you will learn about in the next lesson. For now, even if the sword came with a scabbard, keep it out of any scabbard until you have properly prepared one.

Here are a few rules about keeping the balance with these tools. These may be obvious to some of you and not so obvious to others.

1. Make sure they are never picked up or mishandled by anyone.
   Only the magician should touch or handle the sword.
2. Never *ever* physically strike anything or anyone with the sword, for any reason, ever. If you do, it will break the power within it.
3. Never draw blood from any living creature or person with the sword.
   If you cut yourself and bleed accidentally from the blade, that is ok.
4. Never use the magic of the sword to attack a mortal in vision.
5. Never place poison or anything that could be poisonous in the vessel.
6. If for any reason you want to get rid of them, bury them deeply or cast them into deep water.
   An unbalanced and destructive sword should first be cleansed with fire and then buried deeply.

3. *Task:* Research

Just as an aside, and for your own background understanding of how magical swords work in different places around the world, it is worth doing a bit of research into sacred and magical swords. Below is one example with just a few brief details but enough that you should at least partly recognise what is happening. Tales of swords buried in the ground up to the hilt, or embedded in stone can frequently be found around the world, as can swords that protect king/queenship but must never be used in battle.

An example from Britain is the two swords of king Arthur. One is unnamed and was pulled from a stone, but he used it in a duel and it shattered, which also broke the protection it gave him and the kingdom. The second sword, Excalibur, came from the goddess of the lake, and was used in battle.

Such research can be a fascinating journey, and the more you know from your own magical work the more you will spot in different situations around the world.

> *In Kumasi, Ghana, is the Okomfo Anokye sword which is sacred to the Ashanti people. Buried up to its hilt and protected by a circular high wall that surrounds it, the sword is a symbol of the strength of the Ashanti people. It was planted into the ground three hundred years ago by Okomfo Anokye, a high priest and co-founder of the Ashanti kingdom. Legend states that if the sword is removed from the ground, it will end the Ashanti kingdom.*

I find it interesting that when you look at the legend of the Okomfo Anokye sword, and then think about the Welsh legend of Arthur, there are major parallels. After Arthur pulled the sword from the stone and subsequently misused it, the kingdoms of the Britanni fell apart with the invasion of the Saxons, who Arthur fought with Excalibur.

Here is the source link for the sword in Ghana. This link was still working in 2025, but if it no longer works, the information above is enough for you to research it if you wanted to.

https://nyujournalismprojects.org/africadispatch/2012/06/the-sword-that-cant-be-moved/

Lesson 3
The Shield

In magical terms the shield is often mistakenly believed to be a literal wooden shield with a dogmatic set of symbols and sacred words written on it. While such an object looks very glamorous, it is pretty ineffective in terms of being a real shield. Which brings us to the question of what an actual magical shield is.

A magical shield is, in fact, *two* tools that work in two different ways to offer grounding, anchoring, and protection; and they work in tandem together. One plugs you into your web pattern of fate, which anchors you in who you are, where you are, and what you are doing. The other anchors you deep in the roots of your ancestors, the land, and the female Divine power within the land.

Between these two anchors, you become solid in your stance, which makes it far harder to knock you off-balance. Between these two tools you become like a rock that is very hard to shift or penetrate, if you are working in balance with the land around you and with your fate path. This is far more effective than a dogmatic hand made or store-bought magical shield.

Why? Because a dogmatic, ritualised, sigilised/god-named wooden shield is only as effective as the magician who created it and wields it; and such a shield is very easy to get around by an experienced magician. It is also something that offers no protection in the face of powerful, aggressive beings.

Such shields are often inscribed with God names, angelic names, and a single personal mark or motto that identifies the magician. This completely ignores the polarised divinity within stone/earth, makes no real connection to the fate weave of the magician, and has no connection whatsoever to the beings that naturally work through earth substance.

A magician working deep in the inner worlds who works with such a basic, sigilised shield charged for protection will be overwhelmed very quickly by aggressive forces: there is always something or someone more powerful who knows how to get around such limp protection. It is like using a small child's wooden shield to block an incoming missile instead of drawing on the power of a ten ton granite boulder.

However, a magician who works deep in the inner worlds and who, in addition to working with a shield that amplifies and mirrors their full potential, also engages a second shield that is enlivened with the embodiment of the planetary consciousness and the female divinity within the land itself, presents a much tougher target.

The second shield in particular provides a formidable protection, and one that has been used in temples for thousands of years. The female destroying and creating power, the goddess of life and death herself, is at her most powerful when presented as a stone. This was deeply understood and worked with in ancient times:

goddess temples of the ancient world may have had impressive, tall, beautiful goddess statues, but in the depths of the inner sanctum of the temple, it was an enlivened stone that was the true centre of power. Just as the most powerful manifestation of the male (outputting/future) Divinity in magic is perceived as Divine Breath/wind/utterance/Word, the most powerful manifestation of the female (receiving/birthing and destroying) Divinity is a stone.

The various combinations of the utterance, the stone, the sword, and the vessel give us a wealth of magical lore, legend, and technique that, sadly, is too often cast aside in search of more showy, glittery presentations that are mostly weak and ineffectual.

At the end of this lesson you will find a few key words for research to help you explore the roots of this much forgotten aspect of sacred magic. For example, let me quickly tell you about the use of the goddess stone as a shield/protection/anchor and guardian of Rome.

Cybele

During the second Punic War, the Carthaginian War, Rome was in a mess. There was famine, a failed harvest, and a fearful population after the spotting of many meteors falling across Rome. They were on the losing side of the war with the Carthaginians and things were looking pretty bleak. None of the deities in Rome were of any help as they had been subdivided too much, something you will learn about later in the course, so the Sibylline Oracle was consulted.

The answer came back that the saviour of Rome would be the great Cybele of Phrygian Pessinos, the Magna Mater, the Great Mother of the mountain. Cybele was already at that time considered to be an ancient goddess and was known for her immense power, so a request was sent out to her priests.

Cybele arrived with great pomp and ceremony in Rome – and she arrived not as a statue, as is popularly presumed, but as a black stone. The famine was stopped, the war was won, the harvest was great, and everyone was happy.

There are a few different powerful goddesses around the world, all of whom have, at the depths of their temples, a stone/rock which is not representative of her, *it is her*. The statues give us a face with which to communicate and give the goddess power a humanlike interface for us to interact with. But the pure power that flows through her is expressed in a stone that has been awoken to her power.

The empowered stone has no emotions, no human interface. It is not a deity *per se* but a lump of Divine substance in a purely natural sense. This makes it very powerful indeed, particularly for a priest, priestess, or magician who knows how to tune to that power, draw upon it, and care for it. Through working with the stone respectfully, the magician comes under the protection of the great goddess, and no one could wish for a better shield.

Too many people these days think of the mother goddess as benign, gentle, and sweet. Nothing could be further from the truth. She is loving, but also vicious if crossed.

She is the lioness protecting her young, the tide of destruction that cleans the land. She holds life and death in the balance.

Your work with the stone will introduce you, in a small way, to that power. As your training progresses, you will tread deeper and deeper towards understanding and working with this natural force.

This layer of your work with the stone will be about anchoring, connecting, and protecting you so that you can grow safely as a magician. You will work with a gentle frequency of this power which will give you not only an anchor, but which will start a long process of coming to understand this goddess power, the Divine nature of the land, the ancestors, and your place within that pattern as a human being.

Rather than have me rambling on, it is better that you get straight to work and learn about these two tools by enlivening them and working with them. We will start with the stone, as it is the more powerful of the two. Then the stone can watch your back as you work on the cloth.

1. *Task:* The magical stone

Without realising it (or maybe you did) you have slowly been working towards bringing these tools into your life. The rituals, visions and practical work that you have done have been inching you closer and closer to connecting magically with the tools, while preparing your space and life so that you can accommodate them and work with them.

The work with the land around you, the earth beneath you, the ancestors behind you, your feet on first the Grindstone and Threshing Floor, and then your feet in the Underworld, have been slowly preparing your body and your working space for the stone. It has also been alerting the goddess power that flows through the stone to your existence, and your willingness to work with the powers around you.

That in turn triggers a magical pattern that brings fate threads together into a weave in which you will first find, and then work with, the stone that will become your shield. That magical pattern is also externalised into a cloth where the pattern becomes fixed as a solid anchor that creates boundaries around your life and fate path in order to protect it.

It is wise to note at this point that these magical shields will not protect you from your own stupidity; nor will they protect you from minor magical disturbances or attacks that would serve to teach you wisdom and skill. Rather they will protect you from destructive forces and true dangers: they filter out what you cannot cope with, and allow through what you can, so that you can strengthen and learn.

To begin your work with the stone, you must first find it. Do you remember the work you did with a stone in Module II, Lesson 5? You worked on a stone and then put it back: an act of service for the land. The most likely place you will find your Stone of the Mother is back in the area of land that you gave to in service.

Return back to that patch of land, and start looking for your stone. It should be no smaller than your hand, and may be quite a bit bigger than that. If you are deeply inspired to go elsewhere for the stone, follow your instincts. Take with you the cloth that you have been waiting to work with, so that you can wrap the stone in it when you find it, and your cord to tie up the cloth/stone.

Finding the Stone of the Mother

There are a variety of ways to find the right stone, and the methods are all ones that you have slowly been learning. One will work better for you than another, but try them in the sequence in which I list them: augury, inner senses, inner vision, and divination. Augury is the most natural of the techniques, and divination is the most 'formed' one. So you start with the most natural of the skills and work your way down the list until you get a result.

I will outline these different techniques one at a time, so that you can experiment with which one works for you and which one doesn't. You may strike lucky with the first technique, or you may have to try them all in turn. This exercise will also teach you quite a bit about how your natural inner senses work.

Take: your cloth and cord, your tarot deck, a gift of fruit for the land (if in bear country, take tobacco instead), and a pin to prick your finger (I am sure you are getting sore fingers by now!). Go to the area where you are going to look for your stone, and sit down. Close your eyes, and still yourself with a short meditation.

Technique one: Augury

This is an interesting technique. It works better on lands that are not swamped by city sprawl, and can work really strongly in wilder areas. It triggers more strongly in some people than in others, and relies on your ability to 'spot a message.'

To use this method, go out onto the patch of land where you are expecting to find your rock. Turn off or silence your phone, and have no other electronic devices with you. Take some fruit as a gift for the land, cut it up, and spread it out in an area (if you are in bear country, skip this bit: it could invite trouble so use tobacco instead). Sit down, and meditate for a short while to still yourself. Once you are still, sit and watch the land, the birds, and the creatures for a while.

Once you are truly still and have tuned to the land, get up, and start to wander around the directions. Keep your eyes open for birds, particularly raptors, hovering or diving around a spot. Look for wild animals, spiders, strange things; follow pathways, check out trees. Essentially you are wandering around looking for something that will catch your eye or waiting for something unusual to happen, you just don't know what.

Be prepared for this to take a few hours: it is rare for the land to respond to you quickly. It is a slow unfolding and it takes time, but a magician meditating upon the land often triggers a response of some kind. If you do pay attention and you do get a response, it is a very powerful way to find your stone: nature leads you to the spot.

I have this sort of interaction and help from spiders, birds, mammals – it can come in many forms. You can also combine this technique with the next one: inner senses.

Technique two: Inner Senses

The first stage of looking for the stone is 'feeling out the land.' This technique puts into practice the core skill of inner senses that you learned in Apprentice Module I.

Once you are still, with your eyes closed, be aware of the directions around you and direct your focus of attention to the area to the left of you. Let your awareness focus on that area, and take your time with this. Is it even and calm? Are there any 'bright spots' or feelings of shift/change in a spot to the left of you? If not, bring your focus to the land before you and do the same thing.

Using your mind, 'sweep' the area to your left, then in front of you, then to your right, and then behind you. If one area seems to feel very different to the others, or something catches your attention, open your eyes, get up, and walk slowly in that direction. Look carefully for any larger rocks that catch your attention. If one or more does, sit in front of them and place your hands upon the stone. Close your eyes and once again still yourself. Sit with the stone and be aware of how you feel. Does being there and touching the stone cause a slight shift in your emotions? Does the stone make you feel loving? Powerful? Bright? Hostile? Or do you feel nothing?

These feelings (unless you are naturally sighted) will be very faint, and you will feel them through the interface of your own emotions: take note of any subtle shifts in how you feel.

Work outwards in each direction from where you were sitting until you find a good-sized stone that you feel safe with when you sit with it, with your hands on it, and the feeling from the stone is protective, loving, and strong. If that technique does not work for you and you have spent a long enough time trying, then it is time to move on to technique three.

Technique three: Inner Vision

Sit down on the land and close your eyes. Still yourself with a brief meditation, and when you feel ready, while still working in inner vision, stand up and turn to your left. Walk into that direction away from your body, and look across the land using your inner vision. You are looking for something that is either bright and stands out like a spark, or an inner vision of a lion/lioness. If you walk for a little way and find/see nothing, return to your body, turn, and walk directly in front of your body and repeat the same exercise.

Work around the directions, each time walking away from your body for a little while and looking across that patch of land. If you spot something bright, something that stands out, or you get a brief glimpse of a large cat/lioness/cougar/tiger/bobcat (the Great Mother is always flanked and guarded by her felines), take note of this location in relation to your body. Go back to your body, open your eyes, and walk off in that direction. Slowly scan the ground for the stone that was giving off that power.

Either you will be able to identify it by sight, or you can put your hands on each potential stone and see which one feels right. If you are still not sure, sit in that direction and repeat the visionary search until you narrow down which stone it is.

Technique four: Divination

If all the above techniques have failed then it is time to get your deck out. Go back to the spot where you sat and meditated, get your deck out, place your cloth on the ground to use as a surface, and use the FOUR-DIRECTIONAL READING (use five cards, first one is centre, then east, south, west and north). Ask in which direction is the Stone of the Mother that you are to work with. Look for cards that are earth cards (except Five of earth, which shows poor power), or the Empress (the goddess), the High Priestess (female magical power), The World (the planet is a goddess power) or the Star (the bright planetary power).

Once you have found which direction it is in, then you need to find out how far away from you it is (if there is a Magna Mater stone a thousand miles away in that direction, it will show). So do the same reading again and ask, *"is there a Stone of the Mother with two miles of my position in any direction?"* Either the same direction will show (you are near to a strong stone) or a different direction will show with a weaker card (the strong one is further away, but here is a weaker one that will still work). Once you have identified the direction, then you need to go off and find it.

What to do when you find the stone

Once you have found your stone, pick it up and drip a drop of your blood on the spot when the stone lay. Say thank you to the earth and the land, and sit quietly for a little while, just holding the stone so that you can get used to each other. When you are ready to leave, wrap the stone in the white cloth and wrap your cord around it.

Take the stone home straight away. Go to your work space as soon as possible, light the lights in the directions, open the gates, place the sword by the east altar (blade down to the floor, handle up – prop it against the altar), the vessel in the west and place the stone in the north on the altar. Leave the room for an hour or so and let it all work away. You will feel when it has finished. When you are ready, go back in, close the directions down, place the sword back in its resting place, and leave the stone under the altar or in a north place, still wrapped in the cloth and cord.

2. *Task:* The cloth shield

Once the stone is in position, it is time to do the cloth shield. This cloth will have a variety of jobs/uses. It can be used to stand upon (to anchor your work), to wrap around you when working in a powerful vision that could be dangerous, to lay over you when you are sleeping and are ill or possibly in danger, as an altar cloth for the central altar for particular jobs, and when not in active use as the scabbard for the sword (wrap it around the sword).

The finished cloth is your expression of existence; it is your 'stone' element in ritual form. This form becomes the vessel that encloses the sword (the sword in the stone), a vessel that is uniquely connected to you – your ritualised unique pattern becomes the scabbard for the sword. This is the beginning of forging the unique blend of tools and magician to make one hive, conscious, working magical being.

Making the cloth

You will need:

- The cloth
- A black permanent marker pen and a thick gold marker pen
- Frankincense resin and charcoal
- Your pentagram pattern which you have already worked with
- A charcoal/incense burner
- Something to weigh down the edges of the cloth while you mark it

Get out your notes and the book/lesson for Module III Lesson 8 and re read the task: *Viewing the web ritual, part two of the ritual.* Also read any notes you took from that visionary experience. Remembering that vision is important for the work you are about to do.

Before you start the ritual work, light the charcoal and burn the frankincense resin. Get the cloth from the stone and bathe it well in the smoke of the frankincense. Place the cord on the southern altar. Once the cloth is cleansed with the smoke, clear the floor space in your working room and remove the central altar. Lay the cloth down in the centre of the directions and weigh it down at the edges with small heavy things.

Go around the directions, light the lights, and open the gates. Go again around the directions, stopping at each altar briefly and just being there. Do this circumambulation four times, but do not communicate with any of the contacts there: just bow to acknowledge any that do appear. It is important with this work that you do not ask for help of any kind.

Now the space is tuned and it is time to get to work.

Mark the top of the sheet (south) with a golden hexagram and the centre of the sheet with a golden circle (filled in with gold ink). Change to the black marker.

Ensure that you leave a small border of an inch or two (3 to 5 cm) of blank cloth around all sides. Draw a pentagram using three quarters of the size of the sheet, and ensure there is room above, below, and to the sides of the pentagram to draw things and still leave a small blank edge/border of the cloth. Make sure the gold circle is in the centre of the pentagram.

At the bottom between the two legs of the pentagram draw the symbol for earth. At the end of the left branch of the pentagram draw a downward-pointing sword, as though the arm of the pentagram is holding it. Now draw a vessel/bowl/cup in the 'hand' of the right arm of the pentagram.

On the blade of the sword that you have drawn, draw the sigil that is on your sword. On the vessel you have drawn, draw the sigil of the vessel. Now draw, using the golden pen, small stars (look at Egyptian stars painted on their ceilings; use that shape) in the positions that Saturn, Pluto, Jupiter, Mars, Venus, Mercury, Neptune, Uranus appear on your chart/pentagram pattern, and draw the sigil of each planet above the corresponding star.

Note that neither your name nor any personal identification is placed on this shield; the cloth will hold your fate pattern that inner beings will recognise, but no mortal name that a human will recognise – this is for your safety. A shield which has the name or motto upon it of the magician is a shield that can be *breached* during an attack. (A human name is a bit like a GPS system; a fate pattern is not.)

Now place your magical sword over the sword you have drawn, the vessel where you have drawn a vessel, and the Stone of the Mother over the earth symbol, and go sit in the middle of the cloth, facing south.

Sit in silence and meditate for a short while. Be aware of the stone floor in the Underworld temple beneath you. Be aware of the Divine Breath above you, of the sword to your left and the vessel to your right, the path to your future before you and the Stone of the Mother behind you. Be aware of the magical pattern you sit in the midst of. With your eyes closed, slowly remember the 'Viewing the Web of fate' ritual vision, and recover the visionary detail, the sense/feeling and memory of standing in the centre of your own web of fate. Remember what it looked like, and remember what that vision felt like.

Build the memory until the vision switches back on and you can sense or see the pattern around you, the bright spots of power on your web, the beings that were working on your web and the Sandalphon/Noble One who crossed over the threshold to work with you. Build that vision until it is strong.

You are bathing the cloth in that unique fate power, bathing the cloth in the inner web of your fate. Take your time with this and imagine that web pattern merging with the cloth and the sigils on the cloth.

When you have finished, meditate in stillness for a short while. In that stillness, feel the cloth and the powers around you. Just be with them. When you feel a shift, like a 'locking in' feeling, or a 'normalisation' feeling open your eyes and stand up.

Turn east, bow to the powers of the east, and say thank you. Repeat this action to the south, west and north. Then hold up your arms to the powers above you and say thank you. Lower your arms so that you are holding your hands to the floor and say thank you to the goddess power beneath you.

Quietly leave the room, always stepping clockwise. If the door out of the room is to the left, walk a circle around the directions until you get to east: *always* circle the room clockwise when you come and go in ritual. Let the cloth bathe in the power of the room for a while.

When you feel it is ready, go back into the room, and starting in the east, take the sword and put it on the altar. Do the same with the vessel, and place the stone back under the north altar (or in its resting place in the north). Leave your cord on the south altar. Fold up the cloth, and wrap it around the sword: it will be the scabbard for the sword when you are not working. Close the directions down and put things away (vessel where it lives and the sword where it lives).

Now get your paper pentagram pattern, take it outside, and burn it until nothing of it is left. That was holding a temporary pattern for you: it allowed the inner pattern to build for your shield.

Notice how there is very little ritual and very little directing of power by the magician. When it comes to the power tools, their power flows from inner sources which are freely given to you: there is no need for posturing, demanding, entreating, ritual drama, or grand gestures. It is a subtle but powerful intentional action that brings the power to you, and you to the power.

Ritual when used in magic (as opposed to religious expression, which is different) has to be at the precise balance according to what you are doing. If the magic is not ritualised enough, it does not fully express and externalise in order to do its job. If it is ritualised too much, it blocks the flow of power and the magician gets in the way of the completion of the magic.

Each magical act is different, and while some magic needs a strong solid ritual element to externalise the power, other magical acts need a bare minimum of ritual in order to flow unheeded by the limitations of the magician. So it becomes a delicate balancing act.

The basic rule of thumb is: if the power is being formed and expressed by inner beings, then minimum ritual is needed. The ritual element should only give the magic a simple vehicle or vessel in order to express itself: the magician and his or her actions simply bridge or awaken power, nothing more. If the power and magic is being brought into form by the magician, then more ritual action is needed to give the power boundaries and focus. This is not a hard and fast rule, but is a general overview of the dynamic.

The formation of magical tools is a process that relies heavily on inner beings/spirits/ deities, and therefore needs the magician to get out of the way in order for these powers to do their job. The process, as you will now see, is a slow, subtle march for the magician towards the tools (you started the formation of your tools in Module II) and all that is needed in terms of action by the magician is the providing of vessels for the power to flow into.

3. About the cloth shield

The cloth shield is a very old method of magical working, and is something that is approached in stages. When you very first worked with the pentagram, you were taking the first steps towards this tool. You will notice that once the protective shield was transferred to the sheet, your name or anything directly identifying you was not used. What appears is the planetary alignments, the tools, and the hexagram/pentagram mix (Divinity and Humanity).

The shield becomes matched up to the other tools both through the use of sigil and through the power of resonance: placing the actual tool on its representation in the correct position and on its individual sigil allows a subtle transfer of connection and power between the actual tools and the cloth. Identifying you directly on your paper pentagram connected you into the pattern, not the pattern into you. Now that the shield is fully expressed on cloth that will be used as a tool, you are already now connected to the shield, and having any personal identification upon that shield will only weaken your protection, not strengthen it.

As you progress in magic, you may find that you add to the cloth over time, as different sigils connected to different powers or beings will be made visible to you. The signs that go on the shield are connections to powers that will, through the patterns and combinations, help to protect you.

If you are working with the shield and another magician or a being attempts to hack into your sphere, your work, or your space, two things will happen:

The first is that the hacker will be confronted with a pattern that looks human (the pentagram) but which is surrounded by a variety of different powers and is therefore confusing: the human seems to have no identity and has boundaries that merge with other powers: the hacker sees the shield and not you.

The second thing that will happen is the different powers will switch on when the pattern is approached by an outside influence, and will therefore direct attention to the shield and away from you. The intruder will find themselves surrounded by planetary weaves, land powers, Underworld powers, and the beings that reside in the sword and vessel. That will put off all but the most hardened and highly skilled intruders. The sword will then spring into action.

The shield can also act as *chaff*: when you are working with the shield it becomes very hard for another magician working in vision, or an inner being, to tell which one is you and which one is the shield: when you work with the shield, you merge slightly with it and the boundaries between you and the cloth become blurred.

Don't think, however, that your shield is a bullet proof vest or that it will save you from stupid magical acts, for it will not: the shield is not a *carte blanche* for stupidity. It is a protection, a foundation, and also a guide for an apprentice magician. It will serve you all the way into adepthood, but along the way you will learn to add more strings to your bow in terms of protection and foundation.

And this brings me to the biggest lie in magic: that there is one object, one ritual, or one banishing that will protect you against all things. That is total crap, usually written by armchair magicians who have never been confronted by a real, head-on, powerful magical attack or an aggressive power/being in full flight.

You will learn over time all the different ways of dealing with such situations, where a variety of tools, skills, and knowledge are brought together for effective defensive magic. But none of that defensive magic is recipe book style magic: you cannot look up a ritual or spell or buy a tool that will help you in such a situation.

It is a combination of well-established tools, skills, knowledge, and connections with inner contacts and land beings that saves you in a dangerous situation. The skills you are learning in this module are the foundations that such skills, along with many others, grow from.

4. THE CLOTH AND THE SWORD

While the cloth works mainly as a shield, it is also a scabbard, a vessel, and companion for the sword. The cloth shield holds and contains the power of the sword until it is brought out and released to work.

The cloth and the magician are strongly connected, and the use of the cloth as a scabbard also directly connects you to the sword at a deep level. Slowly over time as you work with the sword and the cloth, you will tune into the sword and the sword will tune to you: you become a working team. The sword protects, guides, and limits you; the cloth contains power and gives you a safe, strong foundation to stand upon.

Once you get to work with these tools you will slowly start to realise how they are all interconnected with each other and with you: they become an extension of you, and you become an extension of them.

5. *TASK:* RESEARCHING THE STONE AND FEMALE DIVINITY

This task is purely to expand your magical understanding and knowledge of the roots and powers of the stone as a magical tool, and also as the mystical focus of female Divinity. The female Divine is a vessel: it is substance, the planet, the body, the rock.

There is no need to take notes in this task unless you want to: it is about following your interest, learning to read between the lines, to spot the magical use and aspect of a sacred object, and to see the connections between these objects around the world. When I suggest research for your own knowledge, take the time to actually do it.

Don't fall into the trap of only doing 'specified tasks', as you will miss so much that you need to learn. This is your path, build it as firmly as you can. Dig in research as much as you can. Look at ancient goddesses and sacred rocks; below is a list to get you started.

Below is also a list of names and terms that you can use for research into the use of a stone as a central focus of the Goddess or the Divine in ancient times. Remember in the midst of that, magic and religion at that time were not separate things: they were heavily woven in together. There was a deep understanding (probably a lot better than we have today) about how power and consciousness can express through substance, and how, as an example of that, a sacred stone was a good direct mediator of the mother goddess power.

Things to research

- Al-Uzzá worshipped with a cubic stone, a pre-Islamic main goddess.
- Palaepaphos/Kouklia stone worshipped out in nature (not in a temple) as goddess of all nature.
- Earliest temple of Artemis of Ephesus was centred on a stone said to have been brought from the stars by Jupiter.
- The stone of Astarte at Sidon.
- The holy stone of the temple of Emesa.
- The Goddess Kali. In the village of Bagnan, Howrah district in West Bengal, India, the goddess Kali is worshiped as a black stone.
- The Huwasi stones of the Hittites.
- The Emesa temple (Syria) to the sun god Elagabalus had a sacred stone (a Baetyl) in the inner sanctum, which also appeared on Roman coins around the 3rd century AD.
- The Baetyl of Aphrodite

There are two stones connected with the mythology of the British Isles that tie sacred stones to the divine kingship: *Lia Fáil* and *The Stone of Destiny* (Scone), they are not the same stone. Also, with the Stone of Scone, if you are interested, look up myths connecting the stone to the isle of Skye. Early descriptions of the stone are that it was a black stone with strange shapes on it with a dip shape that a person could sit in. When Scotland was invaded by Edward I what was placed before him when he demanded the stone (threatening to level Scotland in an effort to find it) was a lump of weathered sandstone from the local quarry.

Lesson 4

Working with the Sword and Cup

The best way to learn about the power of the sword and the cup, and how they work together, is to do practical work with the two tools. Throughout the course you will learn different ways that these tools work alone and together, and how to apply them in different magical situations.

The first, most important step in regards to these tools is to learn how they interact and can affect the constant flow of power in and out of our world. It is pointless learning how to apply the tools in a specific situation or for a specific ritual intent until you know how they operate and engage directly with the ebbs and flows of power that are constantly washing into the world around you, and how that power directly affects you.

Essentially you must learn the skills of working at ground zero, and also how to work with them in an act of cause and effect (which is what magic is) without you having any control over a situation. The reason being that this tide of power/energy that constantly flows though our world also flows through everything in magic: you learn to experience that flow and how to interact with it before you let your conscious mind take a role in the act.

This is a major step in magic: learning how to get your conscious mind out of the way so that you can slowly develop the sense of a power shift without trying to manipulate it for your own agenda. A lot of magical training puts the magician in the driving seat, so to speak, from the early stages. Rituals to make you better or happier, rituals to get you a partner, etc.: all of these magical acts, when done without wisdom and skill, only serve to muddy the waters of your path.

The reason this happens is the average person has little understanding of the long-term patterns of life and fate, so tinkering with such patterns ends up with the magician tied in knots. The magician's conscious mind is always seeking to control, to manipulate, without forethought or understanding; which in turn slowly shuts you down as a magician.

The skill to be acquired is to learn how to step sideways from that low-level, everyday thought/survival mechanism, and engage with the deeper powers directly. That takes us out of survival mode, i.e. wanting resources, sex, companionship, hoarding resources, protecting resources, etc. and puts us into learning and interaction mode.

That survival mechanism is the one that trips up most magicians, and it is the first thing they grab for in magic. The magician uses control and manipulation to operate within the survival mechanism, and they get stuck in a loop. If you think about what many people use magic for, it often stems from that basic survival mechanism that is deeply imprinted within us.

And yet when the magician that steps out of that loop, and as a side effect of doing so, the magician gets the resources they need anyway. The difference is that the magician who is skilled knows what resources they actually *need*, what it is that is driving them, and has the ability to step out of that instinct and into something deeper. In turn what they need flows to them in their outer life as and when it is needed.

When you work with the magical tools, you must always be aware of the survival mechanism that operates within you and potentially drives your actions. Everyone has it, no one ever loses it, but a skilled magician turns it from being an unconscious driving force into a warning/self-checking mechanism.

The work you will do with the tools in this module will move you down the road of acquiring that skill: you learn first to get out of the way of your everyday mind while working with the tools, and from there the tools will teach you how to work with the resource instinct in a conscious and deliberate way – *you* become the driver, not your wants and perceived needs.

And before we get to the practical work, that is also something to think about: the wants and perceived needs of the body. An ordinary person is driven by their body, by their emotions, by the instincts deeply embedded within them, by their brain chemistry, by the bacteria and viruses that make up a major part of their body, and by their learned behaviour.

As the Quareia editor (Michael Sheppard) was reading this section, he offered an anecdote to outline this dynamic:

"In a recent conversation an old friend of mine, who is now a medical doctor, confirmed as reasonable my suspicion that getting glandular fever mellowed me out rather a lot. He took me through the various effects that viruses and bacteria can have on the brain, and how these effects can persist long after the illness itself is gone. Intriguing stuff."

A magician is consciously aware of the difference between what their body is driving them to, what their conscious mind is driving them to, and the voice of the deeper, eternal consciousness of the soul/spirit. Essentially a magician is one who also hears their eternal voice within, and gives that voice equal status and attention along with the drives of their body and their conscious mind.

This is very important when working with the tools: *you* must be operating the tools, not your hormones, your needs, or your everyday mind. That skill does not drop from the sky suddenly, but comes from practice and learning right at the early stages of the magician's training. Working with the tools is one arena where that learning can truly begin, as you will see throughout this module. Where this takes you eventually is a place of intelligently managed resources and skills.

When you are a kid or a teen, the world is simple: if you had tons of money and a fast car, the world is seen as being an open playground; and if you then did a few martial arts lessons, you would be untouchable. The reality of managing resources, of only using skills when necessary, and the long road to acquiring those skills, is something that is little understood at that age.

As you get older, you learn the reality of having to work hard to gain money, that credit is not free money but has to be repaid, and that a few martial arts belts are not going to be of any use to you at 3am in a dark alley confronted by a group of dudes with guns. Or that simply shooting people who piss you off is not socially acceptable. We all go through that painful growing up in one form or another, but somehow it can get missed when a person steps into the magical training.

In magic, we learn that level of maturity by first learning to get out of the way, learning the true power of a skill or tool, so that by the time you have learned those skills fully you have also learned when to engage them and when not to.

The greatest skill an adept learns is when *not* to use magic. But when the adept *does* use magic, it is powerful, focused, and highly effective. So let's get to work and put the two main tools into action.

1. About the practical work

You are going to revisit the ritual patterns you learned in Module II, and you are going to take them to the next level, working with the tools and also with a more developed form of the ritual actions.

After that, you are going to begin the first stage of *working* rather than *practising*: you are going to learn how to actively work with the tools while at the same time learning how to get out of the way of yourself, and why this can be so necessary.

To start with, the revisiting of the second module rituals teaches you how a ritual progresses and steps up its power. You will see how the outer expression of the ritual becomes more contained and limited in order for the inner power to flow better. You will also see how two of the rituals are brought together: you are learning how to link two 'words' together to make a simple sentence.

And this is an important step: in today's world of recipe-style rituals it is easily forgotten that rituals are like poetry. It is not the use of recipes, as is so often believed, but the *linking together* of simple ritual patterns which begins to form a more complex structure that power can flow through. The individual words (rituals) are combined to make a poem (magic).

Throughout your training you will link and interweave more and more ritual elements to create patterns of power. As an adept, you will revisit the very simplistic early rituals of the apprentice, but with the power of the adept behind them. This will expose to you a whole new layer of working with power.

In your regular practice, ensure that you continue to revisit the early rituals occasionally so that they stay second nature to you. And as you build with more complexity, the very simple patterns will slowly reveal to you hidden depths. Don't leave them behind and think you only need to do the more powerful patterns: treat the early rituals as foundational exercises that continue to stabilise your technique.

2. *Task:* Ritual: The Anchor

You will need your sword, vessel, and stone. Have the cord on the south altar. Lay out your work-space with the ritual cloth on the floor (even if you are planning in the future to use it around your shoulders) and the central altar on top of it (ensure that the cloth is positioned so that the central flame is directly over the centre of the cloth). Place the sword on the east altar, the vessel on the west altar, and the stone on the north altar.

Go around the directions starting in the east. Light the flame, stand in silence, see the gates open, acknowledge any contact standing on the threshold, bow, and continue around the directions to finish with the central altar.

Stand facing south with the central altar before you: be aware of the powers above you, your feet in the Underworld, the stone and ancestors behind you, and the two tools on either side of you.

With your right hand, pointing with the first two fingers, starting with your arm outstretched high above you, recite:

"In the name of the Great Father..."

Bring your point down to the right hand corner:

"...and in the name of the Great Mother..."

Trace your point to the left hand corner:

"...and in the name of the Great Spirit."

Trace your point back to complete the triangle.

Immediately use your point to draw a circle from the apex of the triangle and finish the circle at the upper left hand corner, in order to begin the second triangle, the inverted triangle.
Recite:

"In the name of the Great Mother..."

Trace your point across to the high right corner:

"...and in the name of the Great Father..."

Trace your finger down to the low centre of the triangle:

"...and in the name of the Great Spirit."

Trace your point back to the high left corner to complete the triangle.

Walk around the directions, going from the east, and all around until you come back to the east. Stand before the east altar, hold out your arms to the sides, and recite:

> "I call upon the powers of the east to witness the Sword,
> that it may limit and guide me."

Pick up the sword and place it on the east side of the central altar. Step back and bow.

Turn and go to the west altar and hold your arms out to the sides and recite:

> "I call upon the powers of the west to witness the Vessel,
> that it may contain and carry my magic out into the world."

Pick up the cup and place it on the west side of the central altar. Step back and bow.

Turn and go to the north altar. Stand before the north altar, hold down your arms with hands pointing to the floor and recite:

> "I call upon the powers of the north to witness the Stone, the Mother of all;
> may she guide me and root me in her power."

Pick up the stone and place it on the floor in front of the north side of the central altar. It needs to be positioned so that it will be directly between your feet as you stand before the altar. Step back and bow.

Walk a full circle around the central altar and return to standing in front of the central altar facing south. Make sure you are standing with the stone directly between your feet.

Place your left foot on the stone. Using your left hand, trace the upright triangle of the hexagram in the air before you. Recite as you do the action:

> "The Divine Breath that brings life to form flows from the east;
> the Father gives."

Drop your left arm and place your left hand upon the sword. Recite:

> "The Sword that limits and guides me,
> the Grindstone that works me:
> my spirit is ready and willing."

Take your hand from the sword and your foot from the stone. Take a step back, bow, and step forward again.

Place your right foot on the stone. With your right hand, trace the second part of the hexagram, the downward-facing triangle. As you do the action, recite:

> "The Divine Vessel in the west that contains the Breath:
> the Mother receives.
> The wind that blows from the east finds the Vessel of the west."

Drop your arm by your side and place your right hand upon the vessel. Recite:

> "The Vessel that contains and releases my magical actions,
> the Threshing Floor that weighs my harvest:
> my spirit is ready and willing."

Close your eyes. See in your mind's eye the hexagram hanging before you, a centre of stillness, of nothingness, a void from which everything flows. Feel that stillness also within you: clear your mind and be silent.

Then recite:

> "I am born of the Void,
> the Breath that breathes life out of the nothing,
> the Breath that contains everything.
> I step into life with the Divine Breath flowing through me."

Open your eyes. Stand with your feet apart in the pentagram stance.

Note: As you do the recitation for this next step, you will notice it is getting simpler: learn to fix a key feeling or sense of the powers in each direction. So for example as you say 'sword' have a feeling of the real power of the sword, what it is, and what it does. It is important to learn to get beyond words and work more with senses.

Pick up the sword in your left hand and hold your left arm out to the side, sword point facing down. Pick up the vessel in your right hand and hold your arm out to the side: make the pentagram stance with the two tools in your hand.

Recite:

> "Above me, before me and all around me is Divine Power,
> the Father that gives Breath to creation.
> To the east is the power of the Sword.
> Below me is Divine Substance, the Mother that is all creation.
> To the west is the power of the Vessel.
> Before me is the south, the future.
> Behind me is the past, and the angel who guards me.
> Within me is stillness."

Stand for a moment in silence. Feel the powers of the tools around you.

Be aware of the flow down from above, and from below up to you; the weight of the sword in your left hand, the sword that will limit you and push you to work properly and in balance; and the vessel in your right hand that will contain your magic in the future, and whose action of the Scales will weigh your actions.

Be aware of the future before you, the future that you forge through your actions, and not through manipulation. Now place the sword on the east side of the central altar, and the vessel on the west side of the central altar.

Pick up the stone and sit down. Sit in silence, with your eyes closed and the stone in your hands. Be aware that all of your life is supported by the power of the Mother who is beneath you.

Be aware of the very air that you breathe which is always the Divine Breath from the Father.

The Father gives you *life*, and the Mother gives your life *form*.

Sit in stillness. Be aware of the Void, the stillness and nothingness from which all flows, and then sense yourself moving forward into the Void. In the Void, sense yourself spreading beyond the boundary of your human form. Sense yourself in the sword, sense yourself in the vessel, in the stone in your hands, in the room, the walls, the flames, in the air: you are in everything. Sit within that for a while.

When you are ready, open your eyes and stand up, still holding the stone. Bow to the central altar: you are bowing to life itself. Turn around and place the stone on the north altar, then place the sword on the east altar, and the vessel on the west altar.

Starting in the north, go to the altar, see the gates open and bow. Repeat east, south and west. Leaving the lights going, stand at the door to the room, bow to the temple space and leave the room.

Go outside, regardless of whether it is day or night. Find a safe spot near your home (a garden, for example) and just stand outside for a moment. Look at the sky, the power above you, be aware of the ground beneath you, and the air around you. Take in a deep breath and give thanks for your life, and for everything that is around you. Touch the ground in respect for the Mother and then go back indoors.

Starting in the east, say thank you, see the gates close, and put out the candle. Repeat in the other directions, and finish in the centre. Remove the central altar, and roll up the cloth and wrap the sword in it. Put the stone, cord, and vessel away.

3. About the ritual of the Anchor

This is a progression from the ritual forms you learned in Module II. You will notice that the actions of the hexagram and pentagram are brought together: Divinity and Humanity as polarised units. You will also notice it is simplified: you need less recitation, and the recitation that is used is more to the point and has progressed in its understanding. The more you begin to understand the complexity and layers of the powers, the less you need to recite them.

The tools also add another layer of power, and now that you are beginning to understand their different layers there is less and less need to declare or recite. The power switches and increases from simple recitation to a sense of knowing and understanding. Whereas the beginner needs to declare the different aspects and powers of a tool, as the magician starts to gain skills: it is more about a deeper knowing, understanding, and sensing of the power. That is the stage where the power can begin to flow properly. Eventually you will get to a stage where you can pick up an unfamiliar tool blindfolded and sense its power. This sort of deep knowing obviates the need for any declaring, recitation, or ritualisation.

Using the cloth on the floor, regardless of your longer-term plans for its use, infuses the cloth with the power of the ritual. The cloth serves three purposes: a shield, a platform, and a scabbard. You will learn to interchange those actions so that you are proficient in all. Then you will gravitate towards using it in one or more specific ways that suit you as an individual. For now, having it spread out beneath the central altar fills it with the energetic resonance of magic, which in turn brings it more and more to life.

The ritual of The Anchor is just as it says: it works as a *tuning* and *anchoring* ritual that roots you in the ritual patterns and tools. As a progression of earlier, simpler rituals, this will for now become your ritual of use when you need to tune the space, tune yourself, or anchor yourself. You have progressed from earlier tuning rituals, and as you develop, so the rituals develop in power and focus.

4. *Task:* Doing a job

Now it is time for you to learn how to put the tools to work. You can do this straight after your first Anchor ritual, or you can give yourself time and space to prepare to do a job. Before you actually do the ritual visionary work, redo the Anchor to tune yourself and your space for work. The meditation at the end of The Anchor can be as short or as long as you need in order to prepare for work.

In your planning for doing this next task, ensure that you have time afterwards to rest if you need it. Everyone reacts a little differently to magical work. If you feel like you are on a high after the work, do not expend that energy by rushing around: the crash will come. Make sure you have time afterwards to refocus, to sleep if you need to, or to go out for a walk. Don't go straight back into family life or work for a couple of hours after this work.

Don't be surprised if you feel tired the following day, either. This is work, not practice, and there is a big difference. Work makes you tired, as your energies and spirit work hard. But you will regenerate quickly enough. It will be good for you to feel the difference between practice, learning, and actual work: that difference can be big indeed for some. For others it is barely noticeable.

5. The ritual vision of Unknown Service

Prepare the room as per the Anchor ritual. Have a bottle of water on the west altar.

Do the Anchor ritual first and leave the sword and vessel on the central altar, and the stone in position at your feet at the end of the ritual. Leave all the candles burning.

Now pour the water into the vessel until it is two-thirds full (don't fill it all the way) and put the bottle out of the working area. Put a chair on the north side of the central altar for you to sit in as you work, and the stone where your feet will be.

Sit down in the chair and still yourself. Meditate for a few minutes. Pick up the sword and hold it in your left hand, point resting on the floor, then pick up the vessel in your right hand. Hold them in a way that is comfortable for you, as you will be holding them for a while (maybe rest the vessel on your right knee as you hold it). Place your feet upon the stone. Close your eyes.

Be aware of the hexagram above you, the stone beneath your feet, the sword to your left, and the vessel to your right. Using your inner vision, 'see' the hexagram descend to you and flow within and around you so that you are sitting in the hexagram. Be still. Be aware that the hexagram is filled with the Void, the nothing from which all comes. Sit in that nothing, and be aware that you expand beyond your skin: your spirit is like air, and can transcend any boundary.

In that stillness and expansion, utter physically and mentally, the words:

"I wish to serve."

Still your mind once more.

While you sit in stillness, be aware of a faint call for help: someone somewhere is crying out in their minds, or even using their voice, for help. You will not hear it with your ears; you will hear it in your mind. They may be calling on God to help, or just generally calling out in panic or despair.

You are a servant; you will serve. In your mind, focus on the call until it gets louder. In vision, see yourself standing up, holding the tools, and stepping forward, walking through the central altar. Be aware of the central flame on the altar as you step through it: your own inner flame strengthens as you pass through it.

As you step through the other side of the altar you find yourself stepping into a space or room or area. You may not be able to see much, but you will be aware of a person standing in total despair or distress. Do not focus on the person, but focus on the energies around them. Go and stand behind the person. Hold out the tools in a pentagram pattern and as you do so, you will become more aware of different energies flowing around the person. One will be turbulent, possibly aggressive. Hold out the sword, its point down, and you will feel the sword spring to life. The energy within the sword expands. Focus your attention on the sword and ask it to limit whatever energy around this person needs limiting.

See the energy of the sword expand and block the turbulent energy in the space, see it dampen down the turbulent energy and dissipate it: the sword guards the person you are helping. Now turn your attention to the vessel. As you focus on the vessel you see that within the person is a fire energy that does not belong there. It is consuming the person and making them ill. Hold the vessel up to the right shoulder of the person. Using your physical voice and your inner vision, say:

"Power of fire, I command you to enter the Vessel."

See the fire energy flow out of the person's shoulder and into the vessel. Hold that action until all that is left is a simple flame burning in the centre of their body: their inner flame of life. Now step back. Look at the person before you. Now that the turbulent energy around them and the fire energy within them have been dealt with, you will see the person's inner spirit begin to expand in their body: what had been driven into a corner of the body by the invading fire can now stretch back out again and fill them will life force. You have given them a fighting chance. Stand and hold the space for them until they move forward and walk away.

Once they have left the space, turn around and step forward with the intention of stepping into the Void, into nothing. Once you step forward, see yourself in nothing, in peace and stillness: there is nothing to see, nothing to hear, no time, no movement. Stand in the nothing, and be aware of the sword powering down, and be aware of the vessel filled with fire held within the water. In vision, pour the energetic contents of the vessel into the Void, where it vanishes.

Now be still. Be aware of Divine Breath all around you; be aware of the stone beneath your feet – your anchor to the Mother. Feel the Divine Breath flow down into you, replenishing you, feel the Mother beneath you holding you and strengthening you. When you are ready, step forward and find yourself passing through the central altar to your body. Sit down, and when you are ready, open your eyes.

Place the sword on the altar and then immediately get up, take the vessel outside, and pour the water on the ground. Return back to your work room. Put the vessel on the west altar, prop the sword against the east altar and the stone on the north altar.

Starting in the east, go around the directions, thank the powers of that direction, thank the tool in that direction, see the gates closing, put the candle out, and bow. Do all the directions in turn and finish with the central altar.

Pick up the cloth and wrap it around the sword and put the tools away. Wash the vessel with water, a handful of salt, and some unperfumed soap (highly chemically scented soap can interfere with magical processes).

Now go get a bath and pour some salt into the bath; or if you take showers, have a dish filled with salt and as you shower, rub some salt on your forehead, the soles of your feet and wash your hands with the salt and soap. It does not need to be consecrated salt; this is just a general after work clean-up.

Now go rest or do something non-magical.

6. Summary of the job

So what happened there and what did you do? This is the first step of working in service as a magician. Notice that you did not see what the situation was of the person you helped, whether they were a good or bad person, and you didn't battle anything: these are all aspects that the normal human consciousness would want to engage with, and it is precisely those aspects which would cause a magician to make a mistake.

Service, magical service, is about doing what is necessary when it is necessary, and not allowing your cultural conditioning to get in the way. It is not for us to judge, it is not for us to fight battles on behalf of others, and it is not within our limited capability to be able to get a true, clear overview of a situation. There are too many inner and outer variables, and a great potential for misjudgement of a situation.

So the magician makes a clear intention to wish to serve, and that step connects you up to someone who truly needs help. You will never know what time, place or situation you are working in, only that it is necessary.

When a person's spirit calls out for help, (notice it is the spirit, not the human mind/consciousness) that call comes from the depths of a person when they are in true need. There are times when we think we need help and in fact we do not. But when the spirit of a person is truly in unbalanced danger, then the spirit calls out for help, and that call is always answered.

Working unconditionally, and essentially working blind allows you to join the pool of beings who are willing to serve, which can be human, angelic, land beings, whatever; and whoever is best placed to the do the job at that time is directed to the spirit in need. The job you did was for a human in danger. It did not need angelic intervention; a human with tools was all that was needed, and you were matched up with that person in need, wherever and whenever they were. The call goes through the worlds, and someone answers. This time it was you.

So let's look at how the tools got to work.

The sword guards and limits. A person was surrounded by a cascade of power coming at them that was too much for their spirit to cope with. In such circumstances, it is often power coming from magic, or from being in a magical or temple space: it is not a 'natural' flow of power. Sometimes people get badly attacked, sometimes they wander inadvertently into a working temple space and get hit by something, or they stumble into a place that has a terrible tornado of destructive energy, usually as a result of a mass murder that is still imprinted on the space. The variables and situations are endless.

The sword limits the flow of energy around the person, guards them in that instance, and then powers down the energy until it is manageable. The vessel takes power that does not belong in a person, neutralises it, and the power is then composted in the Void and upon the land. The stone ticks away in the background ensuring that your feet are truly upon the power of the Mother so that you are safe as you work, and are properly anchored and rooted in the Underworld.

As soon as the job is done, the person walks away. It is important in such work not to try and connect with the person, not to try and follow them or find out what is happening to them. That need to know is part of a control mechanism that can be very limiting for you as a magician: you need to learn to let go of that need and just do a job, get out, and not be thanked or admired for it. You become a single cog in a very large and complex bit of clockwork.

Occasionally you do get to see a little more, but again, you simply deal with the job in hand and nothing else. I was meditating in the Void one morning, and quite unexpectedly I heard a call for help, a desperate cry. I immediately followed the cry and found myself stepping into an English fish and chip shop. It was clearly in the past and not in my time.

There was a woman behind the counter, middle-aged, tired, overweight, and she was busy serving people. But her heart was in dire distress and she was filled with a deep sorrow that was beyond her ability to cope with. She had cried out in her mind, praying to God for help. That call was passed on through the Void for someone to answer, and it was my turn.

This was not a situation for tools, that much was obvious. So I stood behind her and placed my left hand upon her heart and my right hand upon her shoulder (notice how in some instances you do not work with tools, but the hands become extensions of the tools). Energetically she was 'bleeding out' from profound grief. It was damaging her physical heart: she was truly dying of a broken heart.

My left hand stemmed the flow of emotional and vital force energy from her (limiting), and I found myself cupping her heart in my hand (guarding). I talked to her heart (the organs have their own spirits that you can talk to). I told the heart spirit that it needed to be strong for her.

With my right hand on her shoulder, I used my hand as a bridge for all the terrible pain to flow from her, through my hand, and out onto the floor. Then I simply stood behind her, both hands on her shoulders, and was aware of Divine Breath above, the Mother below, the ancestors behind, and the future ahead. Her colour started to change and stabilise (often the energies will present as colours). Her heartbeat grew stronger and she began to look less burdened. I waited in this position until I felt I could do no more, and as I took my hands off, she took a deep breath (always a good sign) and I could see her central flame burning peacefully in her centre. So my job was done, and I returned back into the Void.

I have no idea what caused her crisis, but looking at the way she was dressed, at a guess I would say a wartime bereavement that was too much to bear, but that is only a guess. Sometimes the service is to do with magic, and sometimes it is not. It really doesn't matter. All that matters is that the job is done, the connection is then broken, and everyone moves on.

This is unglamorous work: there is no result that you get to see, there can be no grandstanding as you really have no clue what it is you are doing, and the person you are helping is not aware of you. But it is necessary work, and something you will do on and off throughout your magical training and later in your magical work.

If you hear a call when you are meditating, then you have the skills to deal with a situation and you have been matched up with the person who needs help. Just ensure that it is actually a call, and not a parasite playing with you – keeping your emotions and *ego* in check is one of the ways of avoiding such. But you will make mistakes, and you will learn from them.

Do not go looking for work; you only work with what is presented to you. And be careful of the pull to become evangelistic about it: you cannot save the world and it is not your job to do so. You only work when you are 'matched' to a job, i.e. you hear the call.

The main risk involved is letting your ego slide in and feel that you are superior or a hero – this work is nothing of the sort. And if you go looking for work either in vision or in the world around you, you will most likely find a mismatched job where either the person really does not need the help as it is their struggle to solve, or you do not have the right skills for the job. The consequence will be a bit of a mess for all concerned.

This at least gives you an idea of how the tools can work and how you can work with them. Obviously this is one small aspect of the tools' work, of which there are many and which vary wildly. As you continue in your training you will learn more and more different applications, and will gain the skills to apply the tools properly and safely.

The base line use of the tools is this:

- The Sword, as you know by now, limits, blocks, guards and warns.
- The Vessel contains, transforms and dispenses, or weighs for judgement.
- The Stone roots, anchors and protects you.
- You will learn about the Cord a little later in another lesson.

The tools can be worked with actively (ritual and vision) or passively: for example placing the sword by your bed when you are under serious threat from an inner source, or leaving it out of its scabbard during dangerous times. Another passive action of a tool is the Scales and your feather: they are continuously working in the background to reaffirm and hold your inner balance.

Lesson 5

Working with the Shield and the Cord

The cloth shield, stone, and cord are what are known as passive tools. Whereas the sword and vessel are very much hands-on, active tools for humans to wield in magical patterns, the shield, stone, and cord are tools that tick away in the background: they do their job so that you can get on with yours safely.

This is part of the balancing act of magic: some tools are actively used, and others work simply by their presence. The sword and vessel are tools that have a wide-ranging application in magic, whereas the passive tools have a narrow but powerful focus to their action.

Of the three passive tools, the stone is the most profound and powerful, as it is a direct connection with the female Divinity, of the land beneath your feet. The cloth shield holds your frequency of power and protects you, and the cord is the measure of your lifespan.

The best way to understand these tools and how to apply them is to look at how they work, why they work, and when you would use them. We will also look at some misconceptions that occur in magic about these tools, so that you can spot an unbalanced or uninformed magical system or pattern should you come across it in your explorations. We will also explore the powers of these tools in ritual work, so that you can engage directly with them: this will give you far more understanding than pages of text would.

1. The cord

Cords and knots feature heavily in folk and ritual magic, and in such settings they are often used to bind, trap, or hold power, energy, a situation, or a person in place. Such uses are much lesser (and messier) applications of the cord, and instead of taking you down the same messy road we will work and learn about the cord from its highest application first. From there, as an initiate and adept, you will learn how to apply cord magic in a powerful but balanced, non-manipulative way.

The specific cord you have is one that was measured in vision by Decima, She Who Measures A Lifespan. The cord power was triggered in that vision, and also by the touch of the Noble One/Sandalphon as he passed over the threshold in the south.

Once the cord has been triggered in vision it slowly builds its energy through resonance with your work, and as you begin to work more actively with it, its power becomes 'fixed.' So what does it do?

Although you will learn lots of different ways of working with various cords and knots in the future, this particular cord is *the measure of your life*. It should be protected in a box which is kept in the south (future), and only used in two ways: either to circle the central flame, or to be wrapped about your right arm or a tool.

The cord[1] magically externalises your life's measure as decreed by the Fates, which in turn makes it much harder for other magicians to use magic against you to shorten your life.

When a magician uses cord magic (or any other type of magic) to limit your lifespan, they externalise your lifespan through a cord and then limit it using that cord. When the cord of your fate has already been externalised, and this externalisation is powerfully infused by the Fates, it obviates any such magic cast against you: there can only be one externalised measure of your lifespan in existence at any one time.

The cord also acts as a passive limiter: if you are working at an adept level and are working powerfully in service, there are times when such work can shorten your lifespan if you are not careful. Remember the hotspots in your fate pattern? If you happen to do a powerful dangerous working and it times in with one of those fate hotspots, it can take you out.

However, if you have a strong, working cord of life on your right arm (your Harvest arm), it will act as a limiter: any magic that seriously threatens your lifespan will be short-circuited. The magic will cease to flow and you will be safe.

There may come a time for some magicians when they know something is likely to lessen their lifespan, but they understand that it must be done anyway, and so they will work without their cord on – the ultimate sacrifice.

The power of the cord is built slowly throughout the training of the apprentice and the initiate: when the magician works magically, they wear the cord around their right arm or they encircle the central flame with it which is the alignment of the central flame and your inner flame. This passive action works through resonance: once the cord is tuned (by Decima) it is worn repeatedly in magical work, and over time its link to your fate grows in strength.

For this reason the cord must be protected and carefully stored so that it does not become lost, damaged, or stolen. It does not matter what it looks like, how simple it is, or what colour it is: its power comes from the inner work and the magical work done upon it and around it. Like all real magical tools the cord is not symbolic: it is a strong, working power tool that an everyday person would probably never give a second glance to.

Most likely there will come a time when the cord becomes damaged, lost, or broken. In such a situation, do not panic. Like all tools, the power can transfer or be renewed by the deities and powers you work with, but it is up to you to protect them as best

---

[1] The Silver Thread of Life.

you possibly can. Your tools can only be replaced so many times, and if you are careless or thoughtless with them, the deities will stop helping you. Deities are not your mother, and they will not wipe your bottom for you.

We will look at what to do in such a situation in a moment, but first here are some practical ways the cord can be worked with as an apprentice.

From now on, wrap the cord around your right arm every time you do magical ritual or visionary work. This is to connect you, your magic, and the cord together deeply, while also protecting your fate. If you are going into a dangerous situation in your daily life, and it is a danger you cannot back away from, wear the cord wrapped around your right arm or wrist, or your right leg/ankle. Do not use it lightly or flippantly in this way; only use it when you know you are going into a dangerous situation.

If you are becoming very ill, wrap the cord around your right foot (the foot that takes you into death). For example, a few years back I had a bout of viral meningitis and kept my cord wrapped around my right ankle until I started to win the battle. From an inner perspective this reiterates your full potential lifespan and gives your measure to the beings that work around death and destruction.

The cord is very specific to you. It is of no use to others, and lest you think it would help a loved one if they wore it, know that by doing this you would simply swap life measures with them. While that may be tempting if, for example, your children are under threat, you have to remember that everyone has their own fate and you cannot fiddle with it in such a way. There are other more efficient ways to protect those who depend on you.

2. Remaking the cord

Should your cord become lost or damaged then you need to make a new one. Make sure the fabric your cord is made out of is robust enough to do the job and will not fray. Stop all magical work except meditation and simple tuning rituals, and do not do anything else until your cord is renewed.

If the cord is just damaged and not lost, place it with the new cord, wrapping them around each other for the resonance to pass from one to the other until you are ready to remake the new cord.

Revisit the ritual you did earlier on your web of fate, where Decima appeared out of the south. Go through the whole process again with your cord, and after that keep it on the south altar or in the south of your space when you are not wearing it, preferably in a box to protect it. Burn the old cord and place its ashes out on the ground outside.

It will take a bit of time for the new cord to build its powers back up, but it will not take as long as the first time. And try to learn the lesson from the old cord: whatever went wrong to make you damage it or lose it, try not to repeat the same mistake.

If it simply fell apart, then for the new one, get a more robust cord. Always try to learn lessons from things that go wrong.

Hopefully now you will see why some types of cord magic can be so vicious, often unintentionally. In modern magic and witchcraft it is popular to employ cords and knots to force someone into a union, to tie them up, or to bind them; or to stack up power and release it though untying a knot.

When you aim this sort of magic at a living being, you are directly interfering with their fate and their lifespan, even if you think it is just a simple spell. Once you have worked with the cord magically with fate, that level of power will trigger in your actions *every time* you work with a cord, and that can get dangerous for others, even if that is not your intention.

Cords and knots can be worked with in conjunction with nature, (storms, etc.) and if you have worked for some time with the cord of fate, such cord use with nature can be powerful indeed. But that is something that comes later in your training; first you must learn the lessons of the cord's power through working with it on your own fate and life.

3. THE CLOTH

The cloth has a variety of uses. It is used to *impress the fate pattern* of the specific magician on their work and work-space; it is used as a *cloak* to protect you (it works as a shield) when you are doing more dangerous work; it can work as an *altar cloth*, a *mobile work space*, and it can also work in *passive protection mode*. By using the cloth as a *scabbard* for the sword, it becomes heavily interlinked with the power of the sword; and as it is specific to your fate, it becomes a proxy for you.

The most powerful scabbard is the stone or the body of the magician, and the cloth takes your body's place as the scabbard: you and the sword become heavily tied in together, and subsequently the cloth and the sword become tightly linked. The sword's power leeches into the cloth, which holds your fate pattern: the sword guards your pattern.

As such, the cloth can be used passively in times of danger. If you are ill, spread the cloth over your bed as you sleep. If later as an adept you are working on something dangerous in service, having the cloth around your shoulders will be one of the layers of protection that will keep you safe.

The cloth can also act as a portable altar if you need to travel and work while you are away from home. Using the cloth in your magical work connects it deeply with your magical pattern, and the pattern of the work-space. When you travel, take the cloth with you and use it either as an altar cloth or as a cloth to stand on as you work. It will carry with it the tuning of the work-space, and this will make it easier for you to do your work. Check the directions of your temporary work-space and make sure the cloth lines up to the directions properly (sword image/left hand in the east, for example).

This magical use of the cloth is also the root of the myths and legends of magical cloaks and coats. At the bottom of the lesson you will find links to various articles and information on these passive tools hidden in mystical/magical myths, and one of them is about a sacred cloak. Read these articles carefully, and you will see how such myths and legends have their roots in magical use.

In the practical work below, you will work with all of these passive tools and put them into action so that you can see how they integrate into magical work.

4. The stone

You should know a fair bit about the sacred, mythic, and legendary use of sacred/magical stones by now if you have done the research I suggested. Finding images that reflect this use of the stone are few and far between, but they are there if you hunt carefully enough. In ancient times and in many different cultures, the depiction of the stone beneath the feet symbolised the relationship between the king/queen or priest/priestess and the sacred land/mother.

The monarch or priest/priestess took on the mantle of service, and in return the sacred land supported them. This was often depicted as that person standing upon a stone, or seated with their feet upon a stone. The understanding of this degenerated down into the belief that the priest king/queen should not have their feet touch the ground, and they would therefore be depicted with a cushion or stone beneath their feet.

This is a misunderstanding and a total reversal of the wisdom. It is only by that direct connection between the sacred king/queen and the land/mother that the monarch ruled in balance. However, saying that, in some magical cultures the magician will not put a bare foot to the ground unless they intend to draw earth power into themselves, or to send magic down into the earth. The rest of the time they always wear something on their feet and will not walk barefoot, even in their own homes.

We also see aspects of the dynamic between mortality, the stone, and the land in Irish faery lore (Tir Na Nog), where a person is carried on a white horse into the faery realm, where they can live forever. If they return to the human world, their feet must not touch the ground (they must not get off the horse), or they will lose their immortality. It is probably a remnant of this belief that plays out in the tradition of monarchs not touching the floor with their feet when ritually sitting on the throne.

To have one's foot connected to the mother through the stone is to reiterate your mortality and offer that term of life in service/learning/governing. In return, the mother upholds your mortal life.

There is a lot in ancient cultures about stones and sacredness. You have already looked at the stones directly connected to the mother, and below, at the end of the lesson, are some research prompts to take and explore, one of which is about a sacred stone of kingship with the dynamic of stone/foot/footprint and the land.

This is a common Celtic theme in Britain, and you will find more instances of this king/feet/stone dynamic if you wish to research it. If you research and read carefully, with what you know of magic in mind, you will see what it was that these ancient people were doing/working with.

5. About the practical work

In this practical work you will do a ritual that is in service to the land around you. It is better for you to learn the skills of the tools by working in such a way, rather than working magically to benefit yourself as too many things can go wrong at this stage of your training. You will learn how the passive tools work in conjunction with the active tools.

Prepare your working space with the cloth on the floor and the central altar directly over the centre of the cloth. Place the tools on the relevant altars, and have a bottle of water on the west altar.

This ritual works like a tiny catalyst in a gentle but powerful way. In our modern world, we have been taught that the use of great force is best for triggering change. In magic, often the reverse is true. It is the subtle but well-aimed and focused action that can trigger a cascade of response, particularly when working with nature. A delicate nudge does not trigger a defensive response, but instead begins a movement that slowly grows, like ripples in a pond.

In this work, you will use the stone, shield, and cord as passive tools that enable you to transfer/mediate levels of power into an element. The use of passive tools allows you to work with greater power levels than normal and guard/protect you as you work.

6. *Task:* The ritual of balancing the water

Spread your cloth shield on the floor and place the central altar over the centre of the cloth. From now on, always place your shield cloth on the floor of your work space when you work.

Start in the east, light the flame, and see the gates open. Bow, and move on to the next direction. Light all the lights, finishing with the central flame. Go around the directions again to tune them by spending a minute or two in each direction in stillness. Now do The Anchor ritual.

When you have finished go around to the south altar, pick up your cord, and wrap it around your right arm. Go to the north, pick up the stone, and place it on the floor in front of the central altar on the west side. Now walk a full circle around the directions clockwise back to the west altar, fill the vessel with the water, and place the bottle beyond the threshold of the work-space.

Now go to the east altar, bow, and recite:

> "I am to serve the land;
> I request your guidance in my words."

Step back, bow once more, and go around the directions to the west altar.

Bow, and recite:

> "Through the power of the west,
> through the power of water,
> through the power of the Scales,
> I wish to assist in the balance of the land."

Stand in silence before the west altar. Be aware of the sword behind you in the east, of the stone in the centre, and the cloth beneath you.

Pick up the vessel. Hold it out, and recite:

> "Through this vessel,
> may the water contain and dispense whatever is appropriate for the land,
> and for the water that flows upon and beneath the land,
> and for the water that falls from the sky.
> Humans have taken from this water, I give back."

Now place the cup on the west side of the central altar.

Standing with your back to the west, place your left foot upon the stone, and hold your right hand over the water. Be aware of the west gate behind you, and the contacts that stand upon the west threshold. Be aware of the east gate before you, and the contacts that stand upon the east threshold. Be aware of the stone under your left foot, and the cord around your right arm. Now still yourself.

Recite:

> "As a magician in service, I allow my body to be used as a bridge:
> I span the outer and inner worlds;
> through me flows whatever is necessary for the land.
> Powers of the west, flow through me
> and place whatever is necessary
> for the health of the waters of the land
> into the water contained within the vessel."

Hold your hand firm over the water, and be aware of power flowing through you from behind you, down your right arm, and into the water in the vessel. Stand for however long is necessary until the flow has stopped. You may feel it in your right hand as heat and tingling – when that stops, drop your hand.

When the flow has finished or you think it has finished, put the vessel down on the central altar, pick up the stone, and walk a full circle around the directions. Finish in the north, turn, bow to the central flame, and sit down, holding the stone.

Clear your mind and be still. In your mind, ask the stone for guidance. You are looking for the best place to dispense the water. Think about what rivers, springs, streams, even storm drains are around you. Think of each one in turn. Do not think in terms of which is nearest or best. Make no assessment or decision; just think about each one in turn, giving equal thought to each one. Ask in your mind where this charged water is most needed, where it will work to its fullest potential. The water needs to go into water, not onto the land.

As you sit quietly, one location will stand out more than the others. When this happens, ask the stone in your hands:

"Mother, is this the place in this area where you need the water the most?"

Be still in listening for the answer. The answer will come through your own inner senses, your emotions, or your mind. If the feeling is blank, then it is somewhere else that needs the water. If the feeling is uncomfortable, then it is not the right place. If the feeling is like a smile, then it is the right place. Take as long as you need to in order to find the right place for the water. It is not an intellectual decision, it is instinctive.

Once you know where the water needs to go, what you do next depends on where that place is. If it is on your property, or very near where you live, then leave the lights going and immediately take the vessel/water to that place.

If it is some distance from your house, you need to close the space down first. Leave the vessel on the central altar. Go around the directions starting in the east, close the gates, put out the candle, and bow. Take off your cord and place it in its box in the south, and return the stone to the north.

Once everything is closed down, pour the water back into the bottle (so that you can transport it), and then wrap the cloth back around the sword.

Pouring the water

If the water is to be poured near your house, go out with the vessel and stand before the water that will receive it. Be aware of the air around you, the power that guides you and limits you. Be aware of the ground beneath you that upholds you, and be still. Hold the water in the vessel close to your mouth so that you can utter over the water. Recite:

"I release you."

Pour the contents of the vessel into the water. Take a step back, bow to the water source, and then return to your work-space and close the directions down.

If the contents of the vessel need to be poured into water some distance from your house, then when it is time to go there (don't wait too long to do this) take the bottle of charged water, the vessel, and your cloth scabbard with you. If possible, do this just before the height of the full moon: the day before the night of the full moon.

When you get to the water source, place the cloth around your shoulders with its markings facing into you. If there are people around, place it around you under a jacket, and if you cannot do that, have it in a backpack on your back. Pour the water into the vessel, utter the declaration of release using the same method as above, and pour the vessel's contents out into the water. Bow to the water source, and leave.

7. *Task:* Observing the results

The subtle catalyst action of this ritual can work in a wide variety of ways depending on what the land and water need. Keep a record for the next six to eight weeks of any major shifts in weather, rain, flooding, etc.

Sometimes the effects are almost immediate; sometimes they come a couple of months later. When they do come it can sometimes be quite dramatic, and it is always unexpected, i.e. it is not something that would normally happen: for example heavy rain in the desert, and it will be directly connected to the water source where you dispensed the charged water. Continue to keep an eye on that water source and what happens to it over the rest of the year.

If you can, go back to the water source a few times just to visit and hang out with the water. If it is a river, lake, dam, or stream, then sing or recite poetry to the spirit of the water: your voice becomes the sword that guards and limits to bring balance, and water always loves the human voice directed at it.

Also write up a summary of your experience with this ritual, and do this in your computer log. If you did return to the water and sang/talked to it, then keep a note in your journal (not your computer log) of the song, poem, or story that you uttered to the water. Use your physical hand to record your utterance to the spirit of the water.

8. Summary of action

To learn the technical aspects of how that ritual worked and how the tools specifically worked, let's just take a moment to look closely at how and why the ritual was put together in that way.

First you used The Anchor to tune yourself and your space in preparation for work. The more you use the Anchor before a ritual or visionary action, the stronger it will become, as each time it is used it focuses the power and the space more and more.

Then you placed the tools in their directions. This energetically reaffirms their working pattern, which will also build over time. The cloth shield on the floor soaks up the magical pattern which in turn tunes and charges it.

The introduction of the water is specific to the action: you need an elemental substance (water) that will act as a carrier for the magic, and because you were working on water courses across the land, you use water to carry the magic: you match element to element for the carrier and recipient.

Why work with water? Land is static, but water flows across the land and dispenses itself throughout the land. It sinks into the land and into the water table, and it is also evaporated into the air as a part of the weather system. It eventually flows to the sea. With these various actions, it spreads the magic far into the environment.

The placing of the water bottle outside of the work area is also important. The bottle is just a bottle: it is not being used magically, and therefore should not be in the space. Because you use it, but in a non-magical way, you must keep it non-magical and not have it within the energy pattern of the work.

Other non-magical things around your working space are unaffected if you do not use them during a magical act. (Though they will become subtly altered by the energy.) But the simple action of having the bottle on the altar and used as a vessel for the water can potentially activate it as a magical vessel. This would just make your work untidy and confusing, so you get it out of the space when it is not being used. This is akin to proper punctuation: keep it tidy and to the point.

You will notice that the sword was kept in its directional position out of the scabbard. This is a passive action: it is there to guard and guide, but it is your use of voice that the active principle of the sword flows through. Your voice becomes an extension of the sword, and standing upon the cloth scabbard reinforces that extension. The cloth also contains the magical space and exteriorises your own fate pattern so that the whole space becomes an extension of you.

The stone, as you will have noticed, can move around the directions: the land is everywhere beneath us. Whatever direction you are working in, if you need the action of the stone, you work with it in the main direction you are working in, which in this case was west/water/dispensing.

By placing your left foot on the stone, you trigger the power of the Grindstone, which is about work and service/outputting power. If the ritual work was about weighing, harvesting, or upon your own scales, then your right foot would be placed upon the stone.

Placing your foot upon the stone grounds you in the land, connects you to the stone floor deep within the Underworld, acts as a strengthener and protector, and connects you to the land as you work in service.

The cord around your arm ensures that you work within the limitations of your mortality, and at this stage of your work it bonds you to the cord and the cord to you. Together, you and the tools, altars, flames, and gates work in harmony as one team, and the constant repetition of this pattern builds it strongly until it becomes second nature to you: it becomes a strong working imprint that you can operate within.

Eventually you will get so used to the pattern and the feel of the energy that, as an adept, you will simply be able to think of that pattern, that energy, and switch it on in your head wherever you are. You will learn to work in any space, without the tools, altars, etc., and you will be able instantly to open the gates and pull the power together. This is important for an adept if they are suddenly confronted by a large tide of power or an incoming magical pattern. You could be in an airport, a shopping mall, the office, or a supermarket, and you will be able to tune instantly into the working pattern in your mind and operate from within that safe structure.

To finish, here are some research prompts for you to look at and research around. Disregard the religious or cultural elements involved in the information: learn to look simply at the energetic or magical action (passive or otherwise) involved. Often what started as something magical became dogmatised into religious patterns, so you just need to look beyond that into the aspects of what is actually going on. Use what information is listed in the research prompts, and using either a library or the internet, see what you can find. As always with magical research, avoid New Age and popularised occult pages. Look for sites on history, mythology, religion, or anthropology, for example. You will have to learn how to draw magical information from non magical sites, but by doing so you will filter out all the made up bullshit that is used to sell product, or is part of a conspiracy theory.

Kingship Stone of Dunadd in Scotland

The Gaelic Kingdom of Dál Riata and the royal centre of Dunadd is a stunningly beautiful hill fort in modern day Argyll, where a footprint in the rock marks the inaugural spot where the Gaelic kings were symbolically married to the land they were to rule. The king would become a consort to the female nature spirit or goddess of the land.

Khirqa Sharif (the sacred cloak)

The sacred cloak is believed to be the cloak that the Prophet Muhammed (PBUH) wore on the famous Night Journey known as the Isrá and Mírag, where the prophet was carried on a white horse in vision up into the heavens. The cloak is kept in a shrine in Kandahar, Afghanistan and is believed to have protective qualities.

The cloak of Elijah in the second Book of Kings[2]

Read the whole passage as it is filled with magical crumbs if you read closely enough, and also at the end it contains a lesson on how not to use such a tool. You will also notice that the magic of Elijah was imprinted into his cloak which became a magical tool in its own right. This text is well worth looking up and reading, and reading it more than once. Move the religion aspect of the text to one side and focus on what is actually happening.

---

[2] 2 Kings 2, Old Testament of the Bible SJV.

On the use of water to heal the land, by Adept Frater Acher

This is a blog post by Frater Acher on magical work he did a few years ago with water to heal the land/restore balance. This blog post gives you an idea of how the simple technique you just learned eventually can be transformed into deep and powerful work in service to the land. You will also notice that the work is quite natural and the magician is just a part of the process, not the conductor of the orchestra. The adept works instinctively within the patterns of magic that are trained into them; yet they are not confined by those patterns.

If the link no longer works (it is functional in 2025) look among his writing and books for mention of his account of the healing work on the land using water.

https://theomagica.com/blog/healing-the-land-part-2.html

Lesson 6
Lesser-known Tools

In Western magic, we tend to think of the obvious tools (sword, wand, cup, shield) as being the only ones applied in magic. This is a devolution of knowledge that crept in with the over ritualisation of magic in the nineteenth century, and then the psychologising of magic in the twentieth century. The result of this devolution is that too many Western magicians no longer use – and are not even aware of – some of the lesser-known tools that can be applied in magic.

These lesser-known tools are often heavily interwoven with, and dependant on, certain skills that are necessary to create or activate them. In this lesson you will start the process of learning those skills and creating tools. These lesser known tools and skills can be misleading as they can appear simple and be easily overlooked, but that would be a mistake. Some of these methods and tools can become very powerful indeed in the hands and work of an adept, so pay close attention to them.

The lesser-known tools escaped the layers of ritualisation and psychology, and as you learn to work with them, it will give you an idea of what magic was like, and how it worked, before it was over organised and became pompous.

Those of you who have studied anthropology or tribal magic will recognise some of these tools and skills: some branches of magic never lost them, and if you study ancient texts you will start to see hints of these skills and when they were applied.

As a magician, it is good to get away from the systemic dogma of modern Western magic, and to understand that tools in magic are many and varied. Some tools are more powerful than others, some have wide-ranging applications, and some have very narrow but useful applications. Together they make a tool kit and a family that you can work with in your magical life.

Some tools are enlivened through direct visionary work, inner contact and ritual patterns, and these tools are the mainstay of the magician's work: the sword, etc. But some tools are crafted or triggered for specific actions, have a certain shelf life, and are then destroyed.

These lesser known tools are loosely connected in their action to the principle tools, and in a way are weaker echoes of their power. Learning how to create and apply these tools will, as a side-effect, give you a deeper understanding of the actions of the principle tools. It will also give you different octaves of power to work with: you do not need a sledgehammer to crack a nut; you need a nutcracker.

So let's have a look at these lesser known tools: what they are, how they work, how you make them, and how you apply them. Like most magic, you will learn one layer of a skill as an apprentice, and that layer will act as a foundation for higher octaves of the skill that you will apply as an adept.

1. Patterns

Physically drawn patterns have a wide range of applications: they can act as spirit traps, containers for magic, vocabulary for communication, and 'skeletons' for power windows (icons for example). When a magician draws a pattern with focus, intent, and knowledge, the pattern starts to form and contain energy. It creates pathways, doorways, and can give form to a spirit consciousness in order for communion and/or communication to occur. Pattern-making is also the root skill of sigil work.

Once you have worked with this skill for a while you will start to look at ancient sacred constructs in a totally different way: you will begin to see that what looks like ornamentation is often not actually ornamentation at all – it is a magical working pattern with a specific purpose.

To create these patterns magically you need a variety of skills. You need to be able to use your hand/pen, (which in the era of computers is a skill that is vanishing fast) get your conscious mind out of the way, (also a vanishing skill) and know what you are doing.

The use of the hand/pen in magic is a much-overlooked and necessary skill; hence you began a handwritten journal right at the beginning of your training. You need to learn how to allow a transfer of power through the hand/pen, and keeping the journal was the very beginning of that. If you can, keep one pen specifically for magical work, just to let resonance build up in it.

Learning how to get out of the way of your mind is also a really important skill, so that beings can communicate or flow directly through you without your conscious mind interfering in the process. In today's world, that is a lot harder than it sounds. This is one of the many reasons why meditation is so important, as it facilitates that skill.

Through learning this technique you will eventually, as an adept, learn not only how to create magical working patterns, but also how to use text in the same way. This will allow beings to 'talk through you' (not channelling!) you will learn how to let a being or inner contact tell you about themselves, or mediate information, and you will learn how to let conscious energy through you as a bridge so that it can communicate. This is known as *contacted writing*, and it will be an invaluable resource to you when you are working in the Inner Library or mediating knowledge that is about to tip into the Abyss and become lost to the human mind. But as I said a bit earlier, this is not what is known as channelling, which is where the magician or person fades into the background and another spirit takes over the mind and body of the person. Bridging is more like interpreting/passing on what you hear/see/feel in a combined effort between you and the being. Sometimes the person and spirit can briefly join but in mutual balanced presence. Once you have learned and practised the skill of creating a pattern tool, then we can look at that tool's various applications and how and when you would use them.

2. Watchers

What I call *watchers* are passive tools that are often used within folk magic in the Near and Middle East. Watchers are simply a pair of eyes, or an eye, that watches over the ritual space and living space of the magician. We see this in use in ancient Egypt with the *Eye of Horus,* and throughout the southeast Mediterranean and the Near East with the *Eye of Fatima.*

Just putting up an eye in a house will essentially do little, if anything. But working with an eye or eyes magically will 'switch them on' so that they work away in the background, keeping an eye on the space and warning you if something is wrong. They can also act as a deterrent to minor, low-level beings that would otherwise try to inch into a space.

It is not always about which eye or what type of eye that is important; it is how you work with them that triggers them. Though using a particular form of eye that has been worked with for millennia[1] makes the job a lot easier, as some resonance flows through the specific pattern. Once you have worked with a resonant eye then you will find it much easier to work with any eye.

Magical students often think that any magical act has a fancy ritual or recitation that makes something work, or a grand calling of angels, saints or other beings. Sometimes that is true, but often it is not, particularly with passive tools. What makes passive tools work is the act of the magician bringing them into a space, focusing his or her intent on them, and then interacting with them.

A magician spends a lot of time creating and upholding patterns, gates, windows, and thresholds. This skill is often applied with direct purpose, but it can also be applied passively in a way that will work strongly. Whereas a non-magician will have no influence over an object, a magician can turn a random object into doorway, a vessel, a window, etc.

You will learn in your practical exercise how to do this with the eyes, and it really is very simple but effective. These passive tools of watchers are not all-powerful or all-seeing, but they add a layer to the space. Slowly the magician builds up a series of layers of magic within a space, each working at different frequencies, in order to create a web of energy/magic that upholds the space.

The eyes in particular literally watch. If a danger, an intruder, or a hostile being should make their way close to or into the space, the eyes will see this and relay the information. That information will be passed to a deity that the magician works with, or to a guardian being, or directly to the magician themselves, and it will surface in dreams, intuitions, or as a direct warning in the mind of the magician. I get my eye warnings through smelling smells that are not physical, and through feeling something is 'off'.

---

[1] Like the Eye of Horus.

The eyes also act as a presence that warns off different types of lowlife beings. Imagine you peer into a window and see a pair of eyes staring back at you. Your initial instinct would be to step back. These eyes work in a similar way with beings who peer into your space. But the eyes cannot defend or attack, they are simply eyes that watch. They can also be further tuned to become the eyes of a specific being, guardian, or deity: it is how you direct your work with them that decides at what level they are going to work.

Sometimes eyes will come to you that are already tuned and working. This has happened to me a few times when I have been in danger: I find an eye and it is already strongly tuned to a specific power that in turn watches over me. I have found these eyes out in the desert around ancient temples, out in fields, etc., and I do not need to do anything magical with them: they are already tuned and ready to work.

You can make your own eye, trigger it to work, and then put it up in your home or temple. In the practical aspect of this lesson you will learn how to trigger them and then apply them and work with them. It is also possible to work with figurines/statues using the same passive technique to trigger them as early warning systems around the house. We will also look at that method in the practical part of the lesson.

3. Bottles and dilution

Bottles as passive tools are a very interesting thing to work with, and the dilution aspect is a method that you apply in conjunction with the bottle. Working with bottles is an extension of the magical vessel/west, and the work with the succussion is a very old stage of true alchemy. It works on the principle of *Similia Similibus* which means similar things take of similar things.[2] The bottle is the tool/carrier, and the content is whatever is wrong (a sick or polluted river for example) which is placed in the bottle and is then highly diluted and impacted repeatedly. This creates a drop of substance that has an energetic signature of the problem. It is then put back into the water that is having the problem. It is this principle that was behind the creation of vaccination.

Each bottle is kept for a specific purpose, and it is not used in any way, magically or otherwise, outside of its key function. So eventually, you end up with a few bottles that are kept for specific jobs.

So for example, remember your work with water, the vessel, and the river/lake that you did in a previous lesson of this module? A next step of that work would be to use a specific bottle during the magical working to store the charged water. The water would be succussed, (we will get to that in a moment) stored, and then dispensed in small drops into the watercourse over a set period of time.

---

[2] *Places in Man*; the Hippocratic Corpus. Hippocrates b.460 BC.

This method of working can be applied to many different scenarios: healing for a specific person, rebalancing a water course, or working with the contacts of the Inner Library to slowly dispense a specific thread of energy for a job.

The resonance of the magic held in the water affects the glass of the bottle, so the magician keeps that bottle specifically for one type of job. The resonance builds up in the bottle until eventually it works with uncharged water: the bottle itself eventually charges the water with the particular energy.

In the practical section, we will look at how to work with and apply this technique in a few different ways. For the practical work with the bottle, you can prepare now by getting a glass bottle with an airtight mental cap/lid.

Succussion is an interesting technique to use with water, and is the mainstay of homeopathic preparations, among other alchemical and magical ways of working. To succuss (impact repeatedly and then dilute) water is to increase the potency of the energy within the water. This works alchemically and imprints the energy of magic or a substance deeper into the water, making it more condensed as an active living energy and pattern. The bottle filled with water is banged repeatedly on a thick book (as it has some 'give') in specific measured impacts, usually one hundred impacts per round of succussion. All but a drop is then poured out, and clean water is added. The action is repeated again at least thirty times. For really highly charged catalyst water, it would be succussed and diluted a thousand times. The result is potentised water that is ready to work, one drop at a time.

Although it seems like a very gentle, dilute way of working, magically the opposite is true: potentised water that has been magically worked with can be a very powerful catalyst, so this method should be treated with respect. Magically, potentised river or sea water can be used in weather magic, or to bring the body of water into better health, or to trigger it's own regenerative actions. But often the resulting rebalancing from the catalyst is not gentle, as water works very closely with the weather. It can trigger huge storms that flood rivers or churn up the seas, or it can change river courses, or it can cause repeated minor flooding that regenerates the flood plains around it. The stronger the potency, the longer the effect takes to manifest physically, and likely the more dramatic it will be.

Succussing and diluting thirty times (and using one hundred impacts per dilution) is a mild to medium potency that will act as a more surface catalyst for change. Succussing and diluting one thousand times is a high potency that is likely to act as a deep catalyst that would be slow to action but dramatic in impact.

This method of dilution and potentisation can also be used with plants and substances. First the plant or substance is turned into a tincture, and then one drop of the tincture becomes the starting point for making the potency. It is also used with magical patterns and rituals – the water is exposed and becomes part of the magical patterning, vision, or ritual, and the magician works to imprint the pattern/magic into the water. Then that water begins the succussion process. The resulting water is basically the energetic essence of the magical working and can be used to dispense the magic in particular ways.

The use of water and a bottle as a vehicle for magic is very old magic and often appears in folk traditions. There was a very famous Irish healer and magical woman by the name of Biddy Early who lived in county Claire in the mid nineteenth century. She always used a blue glass bottle and water from a well close to her house to dispense her healing and magic. She became the most feared and famous healer in all Ireland, with her skills recognised and often condemned by the Catholic Church and also the local judges.

There have been some tales written down about Biddy Early and a couple of books written about her. But in the last few decades I have noticed that the stories about her life and her achievements have been watered down, Christianised, changed or removed to make her appear more acceptable to tourists, and modern locals. This happens a lot in various countries, so keep that in mind whenever you are doing research about a person. Try to find books that are about the subject but are written decades or even centuries apart, and compare them.

4. Short cords

Short cords are tools that can be used to contain an ongoing working and keep you connected with the work or process. If the magician is working on a magical pattern or project that may span weeks or months, they can work with a short cord that acts as an umbilical cord between the work/process and them.

Once it has been worked with, the cord is worn on the relevant wrist (which wrist depends on the type of work) until the work is completed. This acts as a layer of protection and connection between the magician and the work.

It also strengthens the 'warning' dynamic in magic. If the magician is making a misstep in the work, the energy will often become unstable. Sometimes the magician is sensitive enough to pick up on that instability in the energy, and sometimes they are not. If they are not, then the cord can strengthen that subtle instinct in the magician, strengthening the signal so to speak, so that the magician is warned there is a problem or a misstep and can act accordingly.

The cord can also create an energetic link between the ongoing work and the magician, allowing the work to continue to flow strongly even when the magician is at rest or doing mundane things. It can act as a battery for the work, connecting their energies to the ongoing magical work. This is helpful sometimes, but depending on what the magician is doing it can end up draining the magician in an unhealthy way: the magician must learn to check via readings whether using a cord for a particular instance is practical, useful, and safe.

5. About the practical work

For the practical work you will need the following:

For the pattern making:

Paper and pen (preferably a pen which you will use only for this purpose).

For the eye:

Clay and paint to make an eye. A tool to shape the clay (a wax shaping tool is good), phthalo blue acrylic paint and white acrylic paint, optional gold acrylic paint, and a small paintbrush.

Also look for a figurine or ornament of a dog or a cat. Look for something simple but not whimsical: a museum copy of an Egyptian cat, or a figure of a dog with clear, straight-looking eyes and a clear mouth that is not growling or bearing teeth.

For the succussion:

A thick, solid glass bottle or a small, thick glass jar with a screw top or sealable lid (not plastic). Also a thick hardbound book (it is the thickness of the book, not the hardness of the cover that is needed), and a bottle of spring water or sterile water.

For the cord work:

A ball of cotton string.

6. *Task:* Working with patterns

The first stage of working with drawn patterns is learning to 'get out of the way' of the action. Our conscious minds love to take over, and quickly our learned behaviour, our love of control, and our dogmatic thinking comes into play. This immediately disables the action.

So before you learn to apply the skill of patterns in a specific way, first you must learn how to rein in your mind as you work. This is much harder for some people than others, but practice is the only way to prepare the mind for this technique. What follows is a series of exercises that will build your skill in this technique.

Set a time when you will be able to work for an hour or more without being disturbed, get your paper and a pen, and find a comfortable place to work. Do not work with rulers or any other tool; just your hand, the paper, and a pen (not a pencil). Before you start, quietly sit and meditate to still yourself.

Pattern technique one

Once you are still, start to draw a pattern, any pattern, working from the centre outwards. Do not think about the pattern, do not think about the shapes, how it looks, or what it relates to: do it with a blank mind. Let your hand do the pattern while your mind is still.

This is a lot harder than it sounds. Every time you get interested in the pattern or wish to develop it along a particular line or shape it in any way, stop what you are doing. Still yourself, silence your mind, and then continue.

Essentially you are learning to become a conduit. There are two distinct branches of this work: patterns that come from deep within you, and patterns that come from beings around you who speak/draw through your hand. The only way to achieve 'conduit-ness' is first to learn how to surrender control of the pattern, and to learn to be still so that you can mediate through your hand. Don't worry about failing, as you are simply learning the technique at the moment so take your time with it.

Learn to practise this when you are sitting doing nothing: carry a small notepad and pen around with you and when you are sitting in a waiting room, on a train, or in an office when you have no work to do, practise drawing patterns without thinking of the pattern or directing it. Instead of reaching for your phone/tablet and browsing social media, just practise drawing patterns.

Do not correct mistakes (this is really important), and learn to hold back your wish to form a specific pattern – just let it be itself. Not only do you have to learn how to mediate through the use of a pen, you also have to *unlearn* a basic principle you learned in grade school: that what you produce from your pen must be neat, controlled, and make sense. It does not matter what the pattern looks like; that is irrelevant, as you are simply learning to get out of the way of your mind at this stage. Just remember it is a *pattern* you are letting through, not random marks or scribbles.

Keep one or two of your first patterns, and place the paper in your journal so that you can look back to it. These will also be part of your submitted papers for your mentoring. The rest you can just throw away: at this stage there is nothing magical in them, so you do not have to worry about how to dispose of them.

Doing a bit of this every day is really helpful, and should become your doodling habit when bored. I still do it to this day to keep the skill fresh and strong.

Once you are getting fairly good at getting out of the way of yourself, then practise the same thing with your other hand, and be warned, this gets hilarious. You need to learn to *blank pattern* with both hands, as later you will learn to mediate different types of power through different hands.

Once you can blank pattern with both hands, play around with blank patterning while you are blindfolded or with your eyes shut, and don't peek until you have finished.

Some people get good at this quickly and for some it takes a while. Practice these basics intensively for a week or so until you get the hang of it, then move on to the second pattern technique. This practice can be done while you are also doing other practical Quareia work: it is a passive skill and will not interfere with anything else you are doing – it is like practising your alphabet.

Pattern technique two

This is the stage where the technique shifts from being simple practice to the beginnings of a magical act, and that act is the start of learning how to create a magical tool using patterns.

Do this in your working space, and light the east candle. Unwrap the sword from the cloth scabbard and lay out the cloth before the east altar: you will sit on it. Don't worry if the space is not big enough for the pattern on the cloth, it can be folded. It is the presence of the cloth itself that is important. Place the sword by the altar: prop it against the front of the altar, point down.

Meditate to still yourself, and once you are still it is time to get to work. Mark the four directions on the paper, east to the middle left of the paper, south above, etc. Now still yourself again. Be aware of the sword and its power; be aware of the east, the gates, and the power that flows from the east.

Starting from the point where you have marked 'east,' begin a pattern that starts in the east of the paper and build it outwards from the east. Do not let your mind take over and organise the pattern. Every time you feel that creeping in, stop, still yourself, and then continue. Just let the pattern form itself.

Keep your focus on the sword and the power of the east as you draw. As the pattern develops, you may start to recognise what it is or what form it is taking. Just acknowledge that and continue. Don't try and make sense out of it until you have finished.

What you are attempting to do is to give patterned form to an energy that flows out of the east. Once you are able to do this technique clearly, you will then learn how to work with the pattern to contain the energy and then apply that energy to something. So it is important to learn to let that energy take form through your hand.

Once you have done a few patterns for the east, repeat the process using your other hand. It doesn't matter which hand you start with, rather it is important to be able to work with both in turn. Again, be very careful: do not try to repeat the same pattern – you may find that the left hand mediates a totally different pattern for the same energy than the right hand does. This is where your body is learning how to process and interpret the energy in specific ways.

Later, when you come to work more intensely with this technique, you will find that the different hands translate power in very different ways regardless of whether you are right handed or left handed. Practice this a few times until you feel comfortable with it. Watch for micro-actions (remember those?) creeping into the pattern:

don't allow your brain/hand to want to do flourishes with a repetitive pattern, or to do ornamentation. It is important to learn how to mediate the pattern in simple, clear terms, without your mind or brain interfering for its own amusement.

Once you feel you have got the hang of it, pick one east pattern from each hand, put those two pieces of paper in your journal with your first patterns (part of the mentoring assessment), and burn the rest.

Do not just throw the spare patterns away: by this stage, fragments of magical energy will be seeping into them, so you need to dispose of them properly. These patterns can become windows, even at this early stage, and particularly if you are a natural mediator. Having them screwed up in the bin will not stop the flow of that energy, which can become feral if you are not careful. This is also the start of learning magical hygiene: clean up after yourself, and don't leave such things hanging around your space, as they can become troublesome.

Repeat this technique with the other directions (s/w/n/centre). Light that directional candle, place the tool on the altar, and repeat the pattern process using each hand in turn. Keep two patterns from each direction, one from the right hand and one from the left, and place them in your journal. Burn the rest.

This can take some time: map out a schedule for yourself so that you can continue on with your lesson exercises while also practising your pattern technique over a few weeks.

Pattern technique three

This moves the technique on a step but keeps it firmly in the mundane so that you can learn it fully without moving into magical mediation. The reason for this is that it moves from working with patterns to working with words and numbers. This means you have to go back to the beginning of the technique and learn how to do this action without your mind stepping in and interfering.

Just as you practised the initial pattern and doodling, now do the same thing but with random letters (not words) and numbers. At this stage you are not learning to mediate; rather you are learning to train your brain not to get in the way.

When you are bored or waiting for something/someone, get out your small pad and pen. Do not try this on a device; you must use a pen and your hand/paper. Write down lines of random letters and numbers. As soon as your brain starts to make associations or tries to create words, stop, still yourself, and then continue. Practice this until you can write a page of random numbers and letters without interfering or trying to form or control the process.

Once you can do that, practise that skill every so often when you are bored: it is a technique, and like all techniques it must be practised to keep it sharp. This is a preparatory technique which will lead you eventually, as an adept, into learning how to let beings 'talk through you' in a way that is not channelling, and how to do contacted writing.

7. *Task:* Working with watchers

This is a very simple and fun technique, and it is also the beginning stages of an advanced technique that you will learn later, which is to magically and powerfully 'switch on' an object and turn it into a vessel for a being.

Rather than using fancy rituals, which are useless at this task anyhow, this technique works through focused intent and resonance. It slowly builds up through repetitive interaction, like forging a path through brushwood. Once it is strong, it is almost impossible for other magicians to interfere with: there is no specific magical pattern that can be bound, displaced, or dismantled. It is simply a well-worn path and a firmly established 'window' that has grown organically.

There are two foundation techniques in this method, and you will practise both. As you develop in your magical studies you will slowly come to recognise the many variables that can be applied through these foundation techniques, which will in turn allow you to develop specific skills and tools.

The first technique works specifically with eyes. Eyes have always been important in magic, and learning how to create a working eye is the first stage to learning how to give magically enlivened eyes to a deity vessel, i.e. a contacted or 'power-filled' statue of a deity.

The second technique teaches you how to slowly 'switch on' a figurine, image, or statue through a passive magical act. Bear in mind that this exercise is a magical act from the very beginning. It is not like pattern doodling where you can then screw up the paper and throw it away. Anything you work with while practising this technique can potentially become activated magically, and therefore you need to care for the item properly and once you are finished working with it or it gets broken, it must be disposed of correctly.

Technique one: eyes

Get your clay, some water, a tray or something similar to work on (I use an old wooden cutting board) and a shaping tool (I use wax carving tools). Take them into your working space. Set up the four directions with their tools, place the cloth folded up (so you do not get clay on it) on the floor in front of the east altar. Don't bother with a central altar. Light the lights and then sit down in front of the east altar on the cloth with your materials. You sit in the east because you are learning to create.

The reason you do this task in a tuned space is because you are creating something that will have sight: you are essentially creating a vessel, and when you do that there is always the risk that a parasite will try to step into it. Creating it in a working space that is tuned will prevent that from happening.

You do not have to do anything 'magical' in this process: it is a passive technique which simply uses the tuned space as a safe place to work in. Only the beings that should work with you are allowed into your space by nature of the magical imprint of the space, and also by the tools.

You are going to learn this technique by working with a specific type of eye, the *Eye of Horus*. The reason for this is that the Eye of Horus has ancient magic wrapped up in the 'pattern' of the eye: it was used for so long to watch over things that it is a well-used magical image that is easily switched on, and is far less likely to misused by a passing curious being.

This is an important dynamic to learn in magic: well-trodden paths and the use of specific images that have been magically used for millennia are a safe form of sandbox for you to learn with. You will be able to tap into that long line of use, which will help it spring to life.

Figures 4 and 5 are two images of the Eye of Horus. The first is a clear photograph of the actual ancient design for you to copy; the second indicates the colour scheme. Notice it is a *left eye* (east, guarding).

Do not be tempted to be artistic and add on bits, change colours too dramatically, or decorate it in any way. You are working to produce an exact copy to the best of your ability while holding intentional focus. This is not a work of art or an exercise in self-expression; rather this is a magical working that has to be defined and to the point. Any additions or alterations will weaken the flow of power that automatically flows through ancient patterns. Once you have worked with the magic of these eyes for long enough, you will learn what can be changed, and what cannot, and that learning comes from informed trial and error.

Figure 4: Eye of Horus (made by Josephine McCarthy)

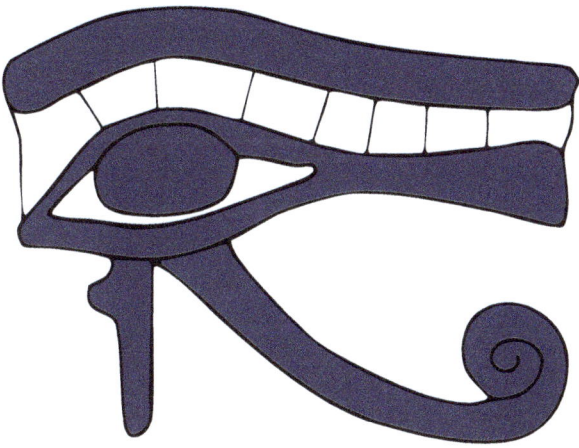

Figure 5: Colour scheme

The first stage of the technique is to make the eye itself. Work in front of the east altar, and using the clay and the shaping tool, and water and a brush to smooth it, make a plaque of the eye. Once it is finished, take it and place it in the oven for a couple of hours with the heat on very low to harden it. If you have no oven leave it for a few days to air-dry, but an oven on low is best. Close the directions down and put the tools away.

Once the eye has dried and is ready to paint, open the directions once more. Work in the east with the tools in the directions for extra tuning, and paint the eye. The blue is a deep lapis blue, and when you are looking for paint, acrylic is probably best to work with, it is called Phthalo blue.

Once the eye is finished place it on the east altar with the lights going and leave the room for a while. When you feel it is ready, come back in, close down the directions, put the tools away, and place the eye in the east of the work room.

Look at the eye and ask it to watch over the space. Do this every time you leave the room in future. By doing so it builds up a pattern of behaviour and tasking, so that over time it will slowly start to switch on and do what you have asked it to do.

Notice that you do not specify what type of being is to look through the eye, nor do you do magic upon it: it is a very passive action. This is another version of 'getting out of the way' and not trying to control a magical act.

The tuning of the magical space and the positioning of the tools creates a frequency in the room which allows only the right type of being into the space, something you should already know by now. By being in that space while it was made, and facing east while you made it, you subtly imprinted that frequency into the eye which acts as deterrent for low-level parasitical beings and instead creates a frequency that will allow helpful beings to work through it.

The eye is activated by your interactions with it. Place it in the east for a short while (a week or so), and every time you enter that room, look at the eye and think: "watching." When you go to leave the room, ask the eye to "keep an eye" on the room for you and let you know if something untoward happens in that space.

After a week or two of being in the ritual space and being talked to by you, the eye will be ready to work in the house in general. Take it and place it opposite a front door, opposite a door of your bedroom, or near a window so that it can look outside and watch the back or front of your house for you.

Because this technique uses passive resonance, every time you pass the eye or see it, think "watching." This tells it what to do. When you go out of the house or go to bed at night, quietly ask the eye to watch over the space and alert you to any danger or intruder.

The strength of this eye as a guardian/watcher will depend on your interactions with it, what type of being decides to help through the eye, or whether it develops as an extension of your own spirit.

Do not try to direct that process either way: learn to let things happen (remember, it's a safe sandbox) so that you can learn whether or not you have the ability to stretch yourself into objects.

Some people naturally can, and some cannot. If you do not have that natural ability, the skill is something you will gain it through training later in the course. In the meantime a being that is within, around, or conducive to your magical work will step into the eye and operate it for you.

This is another magical dynamic that is important to learn. Always give yourself the chance to achieve something by means of your own skills, work, and talents. When you are not able to do something all by yourself, but you have tried, or at least held the door open for that possibility, then beings that work around you in your magic will step in to help you. If you do not leave open that possibility for you to do something by yourself, the beings that work magically around you will see the potential for dangerous dependency on them and they will pull away.

This can be a difficult series of dynamics to get your head around if you have been used to magic that controls, commands, and manipulates. This is the polar opposite method of working. It is about opening safe doors, and allowing power, energy, and consciousness to flow freely back and forth, and into your work and life. This in turn allows you to achieve far more in magic: you are not limited by your lack of understanding, nor by your lack of skill or human limitations. What you cannot do, others step in to do, and by not controlling but getting out of your own way, you allow deeply hidden inherent abilities, latent skills, and knowledge that your spirit carries to come to the fore and make themselves known.

If the eye keeps waking you at night to tell you that something is in the house, such as a mouse, a fly, a spider, etc., which can happen, then you need to talk to the eye and tell it what you consider a threat: a human intruder, a parasite, a ghost, a hostile being, magical attacks, etc.

Sometimes, and this depends on your inner senses' ability, the eye's communications can be very subtle indeed. Something will wake you, or you will waken out of a dream where you saw something that bothered you: that is often the eye trying to communicate with you. I get communications by smell, sound, something in a dream, or sometimes a nagging feeling that something is not right.

If you get an alert and there seems to be no discernible threat, then in the morning do a reading using the TREE OF LIFE LAYOUT and ask if there was indeed something potentially threatening in or around the house that night.

Also, something which I still make the mistake of not doing on some occasions, is, if someone comes to stay at your house, or workmen are coming in for the day, *tell your guardians!* I have had various situations where watchers and guardians have plagued a person that was staying over.

You can also use the tarot to see how the eye works, to understand what it does, and also to ensure that you have communicated with it correctly, i.e. *"Does it understand what to look out for?"*, *"What is the best way for me to receive its communications?"* The power and coherence of the eye builds by you constantly interacting with it: asking it to watch and warn, looking at it, and being aware of it.

But understand that it is just an eye/window, not a being itself. Do not feed it or treat it like a deity; just ask it to watch. It can be moved around the house, but once it is working it will know where it is best to be, or you can do FOUR-DIRECTIONAL READINGS to see where it would work best for you. Letting it settle in one place will allow it to build up a presence so that it slowly gains strength.

Technique two: creatures

This is a similar technique to the eye, but one where you have to be a little more cautious in what you use. As you advance as a magician, you can use more diverse creatures, but to start with it is better to work with creatures that are well known for working and living with humans: dogs and cats.

This technique is not about creating a servitor or a thought-form which are creations of your own mind that are then exteriorised, rather it triggers a vessel for a land being to operate through. These are two very different things.

Like the eye, this technique works by intent and resonance: the land beings (faery beings) are already aware of you via your work in the inner landscape and in your working space. By bringing into the house a figurine with specific features and focusing a particular intent at it, you slowly create a window that a being can use.

The features of the figurine allow the land being to 'behave' and communicate in a specific way: it is almost like a rule-book or a vocabulary. The eyes of the figurine are a filter through which the being watches, the ears filter listening, and the mouth filters warnings. This is why it is important that they are not figures with bared teeth or sharp claws.

Two important points to take note of with this technique are:

1. Do not make the figurine yourself. That will most likely lead to the creation of a thought-form, an extension of yourself. While that is okay if it happens with the eye, when it comes to animal figures it can get messy. The creation of thought-forms is something you will eventually learn, but to do it successfully and safely there are a lot of things that need to be taken into consideration.

2. Be very careful what sort of image you use. It needs to have clear, open eyes, good-sized ears, an attentive stance, no teeth showing, and have nothing dangerous about it. This is really important, particularly if you live with other people or there are pets or children in your house.

I have come across magicians in the past who have used this passive technique with fantasy figures that are bristling with weapons, teeth, claws, and god knows what else, and the spirits that flow through such vessels will often attack a child/pet/person who wanders accidentally into the ritual space.

A few years ago I got into a similar mess. I created the vessel of a dog with huge teeth and big ears and eyes, and asked it to guard me during a round of work I was doing. I didn't create a thought-form; rather I created a vessel that a local faery being could work through.

It was too successful. My then partner started having terrible nightmares every night of a ferocious dog attacking him, and he would wake up covered in scratches. The attacks slowly became more physical, and very intense. The spirit had decided that my partner was a threat to me and that he had to go. Actually, the spirit was right, it just took me a while longer to find out for myself.

So you can see how, if you are successful in your technique, such a figurine can become a serious problem in a household. But getting a figurine like a cat or a dog with no teeth showing, in a form that is clearly a pet, is safe. You do not want them to savage anyone; just to bark or mew if there is a problem, and also act as guardians of your ritual space. They will scare off minor intrusions, and will alert you to any spirits trying to inch into your territory.

The way they alert you is through your inner senses, through sound, touch, and smell. For instance, I used to keep a 'cat' in my work-space. When I would meditate, sometimes I would feel a cat brush up against me.

One day I was deep in meditation when I felt a paw on my leg. I ignored it, but the paw became more insistent. So I opened my eyes to see that a candle in one of the directions had flared pretty badly and was in danger of setting light to a wall hanging. (Big lesson for me: be careful where you put candles!) The spirit operating through the cat used the interface of the cat's behaviour and body (paw) to warn me. The image becomes a shared vocabulary that the spirit can operate through and with.

Here are some images of standard figurines that would work well. The cat and dog have clear eyes, good ears, no teeth showing, and are in awake/alert stances.

Figure 6: Cat and dog figurines

As you see, there is nothing magical about them: no fancy sigils, no ritualisation, nothing. Just cute dog and cat ornaments. This also comes in handy if another magician should try to invade your space: these figurines are enlivened passively, so they do not appear with a magical 'frequency', which in turn makes them invisible to any magician or being trying to invade your space. They just sit on a shelf in your ritual space, are invisible, and do a low-level, subtle job.

The way to activate these figures is very simple and very unglamorous. Once you have your figure or figures, place them in a dish and cover them with salt for twenty-four hours to clean out anything energetically stuck to them.

Then the next time you are opening the directions to do work, once the directions and the gates are open, go and get the figure and place it on the central altar. Let it soak up the frequency of the room and the work that you are doing. Do this when you are simply tuning, doing The Anchor, or something similar. Once you have finished your work, stand in front of the figure and ask it to watch over the room and warn you if an intruder, whether human or spirit, comes near your space.

Pick up the figure and walk around the working space until you find the best place that feels right for it to sit in. Put it where it can see around the room, and like the eye, every time you leave the room, look at it and ask it to watch over and warn.

In return, the spirit that works through the figure gets to partake of a small amount of the energy that is generated by the magic in the room. They will stay for as long as they are happy to stay. You cannot force the spirit to stay there, which would be tantamount to slavery; you simply offer a vessel for them that is a halfway stage towards being in the physical world (which a lot of spirits enjoy experiencing) and in return they warn you when needed.

Often a spirit does not work through the vessel straight away: taking it into the space while the gates are open tunes the frequency in the substance of the figure. Talking to it with intent alerts the beings around you as to what you are trying to achieve. If one is willing, it will step into the figure and operate it. They are not trapped in the vessel, nor are they fully contained in it; it is more like a window for them that provides a two-way access between the spirit world and the human world. The more you interact with the figurine, the stronger that window becomes.

This is not everyone's cup of tea, and it is not a mandatory exercise for the Quareia training, but it is something you can learn a lot from as it builds over the months. If you do this exercise, just make sure that as the ritual space starts to fill up with tools, eyes, figures, images, etc., that you make sure each one is comfortable where it is. Don't, for example, put a bird or spider next to a cat: go by the outer images and how they would act in the physical world.

An adept's household will not look magical at all to an outsider, but when you look more closely you will see that the house is filled with tools, spirits, figurines, images, a deity or two, all placed subtly but carefully. No altars to be seen, nothing showy, just something very subtle but very present.

And to anyone with inner sight, an adept house will show no magical seals, no magical circles, no banishing patterns; just a house full of spirits, beings, enlivened energies, and odd creatures coming and going all the time.

It will not be Fort Knox; it will be more like Grand Central Station. And that is where its strength is. All the members of the household pitch in to help, and in return they get shelter, a human to interact with, and become a part of a balanced community of humans, energies, and spirits.

8. *Task:* Working with bottles, dilution and succussion

To do this practical work, repeat the charging of the water in the way you already learned in the previous lesson, but instead of simply pouring the water, you are going to learn how to *potentise* it.

Before you start, clean your hands with salt, water, and soap. Place a label on the bottle with the name of the watercourse that you intend to work with. Don't work with the same watercourse you worked with in the last lesson, choose a different one so that you can monitor over time the results of the work you did in the last lesson.

Know that the bottle you use must only ever be used on one watercourse: the bottle will build up a particular resonance of the work you do on a specific river/lake/stream.

When you work to charge the water (when you hold your hand over the water), keep the specific watercourse you intend to work on in your mind: when you do the charging, be very clear what watercourse you are charging the water for. Once the water is charged and in the vessel, close down the directions and leave the water on the west altar.

Now comes the alchemical action. Have your clean (unchlorinated) water in a bottle ready to use to dilute, and have a thick book to use for the succussion. Make sure that the glass bottle is very clean and has been swilled out with boiled water.

Also have a large jug to hand: you will be pouring a lot of water away in the dilution process. You can do this part of the work either in your working space, or in a kitchen (not a bathroom).

Pour some of the charged water into the bottle, swill it around, and then pour it out into the jug. Now place ten drops of the charged water into the glass bottle using the glass dropper. Fill the bottle with the clean water almost to the top and put the stopper in/lid on.

Holding the bottle with your thumb on the stopper/lid, now bang the bottle on the book one hundred times (count it). Bang hard enough to make the water jump with energy, but not with such force that it would break the glass. The book will give a bit, which helps the rebound: this is the technique known as *succussion*. When you have finished, take the stopper off, draw a dropper's worth of the water from the glass bottle, and pour the rest of the water away into the jug.

Drop ten drops of water from the dropper into the glass bottle (squirt the rest into the jug), fill it up with the clean water, replace the stopper, and succuss the bottle again one hundred times on the book. Repeat this until the water has been diluted thirty times.

I know that succussion is hard and boring, and many students have been silly enough to skip this part of the lesson. That is a folly indeed. This technique is a very powerful one that can be used for all sorts of different magical applications, and it is a technique that must be worked with as an apprentice so that you are *physically* familiar with it and have full practical experience of it. Do not file it away in the back of your head to 'do when I think I might need it'. Having that attitude to magical learning is a path of failure. There are a lot of things you have been doing that are interlocking together to ensure that you can magically work with this method at this point in your training. And lastly, if you want to work on the environment, this is one of the most potent things you can do for the long term health/survival/fate patterns of water courses. It can also be used in healing, exorcism, construction – its applications are endless, which is something you will realise as an adept. Ok, lecture over.

What you are left with when you have finished your dilutions and successions, is charged and potentised water that has been focused with a specific intent to rebalance a particular watercourse. Place the bottle in the west of your work space where it cannot be knocked off until you are ready to use it. Ensure it is not kept next to strong smelling substances, televisions, wifi routers, computers, phones, etc. Its energetic vibration is very fine indeed, so it needs to be kept in an energetic/

electrical quiet place. One such place would be in a bookcase surrounded by books that would 'buffer' or muffle any incoming energies that could affect it.

As soon as you can, take the bottle and the dropper to the watercourse you intend to work on. From now on, keep both the bottle and the dropper only for use on this watercourse, as they are now tuned to such via the succussion/dilution. It is best dispensed on or just before a full moon, a power peak for water. Conversely, if you feel that the watercourse needs *slow* unfolding of its rebalancing, then do it at a new moon.

When you get to the water course, drop ten drops only of the charged water into the watercourse. There is no need for any ritual act, though singing or talking to the water/river will wake things up. Tell the river these drops are to help it rebalance.

Take the rest of the water in the bottle back home. When you get home, do a reading using the TREE OF LIFE LAYOUT to see if it would be helpful in the long term for the river/water to be given the ten drops at each full moon, or every three months, or whether that one dose was enough. The way to ascertain this is to ask:

> *"Would it help the watercourse for its long-term balance if the drops were dispensed every full moon?"*
>
> *"...every three months?"*
>
> *"...was once enough?"*

The reason you look at the long-term picture specifically is that such charged and potentised water acts as a strong catalyst which can cause a crisis reaction before it finally settles into balance. So the short-term readings may look disastrous, but the longer-term ones would show balance and harmony.

Because the charged water is to be used on a watercourse, do not worry about the water in terms of bacteria growing in it, etc. If you are going to work on the river over a span of a year for example, then the charged water would not be clean to drink, but it will still be fine for the river.

If you wish to work with this method on different watercourses in your area, do no more than three at any one time: it can get too much for you and for the rivers, and could trigger massive local flooding. This act is a tiny magical catalyst, and as such, it can trigger huge reactions if such are needed. It is a dynamic that can be hard for people to understand as many people are used to having to do huge acts to have huge reactions, but in magic often the opposite is true.

Keep a computer log of any changes you notice with the watercourse you are working on, and also any beings that turn up as you are working. Store the bottle(s) away from direct sunlight, keep them in the west, and if you work with more than one bottle, make sure that they are all well labelled: a strong wooden box is a good home for the dilution bottles.

If you wish to experiment further with this technique, choose something you wish to work on, but before you go on to do the work, do readings to see what the short-term and long-term effect will be. Use TREE OF LIFE READINGS, and for longer-term, more in-depth details of the effect, use the LANDSCAPE/DESERT LAYOUT.

Also do readings to see how the work would affect you in the short and long term: this technique can be a strong catalyst at times, so ensure that you are aware of all the parameters before you go ahead with the work. If it seems okay to go ahead, then keep a computer log of your actions and the outcomes.

9. *TASK:* WORKING WITH STRINGS, MEASURING A TERM OF SERVICE

This is a really simple technique and is passive, but it will teach you a bit more about how cords can work. If you are doing a series of workings, like the water drops, for example, you can link yourself to the work by using a cord made of string. Before you start the round of work, cut a length of string that would fit comfortably round your wrist or ankle (left for work, right for fate). Wrap the string around your cord of life and keep it there until you are ready to work.

When you start the magical work and the directions are open and running, take the string and place it on the directional altar that the work is focused on.

Before you close down the directions from the initial working, go to the altar the string is on. Pick up the string and declare verbally that the string is a link, an umbilical cord between you and the work at hand, and that you will wear it until the work is finished. Then put the string on your wrist or ankle and keep it on until the work is finished or until it falls off, whichever happens first.

During the day touch the string and think about your work space. This creates a passive link between you and the work, one that keeps the energy flowing until the work is done. It marks out a term of service, and energetically keeps a line going between you and the work while also deepening that link slightly.

It is a weak, passive, but interesting way to work, and it also teaches you a lot about how cords operate. It is something I have worked with a lot, and I do notice a difference between working with a cord in this way and not using one. The link is subtle but stronger, and in between the active working rituals/visions you can touch the string through the day with the intention to connect with the energy of the ongoing work, which keeps your foot in the door. The cord is powered by the tuning on the altar and by your focused intention.

Again, this is an action you can track in readings. Experiment with it, do readings to see what effect it *will* have, and then when you are actually doing it and wearing the cord, redo the readings to look at what effect it is *actually having*. Not only will that teach you about how cords work, (or not, sometimes), but it will also teach you the difference between a reading of an action that is intended, and an action that is actively being done. Sometimes there are differences. Intention is one thing, but actually doing something often brings in elements that you did not plan or were not expected, and that can change the result. Using readings in this way will teach you a lot about how patterns of magic and behaviour 'fix' once they are set in motion.

10. Summary

Using these lesser, passive tools and techniques will teach you a lot about how magic operates in ways that the official tools will not. It trains you work with resonance and intent, which is something that is not often worked with or talked about in magic these days, and yet is one of the more subtle but powerful ways to approach magic.

It also teaches you to move away from the modern dogma and rediscover a whole avenue of magic that is very personal to you: this form of magic relies very heavily on how you work with your mind and imagination. It will also, once you have worked these methods a few times, teach you the mechanics behind a whole branch of folk magic. Often folk magic becomes dressed over time in top-heavy, ritualised actions, when really very simple dynamics are working underneath that dressing. It will also give you practical experience that will in turn help you to spot when magic is overdressed. Learning the core elements of passive magic will help you see how to strip an overdressed method back to its bones and work with it in a less dogmatic way.

Later in your studies you will learn more controlled and formed magical methods. You will then learn how to fuse together the formed magic with more passive, fluid actions and tools to create a whole solid and balanced magical structure or form.

Lesson 7
Myths as Tools

The form of magic you are learning in Quareia is the underbelly of magical forms that draws on all sorts of streams of magic as opposed to a specific tradition. There is a good reason for this. Many magical traditions, particularly in the West, have slowly been formed into quite rigid orthodoxies which can end up severely limiting the magician.

In the 1960s there was a shift in magical thinking in the West that gave birth to a stream of magic called *Chaos Magic*. This broke apart those narrow ways of thinking and opened up new vistas for magicians. Over time Chaos Magic developed its own orthodoxy in a strange sort of way, but it also profoundly changed how we thought of magic. A great deal of experimentation was done. Some of the new techniques worked well, some did not work, and some worked but with 'chaotic' outcomes.

That enabled magicians to look beyond the parameters of the narrow confines in Western magic and understand that magic has underlying harmonics, patterns, and streams of energy that work well together (and some that do not) regardless of their cultural origins. Over the last forty years, I have spent a lot of time tapping into these various different threads to find which of them work well in combinations, and which do not.

One of the things I discovered was that supposed mythic cultural expressions of magic were not actually connected to a specific culture at all; rather they were connected to certain patterns of power that were sometimes connected with a landmass and sometimes not.

The mythologies and stories that have built up around these power patterns hold keys as to how to interact or tap into a particular type of magic, and use it, if it is compatible, with the land where you intend to work or the situation you find yourself in. This method of approach works with the myths as tools and guides, as opposed to orthodoxies or streams to be immersed in.

Some schools of thought in magic tapped into those mythic streams and immersed themselves within them as an *operating system:* the myth became the backbone and main form of expression for the magic. The magician would strongly identify with a myth and would, by working closely within the mythic pattern over an extended period of time, find themselves 'living the myth.'

The British stream of magic immersing itself in the Arthurian myth is a good example of this. But such immersion is very limiting and can quickly devolve down into psychology. It can also become a limiting cane that the magician leans upon:

"If it's not British and it's not Arthurian, it's not coming in!"

You can see how quickly that narrows down the field of operation of the magician, and how such a practice can become a quasi-religion.

The other problem with such immersion is that often the magician can find themselves trapped in a mythic scenario where they are funnelled into reliving the pattern of the myth, frequently with difficult or sad outcomes.

The key is not to use these cultural myths as an identity or operating system for the magic, but simply use them as magical tools – which is I think what they were intended for in the first place. Rather than immersing themselves in one cultural myth as a magical identity, the magician taps into different myths from different places as they present themselves and when necessary, and works within them as tools for specific jobs. The myths become *maps* or *guidebooks,* and often tell you how to operate the main magical tools (dos and don'ts). And this is how they were first worked with.

The myths often track back to a time before writing, and were oral traditions that were passed unchanged from one generation to the next. As a child you learn the epic stories, but later as a magical adult, you realise that the myth is not just a story, but is an *instruction book* on how to deal with the local powers, not in a dogmatic way, but in a poetic way. The surface story is often hung on a frame of power dynamics that act as indicators for fate patterns, an example of which you will find later in this lesson. Learning to read these myths first as stories, and then through the eyes of the magician, you will come to learn the fragments of working methods, warnings, directions, and paths to take.

As you develop as a magician you will come to realise that stories and myths are extensions of the magical sword and the gate of the east: the act of myth-making and storytelling is a technique, but the myth itself becomes a tool. It can act as a guide/teacher, but as an adept you will also learn how to use myth and story as a magical filter for power to flow through. It is not an enactment of a myth; rather it is using a mythic pattern to contain and dispense energy and power.

And this is where it gets interesting. The magician often does not choose the mythical pattern. Instead, the mythic pattern is indicated to the magician as the appropriate tool for the job by the beings and inner contacts that surround the magician and by the situation they find themselves in. The beings and inner contacts drop very large hints or put the myth in your path for you to find.

Myths are not recipes that you can flick through to find the most useful keys: often the keys that the magician needs are not the most obvious ones. And the myth has to be the right fit for the job. But when there is a particular myth that the magician needs to be working with, the magician will cross paths with that myth. The reason for this is that we humans are fairly limited in what we can perceive when it comes to the bigger picture in magic, whereas spirit beings and inner contacts have a wider overview: they can see which mythic pattern would fit for the magician to do a job. But in turn the inner contacts and spirits do not have physical bodies that can instigate physical actions: the union of magician and beings brings together two sets of very different skills and puts them into action.

This subject matter is complex, and spotting it in action can be even more complicated. Often the involvement of a mythic pattern is subtle enough to pass the magician by, but if you pay attention then the message gets through. Often these mythic patterns are entwined around the stories of traditional magical tools (swords, stones, wands, cups) and their stories tell you about them; other times they tell of more obscure dynamics that the magician can engage with. The appearance of a myth to a magician can also indicate a job that needs doing, or an event that is about to happen, or can tell you that you have just completed a pattern without realising it, and that completion opens the door for the next phase of development or work for the magician.

In the past I was often submerged in a mythic pattern unknowingly, and bumbled my way through it without realising what was happening. It took until the last decade for me to learn to recognise where these patterns were active or had been activated, and how to work consciously with them rather than simply being swept along with them. So hopefully, through this lesson, you will learn far quicker than I did, which may come in very useful for you.

The magician doesn't work with mythic patterns all the time: some magicians will only touch on them once or twice in a lifetime. But some will repeatedly work with different myths at different times of their lives. There are no bullet points for this sort of work; rather the magician has to develop the skill of listening to or reading a story and allowing the keys to emerge through that process. This is why so many ancient systems used mythic stories as their foundations, and why it was considered so important to learn the stories and epic poems – a tradition that still exists to this day in many cultures.

Also bear in mind that when these myths trigger, it is usually because you as a magician are visiting or are living on a land where a job needs doing. Occasionally these myths will trigger to protect you or enable you, so that you can continue doing what you do. This is a dynamic I have spoken about a lot in magic: if you are working in service and doing what you are supposed to be doing, then the inner worlds, spirits, and contacts will step up and help you, protect you, and make sure you have what you need.

1. Two examples of myths as tools in action

Let's take a look at some examples of when this scenario has actually come into play. The best way to tell you about these mythic dynamics is through stories of my encounters with myths. That way you can see from a practical point of view how this works, and how these myths become tools. Bear in mind when you read what follows that I can be extraordinarily dumb sometimes, so often the contacts really have to shove something in my face before I get it.

To show you how these mythic patterns work and interact, I will tell you the stories of what happened first, and then I will give you a breakdown of what was actually happening magically and what that taught me about how to use the myths as tools rather than operating systems.

The first story is not about a traditional tool; rather it is about an act of rebalancing a debt between ancestral lines, faery beings, and the land. At the time I had no clue what the hell was happening, and this strongly illustrates how, as magicians, we can be drawn into these mythic patterns without even realising. Then we will move on to a story about how the pattern of a myth was presented to me in order for me to do magical service in a land area. It shows how magical tools emerge in these myths, and how you use the myth to operate the tool.

2. The story of Ulster and Loughareema

When I first moved back to the UK in 2008 I was invited by some magical friends to go to Ulster in Northern Ireland, and to do some magical work with them. I put all my focus into the magical work, thinking that was what I was going over for. In the past I have worked a lot with magical groups in Ulster, and before that I had spent many a summer there as a child. So I was on very familiar ground when I went over in 2008 to work with fellow magicians. I had planned that we would do a particular round of work and I was all prepared for that.

The inner lot had a different agenda...

After we had finished the magical work we went off to explore the northern coast and various features around Ulster. I have old blood connections with a line in Ulster, and we went around various places connected to those ancestors. I could feel a lot going on, but had no clue as to what it actually was.

The first mythic pattern kicked in, though I didn't realise it at the time, when we visited a cairn of one of my ancestors, who was tied in with the kingship in Ulster (my drop of connected blood comes from his daughter). Before we went to the cairn itself we visited the shoreline. I got a strong urge to pick up a stone to place on his cairn. I hunted around and one stone in particular caught my eye: it was a stone shaped by the sea into the form of a penis. I thought this was hilarious. So I picked it up and took it to the mound.

Once I got to the cairn I went silent and tried to connect with this ancestor. Eventually I got a connection and told him that I had brought a penis stone for him. He told me that was all well and good, but his body was not in the cairn. I asked him where his body was. He pointed in two different, almost opposite directions, and said his body was in pieces and not in the cairn.

I felt bad for him, and asked him if in that case the stone was a waste of time. Should I find his body, or part of it, and put the stone with it? The answer came back as no; I was to place the stone on the cairn as he could still use it. I placed the stone in the centre of the mound, opened my eyes, and talked to the historian that was with us.

He confirmed that there was no body in the cairn: he had been beheaded and his head had gone to Dublin, where it had been placed on a spike outside Dublin Castle. The rest of his body had been buried at Crosskern church above Cushendun. I didn't give the penis stone much more thought, and after spending a little time communing with the ancestor, who was still very much upon and within the land, we left and continued our adventure.

We went to a place called Loughareema, a vanishing lake in the middle of nowhere. It is a curious and magical place where a lake occasionally 'vanishes,' leaving behind an area of mud. It is not tidal; rather it is semi-plugged with mud. When the mud shifts, the lake empties down into the water table and the caverns below. It's a very magical place, with a moon pool, windswept moorland, and a strong sense of land/faery power.

When we arrived the lake had vanished and left behind swirls of mud that reached downwards, a bit like a plughole. I was strongly drawn to the plughole; me and my love of 'red buttons'! The others wanted to explore the moon pool and the ridge beyond.

So off I went, and I climbed down and down, closer to the plughole. As I got close to where the lake vanishes into the Underworld, I got stuck in the mud. At first I didn't think anything of it, and just hauled my way through the mud. Then I realised I was sinking quickly into the mud up to my calves, and it was getting dangerous.

I could just see my friends on the hill, and I waved madly at them. They waved back, smiling. I gesticulated wildly that was I was in trouble and was sinking fast. One of them got the message and came running over. Eventually they hauled me out of the mud and pulled me onto the bank of the lake. My left shoe was left behind, and the mud swallowed it. I staggered out of the mud, with one shoe on, and went to rest on a stone by the moon pool. A really strong contact talked out of the moon pool and asked for my other shoe, which was soaking wet and covered in mud. So I took the shoe off and left it on the stone by the moon pool.

As I took it off, I joked with my friends that the moon pool wanted my shoe. "Of course it does," two of them replied. "The shoes/water is a major connection to the kingship in Ulster." I had, at that time, no idea what they were talking about, but I was happy to be able to do what the pool wanted: give it my shoes.

Looking back, this was a turning point for me in regards to connecting with the land in a powerful way: shortly after this event I was manoeuvred by fate to go live in the very magical place that I now live in. Where I live now is a place steeped in mythic patterns that connect strongly to the pre-Roman Celtic British myths and powers.

So what the hell was going on? I could feel all sorts of powerful things happening, but was totally clueless as to what it meant. First I will tell you the mythic patterns that were triggering, and then what it led to, how it worked, and why it worked.

The mythic patterns

The first pattern that triggered, which I was working within without realising it, is the mythic pattern of *Osiris*. In the myth Osiris, who is an Egyptian deity heavily connected to kingship, is dismembered. Isis cannot find his penis as the fish had eaten it, so she gave him a new one, one she fashioned using magic. This restored the power of the kingship/deity. What would an Egyptian myth have to do with Ireland? Well, besides the fact that there was likely trade between Egypt and Ireland (and also the British Isles) for silver, tin, gold and copper, Ireland has a few mythic stories connected with Egypt, regarding kingship stones. Or it may have triggered because I had been immersed in Egyptian mythos for a while.

The second mythic pattern that triggered was the myth of *Fergus mac Leda and the Wee Folk*.

To cut a long myth short: one morning King Fergus of Ulster finds a faery couple, Bebo (the faery queen) and Lubdan (the faery king) trapped in a cauldron of porridge that was prepared the night before. He cannot believe his luck: he hauls them out of the porridge but will not let them go; he decides to hold them hostage.

Eventually he relents, on the condition that Lubdan give him a special faery treasure (a magical tool or skill) that belongs to Lubdan: the Water Shoes. These will allow the wearer to travel upon and under the water. Lubdan grudgingly gives him the Water Shoes and Fergus releases the couple. As aside, if you are interested in Celtic lore, this story has an interesting poem in it recited by Bebo where Lubdan tells of which tree wood to use for what purpose.

So we have two totally and seemingly unrelated mythic patterns playing out. How and why? Let's have a look.

The mythic patterns in action

The first mythic pattern that kicked in when I visited the cairn of an ancestor was the pattern that can be found in the myth of Osiris. Osiris is cut to pieces by Set, and Isis, devastated, sets out to find his body parts. She cannot retrieve his penis, as the fish have eaten it.[1] So Isis fashions him one using magic and restores him, which in turn restores the inner power of the kingship (Osiris and kingship are tightly linked).

Now this is where we look at the myth as power keys/patterns, not as a story to be followed. The keys in this myth that reflect a pattern which then played out in my visit to Ulster were: the female of a blood line giving the dismembered body of a king a replacement penis, and it is done by a female priest who does not eat fish, I don't, ever, yuck, I won't touch fish. This restores an inner power of kingship:

---

[1] The source of the taboo in Dynastic Egypt for priests, male or female, to not eat fish.

the wrong was righted. My role was as that female: I fitted keys of the pattern. I have a drop of the right blood and also am a consecrated priest, which created a tenuous connection; I found a replacement penis and restored something. What did that job do? I had no idea. But the second mythic pattern gave me a clue.

The second mythic pattern of King Fergus tells of a man taking a faery power under duress while the faery beings were trapped in porridge. (Mud... porridge is like mud.) He held the faery beings to ransom, something which is guaranteed to bring long term bad luck. That leaves a bad feeling between an ancestral kingship line and the faery beings of the land.

By going to a faery lake Loughareema is a faery power spot, and relinquishing my 'watered' shoes under duress while trapped in mud, (I would have died in that sinking mud if I had not been pulled out as I was directly over the hole that the lake vanished into.) I mythically 'gave back' something that had been taken so long ago.

I have direct female blood from the Ulster kingship line, albeit far in the past, and that fact, woven with giving back shoes, in a water situation, trapped in mud, at a faery lake, were the keys that triggered something to happen at a deep level. Note that the myth reversed itself: this time it was the mortal who was 'trapped in the porridge' and had to relinquish the water shoes.

I did not know about this myth at the time I was at the lake, but I knew that I had to answer the demand for my shoes. And I did not give them up lightly. It was March in Northern Ireland, cold, wet, and far from anywhere. I was in cold, muddy, bare feet for a chunk of the day. And no one could find shoes small enough for me. I have faery feet: they are tiny. Even the smallest person in the group had bigger feet than me. So, like the faery king and queen, I had to go without my shoes.

And as an odd aside that ties into this myth for me as a person that fitted the pattern, years before this incident, as a dancer I had danced upon a lake.

As a publicity stunt for a major festival, a platform had been constructed just under the waterline and I was photographed seemingly dancing upon the water, as you can see in Figure 7.

The watery shoes had come from a mortal who had danced upon the water. (See how weird and tenuous the mythic links can be?)

Figure 7: Dancing on water
Photographer: Tim Smith for Bradford UK Heritage Recording Unit

It was not until much later, when I had repeated dreams that replayed that event, that I looked up the myth of Fergus in depth and sort of 'got' what that event had been all about. So why was a pair of cheap, muddy shoes so important? This is how the mythic patterns play out. We place far too much emphasis on what we consider to be the sparkly bits in a myth, and will re-enact them to the letter, when in fact it is often the simple, seemingly innocuous aspects of the story that hold the power keys.

These days we also get into very serious role-play, ritual, and drama around the use of mythic patterns, which causes the magician to totally miss the point. Like fate patterns, mythic patterns are often triggered by simple, seemingly meaningless or random aspects of the myth: if you have the right base ingredients, the right time, place, and people, it clicks a magical pattern into action.

I was in the right place, at the right time, with the right ingredients in my fate pattern to trigger a shift that would bring some sort of deep change in the relationship between the ancestral lines, the living humans, and the land: I fitted the keys of some mythic patterns and was willing to 'give.' I followed my instincts and found a penis, and I followed my instincts to climb down into the vanishing lake, becoming trapped and 'held to ransom.' So it all worked.

What was my link to the Egyptian myth of Osiris? Well, I have worked with Egyptian goddesses for decades, and a lot of my visionary work had connected for years with some of the patterns that flow through Egyptian magic. So I am presuming that is what triggered that myth, along with the pattern of an ancestral kingship power that needed something putting back in place. Also there is the point that the stone of kingship in Ireland, the Lia Fáil, or Stone of Destiny has a myth around it that it travelled to Ireland from Egypt via Spain. And I placed a penis stone on the cairn of the fallen king; like Osiris, his/that power can rise again. As the old saying goes, wheels within wheels, which means there are many layers to the tale. For Ireland, which has been an occupied country for eight hundred years, to find its true nature and balance, first the relationship between the humans, their leaders, the land and the faery race must first be settled before the nation can blossom once more. It doesn't mean that the kingship will be restored as that time went many years ago, rather it is about the relationship between the leaders and the land.

The thing to note in all of this is that the mythic triggering was not for me, or about me: it was for the land and the ancestral connection with the land. Something needed a catalyst to bring change, and I was that bumbling catalyst. We had a 'restoration' and recreation of an organ of the body of a king, righting a wrong and adding to a completion; then a descendant of a king giving back water shoes to a faery place in a reversal of the ransoming, righting a wrong and settling a debt. In return I was given a safe place to live that is steeped in powerful faery contact. But my 'giving' had to be without condition or the expectation of receiving in return.

And hopefully you are now starting to think about magical tools in a different way – they are not just objects, they can be patterns and stories that carry power and flow through objects. A magical tool is something that adds a power point which when triggered brings about magical and often physical change. Magical stories hold power points and patterns that magic can flow through. A lot of magicians ignore such, or label it as 'folk magic' or 'shamanism', which is a form of magical snobbery. Magic flows through a great many different things, and a magician works with what presents that is stable and recognisable; that is how magic evolves.

3. The story of the monster in the lake and Beowulf

This is a story that tells you a lot about the interaction between a magician, a magical tool, and a mythic pattern. I have mentioned this once before in one of my books, but I think it will be most useful to tell it again here. It is a story that shows how these mythic patterns can work even when off their original lands, and it also tells us a lot about magical swords in particular.

When you read what I did, and then read about the different swords of Beowulf, you will start to see how the mythic story of Beowulf passes on wisdoms about how different swords work, and how you are to behave with them. First we will look at my encounter with the Beowulf story, and then look at what it tells us about swords and about beings that can inhabit water and cause problems for us.

When I lived in the USA, there was a time when I lived on the edge of a lake. It was a small community and the land was very powerful in a strange and disturbed way.

Every night I would have nightmares, and my energies got lower and lower: I thought I was getting sick. During this time, when I was at work, people kept talking to me about Beowulf in various ways. I was teaching teens at the time, and different students kept showing me projects, books, paintings, etc. to do with Beowulf. This went on for months and I still did not realise that a large hint was being thrown my way. I had the story more than once as a child, and I just assumed it was turning up a lot because I was dealing with teenagers who were studying it at school.

My weakness got more and more intense, and when I started talking to the locals I found that they all had the same problem: nightmares and feeling very weak all the time. During this time I got a strong message to drop my magical sword into the water.

I did readings to see why, and the reason was obscured from me; but the readings also showed that the instinct was right and had a definite purpose. This magical sword was a working tool, had never shed blood and had never been used in anger: it was used only to limit, guard, and balance. I was quite deeply attached to this sword as it had been through many adventures with me, but I also had a responsibility to answer a magical call. So late one night under the cover of darkness and also the mists that had formed over the lake, a friend and I set out onto the lake in a boat, and I dropped the sword into the lake at the centre, in the deepest part of the water.

At first (because I am dumb) I did not make the connection between the weakness that was affecting everyone who lived by the lake, and the dropping of the sword (duh). But a few days later it did occur to me that something magical was happening. So I started to pay more attention to what was going on by watching the lake in vision, and tuning into the energetic feel of the lake. To cut this part of the story short, I discovered that strange parasitic beings were coming out of the water and literally sucking the life out of people.

I watched this happen repeatedly for a while, and then decided I needed to do something about it. Around that time I was also finally starting to get the Beowulf hint, so I sat down and read the epic poem. I still didn't get it (like I said, dumb). One night, just before a full moon, I decided that this was the night to tackle this problem. I waited until the strange parasitic beings came out of the water and then I went in vision into the lake to see where they were coming from. I dived down and down, and found myself in a strange sort of hall with a huge fat monster-like creature at the bottom of the lake; a massive overfed long term parasite.

The creature was undefended and seemed to ignore me totally, as if I could not possibly be of any danger to it: it was so used to being unchallenged that it had become complacent. It was then that I spotted my magical sword. It was hanging on a 'wall' and beaming brightly. I grabbed the sword and shoved it up to the hilt into the neck of the being, killing it instantly.

I dropped the sword, swam back up to the surface and went back to my body. By my body was one of the strange parasites, and it was dying: they were extensions of the big mother being in the lake, and when it was killed, it killed all of them.

I started to get stronger, the nightmares stopped, and the locals also started to get better. Shortly after that I was 'moved on,' something that used to happen to me a lot: I would do a job in a land area where I lived, and as soon as the job was done I would suddenly be put in a situation where I had to move.

I sat down and read Beowulf again, carefully this time, and finally I spotted what had been going on, why Beowulf had been shoved in my face for so long, and that the mythic poem was in fact a 'how to' myth about dealing with these strange and powerful beings that can reside in lakes and affect people badly. If I had not been so tired and unfocused, I would have picked up on the Beowulf hint a lot earlier, read it, figured out what needed doing, and done it. However it did eventually get done, and thankfully I followed the hidden advice in the poem and heeded the warnings without realising it.

Note how the myth is from a very different land, yet it was still relevant to the situation. These days, if a myth suddenly gets thrust repeatedly in my face, I take the time to sit down and read it. Even if I still do not understand why it has suddenly appeared, the act of reading it a few times puts the keys into your head so that when you come to wield a magical tool in a mythic pattern you heed the advice and warnings, which in turn teaches you about how the tool works.

So let us take a look at the hints and keys that lie hidden in Beowulf, and how they gave directions about how to deal with a magical land issue. And we will look at how the 'patterns' fitted for me so that I could do the job (the same dynamic that played out in the Ulster story).

4. BEOWULF: SOME KEYS

The first key that fitted the lock was that Beowulf, the hero who slays the monster was from 'over the sea' and sailed to Sjælland (Zealand, Denmark). I came to the USA from a place over the sea: I was a stranger that crossed a sea. And just for an added bit of mythic twists and turns, I came to the USA from a land and place (west Yorkshire in northern Britain) that was close to Denmark and was under the Danelaw (Danish kings Rule) for many years. Some of the mythic patterns in the north west of Britain are the same as the Scandinavian ones. I came to a place where a 'monster' lay deep underwater and whose offspring terrorised the locals. The dropping of the magical sword that had shed no mortal blood (magically or otherwise) into the water became the *sword of giants* in the Beowulf poem that eventually worked to kill the monster.

In the battle between Beowulf and Grendel's mother, he takes a sword given to him by Unferth for the task, a sword known as *Hrunting*:

> ...And another item lent by Unferth
> at that moment of need was of no small importance:
> the brehon handed him a hilted weapon,
> a rare and ancient sword named Hrunting.
> The iron blade with its ill-boding patterns
> had been tempered in blood. It had never failed
> the hand of anyone who hefted it in battle...[2]

This is the first lesson that the poem gives: a sword that has been blooded in battle is a battle sword; it is not a magical sword. An inner being (with no physical form) cannot be slain with a blood sword which has torn human flesh or harmed a mortal with magic; it can only be slain by a magical sword that had never been used against a mortal: the *sword of giants*.

The first sword, Hrunting, was a blood sword and so of course it did not kill Grendel's Mother. The giant's sword that he grabbed in the struggle was a magical sword, and so it worked. It hovered aloft near a wall in Grendel's mother's cave, and shone with magic. However, and this is another key in the myth, Beowulf then did something he should not have done: after he decapitated Grendel's Mother with the giant magical sword, he sees the body of Grendel as the monster lay dead. In a rage, he decapitates the corpse of Grendel as a punishment and also to put it on show. As a result, the sword melted and was no more, or in some versions it shatters or breaks in two.

This is an important key with magical swords. It was fair and just to kill the being that had been terrorising and feeding off of others (the locals), but it was not fair and just to then strike a body even though it was dead, and for the reason of rage and revelling in the death. That is an unbalanced use of the sword and went beyond solving a problem: the magical sword is about restoring balance, but nothing beyond that. So the sword was taken from him and its magic dissolved.

Later, when Beowulf had need of a magic sword once more, this time to slay the dragon, it was not there for him. Instead he used *Naegling*, a battle sword of ancient origin, which snapped when Beowulf used it.

The poem relates that Beowulf's strength snapped the sword as he thrust it into the dragon. Beowulf still was not getting that it is the magic in a sword that slays magical beings, not its battle history nor the strength of the fighter: his battle hardness was at odds with the magical element of the situation. This theme also appears

---

[2] Heaney, Seamus. *Beowulf*. USA: Norton, 2000. (Lines 1455–1457).

in the Arthurian story of Caliburn and Excalibur. The magical sword Caliburn is used in battle (big bad mistake) to draw blood, and so it breaks.

From my point of view in the work that I did, the magical sword in the bottom of the lake gave me the weapon to slay the being. I did not then do anything else to the being, i.e. no magical bindings, no attacks or disfigurements, I just left the monster dead, and I also left the sword there. And note that in vision, I saw the magical sword up on a wall and shining in the 'cave' of the monster; that is one of the aspects of the mythic pattern. Note how all the power points in the vision and action I took were ones that were mirrored in the story of Beowulf. When I left that area and moved back to England, another magical sword was waiting for me and was of the same power as the sword I had given to the lake: it came back to me in a strange, roundabout way so that it could be used again in the future.

Let's backtrack and dissect the sequence of events from a magician's perspective so that you can see clearly how these mythic cycles trigger for a magician, and how a magician should spot them and work with them. That way you are more likely to recognise when this happens in your own life and will be able to act accordingly. This is not really apprentice stuff, but these situations can trigger for any level of magician, so it is better that you are able to spot and recognise this dynamic in action from the early stages of your training.

5. Dissection of events at the lake

A myth repeatedly presented itself and was subsequently ignored (my first mistake). The myth presented itself because a magician was in a place of danger, and also in a place where they could work in service to change the dangerous situation.

The magician had a magical tool that would do the work. The myth gave warnings and advice about the use of the tool for a successful outcome. Although I did not use the myth as a proper guide, I had enough inner contact around me to nudge me into the right action.

The myth of Beowulf told me about the situation I was facing (even though I didn't get it at first), what needed to be done, and how to do it. The inner contacts and beings that work around me placed the myth under my nose to give me a guidebook. The pertinent contents of the myth were a lake, a monster and her children terrorising the people around the lake, a magical sword that hung in the cave of the monster, and someone from over the seas, from a land that is connected with Denmark willing to face the monster. I am not sure if the connection with Denmark was necessary or not as it was a weird roundabout connection. But then sometimes magical fate connections can be very odd indeed.

My magical training ensured that I acted to cause just the right amount of impact on the being, without crossing any lines of unbalanced behaviour – something that the myth also outlines strongly: a magical sword slays magical beings, but should not be used to bolster the ego, to dishonour, show off, or attack/harm a mortal.

If Beowulf had stuck to that rule (not decapitated Grendel and dishonoured his body), the giant's sword would not have melted and would have stayed with him to slay the dragon in the future. I was willing to let my sword go for the good of the land, and so it was returned to me. The problem was solved, and everyone moved on.

6. How the magician can use this method

Sometimes the myth is placed in your path by the inner contacts that work around you. This signals that there is a job to be done and that the myth will act as a guidebook to help you, if you follow it. Most of the time for contacted magicians, this is how it works. Sometimes the hints can be very subtle and can come to you via other magicians.

The way to work with these subtle hints that are nudging you towards myths and keys is to think sideways and not try to be logical. Inner hints are like water and will flow through the path of least resistance. A single key will present, and once the magician picks up on that key, if they follow their curiosity without trying to form a logical path, the other keys will start to appear. If you try to nail it down through logical study and analysis, the connection will close down (your logical mind will discount frail connections). Once you know what myth is presenting, read the story and take particular note of the tools/weapons/dynamics and actions in the story. Also take note of the mistakes the hero/heroine makes and understand why they were mistakes, and look at the story of the beast/spirit/deity that is causing the problem.

Once you have those keys then look at your own life and your surroundings and see if there is a connection with something that is happening or has happened around you. Once you join up the dots, follow the advice in the myth regardless of whether or not that myth is local or foreign, and do your job.

One thing to look out for is that sometimes more than one myth at a time will be playing an advisory role. This is because the myth is not an operating system; rather it is working for you as a tool (like in the Ulster story). Fragments of behaviour in different myths tell you various steps that need to be taken in order to achieve something.

This is why it was very important in many magical traditions to spend time in the early phase of training learning diverse mythic poems, stories, and songs from different lands and cultures: it's like learning your mathematical times tables. They are embedded deep in your subconscious so that they can rise back up when needed: a tool is not always something you can hold.

Myths can be like circuit boards: they are pathways that present themselves when certain powers are flowing and operating in a certain way. And this is the thing that often confounds me: humans write the myths to tell a story, but often a landscape or area will present the elements and keys of a myth not only in its natural landscape, but also in the man-made structures upon that land area. So which came first, the myth or the structure?

7. ABOUT THE PRACTICAL WORK

The practical work in this lesson is reading and exploring myths, songs, epic poems, and local legends. Have a notebook handy when you are reading as you will likely come across snippets of text that will tell you something about tools, land, powers, etc. that will come in useful to you. Just note down the snippet and also the myth it comes from. These are not notes to be submitted to mentors; they are just for yourself. However it would be wise to take those notes for your own reference later on.

8. HOW TO RECOGNISE AND WORK WITHIN MYTHIC PATTERNS

The first step to engaging consciously with this process is to learn the myths, legends, and stories of the land area upon which you live. The next step is to look around you. Look at the land itself, and then look at the current happenings in the land/people/communities to see if the myths or fragments of the myths are playing out in any way. If so, are they playing out in a good way (and therefore need no help) or are they playing out in a bad way (like the Beowulf story)?

It is also important not to connect too deeply with the myths: they are tools, not clothing for you to wear. One of the mistakes that people make when working with myths is that they personally identify with the hero/heroine and start to live the mythic life. To do that steps you into the magical current of the myth in full, which in turn will immerse you fully in the challenges, burdens, and dangers of the hero.

If you wish to do that, then all is fine: just realise that you cannot then simply step out of it should it all start going badly wrong. Once you have stepped into a mythic pattern with the intent of living the myth, it is really hard to step back out of it: the mythic struggles start to play out through your life, and you can end up on a hamster wheel of challenges.

This is why many magicians engage with the myths as simple working tools and guidebooks, not as life paths or identities. You can extract the wisdom and advice of a myth without having to live it for the rest of your life. To step into the mythic pattern also steps you out of your own fate and places you in a fate pattern that has played like a bad record for centuries: this is the trap of myths. The role of the magician is to learn how to operate tools, paths, gates, etc. without becoming stuck or tied to any of them in particular: you keep your own fate path, and the tools assist your journey rather than dictate it.

9. *Task:* Research

Look up your local legends and myths, if you can find them. If you cannot find anything on the net, look in your local city library archives. See how they relate to the landscape, see what 'monsters' they tell you about, what tools, what rules of behaviour, what mistakes are made, etc. If you cannot find anything about the land where you live, then look into myths about the land where your family is from.

> Important!
> **Ensure that they truly are ancient or very old myths and legends that come from a culture or peoples. Do not fall into the wide and sharp-toothed trap of using modern hero stories, fantasy stories, or movie themes. Modern fantasy can be used in magic, but in a very different way. It is vitally important to understand the difference between modern fantasy and ancient myth. They can appear similar, but in fact they are very different from a magical perspective.**

In working with traditional myths you are learning the keys of wisdom that were acquired centuries or even millennia ago. They are not just stories; they hold magical skills and knowledge within them in story form so that the wisdom can travel down the ages. Once you have figured out local myths, if you can find them, then start to browse bookshops for other epics, poems, stories, and myths. Look at classical, mythical, and historical sources.

If at all possible, do this with physical books rather than online. The reason for this is it is much easier for inner contacts to guide you and connect you up with the right myths when there is a physical bridge, your hand on the book, for example. However, this dynamic might be different for people who have grown up with the internet, so use your own judgement. But I often find that books will jump out at me from the shelf, sometimes literally (one falling and smacking me on the head).

Don't buy up every mythic book you can find. Remember the flow of water... see where your curiosity takes you, and also be on alert for something that repeatedly keeps showing up, being discussed, or one myth in particular that keeps being presented to you.

Remember, there is still a strong dynamic between the inner pattern of a physical book and its transmission to the magician, which works along the Inner Library pattern. Not only do you read the book, but you hang out with it, sleep with it under your pillow, or keep it close to you.

Once you have absorbed the myths, you may be put to work or presented with a situation straight away, or it may be a matter of you storing the information in your mind ready for something that will come up in the future. Also, many of the mythic patterns have a great deal of information and wisdom that is pertinent to the magician: see what you can spot. You will find that the patterns you have learned in magical practice will turn up in certain myths and will tell you a little more about them.

Lesson 8

Travelling Tools

In today's world we often have to travel a lot and spend time away from home. This can make it difficult for a working magician who uses magical tools, as you cannot drag large swords, vessels, and other paraphernalia around with you on trains, buses, and planes. Usually when you are travelling as a magician there are dynamics that you need to be aware of. One you may have already come across is the problem of visibility.

When you work in magic it is as though a light switches on and glows over your head. You become visible to various spirits and parasites, and you also become vulnerable to localised tides of power that sometimes sweep over an area of land in a destructive way. These are usually (but not always) of minor consequence to non-magicians, but to a magician their effect can become more immediate: you are visible and potentially in the firing line.

That does not mean that every time you travel you are in danger. This is not a time for paranoia. But there will be times when you can be in potential danger simply by the fact that you are a magician, particularly as an apprentice. An adept is better equipped and contacted, and as such is far more able to roll with the punches and not get into too much trouble. But for an apprentice or initiate, sometimes travelling a distance away from home to a land that you do not live on can be an issue.

The solution to this problem is to bring along magical travel tools that serve to guard, warn, limit power, keep you in balance, and assist you on your journey. There are key powers and tools that travel well, which work separately from your regular magical tools. So long as you also do your side of the work, i.e. not diving into dangerous situations beyond your capacity, they will do theirs. So let's have a look at what these travel tools are, and why they are specific tools.

1. The travel tools

The travel tools are kept in a small bag and are always kept away from your magical work space: they are designed for a specific purpose, and once they have been made should never be put in a situation where they would clash with the main working tools. Because of this, you will need a plain waterproof bag to keep the travel tools in, something like a small bathroom bag. Make sure it is a bag with no symbols, shapes, patterns, or images on it.

The travel tools are not copies of the magical tools; rather they are different tools that are related to the core magical tools. It is not wise to have 'copies' of your core tools, as this would subdivide their power: some tools can only have one in existence at any one time. Instead you have tools that are related to the specific aspects of the powers, and you work with them in particular ways while you are travelling and away from home.

The main purpose of the travel tools is to protect you and keep you balanced. We will look in more depth as to how these tools are worked with, and how they work, at the end of the practical aspect of the lesson.

2. The travel sword

The first travel tool we will look at is the sword.

Because it is not viable to travel with a blade, and also because you do not want to make a direct copy of the magical sword, the best way to work with a travel sword is to use a sword pendant. This acts as a little brother or sister of the sword, i.e. not a copy, and will guard/guide you as you travel.

It is different enough in its size and form not to cause the sword to subdivide its power, but at the same time is similar enough for a resonant power of the sword spirit to trigger it to activate.

The usual way to work in this method is to get a sword pendant that you can wear under your clothing. A sword pendant can be very useful, as it is on you all the time, will pass unnoticed (or hidden under clothing), and will not be a security issue.

The best metal to use is silver: silver is an excellent metal for holding resonance and for staying magically clean. It is also a good *hidden* metal: high quality silver does not stand out much in the inner worlds. It casts shadows, obscures, and hides things. It is this quality of silver that aligns it with the moon, not its colour, as is often thought. This is one of the reasons why it was so highly prized in the ancient world, often over and above gold, as gold shouts, silver whispers.

Find a sword pendant that has a good simple blade. It should not be fancy or decorated with dragons, stones or script: it should be like the magical sword – plain, clean, and balanced. Look for one where the blade is a proper length (i.e. longer than the handle), and where the blade is not curved, not grooved, has no gems, no creatures, etc.

Figure 8 is a good example of one.

Once you get the pendant, place it in a bowl and cover it with dry salt for twenty-four hours to strip any energetic impurities out of it. The method to trigger the sword into action is outlined in the practical work section of this lesson. Before you get to that, read about the other travel tools first so that you have a complete overview of what is used and why.

Figure 8: Sword pendant

3. The thread of the fate cloth

As you know, only one fate cloth can exist for you at any one time, but the fate cloth is a powerful and important shield, and you will potentially need its influence when you travel. Chances are the fate cloth is too big for you to drag around as you travel, but there is a compromise method that you can use, and it works well, and also teaches you about resonance in substance.

The compromise method is to extract a small bit of the cloth from its edge, so that you do not cut into the pattern imprinted upon the cloth. It only needs to be a thin strip of the cloth, but by now the substance of the cloth will be deeply infused with the energies of the magic that you have worked, and the pattern of your fate/pentagram outline will be soaked into every thread of the cloth.

This strip of cloth will act as a scabbard for the sword pendant, and can also be laid out on a surface or floor when needed. In the practical section of the lesson we will look more closely at this.

4. The pattern of the Scales/Threshing Floor

The next two tools bring into play a technique that you practised in an early lesson. The first tool is the pattern of the Scales/west/vessel. As you know, a vessel of the west is not always a cup, but can also be a pattern that holds and contains. For your travel vessel you will create a pattern on cloth that will be infused with the power of the Scales/west and the Threshing Floor.

To prepare for this practical work you will need two plain white cotton cloth napkins that you can draw on and two permanent/waterproof ink pens, one blue and one black. The blue ink is for the west cloth and the pattern of the Scales, and the black ink is for the north cloth and the pattern of the ancestors.

5. The shield of ancestors

Just as you create a pattern for the west/Scales/vessel, so you will also prepare one for the north powers. The power that the north pattern will contain is the power of ancestral lines: yours and/or the ancestral lines of the land where you live.

You do not use a stone, as that can get messy very quickly: stones often carry beings within them (like faery beings, for example). They often do not travel well, and if you try and take them along they can get quite pissed off with you; yes, I was that idiot and had an irate faery being attacking me and throwing tantrums at 3am in a hotel room.

Stones are often deeply connected to the land they are living on, and although there are ones that can be quite happily mobile and willing to move, it is usually a willingness to move to another fixed location. Moving them about all the time can sometimes bring a whole host of problems for the magician. They can also be 'fish out of water' on strange land areas: stones and the beings that reside in them are slow connectors, and are not meant to be constantly on the move.

Your bloodlines you carry within you wherever you go: your ancestors are connected to you, not the land, and the human spirit is designed to travel from land to land, and from world to world. So you are less likely to have problems using the napkin method, and more likely to get the help you need when you need it.

In your practical work you will learn how to pattern into cloth a magical structure that is directly connected to ancestral lines that inner spirits can reside within, so that they can travel with you.

It is also a bit like a family tree: it will hold resonant energy from your ancestral connections, and that will in turn inform the powers and spirits of the areas you travel to who you are and who your 'gang' is. This will tend to head off any conflict between land or ancestral spirits where you visit.

Like I said, you will be a bright light that cannot really be well hidden. But with the right tools you will also appear as someone who is well connected, well protected, and therefore less likely to become the target of low-level beings. It is also like a good mannered introduction.

6. Issues when you travel

Before we get to the practical work let's just take a moment to look at what the issues are that can arise when you travel as a magician. You will not have problems every time you travel, and some magicians can travel extensively with no problems or very few. But for some it can be a problem, and sometimes you can just end up in the wrong place at the wrong time. For this reason, and for educational purposes, it is good for you to learn the working method that follows.

I used to travel extensively in my younger days. Sometimes I was perfectly fine, and other times I seemed to step into the midst of World War Three. I used to think it was just me, but over years of talking to other magicians who travel a lot I realised it happened more than I had assumed; hence the development of the travelling tools. It did take me a while to understand what to do and what not to do in terms of these tools.

So what situations am I talking about, and how do the travel tools work?

There are many different types of situations that you can potentially step into as a travelling magician. Some can be externalised energies actively flowing through a physical pattern that you inadvertently step into the midst of, some can be hostile land beings in dispute with the local humans, some can be natural build-ups of waves of destruction or death flowing through a particular place, and some can be hotspots of the fate of that patch of land activating. You can also be a target for parasitical beings in some situations, but the more you do magic, the less of a problem that will become over time.

As a magician, your fate pattern becomes more active and your hotspots become stronger, but you also learn as a magician how to avoid unnecessary problems and how to dodge the bullets. Using the travel tools is a part of that mechanism. The sword pendant will act as a limiter for incoming energies, creating a void around you: you become largely unseen, and anything coming your way gets slowed down so that you can see it.

The thread of your pentagram cloth strengthens your 'story' so that it is harder for something to intrude, and your scales cloth holds the information of your current Harvest. Together the two tools inform any hostile beings or beings dispensing Judgement that you are to be *passed over*. The pattern of your ancestors also solidifies the information around you regarding where you have come from and where you are going, and also acts as an umbilical cord between you and those ancestral beings who are willing to help you.

Essentially the sword guards and protects, the fate and scales cloths are your papers that allow you safe passage, and the ancestral cloth is your backup team. Together they give you safe passage and create a bubble around you that will buffer you and protect you against waves of destruction.

As you travel with them you will learn to listen to them: they act as doorways for beings to contact and warn you, and also as identity papers so that powers and beings who may be destructive, see that you are someone who works with the powers in service and is working in union with the land, the deities, and Divine Power. As such, they will tend to cut you some slack.

I have had many knocks and bruises over the years, but I have always been diverted away from potentially deadly or killer situations. Sometimes I would get direct warnings from the sword; other times I was literally diverted away from a situation where something very destructive happened.

One situation was when a very dangerous spirit was sent to attack a woman I was sharing a room with. It was sent using African magic; it was very powerful and very destructive. It got into the room where we were staying and was able to see both of us. When a being such as this has clear direction, it will usually only see its target. However we both had very similar fate pictures, so it could see us both.

But I had a travel tool with me (my very first) that expressed my scales, which meant that the being was able to differentiate between the two of us as soon as my tool triggered. The being attacked my friend (and destroyed her life) and simply looked at me in puzzlement for a while and then left me alone.

At the time I was not experienced enough to know how to help my friend, I was a young apprentice, but having the tool with me offered me protection not by shielding me, but by *declaring* me: it stopped me becoming collateral damage in the firing line. I have had other times when a sword pendant has warned me to sit tight when I was planning to go on an excursion and would have consequently walked into a disaster. Such a pendant has also guarded me in sticky situations.

In one US city I was exploring a less-than-pleasant neighbourhood and was planning to go to a takeout to get dinner for myself and my friends. I got halfway there and the sword pendant triggered powerfully. I suddenly became very aware of it and could feel a strong sense of danger. So I turned around and went back to the house where I was staying. I called for the takeout but could not get an answer, so I made other plans for dinner. The morning after there was a report in the news that the takeout, at the time I would have been there, had a really bad drive-by shooting in which people were killed and injured as the place was sprayed by bullets. The sword had saved me. I did not need to know what the danger was, only that the danger was ahead, and that I needed to get away from it.

Another example of the tools triggering was a time when I was visiting a friend who lived in a lovely forested area in the US. She had been having problems with her house, so I took my travel tools with me. On the second night I spent there I had terrible nightmares and woke up feeling very bruised and battered. My friend told me that it had been like that for her for months, and it was draining her badly. The following night I laid out the Scales tool and the ancestor tool, and put the pendant on. I had a vivid dream that night in which a group of Indians (Native American) were standing around me. They were very angry about something, but they looked at my tools and decided I was okay, and then they left.

The dream was either showing me ancestral spirits that were still upon that land, or faery/land beings that presented in the dream as 'traditional locals.' Either way the tools provided the 'locals' with enough information to decide that I was not a threat or a problem, nor was I connected to the issue that was making them angry. So they left me alone after that. As an aside, I had also taken my deck with me, and my friend and I looked at the situation. Her house was right on top of an area where it should not have been: it was causing problems for the spirits there. She could not knock her house down, and there seemed to be no way of appeasing the spirits there, so she moved. Her health picked up as soon as she moved, and we both felt bad for the next person who would live in that house. No matter what we thought of to try and rebalance the situation, the readings showed that the only way to stop it was to demolish the house and leave the land. Not really an option in the modern world.

Let's get to the practical work so that you can create your own travel tools. Once you have made them, store them in a part of the house away from your working space, and occasionally wear the sword pendant when you go out of the house so that you can get used to each other.

Do the practical work even if you are not planning to travel or tend not to travel, as it is a good exercise and you will learn a lot by doing it. If at some point in the future you then go on a trip, even if it is just a day trip, take the tools with you to get a feel of how they work.

7. *Task:* Creating a magical sword pendant

Set your work room up with the four directions and the central altar. Go around and light the lights, open the gates, put the tools out on the altars, and put the sword pendant on the south side of the east altar.

Do the Anchor ritual, and when you have finished place the sword on the north side of the east altar. Both the sword and the pendant should have the blades pointing to the central altar and their hilts facing the east gate. Stand at the east altar. Place one hand on the sword and the other on the pendant. Close your eyes. See the east gate, and see a contact standing on the threshold.

In your mind tell the contact that you wish to tune the pendant to the power of the sword so that it can protect you as you travel. Now tell the sword the same thing. Tell the sword that you wish to use the pendant as a sister or brother of the sword when you travel, and ask the sword to release whatever power is necessary and to transfer it though your hands and body into the pendant.

Keep your hands on the two swords, and feel the energy transfer through your left hand, through your body, and into your right hand, and feel it pass into the pendant. Take as long as you need for the transfer to happen. Once you feel it is finished hold the pendant out towards the contact and ask them to complete it so that it will protect, guide, and limit you as necessary when you wear it. In your inner vision, see the inner contact touch the sword or place something within it, and when they withdraw place the pendant back on the altar and open your eyes.

The combination of the energy from the sword and the energy from the contact will create a new tool that is similar to your magical sword, but not exactly the same. Position the main sword so that it lies across the altar, and place the pendant sword over the top of the main sword so that they cross. Step back, bow, and leave the room with all the lights going.

When you feel it is finished, and it may take thirty minutes or so, go back in, place the tools back in their homes, go around the directions and thank them, bow, and put the lights out. Put everything away, and put the pendant on and leave the room. Leave the pendant on for a while so that you and the pendant can get used to each other. Do not wear it when you work in your magical room, and try to avoid going into the magical room with the pendant on from now on.

Wear the pendant when you leave the house for a few times so that you learn to listen to it, and you get used to how it feels, how it communicates, and how it works. Pay attention to the slightest thing that happens around you, how people react around you, how animals act around you, and how it makes you feel. Once you have gotten used to it then put it in the travel bag and use it when you need to. If you are not going to be travelling for a while, put it on occasionally when you go out to keep the connection going.

Module V – The Magical Tools

Do not wear it when you do magic, and do not wear it in the same space as the main sword: it is important to keep them separate and that the pendant learns it is only meant to work when you are away from home. In the home the job of protecting you falls to the main sword: make a very clear distinction between the two tools.

8. *Task:* Creating the pattern of the Scales

This technique draws on methods you have been working with in previous lessons, and is the start of a magical method that develops in very interesting directions. Whereas the sword can trigger a resonance in another sword, the other tools cannot: the sword is the only tool that is not directly linked to your fate, your life, and your actions. Because the other tools have deep connections with you, they can only be worked with in various different forms without duplication.

So for example the vessel you have and the Scales that you have are both of the same directional power, but have slightly different jobs and different forms. The third form a vessel can take is a pattern that contains and measures. You can use the pattern technique in many different ways in magic. In this instance, you will use it to carry information about the overall state of your scales, and to protect your Harvest. This serves to inform beings around you of your actions and intents, and also will identify you as an outsider if you happen to travel into an area that is in the midst of some kind of hostility between inner beings and the humans who live there.

You will not always need this tool, as eventually you will carry the imprint of your scales within you. But until you get to that point it can come in useful. It also carries within it a deeper aspect of the Scales and Justice, which energetically resonates around you from the tool. It will act as a minor protection against injustice, against things that would unbalance your scales through no fault of your own. The more you work with the pattern, the more you will come to understand how it works for you as an individual, as the tools are very personal to each individual magician and will therefore operate in a slightly different way for everyone. Just bear in mind that these are not super-powered tools; they are subtle and just enough for what you need.

Get the white cloth napkin, get something hard to place it on while your draw on it, and a permanent blue marker pen. Place them all on the west altar. Get the tools out and place them on their altars, and the pentagram cloth on the floor. Now go around the directions, get everything going, and then do the Anchor ritual to tune yourself and the space for work. Once you have finished visit the west altar. See the contact on the threshold. Bow to them and ask them for their help in creating a pattern of the Scales for you that you can take with you when you travel. Sit down on the floor in front of the west altar and pick up your cloth and pen.

You are going to use the method you have learned of creating a contacted pattern while staying still and silent: you need to allow a power of the west to flow through you as you work, so don't let your conscious mind get in the way. If you make mistakes, you cannot start again, and you cannot do a pre-run or practise it: it must come out as it is. This is a magical act, not a work of art.

Still yourself and meditate for a little while, and when you are ready, open your eyes. The pattern you are going to create will have two halves with a fulcrum in the middle. Start from the centre of the cloth and make a dot, or a triangle, or draw a line straight down the middle. That is your fulcrum.

Now work out from there and create patterns that flow from this centre and fill the left side of the cloth. Keep in mind that the left side is your ongoing learning and work. That does not indicate specific shapes that you should use, just that you need to focus your mind completely on your work, your learning, your service, and the way you are currently living your life. That will then flow into the pattern.

When you have finished the left side, now it is time to do the right side. The right side is what you have achieved, what you have done/finished, both good and bad, what lessons in life you have learned, and how you have conducted yourself as a human being in this current cycle that you are in.

The work you have done in previous lessons will have addressed your earlier Harvest, so what you are patterning is your current state of affairs. Just keep that in mind as you draw the pattern, and do not let your mind wander: you are mediating what your scales would look like if you were placed at Judgement on that day. The pattern itself can come out as anything. Its shapes do not matter; just let your hand be guided.

When you have finished sit and look at it. When you are away travelling and you have it with you, also take time to spread it out and look at it. Let the patterns talk to you, let them tell your their vocabulary, and let them reflect back to you what you need to work on, what to congratulate yourself on, and what you might not have been aware of that is causing you to be unbalanced.

When you have finished fold up the cloth, leave it on the altar, and go out of the room for a while. When you feel everything has finished, return and go around the directions, put out the lights, put the tools away, bow, and say thank you. Take the scales cloth, fold it up, and place it in the travel bag. When you travel, and before you leave, if you wish to, get your cord and wrap it around the scales cloth as an added boost of protection for your life pattern. Do this in particular if you know you are going into a dangerous area or situation. Sometimes travel without the cord to see if you feel any difference.

9. *Task:* Creating the Shield of Ancestors

The cloth shield of ancestors is made in the same way as the scales cloth. It acts as an umbilical cord to any blood ancestors who work with you or land ancestors that have adopted you through your magical work with the land. It also shows other beings on the land that you are travelling to that you have active ancestors watching your back, so they are more likely to leave you alone.

Set up the room in the same way as you did for the scales cloth, and place the cloth napkin and black pen on the north altar. Put your scales cloth on the west altar. Do the same ritual preparations and Anchor ritual as you did for the scales cloth. When you have finished stand before the north altar and close your eyes. See the ancestral contacts standing on the threshold and ask them if they would help you create a cloth pattern of ancestors to take with you to protect you when you travel. When you are ready sit down in front of the north altar ready for work.

This pattern starts at the top of the cloth. Make a mark that identifies you or a mark either made of your name or a sign that you have come to identify with. From there let the pattern develop outwards and downwards, like the roots of a tree. Certain points of the roots may have their own little pattern that comes out: these mark particular ancestral spirits that work with you. Don't try and preempt that; just let it come out in its own way.

When you have finished stand up and hold the cloth out to the contacts on the threshold. Ask them, using your physical voice, to put into it whatever is necessary to keep you safe and connected while you are away. When they have finished place the cloth folded up on the altar, bow, and leave the room for a while. When you feel it is finished, return to the working space. Before you close everything down you are going to extract a fragment of your pentagram cloth to act as a scabbard for your sword pendant.

Get a pair of sharp scissors and find a small length of the edge of the cloth that is outside of the pentagram pattern so that you do not cut into the pattern in any way. It does not matter if it is a very thin strip. Just clip a small part of the blank part of the cloth's edge. Place it on the central altar. When you have finished go around the directions, thanking the contacts in each direction, bow, put the lights out, and put the tools away.

Take the ancestor cloth, the scales cloth, and the fate thread out of the room. Get your sword pendant and wrap the fate thread around the sword blade. When you can, get a small pouch that the pendant can live in with the slip of cloth wrapped around the blade: this will help you not lose the slip of cloth. Until then wrap the ancestor cloth around the pendant/cloth. Place both patterns and the sword pendant in your travel bag.

10. How to use the travel tools

When you travel, wherever you are going to sleep for the night that is off your own land area, either place the ancestor cloth over your bedspread or under your pillow, or spread it out on the floor beside you. Keep it open and close to you as you sleep. When you are travelling have it in a backpack (watching your back) or keep the travel bag inside your hand luggage.

Put on the sword pendant before you leave your house. The thread of cloth will act as a scabbard, so keep the thread in the pouch while you are wearing the pendant.

Wear it every day while you are away. If you can get a long enough chain it can tuck down under your clothing unseen. When you take it off at night wrap the slip of cloth around the blade (replacing the scabbard). Place the scales cloth on a surface near you as you sleep, and place the sword pendant/cloth thread on top of the scales cloth. You can do this every night, or just use it this way when you feel unsafe, when you are in a place that is not too good energetically, or if you are not sleeping well while away.

In the mornings take the scabbard thread/slip of cloth off the sword and put it in the pouch. Put the pendant on. Fold up the patterned cloths and wrap them around the pouch and place them all in the travel bag. The sword watches over you during the day and the cloth patterns work for you throughout the night.

11. Summary

The techniques you have just learned teach you how the powers of different directional tools work and allow you to carry fragments of their power around with you as you travel. You will not always need these, and in the future, as an adept, you will be heavily contacted and will no longer need to work with travel tools unless it is an extreme situation.

Learning how to impress energy from directional powers into a pattern is the start of a major learning process. It teaches you how to bridge power through a pen and your hand, and it teaches you how energy works well in patterns, as everything around you is simply an energetic pattern. By working this way you are engaging in a very old and powerful technique that you will learn has many layers and depths to it as you progress in magic.

This technique is not only useful for travel, but will unfold in many different ways for you as you progress as a magician, if you pay attention. I will not teach you the many different ways you can use these techniques as it is up to you an as Initiate later in your training to figure out the many different applications of all the techniques you learn in the Apprentice section.

The drawing of the Metatron Cube in an earlier module was the very beginning of that process, and as an adept you will revisit that exercise and be able to reflect the full power of that magical consciousness into a pattern that you can then work with: the contacted patterning is the beginning of the language of 'angels'.

12. *Task:* Documenting the process

Write up your reflections, experiences, difficulties, questions, and insights from this lesson. What was it like drawing the patterns? Have you travelled and used them, and if so what did you experience? What was it like wearing the sword pendant away from the house? Write up your notes in a computer log for future submission to the mentors.

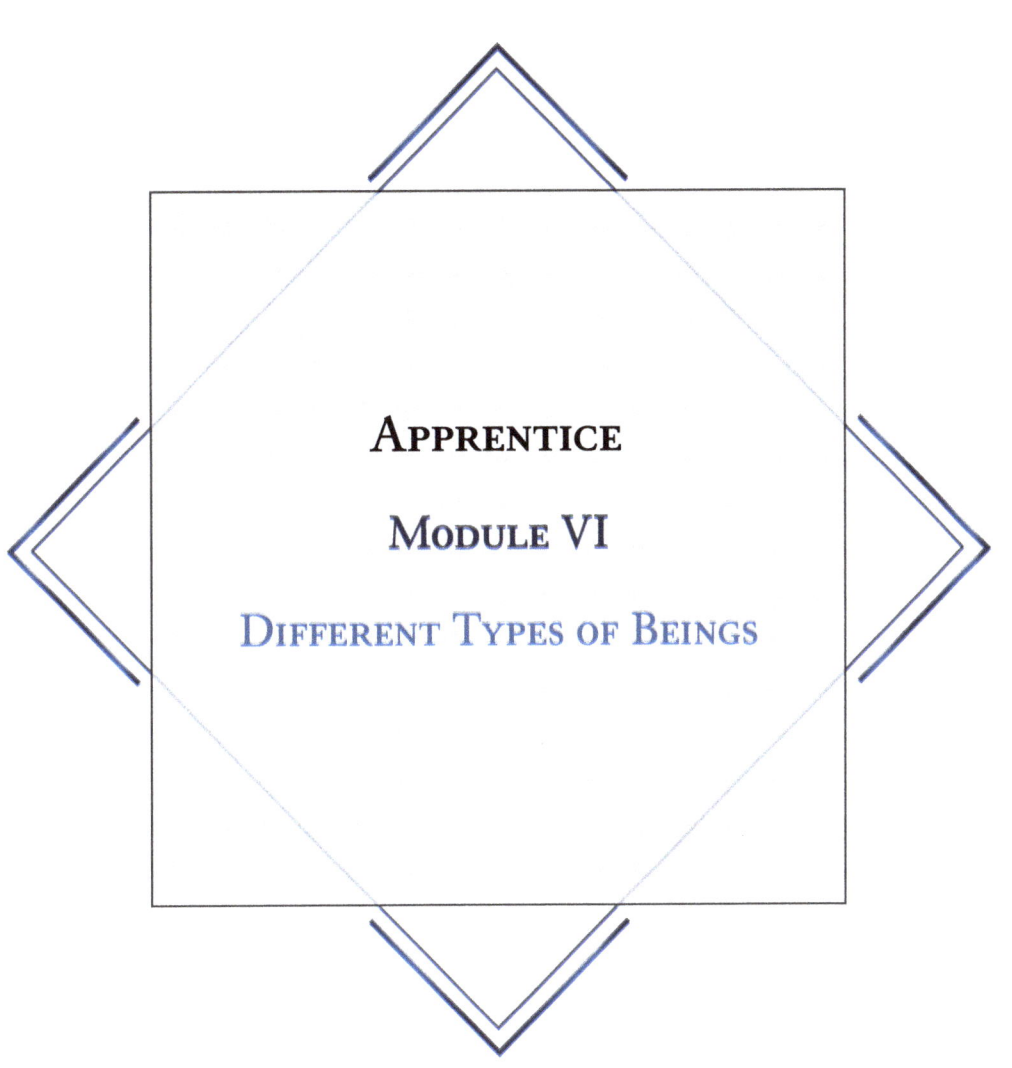

Apprentice

Module VI

Different Types of Beings

Lesson 1
Deities

1. Overview of Module VI

Before we dive into this lesson, I would like to give you a brief overview of Module VI. This will help you understand the various lessons in this module, how they link together, and how their subject matter often shifts from one identity to another. How we view beings in Western cultures is very much coloured by the religions that proliferate in these cultures today. The Abrahamic religions do not recognise deities; rather they 'deify' Divinity, which merges two different streams of power into one. Divinity is given a human consciousness, and is treated like a deity.

This separates people from the complex and diverse kinds of communion that are possible with the different types of beings that exist around us. Instead, these beings are relegated into two camps: good ones and bad ones. The good ones are thought of as angels, and the bad ones are fashioned as evil demons. Everything is squeezed into one of those two camps or else ignored altogether. On the other end of the spectrum from Western cultures, Animist cultures acknowledge consciousness as being present in everything, from a force of nature to a rock or an insect. Everything has a purpose and function, regardless of whether it is bad for humans or good for humans. Many types of consciousness are considered to be a mix of both good and bad. This view is far closer to the 'truth' that magicians work with.

In this module we will look at some of different types of beings, and how the magician works with them, and why. The one thing to start thinking about now is the concept of good and bad. As we go through the lessons, we will look at beings that are considered 'bad' and others that are considered 'good.' It is important as a magician to ask:

"Good or bad for whom?"

This is a fundamental question for magicians as it takes us out of a world centred on humankind and places us in the midst of a community of beings, creatures, forces, and landmasses. We tend to look at the world from a human perspective because we are humans, but what is bad for a human is often good for another being or creature or even for the rest of the inner and outer ecosystem of the world. This human centric perspective, while being an evolutionary influence, is very much strengthened by the Abrahamic belief that 'God created everything for us'. Regardless of your religion or lack of it, the cultural biases and ways of operating in a society are very much shaped by the overall religious influence over hundreds of years; it embeds so deeply into the culture that it is often hard to spot if you live and were raised in that culture.

In the last few decades of the twentieth century and the early twenty-first century, Western societies have moved from being civil societies where everyone contributes towards a greater good, to consumer societies where everyone looks out for themselves. This has also seeped into religion and magic, which has in turn affected how we interact with magic and with everything around us. Although that self-centred perspective has always been part of humanity, it is, after all, a survival mechanism, it has not been quite so polarised or extensive as it is today for quite some time. This has affected how magic is operated, and in turn it has also deeply affected how we interface with everything around us.

So with that in mind, when reading and working with these various lessons, keep that fundamental question in mind: *"good/bad for whom?"*. Also start to look at how your own ideas and attitudes, life habits and assumptions, may have some roots in the religious history of your society. I have lost count of the amount of magicians I have talked to who were shocked when I politely pointed out the religious sources of their 'not religious at all' everyday mindset. It affects our manners, our social norms, our choices, and how we see other people, all of which is unconscious to the magician.

This module does not cover all beings, as that would be impossible and also not necessary at this stage of training. However, the module shines a light on some of the more key types of beings that Western magicians are likely to come across during magical training. This gives you a foundational understanding of different types of beings, which in turn will give you the skills to ascertain and understand other types of beings you may come across that are not listed in this module. As you progress through the course, your understanding of the considerable amount of different beings will slowly widen out as you encounter some of the vastly diverse inner and outer community through your work.

2. Deities

What is a deity? This is a question that must be answered from a magician's standpoint. This is based on direct experience of working with deities rather than reading theoretical, philosophical, or psychological texts. You can theorise and postulate forever, but at the end of the day understanding comes from direct, long-term experience. That is how as a magician, you too will slowly come to an understanding that you can successfully work with.

Asking "what is the nature of a deity?" is like asking "what is the nature of a human?" In one sense it is easy to answer these questions, but in another sense it is almost impossible. Deities are both understandable and confounding at the same time. Rather than delve into a deep discussion about the theory of what a deity could be, I think it far more productive to explore the root, fundamental powers from which most deities flow. That will give you a working platform from which you can launch yourself into your own direct experiences, and those experiences will help you to shape your own understanding.

3. WHAT IS A DEITY?

This is a more complex question than it seems. As you go through your training your understanding of what a deity is (and isn't) will most likely change and develop more than once as you gain more direct experience from interacting with them. For now we will tackle this subject from a basic magical understanding that you can work with, and then it will develop from there.

Essentially a deity is a consciousness that is a part of creation/our world. Divinity is the power from which everything flows, or another way to look at it is that Divinity is the conscious complete whole of everything; the complete pattern of existence. This is a power that we cannot grasp an understanding of. Deities can act as halfway points between Divinity and nature, humanity included: they are the *bridges* between everything in creation and Divine Consciousness.

A magician works with a deity like a window into a consciousness that humans can interface with. For example, rivers tend to have a powerful female consciousness that flows through them. We can interface with that power/consciousness in the form of river goddesses. Deities are not all-knowing and all-powerful, but they are a damn sight more powerful than we are. Over millennia a relationship between deities and humans has been built, for good and for bad, whereby we can connect, communicate, and live alongside these powers.

In the early days of human relations with deities this was more of a classic Animist-style relationship: everything has a consciousness, everything is talked to, and the vocabulary of the powers of nature such as the sound of the wind, the ferocity of the water, the flight of birds, etc., is a channel for communication between the conscious powers of nature and humanity. As humans became more proficient in this vocabulary, we learned how to create vessels that would filter the vocabulary, and we thought it would also filter the power, humans love control.

Staying with the example of a river goddess, such evolution of magical interaction would have gone something like this:

Human recognises great power in the river and relies on the river for life. Human learns that they can communicate with the river and that certain creatures tend to turn up when such communications are active. The human develops a level of communication whereby the river can warn, through augury, that a potential catastrophic flood is coming. This warning comes not only from acute observations of the river's behaviour, but also through dreams, and the signs that the river's creatures display. But the human is still at the mercy of the river. The humans slowly learn that they can create images, in human, animal, or mixed forms, which allow them to communicate far better with the consciousness of the river. They also find that if they create vessels for key animals connected to the river goddess, in the form of statues, they can build a relationship with the spirit/consciousness that flows through these animals.

The human becomes a magician when they learn how to bridge a connection between the power of the river and its animals, and the images/statues, so that the consciousness of the river/animals can talk directly through the images. When a magician creates a deity image in the form of a human or humanlike being, they are teaching the river's consciousness how we see, hear, talk, feel, move. The statue as it is made works magically, so that the ears 'hear,' the eyes 'see,' and so forth. So there is a shift between the human learning the vocabulary of the river, to the river learning the vocabulary of the human. But this still leaves the human at the mercy of the vast power of the river.

The human offers things they feel are of great value to appease the deity. The deity takes the energy from the gift, and also from the heartfelt intent of the human offering it. In return, the deity cooperates more with the human, so that a mutual relationship develops. This forms a delicate basis of balance and order that requires a lot of hard work to maintain. It is worth noting at this point, that the deity would often much prefer the human to work to maintain the health of the river than to shower it with gifts. However, the energy of those gifts can be transformed by the deity in order for that energy to be worked with, so it becomes a trade-off. One day, the human learns that the river wants trash taken out of it, and any potential over fishing stopped. It is at that point that the person stops giving gifts and starts working on the simple things they can do to maintain the river health; they become co-workers with the river.

Of course, as humans become more sophisticated, they begin to resent not only the power that the deity has over them, but also the wealth that has to be offered to the deity. This was a major step in many ancient cultures, and we can see the point at which it occurred quite clearly in their various histories. At this crossroads within the relationship, the human has two choices; become a co-worker with the river which takes care, time and energy, or, work as a magician priest and manipulate the deity vessel to suit the humans better. This is the point at which the magician priests learned how to subdivide the deity forms. What was, for example, a goddess of creation and destruction became two goddesses: one of creation, and one of destruction. Of course, the goddess of creation became more popular, and the goddess of destruction was feared.

This subdivision method was based around the technique of the vessel/image/statue. So in the case of the goddess of creation and destruction, the characteristics that displayed each power in the image were divided: one statue was fashioned with only the creative keys/symbols, and the other with only the destructive keys/symbols. This does not limit the power of the deity, rather it limits the ability of the human and the deity to interface: it vastly shortens the vocabulary of communication.

Eventually even the subdivided goddess was thought to be too powerful and unmanageable. So the images and identities were subdivided further and further until the filter of the deity image no longer allowed any power to flow back and forth with the humans. We ended up with the situation where various cultures had many gods and goddesses and each one of those filters/images allowed only one or two specific powers or characteristics to flow through it.

This was the degenerate end of the ancient world. Rome learned a harsh lesson on why subdividing deities so much was a bad idea. When they got into serious trouble they had to bring in a goddess who had not been subdivided at all: Cybele.

It is not that the subdivision made the deities themselves weaker; rather it over filtered the window of connection until there was really no point to it. Think of it like a sheet of black cloth draped over a doorway, with people in the room beyond. To communicate, if you cannot move the cloth, you would have to shout through the cloth. If there is a big round hole cut in it, the situation is a lot better. You can see into the room and see the people and communicate with them using your voice, your body language, etc. You can see how the people are, what they need, and what is coming at them from behind them.

If that hole in the cloth is sewn up and two smaller holes, spaced apart, are put in, then your view gets worse. You can only see through one hole at a time, and you can only see a part of the room. If you close up those two holes and make a few even smaller ones and space them out, then it becomes almost impossible to see into the room other than in small, snatched glances. The cloth does not stop you existing; it just stops you looking into that room. So you can either walk away, or just go back to trying to communicate by shouting through the cloth. So it is between deities and humans. The deity powers are always there, and were there long before we arrived on the scene. But we created the interfaces and physical forms so that we could have a better, clearer two-way relationship with them in a way we could understand.

Is that method of interfacing still valid? I think my answer would be yes… and no. I have worked for years with deities, and have found that a strong and healthy way forward is using a mix of traditional interfaces, but also working with deities in a less formed way. We will look at that in a bit more detail in the practical work of this lesson.

4. What is *not* a deity?

In more recent times humans have taken to the idea of creating their own deities. Kings/Pharaohs/Emperors becoming gods or sons of gods is one example, and the more modern version is deities that are essentially created out of misunderstandings of texts, or from psychological expressions, or from sheer modern magical fashion, like Lilith for example. These entities can be the most problematic to work with as deities, simply because they are *not* deities; they are something else entirely.

The human-turned-deity is more akin to an inner contact, which we will address later in this module. The modern recreation of what *someone assumes to have been* a deity, and also the creation of a false deity, is essentially working with an unbalanced vessel that a parasite or any other type of being can step into. Again, we will address that later in this module. For now, just be aware that some of the so-called 'deities' that proliferate within magic and paganism are in fact not deities at all, and treating them as deities can trigger all sorts of unwanted issues.

Similarly, different ancient cultures classified the beings they connected with, or were aware of, in different ways. This also can cause untold confusion to the modern magician. What some cultures would call a demon, others would call a deity.

This is often the result of the influence of the Abrahamic religions, particularly Christianity. The Christian religion does not recognise deities, and instead classifies everything as either angel, saint, or demon. This reductionist approach has had a deep and abiding influence on how Western magicians view the inner and outer worlds. That influence has served to cut the Western magician off from the complexity of the various different types of beings, and everything is reduced to good or bad, up or down, for or against. That in turn has also vastly limited how the magician works and what they work with. So as you go through this module, keep the Abrahamic influence in mind as you work. And if you live in the West or your culture has western roots, be aware that even the very basic structure of the Western and Middle East societies are steeped in this influence. That affects how a person raised in that society thinks, learns, how they view the world, and so on, even if they consider themselves not religious. I cannot stress enough how important this is, hence I keep repeating myself when writing around this subject.

The way through this maze can be complex. The way we are going to approach it is through looking at these beings in respect of their power, action, function, and magical presentation. A common vocabulary is needed for the magician to function and discuss the subject matter, so we will work through the lessons using a common, already-known vocabulary, but also look at what is behind that classification. By the time you get to the end of this module, you will have a much better idea of the different types of beings. Always know what you are working with, and also know *why* you are working with them. So let's get back to deities.

5. How and why we work with deities

Deities are the consciousness of the land around us. They flow through the elements, and they also flow through the powers that form in the inner worlds before expressing in the manifest world: powers of creation, destruction, balance, imbalance, judgement, death, etc. For a magician, learning to interact and work with these deities allows us to step into an active role, not only in the upkeep of ourselves, but also in the upkeep of everything around us. The deities and the magician become a major part of a working team.

What can get in the way of that teamwork is when the magician drifts away from working with the *actual* inner power of the deity, and instead spends their time making pretty altars with expensive statues that they cover in jewellery, gold leaf, and other shiny things. This quickly devolves down into a dogmatic religious-style worship, prayers, and impressive photos shared on social media. That dogmatic outer relationship cuts the inner contact. It is a step backwards for magicians, and the 'deity' becomes more of an acquisition, fashion, and plaything than a real contact.

To stop Quareia magicians falling into that trap you will first learn how to work with deities without the outer man-made window and identity filter. This will let you learn the real feeling of what it is like to work with a deity in depth. Once you have that strong foundation it is far less likely that you will get into such problems.

So why do we work with deities? The most helpful, and also powerful, aspect of working with a deity is the protection, guidance, and learning that they can offer. They protect the magician from serious danger. They guide the magician in their magical work, and warn them of things the magician needs to be aware of. Also, many deities will teach you a great deal about their specific flow of power and about magic in general. In return, the magician works in service to assist the deity. We offer our physical capabilities; for example, we can physically move objects from A to B, and sometimes we give them physical substance that they can draw energy from, if they need it for a particular reason.

The key difference between a religious approach and magical approach is the lack of routine and dogmatic behaviour. In a religious interface the magician is told that they must behave a certain way with a deity every day: daily prayers, offerings, etc. Things that always stay the same. But with a magical interface things are far more dynamic: deities go to sleep (vanish) for prolonged periods of time, or suddenly turn up and want you to work with them. They may want food/drink/flame for a short period of time, and then want nothing for ages. They may work seasonally, or they may work erratically: the key for a magician is to learn to be flexible, attentive, and go with the flow. If a magician has a deity statue in the house that demands food, energy, action and/or sacrifice all the time or in return for doing them a magical favour, then it is very likely that what they are interfacing with is not a deity, but a parasite.

The best and truest way to learn how to be with deities is to actually work with them. Once you have become used to working with deities over a period of time, you learn to feel the difference between a true deity and something else that is masquerading as a deity.

6. Meeting the deities

At this stage of your training you are going to work with deities who are foundational element deities that operate through the wind, the sun, the water, and the earth. You will not work with them in a human-formed way, i.e. using known names and dressings that have been created by humans. This is really important: learning to work with the deities as they choose to present to you, not with the dressing or interface that you place upon them, is a major foundation step in magic. Again, this work highlights how important it is for you to learn to get your conscious mind out of the way to allow the deity to present to you in *their* form of interface, not yours. The reason this is so important is that it lets you get to know the real power behind the facade that humans have built up, twisted, and subdivided.

People who are involved in magic have often taken to working with a known deity, for example Isis, Hecate, Thor, Set, etc., but using a modern approach that often clashes with the actual power behind those *façades*. There is also a lot of misunderstanding about many of these deities, and that in turn can cause all sorts of problems.

But if you learn to work with root deities first, with their interfaces and presentations, then it puts you in a position as a magician where you have to learn for yourself. Through your work with them you learn what they are, how they work, and what sort of relationship is best for both you and the deity in question. That in turn teaches you a great deal about how deities operate and what they actually are, which in turn teaches you to how to work properly with the known deities.

It also teaches you how to spot false deities, i.e. human constructs that are operated by parasites and are not actually deities at all. That understanding can save you a lot of wasted time and energy – and also keep you safe and on track as a magician.

This round of practical work is going to take some time, as it is involved work that needs to develop and unfold. Not rushing through this practical aspect of the lesson will give you a firm foundation, and also deity backup, for the problematic aspects of this module that you will encounter. Once you have worked with all of the deities that will present themselves throughout this practical work, they should then become a routine part of your magical work when opening the gates and working in your ritual space. That means anything from simply acknowledging them when you open the gates to working directly with one that may appear or present powerfully when you begin your ritual work.

Go through these workings in sequence, spending at least two weeks on each one, more if you need to, but certainly no less. Remember, this course is not a race, it is a major training. Treat this course in the same way you would treat an undergraduate four-year degree with a possible three-year Ph.D. afterwards – immerse yourself in the work without racing to the finishing post.

7. *Task:* Meeting the Deity of the East

In your work-space, set out the cloth, the central altar, and light the directions finishing with the central flame. Now put the tools out on the directional altars, and go around the directions again, opening the gates. See the contacts on the thresholds, and then do the Anchor ritual. At the end of the Anchor, ensure that the tools are once more on all of their respective altars. The sword should be propped against the front of the altar just off to the left, blade down, tip on the floor.

Stand before the central altar, facing south, close your eyes and be still. Be aware of the Divine Power above you, the consciousness that all of creation comes from. There is no form to use to visualise this power; just be aware of that overarching power, unknowable, ever-present, above, around, beneath, and within you. Once you have built up that feeling, in vision see yourself stepping forward into the central flame and stepping into the Void, the place of nothingness that everything comes from. Feel yourself expand in that nothingness: you have no boundaries; you are everywhere. Feel the absolute peace and stillness of that power, and bathe in that stillness. When you feel still and silent, open your eyes while still feeling that stillness, and go to the east altar.

Stand before the east altar, see the contact on the threshold, bow, and ask if you can meet with the deity of the wind. Sit down in front of the east altar and close your eyes. See the altar before you, and beyond the altar see the contact on the threshold. Repeat in vision the request, if possible, to make contact with the deity of the wind. The contact steps to one side and two creatures come from beyond the gate to the threshold. Just observe what animals/birds/whatever they are, and watch as they separate and stand on either side of the gate on your side of the threshold: they create a gate for the deity of the wind; they are the messengers of the deity.

As you look through the gate, beyond which is mist, you begin to see something moving. You feel a slight breeze on your face, and the mist begins to disperse as a gentle wind moves it around. Something emerges out of the mist, and moves to the threshold of the gates. Let the image form itself. Regardless of whether you can tell what the form is, when you feel the shift in power however subtle, bow your head to acknowledge that power, and ask, using your voice and your mind, if the deity of the wind is willing to work with you, to help you learn about their power, what they do, and how you can work with them in service. Once you have asked, be still. Sit in the stillness with the power before you, and just 'be.' When you feel the power withdraw, open your eyes, stand up, bow, and thank the deity of the wind for visiting you. Go around the directions, starting in the south. Bow, see the gates close, step back, and go to the next direction, finishing in the east. Then go around again and put the lights out, finishing in the east.

Notes on the meeting

This working needs to be done a few times until you have established a defined contact with the wind deity. Take your time, and take however long you need to make a connection that you can recognise for yourself. The deity can present itself as anything from a tornado, to a storm, a bird, an unshaped form that exudes a certain energy, or a humanlike figure. Don't try and preempt how it will appear, as the deity of the wind can appear in many different forms according the particular power on the land where you are working.

If the deity presents as a storm or column of wind, then the best way to work with that deity outside of the working space is by talking to the wind and the storms, or breathing into them as they come over your house. When the wind blows, go outside and talk to the wind deity: that presentation tells you that the main way you can work with them is through the weather and through your voice and breath.

Slowly you will learn how to pick up on changes in that power, so that the wind can tell you of dangerous storms that may be coming. Over time you will also learn how to work with the wind to carry magical utterance to where it needs to go.

If the wind deity presents as a kind of bird, then start to take close notice of that type of bird in the world around you. If you could not tell what type of bird it was in vision, then simply observe closely the birds in your area. The more you watch the more you will see, and the more you will begin to understand when a bird acts oddly.

And of course, feed the birds! As you build up a relationship with the deity power, it is very likely that the birds around you will start to connect with you at key times to warn you, confirm something, or guide you through augury. If they start turning up around you or appearing to you at key times, treat that sign as if the bird was a messenger of the deity.

If you are not sure what the message is, use your tarot deck and ask the following questions one at a time as needed, using the **Tree of Life layout**:

"Is there something that the birds are trying to tell me?"

"Is there danger coming?"

"What is it that I need to know?"

If the deity presents in human form, then this form is the one to be the most careful of. Whenever deities use a human form, particularly if it is a complete human and not half-creature, half-human, then you have to take into account that the deity will filter their power through human emotions and personalities. This is the form that can get the stickiest for an apprentice to work with. For example, a male magician working with a female deity can often have problems if the deity becomes jealous of the magician's female partner/wife (and that does that happen a lot). If a human-type deity appears, use what you know about human relations, emotions, needs, and wants as a reference for how to keep solid boundaries with the deity without pissing them off. Without care and boundaries there is always a risk that the deity will withdraw and a parasitical being will move in. However, the magical method you are using in this lesson is much more likely to connect you to the wind deity at source: as the wind or a creature of the wind/bird. A human form is pretty unlikely to appear using this method.

If the deity presents as half-creature, half-human, take note of which bit is what: if it has the head of a human, then the deity power will filter through a human mind. If the head is a bird, then the deity will filter through the mind of a bird. Paying close attention to human/creature deities, as to what bit is what, will tell you how they work, how they will behave with you, and how you should behave with them.

8. *Task:* Building the connection

Work with the contact ritual/vision over a period of fourteen days, more if needed, until you have built up a good connection with the deity in the east and have an understanding of how to work with them out in nature. Because they are elemental root deities, their strongest action is out in nature, not in temple methods.

The way to start the process of working with them is outside, breathing out to the air while keeping a sense of the contact. Say hello to the wind, even if the deity presented as a bird or something else, work also with the root power, which is wind. Whenever you go outside, keep the wind deity in mind and take note of gusts of wind and changes in the wind. And always quietly acknowledge the wind when it blows.

When a wind storm comes in, go outside and welcome the storm. However damaging they may be to our structures, the storm is doing a job, cleaning the land. Thank the storm for what it brings, tell the storm it is magnificent, and breathe/blow into the wind. This is a baby step towards learning how to interact magically with the weather: instead of doing magic to make the weather how you would like it to be, which is often in conflict with what the weather needs to do, you will eventually learn to work with the wind and storms to get advance warning, to be protected, and to learn how to work with the wind to carry magic from one place to another.

Also acknowledge birds: talk to them and be aware of them. When a bird tries to connect with you in some way, talk to it using your voice, not your mind, and also still yourself. Feel to see if your emotions slightly shift: that is one of the ways of communication, through your emotions. Is the bird warning you of danger? Is it telling you that something good or bad is coming? As you become stronger with your own visionary and communication techniques, you can gently project through image and emotion what your intent is towards the birds – for example when I am going to feed them and they are up in my trees, I project an image of me bringing out food to the bird feeder. Doing that a few times taught them how to communicate with me. So now if they need to warn me or the flock, I will get an image drop into my mind of a 'stranger human'. Sure enough I go outside and a stranger (post or delivery person) is walking down the path and the flock take off and vanish. I use image projection, the sound of my voice (there is no understanding of words but there is of sounds) and the projection of emotion.

Don't just do this as an exercise and then move on: keep up your relationship with the elemental deities throughout your magical life. They are a critical layer to your magical skills, knowledge, and magical communion. And that process starts with these exercises. You need to connect, make friends, and learn to understand these powers before you really start to work with them.

Opening a line of communication between you and the wind deity can be a slow process, but it develops into a powerful one, and is far more potent than invocations and rituals. As an adept, the skills you learn now will flower into your becoming a part of the elements around you. They operate as an extension of yourself: the birds become your communicators, and you learn to look through their eyes, to listen to the warnings on the wind, and to work with the storms.

When a magician interacts with the elements in this way, it is the action of intention to connect with them which triggers them to interact with you in a conscious way. Normally a human would protect themselves against the elements and give no thought to them truly having any consciousness. But for the magician, the first act of reaching out to the elements triggers a response; *Oh, here we have a human who is not deaf, blind, and stupid.* Slowly, over time, the magician and the elements begin to interact, to communicate through emotion, sound and images, and to respond to each other.

In this time of climate change, rather than trying to force the elements to do magically what we want them to do, (magic to bring rain in a drought, for example) we instead ask the elements what they need in magical terms. The need is communicated back, and then it is up to the magician to act intentionally to fulfil that need. That in turn creates necessary change.

These magical acts as an apprentice are simple: use of voice, thought, emotion, and action with intent. As an adept, the magic becomes a catalyst that is worked with in service for the good of the elements. We will cover this more fully in Module VII as you learn to work in service for the elements, and also learn how to work with the elements as magical tools.

9. *Task:* Meeting the Deity of the South

To connect with the deity of the south, you will be working with the deity of the sun. Repeat the same method that you used for connecting with the deity of wind, but this time working in the south. Spend the same amount of time on this direction, and work until you get a strong sense of the deity's consciousness presenting at the south threshold.

The two gatekeepers that will appear first to create the doorway for this deity will be lions. Acknowledge them and respect them. The solar deity can present in a variety of forms, but if it presents as humanlike, just as before, be very cautious. Once you have a strong sense of the deity and have communed with it a few times on the threshold, then it is time to connect with the raw power in nature.

When you go outside, greet the wind, and then greet the sun. If you get up early in the morning, regardless of whether it is sunny or cloudy, greet the sun even if it is hidden, and thank it for ensuring that everything has life, warmth, and strength. When you are rushing to work, look up briefly and thank the sun in your mind. The sun is our battery charger and life support. It has a powerful consciousness and is the root deity for many cultural deities around the world.

The sun, more than any other deity, can become problematic, particularly for men, if it is not worked with equally with the other root elemental deities. The sun's consciousness is pure power, and in history many cultures have become unstuck by priesthoods leaning too much towards a solar deity without the balanced inclusion of the others. When the power of the sun becomes unbalanced in a human (it affects men more than women this way), it tends to lead the male priests/magicians towards war and conquest. It is pure power, but how you work with it will determine if it is balanced power or destructive power.

The simple way that the apprentice learns to connect with the elemental powers ensures a healthy balance between human and the environment. Also, the learning process is a series of small but solid steps that teach you the depths of these powers from the bottom up. When you come to work as an adept with these powers, you will then fully appreciate the beginner steps that you took in this training, even though they currently seem unglamorous and simplistic.

10. *Task:* Meeting the Deity of the West

Again, you will work using the same methods you have learned for connecting with the wind deity.

The guardians that hold the gate open for the deity of the west can appear in many different forms, so just take note of how they appear: they will give you clues as to what aspect of the deity you are connecting with. The deity in the west that you will reach for is the deity of moisture: it is the root deity of the rain, the dew, the rivers, the lakes, and the sea. Spend at least the same amount of time, or whatever is needed to connect with this deity, and be able to commune with them in vision as they stand on the threshold, and also out in nature.

11. *Task:* Meeting the Deity of the North

The deity of the north is connected to you through the land. You have already worked with deeper aspects of this deity in a couple of different forms, such as the Underworld, the stone, and the old woman in the cave. But you also need to learn to connect with the root deity power that is the land all around you.

This deity can present in numerous ways in vision, and that presentation very much depends on the land where you are. Once you have a formed idea from vision as to what presentation you are working with, then keep an awareness of the deity as you go about your life. The deity is all around you in the trees, the rocks, the ground, the mountains, the plains: it is the root deity of the earth from which springs the more localised deities of land features. Be aware of the earth deity in the form it presented to you in your work, and keep that awareness when you connect with the land.

Place your hand on the ground when you are outside and acknowledge the land as your parent, as your foundation. Thank the land power that gives you your body, your food, your shelter. Talk to that power while holding the image or sense of the root deity that presented to you. These actions create a slow but powerful connection to the deity.

Always talk to the land around you and especially when you travel: always connect to the land, place a hand upon the ground and introduce yourself, and say thank you. If you are eating outside, a rushed sandwich for example, give a bit to the land. Just simply break the first bit off and place it on the ground and say thank you. And practise learning to communicate through feeling, image, and sound – language is a very human thing, and sometimes root deities do not connect with language but they do connect with integrity, honesty, inner energy, feelings and intentions.

As you gain more experience of the subtle feeling of the deities around you in the elements, you may find that the unique presentations that they showed you, i.e. how they appeared at the threshold, will slowly start showing up around you. These can presentations that are as silly as a toy, or an image you spot while out driving, or as dramatic as a root creature turning up at your door or presenting to you everywhere you go. I have a raven that turns up at key times and which is connected to the land deity here where I live. This is why it is important for magicians to pay attention to everything around them.

12. Summary

This round of work should take you a minimum of a couple of months. It is designed to plug you into these root deities without any cultural dressing or magical filters, as these can get in the way of a true and pure connection.

Never ever give more attention to one of these deities over the others. This is really important. You must keep the balance between all of the elemental deities at all times. As you work your way around the directions with this work, always 'see' the deities you have already connected with in vision, standing at their thresholds as you work. Once you have finished this round of work, in the future always acknowledge these deities in the directions before you start any magical work in your working space, and acknowledge them all when you go outside.

All the deities that magicians work with have their roots in these core deities. So to truly understand and be able to work with any deity in a balanced and powerful way, you must first be on good working terms with these core deities. This also takes your work right back to the dawn of magic, before it became too overlaid with dressings: you are going back to the source.

Through this work, you will also gradually come to understand that the powers of these deities, which are a dynamic aspect of our planet, are also dynamic aspects of your own body. Our bodies are octaves of the planet, and the deity powers that flow through nature also flow powerfully through us. As you progress in your magical training, you will become more and more aware of this dynamic. It is something that cannot be intellectually understood in real terms; it has to be a direct experience and dawning.

I will leave you with this quote[1] from the earliest mystic in Islam, Ali ibn Abi Talib[2] which demonstrates the deep mystery of our bodies holding octaves of the planet:

> *"You presume you are a small entity,*
> *but within you is enfolded the entire universe."*
>
> — Ali ibn Abi Talib

---

[1] Source: *Diwan al-Imam Ali ibn Abi Talib*. Publisher: Dar al-Kitab al-Arabi. Beirut 2007.

[2] Son in law of the Prophet Muhammad, and the first Shia Imam.

Lesson 2

Angels

Angels appear quite a lot in Western magical and religious texts, as they are major world players in the acts of creation and destruction. As I mentioned in the earlier lesson, some religious/magical systems give angels different names or approach them all as deities or spirits. This can cause a lot of confusion for a magical practitioner, as I am sure you have already discovered. But that is just a matter of semantics: these beings, for magicians, are best identified by how they present, how they operate, and what they do, as opposed to the dressing/identification given to them by systems.

To make it even more complicated, these beings work in tandem and in layers with other beings (deities, elemental spirits, etc.) For example, one magical system may see a storm as an elemental consciousness, another may see it as a deity, and yet another may see it as an angelic or demonic force. In truth, a storm can sometimes have all three: the 'deity' is the fate driver, the angelic or demonic being is the delivery agent of the storm that is acting within a fate pattern, and the elemental consciousness is the intelligence of the storm. A few storms have all three, and sometimes it is just the intelligence of the storm, the combination of wind and water. In some cultures those elements can present as deities.

So for this lesson we will look at what we call angels: what they are, how they present, and what they do. Some information we can glean from magical and religious texts; some we have to find from directly interfacing with these beings.

The problem with magical and religious texts is that although there is a lot of useful information to be found, there are also dogmatic man-made interfaces such as sub divisions, names, colours, numbers, and emotive function that is projected onto the being by humans. These theories are from writers who have never really connected with these beings, and who write from a position of religious manipulation. However, some of these texts also have deep and abiding mysteries outlined in them if the reader knows how to recognise and decipher them.

Once you have built up a strong working relationship with angel beings, which you will have by the time you get to adept-level training, you will easily spot the hidden texts and wisdoms that relate to them. But before you get to that working relationship you need to be sure of what it is you are actually trying to build a relationship with. That is what this lesson is about.

The following is what I have discovered, both through training and practical experience, over the decades. It is not foolproof, it is only from my own experience, and I do not have all the answers, as these beings are in truth way beyond our feeble understanding. But everything written here is a result of direct contact and experience, not theory. And all of it will be approached from a magical perspective, not a religious or cultural one.

1. What are angels?

Angelic beings permeate everything, as they are the building blocks of the inner 'pattern' through which Divine/Universal Power flows in order to manifest in all forms of creation. Angelic beings that are closer to nature/humanity tend to appear in vision in forms that we can relate to, often human, elements or creatures. The further away they are from the details of manifest nature, the weirder they start to look, and the more powerful they become from our perspective.

Besides working as energetic structures for power to flow through, angels are also bridges, guardians, fulcrums, communicators, and deliverers. Some types angelic beings have an extremely focused function that they do not step out of, and often they do not see anything except that which they are tuned to. To me, this type of angelic being is very much like a virus – a virus is not quite a living being but it is essential for life, and viruses have been with us since the very start of the first cell evolution. In evolution viruses enable horizontal gene transfer which is of major importance for genetic diversity.[1] Essentially, besides making us ill which is how most of us become aware of viruses, viruses uphold, diversify life, and bridge 'critical information' from one cell to another, which is basically what 'angels' do between living beings.

Some angelic beings, particularly the ones who work more directly with humanity, tend to have a wider range of action, and they are able to work within a vocabulary that humans can understand and relate to. Angels that work a lot in connection with the human world often 'dress up': they present themselves in a form that we recognise and they will be willing to work within that charade. But charade it often is and such interfacing, if it is too complex or humanised, can limit the human ability to engage fully with, and gain understanding of the angelic being's power. Like viruses, they are not exactly 'living beings' but they are critical to all life on the planet. In early and esoteric Judaism they were/are considered Messengers who have no will of their own and are functional servants of G-D.[2]

2. Historical context

In today's world of magicians, angels abound with many names and are woven by their names into virtually every aspect of magic. This in turn has led to an obsession with names and images that began with post-exile Judaism. What we see in modern magical practices that involve angels/names/colours/hours, etc., with the magician's 'command and control' attitude is yet another example of humanity's need to organise and control. Magically it is pointless and simply attracts parasitical beings.

---

[1] Canchaya C, Fournous G, Chibani-Chennoufi S, Dillmann ML, Brüssow H (August 2003). 'Phage as agents of lateral gene transfer.' Current Opinion in Microbiology. 6 (4): 417–24.

[2] Joseph Hertz: Kommentar zum Pentateuch, hier zu Gen 19,17 EU. Morascha Verlag Zürich, 1984. Band I, p. 164.

Post Judaism was not the only culture or religious pattern to start to name and control these beings, and to humanise them, though it was around the same period from approximately 300 BCE to the 5th century CE.

The need for humanisation of such beings blocked out magical knowledge of the vast array of the many types of these beings and their functions, and also allowed the idea of them as autonomous functioning beings to creep in. In some cases they were presented as deities, such as in the Greek Magical Papryri or as Divine emanations such as in early Kabbalah and also in Zoroastrianism. In Early Zoroastrianism, these emanations were expressions of the Divine will of Ahura Mazda with no will of their own, only the will of the Divine:

> "I invoke the glory of the Amesha Spentas, who all seven have one and the same thinking, one and the same speaking, one and the same doing, one and the same father and lord, Ahura Mazda"[3]

These beings were the bridges, messengers, and deliverers of the Divine Will in the constant dance of creation and destruction within nature – they didn't find parking spaces for you nor get you a job or a girlfriend. Nor would they protect you from your own degeneracy.

That degeneration of thinking is the foundation that modern Western magic sits upon in its method of action. It is really important to realise that, and not to see those early years as some great point in magical history, as the reality was the reverse: that time was the true dawning of the magical Dark Age.

By the time you get to the sixteenth century in Europe the Roman inheritance was in full swing. Everything was about boxing/naming, etc.; and the lure of potentially limitless power, as promised by magic, was a strong pull for anyone who could afford to hire a magician or buy the rare and precious texts. It was a time not unlike today' magical community with its glamorous magical books with fancy sigils and mysterious names, bound in goatskin and inked in 'blood' (i.e. red ink). And the books themselves rarely have anything profound or interesting to say.

But hidden within some of those old texts were gems that whispered, pointing the way to those who paid attention. The clueless searchers would be transfixed by the glamour of strange names, symbols, and difficult rituals. But those who paid attention could find those whispers, break through the glamour, and connect directly with the beings that operate through magic.

And often those whispers truly were whispers. A huge volume may have had only one paragraph that contained all of the magical wisdom that would act as a key to opening up magic for the seeker.

---

[3] The Sacred Books of the East – edited by Max Müller vol 4: the Zend Avesta part 1 translated by James Darmesteter Oxford University Press 1880.

Module VI – Different Types of Beings

A good example of this is found in the *Arbatel of Magic*. On the surface the Arbatel is about connecting to the various levels of consciousness and beings in creation through ritual actions. The magician is told names, numbers, orders, hierarchies, sigils, spells: the recipe is one designed to capture the imagination, and the wish for control, of the magician.

Magicians work with the Arbatel for a number of reasons, some to gain contact with angelic beings, planetary powers, their Holy Guardian Angel, and to discover their own unique purpose and fate. The various magical workings are littered with complex and obscure names, rituals, and so forth.

But underneath that is hidden a profound whisper:

> *There are other names of the Olympick spirits delivered by others;*
> *but they onely are effectual, which are delivered to any one,*
> *by the Spirit the revealer, visible or invisible:*
> *and they are delivered to every one as they are predestinated:*
> *therefore they are called Constellations;*
> *and they seldome have any efficacie above* 40 *yeers.*
>
> *Therefore it is most safe for the young practisers of Art,*
> *that they work by the offices of the Spirits alone, without their names;*
> *and if they are pre-ordained to attain the Art of Magick,*
> *the other parts of the Art will offer themselves unto them*
> *of their own accord.*
> *Pray therefore for a constant faith,*
> *and God will bring to pass all things in due season.*

— *Arbatel of Magic*, Septena Tertia 18

Read that clip a few times and think about it in relation to what you have already learned, and the way you are learning to work with various beings. The Olympic spirits are angelic beings: keep that in mind as you ponder. And also keep in mind that the closed door in magic is kept closed *by the ego of the magician*.

In this course you will learn to work with 'undressed' angels before you move on to work with known ones. This way, just as you did with deities, you will learn the signature feel of an angelic being. As you gain more experience this will allow you to differentiate between an angelic being and something that is not, but that is trying to get you to believe that it is – usually a parasite.

Before we move on, let's just take a little closer look at some different types of angelic functions from a perspective of practical examples, so that you gain a bit more of an understanding before we dig deeper. We will start with the angels that interface more often with humans, and work out from there.

3. Angels close to humans

The angels closest to humans, and which operate around humans, tend to have these functions: they tell you things, show you things, 'open doors' or 'close doors' in your fate path, and facilitate the exteriorisation of power for your birth, death, judgement, health, or sickness: these are angelic beings that act as triggers for key aspects of your life.

As I am sure you are now beginning to understand, everything in the universe works as a series of octaves. Just as an angelic being acts as the filter of the threshold of the manifest world to bring the whole world in to being in an act of constant creation and destruction, so also an angelic being acts upon a threshold that enables *your* creation, your birth, and also your creative output.

From the smallest creation of a plant, an idea, or a fate path, to the creation of the universe itself, an angelic form is present and operating as a filter/bridge/enabler. Before as a magician you dip your toe into the mechanics of the universe, it is wise to understand what is right in front of you.

These angels around humanity are ever-present and usually there is no need for communication: they do their job, you do yours, and everyone is happy. But once a magician steps into magic and opens a conscious dialogue with everything around them the relationship shifts: the magician slowly learns to work alongside, with, and around these angelic beings.

This level of angelic being can present in a variety of ways. How they present to you depends very much on your own understanding and your *ability* to understand, and also on the function of the angel in question, what job they are trying to achieve.

Identifying the angel by function is very important indeed, as it sidesteps a lot of thorny issues for magicians.

A human-created name/image/function is an *interface that the human projects* in order to connect with an angelic being. But if it is over structured then such a projection not only limits the interfacing with the human and becomes a major stumbling-block in the communication, but it can also sometimes create an *empty vessel* a fake identity that a parasite can step into and operate. This happens a lot in magic, more than people realise.

In earlier cultures such as Pre-exile Judaism, Ancient Egypt, etc. the angelic beings were classed simply as angels/spirits who had a particular Divine function and who worked as part of creation: they were known simply by their actions.

They can appear to us in human or semi-human form, often with wings, i.e. showing their ability to flow from one world to another, sometimes with many eyes i.e. sees everything, and with tools for example swords or elements such as flames or wind. This is them projecting images from a vocabulary that they know has relevance to us and that we understand.

Sometimes they will show us things from our own minds in order to convey what they do, e.g. a door, a car, a horse, a cup. What they will not do is give you names or align themselves to planets, substances, times, dates, etc. **those are all man-made constructs**. Behind that angelic vocabulary there is a being of elements, vibrations, sound, and patterns.

People who have taken hallucinogenic drugs have often been thrust before a strange-looking being of colour, sound, patterns, eyes, etc. and the drug has stripped away the human mind's own vocabulary and filter, and exposed the person to the angelic being in its truer form.

Is taking such drugs a good idea? No, not really. Why? Because the mutual simple vocabulary with all its difficulties not only provides a common ground for constructive communication but also provides a filter that protects the human from the impact of the angelic being. These beings carry immense amounts of power within them. Trying to communicate with them without any form of filter can seriously damage a human: think nuclear power. Many hallucinogens bypass or interfere with our natural mind filters, leaving a person over exposed and also unprepared (even when the drug has been taken with ritual preparation).

The simple vocabulary they use in their presentation to us downs the power and filters it into structures of communication and avenues of power that we can cope with. Even so, a powerful angelic being can still impact a human, and this is recounted in magical and religious texts over and over again.

Here is a good example that most of you should already know about: An excerpt from Genesis 32 – Jacob encounters an angel.

> 23 *That same night he arose, and taking his two wives, his two maidservants, and his eleven children, he crossed the ford of the Jabbok.*
>
> 24 *After taking them across the stream, he sent across all his possessions.*
>
> 25 *Jacob was left alone. And a man wrestled with him until the break of dawn.*
>
> 26 *When he saw that he had not prevailed against him, he wrenched Jacob's hip at its socket, so that the socket of his hip was strained as he wrestled with him.*
>
> 27 *Then he said, "Let me go, for dawn is breaking." But he answered, "I will not let you go, unless you bless me."*
>
> 28 *Said the other, "What is your name?" He replied, "Jacob."*
>
> 29 *Said he, "Your name shall no longer be Jacob, but Israel, for you have striven with beings divine and human, and have prevailed."*

30 *Jacob asked, "Pray tell me your name." But he said,* **"You must not ask my name!"** *And he took leave of him there.*

31 *So Jacob named the place Peniel, meaning, "I have seen a divine being face to face, yet my life has been preserved."*

32 *The sun rose upon him as he passed Peniel, limping on his hip.*

— Genesis 32:23–33
This translation was taken from the JPS Tanakh.

Notice in the text how the angel appears to him as a human male, and yet acts as the threshold between Divinity and Jacob. As any magician experienced in working in vision with angelic beings will tell you, communing in depth with an angel feels like you have spent the night wrestling: the physical impact can be quite considerable.

In the Genesis chapter, Jacob spends the whole night in some form of communion with an angelic being, and survives to tell the tale. This changes him forever, which is shown by his change of name.

Not all angels have such an impact upon the human body, but many do, particularly those who are heralds and bridges. A magician spends a lot of time training slowly, building strength, inner vision, roots, and developing filters and tools, so that as they advance they can work and commune with angelic beings safely and without too much impact, unless they overstep the mark.

The modern fantasy idea of what an angel looks like or does, such as a glowing handsome young man in a dress with wings who helps you find a parking space is a perfect 'mind vessel' for a parasite to step into. The same is true also on the 'dark' side of magic that views angelic beings in human styled projections of 'darkness' is also a perfect vessel for parasites. And these various forms are often parasited; they will appear and speak in a way that the hapless magician can easily connect to, and they will be more than happy to engage with the magician as the parasite sucks at the energy of the human.

To sidestep this all-too-common problem with cross-dressing parasites, work with angelic beings by using their *function* as an identity, and allow them to present themselves to you as they wish, not how you think they should look. This also forces the magician to research the true function of specific angels, not just the popular aspect of that angel's function.

Again, as you will have realised by now, it is important for the magician to be able to get out of the way and allow beings to present in their own chosen vocabulary, not one that the magician has plucked from a grimoire. As you progress through the course, the angels that are close to humanity will be beings that you will work with quite a bit; hence it is important at the early stages to be able to get out of the way of your own mind and allow clear communication.

4. Threshold angels

Threshold angels are another type of angelic being that you will work with quite a lot in the latter stages of the Initiate and Adept training. Although you will not work with them as an apprentice it is very useful for your foundational knowledge to know what they are and what they do, just in case one does turn up in your work, which can happen at any stage in a magician's training. Knowledge of them will also help you to understand various ancient texts and spot them in action in those texts regardless of how they are labelled.

For example, in Egyptian texts all beings are labelled as *deities* or *spirits* (Neter). This is not a problem so long as you understand what they *do* and what their *limitations* are. The Egyptians made no distinction between different types of beings, but they did approach the different types of 'deities' in different ways.

To us as modern magicians, labelling different beings with different functions as deities, angels, demons, etc. just makes it easier for us to understand how to approach them and work with them... so long as you do not overcomplicate it in your own mind. But also keep in mind the religious overlay of meanings with these labels, which often have little to do with the actual being.

Threshold angels tend not to turn up in the manifest world, but they can turn up quite a lot in magical vision work depending on what you are doing. They work on 'the other side of the fence,' so to speak, and are a layer removed from the angelic beings that work out in the world with humanity and other creatures.

So for example, where you find an angel who works with the dying, there is also a deeper angelic being in the inner worlds that works with human once they have died. That is a threshold angel. Beyond that threshold angel there is another deeper layer again, with an angel that works with the soul at a more profound level.

Threshold beings work in the Inner Desert, which is essentially the cooking-pot of creation. They combine their patterns to create energetic structures through which power flows from Divinity, forming it in preparation for physical manifestation. These structural angelic beings were also used in the past by priest-magicians for the inner construction of temples and sacred buildings. A good example can be found the Old Testament, for example in the construction of the temple of Solomon in 1 Kings 6: 15-38 KJV.

Remnants of that knowledge survived in aspects of the construction of early Norman cathedrals, but only remnants. If you go to some ancient temples, Karnak in Egypt is a good example, and you sit and go in vision to the inner substance of the temple, you will see the angelic structures embedded within the building.

These beings are involved in far too many aspects of creation to give you a wide overview in one lesson, but from these key details, as you progress, you will be able to spot them.

Another function of the threshold angels is to carry the consciousness of humans to the threshold of Divinity.

One aspect of this function has become very popular in magic and New Age circles, and that is the aspect known as the *Merkaba*. There is so much bullshit around the Merkaba that is it almost comical: everything from UFOs to light vehicles, to complex rituals and actions undertaken to step into some sort of light car and go speeding off to God... good luck with that one.

The reality of the Merkaba is not so flashy, but is far more profound: it consists of threshold angelic beings that provide an access route from the manifest realm to the Divine realm.

You cannot ritually induce it: there is nothing a human can do to force that contact and action. However, it is a natural stage that an adept comes to when they have been working in depth with angelic beings in vision for some time. The angelic beings uphold the human and bridge them across the threshold of the worlds when the time is right for that individual. This is something you will come to learn about in the adept section of the work.

The key to recognising threshold angels is in their presentation and action. They do not appear in the manifest world; they appear only in the inner worlds or at threshold events that involve groups, tribes, or nations: birth, death, destruction, creation, Judgement. At these threshold events a different octave of angelic being will present to the human, but these deeper threshold beings will be working away, literally on the threshold between the worlds.

Visionaries spot them, as do magicians. They appear with many eyes, wings, and flames, with wind, light, darkness, animal heads, etc., and very rarely in any humanoid form that we would recognise. These are not beings to work with in learning, you would get fried, but simply to be aware of so that you can spot them in texts; which in turn will help you understand the hidden meanings in those texts.

5. Angels and the Inner Desert

These angelic beings only work deep in the inner worlds and do not work at all in the manifest world. Their patterns form power that is then passed on to the threshold angels, who in turn pass it on to the angels who work out in the manifest world.

These are the weirdest-looking of all the angels and tend to appear as complex patterns and platonic solids. They are the building blocks or 'code' of creation and destruction.

A good and well-known example of these beings that is passed down through magical texts is the *Metatron Cube*. Many modern magicians think that the Cube is some sort of code to be broken or a pattern that they can manipulate: that is a trap. This pattern is a representation of the angelic structures found at the edge of the Abyss: the first filter that the consciousness and impulse of Divinity passes through as it begins its journey into manifest creation. It is also a modern shape and not an ancient one, and yet it works and does reflect an aspect of these angelic beings.

This is a level of angelic contact that the magician simply observes, and through observation the magician gains insight. If the magician tries to decode this pattern, they get trapped in a loop of 'code-breaking' which shuts them down.

This is the level of contact where the job of the adept is simply to observe, and through that observation, enact their service as 'witnesses.' It is not something for an apprentice to be involved in. Not only would it be fruitless at this stage, but it can also have a massive physical impact, as your body is not yet fully tuned to deal with that level of power. But over time, it is something that you will potentially step into.

6. Bound angels

Some angels that have singular, very powerful actions are often found bound up in a form of sleep until it is their time to release and do their job. These angels only become active at times of major change in the manifest world. As an adept, as you work deeply in the inner worlds, you will potentially come across these bound angels. They are not beings that you would work with magically, but observing and recognising them allows you to spot when one of these powerful beings has been released out into the manifest world.

Usually their job is destruction. We in the West would often consider their actions to be 'demonic,' when in fact they are bringing destruction in order to create balance. Here is a good Biblical example:

> 13 And the sixth angel sounded, and I heard a voice from the four horns of the golden altar which is before God,
>
> 14 Saying to the sixth angel which had the trumpet, Loose the four angels which are bound in the great river Euphrates.
>
> 15 And the four angels were loosed, which were prepared for an hour, and a day, and a month, and a year, for to slay the third part of men.

— *Revelations 9:13*

As magicians we have no business with these beings. Our job is simply to observe and be *witnesses* to these angelic expressions without any personal judgement and without interfering in their processes. But recognising them and spotting them in action brings us a much better, longer-term understanding of what is happening in the manifest world.

If there is massive disaster/war/destruction and we have previously seen one of these bound angels being released, we know that the destruction, however awful it may be, is a necessary function. That in turn tells us not to interfere or get involved unless fate pulls us directly into the firing line.

That can sometimes happen, and has happened to me in the past: you observe the releasing of a powerful angelic being from its bindings and shortly after chaos spills out into the world in some form. You are then suddenly transported right into the midst of the chaos to do a specific task, and then immediately taken back out of the situation. That usually happens where there is a simple job that a human must do in order to assist with the process. Most of the time this is not a magical job, and sometimes it is simply a matter of being there briefly, as a magically switched-on human.

At this level of your training, just be aware of these beings and learn to recognise bound angels in magical and religious texts, as this will tell you a great deal about what was happening and why. This in turn will expand your magical understanding and education, without plunging you into a dangerous area of magic.

I have also come across bound angels that were bound in their actions by human magic. This magic was very old, complex, powerful... and pretty nasty. I do not fully understand the mechanisms by which these beings were bound using magic, but I certainly learned how to take that binding off.

There is a lot of nonsense in modern magical texts about binding angelic beings to 'do your will.' The vast majority of that writing is total bullshit. Binding an angelic being is not impossible, as many would think, but it is a lot harder than most magicians understand it to be. If I had a dollar for every hapless wannabe magician who told me that they had bound the archangel Michael to their arm with a flashy tattoo, to do their will, I would be a rich woman. Not only is this bullshit, it is *infantile* bullshit, which makes it all the more depressing.

Sometimes an overdeveloped human interface for an angel will appear as a magical binding when in fact it isn't: the human structure, i.e. name, image, etc. simply limits the conversation between angel and human so much that it may as well be bound, as it cannot work through such a restricted filter.

7. Developing a working method

By now you will have noticed that the magician does not 'call' angels to himself or herself; rather the magician goes to a threshold level of being where the human and angel can interact in a mutually accessible space. At the apprentice level such a space is the threshold of the directions. Later you will learn to expand that work to deeper visionary work, inner temples, and also out in nature.

This is for a number of reasons, and although the adept will at times call/ask an angel into the manifest working space, most of the time all interactions are in vision. This enables the magician to sidestep all the false dressings and allow full and proper interaction with the angelic being as opposed to random snatches of contact.

This method takes longer in terms of learning and technique development, but it works along more natural paths i.e. vision, dreams, inner senses, which in turn allows for greater and safer communion. By the time you are an adept you will work in both methods.

8. *Task:* Vision work

In this exercise you are going to connect with an angelic being that works through the dynamic known as the Grindstone. You have worked with this influence through your ritual work and through your work with the sword (it is one of the angelic beings that flows with the magic of the sword). This will make it easier for you to make a visionary contact with this angelic being: you sort of already know each other.

Once you have met this being you will slowly start to understand the planetary influence that is connected with/in orbit with this angel. You will also slowly begin to recognise its influence in your life via tarot readings and ritual work. It is a being that works ceaselessly in the manifest world, and is a major component of your magical path.

You do not ask/tell/demand this being to do things for you; rather you learn simply to commune and recognise when it has been triggered in your life. By doing this, the power of the being becomes something that can not only help you understand a situation, but it can also teach you how as a magician to engage fully with its influence in order to achieve your greatest potential: once you know why something difficult is happening, it makes it easier to plough your way through that difficulty, knowing that there is a positive reason for such influence.

Once you have gotten to a stage in your magical training where you are fully capable of taking magical responsibility for yourself, you will then find that this angelic being, along with others, will be more forthcoming in communication with you, and will work more actively with you.

Preparation and work

To prepare for the vision set up the ritual space with the tools in each direction. Prop the sword, point down, against the north side of the east altar. And spread the cloth shield on the floor. Light the lights, open the gates, and do the Anchor ritual. Then go sit down in front of the east altar; spend a short time in stillness meditation.

Once you are still, using your inner vision, see the east gate and the contacts on the thresholds. Ask the contact if you can observe, through the open gate, the power/angelic being of the Grindstone power. Sit quietly and observe in vision. This being can present in a number of ways, so do not try to preempt it in your mind.

When you get a sense of the being, ask if it would be willing to make itself known to you through your dreams, though augury in the outside world, and through any other signs that you could learn to spot. Do not try to limit how this being makes itself known to you, and do not demand anything. The contact is likely to be fleeting and difficult to understand in vision (though not for everybody), so don't expect Ezekiel-like visions; just let it be what it will be.

Your body needs to get used to these deeper powers, so don't push it. Do this vision connection only once, which will trigger further connection out in the manifest world – the safest form of connection at this stage. Working this way, one step at a time, can be frustrating, but it slowly adjusts you so that eventually, as an adept, you will be able to work freely and deeply with these beings. When you have finished the vision, close down the directions in your usual way, and put everything away.

Documenting your observations

Immediately write down your interaction, observations, insights, and descriptions in your journal. Later, type them up in your computer log.

9. *TASK:* TAROT READINGS

Using the LANDSCAPE/DESERT LAYOUT, look to see if this being is having a direct influence in your life at present, and if so, what part of your life and how. Use other layouts if you need to in order to get the information you need.

Do not peer too deeply and do not obsess over it. Simply look, acknowledge, then think about how you may need to step up and fully engage with the situation this being is flowing through in your life.

10. *TASK:* RESEARCH AND PONDERING

Think back to what you learned about the magical sword and how it works out in the world, and also in your own life and magical work. Meditate upon the relationship between the sword and the Grindstone. Write down your observations and conclusions in your computer log.

Read the *Book of Revelation* in the New Testament. Think about the angelic influences that are depicted in the texts, and take notes (computer) as to what you think the underlying work/purpose of these angelic beings are and how you would describe them by function.

Read the *Book of Jubilees* chapter two, verses one to three. This tells you about the different angels involved in nature and creation. Spend some time rereading those short verses and thinking about them in light of what you know.

Lesson 3

Demons

> *"There are places in the Old Testament where some English translations use the word "demon" or "devils".[1] In other places, it is easy for people in the modern world who are accustomed to reading the New Testament to think "demons" when they read things like "an evil spirit," even though the text clearly says that the evil spirit is from God.[2]*
>
> *In spite of the translations, there is no word in Hebrew equivalent to the English word "demon," nor any word that communicates the same meaning that the term communicates in English as a malevolent being in the service of the devil out to destroy humans. That idea today has been shaped by the imagination of medieval Christian writers and popularised in the modern church in terms of evil beings against which Christians need to wage "spiritual warfare." The ancient Israelites lived in a world in which that view of "demons" was not part of their culture or way of thinking.*
>
> *This disparity between our own modern notions and what lies behind the Hebrew terms and concepts often leads to misunderstanding the point of the biblical text and what it communicates. It is always a good idea to read what the biblical text actually says about a topic, and understand the passage against the social and cultural background of ancient Israel and the early church before we impose too many of our modern assumptions and preconceptions about meaning onto Scripture."*
>
> — Professor (retired) Dennis R Bratcher, PhD Theology, Christian Resource Institute USA.

This lesson is a tough one in that its main function is to dispel well-rooted but incorrect myths and instead take the student to a more balanced place of understanding. This is critical to a magician, as without a proper understanding of what a demon is and isn't, there is no proper understanding of how the inner and outer worlds operate from a magical perspective.

In this lesson, which is a read, digest, and research lesson, we can lay dogma to rest and start the process of understanding these powerful beings who exert a direct influence on humanity. This lesson will also lay good foundations of understanding for the rest of this module so that by the end of the module you should have a good basic knowledge of the various beings we come into contact with through magic.

---

[1] Demon: Deut 32:17, Psa 106:37; "goat-demons": Lev 17:7, Isa 13:21, NRSV; "devils": 2 Chron 11:15, AV.
[2] Jud 9:23, 1 Sam 16:14–23.

The majority of Western magicians come from families and communities that are deeply rooted in the family of Abrahamic religions. This most commonly results in magicians who feel that they have divorced themselves from their religious roots, but who continue their religion's ignorance and misunderstanding on this subject into their magical paths without even realising it.

A simple browse through magical books, magical forums and discussions will quickly highlight the baggage that magicians from any culture touched by Abrahamic religions carry around with them. It is time to drop this baggage, and understand what is actually in front of you.

Before we go on to look at the beings who are termed as 'demons' from a magical perspective, let's look at the source of the misunderstanding and how, when fuelled by dogma, it creates a strong barrier against magicians seeking a magical truth.

1. Biblical demons

The New Testament is the first place in which we find the concepts of possession and a world where God, angels, and 'good stuff' are at one end of the Scales, and Satan, demons, and 'bad stuff' are at the other end.

Before that time, in various cultures, including Judaism, as can be seen in the Old Testament, things were a bit more complicated and less polarised: we have mentions of *spirits, deities,* and *Divinity*. The spirits could be good or bad depending on their actions, and the same went for deities.

The key difference is that before the New Testament and the subsequent medieval scaremongering, all ancient texts referred to bad spirits as being part of Divine creation with a role to play in the manifest and inner worlds. Here is a clip from the Catholic Encyclopaedia that describes the change in use of the term *demon* over time within a Catholic theology perspective:

> **Demon:** *Scripture and in Catholic theology—this word has come to mean much the same as devil and denotes one of the evil spirits or fallen angels. And in fact in some places in the New Testament where the Vulgate, in agreement with the Greek, has daemonium, our vernacular versions read devil. The precise distinction between the two terms in ecclesiastical usage may be seen in the phrase used in the decree of the Fourth Lateran Council: "Diabolus enim et alii daemones" (The devil and the other demons), i.e. all are demons, and the chief of the demons is called the devil. This distinction is observed in the Vulgate New Testament, where diabolus represents the Greek diabolos and in almost every instance refers to Satan himself, while his subordinate angels are described, in accordance with the Greek, as daemones or daemonia. This must not be taken, however, to indicate a difference of nature; for Satan is clearly included among the daemones in James 2:19 and in Luke 11:15-18.*

But though the word demon is now practically restricted to this sinister sense, it was otherwise with the earlier usage of the Greek writers. The word, which is apparently derived from daio "to divide" or "apportion", originally meant a divine being; it was occasionally applied to the higher gods and goddesses, but was more generally used to denote spiritual beings of a lower order coming between gods and men. For the most part these were beneficent beings, and their office was somewhat analogous to that of the angels in Christian theology. Thus the adjective eydaimon "happy", properly meant one who was guided and guarded by a good demon. Some of these Greek demons, however, were evil and malignant. Hence we have the counterpart to eudamonia "happiness", in kakodaimonia which denoted misfortune, or in its more original meaning, being under the possession of an evil demon. In the Greek of the New Testament and in the language of the early Fathers, the word was already restricted to the sinister sense, which was natural enough, now that even the higher gods of the Greeks had come to be regarded as devils.

We have a curious instance of the confusion caused by the ambiguity and variations in the meaning of the word, in the case of the celebrated "Daemon" of Socrates. This has been understood in a bad sense by some Christian writers who have made it a matter of reproach that the great Greek philosopher was accompanied and prompted by a demon. But, as Cardinal Manning clearly shows in his paper on the subject, the word here has a very different meaning. He points to the fact that both Plato and Xenophon use the form daimonion, which Cicero rightly renders as divinum aliquid, "something divine". And after a close examination of the account of the matter given by Socrates himself in the reports transmitted by his disciples, he concludes that the promptings of the "Daemon" were the dictates of conscience, which is the voice of God.[3]

The idea of demons being servants of a chief demon called Satan and a gang constantly at war with God and humanity is rooted in the fertile soil of late antiquity Iranian Zoroastrianism and the birth of Christianity as an organised religion.

It is worth taking the time to look in detail at some Judaic texts, particularly early ones, and then to look at the youngest books of the Old Testament. Reading them alongside very early to medieval Christian writings, and also following the progression of Zoroastrianism, you start to see a theme developing; a theme that is not only interesting but critical in the understanding of where the degenerate dogma we have today comes from. That understanding has to be viewed in light of human nature, and also in light of how humans build, expand, and then elaborate upon a subject when there is a void in understanding.

---

[3] New Advent Catholic Encyclopaedia Vol 1 1907, Robert Appleton Publishing company, NY USA.

Here is a quick breakdown of that progression, as the understanding of this process is critical to the development of a magician.

First comes the experience, then comes understanding, and then that understanding solidifies and is worked with. This is the phase, for example, that we see in Old Kingdom Egypt and also in Sumeria in very early texts and image depictions in the period around 2500 BC. Many different civilisations around the world had been building upon their own cultural understanding of the powers around them and had learned to interact and work with them.

Between 2500 BC and 1500 BC in the texts and depictions of various cultures we see a shift in the religious/magical/cultural practices where the emphasis of power is moved from the deities to the kingships. This is all very general and sweeping, but it gives you somewhere to start in your research.

By approximately 400 BC we are looking at huge shifts in the balance of power between neighbouring cultures, and we begin to see a shift in the human understanding of the nature of the world.

The ancient understanding of the world was as a place of order that needs to be maintained through personal and ritual action to avoid it sliding into chaos, for example the Egyptian laws of Ma'at. This understanding gave way to simplified and more degenerate ideas but they were still workable, i.e. a view that there is a constant battle between order and chaos. This is a subtle shift but a critical one. The emphasis has moved from maintaining the creative natural order through the actions of the individual and the community, to defending against evil by one's actions. Almost the same, but not!

Slowly over the next four hundred years the many different spirits and beings that were previously all considered part and parcel of creation, and critical to maintaining balance in the manifest world, became divided into good and evil. Beings who were good for humanity were considered servants of the One God – we were seriously in the throws of monotheism at this point. Beings who were not good for humanity became evil spirits who were hostile to God.

By the time the Jewish sect that became Christianity arrived we were in full flight with demons, angels, and god knows what else. The people who held power, the Kings, priests and people who spoke 'with authority realised that this severe duality had many uses. Demons could be used to scare people into submission, and angels could be used to offer hope to the peasants, which would keep them happy in their miserable lives.

When medieval-flavoured Christianity had gained strength, these simple 'power tools' were used and expanded upon to full effect, and served the feudal system in its various forms around the known Christian world. These 'power tools' were, over time, subsequently taken up by the occultists, philosophers and dabblers, and that is how we arrived at the occult idea of demons today.

"Demons!" is a dogma of control and fear that has proved very popular with and useful to religious and societal organisations. This dogma has infected just about all of Western magic, as well as leaving negative fragments in other religions and magical systems that have been affected by Western culture, in countries that were raided and colonised by the British Empire, for example.

We see examples of this 'infection' of dogma in modern magic not only in the grimoires, but also in the magic of other cultures when it is used by Western magicians. Everything is reduced to 'good' or 'demonic,' which severely limits the magician and plays into the immature power fantasies that many young magicians get trapped in. Hence it is wise to toss all those hierarchies out of the window so that you can get to real study, understanding, and then magic.

2. Demons, destroying angels and parasites – what is what?

So what is a 'demon'? The term we use in magic refers to a being that is *destructive* by its actions or by its nature: we will stick with the name 'demon' for now just for clarity. However, within that definition there are different types of beings that can present in very similar ways. A destroying deity would fall under the heading of 'demon,' just as a destroying or destructive angelic being could be classified as one by nature of its actions.

It is also interesting to observe that in today's world demons are seen as things that corrupt, control, or possess the individual. This is a massive swing from the early idea that 'demons' controlled nations, nature, etc. So also keep that shift in mind as we go along with the lesson: you basically have to shed everything you consider to be a 'demon' in the modern understanding of the word, and instead take a step back and rethink.

Powerful parasites, which we will cover in the next lesson, are also destructive beings. These are usually the ones that pester individual humans. What differentiates a parasite from any other type of destructive being is that a parasite behaves the way that it does in order to feed itself, whereas other destroying beings (deities, angels, spirits) are destructive because that is what they do: their actions and functions are potentially destructive to us, but are not destructive *per se*. In the next lesson we will look in depth at these parasitical beings and their actions when possessing an individual, which is their *modus operandi*. 'Demons' (i.e. destroying beings) do not possess people; parasites do.

So we begin to understand that there are in fact a few different types of beings that fall under the modern heading of 'demon,' and each of these types of beings work in different ways to different ends.

Rather than get wrangled up in the different names and identities, many of which are contradictory or confusing, we will look at the outer manifestations of specific destructive, dangerous, or destroying beings in terms of their actions, their 'signatures,' and their levels of power. This level of being is something that is truly necessary for a magician to understand, for lots of different reasons, as you will come to appreciate through your studies and work.

3. Ones that act on individuals

Truly destructive beings rarely focus their attention on individual creatures, humans included. In ordinary human life a person may be pestered by parasites, land spirits, Djinn, etc., but very rarely by truly destructive forces. So for clarity, most information about the directly negative effects of beings on humans will be handled in subsequent lessons in this module.

A Biblical example can be found in the Book of Samuel – 1 Samuel 16; 14–23. Even though the evil spirit in this text is destructive, it is still within the natural order of life and is acknowledged as such within the text (as it is sent by God).

Once you step out of the ordinary human life and step into powerful magic it becomes more possible for a magician to be directly affected by a powerful destructive being. The deeper and more profound the actions of the magician, the more likely they are to be confronted by a destructive, powerful force. This is not because the magician is 'bad':such understanding is degenerate; rather it is more about visibility, challenge, and being in places that most humans never tread.

Look at it like a mountain climber. As a beginner the climber is challenged by practice walls, small outcrops, etc. where they can test their new-found, developing skills. If they fall it is likely that they will be heavily roped, will fall onto mats, or will not fall very far.

As the climber progresses and takes on harder and harder peaks, so the potential for disaster goes up. When they tackle a peak like K2 they are potentially faced with all sorts of dangers from the forces of nature: not just the peak itself, but the harsh, quickly changing weather and the low oxygen levels. So it is with magic.

The destructive beings an adept can potentially cross paths with are not often aiming particularly at the magician. It is more a matter of a magician getting in the way of such a being, and also the magician can be highly visible. If the adept is working on long-term projects in magic that involve nations, cultures, etc., it is possible that they will either work alongside these destructive beings or they will come face to face with them in some way.

Very rarely, and I mean *really* rarely, one of these very destructive beings can be 'sent after' a magician to destroy them, not only physically, but also spiritually, i.e. locking the human out of the cycle of birth/death and also preventing them from passing deep into death – keeping the magician in stasis so that they cannot act at all.

Many people who dabble in the occult think that this happens a lot, that a 'demon' is sent after a human to destroy them, which exposes the person's lack of knowledge, and that if the dabbler learns lots of complex rituals they will be able to destroy all their enemies, which is very childish. Such events are mainly restricted to the realm of movies and delicate immature egos flavoured by wishful thinking.

Truly powerful destructive magic powered by truly powerful destructive beings is a rare thing indeed, simply because very few Western magicians have the knowledge and power to do such a thing. But in rare cases it does happen: usually when the attacking magician is tied into a specific religious train of thought and feels divinely justified doing such an action. Usually by the time a magician gets to a level of skill where they *can* enact such a thing, they tend to be a bit more intelligent and realise how pointless it is. However, there is always one idiot somewhere...

But when such an event occurs, the magician on the receiving end is like the experienced K2 climber. Having a destroying power aimed straight at you is not automatically destructive. If the person on the receiving end is balanced in what they are doing and is knowledgeable then the destruction is dodged, sometimes engaged with and transformed, and the receiver works with the many different beings around them to restore balance.

In my decades of magic I have seen such a thing unleashed once – and it didn't work. The senders felt justified and were certainly skilled enough, but they were also unwise and unseeing: the power of Divinity works in many different ways, and it is not for us to Judge or be executioner.

The majority of times when magicians fling 'demons' at each other, it is in fact parasites or land spirits working for an energetic fee. This we will look at in the next lesson, along with the issue of mental illness and possession. This lesson is more about the vast powers of destruction: such powers are way beyond the depressed, middle-aged magician in his mother's basement uttering jumbled Hebrew from an elfskin grimoire.

4. The Destroying Ones of Nature

The destructive forces that flow through natural events work in tandem with angelic beings and deities, and are sometimes identified as destroying deities. Some of these destroying deities in nature became reclassified over time into being 'demons.'

Of course wherever there is the word 'demon,' the young modern occultist sits up to attention and reclassifies it again as a 'deity,' but still within their modern fantasy form.

My favourite example of this is Lilith, who started out as Ninlil. We will briefly look at the successive reclassifications of this being as societies and religions cross-fertilised and changed; then we will look at what that power actually is, what it does, and how it works. That will give you a broader scope of understanding, and a better ability to spot these and other destroying powers embedded within ancient texts, when we come to the part of the lesson that looks at destructive powers.

5. Lilith – an example of a destroying power

Rather than just look at this from an archaeological and historical point of view, I thought it better also to weave into that the magical understanding of this power, which will help you in your research into other destructive apparently 'demonic' forces that pop up in magic.

Over the millennia the power we know today as Lilith started out as a powerful creative/destructive deity, and ended up as a pseudo-blow-up doll for frustrated occultists and a fractured, unbalanced role model for female occultists. Throughout the many years everyone projected their own issues, agendas, and fantasies on this identity. As a result the *true nature of this being* is largely ignored, much to the detriment of magicians.

Remember Cybele from your earlier research? The Sumerians had their own version and as the culture developed, so the mythology grew. The great mother goddess became subdivided, and Ninlil emerged.

It is pertinent to note at this point that the names of the deities often changed, switched, or were bound together, for example Mami/Tiamet/Ninlil/Mullitu/Ishtar, and the names drifted along with the twists and turns of societal development. So when you come to do further research, keep this in mind.

Also keep in mind that some (not all) of the early translations and interpretations of the Sumer texts have been rewritten by researchers who assume much by way of their own religious and cultural stances. So you have to dig deep and beyond general articles: you have to go back to university texts. You will know when you spot the quality research... the bells will ring!

Ninlil was the partner of Enlil, the male southern wind, and in the cuneiform texts she is sometimes referred to as the north wind. She also gave birth to the war god of the north wind. Ninlil was also written about as an instigator (north and east), and Enlil was also seen a god of the harvest (south and west). Recognise anything yet? But just to confuse you, one of the forms of Ninlil was also described as the mother of the four winds.

I warn you, there are major switches and turnarounds in the mythologies from the early Bronze Age, through the mid-Bronze Age, to the late Bronze Age. Different attributes and names were constantly switching, so you have to keep your wits about you.

In some versions of the mythos Ninlil was tricked into sex by the deity of the River of Death (the Boatman, who in some variants was Enlil disguised), and so gave birth to Underworld gods.

So here we have a root goddess, referred to in some texts as the Queen of the Heavens and Earth, and as the Mother of the Four Winds; one who guards the entrance to the Underworld, who is also the mother of the Underworld powers. We have a female power who exerts inner and outer influence over the winds, the Underworld, the land, and the stars. As things get out of balance her influence brings destruction in the form of storms, disease, and death to sweep away imbalance.

Over time Ninlil morphed, and by around 600 BC she had become a wind deity who heralded death and destruction: she became sidelined, viewed as something negative, something to be feared. This happened to a lot of the early, powerful female deities in this region: they were either suppressed, for example Asherah, or viewed as evil; the beginnings of demonisation.

The feared wind/destruction deity continued her descent in the eyes of man, until she was identified as Lilith or Lilit, a night monster who ate babies and made men masturbate at night – a good enough excuse as any!

This new 'understanding' is reflected in the Biblical text of Isaiah 34:10–15. It is from the time just preceding the Babylonian exile, when Isaiah prophesied about the coming disaster. In Isaiah, Lilith is referred to by way of a list of animals that signify her presence: ravens, jackals, wild dogs, owls, snakes, and ostriches.

But it didn't stop there. By the time we get to the sixth century AD she appears as a female demon in magical inscriptions on demon bowls and amulets. By the eight century AD, we have another shift in the story of Lilith, as depicted in the *Alphabet of Ben Sirach* – she becomes the errant first wife of Adam.

The *Alphabet of Ben Sirach* was a text from the eighth or ninth century AD that was a mix of old Aramaic proverbs, and newer Hebrew proverbs that were linked to entertaining stories that poked fun at the serious thinkers and rule-makers of the time. It is not a sacred or Rabbinical text; rather it is a text that should be seen in the context of the humour, satire, and vapidity of its time.

It was something that was a bit of a joke, alongside some early wisdom sayings, that has now become a 'sacred text' to be taken literally when it comes to Lilith. One of the satirical and deeply misogynist stories in the book introduces Lilith and gives this imaginary being a back history. The whole book is a collection of different writings and stories that were put together for their jokes, flavour, and the occasional bit of ancient advice. It was never meant to be taken seriously.

Here is a section from the *Alphabet of Ben Sirach* on Lilith:

> *The angels who are in charge of medicine: Snvi, Snsvi, and Smnglof.*
>
> *After God created Adam, who was alone, He said, "It is not good for man to be alone". He then created a woman for Adam, from the earth, as He had created Adam himself, and called her Lilith.*
>
> *Adam and Lilith began to fight. She said, "I will not lie below," and he said, "I will not lie beneath you, but only on top. For you are fit only to be in the bottom position, while I am to be in the superior one."*

Lilith responded, "We are equal to each other inasmuch as we were both created from the earth."

But they would not listen to one another. When Lilith saw this, she pronounced the Ineffable Name and flew away into the air.

Adam stood in prayer before his Creator: "Sovereign of the universe!" he said, "the woman you gave me has run away."

At once, the Holy One, blessed be He, sent these three angels to bring her back.

So within a span of around two thousand years, our understanding of Lilith went from her being a powerful force of nature, a great goddess who spanned the Heaven and the Underworld, to a disobedient wife with a whining husband. But it did not stop even there.

In modern occultism Lilith has been bandied about in all directions as a goddess of lust, sexuality, childbirth, dark moons – you name it, people have projected attributes on to this spirit to make her fit their occult views in accordance with the society fashions of the time. From the end of the Victorian era in Britain to the rise of the wild sixties, Lilith was pointed to as the goddess that flouted the norms of society, or became a nice cuddly mummy goddess who loved women and babies.

Thelema and witchcraft streams in particular have run with the whole sex propaganda. For example, here is a quote about Lilith from Doreen Valiente, a major witchcraft figure:

"*[Lilith] is the personification of erotic dreams, the suppressed desire for delights.*"

It would be hilarious if it were not so sad. And what is truly sad is that the people interested in the occult and these ancient powers only looked as far back as the much later Hebrew texts and pseudo texts, and most certainly did not look in any depth from an inner magical perspective.

Through the actions of these people and their ideas, a massive parasite has built up over hundreds of years that today operates through this window of the occult 'Lilith,' a projection of the female sexual revolution of the 1960s grafted on top of a much earlier projection of a fear of female power, childbirth, disease, and death. To this day, that parasite continues to feed on the clueless projections thrown out by budding occultists.

Besides the archaeological and historical Ninlil deity, what lurks beneath that image that magicians can learn about, recognise, and work with? Let's have a look. And you can use the same research method and understanding as we did with Lilith to look at the other powerful and destructive forces that we will discuss in the rest of this lesson. That way, I do not have to outline every step of history for each power that we look at; you can do that for yourself.

6. Talking to the Wind – The magical power of Lilith

The root of these deities/demons/whatever lies in the power of the elements, and human relationships with those elements. When we look magically at these powers we see more or less three layers: the *angelic structure* that allows the element to express in the manifest world, the *sheer power and action* of the element itself, and then the *deity* that is the human interface and filter for communion between humans and the raw power.

Some magicians work only with the deity and keep very much within the orbit of human action. However that is very limiting, and the relationship quickly becomes a religious and not a magical one. Other magicians work with both the raw power and the deity. Look upon the deity as the *interpreter* and also the *conscious voice* of the element.

The early human settlers in the areas we now call Iraq and Syria quickly learned that a relationship with the elemental powers of the region meant a better chance at survival. The nature of this relationship would likely have been akin to what we see in present day Stone Age tribes around the world. If a storm, flood, earthquake, etc. was coming then the consciousness of that power, by way of its regular interactions with the people, would herald what was to come: Ninlil would whisper, and the people would run for cover.

At the beginning of the Holocene period the elements were very dynamic, with huge shifts in water levels, temperatures, weather fronts, and even the shifting of landmasses from the melting ice further to the north. Today we think of this sort of thing as happening only in isolated places (and further north from Iraq) but in truth, such dynamic action of the elements would have affected everything around these areas, both from an inner and an outer perspective.

People quickly learned to read, listen, and communicate with the elements around them in order to survive. As those skills progressed, people began to communicate formally with the powers around them, to come together as a group voice and communicate with the inner powers of the wind, the land, the creatures, the death and Underworld powers, and the stars above them. We see in this the early forming of temple communication with these raw powers.

A good example of this is probably what we are looking at with Göbekli Tepe, near Şanlıurfa, Turkey, an eleven thousand year old temple construct. There was no city, no settlement around it; rather it was a sacred place where people gathered and then left. The discovery of this vast temple complex pointed the archaeologists towards something that magicians have known for a long time: that these early temples were not born from agriculture or city states; rather they were born from the communion between humans and the powers of nature around them. As that level of communication developed and deities were formed to enable people to communicate indirectly, on more human terms, with the elements, so the 'magic' that we know today was born.

So how would this have translated in terms of Ninlil/Lilith and the human interaction?

People would have worked with Ninlil for danger warnings: "there is a great storm coming that will bring death," "the wind will cease to blow" (in summer that in itself could bring death), "the southern wind will bring dust and heat that will kill." Also disease is carried along on the wind, so the wind can also bring death; you start to get the idea.

Through this interaction over time, it will have become apparent that some people were better at it and more accurate than others. That is the beginning of the magical priest/priestess or shaman type magician who would work with the deity Ninlil, who in turn would give an advanced warning so that they could act accordingly and in time. She would have brought prophecy which is an aspect of the air elemental power, and also the great gifts of rain, gentle wind, and protection from early death or disease. A lot of this interaction could work as a magical dynamic only because the people were mainly nomadic: it is easy to get out of the path of an oncoming storm if you just have to move the tent and goats.

Once city states started to form, getting out of the way of terrible storms and tides of disease-carrying winds, as well as winds that brought anger or triggered hotspots of violence, became almost impossible for all but the lowliest of those societies. So a thread of magic developed to try and bully or appease the dangerous deity in question, or to bring in other deities who would do battle with them: here we see the beginning of the need for control. It was a slow descent for Ninlil, but we can see it happen through the Mesopotamian history. Eventually that power became feared and hated. It was described as being evil and later as being demonic, and so people no longer interacted with her as the interface for the terrible, powerful, and beautiful forces of the elements around them. Is Ninlil still there? Yes, she is. The elements never go away, and their deity interfaces seem to stay around for a very long time. But nobody works with them any more.

Every landmass has their own version of a deity like Ninlil. In some places the power has a predominantly male polarity to it, while in others it is a female polarity. Most land tends to have both polarities present, but one will be stronger than the other, or they will express differently. The polarity and directional power (east wind, north wind, etc.) is not about the external land itself; rather it is an inner directional attribute.

So as a magician who has worked with inner directional powers you will learn to spot the loss of magical knowledge in a culture just by how the directional attribute is attached to a deity. You will see instances where a deity is initially given a magical directional attribute, but this switches, over time, to reflect the actual land/weather directional attribute that flows around the people living in the area.

In the earliest texts, for example, Ninlil is referred to in places as the North Wind (and the partner of Enlil, the South Wind). Magically the north wind is fate, death, and the Underworld, and the south wind is the future, kingship, and prosperity.

But in Iraq the north wind (from a weather perspective) is cooling and brings health, and the southern wind brings heat, disease, and death: the exact reverse of the inner powers that flow from the four winds. This is why outer texts are only helpful up to a point: you also have to have the inner knowledge so that you can see properly what is happening in the texts.

Back to Ninlil and magic. A relationship built with deities like Ninlil is not just a passive one of dodging bad weather. Through the relationship built up between deity and human, the human learns how to mediate the power of the deity through themselves, and also how to *call the winds*. This is not about controlling the power, but about working with the power and asking the power to work with you.

For example, a magician working on the land of Iraq with Ninlil can raise dust storms, fierce winds, winds that carry disease, and can call the wind of death upon the land. They also have the complimentary skill of being able to deflect or modify (but not stop) those naturally occurring events. True power indeed – and much more useful than a magician standing with grimoire in hand calling upon Lilith to bend the neighbour's daughter to their sexual will (yawn). That is how far some areas of magic have devolved. And that is why these powers are considered demonic: because they can kill *en masse* they can reshape the land, destroy a culture, or wipe out a city. And yet it is all part of the natural order and part of the planet's immune system.

These deeper root 'demonic' deities tend to work across the land and not directly on humanity: the humans just tend to get in the way. The magician's job is to be able to talk to these powers and act as an early warning system, or trigger them in to action. This triggering is something that is only done when absolutely necessary, as it can cause extreme fallout. It is worked by the adept using breath, touch upon the land, or through using minute catalysts with water. This type of action is usually only ever called upon by adepts when terrible imbalance has been caused across the land by human intervention: it is rebalancing an imbalance that was caused by man. What we break, we have to fix.

You have been working with these techniques in previous lessons in their kindergarten forms. As you develop a deeper understanding of the land and the elements around you, so you will learn as an adept when to take action and when not to. These magical actions and interactions with 'demonic' deities can be very powerful indeed; hence as an apprentice you need to learn a deep understanding of the powers and elements, their actions and reactions, before as an adept you begin to act magically.

7. The Destroying Ones of Humanity

Just as the powerful root deities act on the land in a constant breathing in and out of creation and destruction, so too do powerful root beings act directly on the species of this planet. Seeing as we are the most destructive and an ever-growing species that is doing the most damage, we tend to be the species on the current receiving end of these destroying ones. The two-way conversation we started with the elements and root deities brought us into an orbit that consists of deities who work directly with humans for both good and bad. That deity interface obviously developed over millennia as a result of persistent attempts at communion between the forces of nature and the group inner consciousness of humanity; societies, and the individual human.

We recognise this today as the pantheon of gods and goddesses that societies work with. Within that pantheon are deities who are presentations for forces of nature that limit and destroy species that get out of control. These beings, and their deity 'presentations' are what are often today classed as demons who bring down cultures. They flow through humanity, nudging group behaviours and feeding power into destructive situations that will bring about some collapse, usually that of the social structure. This type of being often flows through mass epidemics, and also acts as a catalyst in huge and extreme shifts of thinking within populations.

Societies shift and change all the time. Politics flow according to the mindset of the people of the time, and that is often fed by changes in education, sanitation, economics, etc. Those shifts are often confined to single societies or groups of societies that orbit each other either culturally or economically. But beyond that there are more dangerous shifts that happen on a global or nearly-global level. Such shifts, where seemingly unrelated cultures at around the same time all step into destructive behaviours, are usually the result of these powerful destroying beings in action.

Note 2025: *This is a time where such destruction is very much out and about around the world. It has been building for years and was becoming obvious when I first wrote the course starting in 2014, but it is now very obvious to most people who are not sleepwalking through life.*

In our world today virtually every society is undergoing massive change as a result of extreme, polarised thought. Religious and political fundamentalism, from the fascist far right to the communist extreme left, is on a spectacular rise once again. This is nothing new in our world, but this particular tide shift carries a great deal of destruction behind it.

When I first noticed this shift in 2010, and it is a global one not just within the Abrahamic religions and first world nations, I presumed it was the usual swing that happens when societies pitch and fall. But more and more I started to see huge inner build-ups, powerful and very destructive beings backing up in the inner worlds and forming, ready to spill into the outer world. If you have any sense as a magician, when you see something so powerful happening, the first thing you do is to question what you saw and question your interpretation of it.

For quite some time I did not connect the inner build-ups with the outer events that I saw manifesting around the world. I guess I did not want to become a paranoid conspiracy nut. But as I spoke with other adepts around the world and held discussions with them about their own similar experiences, I slowly realised that what I had been seeing was indeed a huge 'demonic' build up of destruction that was soon to be unleashed upon the world.

Now that description is very dramatic and conjures up movie images of Armageddon and the 'end times.' The image of everything coming to an end after a brief struggle between good and bad, an image perpetuated by Hollywood and Bible thumpers, is almost cartoon-like in its simplicity: the terrible thing comes, but is defeated and survived by the 'good' people who then go on to repopulate the world. If only it were that simple. The reality is far more complex, and often does not have a happy short-term ending.

When these waves of destruction express themselves out in the world they flow through humanity as destructive behaviours or destructive diseases. This process is like a slow boil. It happens over decades, and humanity seems not quite to notice as the society around them is slowly dismantled and destroyed. The fall of Rome is a good example of this. This destructive action is not done by something 'out there' like aliens, asteroids, reptilians, etc. It is done by the worst possible common denominator of human nature in all its ugly glory: human evil rising to the surface and finding expression. 'Demonic deities' are not evil; humans are. These beings trigger responses in humanity that either bring out the worst of what it means to be human, or the best.

In ancient societies like the Egyptians this was handled by the rules of Ma'at, whereby everything was a constant job of keeping balance between order and chaos. That job was primarily undertaken by the king, (a topic we have already looked at in previous lessons) but also by the priesthoods, the laws, the temple practice, and everyday life. Every part of society played its role in the upkeep of order, through their own actions and through direct interactions with the forces of nature as expressed through the deities. It was an ideal that was rarely fulfilled, but the surges of effort to try towards that ideal in itself gave balance and protection to society. The civilisation when through various ups and downs in an effort to keep Ma'at, but human nature always messed that up. They would go through a dark fragmented period, and then rise again.

Once that system eventually fell apart in stages, and monotheism rose with all its restrictions, devolving of responsibility, and lack of spiritual interactions with the elements, then societies began to be ruled by swings of destruction, restriction, invasion, corruption, and extremism. The destroying demonic deities lean into that dynamic to bring out either the worst or the best in the individual and the society. But the beings do not cause the destruction; rather they *pour power into the vessel and any crack is split wide open*. Which way we swing on the scale between good and evil is totally up to us as individuals.

Just like well-managed epidemics bring immunity and a fitter, smaller society, so too these beings can potentially bring about a healthier society. But if their actions are neither recognised nor worked with, and humans respond with the lowest, most destructive aspects of themselves, then these beings can bring total destruction. They are not a 'punishment from God,' as we see them through the monotheistic lens; rather they are the deliverers of change, and that can be good, bad, or indifferent, depending on our human responses to them.

Either the evil within a human is brought to the fore, or the human meets the challenge by evolving. Usually the human response is to allow their suppressed evil to surface while justifying it. We can see this throughout history when horrific atrocities are dispensed, usually in the name of good; it gets no more evil than that.

This brings our thinking from 'demons sent to punish us,' or 'demons battling with us,' back to a way of thinking more in common with that of ancient humanity. A deep inner tide of change flows out into the world in a constant act of creation/destruction. We as humans have a responsibility to work with it, to learn from it, and to grow with it, regardless of how hard it is to do this. For an everyday person this is hard thing to accept; but for a magician, an adept who has the ability to look into the distant future, it is something that is accepted, worked with, and learned from.

When a destroying demonic force aims directly at a society and works through its leaders, through nature, and through the collective human consciousness to bring degeneration and destruction this usually results in the collapse of that society. Though occasionally such a force is the salvation of that nation: it all depends on the reactions of the nation's people to the power.

We see such destructive forces as demonic. But what if that society is destructive towards every other living being around it, like modern day societies? What if that society is violent, destructive, gobbles resources, and does nothing to contribute towards the manifestation of nature? Which is more demonic, the society or the being that destroys it in order to create balance?

Which takes us to the question of *what is actually evil?* This is a deeply important question for magicians to think about, and their answers will affect how they act, why they act, and when they act.

Now you begin to see how complex the issues are surrounding these powerful and deadly beings; and why any magical action or work with them should be careful, intelligent, and forward thinking, with the intention to bring about balance for all beings in the long term. Accomplishing this is not easy by any stretch of the imagination and will involve painful choices. Whichever way the magician chooses to go, the choice has to be made from gnosis. That gnosis comes from knowing all the parameters involved. The magician must be aware of those parameters both in a magical sense, and also in an outward, manifest sense. This is why apprentices spend so long learning outer and inner dynamics from the ground up. You cannot be effective as a magician if you do not know what it is you are working with, or why.

We have covered the two biggest forces that the modern world sees as demonic. Now let's look at some of the lesser forces that are sometimes described in modern parlance as 'demons': the composters and choppers.

8. Composters

Composters are beings that gather when something is breaking down. Their influence speeds up the process – a bit like bacteria feeding on a dead corpse. These beings tend not to interact with human consciousness, unlike parasites that can also act in this way. This is a major difference for magicians to take note of. If parasites have gathered to feed on a dying person or situation, they can be removed by a magician. But true composters are a bigger part of the natural process and cannot be gotten rid of. Knowledge of these beings is only useful for magicians in that recognising them in action is important: their appearance tells magicians that a process is in its final stages and should not be interfered with, and most certainly cannot be stopped once it gets to that phase. Composters are generally spotted by magicians when the magician looks at an individual or at a society/group/structure that is undergoing destruction.

Do you remember when you first worked on your web of fate in vision and saw angelic beings working on and maintaining the weave? Composters are the polar opposite of this. They work quietly and diligently, taking something apart and digesting it. They appear only when the inner pattern of something is destroyed to the point that it can no longer survive. The composters take the broken bits apart and absorb them so that the void within whatever is being destroyed can expand: they leave nothing, so that a space is left for something else to fill.

To a magician composters can appear in many different forms, from animal-like to just plain weird. The way to differentiate them from parasites is that a parasite will defend its 'food' and will engage with you if you try to move it: parasites can be communicated with. A magician can either pull them off or bribe them to go away. A composter however will not even be aware of you; and if you try to pull them off you will find that they have become part of whatever you are trying to save. They cannot be communicated with, nor can they be distracted or bribed: they are autopilot beings that just get on with their job.

By the time you get to the latter part of your initiate training you will be placed in situations where you will potentially spot composters. When you do see these beings on a person, place, or society you must realise that no matter how much emotional investment you have in their target, there is nothing you can do to save the situation. You have to learn to step back and simply hold a neutral space for the process to continue.

That can be a very hard thing to do, but it is a necessary thing to learn: there are times, no matter what the situation, where you cannot and should not interfere.

Learning to accept destruction as a part of the universe you live in is a major step for a magician's maturity. The ultimate test of that maturity comes at the end of the adept training, where you will trigger a power of destruction and face it.

9. CHOPPERS

Choppers are another interesting order of beings who are often called 'demonic,' and there is a superb example of them in action in the Ancient Egyptian *Book of Caverns,* a relatively late funeral wall text. *Figure 9* shows an image of one of them from an Egyptian tomb.

Figure 9: Chopper

Copyright and thanks to François Olivier of Meretseger Books
www.meretsegerbooks.com

The choppers are essentially Underworld powers who operate in the death process and are often seen depicted in ancient Egyptian funeral texts as creatures, cats, people or deities holding very sharp knives. They guard the deeper aspects of the realm of death and the Underworld, and attack souls who are degenerate and unbalanced. Remember your work on death and the Underworld, and also your work with the Scales? Well, those areas are where these beings can be found. They hack at the souls they can see clearly, breaking up the human (or animal) pattern of that soul. If the soul weighed upon the Scales of Ma'at has been found to be 'dense' or 'heavy' then it becomes visible to these beings. They respond by hacking away anything that defines that soul in the incarnation it has just come from. In other words that person's image, personality, and identity is torn to pieces.

They can also be observed guarding areas deep in the Underworld and in the Abyss, and they will hack away at anything that breeches those places when it should not be there. In these deep places they have the same function: to prevent some souls from connecting with powers they should not be attempting to connect with.

Say for example that a newly dead soul has somehow managed to get into areas of the death realm where they should not be. They will be abruptly stopped by these beings and potentially have their human pattern destroyed if that is necessary. If an unbalanced but powerful human had used magic to dodge the Scales in the early stages of their death, the choppers would catch that human soul and dismantle it. This is not about punishment but ensuring that unbalanced souls do not reach deep into the inner realms where they could wreak havoc either upon their own eternal souls or the eternal souls of others. They are like the Underworld version of the Sword of Damocles: they are *limiters*.

Similarly, if a living magician tried to gain deep access into the Abyss or Underworld in search of destroying powers to use for their own ends, the choppers will trigger to prevent them from reaching a deep, powerful, and destructive being. If the living magician is attacked by these choppers it is likely that they will die soon after, or lose their minds. There are examples of this in the history of magicians, particularly in the last hundred years, if you look closely.

The choppers are not like the composters in that they are very aware of human consciousness and can be communicated with (if you are dumb enough to try). They often have aspects of different deities within them, and may be an extension of deity powers or beings that work with and for deities. They are not angelic in that they do not dispense patterns and they are not instigators; rather they are the reverse. They block, stop, or limit access to deep areas of the Underworld and death.

But they are beings that we can communicate with if we are careful and wise in our actions. As adepts it is sometimes helpful to stand before one of these beings in vision and ask about what it is they are guarding, why they are guarding it, and why it is so dangerous. If you are a clear and balanced living magician in vision, and your only intent is to learn so that you can serve, then they will either ignore you or they will answer you and teach you what you need to know. If you are an unbalanced magician and you are seeking power, or access to deep power that they are guarding, then they will toast you before you can finish your question. Hence it is recommended that you only connect with these beings when you are an experienced adept and you have a very good, solid, and balanced reason for asking them a question or communing with them. Simple curiosity is not a good reason.

Sometimes it does not matter how balanced you are. As a living magician, if you stretch too far down into the Abyss or the Deep Underworld, the choppers will lash out automatically to guard their space. They will often not warn, nor will they ask. In some areas they can be trigger-happy, terrifying, vicious beings with very sharp knives and a short temper. I found myself lashed once during my thirties when I got a bit too curious and adventurous. I learned my lesson very quickly and did not repeat that mistake twice. And I got off lucky: they essentially fired a 'warning shot', which can happen sometimes.

So you can see how in modern terms these beings can be thought of as 'demonic': all they do is destroy, and they cannot be bargained with, placated, or dodged. If you look carefully at different, very ancient texts and wall carvings, you will spot the different cultural references to these beings as ancient magician-priests spotted them in their visionary experiences. This in turn will give you a lot of real clues as to what the images or text are actually referring to.

10. Guardians of sacred places and temples

Different ancient cultures used what, these days, we consider to be demons as guardians of temple spaces. These beings often appear in many different presentations, but what they have in common are animal features, lots of teeth, staring eyes, big ears, sharp claws, and a powerful body.

Such beings are not created by the temple culture (e.g. thought forms, servitors, or Tulpas). Rather they are powerful spirit beings from the land or the near-to-the-surface Underworld who will work with the inner structure of the temple. When a sacred place is built, first the inner structure is created and inner beings are asked, bargained with, or forced/bound into service to guard the space through time. The forcing or binding of these beings is a degeneration of the original practice, and you can often date a temple's inner construct by seeing how these beings present.

If it is an early temple construction, with possibly newer some construction overlaying it, then these beings will appear in their true, terrifying form, with nothing appearing to limit or bind them. If the inner construct (which comes before the outer construction) has guardians who are leashed, chained, collared, or who have some sacred text or a priest figure limiting them, then you know that you have found a later construction and that its guardians are bound into service.

Often these inner guardians have outer manifestations carved or painted onto the temple or tomb's walls, or there may be statues of them at its entrances. If the inner being is bound into service this will be reflected in their outer form also:

they will be depicted has having a leash or collar, a 'handler' or deity overseeing them, or they will have sacred text written on, above, or beneath them stating that the being/creature is in service to whoever is served by the temple. These beings were employed by temples around the world. In some cases the guardian will appear in a form of a deity, and the only difference between the guardian depicted as a deity and the deity of the temple proper is that the temple will not have a shrine dedicated to the guardian. Bes is a good example of this from ancient Egypt.

Bes did not have his own temple, but he is often depicted in the doorways and thresholds of various levels of the temple complex. Bes is an ancient being indeed, and a powerful land being who was drafted into service in ancient Egypt. He predates human occupation of that land, and is often seen as the protector of women in childbirth. He is also a protector of magicians and magic, and he will guard a temple from magical interference or magical attack. He is depicted as a dwarf, and dwarfs were very highly regarded in Egypt in many ways. Bes is not a warrior, even though many modern people think that these guardians were put there to stop invaders, desecrators, etc. In the latter stages of polytheistic temples it was hoped that these guardians would protect them from such an outer attack. That belief in an overarching guardian is a degeneration of thinking and tends to come in towards the end of priestly culture. These guardians protect against inner attack, inner desecration, and inner interference, acts that were considered far more dangerous than any human atrocity. Even when a society or civilisation falls, its temples for the most part keep functioning and doing their thing.

The guardian spirits ensure that the temple's inner integrity – the inner construct of the temple – stays intact, as that is where the temple's true power lies. The inner longevity of temples ensures that deities, land spirits, and souls of kings, queens, and priesthoods can continue their work upon and within the land, regardless of what happens on the surface. Outer events only trigger temple guardians into action when those events potentially threaten the temple's inner structure. The outer temple can be destroyed or left to collapse into ruin, but the inner temple will maintain its integrity.

For example, the Karnak Temple Complex in Upper Egypt marches through time regardless of what humans do around it. Its power stays intact, its guardians are still in place, and it is still doing its thing in a very powerful way. The land there still serves the deities, and the spirits of the land still abound freely and without restriction. The idea that deities vanish when humans turn away from them is total nonsense; their human like projection/image may fall apart, but the power and consciousness remains. One only has to go as a magician to a place like Karnak and call the wind: the deity reply is still as powerful, beautiful, and responsive as it ever was.

When a true adept walks into one of these places all the inner alarm bells immediately go off. Why? Because you are an unknown quantity and you have the potential to do a lot of damage if you wanted to. So the guardians will trigger, and they will challenge you aggressively. This happened to me a couple of times in Egypt, and each time I responded by going very still and quiet. Then I opened up to allow the guardians to look at every aspect of me; which deities I worked with, what service I did, and what my intentions were. The first time I did this, the guardians simply backed off.

The second time, at a different sacred space, they backed down and agreed to give me safe passage if in return I did a job for them, which I immediately agreed to. (I have a habit of saying yes to a being before asking what it actually wants, which is not always wise!) Luckily the job was within my ability to accomplish, and also within my ethical structure. So I did the job for them, and in return I got free and open access to all of the sites, both inner and outer; I was also given access by officials to sites normally closed to the public, which was a great boon!

Remember, these beings are not evil demons, though having one roaring at you with bared teeth and claws can certainly be a terrifying experience. Some magicians get the full visual display. Others do not see that, but get very clear voices warning them to watch out, and the magician's body will go into full adrenal mode. Once again, you have inner beings who can be very dangerous and destructive, but they are not evil, and they are not 'demonic' in the modern sense of the word.

If you look at pictures of (or even go visit) ancient temple sites around the world you will spot these guardians depicted at the entrances to shrines, temples, inner sanctums, and tombs. Wherever you see an outer depiction there is likely to be an inner guardian, unless it is a relatively 'modern' building in terms of ancient culture. Eventually the inner practice fell apart and the relevant skills were forgotten, but the architects/priests continued to construct the outer images, as that was what a temple was supposed to look like, to their understanding.

Sometimes you get later temples, Roman ones, for example, where guardians are depicted but there are in fact no real inner guardians. Other times you see outer depictions that bear no resemblance to the inner guardian who is actually there. When you come across this you can almost always guarantee that there is the remains of a much older temple underneath the one you are standing in, and the original guardian is still there.

These beings can still be worked with to this day when one is building the inner construct of a temple space, but they are only used by magicians when the space is meant to last through time into the far future. It is pointless doing this sort of work for a temple in a building for a magical group that will most likely not still be there in ten or twenty years, let alone a hundred years time.

These beings are not used to guard residences or outer orders; rather they are guardians of inner temple constructions that are intended to last for *millennia*. As you progress in your magical studies and are exposed to different ancient cultures, their temples, and their magic, you will learn to spot them. Then, if you do visit these sacred places, you will instantly recognise a guardian and know to be open, truthful, and respectful to them, *and also to what it is that they guard.*

Guardians do not only appear in temple cultures, or what we define as temple cultures. I have come across and been challenged by guardians of Stone Age sites who were guarding something very old, very powerful, and very necessary. If you have done some visionary work, which by now you will have started, and you go on holiday and visit a site, then if you find yourself challenged by a spirit like this, do not be defensive, and do not start trying to do banishing. This being is simply doing his or her job. Be respectful, slow down or stop, and become very still. Then, be open with them. Tell them who you are, where you come from, what your intentions are, and that you are willing to abide by the rules of their sacred space.

11. EXTERMINATORS

We looked earlier at 'demons' that flow into societies and affect humans directly *en masse*. Those powers bring to society an overarching power of disease and destruction, but within their orbit are beings who will aim at individuals directly. These are 'classic demons' in that they will directly influence an individual, without possessing them, in order to bring about the destruction that the larger destroying deities are triggering. We see this very clearly in Sumerian texts, and by the first millennium BC they appear as fully fledged 'demons.' However, these beings are not what modern Christians would consider demons, as they do not possess or harass a human; they simply destroy them. Once more, the little detail of *no possession* or *not following the person whispering to them* around tells us that the being in question is not a parasite, but a destroying being simply doing it's job.

A couple of good examples of these exterminators, for that is what they are, can be found in Sumerian texts. One is called Lamashtu, who is the probable source of the Lilith baby-eater idea, and who is also known as Dimme. The other is the well-known as Pazuzu. These beings are not autopilot destroyers like the composters; rather they are deities in their own right, and they have the power to protect as well as destroy. One will often offset the other in an interesting display of polarity.

The destroying deity Lamashtu is described in translations of Sumerian texts as a 'demoness of the four winds'. Note how much flows from the 'winds' and think about this in terms of what you know of the magical direction of air, the sword, and the underlying limiting power of the sword. The job of Lamashtu, along with the other destroying deities found in Assyrian texts, is to limit species. Lamashtu's power is aimed at vulnerable humans; babies, pregnant women, etc. and also at the resources needed for life: she poisons rivers and water sources.

Her presence triggered nightmares in the groups of humans she aimed her power at, and although the modern interpretations of the texts state that she disturbed sleep and caused nightmares, the subtlety of the language used in the translations tells us how far we have fallen in our understanding of these beings, and therefore our ability to survive their activities. A being 'sending you nightmares' implies that it is directly attacking your dreams or your deeper spirit, which is not correct in the case of these destroying deities. The simple presence of these beings will *trigger* nightmares in an individual and in groups of people. These sorts of nightmares happen when your inner immune system's alarm triggers: they tell you that destruction is coming or is already around you and it is up to you to do something about it. This is different from a being directly giving you nightmares on purpose, which is something a parasite would do, but not a destroying deity.

Think back to earlier in the lesson where I discussed the devolution of Ninlil. Humans shifted their relationship with this being from one of understanding that destruction was coming and they needed to get out of the way, to one in which the human became a 'victim of a demon.'

The presence of Lamashtu would trigger when populations were expanding. That deity power would *limit* the population by taking out the weak, the infirm, newborns, or by cutting off or damaging the water supply. Those people who knew the signs would get out of the way or call upon an opposing power to protect them, such as other deities. This dynamic is very important to magicians today: the subtle shifts in how these beings were dealt with, both successfully and unsuccessfully, still apply today, as these beings still flow through and across the land in their various cultural forms.

When Lamashtu triggered, a mother who was magically aware or wise to the local powers would call upon Pazuzu to protect her newborn child, or she would turn to one of the deities within her culture to nurture and protect her baby, while also taking the child to a different area so that the child could grow up safely. Can you see the echoes of this in the story of the Flight to Egypt of Mary, Joseph and the baby Jesus? Fleeing to a different land or sending the child to live elsewhere for their safety was a common theme in ancient stories. But for mother who was not wise or aware, if these types of beings were flowing across the land, and she didn't know how to hide her child, she would potentially lose her baby.

Pazuzu is also a destroying deity, but like most deities he has two sides to him. Pazuzu flowed through the south-west wind. This wind would often bring drought, which resulted in famines, insect infestations, etc. But Pazuzu's 'good side' is that he would often offer protection against terrible sicknesses, and he was the *antidote* to Lamashtu – a bit like catching cowpox so that you do not get smallpox (bad analogy I know, but the best I could think of this morning).

Note that Pazuzu's main (but not only) action is through the land, which in turn affects the humans. Why would Pazuzu trigger in this way? Because he is a deity who protects the land, not the people. Agriculture at the time had good irrigation which enabled bumper crops, but there was poor drainage and too much evaporation, which in turn slowly destroyed the land. Essentially the humans who lived in Mesopotamia at that time created the desert we now see in that region, along with a bit of help from weather changes – think about bad land management and subsequent deities triggering to protect the land.

So let's move sideways and look at this from a nonhuman perspective.

A species settles in an area and begins to affect the land to suit their own need for sustenance. The land becomes the victim of *irrigation salinity,* which essentially destroys everything. This damage to the land, and the subsequent damage to all the other species living on it, will trigger these beings into action. First come the 'big guys' who set the stage for destruction, and then these smaller demonic deities are awoken to action. They bring in powers of limitation, remember the sword/air? In order to attempt a restoration of balance and to stop the unbalanced destruction they will limit the breeding and life capabilities of the offending species. In vertebrates this will often trigger as mass suicides of a species: animals will often, as a group, start to behave in a way that will kill them. This is nature's self-limiting process, and when we observe it from an inner perspective we see these destroying deities in action.

We also see this in humans (though not the suicides). When there is a major overpopulation in humanity and there will likely be a need to limit the population in relation to available resources, female fetuses abort more often. The more you limit the female population, the more you limit population growth. In the reverse, during times of natural disaster when the population is almost wiped out, the male babies abort: it takes many females and very few males to regrow a population.

It makes me wonder if this is the root of the ancient custom of offering the first born to the deity in order to ensure the population at large continued. In a sick sort of way, (to our modern eyes) this would have worked, as it would indeed have limited the population. And it would also have engaged the humans in the limiting process: by the humans taking action themselves, the deities would not need to.

These days we can use contraception: a more humane way of keeping the population under control. And interestingly, contraception was not unknown at least in the Near East from the late Bronze Age onwards, and in Dynastic Egypt it was recommended by the State when the population expanded too much.

So we begin to see that in fact what was considered demonic in the most evil sense of the word was, and is, a *balancing force.* We just don't like it. These beings harm us, so we call them evil. But their intention is not evil; it is actually good: they are nature's pest control workers.

Those people in Sumer who learned how to dodge these beings through common sense, moving, magic, and bargaining would survive. So it becomes not a matter of survival of the fittest, but survival of the *smartest.* Those smart ones would continue living lives in which they interacted with these deities in a respectful relationship, and so they had a better chance of reaching old age.

And this brings us to the dynamic that is so important for magicians: bullet dodging.

12. Bullet dodging

Bullet dodging is where a magician is smart enough to spot an incoming destructive power, and either counteracts it, deflects it, or gets out of its way. In magic this process is sped up, and it acts as a natural selector for magicians. The smart ones learn how to survive, how to interact with all sorts of deities, and learn as adepts how to take their place in the vast community of natural forces. Their lifespan will be safeguarded, though not prolonged, and they will have a much better chance of living their full potential lifespan. Within that preserved life they will live alongside the community of deities and will act in service to the deities and the land. In ancient texts this was seen as daily interactions with the deity to keep the *vessel* of the deity clean and the lines of communication open. Sometimes that would degenerate down to the daily giving of food or gifts to the deity, an action which actively attracts parasites.

In the work I have done with destroying and creative deities it has been made very clear to me that the deities do not want a constant stream of gifts we think they may like; rather they want a worker who will use their human abilities in conjunction with the deities' abilities. The humans provide the window (statue) and the elemental threshold (a flame, water, a stone, etc.) so that the deity in question can inform the humans of what needs to be done in order to maintain or restore balance. The humans do what needs to be done using a human manifest body, and the deities do the jobs which need energetic powers.

The deeper and more powerful the work that the magician engages with, the more powerful the destroying tides will be that flow into the magician's orbit. The adept who successfully dodges those bullets will be one who is of real use to the deities. Smart magicians are useful; stupid magicians are not. And there are varying levels of smart and dumb. At some point, some adept magicians get swept off their feet by a strong tide. However if a magician is simply a dabbler then this dynamic will not kick in, as they are most likely going to be ignored by the deity powers and will end up being playthings of the parasites instead.

In our modern world these powers still flow through the world, both through human populations and through individuals. Each culture has their own names for them, unless its ancient knowledge or texts have been destroyed. Calling upon the name of a Sumerian destroying deity will not help you if you do not live in that region. You will possibly gain some connection to an aspect of that Sumerian deity, or a parasite who has inhabited an image, but you are essentially talking to the governor or limiter of Iraqi lands, not your own. They are not without power when off their own lands, but they are not the most efficient of workers when abroad, either. Just keep in mind that some deity powers can interact with lands and people far away from there base, but many do not. If you know the power of a distant deity and understand that there is also a version of it on your own land, then you can use the very ancient method of connecting with them by their nature, their power, or their descriptive name.

Where I live is fairly exposed to the elements, so all sorts of tides sweep through. I do not go out and chant Sumerian demon names: I talk to the wind and listen to what the wind has to say. Then I act accordingly: Stone Age magic.

13. Having Pazuzu round for tea

It is very fashionable in occult circles to have images of demonic deities around your house. If you know what these beings are in real magical terms, are used to working with that power, and have the intention of working on projects with that power, then all is well. However, many occultists buy statues of destroying demonic deities just because they wish to appear edgy, and they will more or less treat them like special ornaments. They will set them up on altars, reenact rituals that are inappropriate or unconnected in real terms to that deity, and then wonder why their life goes to shit.

When you bring an ornament into the house that is a faithful reproduction of an ancient image or statue, then it will most certainly not be just an ornament: being a magician creates an environment around you that will switch things on. If it has just been made and not used before, and you work with it directly in relation to its true power, then you will have a working window. However, often these destroying powers are very difficult to have around the house, and are best put in hibernation until they are needed. I have an image of an ancient deity who brings rain. Now that I live in Britain, a place where it rains a great deal, she spends most of her time sleeping in her box in the cupboard. If a drought happened I would not just bring her out; first I would talk to the wind, the land, and the trees, and ask if the drought needed help to rebalance. Sometimes a drought is necessary, in which case you do not interfere. But if the land indicated that it did indeed need help then I would bring out the rain deity, wake her up, give her what she asks for, and let her get on with her rebalancing work. Have I worked with her before? Yup, she came out during a drought in the area where I lived in the USA. Within a month a seven year drought was ended. Then the flooding started. Oops. Back in her box she went.

This simple dynamic is a mixture of nature and magic. We as humans deeply affect the land in bad ways, and our religions also have both a negative and positive effect on everything around us. When one of these influences triggers a problem, we can bring in counter powers to help find balance. (Balance, not a cure for something we do not like). So if humans cause a problem, human magic can solve it, if the human knows what they are doing. But sometimes the droughts, storms, and floods are a necessary part of the everyday health of the planet, in which case, you either move or put up with it.

Other times people buy these images and interact with them in the modern fantasy occult way:

"Ooh, a Sumerian demon... smite my enemies for me!"

This tends to attract the parasites who would accompany the work of the destroying deity. For example if a figurine of Lamashtu were brought into the house of some idiotic, immature occultist who started feeding the image and demanding it smite, attack, or whatever; or even tried to have imaginary sex with the 'demon,' then besides having their energy drained off (food source) it is likely that things will get messy and destructive pretty quickly. Each of the destroying deities attracts parasites when they are actively doing their job. When something is destroyed it rots and composts. So the composters are triggered, along with parasites who feed off the emotive/energetic process. Having a destroying demonic deity in the house without knowing what you are doing, and treating it inappropriately, is likely to trigger a very unhealthy situation.

If the image brought into the house has been 'dressed' with more than its original filter image (e.g. a sexier body, teeth, more eyes, different animals, modern weapons, etc.) then it is an unstable vessel that, when triggered magically, can become a vessel for any passing energetic parasite. And then you have a *true* parasite problem. But we will discuss that in another lesson.

14. Other 'Demonic' presentations

This is just a short paragraph (phew, long lesson!) to say there is also a huge collection of beings who appear in animal forms such as scorpions, lions, etc. who are often described as demons but are in fact 'angelic' type beings who work with and through deities. These beings, unlike the types we have been discussing in this lesson, are not destroying beings. They do have the ability to be very dangerous, but also very good, and all the variants in between: they are no more demonic than you or I, unless we get on the wrong side of them.

15. The Abyss

Essentially the Abyss is like a large storage unit for destroying beings once they are no longer necessary or appropriate for the living world. Think dinosaurs: they no longer have a presence in our world, and their deeper consciousness resides in the Abyss in deep storage. You will learn a lot more about the Abyss in later lessons, as I think this lesson is already too long! The whole subject of destructive beings is vast and complex, so breaking it up into different lessons will give you a chance to get your breath and do some thinking and research of your own.

Most of the lessons in this module cover some of the different types of beings that modern occultists and Christians think of as demons. By separating out the different types of these destructive beings into different lessons, it gives you a chance to look a bit more deeply at them, and so hopefully gain a better idea of what it is we are looking at.

16. *Task:* Researching a 'demon' of your choice

Choose a 'demon' from an ancient culture. Find the earliest historical reference to them in texts or wall carvings; then look for how the cultural understanding of them changes over millennia. Look at changes in the culture in relation to changes of how the being is perceived over time. Look at their powers, and maybe try to find out what, if any, element they work through.

Then look at any appearances of the being in modern occultism and compare the original, early historical understanding of them with the popular occult/religious presentation. If there is a massive difference, think about why the being is presented in modern occultism in that way and what effect this would have on magic and magicians.

Also reflect on whether a version of this being exists in your own culture and upon your own land.

Write up your findings and reflections on what you think is happening on computer. Quote your references, embed any images, etc.

Lesson 4

Parasites

Following on from the last lesson, which hopefully gave you some idea of what destroying powers are like and how they work, this lesson will cover the class of beings that modern people tend to think of as demons, but are actually parasites. Why is it important to make this differentiation? Because the way to deal with a parasite, and the way to deal with a destroying being, are two *very* different approaches.

When we watch movies about possession or hear about dramatic Catholic exorcisms, what we are dealing with is parasites, and no amount of religious ranting will get rid of a parasite, any more than it will get rid of fleas, ticks, and worms. But fleas, ticks, and worms are harmless, I hear you say. Not, I answer, if the fleas carry bubonic plague, or the tick carries Lyme disease, or the worm has penetrated into your brain. Then they will potentially kill you.

Parasites are inner beings, i.e. they have no manifest physical body, and they feed off the energy created by emotions or other energetic outputs. They are often very intelligent, very close to humanity, if not actually a part of humanity, and they can operate through your mind and bod to change how your mind and body operates. They can mimic other beings, trick your mind, and push you to do things you would not normally contemplate. They do this by manipulating the parts of your brain and personality that normally give you control over your impulses. These beings, like physical parasites, are a part of creation and are not supernatural scary demons sent from Satan to eat your eyeballs. However most of the time they are not good for us, particularly if they get out of control, which usually happens when there is a major physical, mental, or energetic imbalance in the potential host.

By the time someone reaches the age of twenty-one their system will have had to deal with parasites in one form or another. Most people develop an inner immune response to these beings which affords a certain amount of protection from the heavier, more destructive parasites. When a child catches chickenpox, colds, and other childhood diseases, their immature immune system kicks in and learns how to tackle various viruses. As a result the immune system matures, which gives the adult far greater protection against pathogens that could potentially be fatal. However some children have underlying weaknesses and the immune system does not quite do its job, which in turn leaves that person more vulnerable to disease as they grow up. Essentially, this is a species-limiting process, and also a process of evolution.

The same pattern applies with these inner parasites. As children we are exposed to these beings in our everyday life, and as we mature into adulthood most people develop an inner immune system against them. But some people may have underlying weaknesses or conditions that stop such a maturing of their immune system:

these people are particularly vulnerable to serious parasite infestation. Such an infestation is what presents as 'possessed by demons.'

Magicians are also more vulnerable to parasites simply because they cast their consciousness into areas that most humans do not. Some systems of magic, particularly pre-Christian ones, have dynamics in place that will first protect a magician from parasites, and then slowly help them to develop a good radar and immune system against these beings. But most modern magical systems do not have that inbuilt dynamic of protection that eventually helps the student magician develop immunity through very careful and highly limited/controlled exposure. Some magical systems or schools even have actions and behaviour within them that attract such beings while weakening the student magician. Because of this dynamic, it is wise for apprentices to know what sort of magical actions attract such beings, and which repel them while also strengthening the magician. We have looked at this briefly in previous lessons, so you will already have a basic idea of magic/parasites by now. But the more in-depth detail in this lesson will not only give you a much deeper understanding of how these beings operate, it will also function as primary school for those magicians who will eventually specialise in exorcism.

Every magician should have an elementary understanding of these beings so that they can adjust their work accordingly when necessary, and also so that they do not buy into the very demon hysteria that puts them in the firing line with these beings. These beings are not demonic or evil, but make no mistake about how dangerous and destructive they can be. There does seem to be a mentality in some cultures that if it is not evil, then it is not harmful. This is a stupid and dangerous assumption for a magician to make. Ebola is not evil, but it is deadly and nasty. And the medical analogy is one that can be very useful for magicians: treat these beings like dangerous diseases. They infect, weaken, and then destroy a person, or at least can disable them, sometimes badly. And there is another crossover, in that these parasites can trigger latent diseases within a person, or their predations can run concurrently with a physical or mental illness. Parasites can make recovery from serious illness almost impossible, or they can prolong a serious illness while devastating the inner and outer energies of a person.

These beings also sometimes present as hive beings: when they infest a group or a building, they are often many who are also one. Remember the being I talked about in a previous lesson who lay at the bottom of the lake and sent out its 'children' to feed on the local humans? That is an old, well-established parasite. The range and action of this class of being is wide and deep, and knowledge of how to spot them and get rid of them, or at least limit them in your own body, is the first step towards learning how to deal with them out in the world as a magician and exorcist.

1. Parasites and brains

When an energetic, powerful parasite infects a human, it seems to the outside world that they are 'possessed by a demon.' The symptoms displayed can vary from mild ones which can go unnoticed for years to the highly dramatic. Just like pathogens, the parasites who can feed quietly without causing too much fuss in the host are the ones who have evolved enough to know the importance of keeping its food supply stable and unthreatened.

A parasite who is not quite so clever as that is a bit like a very young, poisonous spider or scorpion: they will cause far more damage because they cannot fully control their 'venom.' A not 'quite so evolved' parasite will trigger energies and behaviours in their host that result in extremes of behaviour that are often dangerous to the host: the host either dies or their infection becomes so obvious that they are 'treated' for it. This in turn limits the food source and lifespan of the parasite.

What does this tell us? It tells us that when we are confronted with a spectacular show of 'possession' with all the bells and whistles, we are dealing with a feral, immature parasite. And even though they are dangerous, they will be easier to get rid of, as they have not as yet developed the skills to hide and cling on.

The more dangerous parasites are the ones who have evolved a system of infection that lets them feed off their host without destroying them or drawing too much attention. These sort are the more common ones present in our societies, and are the most dangerous of all. They will push their host to behaviours that allow a release of energy, while also manoeuvring this behaviour so that the host evades detection: the parasite teaches the host to be clever. If the host does not have a self-destructive personality or a serious imbalance in their brain's reward system, then the relationship between host and parasite can go on indefinitely. But if the host does have a propensity for self-destructive behaviour or a serious imbalance in their brain's reward system, then the parasite can nudge the host to the point of suicide or extremes of self-destructive behaviour. So you begin to see just how dangerous these beings can be.

One word of caution. The presentations of parasite infestation and mental illness are often very similar, to the point that it can be difficult to tell the difference, and there *is* a difference. Sometimes, many times, the two come together, and it is very important for a magician to be able to differentiate between which is which, and why. Someone who is mentally ill and not infested needs to be treated medically. Someone who is infested needs magical treatment. Often times both treatments are needed concurrently.

But as apprentices you are not yet adequately equipped to deal with such a situation. Your job for now is to learn the various presentations, consequences, and magical details. This will help you spot infestations in historical figures, and also identify magical actions or systems that would potentially precipitate such an infestation. In your practical work you will learn a method of inner observation, and this will be your first step in learning how to deal with this type of being.

So let's look in detail at how these infestations occur in individuals, what they do, why, and how. The most common infestations occur via the brain and/or the endocrine system.

When a parasite comes into the orbit of a potential human host, it looks for a weakness that gives it an 'in.' That weakness can be physical, emotional, or psychic. Once infected, the host either has an inner immune trigger response that kicks out the parasite (this can be almost immediate or can take a long while), or they succumb to long-term infestation. It is worth taking the time to identify the various weakened doorways into our systems that these parasites can take, as it can give magicians clues about not only what caused an infection, but also how to get rid of it or protect against it.

2. Physical doorways

The physical doorways that present an opportunity for these beings tend for the most part to involve brain function, endocrine function, or both. The smooth functioning of the human system relies in part on maintaining the balance of substances known as neurotransmitters. Without getting bogged down in biology, these endogenous chemicals form part of a trigger, transport, and communication system that upholds the balance of the body. Neurotransmitters act as triggers or switches: they switch a neuron on or off, or excite or inhibit it. These very simple actions have a profound effect on the body. Think of it in terms of keys and locks. The on-off actions of these chemicals govern, among many other things, emotions, impulse control, and executive controls, and they have a profound effect on hormone regulation. This translates in everyday terms to emotions, actions, reactions, sexual activity, physical movement, and the actions of the autonomic nervous system like breathing, sweating, etc. So you begin to see how important these chemicals are to our health and survival.

When an energetic parasite infects a person, their action often aims directly at these on/off switches. Once they have figured out how to work them, they can effectively govern a person's body, mind, and emotions. In most cases the period of acute infection (the initial stages) is short, and the parasite is kicked out by the human's inner and outer immune system. This often goes unnoticed in most people: only shamanic-type healers and magicians would spot it. The infected person may develop the physical symptoms of a mild virus, while having nightmares or dreams of bugs invading them, and they would experience a short-term problem with mood or impulse control. As their immune system kicks in, the symptoms fade, the parasite is kicked out, and the person's deeper inner system will now be primed, ready and waiting to defend against the next attempt to infest.

Most problematic situations happen when the infected person has a weakness that the parasite can identify and lean on. This makes it harder for the immune system to trigger. Examples of such weaknesses are mild-to-moderate dysfunction of the basal ganglia in the brain, and hormone imbalances (too much or too little testosterone, oestrogen, etc.). If the basal ganglia, one of the favourite sections of the brain for parasites to infest, is targeted by one of these beings, the presentation can be a classic 'demonic possession,' due to the parasite triggering this area of the brain to create an imbalance in neurotransmitter action. Because of that imbalance the human in question can find themselves getting into situations that trigger a food supply for the parasite. If you look up the basal ganglia and read about the wide-ranging effects it has on the body and mind, you will start to see why this area of the brain is such a great place for a parasite to set up its command and control centre. Often we see parasite possession heavily intertwined with a preexisting mental illness, or we see a latent mental illness triggered into action by the parasite's presence.

As I said earlier, most often when a human is infected by a parasite the human's own defence mechanism kicks in and slowly expels it. In the Initiate section of the course you will learn how to spot the more subtle presentations of parasite infestation, and also learn how to get rid of them in people. But before you get to that stage it is easier to learn the more impressive – through rarer – presentations, so that you can spot them in your own community. This phase of your training is about recognition and basic understanding, and from there learning how to keep yourself balanced *before* you attempt to help others. It is also important to learn while you are an apprentice just how complicated these issues are. Grasping that complexity will take you closer to a deeper understanding of how the universe operates around you.

So let's take a look at a stereotypically aggressive and dangerous parasite infestation. This example is based on cases I have worked with, and shows the basics of unravelling the indicators of possession and mental illness so that the exorcist can see which is which.

3. Example

We will call our victim Frank. Frank is an occultist in his mid-thirties with a quick mind and a deep interest in anything ancient. He is of general good health, he has a bit of a nervous tic that has continued from childhood, is pretty psychic, and he had mild bouts of bipolar disorder in his early twenties. He works in an office and has a girlfriend. He likes to take occasional recreational drugs, but nothing heavy, and he has no habit.

Frank started to delve deep into the inner worlds in his magical work. Rather than work with any particular system he flitted around from style to style, mixed his own brand of mythos from his gaming interest into his visionary work, and decided to see if he could connect with 'aliens' in the inner worlds. He felt he had some success in this, and was conversing with beings he felt were aliens. Every time he talked with them in vision he came out feeling amazing, powerful, and full of joy. This is the first potential magical symptom; parasites often give back an emotional release in order to encourage the host into behaviour to its liking. This feeling stayed with him for days. He felt invincible, tall, and his sex drive started to climb (second magical symptom). Because he felt so good after talking to these 'aliens' he started to work in vision almost every day with them.

His workmates noticed that Frank had developed some annoying habits that were starting to get on everyone's nerves. He would constantly tap on his desk, mutter to himself, was unable to focus in his work, and had stopped interacting casually with the office staff. He had stopped eating lunch, was losing weight, and his childhood tic had gotten a lot worse. A couple of weeks down the line his partner began to resent Frank constantly badgering her for sex every morning and night. She also noticed that he had started to make pill-rolling hand movements when watching movies along with a slight hand tremor; symptoms often associated with the onset of motor-neurone diseases. Frank started experiencing quite bad mood swings and would become angry at the slightest thing. He began to obsess over his magical work and started treating his partner with deep suspicion.

At work he took to spending many minutes at a time staring at individuals in the office, pill-rolling with his fingers and muttering to himself. He became paranoid, thought everyone was talking about him, and started breaking out in rashes, sweating a lot, and sneezing constantly. He had also started sexually harassing the women in the office where he worked. He began hearing voices telling him things about the people around him, and his visionary work had become increasingly more bizarre. He started cutting himself, developed strong leg and arm jerks, had bouts of impulsive swearing and diarrhoea, and on occasion declared that he was a demon or god from another planet who was going to destroy everyone. But he did not display violent behaviour.

The house where he lived became difficult energetically. It began to take on the feel of a house that was mildly haunted, with doors slamming, lights going on and off, weird sounds, and a distinct uncomfortable feeling to it. It also felt dirty – no matter how much Frank's girlfriend cleaned the place, she always felt it was dirty. She also found herself waking up at the same time each night and could not get back to sleep, which is an inner defence mechanism. Frank had taken to spending hours lecturing people about magic and different orders of beings, beings that Frank organised into strict hierarchies, with names, numbers, and codes. He became obsessed with numbers, and would spend all night writing numbers out in patterns. He would pace, jerk, shout, scream, and mutter all night.

As you can see, if Frank (or his girlfriend) went to a priest, the priest would likely suspect possession. A psychiatric worker would be thinking a psychotic episode linked to his history of bipolar disorder. They would both be right.

So let us step back and look at this picture, and try to tease out what is what.

4. Breakdown of the picture

Frank has a baseline sensitivity that potentially makes him vulnerable, as he has not learned how to work with his own mind and body type; nor has he learned how to work magically within a system that affords natural protection. He has a double-edged gift of being a natural psychic but with a physical vulnerability, and this is where the basal ganglia hypothesis comes in as he has had bouts of bipolar disorder and has a nervous tic. This tells us that he has a slight vulnerability towards imbalance in his dopamine, serotonin, and/or GABA levels in relation to the receptors, i.e. too many 'locks' for the normal amount of 'keys, or the lock/key mechanism failing somewhere' for example. This problem can be aggravated by taking any drug that causes the inhibition or release of those neurotransmitters. Frank liked an occasional bit of amphetamine on the weekends, which was slowly weakening his system as amphetamine directly triggers a dopamine response.

Frank went in vision in search of aliens. He had a fixed idea in his head of what he wanted to reach. Frank had also taken amphetamine in order to stay sharp and alert so he could work through the night. As he reached out in vision for the aliens he stepped into a level of the inner worlds that is very much about the imagination of humans: it is like a low-level version of the Inner Library; it is the realm of people's group fantasies. Why did he end up there? Because his focused attention was fixed on something straight out of his imagination, a filter built from a childhood of movies and alien toys. He walked straight into a realm of parasites who feed off the energy output from people's fantasy worlds.

These parasites dressed themselves to look how he wanted them to look. They drew nearer to him and saw that areas of his brain were slightly imbalanced and weak, and they would be able to 'get in' in order to feed. Frank's body tried to accommodate their extra presence but could not, which in turn triggered a physical immune reaction. The parasites find that they can trigger areas of his brain that process dopamine and serotonin (among other things). This in turn makes him think and act in ways that produce energy for them to feed off of. They encourage him to work more and more in the inner worlds with them, interactions which allow them to bypass Franks immune system – he essentially 'invited them in.' His body starts to react first with an immune reaction (sneezing and flu-like symptoms), and he begins to show the signs of neurotransmitter imbalance as the parasites interfere with the delicate chemical balance in Frank's brain. This begins to cause the pill-rolling, the leg and arm jerks, the paranoia/psychosis, the increased sex drive, etc.: they essentially trigger his bipolar tendency into a full psychotic breakdown.

As the parasites become well-fed and more turn up for dinner, they gain enough energy to trigger physical actions in the house (lights, noises, etc.) which in turn triggers fear in Frank's girlfriend, an emotion which the parasites then feed off as well. They cannot get into her, as she has a good, balanced inner immune system, but they can trigger fear in her by actions around her, and then feed off the energy of that fear. Essentially the invading parasites in Frank intentionally triggered his bipolar disorder and fuelled it strongly, because his psychosis produced energy that they could then feed from.

Frank would need both medical treatment and magical treatment to stabilise his brain and strip out the parasite. The parasite would need to go first; then after twenty-four hours Frank would be assessed to see what was left behind, which would indicate how much medical treatment was needed. So a magician (working alongside a psychiatrist who was also a magician) stripped Frank of the parasite and temporarily sealed him to prevent it immediately returning, as Frank's inner system would be vulnerable for a while after. The day after, Frank was assessed.

Since the removal of the parasite, Frank had slept for twenty hours. It was the first time he had managed to sleep longer than three hours since the whole thing started. He felt groggy, blank, depressed, not tall, and full of neither power nor sex drive. His hand trembled badly and he felt mentally very slow; his brain no longer had a parasite constantly triggering a chemical response. His girlfriend took him to a cabin in the country for a few days, armed with emergency phone numbers, and she ensured that there were no drugs or alcohol anywhere. Frank wanted to smoke tobacco, a craving that came totally out of the blue. The magician caring for him offered him tobacco, and also herbs that would help him gently. This three-day time-out allows the inner aspect to settle, which then allows any underlying physical and/or mental condition to surface so that it can be properly treated.

After a couple of days away from his home (which was magically stripped and cleaned while he was away), Frank came back feeling very battered and slightly depressed. He was a bit anxious, and was having strange dreams and trouble focusing. But his psychotic behaviour had gone with the parasite, indicating that what had occurred was not a full-on psychotic episode but the result of the parasite's work. If the psychotic behaviour had continued, then Frank would have needed aggressive medical treatment to bring it under control. He was taken to see a doctor who prescribed medication which he took for three months, after which he started to recover. For a few years after this episode, at the same time each year, Frank had an echo of the same situation: it was deeply imprinted on his fate pattern, and it took time to fade. This is a very common experience and also a signal with such a situation; the yearly 'echo' of the event happens frequently after a bad parasite infestation has been removed. I do not know whey this happens only that it does.

The swift change in Frank after the parasite's removal told the magician which symptoms were caused by the parasite and which were the result of Frank's illness. The parasite's removal allowed his body to begin the recovery process, and the doctor was able to properly treat him. If there had been no difference at all after the magical work, this does not mean that the work was weak or wrong; it would have indicated that Frank was not having trouble with the parasite but with his bipolar disorder and was having a psychotic breakdown. Sometimes the parasite invasion can trigger a breakdown, but is not actively causing it: it's like triggering a trip switch.

This is really important to think about. Some exorcists think that when a proper magical or religious working has not worked, then they must be facing a 'really tough, powerful demon.' No; it's a mental illness that has triggered, and the parasite in the victim's body is a side-issue. Parasites do not always cause illness, which we will talk about later in this lesson. Never assume that just because someone has a being living within them (we are essentially made up of beings) that it is causing a problem. Sometimes magic can trigger a mental illness and the being was just hanging out. And remember, no amount of religious prayers or chanting will get rid of a parasite: it is not a 'religious' being, it is just hungry.

Everything in creation works in octaves, like Russian dolls: everything works from the same pattern. The same 'infection' mechanism is in play, whether it is a viral infection or an inner parasite infection. Shamanic magicians (tribal ones, not New Age Western ones) treat a sick person by stripping out the inner aspect of the disease, be it a parasite or some other type of consciousness accompanying the physical illness. This gives the body's own immune system access to its proper energy resources, so it can fight the outer illness. The shaman will then give medicines to clear up the outer infection. Both sides, inner and outer, are dealt with.

5. Identifying the triggers of infestation

Certain things attract parasites. But keep in mind that these beings are part and parcel of our lives, just like catching colds, flu, worms, and fungal infections. You cannot strip the body totally of these beings, as that would become unhealthy. Remember, the body has to learn to cope with these infections as naturally as possible. We will look a bit later in the lesson at symbiotic relationships with these beings, as that is also a natural process. The main triggers (where there is no magic involved) tend to be activities and emotions that provide energetic food. If the host is pretty stable, the parasite will try to dig into their brain in order to unbalance the person and thus provide food. But usually they are kicked out by the inner immune system. The unstable human, even if it is latent or mild, is a lot more vulnerable.

Triggers include: sexual orgasm (huge output of yummy energy), pain, happiness/'bliss,' obsessive and/or compulsive behaviour, anger, feelings of power and control, unusually aggressive behaviour or thoughts, and fear.

These are all normal emotions and activities for a human. What the parasite does is draw near to someone who may be vulnerable, test the waters, and if they can dig in, they will trigger any chemical action in the body they can in order to *enhance* the natural emotion until it becomes unnaturally strong. This sets up a *feedback loop* of triggering stronger and stronger reactions, allowing the parasite to feed off the energy of those reactions.

This is why magicians spend so much time and energy being still and working without emotion. Not only is that the most efficient and stable way to work, it is also the safest.

When magic enters the picture, parasites will be attracted by all of the above, plus they will be attracted by the magician stretching their consciousness in vision into unstable or unbalanced areas, or stretching out their energy in unbalanced or badly constructed rituals that rely heavily on emotive energy, ego, and control. Such working methods leave the magician vulnerable to weak spots in the work, and that will allow a parasite who is intelligent to weave its way into the work unnoticed. They will often dress up out of the consciousness of the magician and reflect back what the magician wishes to see or experience. Banishing rituals[1] have no real effect on these beings at all, as such rituals are easy to get around – that ritual was originally meant as a beginner training ritual. Magicians who work within systems that include deity, angelic, land being, and ancestral powers will usually be protected by them unless they step off-piste without knowing what they are doing.

In such circumstances, if the magician is well trained, they will recognise what is happening and act to get rid of the parasite while also tightening up their working practice. This sort of thing is usually no big deal unless the magician is an egomaniac idiot, in which case he will simply become a long-term yummy meal. Using the health/disease analogy, a parasite can be experienced as anything from the equivalent of a mild cold right the way through to a deadly smallpox infection; which as an aside is a disease that the destroying deities used to flow through. So the situation I outlined above is just one small example in a vast and complicated scenario.

You will learn how to exorcise such beings later on in the course, as by then you will have more inner experience, you will be stronger, and you will know more; therefore you will be able to spot and deal with such situations with more skill and confidence. In the meantime there are a variety of things built into the course that will keep you safe from the nastier parasites, and you are slowly learning magical hygiene.

Now let's look at another parasite issue: buildings being infested. This is becoming a major problem as a result of societal changes.

6. Parasites and buildings

Just as parasites can trot around trying to munch humans (and also animals), they can also congregate in buildings where there is lots of good food to eat. This often means schools, meditation centres, shopping malls, psychiatric units, hospices, etc. Some hospitals also get targeted, though for some reason many hospitals seem to manage to keep their levels of parasites down.

Certain city centres can also get clogged up depending on the people, what happens there, and also the land – rivers that run through cities tend to keep them relatively clean, unless their flow is slowed right down or blocked. Older temples, churches, etc. can also help keep a place clean if they are properly balanced and kept running with regular, ritualised prayer; Catholic, Orthodox, or High Anglican, for example.

---

[1] i.e. Lesser Banishing Ritual of the Pentagram.

The problems occur where there is sluggish land energy (blocked or contained springs, rivers, etc.) or where there are a lot of people gathered who are producing energies that are enticing to these beings. High schools are a good example, as they contain lots of teenagers who are all in various stages of hormonal flux from puberty; as are psychiatric units, with lots of people in various stages of mental illness. The other favourite place for these parasites are New Age centres that do courses on 'dumping and clearing' sessions for people's issues or illnesses: practices that centre on personal psychological issues, the shedding of one's problems, or life games, are particularly attractive to these parasites.

Not all these places are vulnerable, and a lot depends on where they are located and how they are run. But when the conditions are right and a building attracts the attention of parasites, it can quickly turn into a major feeding station that affects all of its occupants to lesser or greater degrees (though some people have a strong natural immunity to such beings). If the parasites have set up a recent feeding station they will defend it, often quite vigorously. If, however, it is well-established, they can become complacent, which makes it easier to break them up and send them packing. Sometimes an experience can teach you more than thousands of words can, so in the practical work of this lesson, we will observe these phenomena in action. Before we get to the practical work we will look at some other aspects of this subject matter.

7. Egregores

In modern magic egregores are thought of as a group mind or group consciousness connected to a group, religion, magical system, etc. It is assumed that they develop naturally through the actions of the participants of the lodge, system, or religion. While that is correct, it is only a fragment of the whole story. Ancient temple priest-hoods and various magical groups also *constructed* egregores rather than letting them develop naturally.

So what actually is an egregore that it can be constructed?

An egregore is an energetic vessel that contains the patterns/structure of energy, knowledge, emotion, and inner action created by a group of people. When egregores develop naturally, without construct or intervention, they become an echo of a group mind: the energy, magic, emotion, and knowledge developed by a group will be collected and shaped into what is termed a 'group mind' or an egregore. Energy created through magical actions also begins to build up a store of energetic resources that can be drawn upon in the future by the next generation of magicians. When an egregore is not deliberately constructed its balance and integrity depends very much on the actions and maturity of the group. Such a natural egregore is only as good as its current group members who are interacting with it.

If a lodge has a poor crop of magicians with ego problems, little knowledge, or who are energetically and psychically immature, the egregore will start to degrade.

When such an egregore starts to degrade, the knowledge, energy, and wisdom stored in it becomes harder to access. The group energy in the degrading egregore becomes more easily accessible to parasites, which invade, feed off of, and then start to control the egregore. Once the infestation has gotten to the level where it is controlling the egregore, the parasites, if they are intelligent, can start to affect and essentially steer the magical group into actions that will facilitate more feeding opportunities.

Some magical groups and many ancient temple cultures constructed their egregores intentionally, creating a vessel for the group pattern, guarding it, and giving it shape so that it operates in a similar way to the Inner Library. The only difference is that the knowledge, experience, energy, and group mind that can be accessed through a constructed egregore is specific to that particular group. The Inner Library, on the other hand, is a vast vessel of human consciousness. In a way, a properly constructed egregore is like a much smaller octave (or smaller version) of the Inner Library.

A properly constructed egregore is well guarded against any intrusion and will also be invisible to parasites. This invisibility comes as a result of the energetic frequency of the construct. Think of it like radio signals: the egregore has to be on a regular human mind's frequency for the parasites to see it. If it is tuned properly the parasites cannot pick up on the frequency, so it remains invisible, not only to parasites, but also to magicians or other humans casually wandering through the inner worlds.

The main issue for you as an apprentice magician is to know that the majority (but not all) of modern magical groups have what are essentially *feral egregores* that are potentially parasited. If someone joins such a group it will not take long before the parasite tries to plug into the individual and have a feed. This will trigger mild-to-medium obsessive behaviour, compulsions, strong emotions, and a loss of impulse control. Sometimes we see this play out in magical wars between groups. Sometimes these 'magical wars' are simply the product of immature, defensive magicians trying to battle over magical superiority. But often the war is driven by parasites who will repeatedly push the humans into conflict in order to keep the aggression going, which in turn provides a food source. When this is the case and the war is well-established, the groups in conflict will often be arguing over some small, insignificant detail, usually connected to 'identity' (ego) and 'authenticity' (control). The psychological, emotional, and magical engagement is often vastly out of proportion to the actual issue.

When challenged politely and intelligently, the involved magicians will often become aggressive (the parasite defending its feeding station). Often they will not be able to tell you what the conflict is actually about: they will simply keep repeating a perceived grievance and will not be able to look at the situation logically. The parasites essentially disengage the magicians from their own balance and perspective; then they trigger the brain chemistry of the magicians into overdrive, which in turn allows the parasites to flow through the group undetected and unchallenged. It can be very difficult for individuals to leave heavily parasited groups. Often threats are involved, along with the parasite triggering a cascade of fear in the person who wants to leave. It can get very messy.

I know of at least two major magical systems that have this serious issue and neither of them address it in any way. This is why it is so important for apprentices to learn about such things before they get to the stage of actually working with them in any depth: being forewarned alerts the apprentice to be attentive and to watch out for such issues as they try to navigate their way through the magical world. By paying attention and using what you know, as you browse through or engage with different magical systems, you will be able to ascertain which systems are healthy and which are not.

Suffice to say, Quareia has an extremely well constructed, well hidden, and well guarded egregore!

8. Symbiotic relationships

Not all parasite infestations are bad. The physical body has many different beings who make up the whole person. Without various viruses, bacteria, etc. we would not survive or exist. Like everything else in creation parasites can be good or bad depending on where they are and what they are doing. Some parasites set up shop in a human and trigger a necessary response in the body of the human which benefits the human and also allows the parasite to feed. If the relationship is advantageous to both parties, then all is good. Just as bacteria in our gut allow us to digest food and extract nutrients, parasites can sometimes be helpful in balancing damaged energy systems in the body: they provide the missing or damaged impulse that allows the person to carry on living.

So it is important to not think that every parasite found in a human must be torn out and destroyed or composted. The exorcist or magician must take their time and be very clear as to what is causing the symptoms and what is not. One should never assume anything without objective clarification. Parasites, for example, can provide bridges for brain impulses, can trigger neurons, and can bridge between veils on behalf of the human in return for a home and a meal. Sometimes that meal is simple and does not harm the human in any way. That is a truly symbiotic relationship between two beings: one of mutual benefit.

A good physical example is the intentional infection of a human with intestinal worms in order to treat autoimmune diseases. There have been some interesting results in various research projects where the infestation of the human by a physical parasite – i.e. intestinal worms – has been shown to limit the flares of inflammation, in inflammatory bowel diseases, for example. The worm gets a home and a meal, and the human gets their inflammatory disease brought under control with few or no side-effects. This could be a major boon in the treatment of autoimmune diseases, as conventional treatment sometimes requires steroids or even chemotherapy in more serious cases.

Module VI – Different Types of Beings

9. *Task:* Vision work

In this practical work you will go and observe a parasite in action over a building. It is important that you stick to the anonymity of this work: you must not try to look at a building that you know. Working this way helps you learn about these beings in action: you can observe them, note their operational methods, see if you can spot their weaknesses, etc. If you try and look at a building that you know then you are very likely to get pulled into the orbit of the parasite living there, and you will end up making the situation worse rather than helping or learning. These beings are clever and will do anything they can to protect their food source. You are of no help to anyone if you get tagged and then pulled into one of these beings, and that is precisely what can happen if you approach them or become visible to them and you do not know exactly what you are doing.

In this vision you will go through the Inner Library, which will afford you protection and will enable you to observe a situation without being seen. You will be placed in an observing position where you watch from a safe distance, and also, as you return through the Library, you will be able to pick up 'learning' from the Library which will lie dormant within you until the time is right for you to begin direct work on these beings. Simply knowing about parasites will trigger processes of inner learning that will mature as you continue to study. It will also help you protect yourself against these beings should you have to spend time in an infested building: *knowing* is a first step of your inner immune system gearing up to trigger protection. It is a bit like vaccination: your immune system gets to see and recognise the parasite, but in a safe way, which in turn triggers a response in your immunity.

Prepare your work space as normal and prop your sword, point down, to the left of your east altar. Do the Anchor ritual and then sit in front of the east altar and still yourself with meditation.

When you are ready, working in vision, pass through the east altar and into the Inner Library as you have already learned to do. Go to the central podium and ask the librarian there if you can be guided to a viewing platform where you can safely observe a parasite infestation over a building. The librarian will guide you to a long, dark corridor that runs off of the central library area, and together you will walk down it until you come to two big bronze doors. Place your hands upon the door. You feel that it is alive: it is a guardian that stops things from the outer world flowing into the Library unchecked. When the guardian is satisfied that you are no threat, the bronze door will swing open and reveal a ledge that looks out over a city. The librarian will hand you a cloak with a hood that you will put on. Pull the hood up and fasten the cloak up properly. When you are ready the librarian will pull a bronze chain that hangs on the door and fasten it to the back of your cloak. They will then step back to allow you to step onto the viewing ledge.

As you stand there, take a minute to get your bearings and look at each building in the city. You will notice that one or more of the buildings seems to have mist around it, obscuring it from view. Choose one of them and look closely at it with intent: you wish to see what is hidden from view. As you focus the mist will begin to clear and you will see that the building is covered by a large being: they are often partially shapeless, a bit like marshmallows, and either there will be one big one with loads of tentacles, or a large one that has smaller versions of itself that extend out and seem to attach themselves either around the building or to the tops of the heads of the people in or around the building.

Take a very close and considered look. Have no emotional reaction to what you see. This is really important: you must feel no emotion whatsoever when you observe these beings. Any hint of anger, fear, loathing, compassion for the people, anything like that will alert the being to your presence and will potentially put you in its orbit. Imagine you are looking at a broken or damaged bit of machinery: you are simply looking to see what the situation is. Look at the being's back, its top... you are searching for its core or its weak spot. Is it very protected with smaller beings guarding it? Does it have spines or armour? Or is it a longstanding being that has no fear of anything interfering with it? If it has lots of smaller beings breaking off or extending from it and feeding off people, your attention should not be on them: these beings are like a hive being or little clones of the main one.

To destroy parasites you look for their core and learn what and where their weak or exposed spot is: a spot without armour, scales, without smaller clones, a spot that goes directly to the heart of them as opposed to a limb. Resist any urge to take action: you are there to learn, nothing more. Some parasites will put out a signal that almost invites humans to attack it: those who do not know how to deal with these beings will be pulled into their orbit and will become dinner. In time you will learn how to dispatch these beings and you will be put to work, but first comes learning and strengthening.

Take your time with your observations and see if you can ascertain what sort of food source is in the building which attracted it. Is it hormone output (teens)? Is it pain and suffering (hospital)? Is it lots of people who have no impulse control (psychiatric unit)? Is it people shedding their baggage and looking for an easy solution, and therefore opening themselves up (meditation group)? Is it greed and adrenaline (stock market traders)? These are all obvious examples, but there are many different food sources that are attractive to parasites. Identifying what the food is can be helpful, but don't worry if you cannot see the trigger, as getting too close in observation will potentially expose you.

Once you have seen all that you need to see, withdraw back through the doors and wait while the librarian takes the chain off and the cloak from you. Touch the door, say thank you to the guardian, and shut the doors. Walk back to the centre of the Library. Ask the librarian to guide you to a shelf of books that cover this subject matter so that you can learn more. When you get to the shelf, run your fingers along the books until you find one that feels brighter or stronger than the others.

Pick up that book and hand it to the librarian, who will push the book into you so that you can absorb its knowledge. When that is done, thank the librarian and bow to them in respect. Then return to your work space.

When you have finished the vision immediately write down everything in your journal that you can remember from the observation, *but do not draw a picture of the being:* to do so will draw it into your space; images can be windows. Once you have finished your write-up in your journal close down the work space, but leave the sword where it is for a while. Go and wash your hands and face with soap and a handful of salt. Leave the sword where it is overnight, and in the morning put it back in its resting place, wrapped up in its scabbard.

10. *Task:* Preparing a report

Using your notes from your journal, write up a summary of your observations in your computer log. Write down how you think these beings might affect the groups of people in the spaces that get infected, and how in turn that might affect society in general. These beings encourage unbalanced behaviour in order to feed, so what are the wider implications for society when groups of people are manipulated in such a way? Also look back at old news reports of teens committing multiple murders in schools. Don't just look at the teen who went on the rampage; look on Google Maps at the school's position in relation to the land around it. Is it in a mountainous area? Parasites that encourage mass murder often (not always) tend to come out of mountainous areas.

Once you have looked at a school situation, step back from the human perspective and see if you think there are any wider reasons that such a thing may have been triggered. Have there been people living in that area for hundreds of years, or is it a fairly new settlement? (Less than two hundred years old.) Is it near or on ancient burial grounds? Is it an area that was settled by native/aboriginal tribes, or was it shunned/avoided by them? Are there any folk legends in that area about dangerous beings? These are all methods where you can start to step back and get a bigger picture of what is happening and why. Sometimes you can identify a specific trigger or collection of triggers. Other times it seems to be simply a matter of a lot of yummy food in one convenient place.

Write up your findings on computer.

11. *Task:* Parasite research

Look up the life cycle of a body parasite, like tape worms, thread worms, etc. Look closely at how they operate. How do they avoid killing their hosts? What cycles do they go through, and when are they at their most vulnerable? The pattern of behaviour in physical parasites will tell you a lot about inner parasites, as they essentially use the same pattern of behaviour. The only real difference is that the physical parasite looks for physical food and an inner parasite looks for emotive energy.

But physical parasites can also interfere with the brain via the Vagus nerve, to manipulate the human into eating foods that create an easier environment for the infestation.

Think about what types of emotive energies would attract parasites and how changes in a society's thinking can make it more vulnerable or more resistant to these beings. Then look at societal inhibitions, rules, and morals. Is it possible, do you think, that some morals and rules of society developed because of the dangers of these beings, and the understanding was lost? Or do they possibly make a society more vulnerable? See if you can spot where societies have developed their own religious or cultural patterns in order to repel or defend against such beings, and how those patterns may have changed human behaviour. Do such developments tip the Scales the other way and become repressive, or are they balanced and protective?

This task is important research for you as an Apprentice magician, and taking the time to think about the complexity of these issues will help you gain a deeper understanding of why societies form themselves in certain ways, how dogmas start, and how wisdoms get lost. It will also teach you the roots of some of the rules within a society, which in turn will help you tease out the wisdom from the dogma so that you can live your own life in a safe, healthy way without succumbing to dogmas, fears, or irrelevant ways of thinking. All of that is of the greatest importance to a magician, as it is often mirrored in the Inner worlds.

Ensure you do the work on computer and provide references from your research.

> Note 2025: **This task was originally optional for the course. However it quickly became apparent that because it was optional, most people did not do it. That is a very stupid way to approach this course – this is not a course simply to pass an exam, this is a course to train you as a specialist. If you do not do this work properly, you put yourself at great risk in magic because of the ignorance that comes from not doing the necessary research and subsequent learning.**

Lesson 5

Titans/Primordial Deities and Vast Land Beings

The understanding of Titans and vast land beings is an important aspect of learning about our planet, our past, and the huge land powers that underpin our world. The term *land being* can cover anything from the consciousness of a rock, to a river or sea, to mountains and continents. It also covers the larger consciousness that operates behind these planetary beings: the Titans.

1. Titans

Many assume, because the Greeks had the Titans within their mythology, that the Titans were Greek. Not so. What has survived in Greek mythology[1] is remnants of their version of understanding regarding these vast and ancient beings. Titans are/were all over the planet. They are also the elemental deity expressions of the planet itself. What came down to us in terms of knowledge were highly constructed stories that outline some of the powers of these beings. The Titans are very ancient deities/consciousness from the dawn of humanity, they are the inner expression of the elements in action around the planet. Were these ancient conscious beings around and active before human consciousness evolved? Who knows, but I suspect that they were, and that they interacted with all life forms on the planet.

The Old Kingdom Egyptians also had knowledge of these powers: they were depicted as the *Ogdoad* Ancient Greek for Eightfold. In Egyptian they were called *ḫmnyw*, pronounced khemenu, also meaning Eightfold or the eight root deities who allowed the world to exist. These eight deities sprang from four powers, and each power had a male and female deity. They were:

- Nu and Naunet
- Amun and Amaunet
- Kuk and Kauket
- Huh and Hauhet

These vast powers set the stage for creation and out of that came the root deities such as Atum, who in turn gave birth to Shu, Tefnut, etc. The Ogdoad or *ḫmnyw* track back to Old Kingdom Egypt, in their cult base of Hermopolis[2] which was originally known as Khemenu (Eightfold) before Greek influence. But the earliest unambiguous mention of them was not until the 18th dynasty (New Kingdom) with a mention in a dedication by Hatshepsut.

---

[1] Our sources are mainly Hesiod; his are the only direct writings about the Titans that have survived.

[2] City of Hermes – the Greek name for the city.

So let's back up a bit and have a closer look at this, as it will give you a much better idea of the formation of deity powers, as well as the understanding the ancients had regarding the formation of our world. The first stumbling block you will come up against is one of semantics. The names and words used in the translation of texts can easily cause misunderstandings from a magical perspective. This is seen, for instance, in the understanding of the primordial waters, Nu and Naunet. 'The primordial waters' essentially refers to the great oceans that life crawled out of: we were born from the sea. This, in various ancient mythologies, is sometimes translated into English as 'the watery abyss,' which then leads some inexperienced magicians to think that the Abyss and the primordial waters are the same thing, which they are not. So tread carefully in your reading and understanding. The 'Nu' is also the inner waters of the Underworld where the dead either 'float, sink or swim in' in some of the funerary texts.

All these deities have the full positive/negative polarity which is expressed as male and female pairings. Here is a brief run-down of them.

1. Nu and Naunet: A power that was the soup (oceans) from which all life crawled out of onto the earth. Nu was/is the roots of the genetics of all species, and this power set the stage ready for various lifeforms to evolve over time. It was also the power that helped create the driving force and catalysts for weather systems, ecosystems, climates, etc. (but not the weather elements themselves). It is also the power that the dead soul drifts in before they awaken to rise out of the depths of the Underworld.

2. Amun and Amaunet: The atmosphere, the 'nothing' between the stars and the earth. The powers of the weather, or air, moisture, sun, etc. play out in the arena which is Amun/Amaunet.

3. Kuk and Kauket: The darkness before the light, the stillness before the action of creation, the chaos out of which order was formed. In this joint male/female form this power is not only the darkness from which sprang the light, but also the light to which the darkness returns: the cauldrons of creation and dissolution.

4. Huh and Hauhet: Infinity, Divine existence before time, the Void from which all creation flows.

In the early creation myth of ancient Egypt there was a massive release of energy that caused a landmass to rise, and that land mass brought Atum to the world. Atum is (and means) 'the complete one': everything was contained within him, and from him came the other deities. Straight away we start to see the knowledge that the ancient Egyptians had of the dynamics of early life on the planet; pretty impressive. Their later imagery shows reptiles (frogs, snakes, etc.) which are very old life forms whose age tells us just how old these deities are in the order of species they connect with. From Atum flowed the deities Shu (wind/life) and Tefnut (moisture/order). From these names you can look up the rest of the creation myths and deities for yourself.

To make sense of all this from the perspective of the magician we will choose one pre-root deity and look at the progression of that power as it steps down enough so that humans can work/interact with it. We will look at the power of air to illustrate how the flow of root deities works.

2. Air

We start with Amun and Amaunet, the undivided power of the air regardless of the chemical make-up that air has. Though today we think of air as being a mix that we can breathe,[3] it has not always been that way on this planet, and the undivided power we know as Amun/Amaunet is the root of *all* the various mixes that our atmosphere has had over time. As an aside, the ancient Egyptians later focused on Amun as a divided male deity of the air – the Unknowable One, who likely set the stage for later Monotheistic ideas in Semitic tribes.[4]

From Amun/Amaunet we step down one notch to Shu: the emptiness that divides the sky and the earth; his two children. Shu is a step closer to our experience of air. He resides in the power of Amun in that Shu is the root consciousness of the air *that moves around us:* the air that we can breathe, as opposed to the total atmosphere that surrounds the planet. He is the power that carries the weather (but not the weather itself) and is the power that enables life to exist. From his children, the earth and the sky, sprang the deities we are more familiar with in Egyptian mythology: Isis, Osiris, Set, and Nephthys. A couple of other key players appear on the scene early on who are essentially bridges between the Ogdoad and the deities closer to our world and our humanity. They are Djehuty and Ma'at. Djehuty is the balance of utterance, the root of communication, magic, knowledge, and the 'accountant of souls,' he who records the results of life. Ma'at, his female counterpart, is the power of balance that flows through everything, order from chaos, and the Scales themselves. In Western magic, Djehuty is the sword/utterance/word, and Ma'at is the Scales.

It is at this level that magicians work with the deities in magical forms, as these deities form a structure that humans can interact with. Trying to work with Amun/Amaunet in deity form is too overarching: you would be plugging into the power of our planet's atmosphere, a vast consciousness that could potentially fry a human mind. It is also too big, too formless, and too expansive for direct, successful communication. Similarly, working directly with Shu is likely to trigger all sorts of weather issues, as he is a deity who flows across continents and rises directly out of the power of the oceans. Shu is not a deity who has a form that magicians can work with. He is the overarching power of air in nature, and is not stepped down enough for us to communicate with him properly; we simply acknowledge and respect his power.

As humans we like to dabble, and we think we know what we are doing, but magically engaging such a deity directly is biting off a bit more than humans can chew.

---

[3] Nitrogen, oxygen, water vapour, argon, and carbon dioxide.

[4] Egyptian territory over time, particularly in the New Kingdom spanned large areas of the Levant.

These powerful forces are acknowledged, respected, and recognised... but not directly plugged into. It's a bit like going round to a friend's house where their grandmother and great grandmother also live. You interact with your friend easily, as they are so similar in age and understanding to you; but you are very polite to their grandmother and great grandmother, and you don't try to sit down and play games with them. These powerful root creation deities flow in fragments through other deities that are closer to our understanding. These other deities, who are stepped-down filters of the overarching powers, are the ones we would connect with magically.

One of these deities is Djehuty. Of the two deities of balance and order, Djehuty is the one that magicians work with directly. Ma'at, who is a power of balance who underpins everything, is recognised, respected, and her laws are adhered to, but a magician would not usually try to communicate directly with her. Instead, the magician would veer towards Djehuty. Why? Partly because Ma'at is a pure concept that is itself. This power was often depicted as a small child, as *truth* is very fragile. There were never any temples to Ma'at and yet she was embedded within all aspects of Egyptian life. Djehuty on the other hand, is a pivotal deity for priests and magicians in that he filters the vast powers of air into a form that is compatible with our existence: the Word. He is a much more active interface for people to understand and work with. In their magical training the priest-magician first learns the powers of magical utterance, limitation that brings balance, and all the powers of magical east/air. At the same time, they learn to connect with the element of air out in nature, not as a deity, but as a 'being-to-being' contact, something you have been doing in your lessons by talking to nature.

As a result of that work, the priest-magician begins to understand the deeper underlying powers that flow through these deities, and slowly inches their way towards the knowledge and understanding of the power of the utterance of creation, and the power of the magical breath upon the wind: the closest we can come to communion with the powerful creation deities that are the consciousness of the air, the weather, and communication.

So where do the Titans come into all this? The Ogdoad are the Titans as understood by the Egyptians, who had a better handle on it than anyone else we know of. Though the Titans are not worked with directly by magicians, they are known of, recognised, honoured, and respected. This keeps their action within your orbit of understanding, and enables you fully to understand the powers that flow around you and through the deities. There are, however, deities like Djehuty who span both the first primordial deities and the language, culture, and magic of humanity. They are a direct filter to these vast powers, and because of their closeness to humanity they can step down or step up the power of their interaction depending on which human stands before them – they can filter their power according to the maturity and capability of the human.

This does not mean that the magician necessarily works with the deity Djehuty unless they are operating within the Egyptian pattern: the bridge power of Djehuty is inherent within all cultures, with all different groups of humans. Djehuty is simply its Egyptian expression. Magicians often make this mistake repeatedly, and will often try to mimic the ancient priesthoods by having statues that they give offerings to, recite prayers to, etc. But this is often done without any understanding of the reasons why these things are done, and it is approached through a modern filter of what the magician thinks a priest would do. For example the *offering of incense* is not a gift to please the deity, it is a working action where the specific resin is burnt around the statue to *keep the statue clean from inner dirt and to discourage parasites.*

But this can become an unbalanced way to work with these powers if you are not careful or don't know what you are doing. If you are an adept working on a specific line of work that is in particular orbit to the Egyptian pantheon, then all is well and good. But that is working with these deities as contacts and tools; it is not a foundation of magical understanding and experience. First the magician must learn to connect with, recognise, and work with those powers without a cultural dressing so that they can find the expressions that flow naturally within the landmass that the magician lives upon. This will also help the magician to recognise those same powers in different cultures around the world. And you have been doing this in small steps. In the first lesson of this module you connected with a deity of the east, of the wind. You were not given a name, a deity form, or an image; rather you were directed to work with the power itself and how it naturally presented itself to you.

When you work in the Library and connect with the beings there, you are connecting with the power that is behind the deity Djehuty, the recorder of all things, the keeper of knowledge, the conversion of the wind into utterance and the Word. The power of the Library is a filter whose overarching power can be approached through the filter of the deity the Egyptians named Djehuty.

So you are already taking the first steps towards working with these powers and understanding them. By doing it this way, not only do you learn the real power without the dogmatic dressing that built up in various cultures over millennia, but you also sidestep the first trap that catches magicians: dogmatic adherence to a decaying understanding. There is no statue to go out and buy, no altar or deity to dress and take pictures of and then show off on social media, no title of priesthood, no special outfit; these are traps laid to catch the unwise.

And yet, once you have come truly to understand the undressed power, you can work with the dressed cultural expression of that power (a named deity) without falling prey to such traps, as you will be able to understand the true function of the deity filter without putting a human-style dressing on it. Then and only then will you be able, as an adept, really to tap into the powers of these deities and work with them properly.

When you worked with your magical tools out in nature you took a first step towards the dynamic of direct contact when you connected with the deity of the river.

Behind this deity is a deeper, more powerful force of water/moisture, and behind this is the power of the ocean and the atmosphere; the two dynamics that form water we can drink. As the magician progresses towards adeptship within their training, when they connect with the river, they would also keep a magical focus on the vast powers *behind* that river. It is like a series of gates: you open the one before you, but you are aware of the other gates behind it, which in turn gives you an understanding of what lies *beyond* the gates.

And here comes the full circle of action: an experienced adept, who is aware of these vast powers beyond the river and may have lightly connected with them magically, will return their focus to the first gate, and approach the river in the same way as an apprentice. The difference is that the adept has a full, in-depth magical understanding of those vast powers, so that when they do a simple act of acknowledging the power of the river, the river responds with the full powers of the root deities behind the river. This dynamic comes into play in all the work an experienced adept does. They have no need to do complex rituals or deep visions; the power in its full depth is immediate wherever they turn their focus.

For you as apprentice magicians, all this translates to first learning the base power of the east, which you have been doing through your ritual and visionary work. As you step into initiate training, the work begins to focus on the deities and powers who translate the power of the east into knowledge of the power of utterance, both in ritual and in nature – the foundations of which you have, again, already started. As you progress, you step into the orbit of deity powers who bridge magical knowledge, structure, and method.

As you step into the work of an adept, you learn to reach through those 'front' powers to recognise and begin to understand, in full magical terms, the forces that lie behind the deities. From there, the adept brings all these vast powers of creation back down to ground level and returns to simplicity. But it is a simplicity full of gnosis: the fool who has traversed the universe and returned to the beginning.

3. LAND BEINGS

In previous lessons and practical work you have been introduced to local land beings around you in a tentative, slow way. As an apprentice your connection to and work with these beings is rudimentary, as such connections need to be taken a step at time. This is because these types of beings do not think or act in the same way as humans, and it is easy to get in a mess by making a misstep with these beings, so the connection is worked with a step at a time. This way, both you and the land beings around you normalise to one another. When you come to work in more depth with them, you will both know each other's working methods, intentions, and you as a magician will have learned not to humanise them.

The major mistake that many magicians make when working and connecting with land beings is approaching and interacting with them as if they were a type of human.

They are not. We expect them to act in human ways and have human emotions, human sensibilities, and human boundaries of behaviour. Nothing could be further from the truth. And by approaching land beings in such a way, the magician can trigger a destructive response without meaning to.

Beyond the local land beings are vast beings of land consciousness that are all around us. Often they are not aware of us as individuals. Within the orbit of these vast beings are many other different layers of being and consciousness that magicians connect to and work with. To get to this stage of fluency you need first to know about these large continental beings, what they do, and how they operate. From there you will be able to connect with the beings that bridge between the huge powers and the local species, humans included. This is akin to the relationship between the Ogdoad and Djehuty: within the vast sphere of land consciousness are beings who can be connected with and worked with as adepts. In some cultures they are viewed as deities and in other cultures they are considered as the consciousness that resides in a mountain, or a chain of mountains, or in the ocean. As magicians, we approach these various bridges of consciousness in a variety of ways, which helps us to recognise these beings depicted in various magical and ancient texts.

Let us first look at some examples of the massive land beings who are so often unaware of humans, just as we are often unaware of insects that live around us. From there you will be able to understand the wide variety of these beings in the landscape.

4. Mountains

We often think of mountains as individual beings of nature, which they are, but they are also deeply connected with all other mountains. The individual mountain is also connected deeply to the range to which it belongs, and the range itself can be approached as an individual land being. But over the years, various magicians have learned that mountain ranges at seemingly vast distances from each other are deeply connected. They can be worked with as a 'family' of ranges: what happens to one range can affect mountains thousands of miles away. From a magical perspective mountains are very active energy-wise. They are often home to many different layers of beings: smaller land beings, deities, ancient sleepers, etc. The energy of a mountain is often volatile; in fact I have yet to come across a mountain or range that is peaceful. If the mountain or range has been worked with for a long time they become *friendly volatile* as opposed to *hostile volatile*. But either way, mountains are rarely, if ever, passive in their energy.

As magicians it is almost impossible to commune directly with the power of a mountain or range, and most of the lesser land beings who inhabit mountains are often hostile or difficult for human contact. Sometimes the difficulty is not about hostility but strangeness, and the presence of a lot of powerful energy that our bodies do not know what to do with. To make more sense out of this for you as an apprentice, we will now look at mountain power in its different octaves and presentations, which hopefully will clarify things a little.

5. Peeling the layers off the mountain

We will start with the smaller beings and work up/down from there. From a psychic energy perspective some mountains are more active than others. So we will look at the dynamic of an 'active' mountain perspective. An active mountain is often populated by a wide variety of land beings who present in a vast array of guises.

The most immediate contacts tend to be nature beings – faery beings. These present as part animal, part human; or as a small or very tall human, or as humanoid beings who incorporate twigs, horns, fur, rock, etc. into their presentation. They are not cute; they are not twinkly with wings and glitter. These are powerful nature beings in their own right, and they will defend their territory quite aggressively if they need to. It is this layer of being that gives humans nightmares or attacks them in their sleep if they feel the human is threatening their territory in any way. Think in terms of folk legends of trolls, Bigfoot, monsters, Krampus, etc.

They can become physically violent: they can throw things, hit people and injure them, or torment the minds of their victims until the humans withdraw from their land. They can also be responsible for the disappearance of humans, and can cause all manner of confusion and disorientation in humans – being 'pixie-led,' for example. 'Pixie-led' is a saying that comes from Britain, and describes how a human can become totally lost on land that they know very well, something that happens when faery beings don't want a human near something, or more often, when a group of faery beings are bored and want some entertainment. Faery beings can reside on the surface of the mountain and can also be found deep in the caves of mountain ranges. They also populate forests and springs.

One step up from these beings, we find beings who can act as *bridges* between the vast consciousness of the mountain/range and humans (or other species). Similar to Djehuty, these *bridge beings* are a part of the larger, powerful force of the land, but are also a consciousness that humans can connect with. These often crop up in mountain cultures as deities who 'come from' or reside in a mountain range. Though they can communicate with humans, they are land beings and as such often do not have human emotions or sensibilities. They are themselves, and it is folly to try and form a relationship with them with the idea that they think emotively, in the same way you do. Often the deities of these mountains appear attended by large predatory animals; or they appear as part-human, part-predatory animal or large-toothed creature (e.g. lion, bear). These deities are essentially the doorkeepers for the deeper powers that reside in the mountains.

Now we get to the vast land being itself: the *mountain consciousness*. Once you get to this level of being you have to switch how you think. The more surface types of beings appear as animals, birds, reptiles, and humans: they mirror the species they have had contact with or are part of. Mountains and ranges do not. They are a totally different form of consciousness and are more closely related to the elements than they are to any species. A curious thing about these powerful mountains, one which many magicians have found when working with them, is that their complimentary element is *air*. I do not mean the air around the mountain, but the air *within* the mountain. This is not a physical manifestation of the element, but an energetic and inner one: air and mountains go together, and are found together magically. We work with that dynamic in a much smaller sense with the sword and the stone. This strange union of the elements shows up when the magician goes deep into the mountain or ranges in vision in a particular way. It also shows in various ancient magical imagery: Moses goes to the top of the mountain to gain the Utterance of God, and the utterance is carved in stone.

In the Western culture's death vision, beyond the river is a mountain range that must be climbed, a mountain of whispers and utterances. As the spirit climbs the mountain, they hear the many dogmas in life that weighed them down or in some way limited them. The link between words/air and mountains varies from an incidental connection, i.e. the Essenes hiding their scrolls in caves, to a deeply mystical one such as the *Cave of the Four Winds*.

For your practical work you will go into the depths of the mountain to find the junction place that joins up mountain ranges, and where the four winds of the Underworld flow together, deep in the heart of land. Before we get to that, and before we move on, let me outline some practical, simple ways you can begin a gentle, outer connection with these vast mountain powers should you live on them, near them, or go visit them. Mountains are vast beings who are often not directly aware of us, and we cannot get into direct contact with the large being itself. But we can use our inherent bridge power to gently tap into their consciousness. We tend not to get a direct answer from the mountain itself in the form of direct magical communication, though sometimes, rarely, that can happen; but we do sometimes get favourable responses from the lesser beings or nature around the mountain, or a rumble of communion from the mountain itself.

The bridging power inherent within humans is the ability to make sound/vibration in a specific way with our voices: it is the quality of 'Djehuty' within humans that allows this trigger to happen. This is done in a very simple way, a way you have already been learning: through the use of your voice in song. Mountains react to human song, and if there is a steady, non-confrontational energy in the song it is usually favourably received. It is akin to our reactions to insects. Most humans do not like earwigs, beetles, woodlice, etc. But we smile when we see a beautiful butterfly. The human voice raised in song elicits a similar reaction from land powers: they pick up on it as something beautiful. We cannot talk directly to the butterfly and hold a conversation with it, but we can admire it; and that admiration often translates to humans planting flowers to give the butterflies food and shelter. And so it is between humans and mountains, if the connection is done properly. Do bear in mind, though, that if a mountain has been attacked by humans, for example through underground bomb testing, mining, blasting, etc. then it is far less likely that you will be welcome.

In such cases connecting with a mountain will trigger a need for balance, and you will be expected to work magically to redress the balance, which can be a lifetime's work of hard and difficult magic. So tread wisely.

The place to sing to the mountain is in its caves so that the sound is within the mountain, not on top of it. Sometimes you sing and there is no response. That doesn't matter: you can continue to sing to the mountain until it notices you, if you are close enough to visit often. Occasionally you can get a huge, or at least interesting, response. When I was a young person I used to do a lot of caving and potholing. When I was deep in a cave system I would often stop for a while and sing to the caves, to the mountain, and to the rocks. At first I got no response at all. And then slowly, after a while, I started to feel a shift in the caves as I went through them. A couple of years later I was caving a long system in Yorkshire that opened out into a huge cavern, and I stood in the centre of the cavern and sang to the hill. I did not get a physical response, but I got a sudden 'opening up', which is the only way I can describe it, of the energy of the cave system: it was like all the energetic lights went on and I was surrounded by a vast consciousness that heard a faint sound. It woke up and was listening. But the energetic output of that brief, simple contact was too much for me at that age, and it overwhelmed me. It was like seeing, from an energetic point of view, the whole range of mountains in the country in one brief flash. I was too young, eighteen years old, to process the experience, and I admit it scared me a little.

Many years later I had a more immediate answer from a mountain. This time I was strong and experienced enough for the contact to be better formed. I went to visit a cave with a group of magicians, a cave within a very powerful and magical mountain. I sat and sang old folk songs from my childhood, and held no intent in my mind other than to sing to the mountain in the same way I would sing to my children at bedtime. As we crawled out of the cave and set off walking back down the mountain, I felt a distinct rumble under my feet. I stopped and listened, and yes, it was like a small earthquake: the mountain was singing back. I am very sensitive to land activity and can often feel very faint earthquakes that others cannot. I asked the others if they felt the quake and everyone said no, and one person pointed out that the mountain range had no active fault lines that they knew of. When I got home I got on to a university website that records all earthquake action, no matter how small. When I was standing on the mountain and felt the rumbling, there was indeed a small earthquake recorded. This was the mountain communicating back at a very low frequency: a rumble. We cannot understand each other, song and rumble; but we acknowledge each other and are aware of each other, and that is enough. Sometimes the teeny tiny action triggers a reaction.

If you go to mountains, find the caves and see if you can safely access one. Sit down and sing songs that trigger either childhood feelings of safety, lullabies, or old folk songs of love, for example. We use these gentle songs because the rhythm and cadence of the song tends to be slightly diffuse and does not hold harsh, regular beats.

The harsher and more regular the song's beat, the more aggressive a response it will trigger. The different responses that humans get from nature in relation to the pitch and beat of a song can vary wildly, and this is something you will learn to work with more directly in your training. As you leave the cave, spend a little time on the hillside listening, watching, and meditating. If you should suddenly be overwhelmed by an unexpected wave of fear or adrenaline, then get off the mountain immediately: the response is aggressive.

If you get a strong compulsion to go back into the cave and sleep there, also get off the mountain immediately: the beings within the mountain want you to leave humanity and go live with them. Going to sleep in such a situation can end up with you dying in your sleep and having your spirit stuck in the mountain as a play companion for the land beings. I am not joking about this, and I have known it to happen before, so be warned. These vast beings and all the other land beings around them are beautiful but also dangerous at times. Their allure can be overwhelming, particularly to sensitive people, so keep your wits about you. The same holds true for any connection with any of these huge land powers: do not be romantic about this as you are dealing with powers that can entwine you and blot you out in a second.

If you do not get such an extreme reaction, but are allowed just to be on the hillside with no major pull either way, enjoy the nature around you and keep a close eye on the birds, the wind, and the weather reactions. If all is good, go back a few times and sing in the caves, but don't overdo it. Spending a lot of your apprenticeship just making friends but not necessarily doing anything pays massive dividends in the future, as you will discover in your own time.

6. Oceans

Oceans, like mountain ranges, are vast beings that hold whole magical inner ecosystems within them as well as their outer ecosystems. The whole body of planetary seawater is one very large being, and the areas where it settles into particular oceans are offshoots of the main consciousness of water on the planet. Each ocean has its own personality and a job that it does, and within that are many beings and contacts. Some of them work with humanity and others do not, or are not even aware of humanity. For us as magicians these ocean consciousnesses are too diffuse and too far removed from humanity for us to interact directly with. But within the oceans are powers that present to us as deities, inner beings, inner priesthoods, and contacts whom we can work with if we need to. Whereas mountains have a strong connection with air and all that air brings to us magically, the ocean brings and takes waves of humanity, and gives us knowledge of life and death, of blood lines, races: it is directly connected with the vessel from which life flows and to which life returns.

Magically the oceans also connect strongly with the magical element of fire,[5] and you will find that many older cultures that live by the sea had numerous fire rituals where fire was gifted to the sea.

Within each ocean is an *undivided deity* form which is still far beyond our ability to reach. These ocean deities are similar in scope and power to the Egyptian Ogdoad, and are treated as such by magicians. One step down from that level of power are more localised powers that we can connect with should we need to. These present as *partially divided deities*[6] who can be connected with where the land meets the sea: at the threshold. Adepts work with these beings as part of work that is connected to the ebb and flow of humanity and the evolution of our species. These beings are not involved or worked with for more mundane magical purposes as their power structure is very specific.

One step down from these threshold deities are beings who present to us as a *priesthood*, male and female, sometimes humanoid, sometimes not, who mediate death and life with the tides of the ocean. It is not individual death; rather it is death connected to species and races. When these contacts appear in magical visions it tells us that we are at a time of major change in our populations, cultures, and even species. Time, and our concept of time, is very different from the concept of time that these large beings have. What can be immediate for them can be hundreds of years for us. This needs to be kept in mind should a magician have any contact from the ocean.

The ocean, as a magical being, is far removed from us: we may live as humans by the sea, but it is not our living environment and as such it is not usually part of the 'family' of beings with whom magicians work. However, some magicians who live by the sea do become deeply linked to the ocean and the being that bridges between the shore and the ocean. For these magicians, work with the ocean often becomes the only work they do, as they align their magical system to become compatible with the sea as opposed to the powers of the land.

And that brings me to an important point for you to remember. Working deep magic upon or with an element you live in or around is generally stable magic and compatible with life. But working deep magic with something like the ocean, something you could not possibly live in, can quickly become dangerous in many different ways. Our bodies and our magic have developed to live and work on dry land. To plunge magically into the ocean with the intent of long-term projects is at odds with our survival as individuals. This can manifest in various ways, from slowly finding it hard to function on dry land, to being swept into the ocean as the being tries to bring you deep into their realm. This almost happened to a magical friend of mine who works deeply with the oceans. One day, while visiting the sea in Ireland, she was suddenly pulled by a freak wave and sucked down off the rocks. She survived, but with a badly

---

[5] South, future, genetics.

[6] They have a specific gender, but undivided power.

broken ankle. The sea recognised her, loved her, and wanted her to join it. With all these large powers the word 'caution' should be tattooed across your forehead so that you look at it every day in the mirror!

But if, as an adept, you are called to work with ocean beings, it is likely that you would work on the threshold, where you would be bridging races or species from the ocean to the land, and from the land to the ocean. This sets up an inner pattern that eventually manifests itself physically. Hopefully we will not need that work in this century, but knowing about it will inform you should you see it in action, or have contact with the ocean in vision or dreams.

7. OTHER LAND FEATURES

The other vast land powers that express in our world are volcanoes, plains, fault lines, and large ice sheets. Smaller powers are expressed in certain valleys, areas of hot springs, etc.

Every one of these has the same kind of structure as mountains and oceans: a vast consciousness with a prime deity expression, a smaller deity form that bridges to humanity, beings who are divided expressions or aspects of the larger consciousness, and then beings who live within that environment. Each land feature will have a central place that acts as a pivot between the inner and outer power. Finding that central place allows the magician to understand how the inner powers, outer powers, beings, and contacts all come together. This is where the visionary magician makes contact, and then works out from.

We will work with a pivotal place in vision in the practical work so that you get an idea of how it all fits together. Later, as an adept, you will work with some of the more volatile, large land beings who manifest through volcanoes, fault lines, etc. But first, by working with the mountains and the vast land being beneath your feet, you will start on the road to acquiring a technique that will enable you to connect with the various land expressions in their more powerful forms.

8. THE LAND BENEATH YOU

In your previous lessons you have worked step by step with various forms of beings and also with nature around you. This in turn has slowly introduced the nearby land powers to you in their lesser forms. It has also introduced you to them. It is important to do this before you attempt to connect with the larger consciousness of the landmass on which you live. Get to know and respect the small guys and make friends before you climb up the corporate ladder! By connecting with the Garden around you, the rivers, the hills, the Underworld, and all in small steps, you have allowed your body and mind to normalise to the land powers, and for the land powers to become aware of you.

You have also learned to work with the power of the stone in various ways. This, too, has prepared you for deeper connection to the land being on the continent where you live. Each landmass, regardless of regional boundaries, holds a huge consciousness that is the being of that landmass. We are less than fleas on the surface of that land, but slowly, step by step, we can make connections with that landmass through the various bridge beings who present upon a land.

The bigger the landmass, the further away from our consciousness the land becomes: it becomes too big and we become too small to make overall contact, so usually magicians work with regional expressions upon a landmass. And that is, for the most part, how you will work. However it is vital to understand the larger power that resides behind the regional presentation, and to start a faint connection to this consciousness, via bridges, if you are to work in any real magical depth as an adept. You at least become vaguely aware of each other, which in turn becomes protective both for you and the land.

If you live on an island, as I now do, it is easier: the landmass is smaller and more contained by the ocean, so the power is more focused, which makes it more accessible. It is harder to make that connection if you live on a large continent (as I have also done), but it is still necessary to attempt that connection in a simple way. Connecting with the overall landmass brings a different layer of meaning and understanding to your relationship with the land, above and beyond the area you usually connect to. Think of it like the politics of a country. There are city and county councils, regional administrations, and a national government. Although the majority of a population do not have a direct role in the running of central government, by casting a vote in a democracy everyone plays a small part, and you, by casting a vote, affect the nation in a tiny way.

So it is with connections with land beings. You work most intensively with the beings directly around you, and you have occasional connections with larger land features like rivers, mountains, etc. You would not usually work directly with the whole consciousness of your continent, but your single voice connecting to the continent does bring about change. Your voice acts as a tiny catalyst that then filters down to the region, the area, and finally your own patch. It is a bit like a chain of command, but not very organised in the way we understand organisation. Slowly you inch your way up the pecking order, say your hello to the being at the top of the power ladder, and then wait for the answer to filter back through the underlings at the bottom.

The way to do this is by intention and focus. You have slowly been expanding your consciousness outwards as you work magically, first through your garden, the wind, and then through regional land features. You would not work in vision or ritual directly with the power of the continent, but by keeping a focused awareness of its presence and the fact that you are its guest, more lights begin to turn on for you magically.

The method for doing this is included in the practical work and is something you should incorporate into your magical work from now on.

9. About the practical work

We will do this work in two stages. The first stage weaves in the start of connection with the continent, and the second stage is the technique for going deep into the pivotal place that connects mountain ranges. Before you start your practical work, there are some things that need saying at this point in your training. Though they may not seem particularly important at this stage, they are the most powerful things in magic you will ever learn. So remember these points: learning them now puts them in your consciousness, and they will unfold in your understanding as you develop as a magician.

What needs saying is this. There are three root powers within a human that are the powers of magic: *observation, resonance, and connectedness*. On the surface these can seem simple things, psychological things, things we already know. But that would be missing the true power behind those three words.

When you *observe* you trigger change.

When you *resonate* at the same frequency as something else, you learn and acquire the skills inherent in whatever you are resonating with.

When you are *connected*, you can change/rebuild/destroy vast patterns with your own small actions.

All magic springs from these three dynamics. But the understanding of these dynamics, in a true sense, comes from direct experience. Remember these three words whenever you do any magic, and you will spot one of these dynamics in action.

10. *Task:* Vision of the Pivot of the Mountains

Stage I

As with all powerful and long visions, if you know you are not going to remember the basic sequence, then record it in your own voice, and follow the recording. Just make sure that in the recording you speak slowly and leave appropriate silences so that you can commune with beings when necessary.

As you prepare to do the ritual to prepare the space for the vision (Anchor Ritual), instead of putting your cloth on the floor drape it round your shoulders. Put out the ritual tools in their place and then stand facing the central altar, facing south. Be aware that in all four directions and below you is the continent that you stand upon. Be aware of it as a conscious being that you live and work upon, and as you keep that awareness remember the drops of blood you have placed on the land in the past, the songs/poems you have sung to the river, and all the land beings you have connected to in various ways.

Hold out your arms and declare, using your voice, that you are a child of that land.

Close your eyes. Be aware that each direction stretches out across that land until it reaches the sea. However large the continent is where you are, allow your mind to reach in all four directions, one at a time, starting in the east. Be aware of how far that land stretches. Roll your consciousness out in the direction until it reaches the sea, pause briefly in that place, and then slowly bring your consciousness back over the land, back to your work-space and then body. The way to do this is through stillness, then expanding your mind/imagination beyond your body in a direction and visualising key elements that are between you and the sea (cities, mountain ranges, vast plains, etc.). As you expand your imagination outwards you also keep a sharp awareness of your body and the room you are working in. As you pull your consciousness back, do it slowly, backtracking the same way you rolled out.

When you have finished kneel down and place your forehead on the floor. Feel your head and your mind touching the land beneath the building where you are. Acknowledge the land as your parent, as the thing that upholds you, as the land that contains every being, element, and society that makes you who you are. Thank the land in your mind for allowing you to live upon it, and imagine that your mind and the land blend thresholds, so that your mind can flow into the land and the land can flow into your mind.

The land becomes your body and your body is the land: what you do to your body is mirrored in the land, and what happens to the land is processed through your body.

Stand in that understanding for a while and just be with it.

When you are ready stand up and begin the Anchor ritual. Keep the vast land being in your mind as you work. Everything that you acknowledge in the directions stands upon the continent; you are all its children, so keep that in the front of your thoughts as you work. Once you have finished the ritual sit down. Choose for yourself where you should sit. Use your energies to feel each direction in turn and decide where you need to be. Now it is time to do stage two of this work, the vision of going to the pivot of the mountains.

Stage II

In vision see an opening in the floor before you. Remember your acknowledgement of the land and ask the land for safe passage into it. Place your hand on the floor and declare that you will treat the land with honour, both in this vision and in your life *and live up to that… no littering, dumping, etc.*

As you look at the opening you see it is a vast, deep, black hole that seems to vanish into the depths of the earth. You are intending to go to the root place from which the breath of the mountains flows. State that intention in your mind, stand up in vision, and look down the black hole. You have to trust the vast land being to take you where you need to go without suffering any harm. Take a step forward and allow yourself to fall down the hole. Stay still in your mind as you fall through the earth with the intention of going to the pivotal place from where the breath of the mountains flows. You will fall down and down in the darkness, you will see nothing in the darkness, no reference point, nothing; just blackness as you fall and fall. You will seem to fall for quite some time until you land on a pile of sand.

Get up. You will find yourself in a small, shallow cave. Before you is a short tunnel with a faint light glowing at the end of it. Follow that light until it brings you into a vast cavern that is circular with four main tunnels, one in each direction, leading off from the centre. In the centre of the circular cavern is a large white crystalline stone that emits a light that shines around the cavern. It also seems to emit sound and vibration. This is the source of the breath of the mountains, and the heart of the vast land beings that we know as mountains.

As you move closer to the stone its sound becomes more like a pressure that you can almost hear but that you can definitely feel. Stand before the stone, kneel down, and place your forehead to the stone. You can feel it pulsing, contracting, as though it was breathing, and with each contraction you can hear a very low vibration like a rumble. Be still. Allow your mind to pulse with the stone. This stone is the beating heart at the root of all mountains. It is the beating heart of the vast consciousness of the mountains, of the land being that your consciousness is currently within. This is one of the elements that you came from, that all of your bloodline and species came from. Though your distant ancestors were birthed from the sea, this stone was the womb that emitted the first spark of life, the first vibration, which then flowed into the ocean before being born. Place your hands on the stone and let your body tune itself to the rhythm of the stone's pulse. Your heart and the heart of the mountains beat together, and for a moment you can feel the body, power, and consciousness of the vast mountain ranges around the world. You can feel the timelessness, the power, and the stillness of these beings. And the beings can feel you: your tiny consciousness encased in a small body, too small for them to register, but your consciousness can expand beyond your body.

Allow your mind to flow outwards. Feel yourself filling the cavern. You have no shape, no body; you are pure consciousness and energy. Feel yourself merge lightly with the rock before you and with the rock walls all around you. The consciousness of the rock feels you, and the vibration emitting from the crystal rock changes and shifts as it becomes fully aware of you. When you feel that shift, slowly bring your consciousness back to your visionary body but retain that stillness and feeling of expansion. Now get up. Wander around the cave and look at the walls. You will notice tiny holes in the walls that seem to be minute tunnels reaching up to the surface world.

Put your hand up to one. You will feel a slight wind on the back of your hand: placing your hand there has interrupted a faint flow of 'air' that is emitting out of the central stone and travelling up these thin tunnels to the surface. Wander around the cave and look at these holes/tunnels in the rock. One will draw you in particular. Put your finger in one of the holes and be still. After a moment you will feel the length of this tunnel, but using your inner senses you will also feel that this reaches up to a mountain or mountain range. An image will flash into your mind of the mountain on the other side of this tunnel where it hits the surface world.

You may recognise the mountain or you may not. As you hold your finger there, in your mind, say hello to the mountain. Then remove your finger so that the breath of the rock can continue its journey unhindered to the surface.

Step back from the wall and wander round the cave again. This time cast your mind to the four tunnels leading off in the four directions. Now is not the time for you to explore these tunnels, but in the future you will. These lead to various beings and consciousnesses who are in long-term service to the land and the mountains. As you edge nearer to one of the tunnels, you will notice that its entrance is covered with a fine spider's web with a spider guarding the centre. Do not disturb her as she will attack: she is guarding the contacts and beings who are deep in the tunnels, constantly working to keep the breath of the central stone healthy and strong. Go back to the central stone and once more place your hands on it. Every time you touch a stone in the future, either in vision or in physical life, remember this central stone. Every time you place your foot upon the stone which is your shield in your magical work, remember that it is connected to the stone floor before the Great Goddess in the Underworld, which in turn is connected to this stone at the centre of all things.

Your focus of thought will renew the connection between them and will strengthen your communication and connectedness with this place. Just stay in silence and stillness with the central stone for a while, and when you are ready, step back. Stand and look at the stone for a while. Watch it gently pulse and notice colours that reflect within the stone, veins of different types of rock and metals that you had not noticed before, as they create a weave pattern over the stone.

Before you leave there is something you can give to the stone. The stone constantly breathes and contracts to keep a flow of energy, vibration, and wind flowing into the mountains. You can do the same for the stone.

Breathe in and out and let your breath flow over the stone: give back a little of the air that it constantly gives out. As you do this, think of the times you have sung for the land, and you will realise that although you were singing to the small land beings and land features, you were also, in a small way, giving back the breath, vibration, and sound to this rock at the centre of all things. This is the rock that birthed mountains, ranges, outcrops, and tiny stones. Its breathing keeps the consciousness of all rock alive and healthy. When you sing to the land you are also singing to this stone, and this stone will always respond: you have breathed together, and you are now connected.

A strong light starts to emit from the stone. It shoots upwards, reaching through a hole in the ceiling you had not noticed. You lean forward to look and you see that the light shoots far up through the rock and will emerge in the surface world: the light of the land. You are drawn to the light, which is purer and brighter than any light you can remember seeing. As you step closer you find yourself stepping into the light. The stone allows you to pass into it and then flow with its light upwards.

The light is like a beam of power that fills you with energy and pulls you upwards, through the ceiling of the cave, through the rock, up and up, until you emerge through the floor of your work space. The light fills your work space and continues to rise through your ceiling and out to the stars.

This is the light of the earth, the true energy and essence of the land, which is always in constant union with the stars. Sit a while and bathe in this light. Slowly its brightness will subside. When you are ready open your eyes and sit quietly for a while. Remember what you saw, and remember what happened. Go and place your hands on your stone shield. Remember the stone at the centre of the deep cave, remember its breathing, its vibration, and how it is connected to this stone. Lift your hands from your stone and place your fingertips very lightly on it so that you are still in contact but hardly touching. Remember the stone in the centre of the cave, how it breathed and vibrated. Feel through your fingertips into the stone, feel it moving, shifting: a feeling that translates more in your mind than in your sense of touch. Spend a little time in communion with the stone.

When you are ready, write your experience down in your journal before you put out the lights and close the gates. Copy the notes from your journal into your computer log when you have time. Whenever you pick up a stone or visit a hill or mountain, remember that deep cave and the white crystalline stone, and spend a few moments in meditation, recovering the feeling of being in that place. It will connect you more deeply with the mountains, hills, and stones around you.

11. *Task:* Researching the Ogdoad

Look up the Egyptian Ogdoad and read about them. Read the creation myth that involves them. Then read the creation myth at the beginning of Genesis in the Old Testament. Keep in mind that the Egyptian writings predate Genesis by a long way.

12. *Task:* Faeries research

If you can, get a copy of the book *The Secret Commonwealth of Elves Fauns and Faeries* by the Rev Robert Kirk. Currently as I write, there are cheap and free PDFs all over the internet if you do not want to buy a paperback. Don't try and read it from cover to cover; rather let your intuition guide you through the pages. If the book is no longer available in any form, do not worry about it. Not reading or looking at it will not affect your studies. However if you can browse through it, it would be interesting for you. This book contains the experiences, observations, and tales of the local folk written down by a seventeenth century Scottish Minister and scholar who worked among them. His book outlines the villagers' experiences of faery beings. It is the best book to read for information on these smaller land beings.

13. *Task:* Research on connecting with faeries

Read *Magic of the North Gate,* chapter five: Faeries and Shrines. This will give you some basic background as to how to connect with the smaller land beings around you in a semistructured way, should you wish to. It is available for you in the appendix of this book.

14. *Optional task:* Researching the bright light

Should you wish to research the bright light that emits from the stone in the deep cave, it is connected to female deities/powers in various cultures. In Britain it was/is Brigh, or Brigit, the Bright One, a goddess who was/is the light of the land. She was eventually dumbed down into Bridget the midwife. But if you dig deeply, you will find much more about her connection with the mountain/cave, and bright light (the word 'bright' and 'Britain' comes from her name). She is also connected with weaponry, being the forger of swords; with white springs; and with thresholds. Her undivided form is the Cailleach, a goddess of life and death, who is the British version of Cybele. She is Brigh in summer and the old hag in winter.

Lesson 6

Spirits of the Body

The spirits that reside within the organs of the body are largely ignored by Western magicians unless they have an interest in acupuncture or Daoism. And yet they are a crucial aspect of our magical power, foundation, and stability: without a good working system in the body/spirit the magician is virtually powerless.

When we are young and full of vital force we tend to ignore our body and inflict all sorts of abuses upon it. Then once we hit middle age and things start to go wrong, we end up paying a bit more attention. But if you can attend, commune, and listen to the spirits of your organs before they get to a state of collapse, you will have an army of workers to tend your home fires while you work. Besides the obvious benefit of looking after your body, there are deeper and more mystical aspects to communing with your body's spirits, something we will look at later in the lesson. But let's start at the beginning.

1. Spirits of the organs

I came across the spirits of the organs through necessity: my body was struggling and I decided to give my various organs a bit of a pep talk in vision. To my shock they talked back. This led me to discover that I had not invented the wheel, but that the Far Eastern cultural systems, Daoism, for example, were well aware of this phenomenon and had been for a very long time. I am always the last to the table!

So I started to read about the Five Spirits of the organs which is a system within Chinese medicine. I realised that some of what I read correlated with what I had experienced, and some of it did not. In this lesson we will only cover what I have found and worked with for myself. From there, you can branch out and study further if you wish. I will say that making this discovery, I guess it is akin to suddenly realising you have a hand... duh, has not only altered how I tend to my body, but it has also vastly altered how I do magic.

The basic outline is this: the organs of the body have their own consciousness and personality. Think of the body as a solar system, not a planet: the organs, the vital force, and the body structure all work together to uphold a physical being who is essentially made up of lots of smaller beings. By consciously working with the beings/spirits of your organs you engage with the various members of your choir to ensure that everyone is singing the right note at the right time. This is vital in powerful magic: if your body is in any kind of serious disharmony the magic will widen the cracks and push the imbalance further. If the magician has had to undertake a magical project that draws heavily on the strength and reserve of their body, which most powerful magic does, then preparing the organ spirits for such hard work and tending to their needs afterwards, ensures that their body survives any knocks well and recovers quickly.

Taking this a step further, an experienced magician can work with an organ spirit as a co-worker in magic, drawing upon the knowledge of the spirit, its wisdom, and its range of action in order to achieve something. So let's have a look at the *who, why* and *how* of work with the organ spirits. Bear in mind I am relaying what I have personally worked with, not the already-formed systems in some Eastern cultures. Be aware that at the time of writing this, I have gaps in my understanding that you may be able to find or fill from further study and your own direct experience. I am still constantly engaging with this work and will do indefinitely as it continues to grow as I work with it.

2. Who are the organ spirits?

From what I have found working in vision, the organ spirits seem to be a part of us and yet also independent of us: if the organ is transplanted into someone else, the unique character of the organ's spirit stays with the organ, not with our eternal spirits. To try and make working sense of this I treat each organ spirit as a unique being in its own right, a being who works with me in order for me to function as a living, breathing being. They work for me, and in turn I care for them.

If you work within Chinese medicine, you may take a different and more complex approach; but like everything else in magic I work from the standpoint of direct experience and then study from there, as opposed to the other way around. This ensures that you gain real, direct experience without taking on board dogmas that other people have built up. If you look at texts regarding the spirits of the organs you will see that attributes, numbers, planetary alignments, and various other connections have been made over a large span of time in relation to the spirit organs. Some of these will be correct, and some will be the inspired or dogmatic intellectual developments that people have added over the years. This is a perennial issue in magic: to truly find powerful ways of working we must pay attention to the findings of others, *but not follow them in an unthinking way.* Their discoveries and ideas are stepping stones that we as individual magicians add to generation by generation. Later generations may find far more powerful and successful ways of doing this work that we could not even contemplate.

The organs I have worked with in vision and had a great deal of success with are the **heart, lungs, liver, kidneys, colon, brain,** (I didn't find a spirit in the brain, but did find the inner landscape) **endocrine glands**, and **stomach**. Some of these are worked with in Chinese medicine and some are not. Some were worked with in ancient Egypt and some were not.

Let's have a look at some of these organ spirits, how they are worked with, and why.

3. Heart

The one thing I do seem to have found that agrees with both the Chinese system and the Egyptian system is the importance of the heart spirit. The heart spirit often appears in vision as a king who sits in an inner sanctum and is surrounded by channels of fluids (blood flow). I found that working in vision with the heart spirit by ensuring he had enough light, that his channels were unblocked, that he was clean, bright, and responsive, had a massive effect on my health and magic. He appeared to be like a ruler of the organs and if he is not happy, nothing else is happy. He ensures that you have the vital force available for your work and that all the nutrients, information, and strength that you need is accessible to you. If the king is tired, dusty, clogged up, or presents in vision as sleeping or wounded, then he needs your immediate attention.

> Note 2025: I have progressed from envisioning a 'king' type being, to passing in to the chambers and talking to the chambers/heart directly. This has given me access to a layer of consciousness in the heart that I had not found before. But going through the stage of giving the spirit an image (king) enabled me to build enough relationship that has in turn given me deeper access to the inner consciousness of the organ. And it has been the same for the other organs. So bear that in mind in your own work – going through the stages are probably important.

The heart spirit is also a voice that speaks on your behalf in the inner worlds, retelling your life without hesitation or avoidance; he is your recorder who tells the Keeper of the Scales of your deeds throughout your life. The voice of the heart spirit also states who you are to other beings in the inner world; one of the things you will eventually realise as a magician, is that who you are, which is to say, *what do you do, how do you behave* is how you are identified to other spirits and deities. If you are a just and honest person, this is your identity before the gods; nothing is more important in the inner worlds than your truth and actions. The ancient Egyptians knew this. As their magical culture began to degrade they developed spells to silence the heart spirit or to force it to lie on their behalf when they stood on the threshold of Judgement. It is much better to listen to the wise counsel of the heart spirit and learn/mature in life rather than try to lie your way through death.

We in the West have retained some of that knowledge in our folklore and in the concept of 'listening to your heart': rather than being driven by emotions, learning to listen to the quiet wisdom of the heart when it speaks is a valuable guide to any magician. In the practical work we will go in vision to talk to the heart spirit, which will in turn give you techniques that you can use to explore, meet, and introduce yourself properly to the other quiet members of your team. But for now, let us look at some of the other organ spirits. Instead of going through all of them, I will pick some who are not usually connected with in the Chinese or Egyptian systems; the rest you can figure out for yourself.

4. Intestines

The intestines are interesting. We think of them simply as processing our food and extracting nutrients. But the digestive system in general, and the intestines specifically, do much more than this: they affect our mood and our immune system. The complexity of the enteric nervous system is something that scientists are only now really starting to look at and unravel. From a magical perspective the intestines appear as something akin to a council of elders who advise the rest of the body and spirit in order to maintain balance and health. When I first came across this 'council' while exploring my body in vision I found it easy to communicate with them, and the advice I was given led me to change a lot about how I maintained my body. And the advice was spot on. It gave the term 'gut feeling' a whole new meaning. It also affected how I did magic. I listened more and more to this group of advisors as I delved into deep exploratory magic. Not only did their advice help in protecting my body, but I also found their group voice joining in with my conversations with inner world beings. It was an interesting experience and really began to change how I interacted with other beings.

5. Brain

The brain is another organ that is not paid attention to by the ancients or the Chinese in terms of spirit. I too have never found an overarching spirit in the brain, but I did find a door into my own inner landscape *via* the brain. I found this very early on in my magical experiments, and spent a few years exploring this inner landscape of the body, learning what to do and what not to do by observing the results triggered by the visionary work.

Essentially I went in vision into my brain with the intention of cleaning it. The cleaning of the inner organs in vision is something I learned in my early days of magic, and has very definite physical results. I would go into my brain in vision armed with a vacuum cleaner and would clean off any build-up I found on its 'wires,' the inside surface of the skull, and the chambers within the brain. One day I came across a door deep in the centre of the brain, and like the curious cat I am I went through the door and found myself in a natural landscape.

Over time I learned not to interfere with the landscape but simply to be there, observe, and acknowledge. There was a deep mystery in this inner landscape. I could feel it, but I was as yet too young, and had not enough experience of magic, to understand fully what I was looking at. I could not understand why it was a natural landscape composed of trees, grass, hills, river, sky, and without a human or a spirit in sight. We will look a bit deeper into this phenomenon soon, but first we need to look at the reasons why you would work with your organs in vision, and how important it is to give these beings the same level of attention that we give to beings in the inner worlds.

6. Why we work with the organ spirits

Besides the obvious health benefits of tending to every aspect of our bodies, there are deeper resonances involving these organ spirits that are of great importance to the magician. The organ spirits do not just work to keep our bodies functioning well; they are also part of our wider consciousness and play an important role in how we communicate with other beings in the inner world and how we interact with the land.

When we work in vision we do not 'leave' our bodies; it is more a matter of stretching and expanding beyond our bodies. When we work in vision we perceive this action as stepping out of ourselves. This visionary technique informs our conscious mind that we are going somewhere, which we are. But we never actually leave our bodies, we don't have to. We have the ability to be in many places at once, to expand beyond our physical boundaries and allow our conscious mind and deeper spirit to flow anywhere. The visionary act of seeing yourself leaving your body is a *training method*. It is a very necessary step that is used for a prolonged period of time, often years, as it helps the physical body, and the organ spirits, to adjust to what is happening. Spreading out too far, too fast, can have a very damaging effect on the physical body. So the magician works in simple steps: these steps train the mind in travelling, and also give the body's spirits and substance warning of what is happening.

Eventually the adept casts their focused mind in a direction and the spirit follows immediately, without the need for visionary steps. In the last lesson you began to take steps towards this expansion of the consciousness, while also working with the visionary sense of 'going somewhere.' Eventually as an adept, the visionary technique will be used far less in your work and the expansive technique used far more. To get to that point takes years of work that cannot be bypassed safely. When the magician takes the visionary action of stepping out of their body, a series of processes kick into action that serve to protect the integrity of their body and to prepare the spirits within the body for the experience. The organ spirits can act a bit like your filing manager, your anchors, and also the manager of your vital force/energy while you work.

When you go in vision into the inner worlds and you meet a powerful being, the first thing the being needs to know is if you are generally balanced. If you are seriously unbalanced you may be a danger to the inner being, so the very first thing that happens upon inner contact is the being casts its mind to your organ spirits. Your heart speaks of your deeds, of who you are, and the spirits of the liver and kidneys speak to the integrity of the physical and inner body and its ability to cope with contact. It is a bit like sitting down in front of a healer who before speaking to you looks at the state of your skin, your eyes, your demeanour, and then makes a first assessment of the state of your health from their observations.

This is how many inner beings work, and it is not your body they look at, it is your organ spirits. If the being can see from your organ spirits that you are ill, about to get ill, or are low in energy or seriously unbalanced, they will immediately break the contact. This is experienced by the magician as being booted out of vision. It is not that you have failed or are being rejected, it is that the contact has seen that communication and work in vision would put you at risk.

Until now, when you have worked in vision you have been unaware of these spirits who are part of the hive which is you. But as you slowly learn to work with them, tend them, and be aware of them, they will communicate to you more as you work and warn you of coming illness. For example when you catch a cold or the flu, it can take a few days from infection to actual illness. During that incubation period doing any deep magical work will weaken you and can make the actual active infection far worse and longer-lasting than it could have been. But if you are used to working with your organ spirits and have built up a relationship with them, the communion between you creates channels through which they can issue you a warning sign. We talk to them as separate beings, and this method creates a pathway for clear communication to flow back and forth.

Each person is different, and you and your organ spirits will find a way to signal/communicate back and forth that works for you both. For example my heart spirit talks to me in dreams, through tarot, and through simply making me aware of him: I will be working and suddenly he will come into my mind. When I focus on him he can then communicate what he needs or wants to say.

My kidney spirits (two very different ones) will 'poke' me with a sudden brief sharp pain. When this first started to happen I thought something was going wrong with my kidneys. But they were fine; it was the spirits trying to get my attention. Once they had done that I learned other ways of allowing them to get my attention without stabbing me! But these experiences are more or less unique to the individual: you will slowly develop your own pathways of communication with these spirits. Just remember that these spirits are housed in organs and not bodies. They do not have eyes and ears, so regular communication with their human can be tricky: you need to find the vocabulary of the organ spirit that also works for you. It can be anything. It could be a shift in your awareness during meditation – by being still and silent the faint voice can be heard.

Your attention will be drawn to an organ if it is trying to communicate with you. It can manifest through dreams, through bodily reactions such as pain, soreness, rashes, or simply by suddenly becoming aware of a part of your body. The better your lines of communication become, the less dramatic the spirits have to be to get your attention. Sometimes they will get your attention because their organ is sick or weak or under threat; sometimes they are telling you that your vital force is low and needs attending to; or they can warn you of magical attacks that directly threaten your organs. They can also alert you to inner contacts/beings who are trying to get your attention: the organ spirit communes with the being, then tries to tell you that you are missing something. This translates into a feeling that you *really are missing something,* and this feeling is generated by an organ spirit to get your attention.

As you become more experienced as a magician, and after you have worked/communed with these body spirits for a while, you will find that they also make very good advisors. They will reflect to you their opinion about an issue from their own standpoint as to how it would directly affect them. For example if an adept was to undertake a major magical project, they would first consult with key organ spirits to see how they would be directly affected, and whether or not they would be able to cope with the impact of the work.

Sometimes this serves to warn the organs of heavy work ahead so that they can gear up for it and be ready. Sometimes the spirits will inform the magician that their organ does not have the strength to sustain such work without damage; or they will advise the magician that they can do the work but that certain organs will need specific support through food, herbs, or other means. The methods of communication for me are; I will envisage something and focus it at the organ. Then as I go about my day I will become very aware of that organ, and it will be accompanied by a feeling of either everything is ok, or no, things are not ok. I used to then use divination to then look further at the organ, but these days I don't need to as the message gets through clearly enough. It is about learning to work as a team and realising that you are not alone in your body. Nor are you an individual unit upon the land; which takes me to the next part of this lesson.

7. Our bodies and the land

The work with your individual organs is something that you can begin to work with and experiment with straight away. There is also a deeper, more profound aspect of you, your body, and the spirits that reside within you; an aspect of mystical magic that takes a life time to unfold, and this is that you and the land around you are truly one and the same being.

This is not something you can switch on and start working with easily, but now is the stage where you simply become aware of it through observation. A lot of your work so far has been edging you to this awareness slowly, and now is the stage where you will really start to look. It will take decades of work to truly just begin to understand it at a deep level: this profound aspect of yourself cannot be grasped by intellect or meditation; rather it comes very slowly in increments that are the results of a series of experiences over time. The first stage of this is to be aware of it. Then the observations unfold over time until you are in no doubt as to the reality of this dynamic. From there, the adept works within the dynamic to affect themselves and everything around them, within them, and above them to bring and maintain balance as a holism.

All different cultural variants of mystical thought express this deep truth, and we can read them and nod wisely, yet we still don't really get it until it is a real body experience. Everything in magic works this way: direct experience brings it home to us in ways that leave no doubt; all we need to do from these experiences is to learn quietly, without needing to become evangelistic about it, which is a trap.

Your path, your learning, your experience, your development are all about you as a living and eternal being, and your experience is going to be different from another person's. Each person is a universe, and they must come to this understanding alone. You can leave pointers, you can guide when asked, you can teach; but in truth, a person walks to this threshold alone and on their own terms.

So let's get back to this connection between the land, you, and your body spirits. For those living in a fast-paced city, spotting the slow connection that develops between land and magician is a tough one, but don't forget that the weather is also part of the land. As you progress in magic and work more and more with land and spirits you will gradually come to notice that your body is affected by the weather in subtle ways. How this manifests is individual to the magician, as we are all very different; but slowly, over the years, you will start to see the connections in no uncertain terms.

This is a two way street, and one that defies everything we know about how the world works. The adept begins to realise that whatever is going on in their body also affects the land and weather around them. This is a dynamic you have already looked at in simple terms: you and the land become one, like the sacred king. If you uphold your inner and outer integrity you also uphold the land. As magical individuals each of us affects everything around us in deep and subtle ways. The adept is the land, and the land is the adept. This is not something you just step into in your early years. But over decades you spot it more and more. I have no logical understanding of this dynamic, only that it 'is.' Intellectually I can look back over history, ancient mysticism, and ancient cultures and see it right there in the writings; but to experience it is something very different, and it confounds logic. But once a magician settles somewhere, usually by middle age, if they are working deeply, they will begin to notice that what they do affects the nature around them and vice versa. This begins with you talking to the land and the land talking back. From there, the process slowly unfolds, and for me it is still unfolding and will continue to do so until I 'fall off my perch', i.e. die.

Remember the mention of inner landscapes in the body? When you go into your body in vision and go into the brain, deep within it is a threshold that when crossed takes you into the inner landscape of the person. But the inner landscape of a human is not an inner person; it is a natural landscape. For years I could not understand why it was the land and not a human inner shape, but I just continued to work with how it presented. I saw that the health of the person could be ascertained by the health of their inner land. It is only very recently that the penny dropped for me: the inner landscape reflects that deep connection between human and land. We are of each other, and this deep inner landscape is the inner pattern for that dynamic. *The energetic and inner health of the soul is expressed as the health of the land in the landscape.*

And that also gives you an idea of how these deeper magical dynamics surface for us. Something presents to you in vision and you have two choices: work with it even though you don't fully understand it, or reject it because it does not make sense.

Modern education has taught us to reject that which does not make sense, but our well of knowledge to draw upon is far too limited for us to instantly recognise and make sense of everything that presents. So the way forward in such a situation is to work tentatively with what presents, and your learning will unfold as is right and balanced for you.

When I come across something like this I have realised that an early step is to check via tarot that it is indeed safe for me to explore. In the past, in my thirties, I would just dive into the unknown and explore. I learned through bitter experience that to do so not only expands your experience and knowledge but can also put you in danger. Eventually I learned, when faced with something unknown, to read up on it to see if it would put me in mortal danger, or severely injure me or anything else. If there was no indication of serious backlash, then I would explore, and take a few knocks along the way. So it is with the unfolding relationship with the land and your body. It can be approached very naturally and simply in the early stages.

Going out into the wind and taking a deep breath while keeping awareness of the spirit of the lungs, the air being Divine Breath, and you being the threshold where the two meet. The wind comes to know you, the spirit of the lungs speaks for you, and the three of you breathe together. Over time, as you get older, that relationship deepens so that you too become the vessel of the wind, and breathing out with intent summons the winds. And in return the wind blows, your breath breathes the wind, and your spirit converts the wind into words: you speak with the wind flowing through you.

When you look up to the sun, be aware of the king of your heart in your centre. The sun and your heart are the same thing: all your organs are mirrored in nature from a magical perspective, and building that relationship between nature and your body strengthens you both. In the practical work there is a visionary exercise that will help get this process started for you.

8. THE POWER NETWORKS

Everything in creation has power networks that interlink: the vital force of the universe. If you try to think of this in such expansive terms it will elude your true understanding; but if you bring your thought and observation down to ground level it is easier to have a direct experience of this, and like all magic we learn from direct experience, not through pondering, philosophising, or hypothesising. Once you have a direct experience of something it becomes embedded deep within you, and it changes you.

We experience power networks in lots of different ways: through our own nervous system, the vital force in our bodies; through moon, sun, and starlight; through electricity; through the pulse and power that flows from the sun to us (coronal mass ejections, solar flares, etc.). Some people have learned to fear such power that we perceive as outside of ourselves, like electricity, for example. And yet they are all a part of us and we adjust around them. We can work with them, adjust to their ebbs and flows, and help our bodies learn to flow with them rather than against them.

The first step of this is to be aware of the power flows within our own body: what the Chinese call *Chi* or *Qi*. This vital force is manifest in everything in creation, and is the root power that enables everything to exist. As magicians, we become aware of this in our own bodies, then in the land, weather, and every other thing that exists. This harmonic understanding allows us to be truly aware of the power and force in everything, and to become consciously joined with this vital force. This is one of the major roots in magic, and where the power of magic flows from. One technique is to expand beyond oneself and join with the vital force that runs through everything. From there the magician can feel disturbance in their own vital force, or disturbance in the vital force of what is around them.

In the previous lesson you expanded yourself in vision to join with the deep cave at the root of the mountains. This technique of achieving stillness and then expanding out to join with everything switches your consciousness on to the understanding that we are not all separate units; rather we are expansions and contractions of the same thing. With this learning, when the body's vital force is slightly disturbed, we can expand outwards to the vital forces of the land, the sun, and the weather. By harmonising with these forces, our own inner force remembers how it should be, and begins the rebalancing process.

If our vital force becomes badly disturbed or run down we become sick, and often the land around us will seem to become disturbed. Then we seek the help of a healer, who can remind our vital force what it needs to do, repair some of the damage, and put us back on our feet. This is why so many magicians work with homeopathy, cranial osteopathy, acupuncture, etc. All these healing modalities reach to the vital force and remind our systems how to heal themselves.

As adepts we often specialise in a particular aspect of magic. Those who focus on healing and working with the land work through a process of learning these subtle healing modalities. At first we work on humans and animals, but eventually we come to realise that these same healing modalities can be applied to the land, the trees, the rivers, etc. You have already begun the learning process for that with your work with charged water and pouring it into the river. As the skills of the adept grow, so they learn to use pressure, minute movement of their hands, transfers of energy, and subtle alchemy (like homeopathy) to heal the land around them. Never fall into the trap of wanting to heal the planet: this is too big a slice of pie for one person to eat. Tend to what is immediately in front of you; that in turn ripples out slowly over time to affect a much wider area.

I have been tending where I live now for the last five years, and the response in nature is wonderful: the land where I live, the little valley, along with all the creatures, are blossoming wonderfully. When I travel I can tell where someone is doing something similar, whether in the countryside or a city. When a patch of land is cared for, regardless of what is on top of it, it blossoms energetically. When the land is ignored, you can also feel it immediately. This reflects in the people and in your own body. We all have illnesses, injuries, and issues: these are normal parts of life. It is how the body deals with those issues that makes the difference. The idea that one can be super-healthy into old age without any trials does not apply to most of us: when this happens it is usually down to good genes. A magician who magically tends the land and their own body will still get illnesses, but their body will adjust, learn, survive, and adapt despite them; just as the land around them may be overcrowded, full of concrete cities, pollution, and god knows what else, but will adapt if it is worked with and tended.

So next time you stand in your work space and begin ritual work, be aware that everything including buildings, people, cities, etc. as it is part of you, and you a part of them, for as long as you live in that area. Be aware of your expansion out in all directions, and be aware that all those directions are mirrored within you, within your vital force, your organs, your spirit, and your flesh. Truly you are the universe and the universe is you. Your intent magically is to serve everything around you, because by so doing you serve the universe and yourself. But if you reverse that and serve only yourself then you shut down that universal connection: it is a paradox.

To truly understand yourself you must expand beyond yourself and flow through everything. Once you have expanded and become part of everything, then the contraction begins, where everything becomes part of you. Everything in the universe expands and contracts, and you are a part of that.

9. *Task:* Meeting the heart spirit

This visionary work needs no ritual preparation, as you are only going into your own body and staying within your own boundary. However, do this work in the room where you normally do magic, and light a candle in the centre of the room or on the central altar. This simple act will switch the room on at a low level and help tune the energy around you.

As with all visions, stay sitting up; do not lie down. Meditate for a few minutes to still yourself.

Once you are still, see yourself in vision stepping out of your body. Turn and look at your body. Pass back into it, and focus on passing into your body at navel level. As your mind flows back into your body, keep the focus that you are investigating and looking, and that your spirit has no shape and is not hindered by size. From the navel flow upwards with the intention of going into your heart. As you move upwards with that intention, see and feel yourself pass into a circular chamber. In this chamber is a circle of columns, and in the centre is a pedestal with a king sitting on it. Around the king, in the floor and inside the columns, are two carved channels for fluid, one on each side. They go round him and join, side by side, in front of him, then vanish out of sight. As you look up you will see skylights above him.

First look at the king. Is he sleepy? Is he dusty? Or does he look bright, full of colour, and acknowledge you when you enter the chamber? (This is how he should look for a healthy heart). Now look at the channels of fluid flowing round him. The fluid in the channels should flow freely and give off vibrant energy. Look up: is light coming through the skylights and falling on him, or are the skylights dirty? Are there plants, flowers, or other signs of nature round him? Once you have assessed what state the king is in, it is time to get to work. The first step is to clear any clogged channels. Scoop up anything blocking the flow of fluids. Take a carrier bag or trash bag from your pocket and place any trash/clog in it.

Go around the chamber. Check the floors, channels, and walls for any build-up of dirt or plaque (it will look like a calcium build-up that you can pick up or scrape off). Make sure the fluid flows freely and brightly. Now start on the king. If he is dusty or covered in crap, reach down to the floor with the intention of reaching for a vacuum cleaner. Pull up a vacuum cleaner with a long arm, and start to vacuum him clean.

Once that is done put the vacuum back, shake the king's clothing to get the air moving around it, then scoop some of the fluid from the channels into your hands and wash his face with it. He cannot move from his throne to wash himself: you must do it for him. As he wakes up, tell him thank you for working so hard, that you really appreciate the life he brings you, and help to tidy him up. Ask him if he needs anything and pay close attention to what he asks for.

Now turn your attention to the skylights above. Stretch up and clean them. See whatever you need to clean them appear in your hands, and clear them until sunlight beams through and falls on the king. Your next job is to ensure that the vital power of nature flows around him. To do this see blossoming trees, flowers, and grasses spring up outside the circle of columns, so that he is surrounded by beautiful nature but inside the circles of columns it is just him and the fluids. When you have finished step back and look at him. He should have sunlight on him, fluids flowing around him, nature around the edges of his shrine, and he should be bright and alert.

Once more thank him: he works very hard for you, and is also the recorder of your deeds in the inner worlds. Ask him again if he needs anything, usually things like a drink of water, which is a prompt for you to drink more water, or for more sunlight, which is a prompt for you to get outside in the sunshine more; or he may ask you to visit him again. When you have finished bow to him, turn round, and leave the chamber by passing through its walls, finding yourself back among your organs. Step forward again with the intention of stepping out of your body and back into your work space. Once you are there, dig a hole in the floor (see it as earth), and place the trash bags in the earth and cover them over so that they will compost.

Turn round and look at your body. Look carefully. Do any areas look dull or strange? If so, take note so that you can attend to them in your next session. Now flow back into your body, feel yourself settle in, and be still. When you are ready, open your eyes.

10. About the previous exercise

Keep an awareness of the king in your heart. As you go about your daily life, every so often, cast your attention to him, to let him know you are thinking of him. Keeping this awareness helps you build up a relationship with him so that if there are problems you will recognise his voice in your body as he tries to get your attention. The actions of cleaning, vacuuming, letting in light, etc., trigger your body's cleaning mechanism into action. Working on the king directly starts the process of building a relationship with that spirit. If you learn to listen, when the heart/body needs more sunlight or more fluids it will tell you.

The heart spirit also acts a bit like the carrier of your resume as you go deeper into the inner worlds. When you are confronted by powerful beings and they want to know who you are and what you are about, it is the spirit of your heart who answers: the truth of your being, your actions, and your intentions are spoken by your heart on your behalf. You will usually not be aware of this while you work in vision, but when a being appears to look closely at you, what they are doing is listening to the vibration and energy that flows from your heart spirit. It is not something you can control or even *should* control: it is the truthful part of you that speaks.

When you are going through a heavy time or are overly stressed or overworked, don't forget the king who is upholding your energies and literally your lifeblood. Go and talk to him, see if he needs anything, and listen closely for what he needs or tells you.

11. *Task:* Going into the inner landscape of the body

The key reason to go into the inner landscape of a body is to observe and gain information about the health of that person and of the land. When in my early thirties I first discovered the inner landscape in a person I became very evangelist about working in a person's landscape to heal them. This will indeed work, but it also obviates their own path through fate.

As an adept there may come a time when you feel it is important enough to take the risk and work on someone's inner landscape, but this should be the very last resort and only done in extreme circumstances. As an apprentice and initiate it is more important to observe the body's inner landscape over time, as you will learn a great deal about it this way. You will also then be armed with enough experience to make the appropriate decision on action, later on. Actually working on an inner landscape takes layers of skill and knowledge. It is a bit like brain and spinal surgery, and because of the risks it carries it is better to spend an extended period of time training, learning to look and recognise what you are looking at, and learning to differentiate between images that make up a person's spirit and images that show something else.

Visionary work within the inner landscape is also balanced with an outer action in order to connect the conscious and subconscious of the person and the land together. The outer action, which you will do after the vision, can be done daily after meditation or before a ritual, or out in life when you feel stressed, under threat, or just in need of touching base with the land.

Read through the vision and look up all the parts of the brain's anatomy that it mentions to ensure that you have a visual understanding of where in the brain you are going.

The vision

To prepare your work space go round the directions, light the lights, open the gates, and as you work in each direction remember the inner landscape of the land beyond each gate. When you are ready sit down before the central candle, facing south with the altar before you. Meditate for a few minutes to still yourself.

Using the same method you used to visit the heart, step out of yourself and look at yourself as this enables you to create a separation between your mind and body so that you can work effectively. Go back into your body via the navel area with the intention of going into your brain. Flow to the back of your body and enter the spinal cord. Flow up the spinal cord until you come to a flap or trapdoor (the medulla). See this area as a tunnel, and as you flow through the trapdoor swim upwards through the tunnel until you find yourself in a small, cave like area which is the third ventricle.

Once you are in the small cave stand up and look around. Directly in front of you are a few steps leading up to a door. Go up the steps and open the door (and close it behind you) and climb the rough-hewn stone steps that lead out onto a landscape. Look around you. Look at the sky, the weather. Is there water in the landscape? (Rivers, streams, sea, etc.) Are there hills, mountains, grassy plains, trees? Take plenty of time to look around. Take note of what type of landscape it is and what condition it is in. If there are trees, are they healthy? What is the weather like? What direction does the weather come from? Take some time to sit in the landscape and observe.

When you are ready to leave go back down the steps to the door. Stop and look at it. You will see that it is breathing and contracting slightly: this door is a guardian being who watches over the threshold deep within you. Place your hands on the door and say thank you to it for watching over this deep threshold for you. Pass through the door, back into the cave-like area. As you look around the cave you will see that one side seems to have a faint light shining through into it. Go towards that faint light. Pass through the living wall of the cave, through an area of lots of sounds and thoughts, and emerge from the area of your forehead just above the bridge of your nose. Step out and away from your body. Turn round and look at it. Remember that your spirit takes the shape of a human body so that you and body fit together well.

Before you step back into your physical body, lift your (spirit's) left hand and look at it. Look at it with the intention that energy will build in it until you see an orange glow in your hand. Once you have that visual, place your glowing hand in front of your body's forehead where you just came out. Transfer the orange glow to your physical forehead and tell it "guard!" The energy will focus on that area and will guard this access route into your deeper self. Now walk round to the back of your body. Again, look at your left hand with the intention of building energy. When you have a glowing orange force in your hand, stick it at the base of your neck. Again, tell it to guard. These actions seal and protect the two entrances to critical areas of you.

When you are ready carefully step back into yourself. Sit for a moment before you open your eyes. Visualise the orange energy glowing from your forehead and the back of your neck. In future, when you meditate, be aware of these orange glows. You can strengthen them if need be simply by focusing on them and telling them to grow stronger. Only do this if it is needed. The orange glow is part of your own vital force, and you must learn to work efficiently with your energies. Never fall into the trap of 'more is better.' It is more a matter of directing your energy where you see it failing or weakening. Before you close the room down, go straight on to the next exercise.

12. *Task:* Mingling inner landscapes

After you have worked with the landscape vision, stand up facing south with your eyes open. Be aware of the inner landscapes over the four thresholds of the room. Now be aware of your own inner landscape.

Hold out your arms to the sides and feel yourself extend beyond your body so that each arm flows into the inner landscape beyond the gates. Feel the land beneath you, and feel your feet upon the land. Feel the sky above you and that your head extends into the air and sky above you. Now feel your own inner landscape extend beyond you like a tide, and feel it flow into the directions all around you: your inner landscape and the land are one. Extend your consciousness out as much as you can, and when you feel it 'peak,' bring the tide back in. Feel the inner land around you mingle with your inner landscape. As you bring the tide back in, feel the quality of the land around you also come back into you. You and the land are both of the same creation. The power of Divinity, the breath of the Universal Power flows through you both as one.

If there is any disturbance in the land, you will feel it. If you do feel that, just be aware of it, and be aware that it will express itself through your breath and your skin or through the wind and the earth. The reverse is also true: disturbance in your body can be expressed upon the land and the weather. At this stage of your training, just be aware of that, pay attention, and experiment with your breath and the wind.

This dynamic of union with the land will slowly grow over the years if you continue to work on this simple tide exercise. As an apprentice, it is important to know about this dynamic and experience it to some degree, but if you wish to work deeply with the land and with creation as an adept, this is where that work starts. This sense of tidal exchange with the land will develop over time until it becomes second nature.

There is no need to work with it in meditation: eventually you will be able to cast your mind to that union and your awareness of it will switch straight on. You will be able to feel into the land, and the land will be able to feel into you.

If you do not want to develop to that level of union with the land, do the tide exercise through your apprenticeship and then re-evaluate from there. If you get the basic skill to a good level of competency in your apprentice training, then you can choose to continue to develop it or leave it once you get to the initiate training. But you will still have the foundation skill in your toolbox. If you do not develop this foundation skill, and if you change your mind about your focus of work later on, you will have to retrain this skill again. Also, through working with this exercise, you will learn how to use this skill of expansion and union with things other than the land.

Throughout the apprentice level, you will be introduced to various foundation training skills, and you will do all of them. Once you get into the initiate training, then you can start to think about where you want your specialist focus to be in adeptship, and narrow down your training accordingly. But to get to that point, learn all the basic skills, so that you will always have access to them in rudimentary forms.

13. *Task:* Affecting your body by communing with the weather

This is really an adept level technique, but again like all magic its roots lie in the apprentice training. Learn first to connect your breath to the wind. When you go outside each day, take a breath and breathe out with intention. Your intention is that your breath and the wind are one.

When there is a storm blowing outside, go outside and again breathe into the wind with the intent that the storm and your breath are one. Learn not to fear storms but to understand them. Some are cleaning the earth and sky, some are watering a dry earth, and some are expressions of anger, of nature hitting back and also trying to rebalance. Think of it in human terms: sometimes you get a cold that makes your cough, sometimes asthma can kick in with allergies, stress, or overwork. Sometimes your breath becomes unbalanced and difficult if you are angry. The land does the same thing. When you feel an angry storm, as I have said before, go outside and tell the storm how much it is respected and that you understand it has a job to do. Tell the wind how beautiful it is, and breathe into that wind to join it.

Similarly if you have breathing problems go outside and take in breaths with intent: allow the sheer power of the air around you to flow into you with deep intent to balance and harmonise you. If you have asthma and use an inhaler, sometimes before you use the inhaler, (unless it is an emergency) take in a breath with the understanding of your connection with the air/wind around you, breathe out, and then use the inhaler. This is something to experiment with. Find your own way of connecting with the elements around you and within you.

This will also slowly change how you think about your body, illness, the weather, and the planet. We have learned to fear bad weather. We have learned to fear illness.

Sometimes both are necessary, and for those necessary storms of nature and body, you must learn how to let them do their job and assist them in any way possible. If the storm or illness is a real danger to you, then your connection with the elements will warn you that you are in danger, and you will be assisted in finding the safe way through the situation. If someone is terminally ill, learning to make this connection with nature at a deep level will help to smooth their passing from an inner perspective. We all have to die at some point, and preparing for that passing with deep connection with the land can bring a deep, settled peace.

14. *Task:* Discover the other organ spirits using vision

Now that you have ventured into your heart and also deep into your brain, it is time to experiment on your own and go to meet the spirits in your liver, kidneys, lungs, etc. Use the technique you have learned for flowing into the body, and use the navel area as an entry and exit point. If you do not know your own anatomy, look it up and learn where the organs are. Choose two or three organs, one session per organ. Go into them, meet the spirits, clean them up if they need it, and ask them if they need anything.

As usual, with all the visions and tasks you have done in this lesson, your notes should be added to your journal and then typed up on computer. Some of the notes from this lesson will be invaluable to you in a few years.

15. *Task:* Read the book Magical Healing

The text of which is provided for you in the Appendix of this book. It has many different aspects of body care, magical body work, and information that is very important for magical students and magicians in general. Do not skip this reading, it is very important and will really help you with the more advanced work you will soon be stepping into.

16. *Optional task:* Read up on the five spirits

> *"Man is in intimate association with Heaven and Earth and the heart is the master. So the ear and eye are the sun and moon, blood and qi are wind and rain."*
>
> — *Huainan zi*, chapter 7, Monkey Press

Read up on the five spirits *Shen, Hun, Yi, Po,* and *Zhi* in Chinese medicine. You will find all sorts of articles in larger libraries and the internet about these spirits. You will also find that in modern articles and books, particularly ones by Western authors, these spirit connections are approached through personal psychology, which is a reductionist approach to a divinely complex universe. As a magician, taking that route (understanding through psychology) will take you down a magical dead end.

Learn to let things be themselves: allow the understanding of individual spirits within a holism to emerge and do not try, particularly at this stage, to analyse them. You do not need to do an intellectual autopsy on everything you experience. Let things be themselves, let them communicate with you on simple terms, and as you gain a lot more direct experience then you can come to your own understanding.

By ploughing through various texts on the five spirits, you will find some information that is useful for you. Some of it may confirm to you your own experiences in vision with the organs, but also remember these texts are a cultural lens, and have been heavily adjusted in modern terms to fit the pseudo-health market in the West.

It is also a good exercise for you to learn how to sift through such writings and extract what you need without taking everything on board. You may feel that you do not need to read through these texts, as you have built up enough of an understanding through your visionary work, and that's fine. The texts come in useful sometimes for confirmation of discovery and to help deepen an understanding.

Once you have worked with the organ spirits you will be able to spot in modern texts where an author has totally missed the point or is waffling around trying to explain something they really don't understand, which is where the psychology usually comes in. Of course these spirits are a part of us, but they are also a part of the land around you, and are also of themselves. They help to process our actions and emotions, but they are not the psychological manifestation of our emotions, those are two very different things. Keep that in mind.

Lesson 7

Sacred Monarchs, Saints, and Priesthoods

These humans in the inner worlds differ from the inner contacts and inner adepts that one finds in the Inner Library. These are humans (well, sometimes not) who are in the orbit of a particular religious/mystical/magical line and who operate specifically through that line. Sometimes they are just humans, and sometimes they have become composites with other beings operating through them. Magicians work with them differently to how they would work with the usual human inner contacts/adepts. It is wise to keep in mind that their human element makes them fallible: they are not all-knowing and all-wise, but they do know things we do not, and if they are worked with magically and within the system that they operate in, they can become useful allies in magical work.

If the magician attempts to work with them outside of their system then problems occur, such as parasited contacts. It has become fashionable in certain quarters of magic to work with this type of human contact in an often out-of-context and near-whimsical way. This exposes the magician to a whole host of problems, and because it is becoming such a widespread magical fashion it is an area of magic that you need to be aware of as an apprentice. In earlier times these contacts were worked with only within their own system, and as a result were not problematic contacts to deal with. But when you form a connection with any being out of its context or system, you disengage all the protective magical patterns within its structure. This makes you fair game for any being who wishes to feed off you, amuse itself at your expense, or, more dangerously, manipulate you for its own agenda.

We are in an exciting time of magical experimentation. With access to the internet we are exposed to all sorts of cultural, religious, and magical systems that only fifty years ago most people were unaware of. This brings great benefit and expansion to magic, but it also brings trouble: it is good to be mutable, but it is also good to approach that mutability with foresight, intelligence, and care. The first step in this experimentation and expansion is an understanding that not everything is as it seems, and not everything in magical fashion is real or stable. Magical fashion, which is often seen as the latest popular deity, saint, or spirit, is a sharp, two-edged sword. On the human side it is often fuelled by a wish to sell product, and on the inner side it receives a parasitical response.

It is easy to become paranoid under these circumstances, but that would be a backwards step. It is better to plough through the dross, with gnosis, and find the gem hidden within the marketing trash. In order to do that, you need a basic understanding of what these saints, kings, queens, and magical priests are, and what they are not. This is the purpose of this lesson. Once the apprentice has a good idea of what surrounds them in the human magical world, they can make informed choices about what and who they work with, and why.

1. Inner priesthoods

We will start with the most common aspect of this magical human contact, the inner priesthoods. The priesthoods who most commonly appear in Western magic tend to be Egyptian, Roman, and Catholic, along with some magical adepts who operate out of specific systems that combine magic with religion. Contacts are not limited to these groups, however; wherever in the world and whenever in time you get a magical/religious mix and a properly built system, you get these inner priesthoods.

When an inner priesthood presents itself to living magicians, key elements are always present to show you they are a real contact. Any well-trained adept of most systems will know, recognise, and understand these keys, and will also recognise when they are missing. But many magicians of various skill levels will neither know nor recognise the keys, or notice if they are missing. Such magicians are vulnerable to being conned, parasited, or lost in a quagmire of glamour, both old and new. Glamour is not a new thing: the early Christian writers were very good at dishing it out.

The term 'inner priesthoods' encompasses a vast range of priesthoods (male or female or transgendered – yes, such has deep and very ancient roots in temple culture) who present through various systems. What all have in common is that they were/are priesthoods in systems that incorporated the Greater Mysteries, which includes magic and mysticism.

Because of where we have taken religion in our modern culture, down the road of social cohesion, making sure people are moral, and that they worship 'the one true god' (and we are overpopulated by 'one true gods' to the point of it being ridiculous), there are precious few real, mystical, magical priesthoods left alive in the West, and only a smattering in the East. The deepest and most profound priesthoods are found in the early ancient cultures. We can track the rise and fall of magical integrity within priesthoods by what those cultures left behind. By the time we get to the Roman era and beyond, the Inner Mysteries were seriously sagging, and only a few fragments survived, mostly in the new and upcoming Roman Christian Church, which eventually morphed into the Catholic Church.

But rather than looking in depth at various specific systems it is better to give you a wider view of the dynamics, patterns, and actions of these inner priesthoods. Then you can spot them yourself in action in various cultures, and also in modern magic.

The first main aspect of the inner priesthoods is the *consecrated line*. This essentially plugs the priest into the deep inner system, and also into the egregore of the system. These days we think of consecration as the transmission of a line obtained via the laying on of hands and through the anointing of the priest. But there were, and are, other methods that would constitute consecration that would tie a human into a system. However a consecration presents itself, a real one steps the person out of their individual fate and opens the path before them to a fate of service within a specific system. The narrower and more defined the system, the narrower and more defined the new fate path of the priest. It is probably wise at this stage to point out that consecration, and initiation are two very different things, and what they do, how they work, and why are also very different indeed.

Just as humans are fallible, so too are many of the consecrated lines. It is not unlikely that you will bump up against a degenerate consecrated line at some point. The line is only as good as the people within it, keep that in mind. For clarity it is best to look at the different variants of this phenomenon and how it has morphed over time. We will start with the earliest form: the sacred king or queen. Then we will return to the priesthood structures.

2. Sacred/magical monarchs

We have to reach pretty far back in our history to find kings and queens who are truly sacred in the real, magical sense. Many of the inner priesthoods sprang from a system that had, or has, a sacred monarch at the spearhead of the line. We have already looked a bit at this concept in previous lessons, but essentially a sacred monarch is a human who has stepped out of their individual life and has become part of the 'We': a part of the land, an aspect of the people, part of the inner consecrated line, in union with other monarchs in the line, and also part of the inner sacred lines of those who serve at the thresholds of creation and destruction. Essentially such monarchs become a fulcrum of balance between Divine Power and creation. We have already looked at their role in life in previous lessons; the Pharaoh upholding Ma'at, for example, but now we need to look at their continued role in death and the inner worlds.

When a sacred monarch dies the link between Divinity and the land/people does not cease; rather it continues as indefinite service. In some cultures the monarch is so closely tied to the land that they continue to walk it, protecting the integrity of the land and the people through the changes of time. But more than that, they continue as protective key aspects of the magical structure. More than anything else they are focused on upholding, protecting, and continuing the flow of power within their specific structure.

We see this at its most visible, as visionary magicians, in Egypt. When you go to certain key places where a king or queen is still active within the system, not only can you switch on the power of the temples and connect with the priesthoods, but you are also made aware, in no uncertain terms, of the collective monarch who upholds it all. When an adept connects with this monarch they will often find themselves connecting with a hive, or group, of successive monarchs who have fused, within the system, into one larger consciousness. This is the root of why many monarchs (and bishops, popes, etc.) refer to themselves as 'We.' They are no longer one person but have joined a stream of consciousness much larger than any individual.

When magicians connect to this stream of consciousness it will often present as just one king or queen. But in fact the wisdom, knowledge, and experience of all the sacred monarchs of a particular stream flows through this one contact: the contact acts like the point of the arrow. The presentation of one king/queen comes either from the reach of the magician (searching for a specific monarch), or from the system itself. The system is essentially the whole magical structure: the inner temple, the lines of priesthoods, the pantheon of deities, the line of monarchs, the land, the deeper inner powers running through that system from the Inner Desert and so forth; as you can see, when I say 'system' I mean a truly complex and powerful whole system that human consciousness can express through.

The only magical purpose of connecting with these sacred inner monarchs is if you are willing to do service for their cause. This is where it can get sticky, and often does. If you are approached, without prompt by one of these contacts it is usually because you have a skill that they need. You have to be aware that service to one of these monarchs is not often a simple or easy task. Nor is the agenda they carry always compatible with what we today consider balanced. These monarchs will approach an adept if the adept is on their land, either living there, or visiting. The further back in time these monarchs existed in life, the more likely their agenda will consist of continued service to the holism of what they ruled over. However the nearer to our time they get, the more weird their agenda sometimes becomes. For example a very ancient monarch may ask you to do a task that will bridge the upholding of the ancient system or pattern across the land or the temple structure. But once we get to monarchs from more recent ancient cultures their plans can often be more about vengeance and war. So keep that in mind. This is not a strict rule; rather it is more of a possibility that you have to watch out for.

I have been approached more than once by an inner monarch. One wanted me to do a job that at the time seemed fairly straightforward, so in my ignorance I stepped straight into it and did what was asked of me. I did not realise that the job, while seemingly straightforward, was actually a huge undertaking from an energetic perspective, and one that would take years to unfold. To this day, part of my vital force continues to do that job, along with other jobs, and I am a bit long in the tooth for that sort of energy deficit. If I had taken the time to do readings beforehand to look at the long-term effects on me, and not just readings to see if it was indeed necessary, which it was, I would probably still have done the work as it was so vital; but I would have been better prepared to tend to my body and the energy drain.

Another time I was approached by a monarch who asked me to have children, specifically a son. The monarch spotted things in my bloodline and when I went on his 'stomping ground' he badgered me relentlessly. Trying to explain to an ancient ancestral monarch that I had been sterilised made for an interesting exchange. Even if I had not been sterile I would still have said no. Not only would this have been a huge, long-term undertaking, it would not have been an appropriate thing to do. Wishing for male bloodlines from a priestess is playing into old tribal wars, jostling for power, and continuing what went so badly wrong with these royal lines. In truth, the bloodline is mostly (but not always) irrelevant: it is the eternal soul of the monarch that is important, not just what flows through their veins while they are alive.

So you can see how sometimes the dynamic of sacred monarchs can be corrupt, can be misused, and can be parasited. Just because an inner monarch approaches you, that does not mean they are balanced and healthy from a spiritual/magical point of view. This is why this area is such a minefield, and not really something a magician should step into unless they really know what they are doing, or they have a death wish.

The other thing to be aware of is that if you are on a land where these sacred monarchs are still active as bridges between the inner and outer worlds, then the whole system that they uphold is also still active, even if the outer culture is long gone. The monarch and the inner priesthoods are all still working away to uphold the system. Most of the time, the upholding of the system is done for the benefit of the land, Divinity, and humanity. When you see this in action it can be very educational as a magician to observe what kicks them into action, and what does not. We think in our modern way, which is often at odds with how these systems operate. For example a system still active on ancient land will not activate or take action against warring people living on that land as that is seen as irrelevant. But they will activate if the people are about to dismantle a key aspect of a temple or a burial where it is vital that the spirit within the burial stays intact.

We would expect them to protect the whole temple or every sacred burial, but it doesn't work like that. I have seen them activate aggressively against a government that was about to demolish key areas of temples, and also to force the government to close and protect certain key tombs. But they didn't interfere with the political turmoil of the living, nor did they interfere with the 'new' religion, nor the excavation of further remains. Just watching how they did activate for certain things and not others taught me what was precious to them in terms of upholding the system, and what was not.

Not all ancient lands still have these systems operating. Many have fragmented, imploded, or the inner priesthoods have withdrawn their influence, often to collapse a corrupt outer system still in operation. Through watching this in various areas I had visited, I began to realise that these inner systems were not interested in the outer manifestations of their system, nor in the larger populations of their lands. Rather they were/are protecting deeper, more profound patterns that allow the flow of power between Divinity and those humans who can pick up on it to continue through time.

If the system has been lightly parasited or threads of power have been disturbed or broken then they will reach out to any passing adept who can hear them and ask for help to restore that sacred balance. They do not want you to join them or their system, and you do not have to be part of that system, though often an adept they ask for help will have been a member at some point in other lives. Once you have worked as a visionary magician and you travel to places that are tied into these sacred monarchs then it is possible one will approach you with a task. Just think very carefully before responding!

On the other end of the scale is the magician that actively seeks out an inner sacred monarch. Sometimes this is done 'just because': this is a stupid reason to approach such an inner contact and is a product of corrupt magical training, or general immaturity. This is rooted in the training exercise of 'summoning a demon' just to see if you can do it and then practise your banishing techniques. This is the most absurd exercise I have ever come across for a myriad of reasons. Above all else, it plants that *modus operandi* into the mind of the magician, and they develop a taste for summoning different beings 'just because.'

Most of the time such behaviour just pulls in cross-dressing parasites. It's much worse if the magician is successful in pulling in contact with a sacred monarch: not only will they be badgered by demands of service and self-sacrifice, but if the magician decides to withdraw in a sulk for some reason, they will find themselves on the receiving end of an enraged line of powerful inner kings or queens, and that is not pretty.

Other times magicians will reach out to sacred monarchs in order to serve the land and the people. This can be good or bad, depending on the understanding of the magician and the agenda of the sacred monarch. Some ancient lines tie into the land to the point where they appear as part-human and part-animal or land (growing out of or embedded within a tree or a rock). These are often powerful sacred monarchs who uphold nature upon the land, and if they are directly approached by a magician, the monarch will expect true service, not just a "hello, how are you" kind of contact. Sometimes they will simply ask for regular remembrance, sometimes they ask you to do specific tasks, and sometimes they will ask you to "slay all the intruders", and that's when it can get awkward. The best rule of thumb for dealing with these sacred lines of consciousness upon the land is to have a damn good reason for approaching them and be willing to do long-term service.

An action that you can do safely as an apprentice magician, if you are aware of ancient monarchs on the land, is simply to acknowledge their presence without direct contact: be aware of them and respect their presence. This opens a simpler, slower line of contact that will develop if needs be. Today in the United Kingdom we often have debates about the relevance of our monarchy, as they hold no real power in the running of the country and are mainly a tourist attraction. For years I was one of the people who felt that they were degenerate and served no real purpose other than to suck money from the people. But when I returned to Britain and started to look at the processes going on at a deep level upon the land, it became clear that they do indeed serve a very important purpose, which surprised me.

The bloodline is irrelevant, and is not British anyhow. But through the process of consecration upon a land which is steeped in power, the sacred line joins and expresses itself through the current monarchy. For the land to be strong, this island needs a sacred monarch. Though our monarchy has long since lost any knowledge of real, deep contact, the outer pattern still exists, which allows the inner system and process to continue. From an inner perspective the monarch serves a great purpose, and having a 'We' monarch, operating within a sacred pattern (Christianity) upon a land steeped in deep inner power, seems from an inner perspective to protect the inner integrity of the land, regardless of what the humans do on the surface. It is an interesting situation: I am guessing that the modern British monarchs have little if any understanding of the inner perspective of the system they operate within, and are purely externalisations that keep the process running. Like all monarchies, you will get good ones where everything flourishes, dumb ones, and bad ones.

3. The priesthoods

The inner priesthoods usually operate in a system that either has a hive monarch or a group of deities, or both. The more ancient ones tend to serve two purposes: to uphold and protect the key sacred places upon a land and to pass on knowledge to living humans who work or will work in their lifetime to uphold balance. That is where we modern magicians come into the picture. There are so few real, physical, mystical, magical priesthoods who are still living operating systems that the priesthoods tend to reach out to adepts who work in harmony with Divinity and with the land. The inner priesthoods will teach the adept, protect them to a certain extent, and also guide their fate to ensure that key moments in their life will be reached in order for them to serve.

These inner priesthoods are not interested in you joining or copying their system. Sometimes adepts do not realise this and will begin to copy the system, becoming an Egyptian or Babylonian 'priest,' for example. This is a glamour trap and when it happens the inner priesthoods will often walk away from the adept and try to find another. Really these priesthoods are interested in the upholding of the magical harmony and the development of aspects of humanity. They will offer you tools, guidance, protection, and education so that you can learn to work in a way that protects and upholds the deeper balance between creation and destruction.

These are the priesthoods we meet when we venture in vision into the inner temples and the Inner Desert. They will download vital knowledge into you that can unfold over your lifetime, knowledge that you can work with and pass on. They will follow your life and intervene when you are seriously threatened, and guide you towards key moments that will open doors for you or allow you to act magically to bring balance to something. Often these priesthoods are active in the life of a human even before that person reaches magic. When an adept who works with these priesthoods looks back over their life they will recognise when these priesthoods were active in their life. Looking back, they were active around me from my childhood; I just didn't realise it at the time.

A magician works with these inner priesthoods in a variety of ways. The adept can go into the inner temples and work directly with them in vision, or they can open gates to allow the inner priesthoods to flow into the work space. They can also work with them on a day-to-day basis in everyday life once that connection has been made. They can also be reached through access points in the remains of ancient temples, if key aspects of the structure are still physically there. If a temple ruin switches on magically when you are there, then you know the system and the inner priesthood is still operating. There are some priesthoods and some priests within lines where, like anything connected with humanity, there is corruption and agenda. The degeneration of these priesthoods happened at various points in human history and in different areas around the world.

These more degenerate inner priesthoods are more interested in the continuation of power and control, of the accumulation of energy, and the aggressive protection of their theology. This often happened when the system/religious structure they operate within was created haphazardly, without proper magical construction, or when they stepped into a preexisting pattern that was decaying and took it over. This does not mean that Divinity cannot flow through such a system as it most certainly can: but it would be a messy system with many dead ends, power traps, parasites, and god knows what else. An adept would have to tread extremely carefully through such an inner system to find the gems hidden within it.

The bottom line with all of this subject matter is awareness and paying attention. The adept must not become glamoured or enveloped within the egregore. They also need to recognise when power, control, division, and hierarchy are apparent within an inner priesthood. In such cases it is better to back away silently. When an adept comes across an inner priesthood or becomes aware of their action in their life, check that the priesthood's main action is the transmission of knowledge, guidance towards balance, and the protection of the adept. Then you know you are plugging into a balanced, powerful, and healthy inner priesthood. In your training you will work with various inner priesthoods and in different ways as an adept. By the time you finish your adept training you will be fully versed in and familiar with many of the inner priesthoods still operating in the inner worlds.

Normally I would introduce the student to inner priesthoods much earlier in the training (it will really start in your initiate training), but we are in difficult times in the world, with a lot of destructive power flowing around, and casting students into that cauldron of fire would not be sensible. It is better to get more training under your belt first, so that when you do step into the deep inner temples to begin work you will be ready and able to deal with whatever you are asked to do.

4. Saints

What we in the West call saints, and other cultures have other names for, are in fact a variety of different types of inner contacts. Some are powerful and have ancient deity roots, others are fragments of the old systems. Some are humans who essentially became inner contacts within their system, and some are parasited shells. Today's concept of a saint came fairly late to the table of the Christian system. Originally, the word saint (*hagioi* in Greek) was used for all early Christians: it meant a believer. By around AD 200 its use had become more or less limited to martyrs, and by the fourth century we see it had become a special title: we have a brief mention of a 'day of saints' in the writings of Ephrem the Syrias.[1]

Honouring saints with particular feast days did not become a mainstream tradition in the Western church until the Roman bishop Boniface IV consecrated the Pantheon at Rome to Christian usage as a church on May 13, AD 609 or AD 610. This was a clever move. The Pantheon was a universally sacred place, whose very name means 'common to all the gods.' By taking it over and consecrating it to *Santa Maria ad Martyres*,[2] that single act turned the focus of prayer away from local deities and contacts and towards the pool of 'saints' within the Christian system: the common folk needed something or someone recognisable to pray to.

At that time the saints were essentially the early martyrs and apostles, with a few 'converted' local deities thrown in for good measure. This process developed and spread out as it became clear that saints were popular with the common folk who could relate to them. The veneration of saints also raised money via pilgrimages. The tombs, relics, and known living places of the saints were visited, and the idea of the saint as a bridge or intercessor between humanity and God took a strong hold. During this time many different, previously unknown people or mythical characters were taken into the fold of sainthood.

The first papal canonisation of a saint took place in AD 993. As the church ran out of martyrs they started turning various ascetics, bishops, and defenders of the church (or people who were wealthy and powerful) into saints. Many of these are parasited shells that continue to feed off people to this day. Why is it important to learn about this? Because in modern magic work with saints pops up in almost all the traditions magicians swim in, and it is vital for a magician to know exactly what they are working with.

The word 'saint' has different connotations for different cultures around the world. Even within Christianity what comes under the heading of saint is a wide variety of different beings and humans. A saint can be a human who achieved greatness in a mystical sense and who continues to work, essentially as an inner contact. This is a true 'saint,' but in reality is one of the rare manifestations of what we call saints.

---

[1] Died AD 373.

[2] St Mary and the Martyrs.

Under the same heading fall older deities and local spirits who have been absorbed into the religious system.

Then we have the nastiest form of saint, which sadly is fairly common. This is where a corrupt priest, bishop, or pope has been canonised (i.e. made a saint through ritual and official recognition) and is then prayed to and rituals (masses) conducted in their honour. This pattern of behaviour essentially creates an unbalanced vessel; it is basically a thought-form structure that a parasite can flow into and operate through. This happens a lot, particularly in aspects of the Abrahamic religions. The more people pray to a parasited 'saint,' the bigger it gets and the more energy it sucks of people. In turn, it gives the pilgrim a small experience of 'the Divine' which opens up the pilgrim to further energetic draining.

But this is only one aspect of saint presentation, and tends to centre around saints who were promoted to powerful bishops, priests, etc. within the system. Not all sainted priests were corrupt and some have morphed into powerful saints; St Francis of Assisi, for example. But because this is such a complex subject, let's break it down into sections so that we can look at the different 'beings' who all fall under the heading of saint.

Also bear in mind that when I use the word 'saint' I am not simply referring to saints within Christianity. Most systems around the world have their version if you look closely. They may call them something different, but we are essentially talking about the same thing. So what you read in this section of the lesson applies to all religions/systems around the world who work with these saints, which are essentially *hybrids*. Once you have looked at this you will have a good idea of the keys that identify a real contact and what signs indicate a parasited presentation. Let us start with the 'saints' who are actually localised or subdivided deities. Then we will look at ancient land powers/spirits as saints, and finally the human presentation of saints, both good and bad.

5. Deities as saints

Sometimes some of the contacts that present in cultures as saints (or immortal ones) are older deity powers that have either been co-opted into a religion or culture or are forces that work through or with deities that are then carried forward into the new religion or culture. These are the most powerful of all 'saints,' and their nature can be often spotted in the iconography used to present them. A popular power that continued into Christianity is that of St Michael. To look at Saint Michael, we also have to look at St George, Apollo, Belinos, and Saint Christina, who are all essentially the same power looked at from different angles. This is an important process for you to learn as a magician, so that you learn to look beyond the surface and truly begin to understand the powers you are potentially working with. Never take things at face value!

To approach this, first strip away the surface presentation: Michael as an angel, George as a soldier, Christina as an early Christian. Then look at the key elements: solar power, the ability to suppress serpent power, the giving or taking of disease, the power of the Scales/Judgement. What we are left with is a group of so-called saints, angels, and pagan gods who are presentations of the same root power that flows through most lands in the northern hemisphere. I have no knowledge of the powers south of the equator, so if you do live down there, you will have to do your own research on the presentations of local deities.

Michael as an archangel is very popular these days and has been in religion and magic for centuries. But here is where caution comes in. The naming and attributions of Christian angels came fairly late to the table in terms of antiquity and they do not present in magical terms as actual angels; rather they tend to present more as deity powers. The angel descriptions in the Old Testament/Tanakh are more correct in their presentation and recounting of angelic beings. The older the book, the closer to real angelic contact the tales become. By the time you get to the New Testament, the angels suddenly appear in the texts with names, human-like personalities, and lists of things that they 'do' with humans (healing, guarding, fighting, gifting, etc.).

As we move further towards our time frame their 'duties' are further expanded and they become angelic heroes who do everything from making the tea to smiting someone who pissed you off. You clearly see the degeneration in thinking and approach through the Christian and magical progression through time. What happened, I think (and it is only my opinion) is that by the time of Christ there was a massive influence in Judea from the polytheistic Greek and Roman cultures, and the monotheistic thinking of the time could not swallow that. So powerful deities became archangels and then later saints. The people who were used to polytheistic thinking could relate to the budding Christian religion much more easily with this collection of angels and saints. Don't forget that the mainstream Christian church of that time essentially became the continuation of the Roman Empire: just slightly different outfits and different names.

So going back to the serpent slayers. As Christianity spread through the decaying Roman Empire, local manifestations of ancient deity land powers were renamed and refigured. Sometimes these deity/land powers were very old and/or were not part of a major pantheon, which prevented any major priesthood battles. But the powers were recognised as important enough to keep them within the new system. Where these powers surfaced in a land or culture, a deity or spirit was identified and worked with. These local and regional cultural interfaces became the new angels and saints.

So how would you work with such saints, knowing they are in fact deities?

The saint presentation is a window you can use to connect with that power. Once connection is made the 'saint' or 'angel' presentation can fall away so you can work directly with the deity itself. To do so, though, takes away the filter which can be useful in safety terms: a solar deity that has the power of sending plague, healing, sun, and battling serpent power is no lightweight deity, and there is a possibility of fingers being burned.

As an apprentice or even as an initiate, there are two ways to approach working with saints. Both can be used concurrently. One is to work with as old a presentation as possible of a saint, (Orthodox icons are best) while also connecting with them through ritual vision or allowing whichever saint wishes to work with you to come forward in ritual vision. This is something you will explore in your practical work.

When you work with the icon remember that it is a presentation that has been *overlaid with a newer religion*. Also remember that often these so-called saints have had skills attributed to them far beyond, or irrelevant to, the actual deity power that flows through the icon. These attributes were often added in order to draw pilgrims, who brought money, gifts, and patronage to a church. So for example the solar serpent-subduing power of Michael (Apollo), which is a major power, is pushed to one side in favour of people praying to him to protect them from their enemies, or to be a soldier who will 'be on their side.' For a magician, ploughing through the outer manifestations and attributes of saints can be a bit of a nightmare, but if you do reach through then what you find underneath can be powerful indeed.

The other thing to be aware of, if you are intending to work magically with a saint that is a deity, is to ensure that the deity power is compatible with the land where you live, and that the spirits, natural deities, etc., who you work with are in harmony with such power.

6. Land powers/beings as saints

Another form of non-human saint is a land spirit/power that has been co-opted into the religion. Often these co-opted land spirits/beings are quite large and powerful, hence the co-opting, and are present over the whole area that was once the Roman Empire, though occasionally you come across localised land powers that have become local saints.

Of the larger land powers, Saint Christopher is a good example. At the turn of the 19th/20th century he was the most popular saint in Britain. Except for the Virgin Mary there were more images of Saint Christopher in churches than any other saint. Christopher has a long reach: from Egypt, Palestine, Greece, all the way to Britain and beyond. He presents as a giant who carries a small child, supposedly the baby Jesus, and he is the patron saint of travellers. I had not given him much thought at all until I started to come across a strange manifestation of land power that would present near seas.

The presentation would be this: a giant humanoid being who carried a small child or dwarf, and who was constantly feeding the child/dwarf. When I asked the giant why he was constantly feeding the child, he told me that it was not a child but a dwarf of great and terrible power, and the only way to keep the dwarf subdued was to feed it. If he didn't, the dwarf would scream, and the screams would summon terrible storms that would kill anyone near or on the sea. So here we have a giant but heroic land spirit who keeps a small but powerfully destructive force under control through service.

When you look at Norse mythology you see parallels between Aegir (Giant) and Ran (delicate but powerful goddess of storms), and a similar dynamic with the goddess Hera and Jason, the chief hero of the Argonauts:

> *Hera's plan was fraught with danger; it would require a true hero. To test Jason's mettle, she contrived it that he came to a raging torrent on his way to Iolcus. And on the bank was a withered old woman. Would Jason go about his business impatiently, or would he give way to her request to be ferried across the stream? Jason did not think twice. Taking the crone on his back, he set off into the current. And halfway across he began to stagger under her unexpected weight. For the old woman was none other than Hera in disguise.*[3]

Again we see the pattern of a hero carrying a small but powerful being in a service connected with water and the suppression of storms. Hera's name is a play on the Greek word for air, *aer*. Her servant, Iris Aellopus, whose name means 'storm-footed,' gives us more clues to her power. She is also known as Juno, and has a habit of sending storms at those who piss her off. So we are looking at a dynamic of a giant land spirit holding a small but powerful deity in order to maintain balance and avert disaster. If we look deeper into the various myths we can also see that when things are out of balance the giant/hero stops service to the deity and all hell breaks loose, which in turn restores whatever was out of balance.

So rather than being a simple Christian saint who dangles from your car's rear-view mirror and stops you bumping into things, we have in St. Christopher an ancient combination of land power and deity working together to balance each other out. And this combo is very much about water, weather, seas, and storms.

A deep female land/inner power (but not deity) who is a popular saint in modern magic is *Santa Muerte* (Death). She is very popular in certain communities in the Americas, and also in modern magical systems. Many occultists flock to working with her because of fashion, and do not realise the sheer force of power behind this being (though some do). Before you enter into a magical interaction with any of these powers, ensure you know everything you should about them, and that you are willing to deal with their powers flowing into your life. Engaging with a force like *Muerte* simply because she looks cool and you want to be edgy, then tossing her to one side when the fashion fades, is not such a great idea. Some will be unaffected by this if they have not made any true magical connection; but if you do and then you turn away in the wrong way you are likely to get a good lashing in some fashion.

---

[3] The story of Jason and the Argonauts is an Ancient Greek myth that was written down in the 3rd century BC by Apollonius of Rhodes who was a scholar and librarian in the Library of Alexandria.

This does not mean you can never back away from such powers; only that it should be done carefully, respectfully, and hopefully by mutual consent. Often these powers flow in and out of your life of their own accord, and that's fine and healthy: it is rare for one of those powers to stick around you indefinitely. But there is a difference between dropping a power because it is out of fashion and easing up on a connection because you both need to move on and whatever was required has been achieved. If you find this subject matter of great interest and you wish to look deeper into saints who are potentially deities or land powers, then take the time to research further. Start with the saint's presentation, and work back through various mythologies in the northern hemisphere, looking at different cultures and their deities. See which ones have the same key powers and present in similar ways. It doesn't mean it is the same deity; only that it is the same deity/land power; there is a difference. This will give you more idea of what it is you are wanting to work with, and also will tell you the best way to work with them.

7. Human saints

The human saints are the ones who really present a challenge to a magician, as they reflect the full spectrum of humanity, from Divinely touched or mystically inspired through to corrupt and nasty while also including a good dose of dumbass.

To find out whether a saint is truly mystical and will work with a magician in service – assuming that the magic is compatible with the saint's own orbit of spirituality; look first at the religious propaganda surrounding them, then at their deeper and, if possible, secular history. The good ones can also be spotted from their legends and the legacy they leave behind. My favourite is St. Francis of Assisi, who in modern terms advocates a low carbon footprint and a full, mystical respect for all of nature. If you are working towards such aims, it is possible that such a saint will be willing to work with you. And this brings me to the practicalities of how a magician would work with a saint who was once human.

The first thing to understand is that however mystical these saints were, they worked within the orbit of a certain religion, and your practice has to be compatible with that. It does not mean that you have to be Christian to work with them, but the underpinning of your practice needs to be compatible with the teachings of the founder of that system: Jesus. This is often where the first mistake is made. The religion we consider Christianity hangs on the structure of the Roman Empire, and also on the system created by Paul (Saul of Tarsus). When true Christian mystics die and flow into the inner worlds, the outer crust of the structure Paul instigated (along with others who added their own agendas) often falls away, and the pure underbelly of the teachings of the founder (Jesus) rise to the surface. This underbelly is much simpler and vaguer, but it is a path that has its keys, and if the keys fit your lock, then all will be good. If not, it is wiser to look to 'saints' who either emerge out of the land where you are, or from a system more compatible with who you are and what you are doing.

Some human saints were mystics who flowed freely with nature, and the Christianity was grafted onto them in one way or another. An example is Saint Bernadette of Soubirous (of Lourdes). She was a simple visionary who eventually found her expression through a Christian monastic life, but her actual visions were far more natural and expressed a much deeper mystery. When Bernadette had visions she described the apparition as 'that.' She heard a strong wind, but there was no wind; then she saw a bright light and then a woman of great beauty. The woman told her to dig and drink of the spring, to wash her face in it, and to eat the herbs that sprung from the ground by the water. When she asked the apparition who she was, after being asked a few times, the lady replied: "I am the Immaculate Conception."

Now the idea of Mary the mother of Jesus as having an immaculate conception was not unknown, but it was not to become true dogma until just after this event. What Bernadette experienced was a female deity power telling her to establish a healing spring, and she told the girl that she was without human creation. I suspect that this apparition was a goddess of brightness, springs, and healing... sound familiar?

Bernadette was plagued with illness, particularly breathing problems. Such physical disability is common among the human saints. It is not that their 'holiness' gave them suffering; rather it is more likely that the burden of visionary mystical ability was a strain on their bodies. Visionary ability and chronic illness (as opposed to dangerous illness) often seem to go together, and we also see this dynamic in many magicians. It seems to be part and parcel of the whole package.

A saint like Bernadette who was very definitely human but who bridged that mystical connection to create something powerful, is essentially an inner contact who a magician can connect to if, again, the agendas of both parties match up. For example if you were interested in working with the female powers of healing springs, the utterance of the water powers, etc., then a saint like Bernadette would be a good person to attempt to connect with in order to learn from and be guided by her.

Even though the main objective of the connection is learning and guidance, Bernadette would not be found in the Inner Library. Nor would she be found in an inner temple. She would be better connected to at healing springs. This is because even though Bernadette operated within a Christian format as an adult, her true and first connection was with a natural force, and that is the root of her power.

Some human saints, even some of the 'big' ones, were simply corrupt, power-hungry movers and shakers, or twisted ascetics who were looked up to because of their extreme behaviour. Others were intellectuals of their time or were princes, nobles, etc. Do not assume that because they are now saints they were balanced or healthy: many were not. If you wish to work with a human saint, first look closely at their behaviour and agenda, not the promises of their gifts that are dangled by the church. Look at their history, and also look closely at why you wish to work with them. Is it because you wish to copy some other magician who has written a book or created a system around them? Or do you have a genuine pull or feeling of connection with this saint?

8. About the practical work

For the practical work of this lesson you will work in visionary ritual to connect with a 'saint' who was once human, who is connected either to your bloodline or to the land where you live and work. Rather than you choosing a saint, this method will let the saint choose you. This is always the better way to work in magic, as we often are blind to the subtle powers around us waiting patiently in the wings.

You will work in your ritual space and will work within a ritual format which will ensure that you are not bothered by a parasite trying to cross-dress and connect with you. This is the reason why, and often before a vision, you do a ritual balancing (The Anchor, for example) it flattens out the space energetically, it tunes the room, and it tunes the energies around you from an inner perspective. Once this is done, low-level beings cannot get into the space, but beings who are compatible with the energy and pattern will be able to flow to you unhindered.

9. *Task:* Meeting a saint

Set up your work space with all five altars. Go around and light the lights, open the gates, and then sit down in the centre to meditate for a few minutes to still yourself. Once you are still, do the Anchor ritual to tune yourself and the space. Once you have finished, with the lights and gates open, stand in front of the central altar, facing south.

Hold the very clear and focused intention in your mind that you wish to reach out to a human saint who is in your orbit somewhere. Look at the central flame while holding that intent, and then utter towards the central flame:

> "I wish to make connection with a human saint."

Still yourself once more. This work will rely on your inner senses, so you need to clear everything out of your mind. Do not have a particular saint in mind: it is important that you approach this work with an open mind and are willing to let whatever saint who may be orbiting within your fate pattern to come forward. Your utterance and focus of intent has already put the call out. You are going to approach the four directional gates one by one to find out from which inner direction the saint will flow. To start the process circle the central altar slowly, keeping a clear mind, then approach the east altar.

Stand before the east altar with your eyes closed and just feel into the space. Is it blank? Is there a power there? Do you feel a pull to that direction for some reason? Or is there nothing? This 'feeling out' with intent creates a contact filter: although there are inner contacts, deities, and land spirits who are often in those directions, because of your specific intent they will fade into the background in order to allow a saint contact to emerge from one of the directions. Take a mental note of any feeling or reaction, but do not respond at this stage; just be aware of it.

Now repeat the exercise in the other directions. Once you have finished in the north, go back to the east and repeat the whole process. Continue with this processing and tuning into the directions with an intent to connect with a saint until you have a very clear sense of one direction being far stronger in energy than the others. It does not matter how many times you have to go round: just make sure you are clear on which direction is really pulling you.

Once you have the direction identified it is time to reach out and make the contact. Go and sit down in front of the altar of the direction you are going to work with. Close your eyes and still yourself. See the gates before you in that direction, and see the flame of the candle on the altar. In vision, see yourself standing up and going to stand before the flame/altar. As you look beyond the flame you will see a figure standing in the shadows on the threshold. Invite them to move out of the shadows and stand on their side of the altar, with the flame between you. Let them look you over. While they do that, look at them. What sex are they? What do they look like? Are they holding anything, or is anything around them?

Do not ask them their name, but ask them what they do. Once they have communicated to you what they do (this could come in words, images, whatever), ask if there is something you can do to assist their work. Again, give them time to communicate to you. They may not directly communicate their need, but they might touch you or blow on you: there will be some bridging of connection that allows them to trigger something within you. If it happens this way, you will be presented with the answer out in life: something will happen or you will come across something that needs doing, and the saint will pop into your mind: that is their signal.

Once that bridging is done, ask them if they are willing to work with you (if you want that) and guide you. If they indicate that they are, then this is the method (vision, candle lit in the direction) you can use to interface with them. When you have finished, thank them for showing up, bow to them, and step back. Once they have withdrawn, starting in the east, go around the directions and close everything down. Note down the details of your contact in your journal so that you can go back and remind yourself of them.

If you wish to continue working with this saint, work in vision in your ritual space, and sit before the direction that they come to you from. Don't just focus on the contact in ritual/vision work; also keep an eye out for their influence in your daily life. Most of your work with the saint will not come just from the visionary contact but in things that you do in outer life, service they may ask of you, and in return their guidance and teaching.

10. *Task:* Documenting your work with the saint

Write up a short summary of your experiences with the saint into a computer log.

11. Advice

If you wish to continue working with the saint, which is your choice, you may not wish to, the way to do this is not through images, candles, offerings, etc., but by keeping them in mind, working with them in vision in the ritual setting, and being aware when they exert some form of influence in your daily life. If this happens, pay close attention to whether they are asking you to do a job or wanting to guide and support you in your work.

At that point, if you wish to have an icon of them, (if you know who it is, and there is an icon of that saint) then just have it in your work space. But do not get into offerings: that is such a parasite trap and also a cop-out. It is easy to toss a few glasses of wine on an altar; it is much harder to join the real work of the saint, which is the greatest offering you can make.

This is how work with saints goes; it is not some glamorous, flashy situation where a dude in robes struts around giving you endless pearls of wisdom in return for a candle and a glass of wine. If you work with a saint you will come closer into their orbit of action; for example Francis' action is in nature, particularly with birds and animals, but also the elements which in turn will put you right into the centre of the saint's work. You become a small part of their work and, as such, those in need gravitate to you: you stand out more.

If you are working with a saint whose orbit of action is teaching/study or medicine/healing, then that is what will be presented to you in your life. It is up to you if you wish to take up that challenge or not. If you do, you will be expected to give as much as you receive, and that giving is not baubles on an altar, it is magical service: work that you as a living human can do that a dead saint cannot do. Whatever that work may be, you must discover it for yourself without explanation from me. You will also receive much in the form of learning, guidance, some protection if it is truly needed, and also a valuable working companion. They will not be around you forever, but the time they do choose to work with you will be rewarding in many ways.

Lesson 8
Apprentice Midterm Summary

Now that you have reached beyond the midpoint of the apprentice section it is time to do a summing up and self-assessment of where you are and how you are working. It is also time to have a bit more direction in how you should be working, how you are preparing your notes, and what to do if you reach difficulties in your studies. Don't skip through this lesson. Read it properly: certain keys are within the text that you will need. This lesson will take you through the various aspects of what you have done so far, how you should be working, what you should be working on, and how to proceed from this point.

By now you should have the beginnings of various skills and some background knowledge on how things work in magic. If you have already worked in magic before, you should now be at a stage where you can strengthen some of the work you have done in the past, and also be able to assess and question certain aspects of the modern magic you have previously worked with. We will go through the key aspects of the training so far so that you can self-assess, adjust your practice if need be, and plan for your ongoing training over the remaining modules of the apprentice section.

1. CORE SKILLS:
   DIVINATION, INNER SENSES, VISIONARY SKILLS, RITUAL SKILLS

Through the first section of the course so far you have been given tasks and placed in situations where you can develop certain core skills that are essential for successful magic. Sometimes those tasks have been repeated in various ways from different angles in order to help you find your own learning style. All these core skills are vital for a good foundation in magic. When you find that you are not instantly 'good' at something it is tempting to cast it aside and focus on what you can do well and easily. This is the first trap of the magical apprentice. Some people will have some of these skills naturally, and some will not. Some people will find it very hard in the early stages of their training to be able to do any of these skills: this is normal. Magic is an art form, and like all art forms it takes a lot of practice to get proficient, then more long-term work to become truly good at it.

It can be disheartening for some if they see others seemingly mastering these skills quickly while they struggle just to get past the first step. Do not measure yourself against others; that is a bad mistake. Your development is unique to you, and no two magicians are the same. Many flash through early training but get stuck later on, some are slow starters but blossom with the later work, and some take their time and digest as much knowledge and experience as they can. **The one thing you should not do under any circumstances is dash through the training. To do so will be a complete waste of time.** Some, many, of the lessons take a long time to absorb as there are lots of inner dynamics working away unseen that are preparing you for handling power. Magic is five percent talent and ninety-five percent hard work and practice. So let's go through these core skills briefly so that you can assess how you are doing for yourself, and also so that you can gain advice, pointers, and a horizon.

Divination

The method of divination used is tarot, and we are using the Rider Waite deck. By now you will have learned various layouts and been set different tasks using tarot. I am sure many of you will have hit problems, usually to do with not understanding the answers you were given. Learning a language takes time, and like all new languages working simply with the vocabulary as a toddler does is the best way to become fluent. Also, working with the Rider Waite deck is a horrible drag as it is not a great deck, but there are reasons why as an Apprentice, you need to work with it. By the end of the Apprentice section you will be able to toss it into the bin if you want to.

This is why, for early tarot readers, I discourage the tarot books that go into the deep philosophical and esoteric meanings and symbolism of the tarot. Tarot then becomes an obtuse language or code that needs to be cracked, and this approach is often the reason why many magicians, even after ten years of study, cannot get a straightforward answer from tarot readings. They may be able to tell you the deepest symbolism in a card, but will not be able to do a straightforward reading to identify a being they are working with. To this end, it is better to have a tarot book that gives a brief outline of each card plus divination key words/meanings: a basic ABC that can then be built upon to fluency.

Once you have a basic fluency in readings, then is the time to study the more in-depth obscurities of the cards. Think of this in terms of learning mathematics: you do not teach a beginner complex mathematical formulas; rather you start with basic addition, subtraction, fractions, basic algebra, etc. This allows their thinking process to develop in a specialised way while teaching them the basic structure of the vocabulary.

The other thing you may have now come up against is the issue of clarity with your questions. If you use vague, emotive questions, you will not get a straight answer. By now you should have the basic skills to be able to step aside of your normal way of thinking and look at your questions objectively. This is a really crucial step in magic: can you step away from your usual thinking pattern and look at your actions, questions, thoughts, emotions, and beliefs in an objective way? By approaching tarot this way you are not only learning tarot skills; you are learning skills of analysis. Remember; work with a Rider Waite deck until the end of the Apprentice section and **always** keep records of readings. Either write them down/draw them out or photograph them.

Now is the time to go back to some of your early notes on readings from the first few modules and see if you would now read them differently? Always in readings, keep it simple, look at the obvious (pictures), and don't try to analyse too deeply. If you get stuck, look at the answer in a poetic sense using the card imagery and key words. And practise divination regularly, lots and lots of practice whenever you have the opportunity. If you have only occasionally done readings so far, you are not pulling your weight in training. Stop whining about it and get to it! Divination skill is like muscle – you have to keep working it for it to develop.

Inner Senses

Inner senses are something you should be working quite a lot with by now. Again these skills vary enormously from person to person, but with work even the least sensitive person can pick up on things. Try to work them at every opportunity by touching things, going places, being near people, pulling away from crowds, and seeing the difference. Every so often throughout your magical life, revisit the inner senses exercises you did in Module I. This is a skill you have to *live* rather than just use occasionally: you are learning to live a magical life as opposed to doing magic on the weekends. As far as the accuracy of your inner senses goes you will likely have more misses than hits; but don't worry about that, you are practising in order to develop. And develop you most certainly will if you work at it. With inner senses it is about learning how to listen to how your body, emotions, and energy changes when you are in certain situations. Learn to listen to your own quiet inner voice.

Visionary skills

With the visionary skills you will have by now figured out whether you are a *visual person* or a *senses person*. Not everyone has visual skills when working in vision; sometimes the person gets the information in other ways, through sensing, for example. If at this stage of the training you are still struggling with visual skills, practise by putting something on the table in front of you, closing your eyes, then using your imagination to visualise whatever is on the table before you. You can practise this skill at work: close your eyes for a moment and just imagine what the room looks like. Use your imagination to visualise what is on your desk/workstation, then open your eyes again. Do this in short bursts when you have a few minutes or even just a minute of spare time. Instead of reaching for social media during a brief break, close your eyes and do this simple exercise. It will prime your imagination to work your visualisation skills better.

If by now you have good visualisation skills but poor senses, then when you work in vision pay attention to how you feel. Does your sense of self shift? Do your emotions shift slightly? Do you feel ease or unease? Paying attention to these subtle shifts in feelings with help your inner senses develop. Do the same at work: if you feel a small shift in your sense of well-being, look around to see if something has caused that.

Has someone come into your space? Is there a shift in the mood of the people around you? Has something just landed on your desk?

These skills develop by paying attention to your own subtle shifts, and also by daydreaming. Daydreaming is something that all kids once did out of sheer boredom, but these days children are inundated with constant stimulation and methods of boredom avoidance, which stops the use of the imagination. Are you constantly filling your time with stimulation and boredom avoidance? If so, you need to adjust to give your imagination time to wander and amuse you.

Ritual skills

Whereas inner senses, visionary skills, and divination are about gaining information, ritual skills are about self-organisation and creating patterns for energy to flow through. If you find that when doing rituals you want to add in little bits, or dress them up a bit, then reel in that temptation: good ritual skills are about self-discipline, order, and accurate, repetitive actions. This is your focusing skill: if you struggle with the order of ritual, you can practise that skill outside of the ritual setting. If you are untidy or slightly chaotic, set yourself a task to have one area of your life that is kept in order. This could be as simple as keeping order in your wardrobe or bedroom, or organising your computer or paperwork. Whatever it is, pick an area of your life and focus on creating order, habit, and routine.

2. Understanding of magic

When most people step into magic or magical training they assume that the specific rituals, grades, incantations, evocations *are* the magic. This is not really true. They are the *filter* that the magic flows through. The magic itself is less defined, less organised, and more natural. The magical systems (Golden Dawn, Goetia, etc.) give a structure for the magic to flow through. This is why you are not learning a system: you are learning the forces and dynamics of the magic itself so that you can then apply it and draw upon it to work with any system. Magic itself is part of creation, part of nature, and as such will flow into anything that has the right filters to allow it through. Never mistake the filter for the magic itself. What you are learning is how to interface fully with magic: how you then apply it is up to you. You can either stay with the freer form you are learning in this course, or you can apply what you have learned to a specific system. Whatever you do, always make sure you know and understand what you are doing and what you are working with.

3. Operational methods

Ritual development

In your ritual practice you will have noticed that in the early modules you were introduced to some ritual patterns (Pentagram, for example) and told "this is it, work with it." And then in later modules it is adjusted, built upon, or cast aside in favour of a different pattern. This is an important dynamic in magic that is often misunderstood, and in certain systems that misunderstanding can result in a beginner exercise being used as a dogmatic 'must always do' ritual; the *Lesser Banishing Ritual of the Pentagram* from the Golden Dawn, for example.

When you learn a ritual pattern it must be 'in the now' for the power to slowly build within you. This means that when you learn it, you think that you are learning a finished product, so to speak. This enables you to immerse yourself within that pattern and draw everything you need to learn from it. If you approach it from the early stages as a simple stepping stone, knowing that something stronger is coming in the future, you will not gain everything you need from that pattern.

This is a dynamic that runs throughout magical practice: you deal with the learning in front of you as if it was the total end product, the complete, full-powered ritual. As the course progresses you will notice this dynamic over and over again. When you do spot it, do not try to second-guess where it is going. Simply work with what is in front of you and immerse yourself within it: this will enable the pattern to unfold at a deep level over time, and it will be a solid brick in your magical structure. As an adept you may go back to some of these early rituals, and then you will truly see the power behind the exercise. But until that point don't try to second-guess where a ritual is going. For example, the Anchor ritual for now is your 'go to' ritual for grounding, tuning, and preparing. It has grown out of your earlier ritual exercises and sits upon those experiences. Know that it will not always be your key ritual, but for now you must treat it as if it will be.

This is also tied into the mystery behind time, time-jumping, and the stretching of time for the magician. Don't always be looking for the next bigger, stronger ritual; rather give your full attention to what is directly in front of you. That work in the now affects both the past and future of your path.

Self-responsibility

In many of the lessons you were introduced to something and told "from now on, include this in your practice." Often these new inclusions are not mentioned again in the lessons. This is to ensure that you pay attention in the lessons and are willing and able to take that information and include it in your practice without further prompting, which in turn is training your self-responsibility in your own magical management. This is partly why casually skipping through the lessons will not work: often key things are mentioned once in the text with a prompt for you to carry it on for yourself, then never mentioned again. If someone browses through the lessons, cherry-picks what work they want to do and ignores the rest, they will miss these subtle prompts and keys. This in turn protects the work and protects the casual browser.

Everything in this course, from the smallest thing to the biggest thing, rests on something else. Because magical work is experiential it cannot in truth be taught by bullet points. This means that a magician must read through everything, take every hint, and work every exercise. I purposely do not shorten things or make them obvious to a casual eye: those who pay attention to detail will build as solid magicians, and the 'pickers and dippers' will be filtered out by their own unwillingness to take the time to read, digest, and work. So be aware that no one is holding your hand. No one is spoon-feeding you. You are expected to pick up every detail, to include the new elements for yourself, and adjust your work accordingly, then decide what is suitable for your own practice and what needs to be rethought as an individual.

By now you should have notebooks/journals for the different modules, and also computer logs, essays, etc. These are your body of reference for you to refer back to in the future, and I can guarantee you that they will become very useful in the years ahead. But they also serve a specific purpose for those magicians who wish to enter into the Quareia mentoring scheme while ever it is still functioning.

But most important of all, the keeping of the journals, essays, readings and notes will become your future teacher; *I cannot stress enough how important this is for a developing magician.* To this day I still keep notes and often look back on very old ones: I learn as much from this process as I do from exploration. And throughout history, the notes of a magician were treated like the gold that they are as they are the results of decades of self training and work. What you didn't understand in a vision you did maybe two years ago, will at some point become very important to you, and being able to look back over your research and work will be a major key for moving forward. This is essentially what true Grimoires were.

Remember, the journals themselves do not need to be flashy. I used old schoolbooks, I have spider handwriting (arthritis in my hands), and my diagrams look like those of a baboon on hallucinogens. The key is that you are using your hands in communication to convey steps of power. Most magicians do not get this dynamic; it passes them by. But the power of infusing an image, written word, or sigil comes in part from your ability to hand-write the transmission of power via communication.

Organise your time but also be flexible: a lot of the practical work in the lessons has repeat exercises to be done with regularity. This is all well and good if you have a simple, straightforward life, which in reality few of us have. The key is to work within your own schedule, with what works for you, and around your responsibilities. I present a framework, and I have to do it in a way that will translate for many different types of lifestyles, cultures, and age-groups. So it will fit exactly with some, and not with many. I understand this, and what I want from you in this training is for you to self-organise and bend the training to fit how you live.

This does not mean skipping the work because you want to spend hours slobbed out in front of a TV; it means that if you have kids, variable work patterns, a crowded household, or you travel a great deal, then use your brains to work out a way to do the exercises that fits within that life pattern. There is a lot of wiggle room in the work if you look closely, and there are also things in the lessons that are not pointed out to you with a big stick, but are there as tools that can be adjusted if you pay attention (the cloth shield for example can be worked with as a portable travel temple just by itself).

Too much magical training these days is spoon-fed to the student, with every single action carefully pointed out in big letters, to ensure that everyone gets it. While this is nice and inclusive it does not train a thinking mind, nor establish independent learning skills, both of which are vital in successful magic. So pay attention!

4. WHAT TO DO IF YOU REACH DIFFICULTIES IN YOUR STUDIES

Everyone will reach a wall in their training, at every level, and this is just normal. Finding things too hard, or feeling like you are restricted, or that you are banging your head against a wall are common situations in any true art training, and it signals that you are on the cusp of a breakthrough. The key to working with that situation is to tread water: keep working slowly, one foot in front of the other, and when in doubt wait, practise, but don't push against the barrier.

From an inner perspective this time is about consolidation and the *test of Saturn:* this is where you are tested to see if you really have the focus and mettle for magic. Can you keep working when you are in a slump or hitting a barrier? This is where real discipline comes in. And that discipline tests you to see if you are capable of handling the larger amount of power and energy that lies beyond the barrier. I always call this time 'waiting at the wall': where you cease trying to push forward, and instead keep practising what you already know in order to refine, deepen, and strengthen your technique and your inner fortitude.

There will also be times when the 'inner weather' of a destructive tide is just too destructive to try and do any magical work at that time. During such a period, step back from your training and put it on pause. Do mundane things like work on your fitness, organise your living space, go out in nature for walks if you can, read up on history, or just rest.

When all the energies within and around you have consolidated into a solid pattern, then the barrier lifts and you leap forward again. If you have ever studied a powerful, physical technique you will recognise what I am talking about. I have hit the wall a few times in magic and many times during my ballet training, and also in life in general. At first I used to thrash against it and even consider giving up, but eventually I learned to wait, practise, and at last the wall would crumble away and I would be plunged into a new round of learning.

5. The inner contacts and keys

By now, whether you are aware of it or not, you will have inner contacts who are in your orbit and working with or alongside you, or in the background. This triggers a dynamic in magical training whereby you are shown things or experience things that are not written about in the course, and sometimes not written about anywhere. Again, this is a normal part of magical development. A teacher or course only shows you sixty percent of the work. The other forty percent comes from your own breakthroughs, which are usually helped along by the inner contacts around you. This can translate into seeing something in vision or finding yourself in a certain place in vision, or suddenly 'knowing something.' It has many different ways of manifesting, depending upon the individual.

When this happens treat it as normal and write it all down, every last detail, regardless of whether or not it makes sense to you. This is the 'passing of inner keys,' and is a hallmark of real training. I or the other Quareia initiates or adepts will point out only so much to you, but there are also many things we will not mention and you will not be taught. This is to allow you to find them for yourself. Remember, this is a lone study as you are learning magic in a very old way.

6. *Task:* Review

Think back over the lessons you have done so far. Were there some that you didn't give much time to, or thought they were useless, or lessons that you found particularly hard? Just look over them and your notes. Think about what was hard, what you didn't get, what you found easy, and what you did get. Think about the experiments and research you have done, and what helped you and what confused you more. List what you think you need to practise more or spend more time on, and list what you think you have understood and absorbed. From there you will be able to self-assess your own strengths and weaknesses. This is a good exercise to do and is worth spending some weeks on, as it will teach you to look at your own work and development with emotional distance. Learn to look for your own weaknesses and strengths, identify your weaknesses, and think about what you need to do to strengthen them. There is no fail or pass with this – no one is testing you. Everyone develops in their own way. Being able to self-assess honestly, without fear of failure, and without grandstanding or ego, is a golden skill for magicians.

Write up a short assessment of where you feel you are at in terms of training, what you need to do more work on, what study you feel you need to return to, and what you feel you have learned so far. What has changed for you? Also ask yourself at this stage: why are you doing magic?

Do this assessment on computer, but also print out a copy and place it with your journals.

Appendix A

Chapters Extracted from
Magical Healing
A Health Survival Guide for Magicians and Healers

Disclaimer

This book is intended to inform and compliment. It is not a replacement or alternative for medical treatment by a healthcare professional.

The medical information in this book is not advice and should not be treated as such.

You must not rely on the information in this book as an alternative to seeking medical advice from your doctor or other professional healthcare provider. If you have any specific questions about any medical matter, you should consult your doctor or other professional healthcare provider. If you think you may be suffering from any medical condition, you should seek immediate medical attention.

You should never delay seeking medical advice, disregard medical advice or discontinue medical treatment because of information presented in this book.

The author makes no representations or warranties in relation to the medical information presented in this book.

Introduction

When I wrote the book *The Magic of the North Gate*, I started to broach the subject of the relationship between the body and magic. I offered general advice to the magician, along with various methods and techniques for tending to the magician's body. Since that time, I have been swamped with letters, emails and requests for a more in-depth look at the issues surrounding a magician and his or her health – hence this book.

Throughout these chapters we will look at the relationship between magic and bodily health, and how the path of magic and the path of body awareness are inextricably linked. We will also look at specific healing modalities, magical impacts on health, consciousness of the body and techniques to maintain body strength. The techniques, ideas and suggestions presented in this book are designed to support you in your magical practice and also to compliment your regular health care provided by your doctor.

When I began to work more powerfully within the sphere of magic I became aware of my body and how it struggled against the strains I was inflicting upon it. I was also aware of how magic strengthened many things within me; a bittersweet relationship. That set me upon a road of deep discovery in terms of magic and the body, which eventually led me to realise that many prominent magicians in the past had also made this powerful connection between magic, body and health. Dion Fortune and her partner Dr Penry Evans were fascinated by this weave of power between body and magic, and Franz Bardon, the Czech adept, also understood the necessity for healing, magic and energetic body awareness to go hand in hand.

In today's world where everything is compartmentalised, this wisdom of the need for a wide breadth of knowledge in the magician is sadly falling by the wayside. Every magician who works with power will come up against a barrier of body and health issues at some point. Hopefully this book will help the magician make solid choices and become responsible for their own energy, health and wellbeing. It will also expose the harsh truth that magic can be a struggle for both body and soul. In today's bullshit world of the New Age movement where everything is always light, fluffy and glowing with health, a reality check is sorely needed.

It is also worth mentioning at this point that I am neither a doctor, nor a qualified health professional. A qualified doctor or health professional should always be your first port of call if you become sick.

The information provided in this book comes from direct experience gained from experimentation, informal study with health professionals, my own educational background, and years of learning, trial and error. I have struggled with a variety of health issues over the years; some are genetic or inherited illnesses, some are the direct result of magic (and my own stupidity), and some were matters of circumstance, accident and disease. Throughout all of these I have endeavoured to find my own solutions where I could, develop my own coping mechanisms, and to learn as much as I can.

This book is the result of my successes and failures. I write it for those coming up behind me on the magical ladder of learning as well as those alongside me who missed this rung. Truly, if I had this book in my hands when I was in my twenties and thirties, I would have avoided a lot of suffering and struggle. If I can help other magicians avoid that same struggle, even in the smallest way, then this book will have been time well spent. Many young magicians never give their bodies a second thought. In their twenties they are full of vitality, health and vigour; health is something for the doctor to worry about as they scour the latest goatskin-bound grimoire looking for another obscure ritual to inflict upon the world. And for many, that total disconnect will continue throughout their adult lives until they hit their forties or fifties, at which point things begin to go badly wrong.

Some magicians become aware early on that the more powerful the magic the bigger the impact on the body, yet they will still ignore the warning signs that their body desperately sends out. A few will get the message and begin to look for ways to maintain their bodies, to lessen impacts, and to treat the body with more respect when it does succumb to illnesses or injuries. This is not a medical or 'health' guide book. Rather, it is a magical approach to health, disease and injury, and it exposes the many interconnected dynamics between the body, soul, energy and magic that we so often blithely ignore.

Our bodies and their reactions are truly unique. While some illnesses have specific symptomatic patterns, others do not and these continue to confound doctors. When you do magic, particularly visionary magic, the symptomatic picture that the body presents when ill often changes: the body shifts how it responds to invaders, imbalances and impacts. Magic does not make you sick *per se*, but not tending to your body and not approaching your magic wisely can eventually make you weak and ill.

So if you are intent on delving deeper and deeper into magic or you are already there up to your knees in power and sporting a really bad headache, it might be worth taking the time to learn more about the body's relationship with magic. To do that, you need to know your own body, how it functions and how it reacts. It is not necessary to learn full human biology, anatomy and physiology, etc., but if you do have those under your belt then they will be useful. I learned these subjects in my late teens and early twenties as part of my training to become a ballet teacher. It served me well in ballet, but even better in magic!

If you want to flourish as an adept it is important to learn a good solid healing modality, and more than one if possible. Through learning a specific form of healing you will also learn about the body and the various ways of approaching its care and upkeep. Taking the time to study, experiment and practise a healing modality not only serves you as a magician, it also serves those around you.

Do not take the advice in this book as an alternative to seeking out medical help: often we need the care and expertise that the medical profession can offer us. Rather, approach this book as a resource that a magician can use to actively engage in their own healing alongside allopathic medical treatment.

It has become fashionable in magical circles to reject all that medicine has to offer: that is true folly. Mainstream medicine does not have all the answers and probably never will, but it does have some pretty awesome aspects and can come in very handy. There are times for mainstream medicine, times for alternative healing and times to use both. Without mainstream medicine, I would not be alive to write this book. In fact I would not have written any books: since my childhood a combination of surgery, medicines and medical care has kept me alive and on my feet. Without hospitals I would have died at the age of ten when my appendix ruptured.

Similarly when I contracted Scarlet Fever, without antibiotic treatment I would not have survived. Throughout my life I have struggled with many illnesses and accidents that have taken me close to death. Many of them were treated with mainstream medicine along with alternative treatments to patch me up afterwards.

On the other hand, magical techniques and alternative therapies have saved my ass when medicine could not. So the moral of the story, and the purpose of this book, is to give you a wider and more grounded understanding of how to navigate through your magical life in a flexible, intelligent and informed way. Magic in its full power changes the goal posts when it comes to our bodies, and a major skill in magic is to know how to react and adapt when your body is under strain.

Do not shun any healing possibility out of an ignorant following of current popular opinion. Nor is it wise to follow any 'magic cure' out of faith, wishful thinking or new age glamour. Educate yourself. Learn how your own body works, and which energy dynamics in magic affect you and which do not. And most importantly of all, listen to your body, use your common sense and take responsibility for yourself.

Chapter 1

Knowing your body: part 1

1. What you need to know about engines

As a magician, your greatest and most precious tool is your own body. If this does not operate properly or is uncared for, then your magic has no foundation to rest upon. The more power you work with, the more important it is to respect your body and attend properly to its needs.

Studying detailed human biology is not necessary, but knowing how your body works in simple terms is very important. You need to know how it processes energy, how its structure is upheld, and how it regulates itself. 'Power in,' 'power maintained' and 'power out': those are the first basics of which you need a rudimentary understanding.

- 'Power in' is the diet, all incoming energies, and all emotions.
- 'Power maintained' is the job of the endocrine system, a delicate structure that is often disrupted by magic.
- 'Power out' is what is expressed through the digestive system, skin, fluids and magical actions.

These are all directly affected for both good and bad by magic; hence it is important to understand them. But remember, the combination of an individual and a specific path of magic makes for a unique picture; there is no 'one size fits all' or 'one pill heals all' scenario.

The path of tending to a magical body is a major stream of magical learning all of itself, so do not neglect it or consider it to be something that is solved with a herbal pill each morning. The body and its reactions to magical work will teach you more about magical power than any fancy grimoire can.

So let's look at a few basic mechanics. We will start with 'power in,' which is essentially anything that goes into your mouth, is put on your skin, or passes into your system via magic. The first 'power in' on that list is the one that is most overlooked: what goes into your mouth. People will talk about magical alchemy in reverent whispers but never give much thought to what they put into their mouths.

When you practise magic, what you put into your body can often have a much more reactive effect than normal and the more powerful the magic, the more of a reaction you will potentially experience. Many magicians report this phenomenon when they achieve powerful levels of working, and yet few think sensibly about it. Many find they are forced to alter their diets or lifestyles, or to give up certain foods or substances, or to otherwise change their relationship with what they put in their mouths or on their bodies.

2. 'Power in'

Food, drink, drugs, sex, magical contact and smelly perfumes

The 'power in' list is one that triggers all sorts of arrogant posturing from soap boxes. There are people who get all evangelical about a diet, a drug, a secret contact or a magical oil. But wherever there is a wonder drug or a special magical substance to be had, there is usually also a price tag, often high, that someone wants you to pay. Whenever the loud posturing is about abstinence, there is often an ego or messiah complex lurking in the background.

Any restriction or issue with a 'power in' substance should be about your individual body and its relationship to a specific magical form – it is about what the body needs and what it does not need. Morals, status or beliefs should have nothing to do with it. Magic does not need a soap box; it needs a tool box, and one that works well.

Sometimes a restriction or an altered body response is directly connected to a deity or a particular line of magical work; in such cases it is wise to take things a step at a time and be willing to be flexible. Often this sort of 'power in' issue is specific to a particular frequency of magical power and once that work is finished then the issue fades away. There will be times when a deity asks you not to eat, drink or partake of certain substances. Again this is not to do with morality; it is most often connected to how their power works in relation to human bodies. Let us look into the background of some of these issues, and how it is best to approach them in order to uphold the magical body.

3. In the beginning

The societal changes in the Western world that have happened over the last hundred or so years have also brought with them subsequent health issues, and many of those issues trace back to diet. Food has moved from being a necessary fuel to being a pastime, a drug, and a substance of indulgence. This is not a new thing for humanity, but it has become far more widespread and normalised since the industrial revolution, before which it was a preserve only of the rich and powerful. Add to that the way food has been chemically and genetically modified over the last few decades, and we have a potential health time-bomb waiting to go off.

Most babies these days are bottle-fed from birth. They are given weaning foods very early on, and are introduced to chemicals and foods long before their bodies are ready to cope with them. As a net result, babies who are sensitive or have inherited a tendency to develop autoimmune issues are being groomed for a life of ill health from birth. Dairy and grains are both major triggers for intestinal imbalances in vulnerable babies, as is the modern lack of bacterial exposure during birth which would normally prime the infant's immune system and digestion in a balanced way. What has this got to do with magic? Everything.

When a magician begins to work with inner or ritual power, the body will make use of that inflow of power to address its own problems. That is the first issue. The second issue is that when power and beings flow from the inner worlds to the outer worlds and pass through or around the magician, the immune system will see them as potential invaders, and this often sets off a small immune reaction.

If the magician has any underlying problems with their immune system these will be triggered, and that will create a series of reactions in the body. Stillness/Void meditation and yoga are two things that will help to lessen this reaction and allow the body to get used to such power without reacting as if it is under attack.

But if the magician was exposed as a baby to foods that affected their intestinal bacteria and immune responses, then that pattern of reaction will already be deeply embedded in their body. The result will be an 'inflammatory flare' within the magician. The older the magician, the more likely such a flare will occur.

This very early exposure to dairy and grains is important to keep in mind when looking for healing and stabilising modalities as a magical tool. The more potential for magic a person is born with, the more there is potential for their body to be sensitive and reactive.

Some of the most useful healing and health support modalities that a magician can use (for example Chinese medicine, homeopathy and herbs) work from the premise that their patient was breast-fed, and usually exclusively for at least the first year of their life. That is often no longer the case. We are living in a world where a new baby is immediately exposed to substances, chemicals, vaccines and foods that its little body was not designed to cope with. This deep shift is changing how our immune systems operate; in turn we must adapt how we treat our bodies.

So if you are a practitioner of acupuncture, herbs, homeopathy, etc., it is helpful to understand that what would have easily rebalanced someone one hundred years ago will not work in quite the same way today. You do not need to abandon the healing modality, but it is wise to understand that some people's systems have been damaged from birth and their immune systems have adapted around that. To compensate, the treatments also need to adapt. You may not always be able to arrive at a still point of health, but you can help the altered body to be the best that it possibly can be within the circumstances.

The first step in supporting a modern body is to pay attention to its unique nutritional needs. There are many books, blogs and courses that teach fad diets or have general food advice. The one fall-down is that no two bodies are exactly alike, and this is particularly true of magical bodies. The more you work with magic, the more unique your body's needs become. The key is learning to listen to your body, to observe, to pay attention and to use your common sense. But there are some general snippets of information regarding magic and food that can be useful. The following section is based upon my own personal experiences (which may be very different to yours) and from treating other magicians over long periods of time.

4. Food and drink

The first thing to be aware of is that the body is constantly changing and renewing itself. A person's immune system shifts and changes over the years, and for a magician that will be all the more apparent. So what will be fine for you in your twenties will not be fine in your late thirties or forties. Things that were not good for your body in your thirties become fine in your fifties... And so on. The key to working with fluctuating patterns like these is the same valuable key we find everywhere in magic: pay attention. Nothing stays the same: the body and mind are immensely dynamic and you truly have to be on the ball to keep up with them. And remember, the more you are involved in magic, the more dynamic the changes become. Let's look first at the foods that create the most reactions, for both good and bad.

5. Carbohydrates

Carbs are your fuel. When you have finished a round of heavy magic, the first thing the body screams for is fuel. A wise magician neither fully indulges the body nor starves it after a magical working: either response will prime the body for problems. The fuel intake needs to be enough to ground the magician and replenish their body's stores of energy without overfeeding it.

In truth, the body is screaming for inner as well as outer energy, so you must attend to both rather than giving it only one fuel source. Inner regeneration comes from sleep, meditation, and from cutting all inner contact. That is easily achieved by doing something which has no inner interaction: something that is passive like watching TV or reading a trashy (non-magical) novel or best of all going for a walk in nature or simply lying in the garden.

The outer fuel should be a light intake of carbohydrate. This is where the first hurdle of immune response should be addressed. Certain carbohydrates will trigger an immune response in a body that has been primed from youth to react to them. The biggest culprit, for those who are sensitive, is grains. If you are not sensitive, then any good quality organic grain will suffice. If you are unfortunate enough to be grain- or gluten-sensitive, then look to root carbs like potatoes. And I mean real potatoes, not the reconstituted mush reshaped into fries and sold in frozen packs or at fast food outlets.

How do you know if you are sensitive to grains? Do you have digestion problems? IBS? Do you have low or high abdominal pain a couple of hours after eating? Do you get brain fog after eating? An easy way to check (and I use the word 'easy' in the loosest possible sense) is to stop eating all grains for a couple of months. If your symptoms settle down, then grains or gluten were at the root of the issue. Reintroducing non-gluten grains first will either confirm or rule out gluten sensitivity. Grains and derivative substances are used to thicken everything from yogurt to stock cubes, so if you are grain-sensitive, you will need to read the labels.

The key is to pay attention, listen to your body and have enough self-discipline to be able to stop eating or drinking something that is ultimately poisonous to your specific body. Discipline is all part of the magical path.

Sugar is a substance that also gets lumped in under the heading of carbohydrates, but it is processed in a slightly different way by the body. It has become the evil aunt of the food groups, but ordinary sugar (the best is unrefined molasses sugar) is of no real harm unless you are well on your way to becoming diabetic, or you also eat a lot of carbs. The body needs a chunk of sugar each day to keep the brain ticking over, most of which it gains from the eating of grains, roots, fruits, and veggies. Sugar in sensible amounts is not evil, and there have been times when my body has really needed it after a heavy round of magic. Like all these things, you have to listen to your body and use your common sense, as everyone is slightly different.

6. Proteins

The way we gain our protein is an issue that is heavily entwined with religious and magical thinking. Some paths and religions demand we eat no animal flesh; others have particular meats that are taboo. These restrictions are often connected either with the worship of a specific deity or philosophy, or to the genetic health issues of a particular group of people.

If you choose to be vegetarian for ethical or health reasons, then it is important to be aware that certain types of magical work will be much harder on your body, and also that certain streams of magic will be far more accessible to you. Depending on how your individual body copes with a meat-free diet, it would be wise to pay very close attention to which areas of magical practice impact you the most, and either avoid them or work around them.

Similarly if you are not willing to go without meat for certain lengths of time, other areas of magic will be limited for you or may be difficult or dangerous to practise. To operate in a wide spectrum of magic requires mutability and a willingness to adapt: that is the first and most important key to staying in one piece over many years of working in the magical inner worlds.

I have been vegan, vegetarian and carnivore, and each switch in my diet was due to my magical practice and health. It also seemed to have a strong correlation to the land power of the specific area where I was living at the time.

The first thing you should do around the protein issue is to step back from all the philosophies and taboos and look at it from your perspective as a magician. The questions you need to ask yourself are: What does your body need (rather than want)? What demands do magical acts put on your particular body? What land are you living on and what are the land spirits like? What deity are you working with? And finally, what specific inner realms are you working with magically? Let's look at these questions one at a time.

Some bodies do not do well with meat. Some do not do well without meat. And there is a whole range of in-betweens. It is important to know your own body, and how it reacts to things. Those reactions will come from a variety of sources: your genetic make up, your childhood upbringing, the land you live on, any conditions you have, etc. Finding out how your body operates normally, outside of magic, will give you a baseline from which you will be able to understand better the various strains and impacts that different types of magic have on your body. The differences are most obvious when it comes to protein intake.

One word of practical caution though – if you are vegan or spending some time being vegan, ensure that you have a full intake of the recommended daily amount of iodine (usually through vegan vitamins). In the USA the salt has added iodine, so it is not so much of an issue. But in other countries a vegan has no source of iodine, and iodine keeps the thyroid functioning normally. Magicians often put their thyroids under strain with magic, so it is wise to ensure you get a proper dose each day (and no more than the daily recommended amount of 150mcg). It is important to understand that religions and philosophies that practise vegetarianism often originated in warm countries where lots of non-animal protein sources were readily available, whereas religions that include meat as a part of their pattern often emerged out of colder climates. We are more racially mixed than our ancestors, we have a wealth of food available, and we are more mobile, so climate and food source availability are not such issues for us.

But the inherited resonances are still within us and they need to be taken into consideration. Some body types just do not do well with certain types of protein, whereas others can eat anything that runs. Find out which proteins feed you and which do not, it is that simple. Forget any other consideration at this point: it is important to know what your needs are so that you can work around them if you have to, such as having to switch diets for magical reasons.

The land that you live on is a major component in the decision of what to eat and what not to eat. As a magician, the land you live on, the land you do magic on, and the land beings that are around you all have a direct influence on what you should eat. The reasons for this are many and varied.

Over the years I have noticed that eating meat on certain lands is needful, whereas when living in other areas eating meat or certain meats causes aggravation. Some land beings cannot see you if you do not eat meat and others will not go near you if you do. Some inner realms are more easily accessed and worked with if you are vegan; other inner realms are downright dangerous if you are not grounded with meat. Over the years I have changed diets back and forth according to what land I lived on, what magical work I was doing, and so forth.

As a magician it is wise to be willing to bend and flex, to be mutable and not to cling to philosophies or ways of thinking that are inappropriate for the path you are walking through life. The key is always within yourself, not in any outside information: your body will tell you if you listen to it.

Sometimes you will find that your body tunes in to a specific magical or religious taboo that involves food, particularly if you are working within a specific religious or magical stream. For example, I cannot eat pork. It makes me sick and makes me feel strange. I do not know why, only that it does. Similarly I cannot eat shellfish, actually I cannot stand even to be around shellfish, I find it repulsive. I do not eat diary, so I do not mix dairy and meats. I had not really thought about this (because I can be incredibly dumb at times) until a Rabbi friend of mine jokingly pointed out that I lived closer to Kosher than some of his family. Whether that is connected with my work in Kabbalah or it is just a coincidence, I don't know.

The more you listen to your body, the more you will hear it speak. If something makes you feel ill, do not immediately reach for the drugs; instead listen to what your body is trying to say to you and find out what is upsetting it.

Specific deities and their demands are another major component in the protein issue. In magic we do not worship a deity; that is the role of religion, not magic. But we do work respectfully with them, sometimes exclusively and intensely. In that tight working relationship, there is sometimes a need to adjust the diet in order to work in more depth with a specific deity power. The reasons for these dietary restrictions or additions has very much to do with how the power of that deity operates, and how your body's energy dovetails with theirs to create a harmonic and balanced power grid that can then be worked with. Sometimes you may well face restrictions that have little to do with any known taboos in connection to that deity; they could instead be specifically related to your body, the land you live on, and how your power operates in conjunction with the deity.

So for example, during the many years I spent working with the goddesses Kali and Durga, I could not eat any animal substance. Once that round of work was over, I was able to eat meat again. Do not assume that what books say about a deity and diet restrictions will be true for you: you must discover for yourself what the appropriate dietary and power relationship is between you and the powers with which you are working. But on the other hand, if the deity demands you become vegetarian while you work with them, and you ignore it and convince yourself it does not apply to you, then you may be in for a major body shock. I can tell you that sometimes these restrictions, be they traditional or individual to you, are there for a damn good reason and it has to do with your body's integrity within the sphere of magic.

7. Drugs, medicines and alcohol

Any substance that affects your consciousness, your brain, or your body's energy processing system is going to affect how you operate within magic, sometimes for the better and sometimes for the worse. Your body is a filter for magical power, so any issues with that filter are going to affect both the flow of magic and the integrity of the body it passes through.

APPENDIX A – MAGICAL HEALING

The first key is to understand how these substances act within the body and how that interaction in turn affects magic. It is also very important to understand how certain beings involved in the flow of power and magic can potentially interact with your body and access your stores of energy when your filters are out of balance.

These substances are entangled with major controversies in our societies, and arguments are constantly being bandied back and forth about ethics versus freedom of choice, and individual versus collective health. However, the wider debate regarding the use of these substances is of no individual concern to the magician: how your body reacts and how your magic works is what is important.

The following list explores different types of substances and the possible effects they may have on your body, your magical actions, and the subsequent interactions with the beings around you. We will also look at reasons for taking these substances, and how those reasons can have a direct affect upon the magicians' life and work.

If a magician finds that they have to take a certain substance, for whatever reason, then it is important to know how it could affect their work and their body, and how to change their practice to accommodate its effects.

8. ANTIDEPRESSANTS

Drugs that alter the level and uptake of serotonin in the body are prescribed for a variety of reasons, not just for depression. Magic uses serotonin as a buffer, or I should say, the body uses serotonin, dopamine and adrenaline to protect itself against magical impact during heavy work, hence the serotonin (and dopamine) 'high' when the inner gates open and the magical work is about to commence.

The human body's neurotransmitter chemistry works rather like a team of a million skilled jugglers all taking part in one mass, interlinked juggle. If just one of them goes out of sync, the whole show will begin to spin out of control. These chemicals are found not just in our brain but throughout our bodies, and they are engaged in a very delicate act of 'keeping balance.' Some neurotransmitters have a wide-reaching effect within the body and some have very specific actions. It does not take much to knock something out of balance.

If a person is depressed, they are prescribed antidepressants. The jugglers are out of balance for some reason: adding magic into that juggling act can help or hinder the rebalancing process depending on the cause of the depression, the way the magician copes with it and the medications that are prescribed.

Everyone gets depressed at some point in their life. But if someone has repeated long-term bouts of depression (bipolar disorder, for example) then their body will not be able to withstand powerful visionary magic, and in fact such magic would aggravate their condition, often to the point of psychosis.

Knowing that there are times when your body will need time out from magic is an important factor in keeping your body strong. If you have been suffering a bout of depression and you are taking antidepressants, then choose to work *with* your body magically, not against it. You can help the antidepressant and speed up the healing process by focusing on stillness meditation and working with the Void in meditation, but nothing more than that in a visionary sense. Any other magical acts should be externalised ritual actions only, and even those should be simple maintenance rituals which do not involve any inner beings.

Some people need to take long term anti-depressants, usually because their own uptake mechanism is lacking something, or they produce too many receptors which means their body is in a constant struggle to produce the necessary serotonin for so many receptors. In such a case, once the person is stable, the medication should not have any adverse effect on their magic, and their magic should not affect them badly. Again, it always goes back to the individual – simply pay attention to your body and do what is right for you as an individual.

Remember that addressing depression is a time of healing, not of learning or work. Any magical work should be about healing and nothing more. Any ritual undertaken should just be about acknowledging the powers around you, tending deities or tending an altar: you are essentially treading water. Working with any beings, action rituals or visions at a vulnerable time like this will only weaken you more in the long term.

A positive way to be useful magically at such a time is to use your hands to make things, or organise things. Creating magical tools, paintings, icons, or shrines are outer magical actions that engage the creative process, which in turn helps the brain to engage its own healing abilities. For a magician, this is also a form of passive mediation. You are still bridging the worlds magically, but because you are not 'working' magically you tap into the inner stream of creative and regenerative power; power which will pass into your body before it goes into whatever it is you are making.

The way to do this is very simple: no magical preparation, no use of sigils, visions, utterances, nothing. Simply begin making whatever it is you are going to make with a clear intent: I am going to make a magical wand, I am going to paint whatever needs painting, etc. It does not matter how it turns out, just let it be itself. Engaging that process will speed up your healing time and you will find that your need for the antidepressant slowly drops as your body begins to regain its sense of balance.

If you insist on doing magic while depressed and on antidepressants (or herbs) the magical action will burn up what available serotonin you have, which can result in a depressive crash the day after, with an added side-order of badly aching muscles and sleep disturbances. Depending on how depleted your body is, that crash could last days or months.

The neurotransmitter dopamine is also tied in with this magical dynamic of boom and bust. When the dopamine has also been burned up and the body is depleted through magic, the magician will develop restless legs, tremors, an out of sync body clock and emotional numbness. Learn to recognise these symptoms of burnout and if any of them appear in your life, it is time to step back from magic and take time out for the body to do its healing.

There is another form of depression which has implications for magicians, and that is the type that is linked to oestrogen and testosterone levels. In late teens until about thirty years old, and later in women, the hormones are at their peak. This can give a magician access to large amounts of power if they know what they are doing. Thankfully, 99.9% of magicians below the age of thirty-five do not really know how to tap into that power in any great depth, though a hormone-inflated ego may think differently.

You will probably have reached your forties before you really learn how to connect with and handle very deep inner power, by which time your body's outer capacity to match that power will have waned. This is a natural mechanism put in place to protect the rest of the world from your own rampant stupidity.

For those of you who are reading this and are in their forties or older, look back to when you were in your twenties. Can you remember how dumb you were, magically and emotionally? How even though you thought you were wise and knowledgeable, mature and grounded, you were actually an immature idiot? I know I was. Can you remember how much emotional power you had? Surges of anger, happiness, arousal, depression – that age-group gets the full stew. Add powerful magic to the mix and watch the bombs go off!

So if you are in that age group and you are suffering from depression as well as the hormone-fuelled wild ride, remember this: it is a harsh but normal phase of life in natural magicians. Use the hormonal power to learn how to operate your body. Give it physical exercise and discipline. This will in turn get you ready to operate the power you potentially could access later in life.

The depression will lift if you put the hormonal fuel to work: dance, martial arts, sports, or hard physical labour. That in turn will get your body ready to handle magical power. A powerful, strong body can take vast amounts of inner power flowing through it. An undernourished or weakly-developed body cannot.

9. Hypnotics, opiates, alcohol, THC and medical marijuana

There will come a time in most magicians' lives when they will use these substances for one reason or another, be it surgery, stress, pain, curiosity, recreation, etc. From a magical perspective it is wise to know that the majority of magicians find these substances lower their ability to mediate power or to handle power. They also loosen the inner boundaries which are there to guide you in visionary work.

That said, with long-term use the body and spirit can learn to adjust around some of these substances, but that long-term application brings with it a whole bag of other problems for the body and spirit. If you are on one of these substances for the long term and you wish to continue visionary magic then there are a few things you should consider.

The first is that any magical work should be done when the substance is least in your system, which means just before the next dose is due.

The second thing to consider is that if you are a long-term user of one of these substances, then it is either because of addiction, illness or injury. If you have any of these conditions, then deep work in the inner worlds will only aggravate them. Working deeply in magical vision involves having large amounts of power flowing through your body, and if that body is ill or broken in some way, it is a cracked vessel as far as many types of inner power are concerned. Cracked vessels leak and fall apart; that is essentially what happens when magicians mix these types of substances with deeper work. It puts a terrible strain on your body, so keep that in mind.

Under such circumstances it is better to shift the working practice to more externalised and naturally-formed non-visionary magic. Visionary work can still be done, but it is best done very rarely, simply, and using well-trodden paths to places in the inner worlds that you know to be safe. The key is only to do what really needs doing, not what you want to do: spend the time learning and consolidating.

Be very aware that if you are on these substances, your focus is likely to be impaired and your boundaries weak, which in turn can make you vulnerable. Many magicians find that when they take such substances the visionary process will just not work. If that happens, do not fight it: it is your body's defence system kicking in to block you out of the inner worlds for your own protection. Listen to your body; it will guide you.

It can be very frustrating for a magician who wishes to work deeply in magic but also has to take medication which disrupts the process; it is wise to think very carefully about what you do to your body and mind. Here is a classic example of how these substances can affect a magician.

A couple of years ago, I had major surgery and was on morphine for quite some time. Morphine in particular can loosen the bond between a person's body and spirit in a potentially dangerous way, and particularly if that person is a visionary magician, for in such cases that bond is already fluid. While I was on morphine I did no magic at all, but every night when I was asleep I turned up in the dreams of my old students, and gave lectures on magical technique. I was completely unaware of this and only found out about it when these former students individually emailed me. Every morning I would wake up exhausted and weak, and my life force was already at a very low ebb from the surgery.

Once I had figured out what I was doing and where my energy was going, I made a talisman to 'lock' my spirit into my body so it could not go wandering off lecturing people every night. I also realised that if my own natural boundaries had become a lot more porous and I was 'leaking out,' then I was also vulnerable to lots of predatory beings who could potentially feed off of my life force.

I set up guardians to watch over my body and put on the locking talisman, and *hey presto!* the visits stopped, and I started to recover. I began to get stronger, to heal faster and to get my energy back. I guess because I was so ill, my spirit felt that I had to pass on as much as I could before I died. That is a natural reaction to a threat to one's life, but it can also speed up the dying process as it uses so much inner energy.

If similar things happen to you, rather than thinking it cool and leaving it at that, think very carefully about the consequences of such behaviour for your life force. If you are a visionary magician, then any drug that sends you into a deep uncontrolled sleep or otherwise dampens your consciousness can put you at risk.

10. Alcohol

Alcohol is in a class of its own when it comes to substances that affect magic. Alcohol has a major dampening affect on your inner boundaries, and leaves you wide open to all sorts of beings taking up residence in your space. Some magicians use it to cut a contact or to dampen down inner sight. It does both those things very effectively, but in more than very small quantities is also leaves you very vulnerable. This is the key reason why many visionary magicians find that the deeper they work in vision, the less tolerance they have for alcohol.

If you find your alcohol tolerance begins to lower (and you are not an alcoholic: lowered tolerance can also be a symptom of physical dependency), then take it as a signal from your body that your defences are going down. Under such circumstances it is wise to stop using alcohol at all.

I cannot drink more that a few mouthfuls before I feel my barriers crumbling and my inner senses decaying. In my teens I used to drink a lot, as it blocked out my ability to 'see' spirits and pick up on subtle energies. I wanted a quiet life, and I did not have the magical knowledge at that time to cope with such contact.

Eventually I realised that by shutting down my senses, I was putting myself in danger and making myself vulnerable. I stopped drinking and within a few months crossed paths with my first teacher who showed me how to handle my senses properly and to work with them magically. I had made a decision to stop hiding, and the inner worlds responded to that decision by guiding me towards someone who could help me develop and grow.

11. Visionary and hallucinogenic drugs

There is a lot of discussion in magical circles about the use of visionary drugs as a tool in magic. Most of this stems from Western interest in the use of hallucinogenic substances in tribal magic, and from the use of LSD. There are a few things to consider here when it comes to visionary magic.

The first is that if you are trying to work with visionary magic, then using these substances will degrade your work considerably. Why? Because visionary magic is about the conscious use of a technique that, when developed and applied, allows you to pass between the different inner and outer realms in a controlled and focused manner. Anything that removes that focus and control is contraindicated.

There are no shortcuts to developing visionary skills, and the use of these substances bypasses all structures, guardians and boundaries that are in place not only to guide you through the inner realms wisely, but also to protect you as you move deeper and deeper into them. Hallucinogenic substances are capable of catapulting you deep into inner spaces where powerful beings who guard life, death and the Abyss reside. Your mind has no interface with which to communicate properly with such beings; you are there without proper context, with no guardians, no guides, and often for no good reason. The chances that things can go badly wrong are huge indeed.

The more visionary magic you have done, the more chances there are for disaster to strike, usually by blowing a fuse in your mind. If you have spent a long time working in the inner worlds, your mind is already pliable. Adding a hallucinogenic chemical to the mix will push your mind deep into the inner worlds and beyond its boundary of capability.

So how come tribal magicians can work well and powerfully using these substances? Well, let's have a look from an outsider's point of view at how they operate.

When a tribal magician uses a visionary substance, whether it is to connect with beings, to heal, to attack, or to protect, they use the substance within a specific context. A tribal magician or shaman (or whatever you want to call them) works within a specific land radius, with particular spirits and beings of the land, with ancestors to which they are deeply connected, and with power spots that are close to the community that they serve. They are deeply tied to the land and its beings by nature of their blood line: generations of tribal magicians will have built up a vocabulary and circle of spirit 'relatives,' along with a deep understanding of the spirit aspects of the visionary plants that are used and worked with.

All of this comes together when a tribal magician works, not only to ensure the success of the endeavour, but to also protect and guide the magician as he or she works. And the work is always done for specific reasons that involve other members of the tribe/community, or the tribal land. Such a tribal magician will also live in a very specific way, eat in a specific way and keep constant vigil over the land, its spirits and its people. This act of service is recognised by the local spirits, which is why they are willing to work closely with the magician.

This is not to say that what tribal magicians do is all sweetness and light – they will often think nothing of killing someone with magic if they are asked to and there is good reason. Tribal cultures tend not to be too infected with the New Age syndrome of thinking that everything is love and light.

The final, most important point is that tribal magicians tend to stay in realms close to our own. They operate within the inner landscape of the land and the threshold of death, and not much beyond that. There is no need to go further: with most of the jobs that tribal magicians do, these realms suffice.

Western visionary magicians however tend to delve far more deeply into the inner realms, passing across thresholds of time, walking deep into the Inner Desert, the Abyss, the Stars, the Angelic Realm, the deep Underworld, and so on.

Once you have trained your mind to go to these places those pathways cannot be closed: any drug can place you anywhere within those realms without warning.

When Western-cultured magicians want to experiment with a tribal visionary substance, they do not think about setting, context, contact, or reason. They are generally in a place where they have little real understanding of the land and spirits around them. Most often the magician is not in direct contact with ancestors or with the spirits around them, and they are not on the land where the substance was grown. When a plant grows on the land, it does not grow in isolation: it is the sum total of all the other plants around it, the spirits around it, and the power of the land it sits upon.

The main reasons I have heard people give for taking such substances in a magical contact are things like 'exploring myself,' 'going on a vision quest,' or just general curiosity. If you are still 'exploring yourself' then you are not at a phase where deep visionary magic is appropriate. If you are 'going on a vision quest' then learn how to do it properly. There are no shortcuts and no excuses. If you want to experiment with your mind and with these substances then that is a personal choice; just don't dress it up as something that it is not.

If you are a ritual magician who does not use visionary magic and has no natural talent in that area then there is a reason to use such substances: if you need to make a direct contact with a specific being. To do this wisely and effectively there are some points to consider:

First you need to find a substance that your body can cope with and which is natural to the land on which you live. Learn as much as you can about the plant/substance, its effects on the body, its history, its mythology. The latter is the most important: the myths and legends surrounding the plant will give you clues as to which beings work with it or are accessed through it.

Then, go out onto the land where the plant grows, and sleep next to where it is growing. This is an important step: by sleeping alongside it, your deeper consciousness gets to know the spirit of the plant and the land beings around it, and they get to know you. It's about making friends with the beings that accompany the effects of the plant. This may offer you some protection when you come to work with the substance.

And most importantly of all, have a damn good reason for doing it, and by that I mean a magical reason, not a personal ego reason. That way, you are more likely to gain some form of protection when you try to contact the being you want to communicate or commune with – though such protection is not guaranteed.

If you simply decide you want to contact a demon to become a living god, use the LBRP to protect yourself and then digest a bag of mushrooms: the most that will happen is that a nearby parasite will be vastly entertained by your antics. It will have a great time telling you it is a demon and acting very 'demonic' for you while it snatches as much energy as it can from you.

Why does this happen? The inner worlds have many traps, boundaries, blocks and heavily-toothed guardians to stop idiots from gaining access to anything remotely powerful. Parasites are about the only beings likely to be connected to under such circumstances. The magician has 'an experience,' their imagination dresses the encounter in suitable 'demonic' dress, and suddenly they feel all-powerful and have become a 'god' in their own lunchtime. If they persist in this behaviour, then the draining-off of vital energy plus the damage inflicted on the brain by repeated use of such substances will result in a fragile, mentally ill egomaniac.

However, if you are a skilled, mature ritual magician with no visionary capacity whatsoever and it is imperative that you have direct contact with an angelic being, demonic being, dead person, etc., then the use of such a substance under the right conditions and done only very occasionally should have no serious magical consequences, unless the substance is toxic and poisons you: then you are screwed. Use of these substances is always a second-best option, as the contact is usually fleeting, nonsensical and hard to use, hence the importance of developing proper visionary skills if you want solid, usable contact.

If you choose to use such substances for entertainment, then that is a different matter entirely and has nothing to do with magic. In my opinion, that is down to personal choice and personal responsibility.

12. Chemical shit-storms

Last on this list of how to blow up your mind and your body are the chemical shit-storms we surround ourselves with every day. A skilled magician uses many different senses of their body and mind in their magical process, and an important and often overlooked one is the sense of smell.

A magician's sense of smell is an invaluable tool with a number of important and hugely beneficial uses. The use of plant extracts and oils, for example, became an integral part of magical practice as soon as we discovered that we could use scent as a magical tool.

As a species, our sense of smell is vital not only for our health and well-being, but also for the way it operates as an early warning system. The detection and secretion of scents and smells plays a key part in our ability to communicate, to remember, to differentiate, to threaten, and so on. But in our rush to be 'civilised,' our societies have tried to manipulate that process through the use of chemical smells to mask, attract or otherwise communicate. Modern living has convinced us that we need to use a vast array of chemicals to survive our daily life. In an average day, a person will use chemical scents or scent maskers when they bathe, wash their hair, brush their teeth, wash their clothing, clean their house, use their makeup, perfumes, colognes, deodorants, drive their cars, etc.

Even women's sanitary products and simple pleasures like toilet rolls are heavily scented these days; it has become a very difficult endeavour to move away from the chemical shit-storm surrounding us.

The effect of this vast array of chemicals, besides their very obvious health issues, is to lock down two of our most vital magical tools: our sense of smell, and our own unique scent that communicates on our behalf.

It would be wrong to think that the complex action of scents works only in the physical realm: that is not true, and it is one of the many skills within magic that is being lost over the years. One's sense of smell can detect inner connections, beings, and dangers as effectively as it can outer connections and threats, and I know from real experience that this is the case.

Magically, the sense of smell is involved in identification on both sides: inner beings can recognise us through our scent, and we can identify various types of inner beings through theirs. When a magician is surrounded by chemical scents all the time, this subtle sense is severely altered and diminished; it can take some time to re-establish the sense and build upon it.

The scents we emit also carry information about our state of health. When we are sick, the subtle scents we emit undergo changes that can be noticed by inner beings (as well as animals), and when an inner contact that we work with detects this slight change in scent, they will often warn us. For us too, when our sense of smell is unhindered by chemicals and is consciously developed, we can detect certain types of disease in other people by their scent.

A classic example is feeling slightly hostile to someone for no good reason. Sometimes this can be caused by a subtle scent the person is emitting which signals that they are diseased with infection, or even that they have a spirit parasite infestation. In this case your hostility towards them is a part of your own body's defence system, and it is trying to ensure that you do not spend enough time around them to risk becoming infected with the same disease. Another curiosity I have discovered is that spirits, beings and ghosts that we work with or are close to can create scents as a form of identification: you learn to become aware of a presence around you by the smell that they emit. Sometimes it is their own scent (like recognising the scent of a person who has died) and sometimes it is a 'signature' scent that the being has learned to present in order to connect with you. Other beings leave a scent trace as a part of their general identity, the classic example (which has become a stereotype but is nonetheless true) being the smell of sulphur when an Underworld or demonic being is present – unless of course your drains are blocked!

So how does a magician develop this sense, along with tending to their own scent? The first step is to rid your body and home of chemical shit-storms. We are told constantly through advertising that we need a vast array of chemicals in order to be presentable, clean and respectable. That is not true, and there are other less damaging ways to have a pleasant smelling house, car and body.

The ways that I have tackled this problem are as follows. For keeping a house generally clean, I use ordinary unperfumed soap in both bars and liquid form. I slowly discovered that despite what the advertisements said, the bathroom, kitchen and the rest of my home could be very well cleaned with soap and water, polished with beeswax, and nothing more. If I really have to use a product that is scented, I use it sparingly and rarely. I use unperfumed shampoo and conditioners, and I do not use deodorants: essential oils are a great alternative if one is needed.

But houses, cars and bodies do get a bit stale sometimes, even in the best conditions. For this there are a number of more natural ways to keep things smelling nice that will not interfere too much with your inner connections. One is to use natural resins or oils in a tea light diffuser. (Incense mixes and sticks are not such a good idea, as many of them contain fixatives and chemical scents.) A pure resin like frankincense (*Boswellia*) is the best form of air freshener, and as a bonus it will eject low-level parasites and other unhealthy beings from your home; a property it shares with many other pure resins.

Living like this can be tough. We are programmed these days to expect a house to be full of chemical scents, and any sort of smell like cooking, tobacco, or animals is badly frowned upon. And yet, when we work with inner beings, those are the smells they expect to find in a home; and the chemical smells we surround ourselves with today are often particularly abhorrent to ancestral contacts. For the car, just a few drops of essential oils on the dashboard will do the trick. Just choose carefully what you use: some can be soporific and that is not a good effect if you are driving! The same goes for scenting the body; if you are going out and want to smell lovely, a few drops of homemade essential oil scent is subtle, smells pleasant, does not knock out everyone around you, and does not interfere too much with magical connections. However, it is a good magical practice to learn to live without constantly covering yourself and your surroundings with added smells.

A good way to make your own magical scent is to start with a base of almond oil (not too much or it will dilute the scent) and add in two or three essential oils. Then drop a few grains of pure resin into the bottle and give it a shake. A nice mix is vetiver (*Vetiveria zizanoides*), frankincense (*Boswellia*) and opopanax (*Commiphora guidottii*) essential oils, with a few grains of frankincense dropped into the bottle.

When you are working magically, particularly in vision, it is best not to wear any oils at all, so that you learn to develop your sense of smell. It is very fashionable to wear oils while working magically, but this is a misunderstanding of how such scents should be used. Most oils and incense resins were used to clear a temple or church and only allow a specific frequency of being to enter the space. If you are working in several different realms, then resins and oils can sometimes hinder rather than help. Specific oils can attract certain types of beings and block others out, but first it is important to re-establish your own sense of smell.

Once you have finished working, it can be very useful to burn pure resins and to use oils to remove any magical residue from the space and from yourself. You can also use them just before any magical process to clear the space. If you are working as an exorcist in a space then it is a different matter altogether: using oils and resins while you work will be very helpful. Also, some deities like the smell of certain resins and oils, and if you are working directly with them an offering of the appropriate incense can earn you brownie points.

Overall it is wise as a magician to learn how to live more naturally, to develop a sensitivity to smells, and to take note of the reactions you have to certain people when you are not dowsed and surrounded by chemical scents. The longer you live in a clear environment, the more sensitive you will become to what is subtly happening around you. Slowly you will learn what type of magical actions need smells and which ones do not.

13. Summary

As a magician living in today's modern synthetic world, it can be very difficult to stay healthy, strong and sensitive without taking specific steps to alter your lifestyle. There is a great deal of pressure on people to conform to unhealthy modes of living and trying to stay healthy and centred in such an environment can be difficult. However, the payback is well worth the effort. It is also wise to ensure that you do not become obsessive or paranoid about everything around you: this requires common sense and understanding that we also have to live in this modern world. Pay attention to your body, educate yourself, and treat your body with the respect it deserves.

Chapter 2

Knowing your body: part 2

1. Checks and balances: energy in, energy out

In today's world of specialisation and compartmentalisation of our knowledge base, it is very easy to become myopic in how we view the reality of magic in our lives. We often see magic as being something 'apart;' the mad relative hidden in the attic only to be visited on special occasions and certainly not included in our everyday lives. This is a big mistake, and one that is often made both in our magical practice and our understanding.

In this chapter we will look at how everyday energy dynamics are affected by the practice of magic, and how magic affects our day-to-day interactions with the world around us. This is of particular importance for visionary magicians and those who work deeply with inner powers and energies. Just as the world around us can affect how and why we do magic, magic can also affect our daily lives, the lives of those around us, and how we operate as humans.

Magic is fuelled by power, and as the decades of magical practice roll by our bodies shift and change how they process that power. On the good side this means that as we age, we become more sensitive and responsive to the inner powers and contacts that are all around us. On the bad side, we also become more vulnerable or reactive to those energies and powers as they express themselves in our everyday lives.

For the average person who is not naturally sensitive, these shifts of energy and power go undetected for the most part, as people tend to develop natural immunities against them from an early age. This is why it can often take a long time for a young magician to learn the foundations of visionary magic: first the filters and blocks that they built in their childhood have to be dissolved.

Every human is different, and how each human responds to energies depends on a complex mix of upbringing, natural senses, health, community, religion, and so forth. There is no hard-and-fast rule, but a fairly consistent one is this: if you live a life of visionary magic, it will alter how you react to and process energy and power. For some this change is dramatic, for others less so. But every magician needs to understand how these energies work, how we react to them, how they can affect us, and how we can learn to consciously navigate a healthier, safer path through life. So what energies and powers am I talking about?

When a lot of people live in close proximity to each other, certain energy dynamics build up. How that energy expresses itself depends on the culture of the people, the land mass they live on, their spiritual coherence, their general health and their overall behaviour.

For example, in a country or area where everyone is more or less involved in the same religious or spiritual practice, a particular energetic dynamic builds up where beings, spirits, ancestors, deities, temple patterns (and so on) all interact in a constant flow of communion and energy with the population. This gives that population a sort of 'herd immunity:' protection from a whole bag-load of parasites and other unhealthy low-level beings. It does not stop them all or stop them completely, but it makes for a less friendly environment for them.

You can test this for yourself. Once you have a good level of energetic sensitivity, go to a place, country, or land mass where everyone is under the umbrella of the same religion. Although the area will have all the same day-to-day issues that any human community has, one thing will become quickly apparent: a lack of 'dirtiness' that you detect in its people, its towns and its buildings. I am not talking about everyday outer dirt, but inner energetic dirt. Places that have a long-term or ancestral spiritual base tend to be magically cleaner simply because of how they operate from an inner point of view. And this tends to happen regardless of the religion's structure or its ethics: the spiritual base blocks out certain levels of beings and energies. (As an aside, such a place will also block out access to certain inner realms that are not conducive to the dominant religious structure: doing magic in such a place is like hacking through a jungle to try and find a path.)

When that spiritual base begins to break down or fragment, inner dirt builds up and more parasitical beings move in (India is a good example). Such a state of fragmentation is what most of us live with in this modern world. This is neither good nor bad, it just is what it is; but it is important as magicians to learn how to adjust and adapt to it. In an energetically dirty city, for example, it is easier to work magically because there are fewer blocks, but it is much harder (though not impossible) to stay clean and centred.

Such challenges are all part and parcel of being a magician and a human, and this is just one example of the wide variety of energetic impacts that we as magicians need to be aware of and adapt around. Let us now look at the aspects of daily living that can affect or impact a magician energetically, and the various ways we have of dealing with them.

2. Living or working in a city

Where you live has a strong influence on how you do magic. If you live in a city you will slowly develop a natural defence against the inner parasites, beings and spirits that live around such large clusters of people. This natural defence has to be taken into consideration when you embark on a path of visionary magic: not only will you have developed a 'thicker skin' that makes working in vision harder in the initial stages, but from the moment you begin working in vision, you will potentially become very visible to every energy-eating inner being for miles around.

This is why any magical system that works with inner vision (as opposed to psychological pathworking) has pretty tight visionary structures for magicians to work through in their first few years of training. These set paths 'tune out' your visibility: you take on a different frequency which in effect makes you vanish. If they cannot detect you, they cannot eat your energies! Many magicians use banishing rituals before they begin to work. But relying on this method, which was originally intended as a simple training exercise for beginners, will obviate the deeper and more powerful protection you can build up through good working practice.

As you work through the set structures, you will begin to make connections with inner contacts, and your interactions with them will bring about various shifts in your energy. Slowly these connections will begin to form new constant protections for you, which will make it a bit safer for you to do magical work in a crowded city.

What you will find, however, is that there are areas of the inner realms where it is unwise for you to work if you are operating in a city. Those areas will vary from person to person and city to city, so as a working magician it bodes well to pay attention to the after-effects of your work. If you find yourself becoming fatigued and slightly ill after visiting a certain realm, try visiting the same place while working out in nature, away from the city where you live. If working there does not present the same problems, then you will know that your city was causing the issue. It is all about experimenting: you gain your own knowledge and wisdom by paying attention and acting accordingly.

Cities can also fluctuate between healthy and dirty, depending on which inner tides are active, what is happening in the city at the time, and what is happening to the land on which it rests. If, for example, rivers are redirected, or springs are dammed up, or burial sites are disturbed, that can change the inner health of the city, sometimes temporarily, and sometimes forever.

As always, the key is awareness: if something shifts and your work is affected, take note of the shift and ask the following questions: has something happened to the land on which the city sits? Or is something powerful happening in the inner worlds, something which most likely has nothing to do with you but is affecting your work? Or is something happening within your body? One of the important skills to develop as a magician is identifying whether the source of a shift in power is within yourself, the inner worlds, or the land around you.

If you are getting drained of energy when you work in the city, then work outside the city, out on the land, and see if that makes a difference. If it does, then it is time to work with divination to see what is happening to the city itself.

The first thing I do when I visit a city that is very dirty (if I am going to be there often) is to 'open the Void' in the city's centre. This is not a cure-all, but it does help to 'tune' the place from an inner perspective. In days past, most if not all cities and city-states had an active temple that allowed a two-way flow of power between the inner realms and the city. The level of 'tuning' the temple provided varied according to what type of temple it was, the deity worshipped there, and how clean or corrupt the priesthood was.

In more recent times in Western societies, churches, mosques, synagogues and monasteries provided this tuning by way of daily mass rituals, daily communal prayer, or the perpetual cycles of prayer that occur in monastic and convent communities. Such tuning does not directly affect how a city's humans behave, but it does level the playing fields somewhat: fewer parasites and low-level inner beings hanging around means less chance that humans are going to be manipulated into behaviour that allows a parasite to feed. The 'tuning' also helps the city's energy to keep flowing so that it does not block up, stagnate and go rancid. Think of waterways and sewers: inner energy works along similar lines.

By opening the Void and tuning it every time you go back to the city (or every day if you live there) you allow a small crack of the Void to remain open and for energy to flow back and forth freely. You cannot single-handedly 'fix' a city, but a daily or regular practice of Void meditation, bringing the stillness into the space and holding it there, allows the tuning process to begin. Soon, other beings within the land and the inner worlds will pick up on what you are doing and assist you. They will not do it *for* you, as the city was built by humans and it is therefore up to humans to clean up the mess. But if you make the effort, then they will help.

If there is a church, temple, cathedral or other place of worship in or near the city centre, then visiting it regularly, sitting quietly and meditating on the Void within the sacred space will help to amplify the effect. It does not matter what religion it is, only that it is a place that uses ritual and prayer in honour of and communion with Divinity.

The older it is the better, and this is because modern sacred buildings tend to be built using architecture that is fashionable rather than sacred and harmonic. If you want a really good example of bad modern architecture for a sacred space and you are in that part of the UK, visit Bristol's Catholic Cathedral at Clifton. If you want to know what trapped and dirty energy feels like, go and stand or sit in that place.

To feel a sacred, tuned space, go from Clifton Cathedral to the main Bristol Cathedral in the centre of town. It is like night and day. Bristol Cathedral is still properly maintained as a sacred space and it has beautiful and harmonic architecture. As a result the energy flows in and out unhindered. It is energetically and physically a very beautiful place to sit and meditate. Just be aware when you visit places like this that they are sacred spaces linked to a specific path to Divinity, and that path must be respected at all times while you are there.

3. Empathy: other people and beings

Most magicians find that the longer they do visionary magic, the more empathic their body becomes. For some this is a natural dynamic, and for others it is something that develops over time. Some magicians never develop energetic empathy, so this will not necessarily be an issue for you. Our interactions with inner beings, realms and powers develop and refine over time. Just as a child has to learn how to interact socially, spot dangers and learn from good or bad experiences, so the magician also has to learn by trial and error how to conduct themselves in the realm of magic.

Just as in everyday life we constantly learn what to do and what not to do, so too will the magician constantly refine and adapt themselves to the flows of power to which magic exposes them. And just as in our outer lives, visionary magic has some basic rules which, when followed, help us to stay safe and healthy. But there are also more complex situations that the magician must address on a case-by-case basis, and a fair number of those involve our energetic reactions to other humans, inner beings, deities, and so forth. We learn by doing, by observing, and by interacting. Direct experience, and how we evolve from such experience, will determine how we develop our own safety mechanisms.

For those who do visionary magic, natural energetic empathy is both a blessing and a curse. The blessing is that you are far more able to reach deep into the inner worlds, to read the inner patterns hidden in the outer world, to detect beings in or around people and places, and to feel illness in others. The downside is that such empathy, if it is strong, can also be very draining and distressing. I am a natural empath, and I have worked with visionary magic for decades. This has strengthened my natural empathy in ways that have caused me numerous problems, but it has also made magical work a lot easier. So it is a double edged sword.

Whenever I go somewhere very crowded, like a cinema, an airport, or a busy part of the city, I can easily become exhausted and overwhelmed by the mix of energies, moods, physical conditions, ghosts, and spirit hangers-on that I encounter. Over the years I have developed a series of coping mechanisms for this, along with making some interesting discoveries about my inner senses. The methods I describe below may or may not work for you, but it will give you a starting-point for your own experimentation should you find that you have similar problems to mine.

4. Inner alarms

The more a magician interacts with inner beings and the inner worlds, the more their inner and outer senses fuse together to become more alert and responsive. When you work regularly and in some depth with visionary magic, your 'inner' sight strengthens and begins to operate in tandem with your everyday faculties, until eventually they fuse together and become indistinguishable.

Say for example that a beautiful person walks towards you, but they appear ugly, out of sorts, or simply 'wrong'. Others do not notice this and would question your observation: they see beauty where you see 'nasty'. What is happening is that you are seeing the inner and outer person at the same time. If their 'spirit' or energy is diseased, has parasites, is unbalanced, or is just plain nasty, your inner sight will pick up on that they will look 'wrong' to you.

Alternatively, you may simply feel hostile to them for no obvious reason. In my early days of visionary work, this was the strongest presentation I got of my inner alarms going off. Occasionally I would meet someone who, although they seemed nice, balanced, etc., just did not feel 'right' to me. I would shrug off the feeling, not trusting it, and continue my interactions with them. Soon enough the odd feeling I had when I first met them would prove to have been right, and they would be revealed as unhealthy, aggressive or destructive in some way.

Like all senses, this one improves with practice, but it is also important to be able to filter it. Otherwise it is easy to become paranoid about everyone around you, and such paranoia left unchecked can be an early sign of mental illness. The line between the development of inner sight and of mental illness is a fine one, but it is nevertheless well defined.

A magician develops this inner sense in tandem with filters for it; a mentally-ill person does not. A normal person will not react to everyone around them; they will walk down a busy street barely noticing most of the people they pass. They will register only the ones who present a potential threat; a mentally-ill person will see potential threat in everyone.

A man following you on a dark night in a predatory fashion is going to put you on alert; someone simply walking past you is not. How do you learn to notice threats? By experience, social learning, maturation, and everyday living. Just as a child slowly learns from their parents, from being a part of society, from being taught and from direct experience, so the magician learns also.

Incidentally, the same mechanism that allows us to spot potential threats also allows us to also spot other magicians, priests/priestesses and mystics. Their inner light will be visible to you: they will shine, look familiar, and will most likely also recognise you.

5. Energetic boundaries

The other major skill a magician develops as a result of visionary magic is a more general energetic empathy, something which can become increasingly pronounced the more inner work the magician does. Their energetic boundaries become looser, which is part and parcel of deeper inner work.

A lot of ritual magic paths make use of daily banishing and protections. This leads to a sterile environment, and as a result the magician is not able to develop much in the way of magical contact skills. This in turn severely limits their capacity to work with any real level of power or to be sensitive to beings and contact.

This 'sterility' also creates another very serious problem: the magician never learns to differentiate between types of beings and powers, or how to adapt and behave around them. As a result, they see all inner beings other than the ones they are invoking as being the 'enemy' that is out to get them. Sadly this is becoming more and more a feature of modern magic. The rules of basic conduct in magic are more or less the same as in daily life: if you lock yourself away and never interact with people, you will never learn social skills, never learn how to tell the difference between good and bad people, and you will never fully be a part of the magical world.

The healthier way to develop as a magician is to slowly learn about the different types of energies, beings and powers, and how best to interact with them. Such learning is also important for everyday life when dealing with people: magic and daily life are part of one another they are not separate.

As you delve deeper into visionary magic, you will slowly develop a heightened level of sensitivity. You will notice that certain people drain you, and others energise you. You will start to pick up a great deal of information about someone by standing next to them, and you will find that you can accommodate them in your energy field if needed. This understanding of the plasticity of our energy fields is a key part of operating properly as a magician.

If someone is ill or parasited, they will drain off your energy. This can be halted in various ways, though it cannot always be stopped. If you are only going to be near them for a few minutes, then there is a simple visionary action that can stop it. First, focus on the Void for stillness, and from there simply visualise a hardened barrier around you. As your skills in visionary magic develop, this action moves from being a psychological visualisation to being an actual magical act. The focus on the Void gives you access to power; visualising a barrier puts that power to work.

If the person causing the energy drain is parasited or possessed by an unhealthy being living within or around them, then that being needs to know it is not going to get a dinner off of you. Mentally wafting sigils at it will work only in about 5% of instances: that language only works if the being understands it. I have found that the clearest and most effective deterrent is to make yourself as inedible and scary as possible.

To do this, after first focusing on the Void, replace that focus with a drawing-up of power from the Underworld through your feet. Once that power is in you, project a demonic mask-face filled with the power of the Underworld. These actions do take visionary skill and magical knowledge, but they scare the shit out of low-level parasites and beings. The ability to focus instantly and then to project such a power image while appearing normal on the outside is a skill in itself. This is why basic visionary exercises done daily are crucial to a magician's development: You must be able to access your power and visionary skills at a moment's notice, anywhere and under any conditions.

This sort of technique will not work against a powerful nasty being hanging around or inside a human, but such an encounter is rare. I have found over the years that if for some reason I am not capable of handling such a being, I am steered away from the encounter by inner contacts. If I do come into contact with such an entity, which has happened to me more than once, then that is a signal that it needs to be dealt with.

The best method I have developed for such encounters is to instantly connect with the Void and then call upon Divinity. I also silently call upon the angelic beings that operate on the threshold of the Void. When I am filled with power, I breathe out with the intention of breathing the pure power of the Utterance into the space around me. I then direct the breath of Utterance at the being. I have found that by doing this, angelic beings will either pull the being into the Void or 'wrap it' to disarm it. The act of using breath with Divine utterance is a passive one: I direct the power at the being in an act of mediation, acting as a bridge between the worlds. I do not direct what the power must do, only where it should go. The angelic beings will do the rest as is needed.

I never take beings out of people unless they ask. It is not the place of the magician to decide who has a relationship with what. I have two exceptions, though: if I find a being in one of my kids I dispatch it, or if a being in a person is driving them to kill, I dispatch it regardless. Such dispatching is not to be done lightly, and certainly not attempted if you do not know what you are doing. You could inadvertently end up as the new host, if you are not careful.

Bridging Divine utterance at the edge of the Void will alert inner beings to the threat, and will trigger an inner response that will unfold over time. Your magical work is to bridge unconditionally the consciousness and power needed to put that being back where it belongs, which you do simply by opening the Void and calling upon Divinity. By initiating that action, you become the catalyst for change.

There will be times in your life as a magician when you will become drained by being surrounded by lots of unhealthy people. It's important to avoid such situations if you can, as the inner beings who work with you will assume that since you know the risk and still choose to expose yourself, then that is your choice. They will not help you or protect you from your own stupidity.

If you have to put yourself in such a situation, it is time to engage the various skills you have learned to protect yourself, and the inner beings who work with you will also do their part to help. It's all about common sense. I have been terribly drained and made ill by sitting in a cinema, an unnecessary place I chose to go to even though I knew it would affect me. But when I have had to visit people in mental institutions, hospices, unhealthy towns and cities I have been perfectly fine because it was something I was doing in service; on those occasions the inner beings I work with helped, guided and protected me where necessary so that I could get on with the job at hand.

6. Talismans

Many people have asked me about using talismans to protect them from being drained by unhealthy beings. The issues around talismans are not straightforward and the use of them is something that, for a number of reasons, should not be done lightly.

If a person is a natural empath but has no wish to develop that skill or to delve into deep magical study, then using talismans will do them no harm and will protect them. Talismans used unwisely will arrest a person's inner development, but if they have no wish to develop further, then it is not an issue.

Similarly, talismans can be extremely useful if a person is at a vulnerable stage in their life (e.g. their childhood or teenage years), if they are suffering from a severe sickness, or if they are living in a dangerous situation like a war zone (in the outer world, not the inner). They are a short-term solution to a problem that eventually must be permanently addressed. When made properly, a good protection talisman will block out anything and everything: it is the equivalent of shrink-wrapping yourself. (By 'good protective talisman' I mean one that is connected to inner contacts and patterns, not some hokey confection sold by internet magicians.)

The downside of talismans is they tend to do a job that you are supposed to do for yourself. The majority of challenges we face are opportunities for us to grow stronger, to learn from, and become part of a larger team of inner beings and outer humans.

When you step onto the path of magic you immediately start to become more visible to inner beings. Some of those beings are helpful, and others are parasitical and unhealthy. Part of your development as a magician involves learning to tell the good beings from the bad ones, and developing the coping mechanisms, inner immune system, and inner social skills you will need to navigate the inner worlds. You may be more vulnerable without a talisman, but such vulnerability will teach you your weaknesses and limits. It is really important that you know your limits, so that you will know when you need to ask for help, and when to not overstretch yourself.

You can only learn those skills through trial and error and through direct experience. If you constantly festoon yourself with talismans and do banishing rituals on a daily basis you will never encounter enough beings to learn which of them are healthy and which are not. Just as a child who is never allowed to mix with other children never learns the skills they need to deal with them, so an overprotected magician never learns how to interact with the vast array of inner beings.

If you are naturally empathic it is even more important that you learn to cope with this faculty, and again the only way is through direct experience. This also helps to toughen up your 'inner skin' so that over time you learn how to filter out and rebuff intrusive low-level beings.

Even so, there are times when any magician becomes overwhelmed: on those occasions it may be better to use a talisman for a few days or weeks to gain some breathing space. The key is to use them rarely, and only when under serious threat or when a major timeout is needed.

7. Protecting and healing within your sphere

This is something that happens often as a magician whether you are doing it consciously or not. When you work in magic, particularly if you are walking a magical path of service, your energetic boundaries become loosened, so that your inner consciousness can flow back and forth in a more fluid way. This allows you to be fully alert in both the inner and outer worlds at the same time. It also enables you to interact more directly, from an inner point of view, with the land and with people around you: the land will recognise you as a magical worker, as will inner beings, ancestors, faery beings, etc.

With the development of civilised living, and as a result of pressure from religions and cultural norms, we are expected to shun anything that cannot be touched, held, and quantified. Imagination is for children, inner senses are silly, and we are constantly told to be in the 'here and now.' That approach culminates in a locked-down adult who finds it very hard to be in touch with themselves, let alone any being or realm they cannot see.

Working magically in vision and practising meditation slowly peels back that hard layer and allows one's spirit to breathe and flow, which is more in line with its natural state: we become more attuned to everyone and everything around us. The more a magician works in vision, the more they are able consciously to affect their own boundary, and one of the benefits of this is the ability to take someone into your boundary of energy.

The magician learns to expand their energy field and to 'wrap it round' a person who is very vulnerable. This is not a skill exclusive to magicians: many natural empaths will nod at the concept of taking someone into your field to protect, heal or energetically feed them.

The question of learning such fluidity takes us back to a very basic working known as the 'vision of the Void,' the key ingredient for so many magical actions. Once still, you expand your field of 'silence' beyond its normal boundary and envelop another living being with it. You will discover that other magical paths and mystical branches of religions have versions of this described in their mystical writings and meditational methods, if you look closely enough.

I use this method to help a child, a pregnant woman, a dying person, a sick animal, etc. that is in need. Standing by them, sitting with them or holding them, expand your energy field beyond the both of you so that they are completely within your sphere. Then, deepen the void within you so that a deep stillness fills you and the person you are holding the space for. The first action brings the person into your frequency, which immediately protects them. The second opens the gates of the Void so that power can flow back and forth. That is all you need do unless you have made the decision (and they have asked you) to give them direct healing or protection.

By holding them and opening the gates of the Void, you act as an intermediary or door for any power, connection, or contact they need. This is an act of service. It is usually done consciously, but it can also happen unconsciously: you often do not realise it is happening until you suddenly feel the stillness all around you. You will be very tired afterwards because it is hard work, and you will most likely need to sleep.

8. SEX

Sex can be draining for a number of reasons besides bedroom gymnastics or prolonged marathon sessions. If one of the partners is ill or badly out of balance, then sex can cause a magician to become quite badly drained (the life is literally sucked out of them) and the out-of-balance partner feels great for a while. Another draining element can happen when parasites are involved, which is a lot more common than people realise, and is not always bad.

I will not go into much detail over this issue because I have written about this subject matter before (in *Magical Knowledge II*) and do not wish to repeat myself. Suffice it to say that if you find your energy becoming badly drained from sex, take a consecrated bath and ritually cleanse your home. If it is a parasite the draining will stop, but will very possibly creep back. If it is your partner, then no amount of cleaning will solve that one. They have to sort themselves out.

If you ritually cleanse yourself and then find that your sex drive drops quite a bit, then you know that a being was feeding on your sexual energy and was also boosting your sex drive so that it could get a more regular supper. Then you have to make a choice... live with the parasite and have a great sex drive but get drained, or have a more natural sex drive and not get drained. Such a decision is a personal choice: sometimes symbiotic relationships with such beings work in a healthy way and sometimes they do not – it's up to you to decide.

9. RAISING KIDS

Having children is probably one of the most draining and rewarding experiences a person can have, and also the most frustrating, mind numbing and hilarious. Besides all the outer effort it takes to raise a child, it also takes a great deal of inner energy to raise one who is balanced and healthy. The ins and outs of the magical dynamics around children would make a book all of its own, and for this book the question of children is very much a side issue. Suffice it to say, if you are a magician and are planning to have children (and this particularly applies to the mother) then prepare for your inner resources to be stretched to the extreme.

Don't for a minute assume that you will be able to conduct a full magical life with a child around, particularly for their first 7 years. Raising a child is a major commitment from an inner point of view and you will find that your inner energies are almost completely devoted to protecting, nurturing, introducing, bridging, fighting off nasties, etc., particularly when they hit their teen years. I was lucky, I had my kids young – I was twenty one when I had my first child, so by the time I was ready to begin deeper magical work, they were past the very vulnerable stage.

If, however, you find that your child suddenly and unusually drains you badly, and it has nothing to do with stress, arguments, etc., then it is probably time to give them a ritual cleansing bath and do a proper cleansing of their bedroom. If that does not work, do a reading to determine if something dangerous is happening. The sudden draining could just be an unhealthy situation like parasites, or it could mean that your energy is being used to protect them or hold them back from a disaster, serious illness or potential accident.

This brings me to the other main reason for a drain of energy, which is working unconsciously to protect someone. This happens automatically with your children, but it can occur whenever you are closely connected to someone. If you have been working on someone who is very sick, then it is possible that your deeper spirit will continue to work on them from a distance. Personally I have found that no matter how I try to cut connections under such circumstances, as soon as I fall asleep I go to the sick person, work on them some more, and then wake up exhausted. My inability to learn how to break connections has led me not to offer to heal (except for my own family/friends, and then only when it is absolutely necessary).

Getting drained is part and parcel of magical service, though not every magician will be called upon to work in protection and healing – it depends on who you are, where you are, and what you do. Some magicians are called into magical inner construction as service, others become guardians, or power weavers, or destroyers. There will always be, times when you will get drained, so learn how to deal with it. Just as working on a construction site at the age of forty five will knock the stuffing out of you, working hard in the inner worlds will tire you out at times.

10. Summary

There are times when the draining of energy is a strong warning that something is amiss. It tends to be my default major alarm signal: I suddenly deflate when something is wrong. An unhealthy landmass can drain you, an out-of-balance city or town can drain you, as can a sick person, a child, an unhealthy object brought into the house, deep magic, an incoming attack, a working tide going out – the list is endless. The key is to find out what is draining you and do something about it. The best way to identify the problem is through observation, and to identify the best solution using readings: look at your options and the situation that surrounds you.

Most of the time, particularly in the early stages of magical development (such as beginner or initiate) getting drained should not be much of a problem unless you are a strong empath. The deeper you go in to magical training the more of an issue it becomes, but it should still not become a major problem. If it does, then there are two possible explanations: either you are working unconsciously on a long-term project and your tide is waaaaay out (discussed in the next chapter), or you have overstretched yourself and are getting sick. Preventing that from happening, and dealing with it when it does happen, is essentially what this book is about.

Chapter 3

Energy and magic

1. Paying the piper: the price of advanced magic

There is no such thing as a free ride, and this is particularly true for magicians. The majority of people who get involved with magic do so out of curiosity, or because they wish to connect deeper with the powers around them (mysticism), or because they wish to control their environment (results magic). All these paths have their own energy dynamics, issues, rewards and problems. Most magicians dabble in all types of magic at some point or other before they settle on what feels best for them and discover what they can cope with.

Part of the learning curve is to discover how the scales of magic work in your own life. Everyone will be different, but there are some inherent power dynamics that it pays to understand as early as possible. Learning by direct experience is always best. It is not so much the experience itself that teaches you, as how you respond to it that will polish or destroy you.

The information in this chapter it is not presented to you in order that you should totally avoid the situations discussed; rather it should give you a better understanding of the parameters involved so that you can make more informed decisions and react logically rather than emotively to some of the impacts that magic can have on your body.

I broached the subject of energy dynamics and magic in my book *Magic of the North Gate* and the following chapter expands on that information, looking in more detail at the energetic ups and downs that occur on the magical path. Forewarned is forearmed: if you have an idea of what could happen to you, then you can practise avoidance magic – otherwise known as the art of dodging bullets!

2. Magic and energy

All magic uses energy of some kind, and the deeper or more powerful the magic, the more energy is used. Different kinds of magic use power/energy in different ways, and the form we practise will determine how that energy will interact with us. The whole picture can become very complex but the basic rule of thumb is this: externalised or ritual magic creates and mediates energetic patterns in this world, and then draws inner power to the pattern. Visionary magic or inner work creates patterns in the inner worlds, and then draws those inner patterns through us before externalising them. Folk magic tends to nudge whatever is already present.

It is crucial to understand how and why these methods affect you in order to learn and grow as a magician. It is good to walk a path with your eyes open, and it is important to have a basic understanding of how to manage the downs as well as the ups of a magical life. Some energetic problems can be avoided with foresight; others cannot. For those that cannot be avoided, it is better to know how to mitigate their effects than to fall victim to them.

In this chapter we will look at the energetic dynamics of some of the various forms of visionary magic that most magicians use, so that we can see how they can potentially affect us.

3. Visionary and inner magic

Visionary magic takes many different forms and is done for a variety of reasons. How, why and where you act magically will determine what effect it will have on you. The sort of effect produced can vary enormously, from being filled with regeneration to being totally trashed, and some forms of visionary magic will have little or no effect on your body. It is all about level, context and content. In general, the deeper or more involved your visionary magic is, the more tired you will be afterwards – not because visionary magic is unhealthy, but because you will have worked hard and your body/mind/spirit is tired.

4. Bridging

This form of magic works with energies closer to the source of their inner pattern, and the magician interacts with powers, deities, inner constructs, contacts, beings and different realms through the use of visionary imagination. Because most of the action happens in the inner worlds, before it can have any effect in the outer world it must bridge through the magician, who acts as a mediator for the power. This simple act can knock the shit out of the strongest magicians, because the power has to pass through your body before it can go anywhere else.

The immediate effect of bridging is to be filled with power and to feel amazing: injuries vanish, your mind becomes crystal clear, your body glows with energy, and you appear youthful and strong. Once the power has passed through you and gone off to do whatever it was supposed to do, you will either return back to your creaky, grumpy old self, or if you are overworking you will dissolve into a puddle on the floor and feel like shit for days. Hopefully you soon recover, ready for the next bout of energy-boxing with the gods.

How much bridging affects a magician depends on what they are bridging and why. When it is an important job that you have been called or guided to do and you are only one of many other beings working on it, the effect is often minimal, even when the overall work is very powerful. Other times, if you are doing inner construction for example, or are working more or less alone, it can feel like you have been wrestling elephants once the power wears off. A magician who persistently overstretches themselves in the inner worlds or tries to grab power can literally end up destroying themselves.

Bridging works with a few different energy dynamics. One is where the power that you are bridging is far greater than your body was designed to hold. Even though you have no intention to hold it and are simply acting as a doorway for that power, it still fills every cell in your body before it passes onward and out into the world. This can be good or bad, depending on what power you are mediating, what that power does, and how healthy your body is at the time.

If you are working with an energy that heals, regenerates and balances, then its effect can be wonderful if you need it, and sometimes it is tempting to try and hold onto it briefly. If you do that but don't actually need any extra energy, it can sometimes 'overfill' the pot of your own energies and trigger an immune reaction which becomes inflammatory. Hence the wisdom of letting the power do its own thing and not interfering with its natural progress.

If you are young and strong, then your body will adapt pretty well to the demands of bridging energy – unless you have already broken through into working with major powers. If that is the case, it is best to be proactive and learn to maintain your body and spirit so that you can withstand the heavy volume of work that awaits you without getting injured or sick. If you are older, it is wise to start keeping a close eye on your health, and be willing to adapt your working methods and actions if necessary.

When you work in the inner worlds, you stretch your spirit in ways that it is not used to: we do not grow up in societies where such inner actions are the norm and therefore practised from an early age. We are the equivalent of thirty-year-olds learning to walk for the first time after three decades of allowing our leg muscles to atrophy. It takes time to build the muscles up slowly, and if you overdo it you will get an injury.

If you are already working on bridging energies and beings, keep a close eye on your health and don't dismiss the subtle little whispers of discontent that a body tends to put out: pay attention, and act accordingly.

The subsequent chapters in this book look at a variety of symptomatic pictures and methods for maintaining and healing the body. No matter how good or strong different healing modalities are, each body works in its own way. Experimenting with different healing forms while tracking your health through readings will show you which forms work best for your body. Also bear in mind that any single healing modality will work for some things and not for others: you may find that you need to use a combination of them to support and heal your body after magical impact. Don't think in terms of constants and consistency, approach it more mutably and go with the flow.

5. Inner study

Working in vision to learn, observe and study has the least impact on the mind and body of all types of visionary magic. This is why it is very important to spend plenty of time as a relative beginner doing regular meditation and work with the Void, and going into well-established and frequently-visited realms to learn. It is also very helpful to connect with a guide so that your mind and body become acquainted not only with the inner pathways, but also the energies of inner contacts.

If you are still finding it a struggle to hold focus and quieten the mind, then you still need to be only practising and learning, not working or doing deep exploration. There is a phenomena to look for which will tell you that your body and mind is going through deep adjustments, and that is where the visionary process falls away and you find yourself deeply still to the point where you think you have fallen asleep or lost consciousness. But it is not the same as simply falling asleep: the deep shift closes off the consciousness as the power flows and yet you surface at the end of the vision.

This happens mostly when someone else is leading you in vision or you are using a recording: your mind is able to let go and the deeper spirit emerges to connect. But if you simply abandon focus on the vision and let go, the power shift does not happen. It is a paradox: by using focus to stay conscious, the consciousness gives up trying to interface with the imagination and the deeper consciousness connects directly with the power.

This is common in the early days of visionary work and it is a sign that you have made the crossing from the simple use of the imagination to an energetic interfacing with the inner worlds. It can still happen occasionally to an experienced magician, and it is often a sign either that the power you are connecting with is either unfamiliar to you, or that you have gone very deep into it.

This 'loss of consciousness' dynamic is very difficult to understand and work with if you are a lone magician, but it is not impossible. When you are working with a group and someone is leading the vision, the group energy upholds you as you work and whoever is leading the vision verbally acts as a beacon. If you do work in a group, it is wise afterwards for everyone to talk through what they saw and experienced. This helps to jog your memory, and even though you may feel like you had passed out during the vision, hearing other people talk it through brings back to you what you actually experienced: most of the time you did not fall asleep, you just went very deep. Whatever you experienced will come back to you when it is ready.

One of the key signatures that you all made it into the inner realms is that you all see the same things even though they are not mentioned by whoever is leading the group. With a psychological pathworking, which is not magical vision, you see what is described and have a few personal experiences as your imagination and personality use the pathworking to address personal issues.

With visionary magic, your imagination breaks through into the inner realms and you all have common experiences that are not described because you are seeing and interacting with what is actually in that realm. An interesting example of this is a group of magicians I know who are all lone practitioners and are scattered at various locations around the world. Recently they were individually drawn to work in the Inner Desert and all experienced an inner contact that I am aware of but have never described. Each one had a startling encounter with a powerful ancient inner contact that has a very specific description and each magician thought that their imagination had made it up. No, they had all tuned into a specific power as it flowed through the inner realms.

From a learning perspective this is why it is important not to second-guess, analyse or dismiss something you see in vision if it is outside your personal experience. For every contact, power and realm described in books, there are many more that are not spoken about; it is very important that you find them for yourself. You will get outside confirmation in one form or other, and you will also feel it in your body: a solid contact interacting with you changes you as you also change them; power/energy interactions between consciousnesses always bring about change. But these learning interactions usually have only subtle effects and not the massive energetic impacts or rushes of power that work interactions can bring. For this reason (and also for obvious other reasons), if you are working as a magician in service in the inner worlds, it is good for your body and spirit to alternate work visits with learning visits, not only to give your body a rest but also to allow for a deepening of understanding both of mind and body.

In today's world of university education, the concept that you go to school for four years to get a degree and then you are an expert has had an effect on how we learn. The age that an undergraduate gets his or her degree tends also to be the age (your twenties) when you know it all and have a delicate ego. This is normal: we have all been there, and at the time most of us were so sick of being looked on as a student that we wanted to be taken seriously as an expert. I know I am being general here, but it is a reoccurring theme: once people have learned how to navigate the inner worlds, they want to get to work. Great. But it pays dividends in the long run also to keep learning. Keep working within the safer inner places like the Inner Library (the inner university for magicians and priests!) because you can never, ever, in a lifetime, learn all there is to be learned from such places.

The constant visiting of these places in order to study also helps the body to stabilise and learn. It is like doing your yoga before breakfast: you don't just do it to learn technique; you do it to maintain the body. Visiting the Inner Library and deep meditation in the Void are both visionary versions of a 'morning yoga routine.' Use the simple visions as a part of your body and mind health routine. They will anchor you, teach you, and help your body regenerate.

6. Observing to bring change: magical exploration

This is a weird one and can have a really long pull upon your energy, or not at all. It is a dynamic that cannot be predicated because of its very nature. This power action is implemented in the Inner Desert (the landscape of the Tree of Life) where time, physical manifestation and death are woven together before spilling out into Malkuth (the world). Standing in the Desert, particularly at the edge of the Abyss and observing the angelic power-patterns come together to create a filter (in Da'at) for the utterance of Divinity to pass through as it crosses the Abyss from Kether and begins its journey down the Tree (through the Desert) is to witness the creation of life itself. By having a living human consciousness observing, the process is altered: we become a part of the process and that inclusion by observation brings change to the pattern.

Our energies interact with the pattern and that interaction can continue long after we have come out of vision and moved on with our lives. It does not happen every time, and there have been times I have observed and then felt no further connection to the process. Other times I have observed and subsequently felt the pull on my energies for weeks or months afterwards.

Through the act of observing we cease to be individual humans for a span of time and instead become timeless beings mediating change at the very edge of creation. If that change is going to manifest as something longstanding, our energies become entwined with the process and will continue to be so until it has reached its peak, at which stage it begins its slow descent into decay. The pattern of death begins at birth.

I discovered this action purely by accident and like everything I find in such a way, I work with it until I understand it a bit more. Over a few years of observing in this manner I have come to understand the process a bit better, though I do realise I am still only grasping one percent of it all. But I have noticed that when I observe a major coming-together of power, my energies can be tied up in it for quite some time. It is not all draining: some of the energy that comes from observing is inspiring and energising – one cannot tell how it will affect anything until it does.

So if you are involved in this type of inner work, just bear in mind that your energy could be tied up for months or longer, though what you stand to learn far outweighs the potential disadvantages. I learned more about magic, power and mysticism from those observations than from any other magical practice. The only thing I would change in retrospect is that I would have timed my interactions better so that I was not partaking of such an act at a time when I needed full access to my energies for everyday life. Saying that, these powerful events have their own time and you fall across them when the time is right for all involved.

The first time I connected to this observation action, I was completely trashed afterwards. But as I lay on my bed staring at the ceiling, all my poor little mind could do was to say "wow... just... wow!" I learned more in twenty-four hours than I had in the previous ten years.

I have come back from such observations filled with power, and that power hung around for weeks. Like all exploration work, you have no real idea what is going to happen until you do it. It did however introduce me to the concept of power in observation, and when I finally learned how to magically observe an event taking place in the outer world, I realised that this brought through an interesting ingredient to the power mix. Not only can you change something simply by observing it, you can also become a passive mediator for power and consciousness to flow through. It is important not to try to direct or shape what flows through you; rather it is enough simply to be a bridge for whatever is coming through into the situation you are observing. You become the human version of the angelic filter that works at the edge of the Abyss, except you are working in Malkuth: we are substance-bound beings working through substance.

By passively observing and being willing to act as a filter in the physical world, you become a lower octave of the same process that is happening all the time in the Inner Desert. And it is important that you are physically there, looking with your own eyes: watching something on a screen does not work. (I know, I tried it.) It is the physical presence of the physical being that makes it work. I also found that I could only act as a filter in Malkuth after I had experienced the process in the Inner Desert in vision; the inner experience primed my spirit to be able to take up the role in the outer world. One startling difference is that while the physical observing triggered a lot of magical energy and 'did things,' it did not trash me the way the inner vision did.

Working in substance in a body on the physical plane may seem like the natural order of things, but I had to go through the inner experiences first to become aware of the act, to understand it energetically and to experience how it felt. Then I could consciously and actively participate in the process as a mediator/magician rather than being completely unaware of what was involved in.

7. Power weaving

Coming from a city of weavers, I found this particular form of visionary magic to be of great interest and took to it like a duck to water. The method of power weaving itself is described in my book *The Magic of the North Gate*, so I will not repeat it here.

Essentially, it is actively working with the weave of energy or power that brings fate, action and events into play. Whereas the angelic pattern filtering at the edge of the Abyss brings form into being (a person, a tree, a building, a genetic race), the weaving brings events and action into place.

When I wrote about power weaving a couple of years ago, I had fallen across it in its raw form and spent a few years essentially 'playing and tinkering' to find out how and why it works. But I had not been working with it long enough to know the prolonged effects it could have, how it affects the energy, the body, etc.

Now, a few years down the line, I have a bit more of an idea. But I suspect that my understanding of this work has not even begun to scratch the surface of its potential application and effects.

So far I have found that, although there seems to be no long-term energetic impact from this work, I get a 'twinge' when another being or magician connects into the power weave that I was working with, as though they nudge a little bell when they interact with the same weave. Working directly with the power weave is hard work, and afterwards I would feel like I had put in a full day's work at the mill. But that feeling quickly faded.

I find the twinges interesting, but am not sure how to interpret them. My guess is simply that once we weave into something energetically, we become a part of that weave and will therefore be aware when anyone else joins it.

It also reminds me of an experience I had many years ago when observing a weaving process between planetary beings. I attempted to hold one of the threads for a split second and suddenly all the beings were aware of me (uh-oh...). But I was too busy feeling like a building had just fallen on top of me to worry about lots of very tall pissed off dudes looking my way. I think I 'twanged' their weave, and I do not think they appreciated it.

If you work with power weaving in the inner worlds, keep notes on your reactions over months and beyond. Both you and everyone else could learn a lot from your experiments and experiences.

8. Energetic consequences of working with deities

The subtitle of this section sounds very doom and gloom, but it's not, although you do need to take certain things into consideration when working with deity powers. Much depends on how you work with them and what your intention is. If you are working with them as priestess or priest in a temple or worship scenario, then their impact or effect on you will manifest in a particular way. If you work with them as a magician, then you will experience a different set of effects. Both ways of working have their advantages and disadvantages.

As I have said before in my books, when you work with deities it is wise to tread carefully and pay close attention to what happens around you. More details on the general ins and outs of working with deities (how they are formed, etc.) can be found in my book *The Magic of the North Gate*.

It is also critical to differentiate between serving them as a priest or priestess and working with them as a magician. For this section I will discuss working with them as a magician and the effects, good and bad, that such work can have on your energy and body.

When you work with a known deity that has been worked with for a long time (i.e. hundreds or thousands of years) the pathways of power that they work through are well established and therefore can have predictable effects upon your body.

The general rule of thumb is to check carefully what energies they work with and what they tend to do with them. Deities are not 'all-powerful all-knowing' beings: they tend to have specialities, limits and a particular focus. Just ensure that you work with one that has both positive and negative attributes, so that they are a balanced power.

Sekhmet, for example, has a balance of healing and destructive aspects, so her power, her knowledge and her applications can go either way. Her positive side also expresses through the goddess Hathor, who is part of the 'Sekhmet' power group. If you want healing, work with Hathor. If you want to know *how* to heal, then you need to learn both polarities of the power, which means working with Sekhmet.

If you work magically with such a power, it will fill you and work on you before it fully engages in magical tasks. So if you are generally healthy but for some reason your body/mind/spirit needs to go through a process of disease in order to mature or balance you, then working magically with such a deity as Sekhmet will trigger the necessary illness. This can be a bummer, but it is important to understand that it is also necessary, so work with it and help the process along.

Similarly, Sekhmet's destructive power can fill you with a sense of power that is beyond your natural capacity. It is important to understand that such power or energy is not your own: you are simply bridging it wherever it needs to go. If you cling on to it, you will spin out in a self-destructive cycle. The more deeply you work in visionary magic with deities, the more powerful your interactions with them become, and the more potential there is for it all to go horribly wrong.

On the positive side, if you work wisely with such power, it will trigger your body's own creation and destruction cycles, which will strengthen your overall healing capacity over time. If however you choose to work with a 'heated' power like Apollo (a solar power) and you have a fire personality or body type, then you are likely to trigger chronic inflammatory conditions unless you properly balance out the work with counter-powers.

Magical work with deities tends not to be draining. If it is, then you are connecting not to a deity but to a parasitical being dressing up as one. But working with deities over a longer period of time can change how your body and immune system works. If you work with a particular power for extended periods, your body's structure, repair mechanisms and fuel begin to change to align more closely with the deity's power. Such changes are usually a good thing, but it is worth observing them closely so that you always know how your body is adjusting.

It is important to be aware of these changes because if you get ill and use alternative healing like homeopathy or acupuncture then it will not work in the usual way. Magic changes how the body responds to illness, and working directly with a deity will make that change far more pronounced and focused.

For example, if you caught influenza, your symptomatic picture would point to a specific set of remedies and treatment. But after a magician has worked in-depth for a while, the regular remedy will often stop working for them. Their body's parameters change, and its reactions cannot be relied on when choosing the right substance to treat the illness. The method of treatment has to be approached in a very different way, often in a more poetic way, by looking at the treatment in the context of the deity's powers and the work that has been recently undertaken with them.

This is where the tarot really comes into its own. You can use a specific spread to look at what is happening in the body and what effect a particular treatment would have. The choice of treatment and its potential action can also be tracked through tarot, and in the process you are often shown very interesting insights into how a substance works and how it relates to your magical activities.

So if you are working in-depth magically for a period of time with an ancient Titan or an ancestral sleeper, do not be surprised if your thyroid starts to run a bit on the slow side!

9. Conditional magic and body effects

Conditional magic is the use of magic for a specific result, and it is usually undertaken for the magician's benefit or by the magician on behalf of someone else. Conditional magic works very well, but like all forms of magic it has its price, and if you choose to use conditional magic then it is wise to know what that price can potentially be. (In this instance I am discussing only the energetic and bodily implications of using conditional magic; its deeper, spiritual implications are a different matter altogether.)

A lot of conditional magic relies on the cooperation, sometimes forced, of a being or beings. If a being is forced to undertake a specific task, then the use of that force requires energy, which is usually drawn from the magician's own reserves. Sometimes that can be an issue; other times the magician rebounds quickly.

The long-term energetic implications of forcing a being's cooperation can sometimes weigh the scales of balance against the magician, as it can divert much-needed energy not only from the resources used for their body's upkeep, but also energy from their fate/life path. The magician often does not notice this until much later in their life: a dangerous situation occurs and the resources that should have been there for them to be able to safely navigate it have been used up and are no longer available. So before you decide to force a being's cooperation for conditional magic, first use divination to look at the long-term implications for you of such an action. Sometimes the price is worth paying, and sometimes it is not.

Another form of conditional magic uses the assistance of beings that freely cooperate with you. Although this is more ethical than forcing a being to act on your behalf, it can have even more damaging consequences if it is not approached knowledgeably. Many of the beings and spirits that will offer you help with conditional magic are parasitical in nature and will work for you very effectively, but for an energetic price. If the bargain and boundaries are not struck properly, then those beings will take their wages by way of your life force, leaving you to slowly weaken and sicken.

Or the energy can be taken from your 'fate pot,' a deeper store of energy that surfaces during potential disasters to help you navigate, survive and learn.

If such energy has been drained from you (and this can happen without your knowledge if you do not know how to keep an eye on it) then your potential for surviving or avoiding fateful disasters or illness is severely reduced. There is no such thing as a free ride, and if you decide to use conditional magic then it is imperative that you state what price you are willing to pay: 'I will give you *this* and no more if you are willing to act on my behalf'. If the being you are working with is a land being, an ancestor, etc., they tend to honour such deals (they will work for precious objects, power substances, etc.). But parasitical beings tend not to be so honourable, and they will take what they want regardless of your boundaries.

When a magician gets into long-term parasitical relationships, it slowly begins to show and what is happening becomes obvious to anyone with inner sight. The magician will slowly begin to look grubby and unhealthy, their mental stability will begin to fragment, and repeated chaotic and destructive incidents or behaviour will become a major feature of their lives. When a person displays these symptoms it does not always mean that they are becoming a victim of their own magical practice: such patterns can emerge for a variety of reasons. But when a magician does conditional magic and is not very careful, such a pattern will very likely emerge.

What type of being is willing to work with you depends on what you are trying to achieve. Not all conditional magic is 'bad,' it is simply a dynamic that can quickly become destructive for your body and your general life if you do not tread carefully. So if you are using conditional magic, ensure you know exactly what you are working with, establish tight boundaries and exchanges, and watch your physical and mental health very closely.

10. Long-term projects

Some magical work, either service or inner construction (of a lodge or temple for example), can have longer-term energetic effects on the magician, often in ways that are unpredictable or unexpected.

When we are asked by inner contacts, deities or ancestors to undertake a task, we are often not aware of the ripples into the future that such action can cause. Similarly what can seem a short-term action or one-off working in service can in truth take years to unfold, and as that unfolding occurs, so our body's energy is woven into that action until its completion.

I did not realise this for many years, and would happily take on major short-term workings in service which at the time did not seem too strenuous at all. (In fact, some powerful actions often feel like not a lot is happening while you are working, so it can be difficult to ascertain just how much power is flowing through an action until it is finished.)

Here is an example. A few years back I was asked to go physically to an ancient temple and do a magical action in service. I did as I was asked and it did not physically feel too demanding as I was working: the contact was very strong, the action went smoothly, and it all made sense. An hour after the ritual finished, the two magicians who were guarding me as I worked suddenly became quite ill, but they recovered after a couple of days and that was that, or so we thought. But no, magic is never that easy.

Things started to change in the manifest world around the temple. Some of the changes were quite dramatic, and each of them had a direct effect on the three of us who had been involved in the ritual. We would suddenly become exhausted for no reason, which each of us separately put down to our health or our workload. It was only when we got together and compared notes that we realised our bouts of exhaustion were happening to all three of us at the same time – and in relation to outer world events around the temple where we had worked.

This is still an ongoing situation. Just when we think it is settling down, it all kicks off again and the three of us lay around drooling for days. Would I change anything in retrospect? No, I do not think I would, except this time I would do readings to look at the long-term effect on all of us before I initiated any action, so that any side-effects can be planned for.

It is not that the work we did at the temple has made us ill, rather that we are still 'working' at an energetic level at key times in the process. So be careful what you sign up for! Just be aware that often magical work has a longer unfolding cycle than we realise; if you have undertaken magical work that is operating directly upon something that is manifesting major change, then your energies are going to go up and down with the tide of power as it flows in and out of the situation, place or construct.

11. Ritualising the action

One way to diminish the impact of powerful inner work is to make sure that if you working in depth with a large amount of power, either alone or in a group, then give your inner work an externalised ritual form to ground it and help bring it out. Do not try to do a lot of advanced power work only in vision. You are the first bridge into substance for the power; ensure that it passes through you and into a ritual pattern which will help it to take form and stabilise before it goes out into the world to do whatever it is going to do. The ritual acts as a substation for the power: any backwash hits the substation (the ritual) before it hits you. The ritual acts as a power buffer.

It is these buffers that are handed down though the generations, and when they fall into the hands of young magicians they think they have found a powerful ritual that will do X. Sadly (or thankfully) for them, all they have is the external substation of the power, not the power button itself.

12. Retirement: knowing when to back out

There will come a time in a visionary magician's life when the body or spirit is no longer able to provide the necessary resources to continue visionary work. This is usually a time of transition, where the magician's work shifts and changes into a different form.

The magic may become more exteriorised through ritual, or it may become a natural flow whereby the magician no longer actively engages in 'magic' but magical power flows through their everyday life in a constant act of 'magical living.'

Working in visionary magic puts a tremendous strain on the physical and spiritual body, and the more adventurous or exploratory the work, the shorter the magician's working life will be. Usually magicians quickly learn that when using deep visionary magic, the actual act of vision does not need to be done regularly: less becomes more in terms of work. It should be just one element of magical practice, not the whole thing.

When it is time to stop, you will know. The idea of going into the inner worlds will fill your body with a sense of dread, and your instincts will tell you that it is time to retire. If you go with the flow, you will experience a shift in your own power over months or a couple of years. The power of the visions will be all around you in everyday life: everything you do will be an echo of the decades of visionary work that you have undertaken. The magic comes to you, finally. A simple ritual act will be filled instantly with power and contact without any conscious need to 'plug in' or work from an inner aspect.

Slowly the magician is taken from being a person who conducts magical acts to being a person who is magical. You turn up somewhere, and change happens. You step onto land you have not visited before and the landscape, creatures and weather react. You have externalised that 'change through observation' dynamic so that you slowly become aware that it is happening all the time, all around you.

This can be a very special time, a beautiful time, when you are able to take a breath, step back, and watch the awesome show that is creation.

13. Summary

Before you can do anything about a problem, you need to know what the problem is. Always keep a working diary so that you can track not only the unfolding of the magical work that you do, but also its effects on your body and mind. To do deeper magic and expect it not to have any physical impact is as much folly as thinking you could hike to the South Pole or build a house without any physical impact. Bruises are going to happen.

The key is to know what is happening and why. Are you tired because you have worked hard? Are you tired because the work is still going on? Did you get injured, or are you still carrying something around and are not aware of it? Have you been impacted, attacked, or has a being ridden back with you?

Have you successfully completed something but taken a knock and your body is out of balance?

Once you have pinpointed the possible cause of the issue and identified the symptoms, it is time to find the appropriate cure or care. It is also wise to know how to avoid such impacts in the future.

Chapter 4

Symptoms, reasons and power dynamics

1. The reactor reaching critical mass

Now that you have a general background of how advanced magic can affect your body, let's look in depth at magical actions and the more specific types of physical backlashes that you may encounter.

Often but not always, the types of physical or mental effects you can suffer as a result of deeper magic work relates directly to the type of being or power you are working with: certain parts of the body are more vulnerable to specific types of power and contact. It is always good to remember that these mental and physical effects are not visited upon you intentionally by beings; it is only a side-effect of their power.

Working in depth in magic is akin to working with volatile and dangerous substances, or to practising an extreme sport: there will be accidents and injuries from time to time but if you work intelligently, with safeguards, these impacts can be kept to a minimum. And if you do take a hit of power that affects you badly, then you need to know how to ameliorate its effects and how to help your body recover.

Similarly, it is important to be able to differentiate between a 'good' magical impact and a 'bad' one. A good impact is where you have successfully achieved a magical action and the body effects are transitory; you have worked hard and you really feel it afterwards. A bad impact is where you have overstepped a boundary, clashed with a being, or reached too far into a power that is not meant to be accessed by a human. Hacking into uncharted territory will often bring a mix of good and bad effects: it takes a lot of energetic effort to break new ground, and it is very likely that you will encounter a being that is hostile or at least incompatible with human contact.

Let's look at the various types of impact, their causes, and how they affect the body and mind. Bear in mind that this is not an exhaustive list, but it will give you a background to work from.

Everything listed here is something I have either experienced myself or treated other magicians for.

2. Magical impacts

Magical impacts are just that: you do magic, you get impacted, and your body suffers the consequence. A direct hit is not something a beginner would normally experience simply because there are too many filters across the inner worlds and deeper powers: someone in the early years of magic will not be able to get anywhere deep enough (usually) to injure themselves.

For more advanced magicians though, it is a different story.

These types of impacts tend not to hit ritual magicians who do not use vision, as they are caused by direct inner contact. Exteriorised magic without use of inner contact or vision by its very nature filters and blocks such impacts because ritual without inner work blocks and filters deep contact. But if you are a visionary magician or a ritual magician who also works in vision, then your chances for getting injured begin to climb as you push deeper into the inner worlds. Such injuries will not happen regularly. They are usually the result of very deep work that is often experimental or 'archaeological' in nature: breaking into old disused patterns, forbidden thresholds, etc. So do not think that you will be injured every five minutes, but it is very likely to happen at some point.

Why does it happen? Magical impact is usually the result of interactions with a power that is beyond your body's capacity to cope with. Just as we humans interact on a subtle pheromone level with each other, so in the inner worlds, beings (including humans) interact subtly at an energetic level. If you are communing with a being that is vast, then the chances are its power will prove too much for your body to cope with.

A similar effect can happen when you are dealing with pure power: when you work magically with power it always flows through and around you. If the power is of a high level, your body will freak out or get 'burned' by it. The other main cause of injury or impact in the inner worlds is moving too quickly: falling through the worlds and literally landing with a bump, or being grabbed by a hostile being.

Let's have a look at some examples of what has happened to magicians (and to myself) when they have been impacted. This allows you to put the information into a context and to see how it unfolds.

3. Examples of impacts

Many years ago, when I was even more stupid than I am now, I was an avid explorer of the inner worlds. I loved pushing boundaries to the extreme, as I always wanted to know what was beyond the horizon. One such round of work took me deep into the Underworld, in search of the ancient power of the planet itself. I wanted to know what made it tick; the nature of the consciousness of the Earth's core. I did manage to make it quite far down (though not as far as I wanted to go) and I had a strange interaction with what I presumed was the consciousness of the threshold of the Earth's mantle. When I came out of vision, I burned. I was so hot my skin was tingling as though I had sat too close to a fire. I lay down for a while to let it pass, but it didn't.

I had to get my act together, as otherwise I was going to be late picking my kids up from school. My kids asked me why I was so red, and when I got home and looked in the mirror, I saw that my face was sunburned – in the middle of winter. I put some aloe vera on my skin before going to bed and thought nothing more of it.

I had experienced something similar a few years before, when I was working with an Underworld deck for the first time. Then, the effect had quickly passed.

That evening I became sick. I developed a fever and I burned all through the night. The following morning I did a Health reading. The picture showed I had something akin to radiation poisoning. So I started taking kelp tablets for iodine, and over a few days the fever finally settled down. This was not a major impact, but it permanently changed how my body reacted to power. The immune response it triggered has become a learned behaviour for my body. Ever since that time, if I come into contact with magic that springs from that Underworld source, I burn, go red, and then have a few days of inflammatory reactions throughout my body.

My big all time idiot impact that changed my health permanently was the bright idea I had to mediate the Goddess Kali into substance. I was young and had absolutely no idea what the hell I was doing. I took four days to do the work, two of which I worked around the clock. To cut a long story short, I ended up with scarlet fever and permanent physical damage, as well as a longstanding pattern of strep infections that were really tough to fight at times.

What caused the illness was my lack of knowledge coupled with my natural ability to tap into power. I had already worked with Kali for a long time, and bridging her into substance (i.e. a physical form like a deity statue or painting) seemed to me a natural progression of my work with her.

Because I did not know what I was doing, I did all of the bridging myself. I did not know at that time how to filter power through other beings, how to work in a line properly with inner priesthoods, or how to prepare my body properly. I just did it.

My body was not ready to have such a destructive force flowing through it, and the power came through unfiltered and hit every little imbalance in my body: it magnified them many times over.

It was a harsh lesson and it took many years to rebalance my body from that impact, but in doing so I learned a great deal about bridging power, what it does, how it works, and so on. After that, whenever I took on a large project, I would first look carefully (through divination) at all the parameters. I would prepare my body properly, ensure that I was working with a team of inner beings, and I would spread the process out over months.

The culmination of that learning process was understanding how structure worked, how inner powers flow from one world to another, how teams worked, and how to anchor the work properly so that my body did not take the full impact. The result of that learning is presented in my book *The Work of the Hierophant*, which goes into depth about bridging and building at an advanced level.

Appendix A – Magical Healing

I have also come out of visions with black eyes, a dislocated shoulder, and a torn ligament. This sounds pretty extreme and the product of an overactive imagination, but it is not. It does not happen that often, but the impact of contact with a powerful being like an angel can certainly knock the body about a bit. It tends to be a direct injury that heals naturally. Think of Jacob wrestling with the angels: he had contact with angelic beings and he got an injury. It is exactly the same dynamic with visionary contact. Usually when I get injured it is because I am either fighting something, carrying something very heavy, or I am doing something stupid. Most of the time after a vision, I feel only the strain of making the contact.

Another interesting example is an impact sustained from an encounter with pure power. This happened to a magician friend of mine that I have a lot of respect for. He is a natural magician and also a very well trained one. But like all of us he makes mistakes, because that is what we do and how we learn.

This magician had been working in depth in the Inner Desert with the land powers around him and with threshold contacts. The work had been slowly building over months, and the power was becoming more and more intense. He was reaching for the formless power, and wanted to bridge it unconditionally from inner to outer. He worked in his temple, opened the gates, and mediated raw power.

What came through was so strong it triggered alarm reactions in various magicians around the world: the power was too raw, too unfiltered, and was full of destructive potential. He quickly closed the contact down and closed the gates, but by then he had already sustained an injury: the power had flowed into him and through him, damaging his brain as it passed through.

Luckily the immediate side-effects were strong enough to drive him to seek help: he began to wake with crushing headaches and a horrible feeling that slowly got worse. He was manifesting a brain injury. Even though nothing had physically touched his body, the impact of power was great enough to elicit a reaction in his body, which reacted as though it had sustained a head injury. If that impact had been left untreated, it would have snowballed into a permanent physical head injury. He was sensible enough to contact another magician who immediately prescribed a series of strong herbal treatments for a head injury (*Hypericum perforatum*). With the use of the herbal treatment the headaches and horrible feeling eased and finally stopped.

Although it was a frightening situation and very painful for him, he learned a great deal about bridging power and how to filter it. It does seem to be a reoccurring theme that we magicians sometimes have to learn the hard way. In this case, it was his first real experience with a major power impact, and in many ways it was very necessary: you can read about it as much as you like, but until you experience a direct hit, the reality of the power levels that magicians sometimes work with are often not understood, accepted or even believed. In every serious magician's life there will be an impact somewhere. The key is to know how to deal with it, learn from it, and adjust accordingly – hence this book.

The most usual form of impact after a work that magicians experience has no lasting effects, and consists of disorientation, followed by vomiting. It only tends to happen after a group working, and therefore the levels of energy being worked with are high.

I do not know the biological mechanisms of why these injuries and reactions happen; only that they do, and that maintaining the body carefully will help to lessen many such reactions.

4. Magical imbalances

This is an area of magic and bodily health that truly fascinates me: the imbalances within the hormone system that can occur as a direct result of magic. The body's hormonal response to power really demonstrates how magic works *through* the body, how the body responds to magic, and how inner power is processed by an outer container (the body).

Understanding the very basics of how the endocrine system functions will help the magician to watch their body carefully and respond to any disturbance brought about by magic. The endocrine system is usually the first thing to react when the power levels worked with are too high, or the work has been done too quickly for the body to assimilate it.

Magicians often presume that a bodily reaction is the result of an attack or injury, when in fact it is simply the body reacting to a power overload. This is why it is important to understand the different ways that the body can react to magic, so that the right steps can be taken to treat it and protect its integrity.

When there is a problem, the first glands to trigger alarms are the adrenals, the thyroid, and (as a result of the thyroid reaction) the ovaries in women, which will affect their menstrual cycle. Let's have a look at each gland's reactions to magical impacts, and the cascade of symptoms that can result.

5. Adrenals

The adrenal glands sit over the kidneys and are our body's early warning and reaction system for danger: they provide us with the cascade of hormones necessary in order for us to deal with a dangerous situation. When we are under threat, the adrenals swing into action and give us quick access to energy, keep us alert, and reduce any inflammation in the body.

When a magician bumps up against a powerful being or a dangerously large amount of power, their adrenals swing into action and provide their body with the resources it needs for 'fight or flight'. When the adrenals are healthy and not overused, an adrenal response during a magical act will feel like being filled with energy – something that also happens as a result of tapping into flows of power.

When the adrenals activate, we become hyper-alert, our heart rate increases, and we feel very aware of any potential danger. This sort of reaction is not a problem unless the magician works regularly with powerful forces and deep contacts: the adrenals will become fatigued by the constant triggering which in turn can weaken them.

One way to avoid such burnout is by regularly working with the meditation of the Void, or with similar meditations where the magician learns to still the body and mind, silence the emergency reactions, and approach power with calm stillness. It is not something that can be achieved easily and it takes practice, hence the need for regular or daily meditation, particularly at the neophyte and initiate levels of work. The initial reaction of the adrenals still happens, but it is muted and quickly dissolved.

If deep work is not approached with stillness then problems will eventually start to surface. Adrenal reactions are also heavily tied to emotional reactions, so if a magician approaches deep and powerful work with an emotional agenda, then detachment and stillness is impossible, as the engine is primed for reaction. Powerful magical work with an emotional agenda, for example to 'fight for the goodies' or 'slay the baddies,' puts the magician into a 'war' situation which puts the adrenals into full swing.

If on the other hand the magician approaches powerful work with the intent simply to do a job that is necessary, or to be a part of a working team with inner beings, then the lack of emotional attachment makes stillness easier to achieve. Anyone would find being in the midst of a riot or battle extremely stressful, regardless of their reasons for being there. Very few people would find cleaning the toilets or the kitchen stressful. How you approach the work will define what frequency of power you find yourself interacting with.

Let's look at a hypothetical example. Let's imagine that a lot of power was building up in the inner worlds, and that the emerging power was destructive. As humans, our understanding of time and of the long-term evolution of a change is very limited, so we cannot tell whether in this case the destructive power is necessary, good, or just plain nasty. But inner contacts that work with a magician – let's call him Fred, tell him that on this occasion, the inner worlds need a human's help. So Fred decides to answer the call and go work in the inner worlds. He builds the ritual structure for the power to flow through which is necessary in order to work deeply, and then he goes into vision. He goes into the inner worlds with an attitude of saving the world from 'nasties' or from destruction – in other words, primed for battle. This approach immediately defines Fred as 'conditional,' that is, he is working towards an outcome that he wishes to define even though he does not fully understand what is happening.

As a result, many of the very powerful beings (usually angels) who work with this sort of massive energetic weaving to bring about change cannot use him as he would become a 'spanner in the works.' And as a result, Fred cannot penetrate the angelic frequency, so he cannot see them.

All that is visible to Fred are the beings mediating the destruction rather than the beings weaving the future pattern, and the former are often demonic, conditional beings. As far as Fred can tell, he has stepped into an inner realm full of powerful demonic beings bent on mediating destruction from the inner to the outer.

That would certainly set anyone's adrenals going. And because of Fred's limited perspective, it would be impossible for him to ascertain who should be worked with or what should be done. His situation becomes akin to a toddler on a battlefield.

The alternative scenario would be Fred answering the call and setting up a ritual pattern to support the work, but this time going into *stillness* before going into vision. By working without emotion or agenda, Fred appears at a frequency of the inner worlds where he sees only what he needs to see. Because he is still, unemotional and without agenda, the angelic beings can work with him without risking a human going feral on them.

Fred appears in the inner worlds and immediately feels all of the power flowing around the destructive pattern. But this time an angelic being appears, hands him a thread, and asks him to take it out to the outer world and anchor it in the land.

Fred does as he is asked; job done. He has experienced no encounters with demonic beings, no fear of the destruction, no battle-ready adrenals – but a powerful act has occurred. A being (human) of physical substance but with the ability to cross into the inner worlds took a thread of power from a destructive pattern, mediated it from the inner worlds to the outer world, and anchored it in substance: as a result the power has become connected to the vessel which is Malkuth. Since the power was mediated by angelic consciousness, whatever expresses itself as a result of that initial magical action is guaranteed to be necessary.

By performing that action unconditionally and in service, Fred has actively engaged in the Divine cycle of creation and destruction. Active engagement without the need to control triggers the octave of Divinity within humanity. That has wide-reaching implications not only for personal evolution, but also for the collective evolution of humanity.

Back to the adrenals. Had Fred acted conditionally, he would certainly have triggered his adrenals in a big way, and by exposing himself to such dangerous and conditional forces, the adrenal reaction would most likely have continued on for some time after the work had finished. His body and mind would have stayed hyper vigilant for days or even weeks, and for good cause: magic does not stop the minute you blow out the candle, finish the ritual or come out of vision – that is the just the beginning. The magician's spirit and mind (in dreams) would have continued to bump up against those powerful beings over a prolonged period of time. Within weeks, the adrenals would have started to show signs of fatigue.

If Fred acted unconditionally, he would still have had an initial adrenal reaction, but it would have been much less intense and would have faded quickly as the work was conducted blind: the mind could not perceive the threat and therefore did not react as much. The adrenals would have reacted to the initial rise in power, but when no discernible threat was identified would have settled back down. The unconditional Fred is more likely to have simply suffered a muscle strain from carrying the thread out into the manifest world.

So how do you know if your adrenals are overworked or getting badly affected? The symptoms of adrenal fatigue caused by magic are the same as those caused by 'normal' adrenal circumstances. First comes the hyper vigilance, headaches and sugar cravings. Then comes the energy crash, craving salt, being tired all the time, a drop in blood pressure, and the inability to cope with any stress. Later, the ankles start to swell from fluid retention, sleep patterns are affected, and allergies become far more pronounced.

These symptoms can also surface if you work unconditionally or blind for too long with large amounts of power. If your adrenals begin to show signs that they are struggling, it is time to back off the inner work and let them heal. If the health of the adrenals falters as a result of magic, then it is important not only to rest them, but to treat them.

If you are working at depth in magic there will be times when you will not be able to avoid triggering an adrenal reaction, but you can still reduce the severity of its effect. It is imperative for an adept to know the signs of adrenal trigger (flight or fight) and adrenal fatigue, and to develop a sensible working practice to minimise any long-term effects.

6. Thyroid

The thyroid gland is another major player in the body, and among many other things is basically your engine's governor. Magic can directly affect the thyroid, though for some reason this more often affects women than men. The thyroid and its hormones control your metabolism, growth, body temperature, muscle strength, and appetite, along with supporting the health of your heart, brain, kidneys, and reproductive system. It is a pivotal gland that needs protecting from any kind of impact.

Magical impact of the thyroid is often insidious and builds up gradually, though I have come across acute impact in a couple of priestesses. Most often the first sign of trouble is a disruption of the menstrual cycle: the power of the inner contact or realm unintentionally 'tweaks' the thyroid which responds with a rapid shift in hormone output, which in turn triggers menstrual bleeding: the woman starts to bleed in time with the magical working rather than her usual cycle. Fascinatingly, the bleeding is often not a result of the magic itself, but happens in preparation for an encounter with power: the priestess begins to bleed on the morning of the magical work, not after it.

This phenomenon is connected with the 'tides of power' that flow out and in with magical work. The power of a major working begins to build the moment the decision is made to do the work, and the magician's body responds to that build-up. I always began menstruating just before a major working or a coming-together of magicians to work, and I understood from very early on that magically-triggered menstruation was connected with the tides of power. But it was years before I linked it to a thyroid impact – I can be a bit dense sometimes.

A thyroid reaction in the form of menstrual dysfunction is a very common magical reaction for many female magicians and priestesses, and seems to be of no major consequence so long as it does not happen on a regular basis or trigger endometriosis, which is a possibility. An easy way to support the thyroid in this type of reaction is to take kelp (iodine) for a few days before a major working and for a week afterwards. This way, the thyroid is supported and does not go into decline from the disruption. Just don't overdo the kelp: too much iodine is as bad as not having enough (and if you live in the USA you will probably not need it or only need one kelp tablet before working, as iodine is added into food salt by law)

In fact, for any magical action that could possibly cause thyroid impact (if you know you are going to be working with deep or heavy powers, for example), take kelp just before, during and after the work. You cannot stop the impact that power has on the thyroid, but you can do a lot to lessen it. In these situations, look on exposure to powerful magic much as you would exposure to radiation: you often cannot get out of its way, but you can lessen its impact by how you attend to your body.

So what happens if the thyroid is not attended to and is regularly hammered by large amounts of magical power? The gland can go in one of two directions when it is impacted. In general, but not always, magical impact will cause a woman's thyroid to slow down, and a man's to speed up. That is a sweeping generalisation: don't forget there are always awkward folks who have to be different… So learn the signs, and watch your body when you do heavy work. Don't assume that because you have testicles, your thyroid will not go on strike.

When the thyroid has been knocked out of balance and has slowed down, the person begins to feel tired all the time, feels cold and hungry, and nothing will warm them up or satisfy their appetite. Their hair begins to look dull and brittle, their nails break, and the distribution of fat in their body begins to shift. Sometimes people get an ache in their lower throat (over their thyroid), and their voice may become deeper.

If you have been doing powerful rounds of work and one day you realise that your body is grinding to a halt, then it is possible that your thyroid is not a happy bunny. That is the time to take action, and also to use divination to look at your thyroid's health, as well as the general health of your endocrine system. Sometimes a slowing thyroid does not indicate a problem with the thyroid itself, but is caused by a magical impact in the pituitary or hypothalamus. The point of impact can sometimes be ascertained through divination (discussed in later chapters), and if it originates outside of the thyroid, you will have to treat the impact-point as well as the thyroid itself.

But the first thing to do in response to a slowing thyroid is to take kelp and to stay on it until your body feels better, however long that takes. Once you are on the kelp, then it is important to work out which healing modality would work best to get the endocrine system functioning again, and to ensure that you attend to it. Also be aware that you can take too much kelp: follow the dosage advice on the bottle.

The thyroid has to be very out of balance before it shows in blood tests, but if you have a severe enough reaction it is wise to see a doctor, have blood tests, and take any necessary treatments. If your thyroid impact is severe, it is very important to have it attended to medically, even if you do not like allopathic medicine. You will not be able to do *anything* without a properly functioning thyroid.

Most of the time such an extreme reaction is rare, and if you use your common sense, spot the early signs, and treat it accordingly, it will never become a major issue. Such careful attention to the body used to be a major survival mechanism, and in pre-industrial times the magician (along with everyone else) would pay far more attention to their body's signs of distress, however subtle they may be. With today's super-baseball-bat steroids, antibiotics, antivirals, vaccines, etc. we have become complacent and tend to ignore or not even notice the body's distress signals. We think that taking a pill will make things better – a sweet honeymoon of medical science that is slowly coming to an end in many areas of medicine. Learn to respect and care for your body!

With men, the thyroid is more often poked in the direction of hyperactivity, and although this is not a common reaction that men have to magic, it can happen in sensitive people. If, after working powerful magic, any man finds that they have difficulty sleeping, develop a fast heart rate, become anxious, and start to lose weight, and these symptoms continue for days and beyond, then the time has come to see a doctor. Do not try and treat a hyperactive thyroid yourself: it is a major health threat and can quickly get out of hand. Such hyperthyroidism in men as a direct result of magic is very rare to see, but I have come across it. As with all things magical, learning comes from first-hand experience and observation and not just studying: without paying attention, there is no progression.

7. Gland summary

The more I have observed physical reactions in magicians, and studied those reactions through readings, observations, etc., the more I have the sneaking suspicion that the hypothalamic-pituitary-adrenal axis is thrown into slight disorder through severe magical impact. When the HPA axis is disturbed, it can cause a cascade effect through the endocrine system, affecting the above-mentioned glands along with disturbing a woman's menstrual cycle and generally causing fatigue, issues with body temperature, metabolism, and so forth.

Similar disturbances can be observed in people with post-traumatic stress disorder, and my guess is that prolonged and profound magical impact, or a serious long-term magical attack, can trigger a similar response to PTSD in the body. I am not a doctor and there are obviously no medical studies that have looked at the physical effects of magical impact, but after years of observation I have seen the similarities too often to come to any other conclusion.

8. Magical catalysts

A magical catalyst is where a magical action triggers a healing crisis within the body. Sometimes this is simply a side-effect of magical work being done, and sometimes it is triggered intentionally by an inner being that sees an imbalance within you and initiates an action that will trigger a healing response.

Often when the body is triggered in this way, it is not simply a passive healing crisis whereby an immune response is triggered, the magician rides out the response, and is all healed at the end. Life is never quite that easy. A magical catalyst will bring unresolved issues with your body or mind into sharp focus, and will awaken or strengthen grumbling problems so that they become more visible. Expect any issues with your body or mind that you have been ignoring, or were not aware of, to be brought right out and shoved in your face.

Examples of this are a grumbling sore throat or a skin issue that suddenly explodes and becomes painfully acute after doing magic. Or a minor allergy to something unhealthy suddenly becomes a major issue. Whatever is out of balance will be magnified: any unhealthy foods or substances that you ingest will start causing major immune reactions.

Essentially, if you are not properly paying attention to your body and it is beginning to struggle, then the issue will be magnified until you 'get it'. This only tends to occur when the problem could eventually lead you down a very bad road: an inner contact or being happens to spot it and they decide to take action.

It is all about personal decision and choice. The balance of self-responsibility versus help from the inner worlds is always a fine set of scales. Inner contacts can show you things, guide you, act as a catalyst for you and so on, but how you choose to respond to their help is up to you, and your decision will dictate your future wellbeing.

So if, for example, a being triggers a response in your body and your immune system subsequently swings into action, you have two choices. You can either deal with it properly, which entails finding out exactly what is wrong, what caused it, and how best to treat it to restore balance; or you can ignore it or suppress it with drugs. The choice is yours.

Usually when an inner being acts as a catalyst for some bodily issue, this indicates that now is a prime time to tackle it. If you do take action, you will tend to find that help is guided towards you, and healers are put in your path who can help you.

APPENDIX A – MAGICAL HEALING

It can often take time and patience to heal imbalances that have been festering for a while, but such diligence pays off in the long term.

The best way I have found to differentiate between an impact and a catalyst situation is through divination. The deck you use is irrelevant, so long as you are familiar with it. What is important is to use a good layout and to phrase your questions carefully. (See Chapter 5: Tarot as a healing tool: layouts, and Chapter 7: Tarot as a healing tool: interpretation).

9. BEINGS AND THE DISTURBANCE OF THE MIND

This is one of the greatest dangers of powerful magic, though thankfully, depending upon how good your magical methods are, it is also a relatively rare problem. I mention it here only because it does sometimes happen and a magician needs to know its signs and symptoms, and what to do if it happens to someone they work with or they recognise it within themselves. Please also bear in mind that some of the symptoms of this problem can also manifest in more common and much less dangerous conditions. Here are some examples.

10. INTRUSION

This rare occurrence is very similar to a real possession (which is also very rare). If a being has half-pushed its way into you and is trying to push you out entirely, and any type of being can do this, it is important to be aware of it. You will feel 'half in' or 'half out' of your body, and you will be aware of a foreign being's presence within you. This is different to mental illness, and none of other symptoms that indicate psychosis will be present. If you catch the intrusion at this stage, it is relatively easy to get rid of it. Music is an excellent tool to ascertain what type of being that you are dealing with: certain pitches or sounds will suddenly become unbearable to you. When you find that sound, play it around you before you go into vision to tackle the intruder: this will loosen the hold the being has over you.

When you are ready, go first in vision into the Void and be still. You will be able to observe the being better while you are in the Void, and you will be able to ascertain without emotion why it is there and how it arrived. From that point, step out into the vision of the Desert and walk to the edge of the Abyss. This is as far as one can get to the foot of Divinity when you are in such a situation. Call upon the Keeper of the Abyss to take the being from your sphere, and then call upon the angelic beings that work in that space to repair your boundary so that it cannot get straight back in again. Once you have done that vision, take a ritual salt bath, and then create a talisman to beef up your boundaries for a week or two.

It is very important to understand how your body acquired a lodger, and how to prevent it from getting another one in the future. At this level of magic there is no step-by-step instruction: these sorts of events form part of your learning process, and it is important for you to learn how to get rid of unwelcome guests for yourself, how to repair yourself afterwards, and how to be more vigilant in the future.

As I said earlier, this happens very rarely, and usually not at all if you have a good magical working practice. Doing a banishing before a working or festooning yourself with protection will not work – if you are so locked-down, you cannot work at the power levels where such an incident could happen anyway.

What can cause such an event is working at a high power level without engaging the inner structures that come with their own inbuilt protection. Going off the beaten track into a high level of power can leave a magician vulnerable to an intrusion unless they are connecting with Divinity and working with the appropriate angelic structures for that realm. The other thing that can make a magician vulnerable to such an intrusion is intent: if you go deep into the inner realms with a self-centred agenda, then the powers that work with creation and destruction will simply ignore you: your wants and needs are totally irrelevant in the deeper realms.

If the being manages to get right into your body and push you out, then your everyday consciousness will not be focused anymore and it will be up to your deeper spirit to fight its way back. The one thing that can save a magician in such a terrible situation is a good understanding of the Qliphoth and its relationship with Divinity. Your body is a Qliphoth – that is to say, a vessel or container – that houses a spark of Divinity, a pattern that was established at your conception. A deep awareness of your relationship with Divinity will act as a safety mechanism, and one that will allow your spirit to re-establish its Divine right to inhabit that shell until your appointed time of death.

Such deep awareness is not a conscious thought that can be engaged like a weapon; rather it is a profound relationship between yourself, your body, and Divinity; a relationship that is established on a daily basis through your recognition of Divinity within you and all around you. That relationship is built up through daily simple meditation, and an awareness of Divinity within all substance.

This is why there are no shortcuts in magic: the simple tasks, meditations, rituals and visions that are used to slowly build a foundation for the magician to stand upon cannot be avoided or circumvented. If you try to do without them, and you still manage to reach deeply into the inner worlds and commune with power, then your lack of foundation could prove your downfall.

Such a foundation does not just come from joining a lodge or learning lessons; it comes from daily simple disciplines, the willingness to take your time to learn skills carefully, and a constant awareness of just how unimportant you really are.

Thankfully most magicians learn well, work carefully, and as a result do not encounter an intrusion; or they are stupid and because of that stupidity, never gain access to the realms of power where an intrusion could happen. But there are always exceptions, however rare, and one must always be prepared.

If you come across a magician who has been pushed out of his body and another being has moved into it, it is pointless to try to fix the situation yourself: the spirit of the magician must engage the rebalancing dynamic for themselves at a very deep level. All you can do is to go into vision and talk to their deeper spirit. You will usually find them at the side of the river of death. They will appear in the same way as many coma patients do: still attached to life via a cord, but unable or unwilling either to move forwards into death or back into life. When you find them, remind them of the Divine allocation of their shell (their body), and tell them that they must call upon the powers of Divinity to guide them back into it. After that, it is up to them. Magic is, above all other things, a school of soul-learning. That learning can be embraced and engaged, or it can be ignored and avoided.

11. Beings meet viruses in your body

This is a weird one, and it is also a fascinating one. It took me a few years to realise this was happening, but once my suspicions were aroused, I started to watch closer, to track the situations through readings, and to treat people accordingly.

What seems to happen is that certain types of inner-world beings also have a presence in our realm, and they have the ability to communicate with and enliven viruses lying dormant within the body. The being triggers the virus, which then activates, and the person gets sick. But as a result of the being's influence the virus acts in strange ways: the symptomatic picture is different, as though the virus had learned different ways to operate within the body, which in turn affects the body in very out-of-character ways.

This seems especially true of the herpes family of viruses. This is very interesting to me, as in biological terms a virus is not technically a life form as we understand it, unlike a bacterium or a fungus. In such situations it seems that either the virus 'changes its programming' in response to the inner being, or the inner being learns how to manipulate the virus to affect the body for its own ends. I'm not sure which it is, but the change in symptoms is very definite, and the virus itself tends to have a much more aggressive impact on the body.

When I first spotted this phenomenon in magicians, I would furiously treat them using my normal homeopathic and herbal methods, but the virus seemed far more resistant to my treatments than usual. When I looked in vision at the infected body, I saw a fascinating interplay between the virus (which appears as the viral structure trying to integrate itself with the nervous system) and another being. It took a while after spotting that (I'm a bit slow at times) to understand that I should try to deal with the being, not the virus, to see if that would settle things down.

So I started to experiment in different ways to eradicate the being, first through ritual bathing and cleaning, which didn't work, and then by having the magician ingest consecrated fluid. When that didn't work either, I went into the body in vision and manually hauled the being out of the magician's body. That did work. After I had removed the being and safely disposed of it, I started to treat the magician in the normal way. Now the treatment worked to a point, but either the pattern of the magician's physical relationship with the virus had changed, or how the virus operated within the body had been permanently changed. So I had to adapt how I chose remedies and treatments. Thinking sideways solved the problem.

Through the years I was confronted with several similar situations in sick magicians, and over time I learned that the best results came from a mixture of visionary work firstly to remove the being, and then more visionary work to communicate with the body. The communication with the body using vision was needed in order to inform the various organs and central nervous system that the virus it thought it was fighting had adapted rapidly, and was now possibly a composite of virus and inner being. After that, I would use homeopathic and herbal treatment.

This combination shifted the body's response mechanism to the virus, and helped it adapt to living alongside the virus without having an immune reaction. This seems to work better than fighting the virus directly and beating it into submission.

When I have used this method, it has usually been to help magicians suffering either from one of the various forms of herpes (it is a pretty large family of viruses) or HIV. But it is also worth considering if you are infected with a strain of hepatitis. In fact, if you live with any dormant virus that could pose a health risk, be aware that certain beings could trigger it back into action, and if that happens you will need to help your immune system to deal with it. It should also go without saying that if you have a potentially serious virus in your system, and it activates, your first action should be to go to a doctor. Magical healing work should always be conducted alongside allopathic medicine when treating moderate to serious illnesses.

I do not know if this relationship with viruses is intentional on the parts of these sorts of beings, or if it is just a matter of 'wrong place wrong time.' When a being has attached itself or has moved into the body (not a possession, but more of an 'infection'), it is important to strip that being out before you do anything else. Often these beings are similar to parasites: they are small, low-level entities and seem to get themselves into other living beings so that they can set up home. They do not necessarily affect the magician's mind or consciousness, but they can affect bodily functions.

Another instance where this can happen, and where it is definitely not deliberate on the being's part, is where the power/energy communion between the magician and the being accidentally activates the virus. This can happen with powerful angelic contact: the power surge that can happen from working with angelic beings in vision can sometimes trigger latent viruses within the body, subsequently swinging them into action.

In these cases, I think that either the immune system gets geared up by the inrush of power and goes off looking for a fight, or the virus is reawakened so that the magician can learn how to work with it. Some of these illnesses cannot be cured, but how the body lives with the virus can be changed: it is often the body's immune reaction to the virus that causes the problem, and so the way forward may be to shift how the body responds, rather than fight the virus.

Most of the time, good working practice usually prevents these sorts of problems, but they can occasionally happen to anyone working in any depth in the inner worlds. Think of it in terms of catching a cold from going into the city and being around a lot of people. Basic hygiene and common sense can usually keep you healthy, but there are still going to be times when you catch something. It is back to the old mantra of pay attention, and act accordingly.

Chapter 8

Visionary healing: part one

1. Going down the rabbit hole

The use of visionary methods to aid the body in the healing and cleansing process is an important skill for the magician to learn. Any human can use the mind in order to trigger a healing or cleansing response, and this action engages the consciousness in an active conversation with the body. However, when such work is done by a magician who is trained or skilled in visionary magic, something very special happens: the consciousness becomes an active participant in an action that goes beyond the individual – it initiates a conversation not only with the body, but with the spiritual beings that flow all around us in the constant universal dance of creation and destruction.

This is one of the hallmarks of visionary work: engaging the conscious mind in a focused way to enable an action or reaction to occur within both the body and the spirit, in union with the many beings that are 'outside' of us.

This working in tandem with inner world beings is what separates visionary work from our own psychology. Psychological therapy uses visionary work or pathworking to achieve a deeper engagement with ourselves. Visionary magic uses visionary work in order to engage with inner beings and realms that are not our own, and which exist independently of us.

When a magician uses such techniques, and works within a magical healing framework or structure, two things happen: firstly, beings that are able to assist us are called upon, and secondly, the magician learns to partially dissociate themselves from their body in order to objectively 'treat' it. Our bodies are our vehicles; they are not our sole identity.

By learning how to work with the body in a team sense as opposed to a 'self' sense, the mind is able to engage healing and regenerative responses without the magician identifying themselves with the process. This is a very important step.

When the body becomes sick from a magical impact, attack or infestation, it is important not to take it personally or to personally identify with the problem. Such isolation pulls the magician away from the more toxic side of psychology that we have developed, and enables the magician to see clearly and without emotion.

Psychology has brought many wonderful things to our door, but it has also brought along many disabling elements, too. Rudolf Steiner began to understand the self's separate existence from the body, and to understand that we stand in line with many other beings that have no physical form, but which nevertheless affect our physical world. Unfortunately the world of science was unable or unready to accept such a concept, and Steiner's experiences were watered down and reinterpreted both by himself and his students in order to protect the awakening science of anthroposophy. But many magicians will look at his paintings, read his words, and nod with recognition at what this talented man was seeing as he peered behind the veil.

If you only reach within yourself for healing, knowledge and wisdom, you will pull from a very limited pot, while many inner beings stand around and observe you with amusement. If however you understand, particularly as a magician, that the world does not begin and end with you, that you are not god, that you are not all beings, and that you do not have a secret stash of wisdom consciousness hidden away in your armpit or somewhere that you could tap into if only you used the right psychology, then such an awakening of understanding will open your eyes to the true vastness of the consciousness that is all around us. We are a very small and insignificant part of the universe, and if we approach the universe properly, we can learn much, gain help and guidance, and become a part of the huge team called creation.

This understanding allows us to surrender our sense of control over everything and ask for help. Through divination, meditation and visionary work we can stand back, ask for advice, and look at the best way forward when we stand at a crossroads. The ability to open our eyes and 'see' is one of the most powerful gifts a magician can have. Magic is not about control; it is about informed choices.

With visionary healing, we engage that power of choice and reach out to the beings all around us to ask for assistance, and of course, we also offer that assistance back when it is needed. It is always a two-way conversation.

2. When to use visionary healing

In this day and age, we are programmed to think in terms of multiple choice questions, and we have a very black-or-white view on most things that we encounter. Life is really not like that, and there are no hard and fast rules as to when visionary healing is the appropriate healing method; often healing the body, soul and mind requires a complex pattern of different healing modalities, selected according to the flow of power both around and within the magician.

This is where divination comes in handy: it is important to work with your body in the way it needs at that specific time. Often those needs will either fluctuate unpredictably or ebb and flow predictably, so it is important to be pliable enough in how you approach your own healing in order to respond appropriately.

So for example, if a magician has taken a major impact or two which has damaged them, or they have become chronically ill, then it is likely that the healing process will include visionary work, herbs, homeopathy, acupuncture, allopathic medicine and rest – though not all at the same time!

The body is a very finely-tuned instrument, and becoming aware of its needs, its language and its energy fluctuations is important so that you can respond and change your healing approach as and when the body asks for it. Do not feel that you can just choose one healing method and run with it, and that such action would suffice; such an attitude is folly, and is a product of our modern 'go to' world. You cannot pop a pill or herb or do a vision and think everything will now be OK; healing is an unfolding process.

Visionary healing is often needed when there has been a major hit on the body, and the emotions, personality or mind have begun to show changes. It is also useful when there is or has been an infestation or a major disease that has an inner being behind it. The visionary work can run concurrent with proper medical care; the inner doctor and the outer doctor! Visionary healing can be overused and can hamper a person's recovery if it is used obsessively, but used properly it can massively speed up the healing process.

The keys to success are as follows: Look through divination: *"will this help the body?"* Work with the appropriate visionary structure, and then let it do its work. If you are not cured after six hours, do not be tempted to try again! Visionary work done on the body takes time to do its work. Sometimes you do feel a massive difference within twenty-four hours; sometimes it needs to bring on a healing crisis.

The methods of visionary healing work from the outside in: first you focus on the structure of the body (i.e. its organs, bones, etc.). From there you step deeper in, and work with the energetic wheels that uphold the endocrine system. Then you move in still deeper to the subtle body and work with the flows of inner power, before finally working upon the inner pattern of manifestation itself that allows you to exist in the physical realm.

Always start from the outside in. Never go straight to the source pattern: to do so can sometimes shock the system. I used to work from the deepest point and then work outwards, but I found that doing so caused an unhelpful overreaction in the body. Working from the outside in allows the deeper energetic body to slowly adjust to the work, thus enabling a steady, stable response.

3. STILLNESS

In all of my books I rattle on about the need to learn how to be within stillness. I am that 'nagging aunt' for a very good reason: without stillness there *is* no visionary work. When you are sick or infested, it is hard to maintain stillness, but it is very important to do a stillness meditation every day, even if only for a few minutes. This also prepares you for visionary work, and allows you to focus on the job at hand. It also gives your mind and body space to begin the cleanup that it needs.

4. CLEANING AND VACUUMING, SEWING AND PATCHING

A lot of visionary healing is very practical in its approach: you imagine the use of tools that you are familiar with in everyday life. If you see yourself cleaning the body out with a vacuum cleaner, you are signalling to an inner being working with you that you are trying to 'clean' the body.

Appendix A – Magical Healing

Often modern spiritual healing methods engage abstract concepts that we do not fully understand, therefore any being trying assist us has no clue what it is we are trying to do. Use your conscious imagination as a vocabulary of communication: if you want to wash something, see yourself with a wet cloth and soap! It is that simple.

Often when the body is impacted from magic, or you have travelled in vision to an unhealthy place, there is a good chance that you are covered in spiritual dirt, gribblies (a highly-technical term for low-level parasitical beings!) etc. You may have been injured, torn something, or had a piece bitten out of you. In such cases visionary magic would be the first port of call, after which it would be wise to use herbs to mop up the residue and trigger healing.

This method can also be used when you have gone into a very bad place in the outer world, and have taken an energetic impact as a result. If the impact is big enough, a ritual cleansing bath will not be enough: you will also need to do an internal visionary cleaning. So how do you do it? Quite simply, really.

Light a candle, and do a stillness meditation. After a few minutes, call upon the deity you work with, or upon Divinity and the angelic beings that work between Divinity and humanity, or upon the Goddess within the land to guide and protect you as you work. This is an important step, as it immediately signals an intention to work with Divine forces which in turn alters the energetic frequency around you: this keeps you safe while you work.

Note: Do not call upon specific named angels – simply ask 'The Angels of Divinity' or 'Angels of the Lord' to assist you. This allows the appropriate angel to step in, the one who is best suited for the job.

There is no need for impressive rituals and callings. As a magician, simply stating your submission to the Divine force is enough to engage it at a passive level. If, however, you are working on something far more powerful than dirt and gribblies, then you will need a more targeted approach.

Close your eyes, and see the room around you in your mind. Step out of your body and stand before it in vision. Call upon the Father and the Mother to guide and watch over you as you work. See a tool kit and cleaning kit at the side of your body.

As you begin to work, you may become aware of beings working with you, handing you tools and taking the dirt away. It is also good to note that what you see as a vacuum cleaner is actually a being you are working with – the vacuum imagery simply enables you to work quickly and allows the being to get on with its job.

Look into the body to see any dark areas, small beings clinging onto the spine or neck, or around the pelvic region or genitals. Look for grubs, eggs, and anything that looks like it should not belong there, and start to take them out using a vacuum cleaner. Vacuum throughout the body, making sure you get into all the corners, and pay particular attention to the spine and the brain.

When you are done with the vacuum, then get out the hosepipe and flush the body clean. If you see rips or tears in or around the body, sew or glue them back up. When you have finished cleaning the body, see yourself digging a hole in the floor down into the earth, and empty the vacuum bag into the land where it will compost. Once finished, come out of vision and immediately take a ritual salt bath.

This is the first stage of visionary healing, and it is the method used to clear the decks of low-level dirt and beings so that you can begin to work on what is *underneath* all that dirt, and to also begin to work on the body itself. This method of work is very 'shamanic' in its application; such an approach works well with the body, and there is no need for anything more ritualised or spiritualised. It is a matter of rolling your sleeves up and getting on with it.

5. THE GUARDIANS OF THE ORGANS

As you will have noticed, visionary healing starts from the outside and works in. Rather than going straight into deep spirit and working with the life force, it is better to start at the surface by cleaning up the body, ensuring that its physical substance is worked on before moving deeper into the more powerful thresholds within the body.

The reason for working from outside to inside, from mundane to spirit, is because such a graded process allows the body to adjust energetically at every step, and it therefore does not shock or burden the body. In today's world, we often think that more and stronger is better, which is not always the case, particularly where the body is concerned. The human body often responds far better to subtle hints than it does to shouting.

After the body has been cleaned, it is time to talk to the Guardians. You can talk to your own or you can talk to someone else's: like all of this work, it is both for personal use and for use in service to fellow magicians. Working with the Guardians of the Organs essentially means talking to the organs and to the spirits that reside within them.

This is an alien concept to us in the West, and I fell across it while reading texts about acupuncture. When it comes to an unfamiliar magical technique, I first work with it practically to see if it does work, and then if it does, I explore further to see how it works, why it works, etc. And I can tell you, boy does this one work! It is also very interesting, and what it revealed certainly changed how I viewed my body. Who said you cannot teach an old dog new tricks...

Using visionary focus, sit quietly and meditate for a little while to settle everything down and become still. Once you are nice and quiet, be aware of yourself and of your body, and be aware of where your organs are and what they do. Focus first on the organ you feel is under the most stress, and using the same technique as 'cleaning your body,' go into your body in vision and look at the organ. Imagine the organ as a person, or a chamber with a person in it. This focused imagination creates an interface which allows you to interact with the spirit guardian or consciousness housed within the organ.

Look at what state they are in. Are they tired? Do they look ill? Do their surroundings look dusty or damaged? Talk to the guardian and tell them that you want to help. Clean up their area, wash them, and visualise them as full of power, well-dressed, and with a light or sunlight streaming into their space.

Work instinctively. When I worked with my heart, he looked like a tired old king in a dusty hall. I cleaned up the hall and imagined sunlight reaching him. As I was working, I got the strong impression that there were channels running around him that should be filled with water, but which were dry. I imagined the channels filling with fluid and flowing all around him.

Suddenly the old king woke up, and began to shine and look very regal. (And I felt the positive effect from that vision within an hour of finishing it.) I talked with him and checked that he was happy before I moved on to another organ.

Rather than look up any organ's attributes in the Five Spirit texts on acupuncture, I simply allowed the spirits to present themselves. By imagining a human interface, it lets the spirit interact with you and use your mind to create a common language. I did find, after I went back to the texts, that what I had 'imagined' corresponded pretty closely with what had been written. This is always the best way to work – find out for yourself what is there, and then check your observations with the textbooks.

After a few months of working this way and once communication was established, if a particular organ was struggling, it would 'tell' me: I would become very aware of the organ in question while going about my everyday life, and when that 'alarm' awareness happened, I would go in vision as soon as possible and talk to it. Often it needed some help or interaction.

This might all sound very strange, but hey – magic *is* strange, and it is important in magic to explore and find things out for yourself, rather than either dismissing a claim out of hand, or taking it on board without direct, personal experience.

I was quite astonished at the simplicity but also the effectiveness of this technique, but when I sat and thought about it, it did occur to me that we are, in fact, made up of many different beings. The human body houses masses of different bacteria, viruses, fungi, and God knows what else: we are a collective, and between us all we keep the body going. So it pays to know who your close neighbours are!

6. Colouring with the organs

This is closely connected with the concept of talking with the organs, but this particular technique looks at the energy around and within the organ. Essentially, the energy fluctuations of a body part can be perceived by visionary magicians in terms of colour. The identification of an energy by its colour is an old technique and one that has been long used in magic, but many magicians think of it as an intellectual attribute rather than a literal 'colour.' Nothing could be further from the truth. All energy vibrates at a particular frequency, and our brains can translate that frequency into colour or sound.

If an organ appears to have a red glow around it, then the chances are it is infected or inflamed. If it is grey, then it is probably lacking in energy and is breaking down. If the kidneys and adrenals are under stress, they too may appear red: allow your instincts to kick in when interpreting the colours rather than using any intellectual form.

If the organ is displaying a colour that is not right, simply imagine washing it with a colour that is healthier, calmer and more vital. When you have finished with the vital organs, imagine your body with all these different colours flowing in and around it. If you can, go have a sleep after doing this work, so that the power can integrate properly and the organs can begin their regeneration processes.

If you practise this technique, you will find that it is very handy when you are suddenly under stress or fall ill; you can immediately direct the right frequency of energy to a particular organ to assist it in its rebalancing process.

7. Working with the endocrine system

This part of the human body can really take a hit from various forms of visionary and ritual magic if the work is prolonged and powerful. One of the various ways of healing such an impact is to work in vision directly with the glands themselves. Unlike the organs, the endocrine glands do not seem to have 'spirit guardians' so much as a dynamic that in Eastern meditation is known as the chakras. 'Chakra' means 'vortex' or 'wheel,' and that is exactly what appears in vision over the major glands. These wheels can be worked with and strengthened if the magician has good visionary skills.

A word of caution: if you are using this work on someone else to assist in their healing, and if they are very sensitive, be careful not to overstimulate these power glands. I once inadvertently overstimulated a thyroid gland in a sensitive visionary by being too enthusiastic in the work I did on them.

The magician was suffering from an impacted thyroid which had become very slow. I stimulated the gland, and twenty-four hours later I had a frantic magician at my door who was whizzing around like a hummingbird – oops. So tread carefully. You can always do a bit more work on a gland if it doesn't respond, and it is easier to give a gland more impetus than it is to slow it back down again if you overstimulate it.

The wheels work down the body from above the head to the groin, and then finally down to the earth. The first wheel, which appears over the top of a person's head, is in magical terms an energetic anchor that filters that person's future. The second wheel appears at the forehead, and stimulates the hypothalamus, pineal and pituitary glands.

These three glands work in tandem, and the pineal in particular is more active in visionary magicians than in the ordinary person in the street. The pineal seems to work as a primal anchor, with the hypothalamus and pituitary busying themselves with keeping stasis and filtering power.

The next gland to have a wheel over it is the thyroid, and then below that the thymus. Just under the sternum is the pancreas which also has a wheel, and in the position of the umbilicus is the wheel that affects the adrenals. The groin also has a wheel which governs the sexual organs, and the final wheel, which often does not appear on Eastern medicine charts, is the grounding wheel which appears just under the feet.

These wheels chart a line through the body and beyond, and linked together they form a power highway axis that the rest of the body operates around. They work in tandem, and should all be running at the same speed. When working in vision with these wheels, if you find one that is not running at the same speed as the others, it identifies a problem in that area of the body.

To work in vision with these wheels, lie down and still yourself. When you are sure you are still, visualise yourself within the body and be aware of these wheels. To some they appear within the body, but for me they always appear just above its surface, hovering over my skin.

I have developed a visionary language so that I can interface with these wheels, and that visionary language is to see them as mechanical wheels with cogs at their base and a setting indicator at the top. The indicator dial has twelve settings, with the sixth setting at twelve o'clock: this is the default setting that they should all run at to be healthy.

The wheels all have their own unique energetic 'light' and colour, which seems to vary from person to person. Using your imagination, start with the wheel above your head, and build an awareness of its brightness and setting. If it is dark, it will need cleaning and light bringing into it to energise it. I imagine a well of energy at my umbilicus that I can draw from to brighten up dull wheels.

When I have worked on these wheels both on myself and other people, I did notice that the first and last (over the head and under the feet) had no setting range, just brightness and colour. So start from the top wheel and work on its colour and brightness. As you work to energise it, you will instinctively become aware if its colour is not right: trust your instinct and experiment – it is the best way to learn!

When you move down to the wheels that are over the glands, you will become aware of their settings, cogs, base, etc. If the setting is too low or too high, adjust it (I see myself turning a knob until the pointer is at midpoint). If it will not move, it may have a blockage. If that is the case, then imagine getting into the cog underneath the wheel where it 'plugs' into the body, and see if there is any stuff blocking it.

I say stuff, because when I see it, it is like dirty glue or a calcified build-up. I just clean it off, grease the mechanism down, and set it off again. Work with the imagination in ways that are familiar to you: imagine cleaning cogs and wheels, washing things down, brushing them, and if the energy is low, imagine a hosepipe from the stars that runs to your energy pot in your umbilicus to 'fill the tank' back up. By using such familiar images, your body, spirit, and any other beings around you know what it is you are trying to do.

Work your way down the body, take note of ones going too slow or too fast, reset them and finish with the energetic one under your feet. If one is going slow and refuses to speed up, then it is probably going slow for a reason. If there is infection or something invasive going on in that region of the body, the wheel that sits over or close to it will slow down as the body tries to fight whatever it is fighting. I am guessing here, but chances are it is slowing down to stop any invader having access to the energy it dispenses.

A few times when I have worked on people, one of their wheels would just not budge its speed even after it had been cleaned and energised. Without fail, a few days later that person would get sick, and the sickness would focus on the area near the slowed wheel. After their immune system had done its job and suppressed the invaders, the wheel would speed up again. I found that absolutely fascinating.

To me (and I may be stating something that everyone except me already knew) it would seem that these wheels are like an energy highway for the body. Just as the endocrine glands function as controllers, communicators and governors, the 'inner' endocrine system (these wheels) distribute energy to those glands and their surrounding organs in order to help them work.

If when you are working on these wheels you find that one of them is out of rhythm, use the method of going into the body in vision, and look around the affected area: look at the organs, nerves and bones, and see if you can find where the problem lies.

8. The inner landscape

This technique is an interesting and powerful way to look at the overall health of a body, to spot disturbances at a deep psychic level, to see if there are any unwelcome spirits deeply embedded within the container of the body, and to look at the deeper personality or the soul of the person.

To access the inner landscape I use a simple visionary interface: I use vision to go into the body, up the spine and into the brain. I move deep into the centre of the brain, and there I 'see' a doorway. I go through the doorway, and up some old stone steps which open out onto a landscape.

When I first came across this level of the body's consciousness, I worked within people's landscapes to initiate healing; but I gradually found that making changes in this place seemed to shortcut their long-term, deep soul learning. I learned eventually not to tinker with a person's inner landscape, but to merely observe and take note: it would give me a great deal of detail about how deep the damage was, and that information would then guide me as to what sort of healing was necessary.

The inner landscape does not appear as an inner body; rather it appears as a nature landscape. For years I could not understand why it should appear this way, but the deeper I delved into visionary Kabbalah, the more it made sense. The landscape is Malkuth: the container of the Divine Spark, the manifest world, and everything that physically appears in the physical realm. Every physical thing that manifests is a container for Divinity, and the first expression of that manifestation is the land. The living beings all sprang from the landscape – we truly are children of the Great Mother.

When you look at a person's inner landscape, take note of the weather, of the land itself, the nature that is alive (trees, plants, water, rock) and any beings that are present besides the person themselves. Most people appear in their landscapes, and how they appear will tell you a great deal about the state of their deeper spirit.

Do they appear as children? Do they appear old or young, healthy or ill, strong or faint? What type of landscape do they have? Is it barren, fruitful, balanced with land and water; is it a garden, is it in a state of nature, or is it a harsh and lifeless landscape?

I found over the years that bad weather such as storms would herald illness or infection, a lacklustre landscape indicated low energy, and a lack of landscape or a chaotic one would often indicate more serious mental issues. I have come across landscapes that do not have any nature within them at all, and I eventually learned that such people seemed 'new' to humanity, as if they did not understand nature or humanity at all; it is as if they came from some other realm that had little or no connection with humanity.

Occasionally I came across other beings in a landscape, and I learned that often they were trying to move into a person and establish themselves. Often a sharp telling-off and showing them 'the door' would get rid of them, but by doing this I bypassed the person's own inner immune system, and they did not learn how to defend themselves from such an invasion. I eventually figured out that it is better to work at a more 'surface' level with the endocrine system, organs, brain, and nervous system, followed by ritual bathing, so that the body itself expelled the intruder.

I also found, mainly in more vulnerable teens and young adults, that occasionally when a person was in an abusive relationship, their abuser would appear in their landscape, as if they had bypassed the natural boundaries of the spirit and were operating energetically at a deep level in the victim's psyche. Obviously this is not intentional on the abuser's part, but that type of person seems to have a natural ability literally to 'invade' someone. In such cases I simply took note and worked at more outer levels to strengthen the person emotionally, so that they could eventually break the connection for themselves. That way, their own inner immune system could learn and mature.

If you are working within your own landscape it is a slightly different situation. There are times when it is okay to work on your own landscape, and there are times to simply observe, take note, and act from an outer approach. If you do find a being wandering about your inner landscape, simply tell it to fuck off out (ancient ritual words!) and then work from a more outer perspective to strengthen your mind, body and energy so that it cannot happen again.

As with all deeper magic, there are no hard and fast lists of rules to follow. You must learn the basics first, and then work instinctively, use divination to track your progress and options, and learn by practical experience. The more you work, the more you will learn for yourself and discover your own vocabulary of practice.

Every culture around the world has its own versions of this type of work in their mystical texts; the key is to not be dogmatic but to understand that they are talking from their own time and culture, and that none of us have all the answers. It is better to use texts as signposts but walk the path yourself, and adjust your work according to what you find, how it works, and what reactions you have to it.

9. Working with the patterns of life force

This is the deepest form of visionary healing that can be done on a person, and it works at the threshold where the spirit and the body come together to exist as a living human. This level of visionary healing works with the power of the weaver: a pattern within the Mysteries that presents itself in the Inner Desert at the edge of the Abyss in the form of a web of geometric patterns made up of angelic beings.

Those beings create thresholds and filters for the Utterance of Divinity to flow through into manifestation. Everything in creation has octaves, and the web pattern found deep in the inner worlds as a filter for manifestation also presents at a lower octave in our bodies. We too have a threshold pattern that allows the Utterance of Divinity to flow into us, giving us our life force. Sometimes, that web can get damaged and needs attending to.

In the ordinary everyday person, such a breakdown of the pattern is connected with ageing and long-term disease: it is a part of the destruction process that will eventually lead someone to their death. In a magician, such damage to the pattern can also come about from magical impact, attack, or a power issue. In these cases it is important to repair the damage at the deepest level.

If a magical impact or attack damages the pattern at this level, no matter what other healing is done, the magician will neither fully recover nor have their power restored if their pattern of life is torn. The best way to tell if the magician is damaged at this level is to look via readings.

To work at this level of healing it is useful to plug into something more powerful than yourself. Whereas all the other healing methods rely on the magician and the usual beings around him or her, working with the pattern of life is far more effective if the magician plugs themselves into the deeper pattern at the edge of Abyss. This involves working in two places at once and bringing the octaves together.

It requires a good working knowledge of the Kabbalistic Inner Desert, a familiarity with working at the edge of the Abyss with the pattern of manifestation, and the ability to work with angelic beings in vision.

The first step of this work is to go in vision into the Inner Desert and walk to the edge of the Abyss. Turn around to face down the Desert/Tree of Life with the intention of working with the pattern of manifestation. This pattern appears at the edge of the Abyss and is akin to watching angelic beings play cats cradle. Walk through the pattern (doing this triggers your own pattern), and continue walking within the pattern as you move down the Desert/Tree and step over the threshold of Malkuth.

See yourself walking into mist with the intention of going to your own body or the body you will be working on. Also be aware of angelic beings walking behind you as you emerge out of the mist. You do not need to communicate or interact with them; rather your approach and intention tells them what you are about to do.

As you walk out of the mist, the building where your body is emerges in front of you: step into the building, go to the body, and look at it. Give yourself time to adjust as you look into the body: have the intention of seeing the web pattern of manifestation in the body – it usually fans out from the umbilicus in all directions. Look for breaks in the pattern, frayed bits, or signs of tearing or impact. One of the angelic beings will position themselves behind you and will work through you, their arms through your arms.

Don't allow your intellect to intervene; it is better to work instinctively so that the beings behind you can work properly through you. Let your hands work like a spider, reweaving and reattaching, with threads coming out of your hands as you weave. Make sure that all the threads coming out of the umbilicus are reattached to where they should be, and that all the lines that were broken are rewoven. Once you have finished, it is then time to ensure that life energy can run properly through the pattern.

Look at the point from which all the threads originate, the point of the umbilicus. If you look closely, you will see that they seem to emerge from a small well. Make sure the well is clear of blockage so that power can flow properly.

There are two actions that can be done now to ensure the strength of life flows properly through the person. The first is to energise the pattern itself, to fill it with life force. Reach down into the tiny well at the umbilicus until you feel the life force, and pull it up to the surface. The pattern should immediately light up and glow brightly. This will also show you if there are any hidden tears that you missed.

The second action is to strengthen the person's spirit so that they are properly seated in their energetic and physical body. To do this, go behind the body and look at the back of the neck.

An angelic being will understand what it is you are about to do and will stand behind you. As you look at the base of the neck, you will notice a small opening that looks a little like a mouth: place your lips just in front of the mouth and you will feel the angel doing the same behind you. The mouth on the back of the neck of the body will react to your presence and will open slightly.

A noise will build up behind you, like muttering and singing. You will feel the angelic being placing their mouth on the back of your neck and breathing: this will cause an immediate build-up of power within you, a power that vibrates like a lot of voices. Open your mouth and let that power/vibration flow through your neck and out through your mouth: it will flow straight into the neck and body that you are working on.

The power pattern of the body will begin to vibrate and produce its own sound, and the sound that has flowed through you will join in. It becomes a symphony of life: all life is a vibration or frequency of power, and this action refocuses, reaffirms and reawakens the deepest part of a person, reminding them who they are. This action is a much lower octave of the Divine action of uttering a being into life, what is known in the Bible as 'The Word.'

This magical action is a profound and difficult one, which will leave you tired. It is important to sleep after doing this work, regardless of whether you do it on yourself or on someone else. It is not to be done lightly, and must only be done when absolutely necessary.

10. Summary

Visionary magic that focuses specifically on working directly with the body and within the body can be a powerful tool in the healing process. It gives the healing process a strong energetic foundation that the outer healing can stand upon: no matter what concoctions you give a person, if they have low vital force or are damaged at an inner level, the healing will not be successful or sustained until the deeper healing is done.

The methods of visionary healing that we looked at in this chapter work directly between magician and body. Sometimes we need a little more help if we have been knocked heavily, or the healing work needs to be done in a more structured visionary form. This is when the magician goes in vision to various realms to work with beings or deities who will intervene and assist in the healing process. That is what we will discuss in the next chapter.

Chapter 9

Visionary healing: part two

1. The call for help

Sometimes a magician can get so battered down from working powerfully in magical service that they need a helping hand from the inner worlds. A major impact cannot be fixed by doing a single vision, but working carefully with a deity both in vision and through protection magic over a period of time can assist dramatically with the healing process.

If the magical impact has caused chronic infection or a sustained immune response, then it is best to work with Underworld deities and visions in order to help the body fight the infection. If the inner pattern of the magician has been damaged, then one method of approaching that problem is to work with angelic beings and the patterns of life itself while in vision. None of these methods are a replacement for wise actions, medicine, and caring correctly for the body, but they are among many of the tools that an experienced magician can use to help repair and regenerate it.

If you are planning to work with a deity in vision for deep healing, then it is a good idea to know what power you are working with, and whether it is the right power for what you are trying to achieve. Most of the deities that work well in this type of visionary healing are the ancient and Underworld goddesses: they are vessels who hold both regeneration and destruction within their power. The older and more stable the goddess, the more successful the work will be.

I work a lot with Sekhmet, who is a goddess of both destruction and regeneration (her most regenerative healing aspect also appears as Hathor). She poisons and spills epidemics out into the world, but she also carries the cures for such calamities: every powerful deity will have both sides of a power dynamic within their repertoire.

If a magician has been working deep in the Underworld or the Abyss, or has been attacked by beings or forces that are generated in these places, then the most likely presentation of illness from such contact will be an infection of the mind or body. In such a case it is to the Underworld that we turn to for help: always work with powers that are familiar with the issue.

In this chapter we will look at a specific visionary pattern for Sekhmet, before going into broader, less-defined areas of visionary healing. The vision that works with Sekhmet will show you how the structure works when you approach a powerful deity for healing. The other forms of visionary healing in this chapter have a broader sweep that the magician can adjust as needed for their own personal work.

2. Working with Sekhmet

Why Sekhmet? Most magic we encounter in the Western world has deep roots in the land of Egypt and the surrounding areas of Mediterranean North Africa, the Near East, and Southern Europe. Sekhmet is a very old deity and a form of the Underworld Goddess who appears within the land throughout Europe, North Africa, and the Near and Middle East. Neolithic portrayals of her have been found in Europe, and she is a power who presents herself often in deep magical work.

Her Egyptian form as Sekhmet is an interface that has been used for millennia, and her temple images still stand *in situ* – this is very important when reaching for an ancient deity: if the outer magical and ritual structure is still there, it is much easier to tap into the contact.

If you wish to work with her, it is wise to have good manners as she is a powerful and fierce goddess (alternatively you can work with Hathor; go where your instinct tells you to go). Having an image of her at home or in your temple where you can sit and talk with her, work with her, and give her offerings (a lit candle, a bowl of water, etc.) will create a good working relationship. It is not about worship but respect, and honouring a power that is far greater than you are.

By first building a relationship with Sekhmet in such a way, it not only makes it easier to work with her in depth in vision, but it also gives you brownie points: she is more likely to be willing to help you if you honour her properly.

To approach her in vision in her Underworld temple (as opposed to visiting her in a surface-world temple) is to meet her at her most powerful. Be aware that nothing can be hidden from her, and a deep undercurrent of Ma'at runs through her: she is the defender of Ma'at, and of the order of life and death. If you approach her with selfishness, with hidden unbalanced intent, or to greedily ask for power, she will tear you apart. But if you approach her with openness, seeking her help after being damaged while acting in service, then she will become both Sekhmet and Hathor: the defender and the healer.

Because of the primal depths of Sekhmet's power and the strands of life that she holds, it is important that you place yourself before her at some point in your magical life, no matter how scary she can be. The vision of Sekhmet works on two different levels. The first level connects you to the formalised temple structure that has been built around her, and the second level of the vision takes you into direct contact with her power before it became too heavily formalised.

3. Vision of Sekhmet

For effective use, record this vision or have someone record it for you, and follow it passively for the first time or two. This enables you to learn the 'path' to Sekhmet. Once you know the way there, then it is important to be able to do the vision for yourself without recordings or help from others.

To prepare for the vision, have a candle lit before a traditional or ancient image of Sekhmet, and sit down quietly. Do not lie down, as it is important not to fall asleep during this vision. Close your eyes and go into the stillness. Meditate for a few minutes to totally still yourself and prepare for work.

With closed eyes, imagine that you can see the candle flame before you using your inner vision. As you look at the flame, remember your intent to visit the Underworld temple of Sekhmet. As you think about that temple, a large hole opens up in the ground before you and the candle plunges down it, deep down into the land. You watch the candle fall, and decide to follow it. Jump into the hole. Do not fear it, or fear falling: trust, and jump.

Your body turns and tumbles as you fall deeper and deeper into the land, and the light of the surface world vanishes above you, leaving you to fall in darkness. You fall and fall, deeper and deeper into the land, entering the Underworld as you fall. You can hear water running around you, but you see nothing as you fall down and down. A wind comes up from beneath you, and seems to slow your falling until you almost come to a stop. You land in water, finding yourself surfacing and swimming in an underground lake, but it is dark, and you can barely see anything. The only source of light is a flame in the distance, and you swim towards it.

The closer you get to the flame, the lighter the cavern becomes, and more flames appear. As you look around, you see that you are in a deep Underworld temple that is vast. The ceilings of the cavern are all painted deep blue with golden stars, and the closer you get to the lights, the more you notice large stone columns appearing on either side of you. The lights guide you to some rough-hewn steps that lead you out of the water and into the temple.

Climbing out of the water, you stand and look in awe at the vast ancient place in which you find yourself. Before you is a parade of colossal columns, all beautifully and colourfully decorated. The columns seem to go on forever and vanish into clouds of steam and smoke in the distance.

Something draws you to the smoke, which smells strongly of tree resins, and as you walk into the smoke you are bathed in the sacred perfume of temple incense in preparation for meeting the great Sekhmet. Something pushes you to move forward, and as you emerge out of the smoke you find yourself standing before a vast statue of Sekhmet that seems to be a hundred feet high. Between her colossal feet is a doorway, and in front of the doorway is a stone table or oblong altar.

Bow deeply to the ancient goddess and reach into your pocket. Whatever you find there, you offer to her.[1] As you place the offering before her, the doors between

---

[1] If the object in your hand is something you own in your everyday life, then after the vision it must be given to her either by burying it, throwing it into a lake or river, giving it away to someone, or by burning it. It does not matter how valuable it is, you must give it to her. If it is something like your house keys, then be willing in your heart and mind to let it go. If you lose your house under such circumstances, then it is a good thing out of a bad – you no longer belong there and it is holding you back. It is important to learn to let go, to trust, and not to cling.

her feet open, and priests comes out. They indicate for you to get onto the altar, and to lie down. Once you lay down, they begin to work on your body by pulling things off of you, cleaning you, using medicines on your skin, and working energetically on you. Be still and let them work for however long it takes.

When they have finished, they step back and indicate for you to get off the altar and to enter the doorway between the feet of the goddess. As you step over the threshold of the door, you peer inside the chamber: it is dark, you can hear water dripping, and it smells strange. A hand pushes you from behind, and you stumble into the space as the doors slam shut behind you.

You find yourself in total darkness, but you can hear and smell a great deal. There is water all around you, and you can hear panting, like a large animal. A strong smell of lions fills the air, along with the smell of moss, damp stones, and earth. A light appears like a small oil lamp, and you gravitate towards it, treading carefully.

The lamp's flame slowly grows bigger so that you begin to see the cave in which you are standing. As you look around, you see a large, rough cave with many ancient primitive drawings painted on its walls. A small stream of water runs through the cavern, and the ground is littered with moss-covered rocks.

At the far end of the cave is a deep recess, and a fleeting movement in it catches your eye. Drawing closer you see an outline emerging, but it is not until you are very close that you see the two flashing lion eyes and the large outline: before you sits a tall black woman with the head and paws of a lion and the torso and limbs of a human. She is watching you to see how you will react to her. No matter how scared you are, inch closer and bow to honour her: this is Sekhmet in her true and most powerful form.

As you bow before her, she reaches out with a claw and scratches you deeply on the forehead. Blood runs down your face, and she moves closer to you to lick your face clean. The scratch has opened something in you, and you feel a deep shift in your body and mind. Sekhmet leans over you and breathes over the wound on your forehead, her breath reaching deep into your brain.

She sits back into the shadows as waves of darkness engulf you. You find yourself falling into darkness, tumbling around your memories and thoughts. The thoughts and memories slowly fade away as you fall through the darkness, until finally you stop falling and your mind moves into stillness and silence. There is no movement, no breath, no time, no thought: you drift in silence and your mind is calm, still and centred. This state fills you with peace and stability. Nothing intrudes, nothing demands; you simply *are*.

Within that stillness you slowly become aware of earth and rock all around you, of the roots of trees, the trickle of underground water, and the sleep of the ancestors who lie beside you. You are deep in the earth, at peace, in stillness – and yet you are still at the feet of the most ancient Lioness Goddess. A noise distracts you from the stillness. Someone is calling your name.

Your mind follows the sound, the sound becomes a pattern, and the pattern becomes a web that you can traverse. You follow the path of the web which takes you from that deep, still place in which you were drifting to a place where you stand before a seated human.

It takes a moment for you to realise that you are standing before your own body. You see the threads of the web that stretches from your body and falls deep into the Underworld: you are anchored in the presence of Sekhmet, and yet you are back in your own world before your own body. Step back into your body, and sit for a moment before opening your eyes: get used to the feel of being connected deep in the earth while still being conscious in your body. When you are ready, open your eyes, and meditate for a short while.

The deep vision of Sekhmet (which you should take your time with) is a long and difficult vision, but it connects you back to the ancient consciousness within the land, which in turn gives you an anchor that helps you to rebuild your strength. It also opens the gate within you to the most ancient goddesses within the land who hold this lioness power, a gate through which power, service and healing can run in both directions.

You must never place yourself at Sekhmet's feet if you are not willing to be aware of the Divine consciousness within the earth, and to offer service to the ancient powers that reside in the land. These powers will assist you if you are willing to be of service to the land, and to the Titan powers that run through it: one day you may be asked to work magically to support these deeper powers as they emerge within humanity, or to work with the elements to support the land in its recovery from the damage that humans have wrought.

4. Repairing the pattern

In the previous chapter, one of the magical acts of healing that we looked at was the action of repairing the inner pattern that allows you to manifest as a living being. Sometimes if a magician takes a big enough hit, the strain of working upon ones own pattern is too much of an energetic burden: if you are very low in energy but are still able to work in vision, then it is good to go and get some help.

The safest place to have your inner pattern worked on while you are vulnerable is in a star temple which can be found hidden within the Inner Library. The Inner Library is a magical realm that is extremely stable, well guarded, and has endless branches connecting it to temples and priesthoods throughout time.

There is a part of the Inner Library that houses a fragment of the consciousness of arch-angelic beings that build, hold, and destroy the patterns of physical manifestation: they work to the rhythm of the Fates and the Weaver.

If you go in vision to the Inner Library with the express intent to work with these beings, you will be guided through the library's many different areas to the great circular door that is the threshold of these beings.

Once you step inside that chamber, you will be confronted by vast beings that seem to be holding complex patterns of threads in place, a bit like cat's cradle. Walk under the threads to the far side of the hall, and you will find slightly smaller angelic beings who will be able to help you. They will ask you to lie down while they stand over you and begin to reweave you, repair tears, etc.

You might well have to return to this place a few times to have the repairs done bit-by-bit. Follow your instincts, and do not waiver from your path to this chamber; do not get distracted in the Library. It is important to be focused and yet to surrender control over what is done to you in this place.

I had to use this method after I sustained a major magical impact when my energies were already low. I went in to the vision once every seven days for three weeks to have the repair-work done. After my first visit to this chamber, nothing much happened that I could notice: I did not seem to feel any different. But after the second and third visit, I noticed that I was starting to get an immune response: I got a really bad cold. I thought I must have been working in the wrong way, but the inner advice I was getting was to continue with the visions.

After the last visit, my cold resolved and I really started to feel good and strong. I ate like a horse and slept like the dead for a week, after which I emerged in full fighting form once more.

Something that we have lost touch with in this day and age of treating symptoms rather than the disease is that the body often needs to go through a healing crisis, where things are brought to a head and resolved. This is something that our forefathers understood very well, but it is a wisdom we have all but lost through our habit of seeking a drug that will instantly make us feel better, but which often just masks the disease by suppressing the symptoms. For true healing, our bodies need to go through various stages of acute symptoms while the body gears itself up, followed by a phase of slower recuperation as the dust settles.

If after doing this work you have a similar reaction to mine, just go with the flow: let your body do what it needs to do, and support it without suppressing any of the shifts it is attempting to make. Once the body is on its way to the resolution phase of the healing process, then you can begin with herbs, rest, acupressure, etc. to support the healing without stopping the shifts that need to happen.

5. Finding the right realm and contacts for the job

Using vision to seek assistance is a major way of repairing underlying damage to the body and spirit, which then leaves the more surface manifestations to be dealt with using herbs and more body-based, externalised healing methods. A vast number of realms, deities, and inner contacts can be connected to for such healing, and which ones you should use largely depends on what land you live upon, what magical work you do, and what deities you are already connected to.

It is a good idea to seek help from within the circle of inner contacts and realms that you regularly work with. So, for example, if your magical work is very much geared towards faery and land-based magic, then that should be your starting-point. If you work as a Kabbalist, then the inner structures of the Desert, inner temples, and angelic beings would be the place to begin. For the magician who works within a set tradition with deities, then looking for the appropriate deity within that tradition will bear good fruit. It is all about using your common sense.

However if you are an eclectic magician (as I am) and have moved beyond traditional paths, then you will probably find that one area of your practice will shout loudly for you to use that method or contact. Using divination to decide the right course of action goes without saying, and the level of power contact you decide to approach should be proportional to the level of damage you have sustained.

So, for example, curing a minor impact does not need a huge, powerful angel: an inner contact in the Library will be able to help with that. Conversely, a massive, life-threatening impact cannot be adequately handled by a local faery being.

Use your common sense, and if you are still not sure, turn the situation around in your mind and view it in terms of everyday life. Would you go to the local Reiki healer if you had a compound fracture? No, you would go to a hospital.

The one thing I will caution you about is to not use these methods to 'heal yourself' if what you are suffering from is simply a matter of you having a shit time in life, where 'no one loves you and the world is all against you.' If you have issues, stop looking in your navel, and sort your life out by direct engagement and action.

These powerful methods and contacts are not there to take your hand and baby you, or to deal with your own emotional and mental inadequacies. It is up to you to do everything in your power to sort yourself out and to get yourself back on your feet. You deal with your own personal dramas; the inner lot deal with energetic impacts that could potentially kill you or disable you.

6. Approaching a contact for healing

Once you have decided which deity or contact to approach for healing, you need to think carefully about what type of visionary interface to use in order to obtain the healing that you need. Rather than constructing a new interface, which takes a lot of time and energy which you most probably do not have, look to use an interface that is well-established.

Choose the interface (Underworld, Inner Library, Desert, faery realm, etc.) and before you do anything in vision, spend some time in a stillness meditation. From that stillness, pass into the visionary interface, and do not be distracted or allowed to be led into a different space: if you are weak, then you are vulnerable. If the interface you are working within has known guardians you can call upon, then do so.

Allow the deity or contact to work upon you, and when they have finished, leave a gift for them or agree to return the favour when called. Ensure that you stick to the bargain, and if you leave a gift in vision, ensure that whatever it was that you gave them is also given up in the material realm. So, for example, if you gave your favourite ring to the Goddess, then once you are out of vision you must get that ring and throw it in the nearest river. It does not matter how expensive it is: a gift is a gift.

When giving a gift, do not think about what you can get away with: if you hand opens and something of great value (financially or emotionally) appears, do not even for a second think about changing it to something of less worth to you. Letting go is an important dynamic for magicians to learn, and there is also an interesting connection with what appears in your hand and what you need to learn to let go of.

After you have finished the vision, go and sleep. This is an essential part of visionary healing: the work continues in your body long after the vision has ended. By sleeping, you allow the powers to deepen within you.

7. Summary

Visionary healing is about dealing with energetic/magical injury and impact at the deepest level. On its own it is not a cure-all; but it will repair your foundations and reconnect your body and spirit back with your energetic resources so that your healing process can begin properly. Once you have worked on yourself in vision, give the body some time (i.e. a week or so) to absorb the experience before beginning more surface levels of treatment such as alternative medicine or even allopathic medicine.

Also be aware that deep magical impacts often have return resonances, whereby each year to the date of the original impact, the body experiences an echo of the event. You may get flare-ups of old injuries, dreams that put you back in the situation, or a lesser but similar event happening. Don't worry too much about this if it happens, as it is very common and perfectly normal. Just take note and see if there are any loose ends that need attending to. The echo will fade over time, but it may take two or three years to pass if the original event was a big one.

Chapter 12

Approaches to self-healing and maintenance

1. Magical, emotional, and physical considerations

Working within magic brings about change; it is as simple as that. How we handle the changes to our lives, our health, our minds, and our spirit determines what harvest we will reap. The longer we operate within magic, the more we become exposed to the complexity of how power, life, and our role within the manifest world all hang together.

Once the fallacy of 'magic gives you what you want' falls away, then we are left staring at ourselves in the mirror, and we begin the long walk towards understanding just how complex, powerful, beautiful, and difficult magic really is. That walk takes a lifetime, and the further down the road we walk, the more we realise just how little we know and how little we can truly control.

2. Emotional baggage

The dawning of magical awareness brings with it changes to our health as our minds struggle to let go of the unhealthy things that we cling to. The more we let go of our emotional baggage, the more our body engages with the process and attempts to rebalance itself by cleansing itself of emotional and physical toxicity.

Sometimes that rebalancing works, and sometimes the body or mind is too damaged or toxic to achieve such a wondrous goal. We cling to a sense of victimhood, and feel a need for 'justice' to be done in matters both tiny and great, and this clinging to emotional need buries itself within the body's structure and churns silently away until the body is no longer able to hold it.

When we are badly hurt physically or emotionally by others, it is part of the psychological process to want justice or revenge, and there is nothing wrong with those feelings. Where it becomes a problem for a magician is when those feelings trigger energetic ties that feed back and forth in a continuous cycle.

That energetic structure builds on itself, and becomes an automated loop of emotion that the magician can get badly tangled within. Parasites become attracted to the energy feed, which they see as a free lunch, and the magician becomes caught in an energetic relationship that connects them to their attacker in a constant energy loop upheld by beings that are enjoying the meal.

Walking away from that dynamic is very hard and is best done in increments, depending on just how much emotional damage you have sustained. Turning your focus away from others, and instead investing your energy in healing yourself, moving forward, and getting on with life frees up all of that trapped energy that is rotting within you.

Being able to let go of things is a major ingredient towards maintaining our physical, mental, emotional, and magical health. Someone does terrible things to you, and you want justice. Learning how to let go of that need for justice, and being able to focus upon sorting yourself out regardless of the actions of others, enables your deeper energies to let go of all the threads and connections, and instead focus on moving forward to heal, learn, and grow. This growth is not only emotive or spiritual; it flows deep down into the body as well, teaching each cell how to patch up, move on, and not be dragged back into a cycle of holding, waiting, and festering.

I do not say this lightly, or from a place of theory or ignorance. I have been around for a while now, and have experienced many unpleasant things done to me in my time. The greatest lesson I have drawn from those experiences, some of which were severe, is an understanding that letting go, moving forward, and flowing around the 'punches' frees up the spirit and the body. Only then can the body focus on dealing with the necessary repair, which in turn enables us to engage fully with magic.

For a magician those 'punches' can come hard and fast over a prolonged period of time, simply because of the power dynamic of magic. The more you learn, the more challenges you are presented with, and the more the *façades* of life fall away to expose a deeper truth.

Regardless of the irreparable damage the body may have in later years, healing and then maintaining ones health starts from within, deep in your spirit centre. And such deep healing comes from letting go.

Only you can do that. No healer, no teacher can be with you in that process: it is something you must do a day at a time, a situation at a time. It cannot be accelerated by meditation or counselling; it is a tactile experience that tiptoes up on you if you are willing and able to see the opportunities that present themselves.

Once you are willing to engage that process consciously, then a path will open up before you that slowly walks you through deeper and deeper octaves of the experience, until the letting go allows your emotive, ego-driven needs to slowly but surely dissipate. That in turn leads you to deeper parts of yourself, and from those depths you are able to access the strength needed to wield magical power.

Letting go of the emotional need for revenge, recognition and justice is not a coward's way out: it takes considerable strength to walk away from such dynamics, and it does not mean that justice will not be served. As you move deeper into magic and begin to learn the power of balance, of the scales of Ma'at, you will slowly see how things have a way of sorting themselves out.

Besides the deeper and more spiritual, emotional aspects of the body's healing mechanism, it is also important to deal with the more surface presentations of *dis-ease*, which we have looked at in depth in this book. In between those two aspects is the maintenance of the body and its energy within the flow of magic, which is what this chapter is about.

3. Magical maintenance

No checklist or recipe exists for maintaining your health while walking a magical path; magic, power, and the interweaving of those energies with life is not that simple. In truth, there is no 'clearing and cleansing' ritual that will sweep away every nasty from your path on a daily basis when you are a magician working with deeper aspects of power.

Maintaining a healthy spiritual, physical, and environmental balance is simple, and yet profoundly complex. It is the root principle of true magical self development, and the mystery most damaged by psychology. However, some basic principles can help a magician establish a strong, healthy foundation to stand upon. Some of the recommendations I am about to make might seem to come from a moralistic standpoint; that would be an incorrect assumption.

Sadly, magical and mystical dynamics and wisdom have long been twisted in their application by unscrupulous, ignorant and manipulative priesthoods within religions. Our vast wealth of magical, spiritual and mystical texts have been constantly rewritten or altered to manipulate and subjugate in line with dogmas and misunderstandings of the deeper mysteries.

Those manipulated 'truths' become moralistic dogma, and any intelligent person can see the emptiness in such falsehoods. As a result, the moral dogma is rejected along with the original dynamics of the mystical truths hidden within the texts. So please bear that in mind when you read the following information... None of it has anything to do with morals, but it has everything to do with how magical energy works.

4. Keeping clear of tangles

One of the single biggest drains on a magician and their health is energetic tangles. These tangles are created by magical action, and the more emotional investment is put into the action, the stronger and more complex the tangle becomes. Some of these tangles or links are a necessary side-effect of essential magical work, but many are totally unnecessary and usually counterproductive in the long term. And it is the long-term consequences of magical action that are usually the most overlooked, especially by younger and less experienced magicians.

Any magical action has a short-term, medium-term and long-term effect, both on the target of the magic and on the magician themselves. The long-term effects can also spill out into the local community or family of the magician, and the consequences of this continued ripple of power usually pass unseen by novice magicians.

That is why magicians do less and less magic as they learn and mature, but when they do take action it is focused, powerful, and necessary.

Let's have a look at a practical example. Two young magicians clash on some matter (which is a daily occurrence these days). One magician thinks that the other magician is dangerous or 'bad,' and they decide to bind the ritual words, actions, thoughts, and visions of the offending magician. The short-term effect on the magician doing the binding is to be drained from the work, but such an effect is transient. The short-term effect on the victim is to suddenly find him or herself unable to get into vision, or unable to do rituals. They forget rituals, lose tools, or find they cannot get a clear mind to go into vision.

The medium-term effect of this binding on the victim is a slowing-down of their magical and spiritual development: they are not able to do any magic, therefore they are not able to learn from mistakes; they are not able to see the consequences of any action, nor are they able to commune with beings who could steer them onto a more solid path.

In effect, the binding has stunted their spiritual and magical growth. If they persist in trying to continue magical actions despite the bindings, then their immune system will begin to react to the binding and they will become ill. This in turn begins to pull on the energy of the magician who did the binding. The arresting of the spiritual development of another human being has many energetic consequences: it takes a lot of energy to stop a person walking towards Divinity and spiritual development.

Even though that was not the original intent of the magic, it is a direct consequence which draws more and more energy into the process as it unfolds. So the magician who did the binding becomes energy deficient as their resources are drained off. This can go on for some time without being fully noticed if the magician had good energy reserves to begin with: it is only when the pot is almost empty that the body's alarms go off.

So at this point in the story, we have one magician who is spiritually and magically arrested, and another who is in energy deficit. It is very likely that neither of them is aware of the source of their problems. They may limp on like this for years without fully realising what is happening to them.

The long-term consequences of this type of binding are very sad indeed. For the magician who was bound, it is most likely that their magical and spiritual life will grind to a total standstill. Instead of slowly developing and maturing, the person is almost essentially 'locked' into their body, and yet the spirit will still strive for power, which is the usual emotive catalyst that takes people to magic in the first place.

That striving for power will instead be focused on their everyday life, which can manifest as a constant attempt to exert control over the people closest to them. This is not a good dynamic, and it often creates egomaniac manipulative control freaks who make other people's lives a misery.

This scenario does not tend to happen if the initial catalyst for magic in the victim's life was a wish to commune with Divinity. In such cases the communion will still happen in a limited way, even though they are magically bound, but such a dynamic will often cause profound suffering in their body.

On the other end of the seesaw is the magician who did the original binding. A couple of decades or more down the road of life, and the threads of the magician's energy tied up in the binding action are getting heavier and heavier. By doing the binding they 'created' a life-path for their victim. As its 'creator' they are energetically upholding all the threads of action, energy exchange, and the weight of the web pattern of the victim's life.

The fact that the victim did not manage to fulfil their potential spiritual development through experiential learning is one burden to be carried. The suffering of subsequent victims caused as a result of the bound magician turning into an oppressor also becomes an energetic burden: those threads have to be upheld too. You are responsible for the monsters you create.

Let's go back to the beginning of this story to see how magic could and should have been used. The 'when and where' of magic is even more important than the 'how,' but that understanding can often come quite late in a magicians development, as these days magic is often taught from an egocentric point of view. The modern approach to many forms of Western magic is a result of the post-Victorian magicians: it is about ones 'will' and 'control,' which is very much a 'toddlers' perspective, as opposed to 'need' and 'participation.'

Back to the beginning. There is a young magician who is throwing their weight around in an unhealthy way, or so it is perceived by another young magician. The first step is to use divination to look at the long-term consequences for the people, beings and land around the offending magician. If they are simply going to blow themselves up or degenerate down into a pile of shit, then that is their choice and their business: most of the time, these sorts of issues have a way of working themselves out.

If it looks like their actions are going to have severe long-term consequences for others, then the next step would be to look at the situation through divination to ascertain whether or not such disaster is indeed fated and necessary. It is possible that the negative actions of the magician are providing a conduit for the power of Ma'at to flow through, and bring about a balancing of scales. If this is the case, then it is not your place to interfere (remember, destruction lives alongside regeneration and creation). But if it is not a necessity, then it may be wise to act.

The next step, to take necessary magical action without being personally tied to the fate pattern of the person, is to work unconditionally with the angelic beings that pattern the future. That means you act as a human catalyst for whatever is necessary to bring about a healthier pattern to the situation. That might indeed mean the 'bad' magician is blocked from magic, or that they drop dead, or that they cross paths with someone who changes them, or that they have an experience that changes their life and therefore their magic.

Another, more conditional form of magic that could be appropriate to use under certain circumstances (though not all, so check through divination first) is to indeed bind the magician, but use your words and intent carefully and specifically: bind them only from using magic that specifically hurts other humans and beings. This still carries some energetic tangles with it, but not many. It will not arrest the other magician's potential for development, but it will stop them using magic to kill, rape, or destroy others.

Taking this approach requires the magician who instigates the action to be removed from any ego-driven agenda or emotive action. If the magician feels that 'they are right', that is their ego talking. If they want the person out of their life because the bad magician is an annoyance, then their ego is sitting in the magical driving seat. The variables are many, but you get the idea. Which takes us back to the earlier conversation in this chapter about being able to step away from emotional and ego-driven wants and needs: hopefully now you can see the immense tangles that magicians can become caught up in.

5. Everything has its own time for resolution

Before I plough into paragraphs about how to maintain the physical and emotive body, there is one more thing that would be useful for a magician to know and understand in regards to managing their health. And that is the dynamic of timing.

Everything that magic touches has its own 'time.' It is a really interesting dynamic, whereby any energetic magical process that has been set into motion already has its time of resolution patterned into the process. What this means for a magician is that healing will come at the right time, in the right place, and not before. This is important to keep in mind when you are trying to bring healing to a body, specifically when that body is involved with magic. The same dynamic also works for major magical projects.

So for example, say a magician has been undertaking a long, drawn-out series of magical workings, and his body has also been struggling with illness. Everything that the magician has done to try and bring healing, be it vision, herbs, etc. has only worked up to a point. The magician gets to their breaking-point, and feels that they cannot carry the burden any longer, as their body and mind is beginning to collapse under the strain. The magician may feel that their ability to 'divine' a solution is clouded, and that they are thrashing about in the dark.

One day, without warning, the solution appears: the resolution of the suffering and the resolution of the work turn up together. Energy rushes into the magician to patch up the deficit, and suddenly everything moves forward. In retrospect, the magician looks at their astrology chart and sees how there was a particular alignment that was favourable to such a leap forward. Remember that magic is a process: it will not be hurried, but it will not forget you or leave you behind.

6. Energetic resources

The magical understanding of energy resources and how to manage them is little known about in today's world of magic. To put it in a nutshell, imagine that when you are born you have a series of 'energy pots' that have varying capacities for holding and distributing energy. Some pots are larger than others, and some have a greater carrying capacity than others. These 'pots' are stored within your 'house of life' and are managed by your guardian angel. This is a very simplistic description, but it gives you a general idea of how the dynamic works.

Having an understanding of your accessible resources and using them wisely is of paramount importance in magic, as is learning not to interfere with them – a lesson I learned in an immediate and very harsh way. I learned about these 'pots' from an inner contact while I was working magically in Egypt, and I was fascinated.

I decided to experiment with these pots, to see if I could move resources from one pot to another. The inner contact had shown me my 'house of life,' and I saw that my 'pot of health' was looking very low in its energy capacity, but my 'pot of outer resources' (wealth) was more or less unused. I decided to move energy from my 'wealth pot' and put it into my 'health pot'.

The effects were immediate. Suddenly I was filled with energy and was annoying everyone around me by bounding about full of beans: I became super efficient and glowing with health. Two days later I lost my job, and I was suddenly without any income of any kind.

I went in vision to my 'house of life' to talk with my guardian angel. I got a long lecture about human stupidity and short-sightedness, and was forced to reverse the magic that I had done. The angelic being said it was its job to move resources about as necessary, in accordance with long-term patterns within my life and fate.

I did not like that sense of personal inaction, and I asked the angelic being what action I could take to help facilitate the best use of my remaining resources. The angel showed me the various foolish actions I had done in the past which had wasted precious energy. I was also shown how magically taking or asking for energy from other places outside of my own resources could affect my own energy stores: the deficit caused elsewhere would be balanced using my own energy – there was no free lunch.

I worked in vision over a series of weeks to commune with the angelic being to learn as much as I could, and then spent time looking back over periods of my life that the angelic being had identified as times when I had foolishly squandered precious power, and other periods where I had used my power wisely.

I saw that sometimes the creation of a deficit was necessary, and how at those times the other unused resources were shared out to compensate. This in turn led me to look at magical energetic dynamics in a different way, and to understand just how complex magical actions can really be.

It also showed me how some magicians have 'deeper pockets' than others in terms of resources to draw on, and that such dynamics are personal to you and cannot be compared to others. Each magician is born with the potential resources they need in order to achieve whatever it is they need to achieve. Whether they are successful or not depends on how they approach life, what they do magically, and how their decisions affect the balance of their resources.

Squandering resources creates a deficit, while hoarding them stunts the magician's inner growth: neither is helpful and the way forward is somewhere in the middle. The first important step is to find out which resources you have in abundance, and of which ones precious little remains. Learning how to use them wisely is the second step. Where we have an abundance of resources we can share, help others, and use them in long-term service. The resources we have precious little of we must protect and use wisely.

By sharing our abundant resources, we create a pattern between ourselves, humans, and other beings (and the land, etc.) that supports rather than entangles: we connect into the communal web that is creation. It also lets us tap into the great energetic recycler, which is in effect an energetic web that interconnects us. When we give freely of our energetic wealth when it is needed by others, the web upholds us when we are in deficit: by giving, we receive. This does not happen automatically: first we have to be willing to share our resources as magicians. When we do share, that connects us to this larger energy community, and power flows to and from us as is needful: we become an energetic collective rather than standing alone. This interaction in turn forces us to make connections: we support each other in various ways where there is true need, both consciously and unconsciously, physically and energetically. What this collective will not do, however, is uphold you when you have squandered resources unwisely: first and foremost you must be responsible for your own energy.

To cut a very long story short, the most useful advice is to be aware that all of your resources, be they health, financial, emotive, magical, or prophetic are all limited and should be used wisely. They can be interchangeable, and you are likely to have strong resources in some aspects and weaker ones in others. Recognising where your weaknesses lie and protecting those areas by not squandering their energy is an important part of keeping your mind and body together in magic. Recognising where you have a lot of resources is probably your key to where your path of service lies.

These pots of resources can also be affected by bindings placed on you by other magicians in an attempt to limit you, just as your angelic being can limit your access to a good resource until the time when it is truly needed. So it pays to keep an eye on them to ensure they are not being interfered with.

What I took away from this experience is the need to learn how to trust, and also how to be responsible for myself energetically. If you waste a lot of your resources over decades and then cry for more, your cries will be met with a stony silence.

If you try to take more from other places, you will slowly spiral into more and more deficit (think credit card debt).

If, however, you recognise that you have squandered (which we all do at some point, particularly in our youth) and work magically from an understanding that you will now have some limitations, then you will find that between your focus of action and the overseeing of your energy management by your angelic being, you will find ways to operate very efficiently.

Also, if you learn from your youthful mistakes and engage in proper resource management with your guardian angel, and you are committed to long-term magical service of some kind, then you will benefit when necessary from the scale rebalance and the communal web. This usually comes in terms of mundane resources like food, shelter, skills, etc. What you do not have will come to you through various outer channels as and when you need it.

Those who have an abundance of resources pass their surfeit on to those in deficit. In turn that resource is used for magical service that benefits the wider future. This is turn weaves a web of communal cooperation and support. The Inner Library is one manifestation of that communal web: it is the communal collection of energetic resources that we use as knowledge.

The visionary image of the house of life and the energy pots is simply an interface that we can use to tap into that energy dynamic. It seems to have been something the ancient Egyptians knew about, and at some point in time I would like to return to Karnak to search for remnants of this mystery in the paintings and architecture. Once you have experienced this visionary interface directly, then you will begin to recognise it in mystery texts.

These limited resources are another reason to think carefully about using magic to get laid, get a car, a healthy bank balance, etc. The powers that flow through magic are profound, and we are inextricably linked into the complex web of energy/power: to squander such precious resources on things that we could achieve for ourselves without magic is a folly and can be a very expensive folly in energetic terms.

7. Scapegoating

This is another energy dynamic that I have talked about in some of my other books, but here is a brief summary. If you are involved in a magical group, lodge, or organisation, then there is a possibility that you could be used as a scapegoat for magical rebound. What this means is that your group's leader or leaders can initiate magical actions that would normally result in an energetic backlash on them. To avoid that backlash, the leader magically assigns (usually without the victim's knowledge) a member or members of the group to act as a scapegoat for the backlash. This neophyte not only suffers a loss of energy, but also the energetic consequences of their leader's magical action, while the leader gets off Scot-free.

This does not happen too often, as many magicians these days do not know how to do it. But it does happen, and it is nasty. This can be identified by observing changes to your energy and health when you are involved in a group. If you join a lodge or group and find that you slowly become sick, drained or depressed, and unhealthy things are happening around you, then it is time to use divination to find out if indeed you are being scapegoated.

Such a collapse of your health and life pattern upon joining a lodge can be for a variety of reasons, not just scapegoating, so do not jump to conclusions. Sometimes initiation can throw your life up in the air to rearrange you: you are broken down before being rebuilt.

It can also happen if the group is unhealthy: you begin to get dragged down by the parasites that usually frequent unbalanced lodges. The way to tell what is happening under such circumstances is to use divination (the **Tree of Life layout** is best for **yes/no answers**), and clearly ask *"am I being scapegoated?"* If the answer is **no**, then the next question should be, *"is this destruction necessary for my development?"*

If you find yourself in a scapegoat situation and it is making your body ill, then the magical impact has already embedded itself within your physical structure. The way to remove such embedded bindings is to do a visionary body cleanup, and then take a consecrated ritual bath where you specifically direct the ritual to remove the bindings of the scapegoat.

Keep a close eye on the effects a group is having on you, which in turn will enable you to make more informed decisions about your membership of that group. Part of the overall maintenance of a magician's health and strength is proactive awareness.

8. Physical maintenance

The best way to keep your body in good (or at least reasonable) health is a basic, old-fashioned common-sense rule that we often forget in today's crazy world. Sunshine is one of the greatest healers, and the sun gives us strength physically and magically. Most often these days we spend a lot of time indoors, and are told that the sun will give us cancer. Too much of anything is bad for you, but where sunshine is concerned we tend to go to the other extreme in avoidance.

As a magician, going out each day for a walk, being in sunlight, greeting the sun, and sitting in its power are some of the most powerful things you can do to uphold your health. You should bathe in the sun, the air, and the nature around you on a daily basis. If that is not possible, perhaps because of work commitments, then do it as often as you can. Exposure to sunlight is not a magic pill to make you better, but it is a major element of healing and maintenance for magicians.

The same goes for eating food that has life in it, and keeping to healthy sleep cycles. If you regularly stay up through most of the night, then do not be surprised if your immune system, heart and central nervous system eventually begin to falter.

Resetting and repairs to the body are done at specific times through the night, and daytime sleep does not work in the same way. The body works with tides, with the moon, with the seasons, with day, and with night: we happily pour over tables and correspondences for magic, but few apply the same diligence to their own bodies.

Magic and life are not separate: they are of one another. The repair cycle for your body begins around midnight and continues until dawn. Give your body the sleep that it needs, and don't forget that a lot of magic happens or continues in your sleep.

9. Getting maintenance work done

In the previous chapters we looked at a couple of healing modalities that a magician can learn and apply to themselves. Sometimes, however, it is needful to go to someone for treatment or to have maintenance work done on your body to keep you on your feet. There are lots of different forms of healing out in the world, and everyone will find one that suits their body best. As always, remember that each body is different, and what works well for someone may not necessarily work well for another.

The two main forms that I have found the most helpful for me are acupuncture and cranial osteopathy (not cranial sacral therapy). Both of these healing forms work deep into the body, and access the levels within you that are active in magic. Whichever form of healing you look to, ensure that it has a physical element to it: the treatment needs to ground within the body itself as well as operate within the energetic sphere. Simply manipulating a person's energy through spiritual or energetic healing will not help a magician as much as something that has a physical element to it: magic goes through the whole body from energy to physical substance. Any healing needs to follow those same paths.

When a body is not involved in magic, it is not pliable energetically, so energy healing can truly balance such denseness. But once the body, spirit, and energy of a person has worked within magic and has become looser in its boundaries, then it becomes really important to ensure that any healing form spreads across all aspects of a person.

With acupuncture, once the body has learned how the system works, it can be useful to learn the basic channels and points so that you can manipulate them through finger pressure after magical workings: sometimes a flow of energy becomes stuck or clogs up from the magical impact. The points affected will become sore, and if that happens, rubbing or pressing on them can help to free things up. This is not a replacement for proper treatment, but it helps, particularly if you have no money for a treatment.

10. Astrology

It can be very useful to learn the basics of how to look at a chart and recognise specific transits that are occurring for you. Rather than plan actions around specific astrological events, it is better to 'go with the flow' and look in retrospect.

Astrology can also be used in maintaining your energy levels within magic, and protecting your health. If your emotional or physical health takes a dive, or your outer life is a bit turbulent, it pays to look at your own chart with transits to see what dynamics are currently at play. Sometimes it is a development process you are going through, and astrology can highlight the specifics for you. Once you know what process is unfolding and what planets are involved, then you can actively engage with the process and with the powers flowing through your life, which in turn enables you to get the most out of the transient powers.

There are a variety of websites that offer free chart drawing, with current transits listed along with explanations. It is a useful learning tool to keep track of your chart, and it also helps you to understand a little bit more about the consciousness that flows through the planets and how they can affect you. It is not necessary to learn astrology in depth, but a rudimentary understanding is very helpful.

11. Lose the New Age bullshit

This in itself can be a major help when it comes to maintaining your body and spirit. The whole 'New Age' industry makes billions out of telling people what they want to hear, and not what they should hear. This is particularly true in regards to health and energy issues.

We are told repeatedly that if we live as clean spiritual beings, we will never be sick. This is total tosh, and is a shining example of how wisdoms can be twisted into dogmas. This perpetuated lie has caused untold suffering to many people who have been treated as spiritual exiles because they are sick.

Bodies get sick. Bodies get into accidents, have inherited disease, and have stress; the list of what can affect our health is endless. Some sicknesses can be treated medically; others can be treated through alternative medicine and energy healing. Some illnesses and disabilities cannot be fixed, and the magician has to learn how to continue operating within their limitations.

Magicians who innovate and explore are more likely to take constant body hits or end up with chronic illness than those who trot along comfortably in a teaching group. The true key to magical health is about upholding, maintaining, listening to the body, and making the best of what you have.

The other New Age bullshit bullet to dodge is the constant aggressive sale of 'wonder nature cures.' Some are no better than snake oil, but others are true healing substances taken out of context, refined, and made into a supplement that you are told you must take every day (at great expense). Don't get sucked into the bullshit. Learn about your own body, learn about substances and how they work, and do not get trapped in the endless New Age loop of pseudoscience.

12. Summary

Keeping your mind and body together in some form of good condition, while going through the trials of magic, is indeed a trial in itself. A major aspect of such maintenance is ensuring that you tend to the magical, energetic, emotive and physical parts of you: all of these aspects of your existence are interwoven and cannot in truth be separated out. One affects the other, and they are all interdependent on each other.

Whenever you are in doubt as to the wisdom of a magical action in relation to your health or energy, and you cannot find a magical reference to guide you, then use your common sense. Relate your experience to an outer paradigm. For example, imagine that you are not in the greatest of health and you want to work magically in vision and ritual with stellar powers. In everyday life, a magical endeavour like that would equate to climbing Everest while you have flu and a health condition. Not the wisest of choices!

Magic will affect your health, and your health will affect your magic. Always keep that in mind, and any magical teacher who tells you that you can do anything you want magically, and that you will have no consequences, is either an idiot or a magical criminal.

Be kind to your body: it carries you faithfully, powerfully, and adapts to the craziest things you feed it, clothe it in, or do with it. If you work with it, even if you make huge and glaring mistakes (as I have), it will adapt and work hard to carry you through life, until the time when the angel of death stands before you.

Appendix B

Chapter Extract from
Magic of the North Gate
Powers of the Land, the Stones and the Ancients

Chapter 5

Shrines on the land

Land spirits, faeries, deities; having friends around for tea

Part of the work of a magician is the building of shrines. This is done in various ways for lots of reasons, but the biggest reason is to create a point of contact and place to exchange energies. How and where you build the shrine depends largely on what types of beings you are trying to work with, where you are working, and why.

If you live in an area that is a strong faery/land spirit area, then it makes sense to work with those beings and use a shrine as a place of exchange. If you are working more in a place where deities are flowing back and forth, then a shrine to work with the local deity would be productive. It also really depends on what work you are trying to achieve.

It is also important to understand that as we change and develop, so the beings we work with and the work we attempt also changes. Everything has a time and place, and it is wise to bend and flex with that change. So for example you may find yourself working for a span of time with nature/faery beings only to find the work evolving to a point where it needs the input of deities or larger powers. There are vast bodies of work, however, that do not require shrines and such a physical level of contact: it is all about using the right tools, the right contacts, and the right approach for what you are trying to achieve.

1. Faery/Land spirit work

Shrines for land spirits/faery beings are good bridge builders for friendship and working relationships with the land and the elements.

If you are trying to clean up the land, balance out the impact of civilisation/buildings/pollution, learn about plants and their power, work with animals, and generally learn about the land/beings where you live, then a faery/spirit shrine would be useful. They are also good allies when it comes to healing and protection, and for developing an early warning system and your inner sight. The work they ask for in return is usually simple in human terms, and consists of moving things from one place to another, fostering certain plants, cleaning up the land, offering food, and generally being social with them.

In such a case the shrine would be used to make contact and develop a relationship and a place for work. You and the spirits that inhabit or pass through the shrine will slowly build a method of interaction and exchanging energy, and eventually friendships will develop.

When working with land spirits/faery beings it is important to understand that they can be unpredictable. They do not think the same way that you do, and they are partial to practical jokes. They anger easily, but they are also generous when they see clear and good intent. If you wish to work with such beings, then it will pay great dividends to do your homework. Find out about the local faery beings through local legends and stories. Research stories and myths of other countries in the same hemisphere, as you will find the same stories repeat across many different countries. Many key elements are the same, and will teach you operating methods of working with these beings.

Before you start to build the shrine, step out of your normal way of thinking and assess each step of practically building it. And think about how it will impact the local environment. This is a very important magical step: think about the construction in terms of the beings that will use it, not your own convenience and satisfaction. For example, shrines are becoming a major fashion at the moment thanks to an interest in Voodoo and similar traditions. People are furiously building shrines and filling them with plastic images, toxic substances, and ornaments. If this is in your home, at least you can do no damage. But if you do that out in nature then you will get a hostile response or no response at all. Why? Because these materials poison the land and are meaningless or useless to the land spirits. Really such shrine-building is more about a grown up playing at 'doll house': something done for their entertainment and enjoyment rather than to help build a working relationship with land spirits.

Faery/spirit shrines out in nature need to be compatible with nature. They need to be focal points of land energy for creatures and spirits, so their contents need to enhance that, not inhibit or detract from it. So their structure needs to be made of wood or woven sticks, stone, or earth: things that are of nature and cannot poison the land. Stay away from plastic and nylon, or anything that is chemical-based and does not degrade. The shrine *needs* to degrade slowly through time, as it should not be permanent. Also veer away from metal: various metals have specific, usually blocking influences around land spirits.

If you wish to work with herbs in the shrine, then dried herbs will cut no ice, as they have no life left in them. But planting herbs around the shrine will be well received, so long as they are herbs that grow naturally on that land. Let weeds grow around them, but keep them in check: don't let anything overgrow the shrine. I work with a shrine by my house: it is a simple large stone with a flat stone before it that receives the offerings. Flowers and herbs have sprung up around it, and local birds visit it frequently to partake of the offerings.

Unlike a deity shrine, it is unnecessary – unhelpful, even – when trying to attract land/faery spirits, to have an image or statue in the shrine. As any image or statue can be walked into by a land spirit if the statue is not tuned to a deity, you may end up with a bit of a problem if you get a bully: once they have a face and a humanoid form to play with, things can get a bit tricky. Faery beings are best worked with, and are more stable, when they are themselves and are not given access to a humanoid interface.

It takes longer to learn how to interface with spirits if you have no point of reference like a statue, but perseverance really pays off. Once the spirits have figured out how to communicate with you, then the contact becomes much deeper than the type of contact you get when it is filtered through a statue.

Use the shrine to leave food and offerings. Sweet foods like honey, breads, milk, fruit and nuts are generally good: you will slowly get a feel for what the spirits like and do not like. The more powerful the substance you leave, the more they can draw on its energy and use it for good or bad. One way to operate is to regularly take out food offerings, but when there is some powerful work to be done, give them power substances like coffee and alcohol. Just make sure these substances cannot be accessed by birds or animals, and take them away after a day. Do not give them power substances on a daily basis, or you may end up with a caffeine-crazed land spirit that wants to mate with you or move into your house and take over – this is also a good reason why it is best not to have a faery shrine in your house.

The work would go a little like this: build a shrine out of wood, bark, stones, etc., and have a large stone for the beings to reside in. Every day take out food and drink (the local creatures may eat this up, which is not a problem) and sit with the shrine. Talk to the shrine as if the being was there (this action starts an inner calling process) and tell them what you are trying to achieve and why. Do this every day for a full cycle of the moon so that the contact has a chance to build up slowly. After you have been feeding the shrine for a month, on your next visit, sit in silence/meditate in stillness, and when you come out of that, take note of what is around you. What creatures are appearing nearby; how does the shrine 'feel,' how do you 'feel'? If you have developed your inner senses, then just listen to see if anything is trying to reach out to you. If you have problems with such sensitivity, or if it is not normal for you, then you need to develop an inner form of communication which is done in vision using the imagination.

To do this, simply be still. Once you are still, then use your imagination to see yourself stepping out and standing next to your body. Imagine the shrine before you, and look at it through your imagination. See what looks different, see what seems to shine and what does not. Then look at the area around the shrine. See the bushes, trees, water, etc. nearby. If any inner beings have been attracted to the shrine, then they will begin to understand that you are using your imagination as an interface: they will start to develop ways to contact you through your visionary action as well as through dreams and nature cues. At first it will be difficult to tell what is simply your imagination, and what is a real contact. The key to overcoming this is to treat *everything* as if it were real unless it is obvious that it is not (like Mickey Mouse appearing, or cute butterfly wing faeries).

This will strengthen the interface and stop you second-guessing yourself. There will come a crossover point where it becomes obvious what is real and what is not. You will see something strange, something you had not expected, and you will question yourself. But then you will pick up a book on spirits or local legends, a book that you have not read before, and you will see a description of exactly what you experienced. This is because it is an image interface they have used before with other humans who have then gone on to describe it.

After establishing contact, you will be able to interface with the spirits through vision, dreams, and through instinct and outer happenings. You will notice simple things like a certain bird or creature always appearing when things are getting powerful. The same creature will start to appear in your dreams, or away from the shrine. This is where the contact is starting to strengthen, and they are beginning to work with you.

Working at this level with faeries and land spirits is evocative, imaginative, and just plain odd. For a magician who is used to more ordered work and contact it can take some getting used to, but it is rewarding and interesting work. It does have its limits, though. Local beings tend to be active only in a certain area and have certain skills. They do not have the reach and power that a land deity would have, but if you are searching for a more down-to-earth coworker, they are great to work with.

I worked in this way when my children were little and had illnesses. I worked with local land beings, and had a gift area (but not a shrine) where I left things for them and I would sit and talk to them. If my daughter became sick then I would ask for their help and advice, which would be given. In return they would ask me to plant certain things, move certain things off the land, or pick up trash: all simple stuff for a physical body to do, but hard for a spirit to do. They would provide a protective barrier around the children and help their energetic bodies when they were ill. They would also warn me if there was a problem with one of the children, or if there was danger around.

Here is a solid example of a not particularly good way of doing shrine work. Unfortunately this was retrospective work: work to rebalance a wrong done on an area of land. A few years ago I was asked to help a family. The grandmother was ill, but the doctors could find no reason for her pain. I went along and found that the old lady had chopped down a bush at the back of the property which had angered some local spirits. This was a wild part of the country in Montana where the spirits were strong and still not used to human interaction. They had launched an attack on her to punish her for cutting down one of their 'houses.'

I managed to negotiate a truce with them. Another bush in the garden would be allowed to grow wild, and sweet foods would be placed at the base of the tree every week. They also wanted a gift from her to be buried in the base of the bush. She gave a little medicine wheel she had made, and the children buried it for her at the base of the bush. Food was left out and the bush was not touched. Her pains stopped immediately and she started to get better. I called each week for a month and all was going well.

Six months later I got a call from the family. It had all started up again. I visited the grandmother and she was in pain again. I asked about the routine with the bush, and I was told that some flowers had been cut from the bush to put in the house, and they had stopped putting out food as they felt it attracted bears. She had broken her agreement. The family asked if I could renegotiate for them. The spirits in the bush were very angry and refused to make any other agreement: the flowers had been cut from the bush, which to them was a crime, and the food had stopped which was a breaking of the bond. They felt the family could not be trusted, and had not kept up their bargain.

I explained all this to the family. I asked why they had cut flowers from that bush where there were tons of flowers on the other bushes which they could have cut with no harm done. The daughter replied that the special bush gave off the best flowers. They did not understand that the best flowers, for whatever reason, were to be protected for the land spirits and were not for humans to touch. That had been the deal: there was to be no cutting of that bush in any way.

As for the food, the shrine was far enough away from the house for it to not be a major bear problem, and bears were part of the pattern of nature there. Bears came through all the yards in that area anyhow: we were sat right on the edge of the wilderness. I asked if the food had drawn bears into their yard and they said no and admitted they just got lazy and didn't want to go out in the cold to put the food out.

There was nothing I could do. I had set up a way for the humans and spirits to coexist, but the humans had not kept up their side of the bargain. Land spirits don't do 'sorry': if you break a promise then the deal is off. Sad to say the grandmother then suffered pain constantly from that time on, and there was nothing anyone could do about it. It was a harsh lesson for her, and a major lesson for me also. It taught me a lot about working with land spirits and what they can do, but it also taught me a great deal about personal responsibility and acting as a mediator. You can only set up the conditions, but the people themselves have to keep their side of the bargain, and often they do not. They wanted me to fix it again, but magic does not work like that: a major component of magic is responsibility and keeping your word.

I felt really bad about walking away knowing that an old lady was in constant pain, but she had had the power in her own hands to fix that, and she chose not to. A harsh lesson was learned by all concerned.

This situation does illustrate how shrines can be used, and the dangers involved when dealing with strong land spirits. Always keep your word and keep up your end of the bargain. Land/faery beings will do something for you, but for a price and you must be able and willing to pay that price. Before you agree to do something with a shrine, make sure you can keep up your end of the agreement. If necessary, give a time limit of what you are able to do. Think carefully about what you are willing to undertake, and stick to it.

A shrine to land spirits brings the contact in sharp focus, which in turn intensifies the contact and the work. This can allow you to achieve and learn a great deal, but it is a responsibility that needs thinking about before you undertake it.

When I had faery gift areas on my land, I always agreed to uphold it for as long as I lived in that place, and when I moved on I would stop working with it. That was part of the agreement I made. It's just a matter of stating your boundaries and them stating theirs.

2. Deity shrines

Working with deities on the land can be very powerful and a good source of great learning. There are two main ways to approach it: one is to work with a known deity and the other is to reach out to a deity that is still within or on the land but has fallen into obscurity.

Working with a known deity involves a bit of background research. It is important to know if that deity is compatible with the land and community, and to know what power the deity mediates. In some countries like the UK, deities were brought in from other countries to protect and assist invaders, immigrants, etc. Some blended well, and some did not. It is wise to question your motives in setting up work with a specific deity: is it because you wish to work with and learn from a particular power, or are you simply following a current occult fashion?

Working with a deity who is not directly involved with nature is pointless in an outside shrine. For example Athena, a goddess who was fashionable for a time, is a power that works in temples, in cities, and with male warriors. It is pointless having a nature shrine out in the countryside and putting an urban goddess in there. Whereas a deity connected to creatures or the fertility of the land would be ideal.

Are you wishing to work with a deity, or worship them? If it is the latter, then it is better to work within a religious setting rather than a purely magical one. I work with deities magically but not religiously, so my techniques will not be best for someone wishing to become a devotee of a particular deity. There is a clear distinction between the two approaches, and they have different outcomes.

3. Known deity shrines

If you are wishing to build a shrine to a deity out on the land, first make sure they would be happy to be worked with out on the land. Ensure that the land spirits would be compatible with the deity so that you do not inadvertently create conflict in an area.

Correct choice of deity pays great dividends. If the god or goddess is from another land, use vision or readings to see how your land would react to them. It is also a good idea to see what elements or powers would balance the deity so that you do not end up working with a lopsided power. If you research well, which is easy these days with the internet, then look into what companions, what tools, and what spirits are depicted with a particular deity. Instead of just working with text, let your instincts contribute as well. It can be a interesting learning experience.

The first step, once the deity is chosen (or they have chosen you) is to build the outer shrine on a chosen patch of land like in a garden or yard. Again, care needs to be taken with what materials you use to make sure that you do not put the local wildlife or land at risk. Natural materials are good; bits of plastic are bad.

Take care to build according to what the deity needs and the tools you wish to work with, as opposed to building in a way that simply looks good. A shrine is not a New Age display: it is a working space and needs to be constructed with that in mind. Once the construction is in place, introduce the image of the deity to the shrine so that the interface is ready for activation.

The next step is the inner opening of the shrine. This work is done in vision. It allows the inner flow of power across the land to integrate with the shrine and the intermediary powers of the deity to flow into the image. A simple way of doing this is to sit before the shrine and still yourself. Using meditation, still yourself until your mind has settled, and slowly become aware of your surroundings in vision. With your eyes closed, see the space around you and see yourself walking around the land space. You may notice that your home or building does not appear on the land: this is normal if it is a modern building. Buildings, unless they are consecrated spaces or temples, tend to take hundreds of years to fully appear in the inner landscape of the land.

When you have a clear vision of the land around you, slowly imagine the shrine building up on the land until it clearly appears on the inner landscape. It may take more than one session to build the inner image strongly enough for it to stay. The building of the shrine is done only through physical construction and then imaginary imprint. This is different from constructing a temple, which involves many different beings and working with visionary magical construction. Building a shrine is akin to setting up a telephone line to a deity as opposed to a fully constructed workspace like a temple.

When the shrine is clear in your mind on the inner landscape, then it is time to 'open the doors' to call the deity in. Sometimes this happens naturally with shrines, and the deity power will almost immediately begin communicating with you. Other times you need to open the door. This is done by lighting a candle in front of, or within, the shrine (when it is windy, putting a tea light in a glass jar works well) and working the shrine like an altar. 'See' the flame with your inner vision, and see the shrine as a gateway. Using inner vision, call through the gateway for a priest or priestess of the deity to work with you as an inner contact to activate and guide you in the work of the shrine. A figure will be drawn to the shrine and will appear to you in vision. Talk with them and ask them to work with you and guide you.

That is all that is needed from a visionary magic point of view. The key is to try and maintain contact with the priest or priestess in the way that works best for you, either through vision, dreams, or instinct. The inner contact will act as a slow door opener and mediator for the deity power to flow into the shrine, a bit like an interpreter.

Working regularly with the shrine, working with it as an altar and a place of offerings, will slowly open the door wider, and allow a natural interaction to develop.

Take note of how the animals, birds, and plants respond to the shrine. If the power is unbalanced then it will negatively affect the wildlife around it. If it is positive then you will notice that plants flourish, more birds visit, and the wildlife becomes more noticeable. The shrine will become a working point of focus that can be used for all manner of nature work in conjunction with the deity. Often shrines take on a life of their own and teach you how to work with and for them.

4. Local deities and ancient powers

The actual construction method of the shrine would be the same as the method above, but there are unlikely to be images available of the local deity: most ancient gods and goddesses in Europe, for example, were overlaid and forgotten. If this is the case then your detective work has to be mainly in vision. Take your time when working in vision and repeatedly walk through the inner landscape: this will enable you to connect with any ancient deities that are still accessible on or within the land. For example in one place where I lived, I wanted to know who and what the local deity powers were. I lit a candle, sat down, and went into vision, seeing myself walking out of my house, down the road, and into the fields and the forest. I did this a few times and slowly got used to the land I had moved to. I also became aware of local spirits, ancestors, and a large burial mound with guardians that appeared in the inner landscape but not in the outer landscape. There was no burial mound anywhere nearby that I was aware of.

The next time I went in vision, I talked to the guardians who told me that the Mother of this land was sleeping in the mound and had been trapped there for a long time by human magic from another land. I went to the doorway of the mound that the guardians showed me: the door had a crucifix on it and behind that, lots of script and strange-looking symbols. The guardians told me that people had locked the goddess in the mound a long time ago, and though they still guarded her, they could not set her free: only a human could undo what a human had done.

I decided to take the job on and spent time repeatedly going in vision to clear things off the door before slowly dismantling the door/blockage step by step. Eventually I managed to get the door open and go inside. A goddess was sleeping on the ground, surrounded by black dogs. One of the dogs woke up and barked, which woke her up. She was very angry, not at being woken, but at humans magically sealing her in the mound.

I apologised for how she had been treated in the past, and I agreed to help her leave. In retrospect, this was not such a good idea. She was angry, very angry, and she wanted revenge. It took a lot of negotiating to calm her down. One of the terms of our treaty included a shrine, offerings, and adjustments to the surrounding land and to how I lived on it. She is really a warrior goddess, specific to a small area, essentially the village and surrounding land, and she has a very fixed idea about how humans should interact with her.

Such local deities can be difficult to work with, and they seem to be a combination of deity, ancestral consciousness, and land spirits. As a result of my experience with this goddess, nowadays I am wary of this level of deity, as they are so unpredictable and difficult to work with. But such work is not impossible if you work with a bit more care than I did, and find out a lot more about the local deities before interacting with them. In retrospect I should have consulted with local ancestors, inner contacts, and land spirits to learn more about the deity power before deciding to hack down a magical barrier. That way I would have been better prepared to interact with her and would have been better able to counter any danger posed by opening an ancient contact of power.

If you do decide to build a shrine to a local deity, keep it simple and use it as a point of contact and offerings. The more you work with it, the more they will get the idea that it is a place to meet and work, and they will keep their interactions with you confined to that shrine: there is nothing worse than having a local spirit, ancestor, or deity tramping through your home at all hours of the day and night. Which brings me to another point: this method of outdoor shrine building can also be used as a meeting place of contact for local ancestors: really a shrine is a magical meeting point for you to connect with local spirits/beings. It is the intent that counts: the slow building, both in vision and in ritual action, will tune the shrine and get it in focus.

When you have come to the end of working with a shrine, or you are going to move, you should bury any deity image (unless you are taking it with you), break up the shrine, and let it go back to nature. Leave a last gift and tell the spirits that you are going, why you are going, and where you are going. If they are long-range beings, they may be waiting for you in your new home, whether you like it or not. Putting down boundaries at the beginning of the relationship ("I will only work with you here") can be a good idea!

5. **Befriending local spirits and ancestors, and having them live with you**

This is an interesting way of working should you cross paths with local ancestors in the area where you live. If you live in a city, you are more likely to get confused ghosts that find you and seek refuge with you: magic switches all the lights on and draws them in. In such instance they will either want help passing in and through death, or they will want a place to hide and rest.

If you do end up with a resident ghost that is not ready to move on, then living with them can be simple: just state your boundaries and give them a safe corner of the house to 'reside' in. As long as they do not cause problems and do not drain energy from you (in which case a parasite is masquerading through a ghost shell), then they will live happily in an area of the house and will leave when they are ready.

Under these circumstances it is not a good idea to work magically with them or interact too much. Remember, this is a stranger who is unbalanced or needy: giving them shelter is enough. Much more than that can cause problems for the living and the dead. Often they will suddenly vanish in a magical working: the gates open and they will be pulled through into death.

When my cousin died after a long and terrible illness, he hung out with my partner and I for a while. He would not cause problems other than blowing the light bulbs on a nearly daily basis: he was terrified of death, and in his terror he latched onto our home and hid there. Slowly he began to relax as he realised that he still existed, and I was not going to attempt to move him on. For a dead person, coming to understand their new state and form of existence is a major shift of awareness, and if they can make that shift themselves it will be a major part of their learning and evolution as a soul. So let them have some time to get used to the idea of their being dead.

After a while we were due to go and work with a magical group in Bath so off we went, and my cousin came too. He sat in the back of the car, which felt a bit odd, came with us to the working, and sat in a chair as we opened the gates. He sat through a couple of the magical workings and was picked up on by one of the magicians ("I can smell alcohol," said one worker: my cousin was an alcoholic.) The major working of the day was underway when suddenly he just vanished through the gates. That was it. He had overcome his fear, seen where he was supposed to be and not supposed to be, and had moved on of his own accord, with his own understanding.

This is a bit different to moving in a house that has a resident ghost. Usually this is someone who is trapped, or is a parasite, or is an echo. These must be dealt with in a specific way.

A different type of ancestral work is where you cross paths with an ancient ancestor who is purposely staying in our world for a specific reason. They will find you, often through strange routes. It tends to happen more frequently out in the country where there is less 'civilised psychic noise.' Because we know so little of the culture and beliefs of our ancient ancestors, you really have to play this by ear.

As I have discussed in my books before, when I move into an area, I go to the local burial ground or cemetery and make friends with the people buried there. I show respect and honour those who have lived on the land before me. Often that is enough, but on one occasion something interesting happened.

I slowly began to make friends in the local village where I was living and my neighbour began to understand that I was a little bit, well, odd. Her family had lived in that area as farmers for at least a thousand years that they knew of, and they were closely connected to the land. One day she came to me with a bundle and sat down to tell me a story about her grandfather. He was a local farmer and had begun to expand his farm decades ago, by ploughing rough land that they owned but had never touched.

The ploughing dug up a body, an old skeleton from one of the mounds in the rough field. His friend who was a doctor looked at the body and said it was old, not a recent one. The grandfather took the skull, which was the best preserved part of the remains, and gave it a home in his house, where it lived quietly in the corner for decades. When he and then his son died, his granddaughter was clearing the house out and came across the skull. She remembered the story of it from when she was a little girl. She did not want to throw it away or pass it on to historians who would not respect it. So she brought it to me, after having a strong instinct that I would look after it.

After she left, I placed the skull on the table and tentatively felt around it for any presence. Many remains do not have any connection to their original owners, but some do. I was also aware of something my first teacher told me, which was that when you work magic, things happen for a reason. Things find their way to you for a reason, and one must find out what that reason is. She was clear about this and saw reason in everything. I was not that convinced, and I still feel it is important to differentiate between everyday happenings and magical jobs and events... but never take anything for granted either way.

So I felt around the skull and yes, there was a faint something, like a whisper. I went in vision with my hands on the skull and came across a young girl, young, maybe twelve or thirteen years old. She was strong, present, and was showing me birds. She tried to convey to me that she worked with birds, in what we would call a magical way, though to her it was normal. I told her I too had worked with birds and she nodded, saying that was why she wanted to come and live with me.

I questioned myself: I was not sure how much of this was just my own imagination, as it was a slightly different way of working to what I am used to and I was on uncertain ground. I found her a place in the house to live, on a shelf with my birds, feathers, etc. that I had collected. She seemed happy enough.

Over time I began to learn a lot from her about local birds: how to call them in, how to 'fly' with them in my mind, and how the local winds worked. A friend came to visit me who is an archaeologist, and he took a look at the skull. Without doing tests he said it was difficult to confirm, but his opinion was a child aged somewhere between 12 to 14, and it was *old*. Hmmm.

So I worked with her for a couple of years, then one day she wanted to go to sleep. I did not quite understand what she meant, and it took me a week or two to figure it out. In the meantime she was getting frustrated and was beginning to get disruptive. Things were flying off the shelf and birds were hitting the window or pecking at the window: it was the Inner Worlds crying out for attention.

Eventually I figured it out and got her a casket. I put the skull in the casket and did a reading to find out where she wanted to be buried. She did not want burying; she wanted to sleep where I slept. So she was moved into the bedroom, still in her casket, and was placed beneath a bit of furniture so she was hidden. She sleeps for certain lengths of time but occasionally she will wake up and ask to come back out among the living for a time.

I do not know why she does not want burying, or even how her spirit had managed to hold onto her skull for so long. It is all part of an ongoing learning experience for me, and we are in such a magical dark age that we need to find our own way through the dark and figure it out as we go along.

I have learned a great deal from her, and she has found sanctuary: a good trade! I began to think about how magicians use skulls, often without respect and without care for the person to whom the skull belonged. There seems to be little emphasis on trying to find out if the skull is still connected to a spirit and what that spirit may need. It has become a fashion to have a skull along with a glamorous grimoire, and it makes me wonder what effect this is having on the magicians and the ancestors that are still connected to those skulls.

I certainly learned to be far more conscious and compassionate towards body remains, and I learned that there is a lot more to working with skulls than meets the eye: sometimes those skulls might not want to work, they may want to sleep.

So if some remains come your way, particularly unexpectedly, and you are a magician, then step back before including the skull in your work. Take time to try and find out who they are and what they need. Why did they come to you? Find out what you can do for them before asking what they can do for you.

6. Summary

Working with the land and the powers that flow through the land is ideally a natural, instinctive interaction with everything around you: no dressing, no shrines, just you and nature. This works immediately for some and not for others. For those who find such formless work a bit overwhelming or difficult to penetrate, then working with shrines, offering areas, and key places on the land is an intermediary step towards building up a relationship with the powers around you.

I still work with an outside offering area that houses a large stone, not only to keep in touch with the land beings, but also to feed the birds and creatures in winter. Building up a relationship with the land involves connecting to the land spirits and deity powers, as well as the local creatures, birds, waterways, springs, hills, and rocks.

Differentiating between temple-based deities and land spirits/ancient deities of nature is important: know who you are working with and why. Temple based deities work best with you through temple spaces, altars and other interfaces, and usually have heavily formed rituals. Nature deities connect with you through the elements, the creatures, and the land. They connect directly with you, and they can certainly pack a punch!

Working in such a way is an interesting and good training exercise for a magician: we can get too locked into a system and end up shutting out all the powers around us. It is better to learn different ways of working, different types of contacts, etc., as it is all part of the bigger picture and creates a well-rounded magician. We are in a culture of specialisation and magic can get sucked into that mentality too.

Learn the basic structures through one path, then branch out and learn in as many directions as possible so that you gain experience and allow for the right skill set to find you. After many years you will find that you naturally start to specialise, once you have learned many different skills. That specialisation 'wires' you to a focus point so that you become 'adept' in a certain area. But specialising too much too early has the opposite effect. Let it happen naturally and in the meantime, if you are a heavily ritualised magician, get out on the land. If you are more shamanic in your practice, learn how to work within a temple setting. The learning never stops!

Quareia

A New, Free School of Magic for the 21st Century

*Advancing education in Mystical Magic
and the Western Esoteric Mysteries.*

www.quareia.com

Quareia is a practical magical training course written in its entirety by adept Josephine McCarthy, and presented freely through an online school, Quareia, founded by Josephine and Frater Acher.

It is a complete and freely available course designed to develop a student from a complete beginner into an adept. There are no barriers to entry: the course is accessible regardless of income, race, gender, religion, or spiritual beliefs.

Quareia is aligned to no particular school or specific religious, mystical, or magical system; rather it looks at and works with various magical, religious, and mystical practices that have influenced magical thinking in the Near Eastern and Western world from the early Bronze Age to the present day.

The entire course is free and openly available without any registration on the Quareia website.

www.ingramcontent.com/pod-product-compliance
Lightning Source LLC
Chambersburg PA
CBHW061235070526
44584CB00030B/4138